ANGLICAN HYMNS OLD & NEW

kevin
mayhew

Acknowledgements

The publishers wish to express their gratitude to the copyright holders who have granted permission to include their material in this book.

Every effort has been made to trace the copyright holders of all the songs in this collection and we hope that no copyright has been infringed. Apology is made and pardon sought if the contrary be the case, and a correction will be made in any reprint of this book.

For additional information on the copyright holders please contact the Copyright Department at Kevin Mayhew Ltd (copyright@kevinmayhewltd.com)

First published in Great Britain in 2008 by
KEVIN MAYHEW LTD, Buxhall, Stowmarket, Suffolk IP14 3BW
www.kevinmayhew.com
© Copyright 2008 Kevin Mayhew Ltd

Full Music edition
ISBN 978 1 84417 837 7
ISMN M 57024 790 5
Catalogue No: 1413803

Melody edition
ISBN 978 1 84417 836 0
ISMN M 57024 791 2
Catalogue Number 1413802

Words edition
ISBN 978 1 84417 835 3
ISMN M 57024 792 9
Catalogue No: 1413800

Large Print edition
ISBN 978 1 84417 834 6
ISMN M 57024 793 6
Catalogue Number 1413801

20 19 18 17 16 15 14 13

Cover design by Sara-Jane Came

Printed and bound by
CPI Group (UK) Ltd,
Croydon, CR0 4YY

FOREWORD

Like its predecessors, this new and enlarged edition of *Hymns Old & New* is offered to congregations, clergy and musicians in the sincere hope that it will unite the whole Church community in praise of God.

It contains a wealth of both traditional and modern hymns and worship songs, and we hope that everyone who uses it will find their own favourites here as well as discover new and refreshing material.

Texts have been carefully chosen and edited so that their language is inclusive, and archaic forms have been avoided where possible. An asterisk indicates that a verse may be omitted.

Many tunes appear in a choice of keys so that the requirements of specific congregations may be taken into account. Except when unavoidable, no tune goes above E flat or below B flat. Sensitive musicians will know which key to choose.

'Those who sing pray twice' was the oft-quoted encouragement of Augustine of Hippo.

John Wesley would have added that those who sing out of tune also pray twice, as this quotation from a lecture of 1862 confirms:

> One good man sang out of tune, to the offence of Mr Wesley's delicate ear. 'George,' said he, 'you do not sing in tune.' The man stopped, but soon began again. The rebuke was repeated. 'Please, sir, I sing with my heart,' was the sufficient reply. 'Then sing on,' said Mr W.

May *Hymns Old & New* encourage all singers, tuned or untuned, to 'sing with joy in your hearts to the Lord' (Colossians 3:16).

Kevin Mayhew

1
Percy Dearmer (1867-1936)

1. A brighter dawn is breaking,
   and earth with praise is waking;
   for thou, O King most highest,
   the power of death defiest.

2. And thou hast come victorious,
   with risen body glorious,
   who now for ever livest,
   and life abundant givest.

3. O free the world from blindness,
   and fill the earth with kindness,
   give sinners resurrection,
   bring striving to perfection.

4. In sickness give us healing,
   in doubt thy clear revealing,
   that praise to thee be given
   in earth as in thy heaven.

2
St Germanus (c. 634-c. 734) trans.
John Mason Neale (1818-1866)

1. A great and mighty wonder,
   a full and holy cure!
   The Virgin bears the infant
   with virgin-honour pure:

   Repeat the hymn again!
   'To God on high be glory,
   and peace on earth shall reign.'

2. The Word becomes incarnate,
   and yet remains on high;
   and cherubim sing anthems
   to shepherds from the sky:

3. While thus they sing your monarch,
   those bright angelic bands,
   rejoice, ye vales and mountains,
   ye oceans, clap your hands:

4. Since all he comes to ransom
   by all be he adored,
   the infant born in Bethl'em,
   the Saviour and the Lord:

3
Somerset Corry Lowry (1855-1932)

1. A man there lived in Galilee
   like none who lived before,
   for he alone from first to last
   our flesh unsullied wore;
   a perfect life of perfect deeds
   once to the world was shown,
   that people all might mark his steps
   and in them plant their own.

2. A man there died on Calvary
   above all others brave;
   the human race he saved and blessed,
   himself he scorned to save.
   No thought can gauge the weight of
      woe
   on him, the sinless, laid;
   we only know that with his blood
   our ransom price was paid.

3. A man there reigns in glory now,
   divine, yet human still;
   that human which is all divine
   death sought in vain to kill.
   All power is his; supreme he rules
   the realms of time and space;
   yet still our human cares and needs
   find in his heart a place.

4
v. 1 unknown, based on John 13:34-35
vs. 2-4 Aniceto Nazareth, based on John 15 and 1 Cor. 13
© 1984, 1999 Kevin Mayhew Ltd

A new commandment I give unto you:
that you love one another as I have
   loved you,
that you love one another as I have
   loved you.

1. By this shall all know
   that you are my disciples
   if you have love one for another.
   (Repeat)

Continued overleaf

2. You are my friends
   if you do what I command you.
   Without my help you can do
   nothing.
   (Repeat)

   A new commandment I give unto you:
   that you love one another as I have
   loved you,
   that you love one another as I have
   loved you.

3. I am the true vine,
   my Father is the gardener.
   Abide in me: I will be with you.
   (Repeat)

4. True love is patient,
   not arrogant nor boastful;
   love bears all things, love is eternal.
   (Repeat)

5 Dave Bilbrough
  © 1977 Thankyou Music

   Abba, Father, let me be
   yours and yours alone.
   May my will forever be
   more and more your own.
   Never let my heart grow cold,
   never let me go.
   Abba, Father, let me be
   yours and yours alone.

6 Henry Francis Lyte (1793-1847)

1. Abide with me,
   fast falls the eventide;
   the darkness deepens;
   Lord, with me abide:
   when other helpers fail,
   and comforts flee,
   help of the helpless,
   O abide with me.

2. Swift to its close
   ebbs out life's little day;
   earth's joys grow dim,
   its glories pass away;
   change and decay
   in all around I see;
   O thou who changest not,
   abide with me.

3. I need thy presence
   every passing hour;
   what but thy grace
   can foil the tempter's power?
   Who like thyself
   my guide and stay can be?
   Through cloud and sunshine,
   Lord, abide with me.

4. I fear no foe
   with thee at hand to bless;
   ills have no weight,
   and tears no bitterness.
   Where is death's sting?
   Where, grave, thy victory?
   I triumph still,
   if thou abide with me.

5. Hold thou thy cross
   before my closing eyes;
   shine through the gloom,
   and point me to the skies;
   heaven's morning breaks,
   and earth's vain shadows flee;
   in life, in death, O Lord,
   abide with me.

7 Lenny LeBlanc (b. 1951) and Paul Baloche (b. 1962)
  © 1999 Lensongs Publishing/Integrity's Hosanna! Music

   Above all powers, above all kings,
   above all nature and all created things;
   above all wisdom and all the ways of
     man,
   you were here before the world began.

Above all kingdoms, above all thrones,
above all wonders the world has ever
  known;
above all wealth and treasures of the
  earth,
there's no way to measure what you're
  worth.
Crucified, laid behind the stone;
you lived to die, rejected and alone;
like a rose, trampled on the ground,
you took the fall, and thought of me,
  above all.

8 Taizé Community
© *Ateliers et Presses de Taizé*

Adoramus te, Domine

1. With the angels and archangels:

2. With the patriarchs and prophets:

3. With the Virgin Mary, mother
   of God:

4. With the apostles and evangelists:

5. With all the martyrs of Christ:

6. With all who witness to the Gospel
   of the Lord:

7. With all your people of the Church
   throughout the world.

9 Robert Bridges (1844-1930) from J. Heerman (1585-
1647) alt. based on an 11th-century Latin meditation

1. Ah, holy Jesu,
   how hast thou offended,
   that so to judge thee
   mortals have pretended?
   By foes derided,
   by thine own rejected,
   O most afflicted.

2. Who was the guilty?
   Who brought this upon thee?
   Alas, O Lord,
   my treason hath undone thee.
   'Twas I, Lord Jesu,
   I it was denied thee:
   I crucified thee.

3. Lo, the good shepherd
   for the sheep is offered;
   the slave hath sinnèd,
   and the Son hath suffered;
   for our atonement
   Christ himself is pleading,
   still interceding.

4. For me, kind Jesu,
   was thy incarnation,
   thy mortal sorrow,
   and thy life's oblation;
   thy death of anguish
   and thy bitter passion,
   for my salvation.

5. Therefore, kind Jesu,
   since I cannot pay thee,
   I do adore thee,
   and will ever pray thee,
   think on thy pity
   and thy love unswerving,
   not my deserving.

10 William Henry Draper (1855-1933) alt. based on
the 'Cantico di Frate Sole' of St. Francis of Assisi
(1182-1226)

1. All creatures of our God and King,
   lift up your voice and with us sing
   alleluia, alleluia!
   Thou burning sun with golden beam,
   thou silver moon with softer gleam:

   O praise him, O praise him,
   alleluia, alleluia, alleluia!

Continued overleaf

*2. Thou rushing wind that art so
  strong,
  ye clouds that sail in heaven along,
  O praise him, alleluia!
  Thou rising morn, in praise rejoice,
  ye lights of evening, find a voice:

*O praise him, O praise him,
alleluia, alleluia, alleluia!*

*3. Thou flowing water, pure and clear,
  make music for thy Lord to hear,
  alleluia, alleluia!
  Thou fire so masterful and bright,
  that givest us both warmth and light:

4. Dear mother earth, who day by day
  unfoldest blessings on our way,
  O praise him, alleluia!
  The flowers and fruits that in thee
    grow,
  let them his glory also show.

5. All you with mercy in your heart,
  forgiving others, take your part,
  O sing ye, alleluia!
  Ye who long pain and sorrow bear,
  praise God and on him cast your
    care:

6. And thou, most kind and gentle
    death,
  waiting to hush our latest breath,
  O praise him, alleluia!
  Thou leadest home the child of God,
  and Christ our Lord the way hath
    trod:

7. Let all things their Creator bless,
  and worship him in humbleness,
  O praise him, alleluia!
  Praise, praise the Father, praise the
    Son,
  and praise the Spirit, Three in One.

11 William John Sparrow-Simpson (1859-1952) alt.
  *© 1887, 1915 Novello & Co. Ltd.
  Revised edition © 1999 Novello & Co. Ltd*

1. All for Jesus! All for Jesus!
  This our song shall ever be;
  for we have no hope nor Saviour
  if we have not hope in thee.

2. All for Jesus! thou wilt give us
  strength to serve thee hour by hour;
  none can move us from thy presence
  while we trust thy love and power.

3. All for Jesus! at thine altar
  thou dost give us sweet content;
  there, dear Saviour, we receive thee
  in thy holy sacrament.

4. All for Jesus! thou hast loved us,
  all for Jesus! thou hast died,
  all for Jesus! thou art with us,
  all for Jesus, glorified!

5. All for Jesus! All for Jesus!
  This the Church's song shall be,
  till at last the flock is gathered
  one in love, and one in thee.

12 St Theodulph of Orleans (d. 821)
  trans. John Mason Neale (1818-1866)

*All glory, laud and honour,
to thee, Redeemer King,
to whom the lips of children
made sweet hosannas ring.*

1. Thou art the King of Israel,
  thou David's royal Son,
  who in the Lord's name comest,
  the King and blessèd one.

2. The company of angels
  are praising thee on high,
  and mortals, joined with all things
  created, make reply.

3. The people of the Hebrews
  with palms before thee went:
  our praise and prayer and anthems
  before thee we present.

4. To thee before thy passion
   they sang their hymns of praise:
   to thee now high exalted
   our melody we raise.

5. Thou didst accept their praises,
   accept the prayers we bring,
   who in all good delightest,
   thou good and gracious king.

13 Dave Bilbrough
© 1987 Thankyou Music

All hail the Lamb, enthroned on high;
his praise shall be our battle cry;
he reigns victorious, for ever glorious,
his name is Jesus, he is the Lord.

14 Edward Perronet (1726-1792)
adapted by Michael Forster (b. 1946)
© This version 1999 Kevin Mayhew Ltd

1. All hail the power of Jesus' name,
   let angels prostrate fall;
   bring forth the royal diadem
   and crown him, crown him,
   *   crown him,*
   crown him Lord of all.

2. Crown him, all martyrs of your God,
   who from his altar call;
   praise him whose way of pain you
   trod,
   and crown him . . .

3. O prophets faithful to his word,
   in matters great and small,
   who made his voice of justice heard,
   now crown him . . .

4. All sinners, now redeemed by grace,
   who heard your Saviour's call,
   now robed in light before his face,
   O crown him . . .

*5. Let every tribe and every race
   who heard the freedom call,
   in liberation, see Christ's face,
   and crown him . . .

6. Let every people, every tongue
   to him their heart enthral:
   lift high the universal song
   and crown him . . .

Tune 2:

1. All hail the power of Jesus' name!
   Let angels prostrate fall;
   let angels prostrate fall;
   bring forth the royal diadem,

   and crown him, crown him,
   *   crown him,*
   crown him, and crown him Lord of all.

2. Crown him, all martyrs of your God,
   who from his altar call;
   who from his altar call;
   praise him whose way of pain you
   trod,
   and crown him . . .

3. O prophets faithful to his word,
   in matters great and small,
   in matters great and small,
   who made his voice of justice heard,
   now crown him Lord of all.
   now crown him . . .

4. All sinners, now redeemed by grace,
   who heard your Saviour's call,
   who heard your Saviour's call,
   now robed in light before his face,
   O crown him . . .

*5. Let every tribe and every race
   who heard the freedom call,
   who heard the freedom call,
   in liberation, see Christ's face,
   and crown him . . .

6. Let every people, every tongue
   to him their heart enthral:
   to him their heart enthral:
   lift high the universal song
   and crown him . . .

15 Tricia Richards
© 1987 Thankyou Music

1. All heaven declares
   the glory of the risen Lord.
   Who can compare
   with the beauty of the Lord?
   For ever he will be
   the Lamb upon the throne.
   I gladly bow the knee
   and worship him alone.

2. I will proclaim
   the glory of the risen Lord.
   Who once was slain
   to reconcile us all to God.
   For ever you will be
   the Lamb upon the throne.
   I gladly bow the knee
   and worship you alone.

16 Graham Kendrick (b. 1950), based on
Philippians 3:8-12. © 1993 Make Way Music

1. All I once held dear, built my life
   upon,
   all this world reveres, and wars to own,
   all I once thought gain I have
   counted loss;
   spent and worthless now, compared
   to this.

   Knowing you, Jesus, knowing you,
   there is no greater thing.
   You're my all, you're the best,
   you're my joy, my righteousness,
   and I love you, Lord.

2. Now my heart's desire is to know you
   more,
   to be found in you and known as
   yours.
   To possess by faith what I could not
   earn,
   all-surpassing gift of righteousness.

3. Oh, to know the power of your risen
   life,
   and to know you in your sufferings.
   To become like you in your death,
   my Lord,
   so with you to live and never die.

17 Traditional

1. All in an Easter garden,
   before the break of day,
   an angel came from heaven
   and rolled the stone away.
   When Jesus' friends came seeking,
   with myrrh and spices rare,
   they found the angels at the door,
   but Jesus was not there.

2. All in an Easter garden,
   where water lilies bloom,
   the angels gave their message
   beside an empty tomb:
   'The Lord is here no longer,
   come, see where once he lay;
   the Lord of life is risen indeed,
   for this is Easter day.'

18 Stuart Townend (b. 1963)
© 1998 Thankyou Music

1. All my days I will sing this song of
   gladness,
   give my praise to the Fountain of
   Delights;
   for in my helplessness you heard my
   cry,
   and waves of mercy poured down on
   my life.

2. I will trust in the cross of my
   Redeemer,
   I will sing of the blood that never fails,
   of sins forgiven, of conscience cleansed,
   of death defeated and life without end.

Beautiful Saviour, Wonderful Counsellor,
clothed in majesty, Lord of History
you're the Way, the Truth, the Life.
Star of the Morning, glorious in holiness,
you're the Risen One, heaven's champion,
and you reign, you reign over all!

3. I long to be where the praise is never-
   ending.
   yearn to dwell where the glory never
   fades,
   where countless worshippers will
   share one song,
   and cries of 'worthy' will honour the
   Lamb!

19 Robert Bridges (1844-1930) alt., based on 'Meine Hoffnung stehet feste' by Joachim Neander (1650-1680)

1. All my hope on God is founded;
   he doth still my trust renew.
   Me through change and chance he
   guideth,
   only good and only true.
   God unknown, he alone
   calls my heart to be his own.

2. Human pride and earthly glory,
   sword and crown betray his trust;
   what with care and toil he buildeth,
   tower and temple, fall to dust.
   But God's power, hour by hour,
   is my temple and my tower.

3. God's great goodness aye endureth,
   deep his wisdom, passing thought:
   splendour, light and life attend him,
   beauty springeth out of naught.
   Evermore, from his store,
   new-born worlds rise and adore.

4. Still from earth to God eternal
   sacrifice of praise be done,
   high above all praises praising
   for the gift of Christ his Son.
   Christ doth call one and all:
   ye who follow shall not fall.

20 Roy Turner (b. 1940)
© 1984 Thankyou Music

1. All over the world the Spirit is moving,
   all over the world,
   as the prophets said it would be.
   All over the world
   there's a mighty revelation
   of the glory of the Lord,
   as the waters cover the sea.

2. All over this land the Spirit is
   moving . . .

3. All over the Church the Spirit is
   moving . . .

4. All over us all the Spirit is moving . . .

5. Deep down in my heart the Spirit is
   moving . . .

21 William Kethe (d. 1594) from Day's *Psalter* (1569) alt.

1. All people that on earth do dwell,
   sing to the Lord with cheerful voice;
   him serve with fear, his praise forth tell,
   come ye before him and rejoice.

2. The Lord, ye know, is God indeed,
   without our aid he did us make;
   we are his folk, he doth us feed
   and for his sheep he doth us take.

3. O enter then his gates with praise,
   approach with joy his courts unto;
   praise, laud and bless his name always,
   for it is seemly so to do.

4. For why? the Lord our God is good:
   his mercy is for ever sure;
   his truth at all times firmly stood,
   and shall from age to age endure.

5. To Father, Son and Holy Ghost,
   the God whom heaven and earth adore,
   from us and from the angel-host
   be praise and glory evermore.

22 Charles Wesley (1707-1788)

1. All praise to our redeeming Lord,
   who joins us by his grace,
   and bids us, each to each restored,
   together seek his face.

2. He bids us build each other up;
   and, gathered into one,
   to our high calling's glorious hope
   we hand in hand go on.

3. The gift which he on one bestows,
   we all delight to prove;
   the grace through every vessel flows,
   in purest streams of love.

4. E'en now we think and speak the
      same,
   and cordially agree;
   concentred all, through Jesu's name,
   in perfect harmony.

5. We all partake the joy of one,
   the common peace we feel,
   a peace to worldly minds unknown,
   a joy unspeakable.

6. And if our fellowship below
   in Jesus be so sweet,
   what heights of rapture shall we know
   when round his throne we meet!

23 Francis Bland Tucker (1895-1984)
based on Philippians 2:5-11
© *Church Publishing Inc.*

1. All praise to thee, for thou, O King
      divine,
   didst yield the glory that of right was
      thine,
   that in our darkened hearts thy grace
   might shine: alleluia!

2. Thou cam'st to us in lowliness of
      thought;
   by thee the outcast and the poor were
      sought,
   and by thy death was God's salvation
   wrought: alleluia!

3. Let this mind be in us which was in
      thee,
   who wast a servant that we might be
      free,
   humbling thyself to death on
      Calvary: alleluia!

4. Wherefore, by God's eternal purpose,
   thou art high exalted o'er all creatures
      now,
   and given the name to which all
      knees shall bow: alleluia!

5. Let every tongue confess with one
      accord
   in heaven and earth that Jesus Christ
      is Lord;
   and God the Father be by all adored:
      alleluia!

24 Sebastian Temple (1928-1997)
© *1967 OCP Publications*

1. All that I am, all that I do,
   all that I'll ever have, I offer now to
      you.
   Take and sanctify these gifts
   for your honour, Lord.
   Knowing that I love and serve you
   is enough reward.
   All that I am, all that I do,
   all that I'll ever have, I offer now to
      you.

2. All that I dream, all that I pray,
   all that I'll ever make I give to you
      today.

Take and sanctify these gifts
for your honour, Lord.
Knowing that I love and serve you
is enough reward.
All that I am, all that I do,
all that I'll ever have, I offer now to
you.

25 Michael Cockett (b. 1938)
© McCrimmon Publishing Co Ltd

All the nations of the earth,
praise the Lord who brings to birth
the greatest star, the smallest flower.
Alleluia.

1. Let the heavens praise the Lord,
   alleluia.
   Moon and stars, praise the Lord,
   alleluia.

2. Snow-capped mountains, praise the
   Lord, alleluia.
   Rolling hills, praise the Lord, alleluia.

3. Deep sea water, praise the Lord,
   alleluia.
   Gentle rain, praise the Lord, alleluia.

4. Roaring lion, praise the Lord, alleluia.
   Singing birds, praise the Lord,
   alleluia.

5. Earthly monarchs, praise the Lord,
   alleluia.
   Young and old, praise the Lord,
   alleluia.

26 Cecil Frances Alexander (1818-1895)

All things bright and beautiful,
all creatures great and small,
all things wise and wonderful,
the Lord God made them all.

1. Each little flower that opens,
   each little bird that sings,
   he made their glowing colours,
   he made their tiny wings.

2. The purple-headed mountain,
   the river running by,
   the sunset and the morning
   that brightens up the sky.

3. The cold wind in the winter,
   the pleasant summer sun,
   the ripe fruits in the garden,
   he made them every one.

4. The tall trees in the greenwood,
   the meadows for our play,
   the rushes by the water,
   to gather every day.

5. He gave us eyes to see them,
   and lips that we might tell
   how great is God Almighty,
   who has made all things well.

27 Percy Dearmer (1867-1936)
after John Bunyan (1628-1688) alt.

1. All who would valiant be,
   'gainst all disaster,
   let them in constancy
   follow their Master.
   There's no discouragement
   shall make them once relent,
   the first avowed intent
   to be a pilgrim.

2. Those who beset them round
   with dismal stories,
   do but themselves confound –
   their strength the more is.
   No foe shall stay their might
   though they with giants fight:
   they will make good the right
   to be a pilgrim.

Continued overleaf

3. Since, Lord, thou dost defend
   us with thy Spirit,
   we know we at the end
   shall life inherit.
   Then fancies flee away,
   we'll fear not what they say,
   we'll labour night and day
   to be a pilgrim.

28 18th-century Latin
   trans. Edward Caswall (1814-1878) alt.
   © This version 1999 Kevin Mayhew Ltd

1. All you who seek a comfort sure
   in trouble and distress,
   whatever sorrow vex the mind,
   or guilt the soul oppress.

2. Jesus, who gave himself for you
   upon the cross to die,
   opens to you his sacred heart;
   O, to that heart draw nigh.

3. You hear how kindly he invites;
   you hear his words so blest:
   'All you that labour, come to me,
   and I will give you rest.'

4. What meeker than the Saviour's
   heart?
   As on the cross he lay,
   it did his murderers forgive,
   and for their pardon pray.

5. Jesus, the joy of saints on high,
   the hope of sinners here,
   attracted by those loving words
   to you I lift my prayer.

6. Wash then my wounds in that dear
   blood
   which forth from you does flow;
   by grace a better hope inspire,
   and risen life bestow.

29 vs. 1-4 unknown, vs. 5-7 Damian Lundy (1944-1997)
   © Additional words 1996, 2007 Kevin Mayhew Ltd

1. Alleluia . . .

2. Jesus is Lord . . .

3. And I love him . . .

4. Christ is risen . . .

   *Additional verses may be composed to
   suit the occasion. For example:*

5. Send your Spirit . . .

6. Abba, Father . . .

7. Come, Lord Jesus . . .

30 Owen Alstott
   © 2002 Owen Alstott

   Alleluia! Alleluia!
   Raise the Gospel over the earth!
   Alleluia! Alleluia!
   Peace and justice bringing to birth!

1. Blessed those whose hearts are gentle.
   Blessed those whose spirits are strong.
   Blessed those who choose to bring forth
   right where there is wrong.

2. Blessed those who work for justice.
   Blessed those who answer the call.
   Blessed those who dare to dream of
   lasting peace for all.

3. Tremble, you who build up riches.
   Tremble, you with opulent lives.
   Tremble, when you meet the poor and
   see Christ in their eyes.

4. Tremble, you who thirst for power.
   Tremble, you who live for acclaim.
   Tremble, when you find no comfort
   in your wealth and fame.

5. Glory like the stars of heaven.
   Glory like the sun in the sky.
   Glory shines upon all people,
   equal in God's eyes.

6. Glory to the Word of Justice.
   Glory to the Spirit of Peace.
   Glory to the God of Love whose
   blessings never cease.

31
Donald Fishel (b. 1950) alt.
© 1973 Word of God Music. Administered by CopyCare

Alleluia, alleluia,
give thanks to the risen Lord,
alleluia, alleluia, give praise to his name.

1. Jesus is Lord of all the earth.
   He is the King of creation.

2. Spread the good news o'er all the earth.
   Jesus has died and is risen.

3. We have been crucified with Christ.
   Now we shall live for ever.

4. God has proclaimed the just reward:
   'Life for us all, alleluia!'

5. Come, let us praise the living God,
   joyfully sing to our Saviour.

32
Christopher Wordsworth (1807-1885)

1. Alleluia, alleluia,
   hearts to heaven and voices raise;
   sing to God a hymn of gladness,
   sing to God a hymn of praise:
   he who on the cross a victim
   for the world's salvation bled,
   Jesus Christ, the King of Glory,
   now is risen from the dead.

2. Christ is risen, Christ the first-fruits
   of the holy harvest field,
   which will all its full abundance
   at his second coming yield;
   then the golden ears of harvest
   will their heads before him wave,
   ripened by his glorious sunshine,
   from the furrows of the grave.

3. Christ is risen, we are risen;
   shed upon us heavenly grace,
   rain, and dew, and gleams of glory
   from the brightness of thy face;
   that we, with our hearts in heaven,
   here on earth may fruitful be,
   and by angel-hands be gathered,
   and be ever, Lord, with thee.

4. Alleluia, alleluia,
   glory be to God on high;
   alleluia to the Saviour,
   who has gained the victory;
   alleluia to the Spirit,
   fount of love and sanctity;
   alleluia, alleluia,
   to the Triune Majesty.

33
William Chatterton Dix (1837-1898) alt.
This version © 1999 Kevin Mayhew Ltd

1. Alleluia, sing to Jesus,
   his the sceptre, his the throne;
   alleluia, his the triumph,
   his the victory alone:
   hark, the songs of peaceful Sion
   thunder like a mighty flood:
   Jesus, out of every nation,
   hath redeemed us by his blood.

2. Alleluia, not as orphans
   are we left in sorrow now;
   alleluia, he is near us,
   faith believes, nor questions how;
   though the cloud from sight received
   him
   when the forty days were o'er,
   shall our hearts forget his promise,
   'I am with you evermore'?

Continued overleaf

3. Alleluia, bread of angels,
here on earth our food, our stay;
alleluia, here the sinful
come to you from day to day.
Intercessor, friend of sinners,
earth's redeemer, plead for me,
where the songs of all the sinless
sweep across the crystal sea.

4. Alleluia, King eternal,
he the Lord of lords we own;
alleluia, born of Mary,
earth his footstool, heaven his throne;
he within the veil has entered
robed in flesh, our great High Priest;
he on earth both priest and victim
in the Eucharistic Feast.

34 vs. 1-4 John Newton (1725-1807) alt.
v. 5 John Rees (1828-1900)

1. Amazing grace! How sweet the sound
that saved a wretch like me.
I once was lost, but now I'm found;
was blind, but now I see.

2. 'Twas grace that taught my heart to
fear,
and grace my fears relieved.
How precious did that grace appear
the hour I first believed.

3. Through many dangers, toils and snares
I have already come.
'Tis grace that brought me safe thus far,
and grace will lead me home.

4. The Lord has promised good to me,
his word my hope secures;
he will my shield and portion be
as long as life endures.

5. When we've been there a thousand
years,
bright shining as the sun,
we've no less days to sing God's praise
than when we first begun.

35 Fred Pratt Green (1903-2000)
© 1974 Stainer & Bell Ltd

1. An upper room did our Lord prepare
for those he loved until the end:
and his disciples still gather there,
to celebrate their risen friend.

2. A lasting gift Jesus gave his own:
to share his bread, his loving cup.
Whatever burdens may bow us down,
he by his cross shall lift us up.

3. And after supper he washed their feet
for service, too, is sacrament.
In him our joy shall be made complete –
sent out to serve, as he was sent.

4. No end there is! We depart in peace,
he loves beyond the uttermost:
in every room in our Father's house
he will be there, as Lord and host.

36 Charles Wesley (1707-1788)

1. And can it be that I should gain
an interest in the Saviour's blood?
Died he for me, who caused his pain?
For me, who him to death pursued?
Amazing love! How can it be
that thou, my God, shouldst } *(x2)*
die for me?

2. 'Tis mystery all! the Immortal dies:
who can explore his strange design?
In vain the first-born seraph tries
to sound the depths of love divine!
'Tis mercy all! Let earth adore,
let angel minds inquire no } *(x2)*
more.

3. He left his Father's throne above
so free, so infinite his grace;
emptied himself of all but love,
and bled for Adam's helpless race;
'tis mercy all, immense and free; }
for, O my God, it found } *(x2)*
out me.

4. Long my imprisoned spirit lay
   fast bound in sin and nature's night;
   thine eye diffused a quick'ning ray,
   I woke, the dungeon flamed with light;
   my chains fell off, my heart
     was free;
   I rose, went forth, and
     followed thee. ⎫ *(x2)*

5. No condemnation now I dread;
   Jesus, and all in him, is mine!
   Alive in him, my living Head,
   and clothed in righteousness divine,
   bold I approach the eternal
     throne,
   and claim the crown, through
     Christ my own. ⎫ *(x2)*

37 William Blake (1757-1827)

1. And did those feet in ancient time
   walk upon England's mountains green?
   And was the holy Lamb of God
   on England's pleasant pastures seen?
   And did the countenance divine
   shine forth upon our clouded hills?
   And was Jerusalem builded here
   among those dark satanic mills?

2. Bring me my bow of burning gold!
   Bring me my arrows of desire!
   Bring me my spear! O clouds unfold!
   Bring me my chariot of fire!
   I will not cease from mental fight,
   nor shall my sword sleep in my hand,
   till we have built Jerusalem
   in England's green and pleasant land.

38 William Bright (1824-1901)

1. And now, O Father, mindful of the love
   that bought us, once for all, on
     Calv'ry's tree,
   and having with us him that pleads
     above,
   we here present, we here spread forth
     to thee
   that only off'ring perfect in thine eyes,
   the one true, pure, immortal sacrifice.

2. Look, Father, look on his anointed
     face,
   and only look on us as found in him;
   look not on our misusings of thy grace,
   our prayer so languid, and our faith
     so dim:
   for lo, between our sins and their reward
   we set the Passion of thy Son our Lord.

3. And then for those, our dearest and
     our best,
   by this prevailing presence we appeal:
   O fold them closer to thy mercy's
     breast,
   O do thine utmost for their souls'
     true weal;
   from tainting mischief keep them
     pure and clear,
   and crown thy gifts with strength to
     persevere.

4. And so we come: O draw us to thy
     feet,
   most patient Saviour, who canst love
     us still;
   and by this food, so aweful and so
     sweet,
   deliver us from every touch of ill:
   in thine own service make us glad
     and free,
   and grant us never more to part with
     thee.

39 James Montgomery (1771-1854)

1. Angels from the realms of glory,
   wing your flight o'er all the earth;
   ye who sang creation's story
   now proclaim Messiah's birth:

   Come and worship
   Christ, the new-born King:
   come and worship,
   worship Christ, the new-born King.

2. Shepherds, in the field abiding,
   watching o'er your flocks by night,
   God with us is now residing,
   yonder shines the infant Light:

3. Sages, leave your contemplations;
   brighter visions beam afar:
   seek the great Desire of Nations;
   ye have seen his natal star:

4. Saints before the altar bending,
   watching long in hope and fear,
   suddenly the Lord, descending,
   in his temple shall appear:

5. Though an infant now we view him,
   he shall fill his Father's throne,
   gather all the nations to him;
   every knee shall then bow down:

40 Francis Pott (1832-1909) alt.

1. Angel-voices ever singing
   round thy throne of light,
   angel-harps for ever ringing,
   rest not day nor night;
   thousands only live to bless thee,
   and confess thee Lord of might.

2. Thou who art beyond the farthest
   mortal eye can see,
   can it be that thou regardest
   our poor hymnody?
   Yes, we know that thou art near us
   and wilt hear us constantly.

3. Yea, we know that thou rejoicest
   o'er each work of thine;
   thou didst ears and hands and voices
   for thy praise design;
   craftsman's art and music's measure
   for thy pleasure all combine.

4. In thy house, great God, we offer
   of thine own to thee;
   and for thine acceptance proffer
   all unworthily,
   hearts and minds and hands and
      voices
   in our choicest psalmody.

5. Honour, glory, might and merit,
   thine shall ever be,
   Father, Son and Holy Spirit,
   blessèd Trinity.
   Of the best that thou hast given
   earth and heaven render thee.

41 18th century

1. As Jacob with travel was weary one
      day,
   at night on a stone for a pillow he lay;
   he saw in a vision a ladder so high
   that its foot was on earth and its top
      in the sky:

   Alleluia to Jesus who died on the tree,
   and has raised up a ladder of mercy for
      me,
   and has raised up a ladder of mercy for
   me.

2. This ladder is long, it is strong and
    well made,
    has stood hundreds of years and is
    not yet decayed;
    many millions have climbed it and
    reached Sion's hill,
    and thousands by faith are climbing
    it still:

3. Come let us ascend! all may climb it
    who will;
    for the angels of Jacob are guarding it
    still:
    and remember, each step that by faith
    we pass o'er,
    some prophet or martyr has trod it
    before:

4. And when we arrive at the haven of
    rest
    we shall hear the glad words, 'Come
    up hither, ye blest,
    here are regions of light, here are
    mansions of bliss.'
    O who would not climb such a
    ladder as this?

42 Psalm 42 in *New Version* (Tate and Brady, 1696)

1. As pants the hart for cooling streams
    when heated in the chase,
    so longs my soul, O God, for thee,
    and thy refreshing grace.

2. For thee, my God, the living God,
    my thirsty soul doth pine:
    O when shall I behold thy face,
    thou majesty divine?

3. Why restless, why cast down, my soul?
    hope still, and thou shalt sing
    the praise of him who is thy God,
    thy health's eternal spring.

4. To Father, Son and Holy Ghost,
    the God whom we adore,
    be glory, as it was, is now,
    and shall be evermore.

43 Martin Nystrom (b. 1956), based on Psalm 42:1-2
    © 1983 Restoration Music Ltd/ Sovereign Music UK

1. As the deer pants for the water,
    so my soul longs after you.
    You alone are my heart's desire
    and I long to worship you.

    You alone are my strength, my shield,
    to you alone may my spirit yield.
    You alone are my heart's desire
    and I long to worship you.

2. I want you more than gold or silver,
    only you can satisfy.
    You alone are the real joy-giver
    and the apple of my eye.

3. You're my friend and you are my
    brother,
    even though you are a king.
    I love you more than any other,
    so much more than anything.

44 Percy Dearmer (1867-1936)

1. As the disciples, when thy Son had
    left them,
    met in a love-feast, joyfully conversing,
    all the stored mem'ry of the Lord's
    last supper
    fondly rehearsing;

2. So may we here, who gather now in
    friendship,
    seek for the spirit of those earlier
    churches,
    welcoming him who stands and for
    an entrance,
    patiently searches.

Continued overleaf

3. As, when their converse closed and
supper ended,
taking the bread and wine they made
thanksgiving,
breaking and blessing, thus to have
communion
with Christ the living;

4. So may we here, a company of faithful,
make this our love-feast and
commemoration,
that in his Spirit we may have more
worthy
participation.

5. And as they prayed and sang to thee
rejoicing,
ere in the night-fall they embraced
and parted,
in their hearts singing as they
journeyed homeward,
brave and true-hearted;

6. So may we here, like corn that once
was scattered
over the hillside, now one bread
united,
led by the Spirit, do thy work rejoicing,
lamps filled and lighted.

45 John Daniels. © 1979 Authentic Publishing.
Administered by CopyCare

As we are gathered, Jesus is here;
one with each other, Jesus is here;
joined by the Spirit, washed in the
blood,
part of the body, the church of God.
As we are gathered, Jesus is here;
one with each other, Jesus is here.

46 William Chatterton Dix (1837-1898) alt.

1. As with gladness men of old
did the guiding star behold,
as with joy they hailed its light,
leading onward, beaming bright;
so, most gracious Lord, may we
evermore be led to thee.

2. As with joyful steps they sped,
to that lowly manger-bed,
there to bend the knee before
him whom heaven and earth adore,
so may we with willing feet
ever seek thy mercy-seat.

3. As their precious gifts they laid,
at thy manger roughly made,
so may we with holy joy,
pure, and free from sin's alloy,
all our costliest treasures bring,
Christ, to thee our heavenly King.

4. Holy Jesu, every day
keep us in the narrow way;
and, when earthly things are past,
bring our ransomed souls at last
where they need no star to guide,
where no clouds thy glory hide.

5. In the heavenly country bright
need they no created light,
thou its light, its joy, its crown,
thou its sun which goes not down;
there for ever may we sing
alleluias to our King.

47 Unknown

1. As your fam'ly, Lord, see us here,
as your fam'ly, Lord, see us here,
as your fam'ly, Lord, see us here,
O Lord, see us here.

2. At your table, Lord, we are fed;
   at your table, Lord, we are fed;
   at your table, Lord, we are fed;
   O Lord, feed us here.

3. Fill our spirits, Lord, with your love,
   fill our spirits, Lord, with your love,
   fill our spirits, Lord, with your love,
   O Lord, give your love.

4. Make us faithful, Lord, to your will,
   make us faithful, Lord, to your will,
   make us faithful, Lord, to your will,
   O Lord, to your will.

5. As your fam'ly, Lord, see us here,
   as your fam'ly, Lord, see us here,
   as your fam'ly, Lord, see us here,
   O Lord, see us here.

48 Peter West, Mary Lou King and Mary Kirkbride-Barthow. © 1979 Integrity Music Europe Ltd/ Sovereign Music UK

Ascribe greatness to our God,
   the Rock,
his work is perfect and all his ways
   are just.
A God of faithfulness
and without injustice,
good and upright is he.

49 Henry Twells (1823-1900) alt.

1. At even, ere the sun was set,
   the sick, O Lord, around thee lay;
   O in what divers pains they met!
   O with what joy they went away!

2. Once more 'tis eventide, and we
   oppressed with various ills draw near;
   what if thy form we cannot see?
   We know and feel that thou art here.

3. O Saviour Christ, our woes dispel;
   for some are sick, and some are sad,
   and some have never loved thee well,
   and some have lost the love they had.

4. And some have found the world is
   vain,
   yet from the world they break not free;
   and some have friends who give them
   pain,
   yet have not sought a friend in thee.

5. And none, O Lord, has perfect rest,
   for none is wholly free from sin;
   and they who fain would serve thee
   best
   are conscious most of wrong within.

6. O Christ, thou hast been human too,
   thou hast been troubled, tempted,
   tried;
   thy kind but searching glance can view
   the very wounds that shame would
   hide.

7. Thy touch has still its ancient power;
   no word from thee can fruitless fall:
   hear, in this solemn evening hour,
   and in thy mercy heal us all.

50 'Stabat Mater', ascribed to Jacopone da Todi (d. 1306) trans. Edward Caswall (1814-1878) adapted by Michael Forster (b. 1946) © This version 2004 Kevin Mayhew Ltd

1. At the cross she keeps her station,
   treading, in her contemplation,
   every step his feet have trod.

2. Now she hears the sentence spoken,
   feels her heart by sorrow broken,
   mother of incarnate God.

3. As he lifts his cross, she senses
   all the weight of earth's offences,
   vaunted pride and broken trust.

Continued overleaf

4. Now she sees his body falling,
   hears his anguished spirit calling,
   God-is-with-us in the dust.

5. On his walk of pain she meets him,
   with a kiss of peace she greets him,
   in the midst of cosmic strife.

6. Then she sees a passing stranger
   share his burden, pain and danger,
   on the road to death and life.

7. One kind face among the rabble,
   one kind act amid the babble,
   sets the image of his face.

8. Once again she sees him stumble,
   watches earth its maker humble,
   sees the majesty of grace.

9. Even now, the Man for Others
   hears the cries of anguished mothers,
   weeping for a world of pain.

10. Mother shares the pains that grieve
    him,
    feels the stony ground receive him:
    earth's Redeemer falls again.

11. Then she sees them strip his body,
    wearing still their splendid shoddy,
    lest the naked truth be told.

12. Spear-like nails that wound and gore
    him
    pierce the very wound that bore him
    – love so warm, with steel so cold.

13. Yet she stays to see his dying,
    hears his voice triumphant crying,
    share the agony of grace.

14. Take away the body, slighted,
    lest the festival be blighted
    by God's ugly, suffering face!

15. Then amid his mother's sorrows,
    someone else's grave he borrows,
    nowhere still to lay his head.

16. All creation waits and wonders,
    God the final curtain sunders:
    life abundant with the dead!

51 'Ad regias Agni dapes'
trans. Robert Campbell (1814-1868)

1. At the Lamb's high feast we sing
   praise to our victorious King,
   who hath washed us in the tide
   flowing from his piercèd side;
   praise we him, whose love divine
   gives his sacred blood for wine,
   gives his body for the feast,
   Christ the victim, Christ the priest.

2. Where the paschal blood is poured,
   death's dark angel sheathes his sword;
   faithful hosts triumphant go
   through the wave that drowns the foe.
   Praise we Christ, whose blood was
   shed,
   paschal victim, paschal bread;
   with sincerity and love
   eat we manna from above.

3. Mighty victim from above,
   conquering by the power of love;
   thou hast triumphed in the fight,
   thou hast brought us life and light.
   Now no more can death appal,
   now no more the grave enthral:
   thou hast opened paradise,
   and in thee thy saints shall rise.

4. Easter triumph, Easter joy,
   nothing now can this destroy;
   from sin's power do thou set free
   souls new-born, O Lord, in thee.
   Hymns of glory and of praise,
   risen Lord, to thee we raise;
   holy Father, praise to thee,
   with the Spirit, ever be.

52

Caroline Maria Noel (1817-1877) alt.

1. At the name of Jesus
   every knee shall bow,
   every tongue confess him
   King of glory now;
   'tis the Father's pleasure
   we should call him Lord,
   who, from the beginning,
   was the mighty Word.

2. At his voice creation
   sprang at once to sight,
   all the angels' faces,
   all the hosts of light,
   thrones and dominations,
   stars upon their way,
   all the heavenly orders
   in their great array.

3. Humbled for a season,
   to receive a name
   from the lips of sinners
   unto whom he came,
   faithfully he bore it,
   spotless to the last,
   brought it back victorious
   when from death he passed.

4. Bore it up triumphant
   with its human light,
   through all ranks of creatures
   to the central height,
   to the throne of Godhead,
   to the Father's breast,
   filled it with the glory
   of that perfect rest.

5. In your hearts enthrone him;
   there let him subdue
   all that is not holy,
   all that is not true;
   crown him as your captain
   in temptation's hour;
   let his will enfold you
   in its light and power.

6. Truly, this Lord Jesus
   shall return again,
   with his Father's glory,
   with his angel train;
   for all wreaths of empire
   meet upon his brow,
   and our hearts confess him
   King of glory now.

53

Martin E. Leckebusch (b. 1962)
© 1999 Kevin Mayhew Ltd

1. At this table we remember
   how and where our faith began:
   in the pain of crucifixion
   suffered by the Son of Man.

2. Looking up in adoration
   faith is conscious – he is here!
   Christ is present with his people,
   his the call that draws us near.

3. Heart and mind we each examine:
   if with honesty we face
   all our doubt, our fear and failure,
   then we can receive his grace.

4. Peace we share with one another:
   as from face to face we turn
   in our brothers and our sisters
   Jesus' body we discern.

5. Bread and wine are set before us;
   as we eat, we look ahead:
   we shall dine with Christ in heaven
   where the Kingdom feast is spread.

6. Nourished by the bread of heaven,
   faith and strength and courage grow –
   so to witness, serve and suffer,
   out into the world we go.

54
Graham Kendrick (b. 1950)
© 1988 Make Way Music

At this time of giving,
gladly now we bring
gifts of goodness and mercy
from a heavenly King.

1. Earth could not contain the treasures
   heaven holds for you,
   perfect joy and lasting pleasures,
   love so strong and true.

2. May his tender love surround you
   at this Christmastime;
   may you see his smiling face
   that in the darkness shines.

3. But the many gifts he gives
   are all poured out from one;
   come, receive the greatest gift,
   the gift of God's own Son.

Last two choruses and verses:

Lai, lai, lai . . . etc.

55
Charles Wesley (1707-1788)

1. Author of life divine,
   who hast a table spread,
   furnished with mystic wine
   and everlasting bread,
   preserve the life thyself hast given,
   and feed and train us up for heaven.

2. Our needy souls sustain
   with fresh supplies of love,
   till all thy life we gain,
   and all thy fullness prove,
   and, strengthened by thy perfect grace,
   behold without a veil thy face.

56
John Raphael Peacey (1896-1971)
based on Ephesians 5:6-20 alt.
© By kind permission of the Revd M. J. Hancock

1. Awake, awake: fling off the night!
   for God has sent his glorious light;
   and we who live in Christ's new day
   must works of darkness put away.

2. Awake and rise, in Christ renewed,
   and with the Spirit's power endued.
   The light of life in us must glow,
   and fruits of truth and goodness show.

3. Let in the light; all sin expose
   to Christ, whose life no darkness
   knows.
   Before his cross for guidance kneel;
   his light will judge and, judging, heal.

4. Awake, and rise up from the dead,
   and Christ his light on you will shed.
   Its power will wrong desires destroy,
   and your whole nature fill with joy.

5. Then sing for joy, and use each day;
   give thanks for everything alway.
   Lift up your hearts; with one accord
   praise God through Jesus Christ our
   Lord.

57
Thomas Ken (1637-1711) alt.

1. Awake, my soul, and with the sun
   thy daily stage of duty run;
   shake off dull sloth, and joyful rise
   to pay thy morning sacrifice.

2. Redeem thy mis-spent time that's past,
   and live this day as if thy last;
   improve thy talent with due care;
   for the great day thyself prepare.

3. Let all thy converse be sincere,
   thy conscience as the noon-day clear;
   think how all-seeing God thy ways
   and all thy secret thoughts surveys.

4. Wake, and lift up thyself, my heart,
and with the angels bear thy part,
who all night long unwearied sing
high praise to the eternal King.

5. Glory to thee, who safe hast kept
and hast refreshed me whilst I slept;
grant, Lord, when I from death shall
wake,
I may of endless light partake.

6. Lord, I my vows to thee renew;
disperse my sins as morning dew;
guard my first springs of thought and
will,
and with thyself my spirit fill.

7. Direct, control, suggest, this day,
all I design or do or say;
that all my powers, with all their
might,
in thy sole glory may unite.

8. Praise God, from whom all blessings
flow,
praise him, all creatures here below,
praise him above, angelic host,
praise Father, Son and Holy Ghost.

58
Isaac Watts (1674-1748) based on Isaiah 40:28-31

1. Awake, our souls; away, our fears;
let every trembling thought be gone;
awake and run the heavenly race,
and put a cheerful courage on.

2. True, 'tis a strait and thorny road,
and mortal spirits tire and faint;
but they forget the mighty God
that feeds the strength of every saint.

3. The mighty God, whose matchless
power
is ever new and ever young,
and firm endures, while endless years
their everlasting circles run.

4. From thee, the overflowing spring,
our souls shall drink a fresh supply,
while such as trust their native strength
shall melt away, and droop, and die.

5. Swift as an eagle cuts the air,
we'll mount aloft to thine abode;
on wings of love our souls shall fly,
nor tire amidst the heavenly road.

59
Original text: William James Kirkpatrick (1838-1921)
Alternative text, vs. 2 & 3: Michael Forster (b. 1946)
Alternative verses 2 and 3 © 1996 Kevin Mayhew Ltd

1. Away in a manger,
no crib for a bed,
the little Lord Jesus
laid down his sweet head.
The stars in the bright sky
looked down where he lay,
the little Lord Jesus,
asleep on the hay.

2. The cattle are lowing,
the baby awakes,
but little Lord Jesus
no crying he makes.
I love thee, Lord Jesus!
Look down from the sky,
and stay by my side
until morning is nigh.

3. Be near me, Lord Jesus;
I ask thee to stay
close by me for ever,
and love me, I pray.
Bless all the dear children
in thy tender care,
and fit us for heaven,
to live with thee there.

Continued overleaf

An alternative version

1. Away in a manger,
   no crib for a bed,
   the little Lord Jesus
   laid down his sweet head.
   The stars in the bright sky
   looked down where he lay,
   the little Lord Jesus,
   asleep on the hay.

2. The cattle are lowing,
   they also adore
   the little Lord Jesus
   who lies in the straw.
   I love you, Lord Jesus,
   I know you are near
   to love and protect me
   till morning is here.

3. Be near me, Lord Jesus;
   I ask you to stay
   close by me for ever,
   and love me, I pray.
   Bless all the dear children
   in your tender care,
   prepare us for heaven,
   to live with you there.

60 Morris Chapman
© 1983 Word Music. Administered by CopyCare

Be bold, be strong,
for the Lord, your God, is with you.
Be bold, be strong,
for the Lord, your God, is with you.
I am not afraid, I am not dismayed,
because I'm walking in faith and
   victory,
come on and walk in faith and victory,
for the Lord, your God, is with you.

61 Unknown, based on Psalm 46

1. Be still and know that I am God. *(x3)*

2. I am the Lord that healeth thee. *(x3)*

3. In thee, O Lord, I put my trust. *(x3)*

62 David J. Evans (b. 1957)
© 1986 Thankyou Music

1. Be still, for the presence of the Lord,
   the Holy One, is here.
   Come, bow before him now,
   with reverence and fear.
   In him no sin is found,
   we stand on holy ground.
   Be still, for the presence of the Lord,
   the Holy One, is here.

2. Be still, for the glory of the Lord
   is shining all around;
   he burns with holy fire,
   with splendour he is crowned.
   How awesome is the sight,
   our radiant King of light!
   Be still, for the glory of the Lord
   is shining all around.

3. Be still, for the power of the Lord
   is moving in this place;
   he comes to cleanse and heal,
   to minister his grace.
   No work too hard for him,
   in faith receive from him.
   Be still, for the power of the Lord
   is moving in this place.

63

Katherina von Schlegel (b. 1697)
trans. Jane L. Borthwick (1813-1897), alt.

1. Be still, my soul: the Lord is at your
   side;
   bear patiently the cross of grief and
   pain;
   leave to your God to order and provide;
   in every change he faithful will remain.
   Be still, my soul: your best, your
   heavenly friend,
   through thorny ways, leads to a joyful
   end.

2. Be still, my soul: your God will
   undertake
   to guide the future as he has the past.
   Your hope, your confidence let
   nothing shake,
   all now mysterious shall be clear at last.
   Be still, my soul: the tempests still obey
   his voice, who ruled them once on
   Galilee.

3. Be still, my soul: the hour is
   hastening on
   when we shall be for ever with the
   Lord,
   when disappointment, grief and fear
   are gone,
   sorrow forgotten, love's pure joy
   restored.
   Be still, my soul: when change and
   tears are past,
   all safe and blessèd we shall meet at
   last.

64

Alan J. Price
© 1990 Daybreak Music Ltd

1. Be the centre of my life, Lord Jesus,
   be the centre of my life, I pray;
   be my Saviour to forgive me,
   be my friend to be with me,
   be the centre of my life today!

2. Let the power of your presence,
   Lord Jesus,
   from the centre of my life shine
   through;
   oh, let everybody know it,
   I really want to show it,
   that the centre of my life is you!

65

Isaac Williams (1802-1865)

1. Be thou my guardian and my guide,
   and hear me when I call;
   let not my slipp'ry footsteps slide,
   and hold me lest I fall.

2. The world, the flesh, and Satan dwell
   around the path I tread;
   O save me from the snares of hell,
   thou quick'ner of the dead.

3. And if I tempted am to sin,
   and outward things are strong,
   do thou, O Lord, keep watch within,
   and save my soul from wrong.

4. Still let me ever watch and pray,
   and feel that I am frail;
   that if the tempter cross my way,
   yet he may not prevail.

66

Irish 8th century, trans. Mary Byrne (1880-1931)
and Eleanor Hull (1860-1935)

1. Be thou my vision, O Lord of my
   heart,
   naught be all else to me save that
   thou art;
   thou my best thought in the day and
   the night,
   waking or sleeping, thy presence my
   light.

Continued overleaf

2. Be thou my wisdom, be thou my
   true word,
   I ever with thee and thou with me,
   Lord;
   thou my great Father, and I thy true
   heir;
   thou in me dwelling, and I in thy care.

3. Be thou my breastplate, my sword for
   the fight,
   be thou my armour, and be thou my
   might,
   thou my soul's shelter, and thou my
   high tower,
   raise thou me heavenward, O Power
   of my power.

4. Riches I need not, nor all the world's
   praise,
   thou mine inheritance through all
   my days;
   thou, and thou only, the first in my
   heart,
   High King of heaven, my treasure
   thou art!

5. High King of heaven, when battle is
   done,
   grant heaven's joy to me, O bright
   heaven's sun;
   Christ of my own heart, whatever
   befall,
   still be my vision, O Ruler of all.

67 Graham Kendrick (b. 1950)
    © 1993 Make Way Music

1. Beauty for brokenness,
   hope for despair,
   Lord, in the suffering,
   this is our prayer.
   Bread for the children,
   justice, joy, peace,
   sunrise to sunset
   your kingdom increase.

2. Shelter for fragile lives,
   cures for their ills,
   work for the craftsmen,
   trade for their skills.
   Land for the dispossessed,
   rights for the weak,
   voices to plead the cause
   of those who can't speak.

God of the poor,
friend of the weak,
give us compassion, we pray,
melt our cold hearts,
let tears fall like rain.
Come, change our love
from a spark to a flame.

3. Refuge from cruel wars,
   havens from fear,
   cities for sanctuary,
   freedoms to share.
   Peace to the killing fields,
   scorched earth to green,
   Christ for the bitterness,
   his cross for the pain.

4. Rest for the ravaged earth,
   oceans and streams,
   plundered and poisoned,
   our future, our dreams.
   Lord, end our madness,
   carelessness, greed;
   make us content with
   the things that we need.

5. Lighten our darkness,
   breathe on this flame,
   until your justice
   burns brightly again;
   until the nations
   learn of your ways,
   seek your salvation
   and bring you their praise.

68 Isaac Watts (1674-1748) based on Psalm 100

1. Before Jehovah's aweful throne,
   ye nations, bow with sacred joy;
   know that the Lord is God alone:
   he can create, and he destroy.

2. His sovereign power, without our aid,
   made us of clay, and formed us then;
   and, when like wand'ring sheep we
      strayed,
   he brought us to his fold again.

3. We'll crown thy gates with thankful
      songs,
   high as the heavens our voices raise;
   and earth, with her ten thousand
      tongues,
   shall fill thy courts with sounding
      praise.

4. Wide as the world is thy command,
   vast as eternity thy love;
   firm as a rock thy truth must stand,
   when rolling years shall cease to move.

69 'Te lucis ante terminum' before 8th century
   trans. John Mason Neale (1818-1866)

1. Before the ending of the day,
   Creator of the world, we pray,
   that with thy wonted favour thou
   wouldst be our guard and keeper now.

2. From all ill dreams defend our eyes,
   from nightly fears and fantasies;
   tread under foot our ghostly foe,
   that no pollution we may know.

3. O Father, that we ask be done,
   through Jesus Christ thine only Son,
   who, with the Holy Ghost and thee,
   doth live and reign eternally. Amen.

70 Charitie L. Bancroft (1841-1923), *adapted by Vikki Cook.* © *1993 PDI Worship. Administered by CopyCare*

1. Before the throne of God above
   I have a strong, a perfect plea,
   a great High Priest whose name is
      Love,
   who ever lives and pleads for me.
   My name is graven on his hands,
   my name is written on his heart;
   I know that while in heaven he stands
   no tongue can bid me thence depart,
   no tongue can bid me thence depart.

2. When Satan tempts me to despair,
   and tells me of the guilt within,
   upward I look and see him there
   who made an end to all my sin.
   Because the sinless Saviour died,
   my sinful soul is counted free;
   for God, the Just, is satisfied
   to look on him and pardon me,
   to look on him and pardon me.

3. Behold him there! The risen Lamb,
   my perfect, spotless righteousness;
   the great unchangeable I AM,
   the King of glory and of grace!
   One with himself I cannot die,
   my soul is purchased with his blood;
   my life is hid with Christ on high,
   with Christ, my Saviour and my God,
   with Christ, my Saviour and my God.

4. I bow before the cross of Christ,
   and marvel at this love divine;
   God's perfect Son was sacrificed
   to make me righteous in God's eyes.
   This river's depths I cannot know
   but I can glory in its flood,
   the Lord Most High has bowed
      down low
   and poured on me his glorious love,
   and poured on me his glorious love.

71

Thomas Pestel (1585-1659)

1. Behold, the great Creator
   makes himself a house of clay,
   a robe of virgin flesh he takes
   which he will wear for aye.

2. Hark, hark! the wise eternal Word
   like a weak infant cries;
   in form of servant is the Lord,
   and God in cradle lies.

3. This wonder struck the world amazed,
   it shook the starry frame;
   squadrons of spirits stood and gazed,
   then down in troops they came.

4. Glad shepherds ran to view this sight;
   a choir of angels sings,
   and eastern sages with delight
   adore this King of kings.

5. Join then, all hearts that are not stone,
   and all our voices prove,
   to celebrate this Holy One,
   the God of peace and love.

72

Elizabeth C. Clephane (1830-1869) alt.

1. Beneath the cross of Jesus
   I fain would take my stand,
   the shadow of a mighty rock
   within a weary land;
   a home within a wilderness,
   a rest upon the way,
   from burning heat at noontide and
   the burden of the day.

2. O safe and happy shelter!
   O refuge tried and sweet!
   O trysting place where heaven's love
   and heaven's justice meet!

As to the holy patriarch
that wondrous dream was given,
so seems my Saviour's cross to me
a ladder up to heaven.

3. There lies, beneath its shadow,
   but on the farther side,
   the darkness of an awful grave
   that gapes both deep and wide;
   and there between us stands the cross,
   two arms outstretched to save;
   a watchman set to guard the way
   from that eternal grave.

4. Upon that cross of Jesus
   mine eye at times can see
   the very dying form of One
   who suffered there for me;
   and from my stricken heart, with tears,
   two wonders I confess –
   the wonders of redeeming love,
   and my unworthiness.

5. I take, O cross, thy shadow
   for my abiding place!
   I ask no other sunshine than
   the sunshine of his face;
   content to let the world go by,
   to reckon gain as loss –
   my sinful self, my only shame,
   my glory all – the cross.

73

Bob Gillman (b. 1946)
© 1977 Thankyou Music

Bind us together, Lord,
bind us together with cords
that cannot be broken.
Bind us together, Lord,
bind us together, Lord,
bind us together in love.

1. There is only one God,
   there is only one King.
   There is only one Body,
   that is why we sing:

2. Fit for the glory of God,
   purchased by his precious Blood,
   born with the right to be free:
   Jesus the vict'ry has won.

3. We are the fam'ly of God,
   we are his promise divine,
   we are his chosen desire,
   we are the glorious new wine.

74 Taizé Community, from Psalm 103
© Ateliers et Presses de Taizé

Bless the Lord, my soul,
and bless God's holy name.
Bless the Lord, my soul,
who leads me into life.

1. It is God who forgives all your guilt,
   who heals every one of your ills,
   who redeems your life from the grave,
   who crowns you with love and
      compassion.

2. The Lord is compassion and love,
   the Lord is patient and rich in mercy.
   God does not treat us according to
      our sins
   nor repay us according to our faults.

3. As a father has compassion on his
      children,
   the Lord has mercy on those who
      revere him;
   for God knows of what we are made,
   and remembers that we are dust.

75 Frances Jane van Alstyne
(Fanny J. Crosby) (1820-1915)

1. Blessèd assurance, Jesus is mine:
   O what a foretaste of glory divine!
   Heir of salvation, purchase of God;
   born of his Spirit, washed in his blood.

   This is my story, this is my song,
   praising my Saviour all the day long.
   (Repeat)

2. Perfect submission, perfect delight,
   visions of rapture burst on my sight;
   angels descending, bring from above
   echoes of mercy, whispers of love.

3. Perfect submission, all is at rest,
   I in my Saviour am happy and blest;
   watching and waiting, looking above,
   filled with his goodness, lost in his
      love.

76 Beth Redman and Matt Redman
© 2002 Thankyou Music

1. Blessèd be your name
   in the land that is plentiful,
   where your streams of abundance flow,
   blessèd be your name.
   And blessèd be your name
   when I'm found in the desert place,
   though I walk through the wilderness,
   blessèd be your name.
   Every blessing you pour out
   I'll turn back to praise.
   And when the darkness closes in, Lord,
   still I will say:

   Blessèd be the name of the Lord,
   blessèd be your name.
   Blessèd be the name of the Lord,
   blessèd be your glorious name.

Continued overleaf

2. Blessèd be your name
when the sun's shining down on me,
when the world's 'all as it should be',
blessèd be your name.
And blessèd be your name
on the road marked with suffering,
though there's pain in the offering,
blessèd be your name.
Every blessing you pour out
I'll turn back to praise.
And when the darkness closes in, Lord,
still I will say:

Blessèd be the name of the Lord,
blessèd be your name.
Blessèd be the name of the Lord,
blessèd be your glorious name.

You give and take away,
you give and take away.
My heart will choose to say,
'Lord, blessèd be your name.'
(Repeat)

Blessèd be the name of the Lord,
blessèd be your name.
Blessèd be the name of the Lord,
blessèd be your glorious name.

77 Latin, before 9th century
trans. John Mason Neale (1818-1866)

1. Blessèd city, heavenly Salem,
vision dear of peace and love,
who of living stones art builded
in the height of heaven above,
and with angel hosts encircled
as a bride dost earthward move.

2. Christ is made the sure foundation,
Christ the Head and cornerstone,
chosen of the Lord, and precious,
binding all the Church as one,
Holy Sion's help for ever,
and her confidence alone.

3. To this temple, where we call thee,
come, O Lord of hosts, today;
with thy wonted loving-kindness,
hear thy servants as they pray;
and thy fullest benediction
shed within its walls alway.

4. Here vouchsafe to all thy servants
what they ask of thee to gain,
what they gain from thee for ever
with the blessèd to retain,
and hereafter in thy glory
evermore with thee to reign.

78 Gary Sadler and Jamie Harvill
© 1992 Integrity's Hosanna! Music/Integrity's Praise!
Music/Sovereign Music UK

Blessing and honour, glory and power
be unto the Ancient of Days;
from every nation, all of creation
bow before the Ancient of Days.

Every tongue in heaven and earth
shall declare your glory,
every knee shall bow at your throne in
worship;
you will be exalted, O God,
and your kingdom shall not pass away,
O Ancient of Days.

Your kingdom shall reign over all the
earth:
sing unto the Ancient of Days.
For none shall compare to your
matchless worth:
sing unto the Ancient of Days.

79 vs. 1 and 3 John Keble (1792-1866)
vs. 2 and 4 William John Hall (1793-1861)
Psalms and Hymns (1836) alt.

1. Blest are the pure in heart,
for they shall see our God;
the secret of the Lord is theirs,
their soul is Christ's abode.

2. The Lord who left the heavens
   our life and peace to bring,
   to dwell in lowliness with us,
   our pattern and our King.

3. Still to the lowly soul
   he doth himself impart,
   and for his dwelling and his throne
   chooseth the pure in heart.

4. Lord, we thy presence seek;
   may ours this blessing be:
   give us a pure and lowly heart,
   a temple meet for thee.

80 'Lucis Creator Optime'
trans. unknown

1. Blest Creator of the light,
   making day with radiance bright,
   thou didst o'er the forming earth
   give the golden light its birth.

2. Thou didst mark the night from day
   with the dawn's first piercing ray;
   darkness now is drawing nigh;
   listen to our humble cry.

3. May we ne'er by guilt depressed
   lose the way to endless rest;
   nor with idle thoughts and vain
   bind our souls to earth again.

4. Rather may we heavenward rise
   where eternal treasure lies;
   purified by grace within,
   hating every deed of sin.

5. Holy Father, hear our cry
   through thy Son our Lord most high,
   whom our thankful hearts adore
   with the Spirit evermore.

81 Geoffrey Ainger (b. 1925)
© 1964 Stainer & Bell Ltd

1. Born in the night, Mary's child,
   a long way from your home;
   coming in need, Mary's child,
   born in a borrowed room.

2. Clear shining light, Mary's child,
   your face lights up our way;
   light of the world, Mary's child,
   dawn on our darkened day.

3. Truth of our life, Mary's child,
   you tell us God is good;
   prove it is true, Mary's child,
   go to your cross of wood.

4. Hope of the world, Mary's child,
   you're coming soon to reign;
   King of the earth, Mary's child,
   walk in our streets again.

82 John L. Bell (b. 1949) and Graham Maule (b. 1958)
© 1989 WGRG, Iona Community

1. Bread is blessed and broken,
   wine is blessed and poured:
   take this and remember
   Christ the Lord.

2. Share the food of heaven
   earth cannot afford.
   Here is grace in essence –
   Christ the Lord.

3. Know yourself forgiven,
   find yourself restored,
   meet a friend for ever –
   Christ the Lord.

4. God has kept his promise
   sealed by sign and word:
   here, for those who want him –
   Christ the Lord.

83 Josiah Conder (1789-1855)

1. Bread of heaven, on thee we feed,
   for thy flesh is meat indeed;
   ever may our souls be fed
   with this true and living bread;
   day by day with strength supplied
   through the life of him who died.

2. Vine of heaven, thy blood supplies
   this blest cup of sacrifice;
   Lord, thy wounds our healing give,
   to thy cross we look and live:
   Jesus, may we ever be
   grafted, rooted, built in thee.

84 Reginald Heber (1783-1826)

1. Bread of the world in mercy broken,
   wine of the soul in mercy shed,
   by whom the words of life were
       spoken,
   and in whose death our sins are dead.

2. Look on the heart by sorrows broken,
   look on the tears by sinners shed;
   and be thy feast to us the token
   that by thy grace our souls are fed.

85 Michael Forster (b. 1946)
© 1993 Kevin Mayhew Ltd

Break the bread and pour the wine,
break the bread and pour the wine,
break the bread and pour the wine,
share a meal with Jesus,
share a meal with Jesus.

1. Come and meet around the table,
   God prepares the holy food;
   we can share with one another
   everything we have that's good.

2. Come and meet around the table,
   God provides the wine to share;
   we enjoy a meal together,
   show each other how we care.

86 v. 1 Mary Artemisia Lathbury (1841-1913)
vs. 2 & 3 Alexander Groves (1842-1909)

1. Break thou the bread of life,
   O Lord, to me,
   as thou didst break the loaves
   beside the sea.
   Beyond the sacred page
   I seek thee, Lord;
   my spirit longs for thee,
   O living Word!

2. Thou art the Bread of Life,
   O Lord, to me,
   thy holy word the truth
   that saveth me;
   give me to eat and live
   with thee above;
   teach me to love thy truth,
   for thou art love.

3. O send thy Spirit, Lord,
   now unto me,
   that he may touch my eyes,
   and make me see;
   show me the truth concealed
   within thy word,
   and in thy book revealed
   I see thee, Lord.

87 Edwin Hatch (1835-1889) alt.
This version © 1999 Kevin Mayhew Ltd

1. Breathe on me, Breath of God,
   fill me with life anew,
   that as you love, so may I love,
   and do what you would do.

2. Breathe on me, Breath of God,
   until my heart is pure:
   until my will is one with yours
   to do and to endure.

3. Breathe on me, Breath of God,
   fulfil my heart's desire,
   until this earthly part of me
   glows with your heavenly fire.

4. Breathe on me, Breath of God,
   so shall I never die,
   but live with you the perfect life
   of your eternity.

88 Richard Mant (1776-1848)

1. Bright the vision that delighted
   once the sight of Judah's seer;
   sweet the countless tongues united
   to entrance the prophet's ear.

2. Round the Lord in glory seated
   cherubim and seraphim
   filled his temple, and repeated
   each to each the alternate hymn:

3. 'Lord, thy glory fills the heaven;
   earth is with its fullness stored;
   unto thee be glory given,
   holy, holy, holy, Lord.'

4. Heaven is still with glory ringing,
   earth takes up the angels' cry,
   'Holy, holy, holy,' singing,
   'Lord of hosts, the Lord most high.'

5. With his seraph train before him,
   with his holy Church below,
   thus unite we to adore him,
   bid we thus our anthem flow:

6. 'Lord, thy glory fills the heaven;
   earth is with its fullness stored;
   unto thee be glory given,
   holy, holy, holy, Lord.'

89 Reginald Heber (1783-1826)

1. Brightest and best
   of the suns of the morning,
   dawn on our darkness
   and lend us thine aid;
   star of the east,
   the horizon adorning,
   guide where our infant
   Redeemer is laid.

2. Cold on his cradle
   the dew-drops are shining;
   low lies his head
   with the beasts of the stall;
   angels adore him
   in slumber reclining,
   Maker and Monarch
   and Saviour of all.

3. Say, shall we yield him,
   in costly devotion,
   odours of Edom,
   and off'rings divine,
   gems of the mountain,
   and pearls of the ocean,
   myrrh from the forest,
   or gold from the mine?

4. Vainly we offer
   each humble oblation,
   vainly with gifts
   would his favour secure:
   richer by far
   is the heart's adoration,
   dearer to God
   are the prayers of the poor.

90

Janet Lunt (b. 1954)
© 1978 Sovereign Music UK

*Broken for me, broken for you,
the body of Jesus, broken for you.*

1. He offered his body, he poured out
   his soul;
   Jesus was broken, that we might be
   whole.

2. Come to my table and with me dine;
   eat of my bread and drink of my wine.

3. This is my body given for you;
   eat it remembering I died for you.

4. This is my blood I shed for you,
   for your forgiveness, making you new.

91

Richard Gillard (b. 1953)
© 1977 Scripture in Song, a division of Integrity
Music/Copycare

1. Brother, sister, let me serve you,
   let me be as Christ to you;
   pray that I may have the grace to
   let you be my servant, too.

2. We are pilgrims on a journey,
   fellow trav'llers on the road;
   we are here to help each other
   walk the mile and bear the load.

3. I will hold the Christlight for you
   in the night-time of your fear;
   I will hold my hand out to you,
   speak the peace you long to hear.

4. I will weep when you are weeping;
   when you laugh, I'll laugh with you.
   I will share your joy and sorrow
   till we've seen this journey through.

5. When we sing to God in heaven,
   we shall find such harmony,
   born of all we've known together
   of Christ's love and agony.

6. Brother, sister, let me serve you,
   let me be as Christ to you;
   pray that I may have the grace to
   let you be my servant, too.

92

David Adam (b. 1936)
© SPCK

Calm me, Lord, as you calmed the
   storm;
still me, Lord, keep me from harm.
Let all the tumult within me cease;
enfold me, Lord, in your peace.

Last time:
Lord, enfold me in your peace.

93

From the Liturgy
© 1985 Fintan O'Carroll

Alleluia, alleluia,
alleluia, alleluia.

94

Ascribed to St Patrick
trans. Cecil Frances Alexander (1818-1895)

1. Christ be with me, Christ within me,
   Christ behind me, Christ before me,
   Christ beside me, Christ to guide me,
   Christ to comfort and restore me.

2. Christ beneath me, Christ above me,
   Christ in quiet, Christ in danger,
   Christ in hearts of all that love me,
   Christ in care of friend and stranger.

95

Samuel Wolcott (1813-1886)

1. Christ for the world we sing!
   The world to Christ we bring
   with fervent prayer;
   the wayward and the lost,
   by restless passions tossed,
   redeemed at countless cost
   from dark despair.

2. Christ for the world we sing!
   The world to Christ we bring
   with one accord;
   with us the work to share,
   with us reproach to dare,
   with us the cross to bear,
   for Christ our Lord.

3. Christ for the world we sing!
   The world to Christ we bring
   with joyful song;
   the new-born souls, whose days,
   reclaimed from error's ways,
   inspired with hope and praise,
   to Christ belong.

96 'Urbs beata Jerusalem' (c.7th century)
trans. John Mason Neale (1818-1866) alt.

1. Christ is made the sure foundation,
   Christ the head and cornerstone,
   chosen of the Lord, and precious,
   binding all the Church in one,
   holy Zion's help for ever,
   and her confidence alone.

2. To this temple, where we call you,
   come, O Lord of hosts, today;
   you have promised loving kindness,
   hear your servants as we pray,
   bless your people now before you,
   turn our darkness into day.

3. Hear the cry of all your people,
   what they ask and hope to gain;
   what they gain from you, for ever
   with your chosen to retain,
   and hereafter in your glory
   evermore with you to reign.

4. Praise and honour to the Father,
   praise and honour to the Son,
   praise and honour to the Spirit,
   ever Three and ever One,
   One in might and One in glory,
   while unending ages run.

97 Latin, before 9th century
trans. John Chandler (1806-1876)

1. Christ is our cornerstone,
   on him alone we build;
   with his true saints alone
   the courts of heaven are filled:
   on his great love our hopes we place
   of present grace and joys above.

2. O then with hymns of praise
   these hallowed courts shall ring;
   our voices we will raise
   the Three in One to sing;
   and thus proclaim in joyful song,
   both loud and long, that glorious
   name.

3. Here, gracious God, do thou
   for evermore draw nigh;
   accept each faithful vow,
   and mark each suppliant sigh;
   in copious shower on all who pray
   each holy day thy blessings pour.

4. Here may we gain from heaven
   the grace which we implore;
   and may that grace, once given,
   be with us evermore,
   until that day when all the blest
   to endless rest are called away.

98 Timothy Rees (1874-1939)
© Continuum International Publishing Group Ltd

1. Christ is the heavenly food
   that gives to every famished soul
   new life and strength,
   new joy and hope,
   and faith to make them whole.

2. We all are made for God alone,
   without him we are dead;
   no food suffices for the soul
   but Christ, the living bread.

Continued overleaf

3. Christ is the unity that binds,
   in one the near and far;
   for we who share his life divine
   his living body are.

4. On earth and in the realms beyond
   one fellowship are we;
   and at his altar we are knit
   in mystic unity.

99 G. K. A. Bell (1883-1958)
© *Oxford University Press*

1. Christ is the King! O friends rejoice;
   brothers and sisters with one voice
   tell all the world he is your choice.
   Alleluia, alleluia, alleluia.

2. O magnify the Lord, and raise
   anthems of joy and holy praise
   for Christ's brave saints of ancient days.
   Alleluia.

3. They with a faith for ever new
   followed the King, and round him
     drew
   thousands of faithful hearts and true.
   Alleluia.

4. O Christian women, Christian men,
   all the world over, seek again
   the way disciples followed then.
   Alleluia.

5. Christ through all ages is the same:
   place the same hope in his great name,
   with the same faith his word proclaim.
   Alleluia.

6. Let love's unconquerable might
   your scattered companies unite
   in service to the Lord of light.
   Alleluia.

7. So shall God's will on earth be done,
   new lamps be lit, new tasks begun,
   and the whole church at last be one.
   Alleluia.

100 Fred Pratt Green (1903-2000)
© *1969 Stainer & Bell Ltd*

1. Christ is the world's Light, he and
     none other:
   born in our darkness, he became our
     Brother;
   if we have seen him, we have seen the
     Father:
   Glory to God on high.

2. Christ is the world's Peace, he and
     none other;
   no one can serve him and despise
     another;
   who else unites us, one in God the
     Father?
   Glory to God on high.

3. Christ is the world's Life, he and
     none other;
   sold once for silver, murdered here,
     our Brother –
   he who redeems us, reigns with God
     the Father:
   Glory to God on high.

4. Give God the glory, God and none
     other;
   give God the glory, Spirit, Son and
     Father;
   give God the glory, God in Man my
     Brother:
   Glory to God on high.

101

Ascribed to Rabanus Maurus (776-856), trans.
C. S. Phillips (1883-1949)
© Hymns Ancient & Modern Ltd

1. Christ, the fair glory of the holy angels,
   ruler of all, and author of creation,
   grant us in mercy grace to win by
       patience
   joys everlasting.

2. Send thine archangel, Michael from
       thy presence;
   peacemaker blessèd, may he hover
       o'er us,
   hallow our dwellings, that for us thy
       children
   all things may prosper.

3. Send thine archangel, Gabriel the
       mighty:
   on strong wings flying, may he come
       from heaven,
   drive from thy temple Satan the old
       foeman,
   succour our weakness.

4. Send thine archangel, Raphael the
       healer:
   through him with wholesome
       med'cines of salvation
   heal our backsliding, and in paths of
       goodness
   guide our steps daily.

5. Father almighty, Son, and Holy Spirit,
   Godhead eternal, grant us our petition;
   thine be the glory through the whole
       creation
   now and for ever.

2. He who gave for us his life,
   who for us endured the strife,
   is our paschal Lamb today;
   we too sing for joy, and say:
   Alleluia.

*3. He who bore all pain and loss
   comfortless upon the cross,
   lives in glory now on high,
   pleads for us, and hears our cry:
   Alleluia.

*4. He whose path no records tell,
   who descended into hell,
   who the strongest arm hath bound,
   now in highest heaven is crowned.
   Alleluia.

*5. He who slumbered in the grave
   is exalted now to save;
   now through Christendom it rings
   that the Lamb is King of kings.
   Alleluia.

6. Now he bids us tell abroad
   how the lost may be restored,
   how the penitent forgiven,
   how we too may enter heaven.
   Alleluia.

7. Christ, our paschal Lamb indeed,
   you, your ransomed people feed;
   take our sins and guilt away;
   let us sing by night and day:
   Alleluia.

102

Michael Weisse (c. 1480-1534)
trans. Catherine Winkworth (1827-1878) alt.

1. Christ the Lord is ris'n again,
   Christ hath broken every chain.
   Hark, angelic voices cry,
   singing evermore on high:
   Alleluia.

103

Michael Saward (b. 1932)
© Michael Saward/Jubilate Hymns

1. Christ triumphant, ever reigning,
   Saviour, Master, King.
   Lord of heaven, our lives sustaining,
   hear us as we sing:

Continued overleaf

Yours the glory and the crown,
the high renown, th'eternal name.

2. Word incarnate, truth revealing,
   Son of Man on earth!
   Power and majesty concealing
   by your humble birth:

3. Suffering servant, scorned, ill-treated,
   victim crucified!
   Death is through the cross defeated,
   sinners justified:

4. Priestly King, enthroned for ever
   high in heaven above!
   Sin and death and hell shall never
   stifle hymns of love:

5. So, our hearts and voices raising
   through the ages long,
   ceaselessly upon you gazing,
   this shall be our song:

105 Charles Wesley (1707-1788)

1. Christ, whose glory fills the skies,
   Christ, the true, the only light,
   Sun of Righteousness, arise,
   triumph o'er the shades of night;
   Dayspring from on high, be near;
   Daystar, in my heart appear.

2. Dark and cheerless is the morn
   unaccompanied by thee;
   joyless is the day's return,
   till thy mercy's beams I see,
   till they inward light impart,
   glad my eyes, and warm my heart.

3. Visit then this soul of mine,
   pierce the gloom of sin and grief;
   fill me, radiancy divine,
   scatter all my unbelief;
   more and more thyself display,
   shining to the perfect day.

104 F. Bland Tucker (1895-1984)
© *Church Publishing Inc.*

1. Christ, when for us you were baptised
   God's Spirit on you came,
   as peaceful as a dove,
   and yet as urgent as a flame.

2. God called you his belovèd Son,
   called you his servant too;
   his kingdom you were called to preach,
   his holy will to do.

3. Straightway and steadfast until death
   you then obeyed his call,
   freely as Son of Man to serve,
   and give your life for all.

4. Baptise us with your Spirit, Lord,
   your cross on us be signed,
   that likewise in God's service, we
   may perfect freedom find.

106 Colin P. Thompson
© *C. P. Thompson*

1. Christian people, raise your song,
   chase away all grieving;
   sing your joy and be made strong,
   our Lord's life receiving;
   nature's gifts of wheat and vine
   now are set before us:
   as we offer bread and wine
   Christ comes to restore us.

2. Come to welcome Christ today,
   God's great revelation;
   he has pioneered the way
   of the new creation.
   Greet him, Christ our risen King
   gladly recognising,
   as with joy we greet the spring
   out of winter rising.

107 John Byrom (1692-1763) alt.

1. Christians, awake! salute the happy
   morn,
   whereon the Saviour of the world
   was born;
   rise to adore the mystery of love,
   which hosts of angels chanted from
   above:
   with them the joyful tidings first begun
   of God incarnate and the Virgin's Son.

*2. Then to the watchful shepherds it
   was told,
   who heard th'angelic herald's voice,
   'Behold,
   I bring good tidings of a Saviour's
   birth
   to you and all the nations on the earth:
   this day hath God fulfilled his
   promised word,
   this day is born a Saviour, Christ the
   Lord.'

*3. He spake; and straightway the
   celestial choir
   in hymns of joy, unknown before,
   conspire;
   the praises of redeeming love they
   sang,
   and heaven's whole orb with alleluias
   rang:
   God's highest glory was their anthem
   still,
   peace on the earth, in every heart
   good will.

*4. To Beth'lem straight th'enlightened
   shepherds ran,
   to see, unfolding, God's eternal plan,
   and found, with Joseph and the
   blessèd maid,
   her Son, the Saviour, in a manger
   laid:

then to their flocks, still praising
   God, return,
   and their glad hearts with holy
   rapture burn.

5. O may we keep and ponder in our
   mind
   God's wondrous love in saving lost
   mankind;
   trace we the babe, who hath
   retrieved our loss,
   from his poor manger to his bitter
   cross;
   tread in his steps, assisted by his grace,
   till our first heavenly state again
   takes place.

6. Then may we hope, th'angelic hosts
   among,
   to sing, redeemed, a glad triumphal
   song:
   he that was born upon this joyful day
   around us all his glory shall display;
   saved by his love, incessant we shall
   sing
   eternal praise to heaven's almighty
   King.

108 John E. Bowers (b. 1923)
© *John E. Bowers*

v.1 is repeated as a Refrain after vs. 2-7.

1. *Christians, lift up your hearts,*
   and make this a day of rejoicing;
   God is our strength and song;
   glory and praise to his name!

2. Praise for the Spirit of God,
   who came to the waiting disciples;
   there in the wind and the fire
   God gave new life to his own:

Continued overleaf

3. God's mighty power was revealed
   when those who once were so fearful
   now could be seen by the world
   witnessing bravely for Christ:

   Christians, lift up your hearts,
   and make this a day of rejoicing;
   God is our strength and song;
   glory and praise to his name!

4. Praise that his love overflowed
   in the hearts of all who received him,
   joining together in peace
   those once divided by sin:

5. Strengthened by God's mighty power
   the disciples went out to all nations,
   preaching the gospel of Christ,
   laughing at danger and death:

6. Come, Holy Spirit, to us,
   who live by your presence within us,
   come to direct our course,
   give us your life and your power:

7. Spirit of God, send us out
   to live to your praise and your glory;
   yours is the power and the might,
   ours be the courage and faith:

109 John E. Bowers (b. 1923)
© John E. Bowers

1. Christians, lift your hearts and voices,
   let your praises be outpoured;
   come with joy and exultation
   to the table of the Lord;
   come believing, come expectant,
   in obedience to his word.

2. See, presiding at his table,
   Jesus Christ our great High Priest;
   where he summons all his people,
   none is greatest, none is least;
   graciously he bids them welcome
   to the eucharistic feast.

3. Lord, we offer in thanksgiving
   life and work for you to bless;
   yet unworthy is the off'ring,
   marred by pride and carelessness;
   so, Lord, pardon our transgressions,
   plant in us true holiness.

4. On the evening of his passion
   Jesus gave the wine and bread,
   so that all who love and serve him
   shall for evermore be fed.
   Taste and see the Lord is gracious,
   feed upon the living bread.

110 John L. Bell (b. 1949) and Graham Maule
(b. 1958). *© 1989 WGRG, Iona Community*

1. Christ's is the world in which we
      move,
   Christ's are the folk we're summoned
      to love,
   Christ's is the voice which calls us to
      care,
   and Christ is the one who calls us here.

   To the lost Christ shows his face;
   to the unloved he gives his embrace;
   to those who cry in pain or disgrace,
   Christ makes with his friends a
      touching place.

2. Feel for the people we most avoid,
   strange or bereaved or never employed;
   feel for the women, and feel for the
      men
   who fear that their living is all in vain.

3. Feel for the parents who've lost their
      child,
   feel for the women whom men have
      defiled,
   feel for the baby for whom there's no
      breast,
   and feel for the weary who find no rest.

4. Feel for the lives by life confused,
   riddled with doubt, in loving abused;
   feel for the lonely heart, conscious of
   sin,
   which longs to be pure but fears to
   begin.

111 Samuel Johnson (1822-1882) alt.

1. City of God, how broad and far
   outspread thy walls sublime!
   Thy free and loyal people are
   of every age and clime.

2. One holy Church, one mighty throng,
   one steadfast, high intent;
   one working band, one harvest-song,
   one King omnipotent.

3. How purely hath thy speech come
   down
   from earth's primeval youth!
   How grandly hath thine empire grown
   of freedom, love and truth!

4. How gleam thy watch-fires through
   the night
   with never-fainting ray!
   How rise thy towers, serene and bright,
   to meet the dawning day!

5. In vain the surge's angry shock,
   in vain the drifting sands;
   unharmed upon th'eternal Rock
   th'eternal city stands.

112 Jimmy Owens (b. 1930)
© 1972 Bud John Songs/EMI Christian Music
Publishing. Administered by Kevin Mayhew Ltd

Clap your hands, all you people.
Shout to our God with a voice of
   triumph.
Clap your hands, all you people.
Shout to our God with a voice of
   praise!
Hosanna, hosanna.
Shout to our God with a voice of
   triumph.
Praise him, praise him.
Shout to our God with a voice of
   praise!

113 John L. Bell (b. 1949) and Graham Maule
(b. 1958). © 1987 WGRG, Iona Community

Cloth for the cradle,
cradle for the child,
the child for our every joy and sorrow;
find him a shawl that's woven by us all
to welcome the Lord
of each tomorrow.

1. Darkness and light
   and all that's known by sight,
   silence and echo fading,
   weave into one a welcome for the Son,
   set earth its own maker serenading.

2. Claimant and queen,
   wage earners in between,
   trader and travelling preacher,
   weave into one a welcome for the Son,
   whose word brings new life to every
   creature.

3. Hungry and poor,
   the sick and the unsure,
   wealthy, whose needs are stranger,
   weave into one a welcome for the Son,
   leave excess and want beneath the
   manger.

4. Wrinkled or fair,
   carefree or full of care,
   searchers of all the ages,
   weave into one a welcome for the Son,
   the Saviour of shepherds and of sages.

114

Sue McClellan (b. 1951), John Paculabo
(b. 1946), Keith Ryecroft (b. 1949)
© 1974 Thankyou Music

1. Colours of day dawn into the mind,
   the sun has come up, the night is
   behind.
   Go down in the city, into the street,
   and let's give the message to the
   people we meet.

   *So light up the fire and let the flame
   burn,*
   open the door, let Jesus return,
   take seeds of his Spirit, let the fruit grow,
   tell the people of Jesus, let his love show.

2. Go through the park, on into the
   town;
   the sun still shines on; it never goes
   down.
   The light of the world is risen again;
   the people of darkness are needing
   our friend.

3. Open your eyes, look into the sky,
   the darkness has come, the sun came
   to die.
   The evening draws on,
      the sun disappears,
   but Jesus is living,
   and his Spirit is near.

115

Richard G. Jones (b. 1926)
© Richard G. Jones

1. Come, all who look to Christ today,
   stretch out your hands, enlarge your
   mind,
   together share his living way
   where all who humbly seek will find.

2. Come, all who will from every race;
   to lose self-will as Christians should
   then find the Spirit's strong embrace
   which binds us to the common good.

3. Come, young and old from every
   church,
   bring all your treasures of prayer,
   join the dynamic Spirit's search
   to press beyond the truths we share.

4. Bring your traditions' richest store,
   your hymns and rites and cherished
   creeds;
   explore our visions, pray for more,
   since God delights to meet fresh needs.

5. Come, trust in Christ and live in peace,
   anticipate that final light
   when strife and bigotry shall cease,
   and faith be lost in praise and sight.

116

Nick Fawcett (b. 1957)
© 2004 Kevin Mayhew Ltd

1. Come and celebrate, my friends,
   sing of love that never ends.
   Let go of all that holds you back,
   receive the joy and peace you lack,
   live the life your Father sends.

2. Come and celebrate today,
   put your cares and fears away.
   Give thanks, rejoice in all you do,
   God's love is watching over you,
   light and life are here to stay!

3. Come and celebrate with me,
   Christ the Lord has set me free.
   He tore the chains of doubt apart,
   put living hope within my heart.
   Trust in him and you will see.

4. Come and celebrate his call,
   bring your talents, great and small.
   In faith commit to him your days,
   entrust your lives in grateful praise.
   Love like this demands our all.

117
Valerie Collinson (b. 1933)
© 1972 High-Fye Music Ltd

Come and join the celebration.
It's a very special day.
Come and share our jubilation;
there's a new King born today!

1. See the shepherds
   hurry down to Bethlehem,
   gaze in wonder
   at the Son of God who lay before
       them.

2. Wise men journey,
   led to worship by a star,
   kneel in homage,
   bringing precious gifts from lands afar.
       So:

3. 'God is with us,'
   round the world the message bring.
   He is with us,
   'Welcome,' all the bells on earth are
       pealing.

Deep wounds of love
cry out, 'Father, forgive.'
I worship, I worship
the Lamb who was slain.

2. Come and weep, come and mourn
   for your sin that pierced him there;
   so much deeper
   than the wounds of thorn and nail.
   All our pride, all our greed,
   all our fallenness and shame;
   and the Lord has laid
   the punishment on him.

3. Man of heaven, born to earth
   to restore us to your heaven.
   Here we bow in awe
   beneath your searching eyes.
   From your tears comes our joy,
   from your death our life shall spring;
   by your resurrection power
   we shall rise.

118
Graham Kendrick (b. 1950)
© 1989 Make Way Music

1. Come and see, come and see,
   come and see the King of love;
   see the purple robe
   and crown of thorns he wears.
   Soldiers mock, rulers sneer
   as he lifts the cruel cross;
   lone and friendless now,
   he climbs towards the hill.

We worship at your feet,
where wrath and mercy meet,
and a guilty world
is washed by love's pure stream.
For us he was made sin –
oh, help me take it in.

119
Christopher Idle (b. 1938),
based on Revelation 4, 5
© Christopher Idle/Jubilate Hymns

1. Come and see the shining hope
   that Christ's apostle saw;
   on the earth confusion,
   but in heaven an open door,
   where the living creatures
   praise the Lamb for evermore:
   Love has the vict'ry for ever!

Amen, he comes! to bring his own
*   reward!*
Amen, praise God! for justice now
*   restored;*
kingdoms of the world become the
*   kingdoms of the Lord:*
Love has the vict'ry for ever!

Continued overleaf

2. All the gifts you send us, Lord,
   are faithful, good, and true;
   holiness and righteousness
   are shown in all you do:
   who can see your greatest gift
   and fail to worship you?
   Love has the vict'ry for ever!

   Amen, he comes! to bring his own
   reward!
   Amen, praise God! for justice now
   restored;
   kingdoms of the world become the
   kingdoms of the Lord:
   Love has the vict'ry for ever!

3. Power and salvation
   all belong to God on high!
   So the mighty multitudes of heaven
   make their cry,
   singing Alleluia!
   where the echoes never die:
   Love has the vict'ry for ever!

3. Let holy charity
   mine outward vesture be,
   and lowliness become mine inner
      clothing;
   true lowliness of heart,
   which takes the humbler part,
   and o'er its own shortcomings weeps
      with loathing.

4. And so the yearning strong,
   with which the soul will long,
   shall far outpass the power of human
      telling;
   nor can we guess its grace,
   till we become the place
   wherein the Holy Spirit makes his
      dwelling.

120 'Discendi, amor santo' by Bianco da Siena (d. 1434), trans. Richard F. Littledale (1833-1890) alt.

1. Come down, O Love divine,
   seek thou this soul of mine,
   and visit it with thine own ardour
      glowing;
   O Comforter, draw near,
   within my heart appear,
   and kindle it, thy holy flame bestowing.

2. O let it freely burn,
   till earthly passions turn
   to dust and ashes in its heat
      consuming;
   and let thy glorious light
   shine ever on my sight,
   and clothe me round, the while my
      path illuming.

121 Michael Forster (b. 1946) © 2000 Kevin Mayhew Ltd

1. Come, faithful pilgrims all,
   give God the glory.
   Let all who hear his call
   tell out his story:
   how he set Israel free
   from Egypt's slavery,
   and called them out to be
   a pilgrim people.

2. Out on the desert way,
   in all its starkness,
   faith led them through the day,
   and lit their darkness.
   No written guarantee,
   no easy certainty,
   just God's great call to be
   a pilgrim people.

3. Let all the world rejoice
   in exultation
   let every silent voice
   sing of salvation.
   Loose all the chains that bind,
   set free both heart and mind,
   and make all humankind
   a pilgrim people.

122 S. Browne (1680-1732) and others

1. Come, gracious Spirit,
   heavenly Dove, with light and
      comfort from above;
   be thou our guardian,
   thou our guide, o'er every thought
      and step preside.

2. The light of truth to us display,
   and make us know and choose thy
      way;
   plant holy fear in every heart,
   that we from God may ne'er depart.

3. Lead us to Christ, the living Way,
   nor let us from his pastures stray;
   lead us to holiness, the road
   that we must take to dwell with God.

4. Lead us to heaven, that we may share
   fullness of joy for ever there;
   lead us to God, our final rest,
   to be with him for ever blest.

123 Charles Wesley (1707-1788)

1. Come, Holy Ghost, our hearts inspire,
   let us thine influence prove;
   source of the old prophetic fire,
   fountain of life and love.

2. Come, Holy Ghost – for, moved by
      thee,
   thy prophets wrote and spoke –
   unlock the truth, thyself the key,
   unseal the sacred book.

3. Expand thy wings, celestial Dove,
   brood o'er our nature's night;
   on our disordered spirits move,
   and let there now be light.

4. God, through himself, we then shall
      know,
   if thou within us shine;
   and sound, with all thy saints below,
   the depths of love divine.

vs. 1-3, 5 John Cosin (1594-1672)
after Rabanus Maurus (c. 776-856) alt.
124 v. 4 Michael Forster (b. 1946)
v. 4 © 1993 Kevin Mayhew Ltd

1. Come, Holy Ghost, our souls inspire,
   and lighten with celestial fire;
   thou the anointing Spirit art,
   who dost thy sevenfold gifts impart.

2. Thy blessèd unction from above
   is comfort, life, and fire of love;
   enable with perpetual light
   the dullness of our blinded sight.

3. Anoint and cheer our soilèd face
   with the abundance of thy grace:
   keep far our foes, give peace at home;
   where thou art guide no ill can come.

4. Show us the Father and the Son,
   in thee and with thee, ever one.
   Then through the ages all along,
   this shall be our unending song.

5. 'Praise to thy eternal merit,
   Father, Son and Holy Spirit.'
   Amen.

125
Michael Forster (b. 1946)
based on 1 Corinthians 12:4-11
© 1992 Kevin Mayhew Ltd

1. Come, Holy Spirit, come!
   Inflame our souls with love,
   transforming every heart and home
   with wisdom from above.
   O let us not despise
   the humble path Christ trod,
   but choose, to shame the worldly-wise,
   the foolishness of God.

*2. All-knowing Spirit, prove
   the poverty of pride,
   by knowledge of the Father's love
   in Jesus crucified.
   And grant us faith to know
   the glory of that sign,
   and in our very lives to show
   the marks of love divine.

*3. Come with the gift to heal
   the wounds of guilt and fear,
   and to oppression's face reveal
   the kingdom drawing near.
   Where chaos longs to reign,
   descend, O holy Dove,
   and free us all to work again
   the miracles of love.

4. Spirit of truth, arise;
   inspire the prophet's voice:
   expose to scorn the tyrant's lies,
   and bid the poor rejoice.
   O Spirit, clear our sight,
   all prejudice remove,
   and help us to discern the right,
   and covet only love.

5. Give us the tongues to speak,
   in every time and place,
   to rich and poor, to strong and weak,
   the word of love and grace.

Enable us to hear
the words that others bring,
interpreting with open ear
the special song they sing.

6. Come, Holy Spirit, dance
   within our hearts today,
   our earthbound spirits to entrance,
   our mortal fears allay.
   And teach us to desire,
   all other things above,
   that self-consuming holy fire,
   the perfect gift of love!

126 Unknown

1. Come into his presence, singing,
   'Alleluia.' (x3)

2. Come into his presence, singing,
   'Jesus is Lord.' (x3)

3. Come into his presence, singing,
   'Glory to God.' (x3)

127 Isaac Watts (1674-1758) alt.

1. Come, let us join our cheerful songs
   with angels round the throne;
   ten thousand thousand are their
      tongues,
   but all their joys are one.

2. 'Worthy the Lamb that died,' they cry,
   'to be exalted thus.'
   'Worthy the Lamb,' our lips reply,
   'for he was slain for us.'

3. Jesus is worthy to receive
   honour and power divine;
   and blessings, more than we can give,
   be, Lord, for ever thine.

4. Let all creation join in one
   to bless the sacred name
   of him that sits upon the throne,
   and to adore the Lamb.

128 Charles Wesley (1707-1788)

1. Come, let us use the grace divine,
   and all, with one accord,
   in a perpetual cov'nant join
   ourselves to Christ the Lord.

2. Give up ourselves, through Jesu's
        power,
   his name to glorify;
   and promise, in this sacred hour,
   for God to live and die.

3. The cov'nant we this moment make
   be ever kept in mind:
   we will no more our God forsake,
   or cast his words behind.

4. We never will throw off his fear
   who hears our solemn vow;
   and if thou art well pleased to hear,
   come down, and meet us now.

5. To each the cov'nant blood apply,
   which takes our sins away;
   and register our names on high,
   and keep us to that day.

129 Charles Wesley (1707-1788)

1. Come, let us with our Lord arise,
   our Lord, who made both earth and
        skies:
   who died to save the world he made,
   and rose triumphant from the dead;
   he rose, the Prince of life and peace,
   and stamped the day for ever his.

2. This is the day the Lord has made,
   that all may see his love displayed,
   may feel his resurrection's power,
   and rise again, to fall no more,
   in perfect righteousness renewed,
   and filled with all the life of God.

3. Then let us render him his own,
   with solemn prayer approach his
        throne,
   with meekness hear the gospel word,
   with thanks his dying love record,
   our joyful hearts and voices raise,
   and fill his courts with songs of praise.

4. Honour and praise to Jesus pay
   throughout his consecrated day;
   be all in Jesu's praise employed,
   nor leave a single moment void;
   with utmost care the time improve,
   and only breathe his praise and love.

130 Howard Charles Adie Gaunt (1902-1983)
© *Oxford University Press*

1. Come, Lord, to our souls come down,
   through the gospel speaking;
   let your words, your cross and crown,
   lighten all our seeking.

2. Drive out darkness from the heart,
   banish pride and blindness;
   plant in every inward part
   truthfulness and kindness.

3. Eyes be open, spirits stirred,
   minds new truth receiving;
   make us, Lord, by your own word,
   more and more believing.

131 George Herbert (1593-1633)

1. Come, my Way, my Truth, my Life:
   such a way as gives us breath;
   such a truth as ends all strife;
   such a life as killeth death.

2. Come, my Light, my Feast, my
      Strength:
   such a light as shows a feast;
   such a feast as mends in length;
   such a strength as makes his guest.

3. Come, my Joy, my Love, my Heart:
   such a joy as none can move;
   such a love as none can part;
   such a heart as joys in love.

132 Brian Doerksen (b. 1965)
© 1998 Vineyard Songs (UK/Eire)
Administered by CopyCare

Come, now is the time to worship.
Come, now is the time to give your
   heart.
Come, just as you are to worship.
Come, just as you are before your
   God. Come.

*One day every tongue will confess you
are God.*
One day every knee will bow.
Still, the greatest treasure remains
for those who gladly choose you now.

133 Marty Haugen (b. 1950)
© 1999 GIA Publications Inc.

1. Come now, the table's spread,
   in Jesus' name we break the bread,
   here shall we all be fed
   within the reign of God.
   Come, take this holy food,
   receive the body and the blood,
   grace is a mighty flood
   within the reign of God.

Blessèd are they who will feast in the
   reign of God!
Blessèd are they who will share the
   bread of life!
Blessèd are they who are least in the
   reign of God!
They shall rejoice at the feast of life!

2. Stand up and do not fear
   for Christ is truly present here,
   sing out, and cease your tears
   within the reign of God.
   Welcome the weak and poor,
   the sinner finds an open door,
   none judged, and none ignored
   within the reign of God.

3. Here shall the weary rest,
   the stranger be a welcome guest,
   so shall we all be blest
   within the reign of God.
   Now at this wedding feast,
   the greatest here shall be the least,
   all bonds shall be released
   within the reign of God.

134 Charles Wesley (1707-1788)
based on Genesis 32:24-30

1. Come, O thou traveller unknown,
   whom still I hold, but cannot see;
   my company before is gone,
   and I am left alone with thee;
   with thee all night I mean to stay,
   and wrestle till the break of day.

2. I need not tell thee who I am,
   my misery or sin declare;
   thyself hast called me by my name;
   look on thy hands, and read it there!
   But who, I ask thee, who art thou?
   Tell me thy name, and tell me now.

Duston & Upton Parish

— St Francis' Church † St Michael's Church † St Luke's Church —

Duston & Upton Parish Office, St Francis' Church, Eastfield Road, Northampton. NN5 6TQ
www.dustonanduptonparish.org.uk

The Baptism service is <u>free of charge</u>. There is only a nominal charge of made for a Baptism Certificate. We would, however, like to ask for a donation as there are significant costs associated with serving the whole community in this way, which are covered only by those who regularly come to church. You can put cash in the collection plate or write a cheque to 'Duston & Upton PCC'
Thank you.

APPLICATION FOR INFANT BAPTISM
(PLEASE COMPLETE USING BLOCK CAPITALS)

<u>Your Child's Details</u>

Child's full name ...... MIRACLE CHIOMA EGONU ...... Boy or Girl?

Date of Birth ...... 29 JULY, 2019

<u>Date & Place of Baptism</u>

Requested Baptism date* ...... 23rd ~~02~~ FEB, 2020

*Your baptism date will be confirmed by the Parish Office after receipt of this form. **Please do not make any further family arrangements until we have confirmed your Baptism date, place and time.**

Please indicate the Church and time in which you wish your child(ren) to be baptised:

St Luke's Church: 1st Sunday of the month only: 10am   2nd Sunday of the month: 12 midday

✓ St Francis' Church: 4th Sunday of the month only: 10am ✓

1

<u>Agreements</u>
Please tick to confirm your acceptance of these important points:

- **Preparation:** I/we confirm that I/we have attended Baptism Preparation in the Parish for the child that you are bringing for Baptism. If you have not you should contact us ASAP. Tick here to confirm: ☑

- **Cost:** I/we understand that the Baptism service is free of charge. There is only a nominal charge made for a Baptism Certificate of £14 for 2019. I /we understand that there are significant costs associated with serving the whole community, which are covered only by those who regularly come to church. You can donate by cheque/cash. Thank you. Tick here to confirm you have read this: ☑

- **Minimum Service Attendance:** I/we also understand that in addition to attending the Baptism Preparation morning I/we are expected to attend AT LEAST the following 3 services in our churches in advance of the baptism. Tick here to confirm: ☑
  1 – 1st Sunday of the month All Age Holy Communion at St Luke's Church at 10am
  2 – 3rd Sunday of the month Kidz Club at St Luke's Church at 10am
  3 – 4th Sunday of the month All Age Service at St Francis' Church at 10am

- **Commitment:** In signing below I/we understand that as we bring our child for Baptism I/we freely undertake to help my/our child grow up as active members of the Church. Tick here to confirm: ☑

- **Keeping your Promises:** I/we confirm that we are happy to be added to an email list for Baptism & Thanksgiving Families. You will receive occasional emails about services, events and other resources to help you keep the Baptism promises you make in church. Tick here to confirm: ☑

- **Data Protection:** You need to also fill out and return the attached Contact and Data Consent Form. Tick here to confirm you have filled this out and attached: ☑

Please note that there is to be NO parking in Church Way by you or any of your guests. Alternative parking may be found in surrounding streets and there is usually some availability at the Rectory at 3 Main Road.

Father: ....

Mother: ....

The best way to help your child(ren) grow in faith is to be growing in faith yourself. Various opportunities are publicised at www.dustonanduptonparish.org.uk. You would be warmly welcome to join any.

When complete please return this form with your certificate fee (£14 – cheques to 'Duston & Upton PCC') and any donation to the Parish Office at the address above or by email at: office@dustonanduptonparish.org.uk. Thank you.

22072019

Address	Nigeria
Date and Place of Baptism (& Confirmation if applicable)	

Godparent's Full Name	MISS CAROLINE ADAORA EZEUGWU
Email Address	EZEUGWU.adaora @ yahoo.com
Address	32 Galapagos Grove Newton leys MK35NX
Date and Place of Baptism (& Confirmation if applicable)	11/02/2005 Germany

Godparent's Full Name	MATSHELISO SUSAN MABENA DUBE
Email Address	
Address	South Africa
Date and Place of Baptism (& Confirmation if applicable)	South Africa

3

Please indicate the number of children you expect to be present in church on the day of the Baptism and approximate ages:

....

Please also indicate the number of adults expected in your party: ....

Parent Details

Father's full name ...WILLIAM CHUKWUGOZIE EGONU...

Baptised? ...YES... Confirmed? ...YES

Mother's full name ...CHIDMA JOSEPHINE EGONU...

Baptised? ...YES.. Confirmed? ..YES

Address ...51 LICHFIELD DRIVE, NORTHAMPTON

......NN4 0QU

Tel No...07828190386......Email...WEGONU@YAHOO.CO.UK
07828248815

Father's occupation ...TRAIN DRIVER...

Mother's occupation ...NURSE...

Godparent Details

- 3 Godparents is the accepted 'norm'.
- Note that Godparents <u>do not</u> automatically become legal guardians.
- <u>Please note that ALL Godparents must be baptised. If any are not you must tell us ASAP before proceeding</u>

Godparent's Full Name	MISS CHICHEREM EZEONU
Email Address	

3. In vain thou strugglest to get free;
   I never will unloose my hold.
   Art thou the man that died for me?
   The secret of thy love unfold:
   wrestling, I will not let thee go,
   till I thy name, thy nature know.

4. Yield to me now, for I am weak,
   but confident, in self-despair;
   speak to my heart, in blessings speak,
   be conquered by my instant prayer.
   Speak, or thou never hence shalt move,
   and tell me if thy name is Love!

5. 'Tis Love! 'tis Love! Thou diedst for me!
   I hear thy whisper in my heart!
   The morning breaks, the shadows flee;
   pure universal Love thou art:
   to me, to all, thy mercies move;
   thy nature and thy name is Love.

136 Graham Kendrick (b. 1950)
© *1986 Thankyou Music*

Come on, let's get up and go.
Let everyone know.
We've got a reason to shout and to
   sing,
'cause Jesus loves us
and that's a wonderful thing.

Go! go! go! go! get up and go.
Don't be sleepy or slow.
You, you, you, you know what to do.
Give your life to him.

Come on, let's get up and go.
Let everyone know.
We've got a reason to shout and to
   sing,
'cause Jesus loves us
and that's a wonderful thing.

135 Patricia Morgan and Dave Bankhead
© *1984 Thankyou Music*

Come on and celebrate
his gift of love, we will celebrate
the Son of God who loved us
and gave us life.
We'll shout your praise, O King,
you give us joy nothing else can bring;
we'll give to you our offering
in celebration praise.

Come on and celebrate, celebrate,
celebrate and sing,
celebrate and sing to the King!
(Repeat)

137 George Wallace Briggs (1875-1959)
© *Oxford University Press*

1. Come, risen Lord, and deign to be
   our guest;
   no, let us be thy guests; the feast is
   thine;
   thyself at thine own board make
   manifest,
   in thine own sacrament of bread and
   wine.

2. We meet, as in that upper room they
   met;
   thou at the table, blessing, yet dost
   stand:
   'This is my body': so thou givest yet:
   faith still receives the cup as from thy
   hand.

Continued overleaf

3. One body we, one body who partake,
one Church united in communion
blest;
one name we bear, one bread of life
we break,
with all thy saints on earth and saints
at rest.

4. One with each other, Lord, for one
in thee,
who art one Saviour and one living
Head;
then open thou our eyes, that we may
see;
be known to us in breaking of the
bread.

138 Martin E. Leckebusch (b. 1962)
© 1999 Kevin Mayhew Ltd

1. Come, see the Lord in his
breathtaking splendour:
gaze at his majesty – bow and adore!
Enter his presence with wonder and
worship –
he is the King, and enthroned
evermore.

2. He is the Word who was sent by the
Father,
born as a baby, a child of our race:
God here among us, revealed as a
servant,
walking the pathway of truth and of
grace.

3. He is the Lamb who was slain to
redeem us –
there at the cross his appearance was
marred;
though he emerged from the grave as
the victor,
still from the nails and the spear he is
scarred.

4. He is the Lord who ascended in
triumph –
ever the sound of his praises shall ring!
Hail him the First and the Last, the
Almighty:
Jesus, our Prophet, our Priest and our
King.

5. Come, see the Lord in his
breathtaking splendour:
gaze at his majesty – bow and adore!
Come and acknowledge him Saviour
and Sovereign:
Jesus our King is enthroned evermore.

139 Stephen Langton (d. 1228)
trans. Edward Caswall (1814-1878) alt.

1. Come, thou Holy Spirit, come,
and from thy celestial home
shed a ray of light divine;
come, thou Father of the poor,
come, thou source of all our store,
come, within our bosoms shine.

2. Thou of comforters the best,
thou the soul's most welcome guest,
sweet refreshment here below;
in our labour rest most sweet,
grateful coolness in the heat,
solace in the midst of woe.

3. O most blessèd Light divine,
shine within these hearts of thine,
and our inmost being fill;
where thou art not, we have naught,
nothing good in deed or thought,
nothing free from taint of ill.

4. Heal our wounds; our strength renew;
on our dryness pour thy dew;
wash the stains of guilt away;
bend the stubborn heart and will;
melt the frozen, warm the chill;
guide the steps that go astray.

5. On the faithful, who adore
   and confess thee, evermore
   in thy sevenfold gifts descend:
   give them virtue's sure reward,
   give them thy salvation, Lord,
   give them joys that never end.

140 Charles Wesley (1707-1788)

1. Come, thou long-expected Jesus,
   born to set thy people free;
   from our fears and sins release us;
   let us find our rest in thee.

2. Israel's strength and consolation,
   hope of all the earth thou art;
   dear desire of every nation,
   joy of every longing heart.

3. Born thy people to deliver;
   born a child and yet a king;
   born to reign in us for ever;
   now thy gracious kingdom bring.

4. By thine own eternal Spirit,
   rule in all our hearts alone:
   by thine all-sufficient merit,
   raise us to thy glorious throne.

141 Martin E. Leckebusch (b. 1962)
© 1999, 2004 Kevin Mayhew Ltd

1. Come, wounded healer, your
   sufferings reveal,
   the scars you accepted, our anguish
   to heal.
   Your wounds bring such comfort in
   body and soul
   to all who bear torment and yearn to
   be whole.

2. Come, hated lover, and gather us near,
   your welcome, your teaching, your
   challenge to hear:
   where scorn and abuse cause rejection
   and pain,
   your loving acceptance makes hope
   live again!

3. Come, broken victor, condemned to
   a cross –
   how great are the treasures we gain
   from your loss!
   Your willing agreement to share in
   our strife
   transforms our despair into fullness
   of life.

142 Job Hupton (1762-1849)
and John Mason Neale (1818-1866) alt.

1. Come, ye faithful, raise the anthem,
   cleave the skies with shouts of praise;
   sing to him who found the ransom,
   Ancient of eternal days,
   God of God, the Word incarnate,
   whom the heaven of heaven obeys.

2. Ere he raised the lofty mountains,
   formed the seas or built the sky,
   love eternal, free and boundless,
   moved the Lord of Life to die,
   fore-ordained the Prince of princes
   for the throne of Calvary.

3. There, for us and our redemption,
   see him all his life-blood pour!
   There he wins our full salvation,
   dies that we may die no more;
   then arising, lives for ever,
   reigning where he was before.

Continued overleaf

4. High on yon celestial mountains
   stands his sapphire throne, all bright,
   midst unending alleluias
   bursting from the saints in light;
   Sion's people tell his praises,
   victor after hard-won fight.

5. Bring your harps, and bring your
      incense,
   sweep the string and pour the lay;
   let the earth proclaim his wonders,
   King of that celestial day;
   he the Lamb once slain is worthy,
   who was dead and lives for ay.

6. Laud and honour to the Father,
   laud and honour to the Son,
   laud and honour to the Spirit,
   ever Three and ever One,
   consubstantial, co-eternal,
   while unending ages run.

143 St John of Damascus (d. c. 754)
trans. John Mason Neale (1816-1866) alt.

1. Come, ye faithful, raise the strain
   of triumphant gladness;
   God hath brought his Israel
   into joy from sadness;
   loosed from Pharaoh's bitter yoke
   Jacob's sons and daughters;
   led them with unmoistened foot
   through the Red Sea waters.

2. 'Tis the spring of souls today;
   Christ hath burst his prison,
   and from three days' sleep in death
   as a sun hath risen:
   all the winter of our sins,
   long and dark, is flying
   from his light, to whom we give
   laud and praise undying.

3. Alleluia now we cry
   to our King immortal,
   who triumphant burst the bars
   of the tomb's dark portal;
   alleluia, with the Son,
   God the Father praising;
   alleluia yet again
   to the Spirit raising.

144 Henry Alford (1810-1871) alt.

1. Come, ye thankful people, come,
   raise the song of harvest-home!
   All is safely gathered in,
   ere the winter storms begin;
   God, our maker, doth provide
   for our wants to be supplied;
   come to God's own temple, come;
   raise the song of harvest-home!

2. We ourselves are God's own field,
   fruit unto his praise to yield;
   wheat and tares together sown,
   unto joy or sorrow grown;
   first the blade and then the ear,
   then the full corn shall appear:
   grant, O harvest Lord, that we
   wholesome grain and pure may be.

3. For the Lord our God shall come,
   and shall take his harvest home,
   from his field shall purge away
   all that doth offend, that day;
   give his angels charge at last
   in the fire the tares to cast,
   but the fruitful ears to store
   in his garner evermore.

4. Then, thou Church triumphant,
   come,
   raise the song of harvest-home;
   all be safely gathered in,
   free from sorrow, free from sin,
   there for ever purified
   in God's garner to abide:
   come, ten thousand angels, come,
   raise the glorious harvest-home!

145
Psalm 118
© 1981 Ateliers et Presses de Taizé

Confitemini Domino quoniam bonus.
Confitemini Domino. Alleluia!

*Translation: Give thanks to the Lord
for he is good.*

146
Martin E. Leckebusch (b. 1962)
© 1999 Kevin Mayhew Ltd

1. Creation sings! Each plant and tree,
   each bird and beast in harmony;
   the brightest star, the smallest cell,
   God's tender care and glory tell –
   from ocean depths to mountain peaks,
   in praise of God, creation speaks!

2. Creation speaks a message true,
   reminds us we are creatures, too:
   to serve as stewards is our role,
   despite our dreams of full control –
   when we disparage what God owns,
   in turmoil, all creation groans.

3. Creation groans to see the day
   which ends all bondage, all decay:
   frustrated now, it must await
   the Lord who comes to recreate
   till round the universe there rings
   the song his new creation sings!

147
Donald Wynn Hughes (1911-1967)
© Mr P. Hughes

1. Creator of the earth and skies,
   to whom the words of life belong,
   grant us thy truth to make us wise;
   grant us thy power to make us strong.

2. Like theirs of old, our life is death,
   our light is darkness, till we see
   th'eternal Word made flesh and
      breath,
   the God who walked by Galilee.

3. We have not known thee: to the skies
   our monuments of folly soar,
   and all our self-wrought miseries
   have made us trust ourselves the more.

4. We have not loved thee: far and wide
   the wreckage of our hatred spreads,
   and evils wrought by human pride
   recoil on unrepentant heads.

5. For this, our foolish confidence,
   our pride of knowledge and our sin,
   we come to thee in penitence;
   in us the work of grace begin.

6. Teach us to know and love thee, Lord,
   and humbly follow in thy way.
   Speak to our souls the quick'ning
      word
   and turn our darkness into day.

148
7th century
trans. John Mason Neale (1818-1866) alt.

1. Creator of the starry height,
   thy people's everlasting light,
   Jesu, redeemer of us all,
   hear thou thy servants when they call.

*2. Thou, grieving at the helpless cry
   of all creation doomed to die,
   didst come to save our fallen race
   by healing gifts of heavenly grace.

Continued overleaf

*3. When earth was near its evening hour,
thou didst, in love's redeeming power,
like bridegroom from his chamber,
    come
forth from a Virgin-mother's womb.

4. At thy great name, exalted now,
all knees in lowly homage bow;
all things in heaven and earth adore,
and own thee King for evermore.

5. To thee, O Holy One, we pray,
our judge in that tremendous day,
ward off, while yet we dwell below,
the weapons of our crafty foe.

6. To God the Father, God the Son
and God the Spirit, Three in One,
praise, honour, might and glory be
from age to age eternally.
(Amen.)

149 Ray Simpson (b. 1940)
© 1995 Ray Simpson

1. Creator Spirit, come,
renew the face of the earth;
creator Spirit, come,
renew the face of the earth.

2. Kindling Spirit, come,
inflame our waiting hearts;
kindling Spirit, come,
inflame our waiting hearts.

3. Anointing Spirit, come,
pour forth on us anew;
anointing Spirit, come,
pour forth on us anew.

150 Matthew Bridges (1800-1894)

1. Crown him with many crowns,
the Lamb upon his throne;
hark, how the heavenly anthem
    drowns

all music but its own:
awake, my soul, and sing
of him who died for thee,
and hail him as thy matchless King
through all eternity.

2. Crown him the Virgin's Son,
the God incarnate born,
whose arm those crimson trophies won
which now his brow adorn;
fruit of the mystic Rose,
as of that Rose the Stem,
the Root, whence mercy ever flows,
the Babe of Bethlehem.

3. Crown him the Lord of love;
behold his hands and side,
rich wounds, yet visible above,
in beauty glorified:
no angel in the sky
can fully bear that sight,
but downward bends each burning eye
at mysteries so bright.

4. Crown him the Lord of peace,
whose power a sceptre sways
from pole to pole, that wars may cease,
absorbed in prayer and praise:
his reign shall know no end,
and round his piercèd feet
fair flowers of paradise extend
their fragrance ever sweet.

5. Crown him the Lord of years,
the Potentate of time,
Creator of the rolling spheres,
ineffably sublime.
All hail, Redeemer, hail!
for thou hast died for me;
thy praise shall never, never fail
throughout eternity.

151

John L. Bell (b. 1949) and Graham Maule (b.1958)
© 1987, 2002 WGRG, Iona Community

Dance and sing, all the earth,
gracious is the hand that tends you:
love and care everywhere,
God on purpose sends you.

1. Shooting star and sunset shape
the drama of creation;
lightning flash and moonbeam share
a common derivation.

2. Deserts stretch and torrents roar
in contrast and confusion;
treetops shake and mountains soar
and nothing is illusion.

3. All that flies and swims and crawls
displays an animation;
none can emulate or change
for each has its own station.

4. Brother man and sister woman,
born of dust and passion,
praise the one who calls you friends
and forms you in his fashion.

5. Kiss of life and touch of death
suggest our imperfection:
crib and womb and cross and tomb
cry out for resurrection.

2. In simple trust like theirs who heard,
beside the Syrian sea,
the gracious calling of the Lord,
let us, like them, without a word,
rise up and follow thee,
rise up and follow thee.

3. O Sabbath rest by Galilee!
O calm of hills above,
where Jesus knelt to share with thee
the silence of eternity,
interpreted by love!
Interpreted by love!

4. Drop thy still dews of quietness,
till all our strivings cease;
take from our souls the strain and
stress,
and let our ordered lives confess
the beauty of thy peace,
the beauty of thy peace.

5. Breathe through the heats of our
desire
thy coolness and thy balm;
let sense be dumb, let flesh retire;
speak through the earthquake, wind
and fire,
O still small voice of calm!
O still small voice of calm!

152

John Greenleaf Whittier (1807-1892)

1. Dear Lord and Father of mankind,
forgive our foolish ways!
Re-clothe us in our rightful mind,
in purer lives thy service find,
in deeper rev'rence praise,
in deeper rev'rence praise.

153

Johann Franck (1618-1677)
trans. Catherine Winkworth (1827-1878)

1. Deck thyself, my soul, with gladness,
leave the gloomy haunts of sadness;
come into the daylight's splendour,
there with joy thy praises render
unto him whose grace unbounded
hath this wondrous banquet founded:
high o'er all the heavens he reigneth,
yet to dwell with thee he deigneth.

Continued overleaf

2. Now I sink before thee lowly,
filled with joy most deep and holy,
as with trembling awe and wonder
on thy mighty works I ponder:
how, by mystery surrounded,
depth no mortal ever sounded,
none may dare to pierce unbidden
secrets that with thee are hidden.

PART TWO

3. Sun, who all my life dost brighten,
light, who dost my soul enlighten,
joy, the sweetest heart e'er knoweth,
fount, whence all my being floweth,
at thy feet I cry, my Maker,
let me be a fit partaker
of this blessèd food from heaven,
for our good, thy glory, given.

4. Jesus, Bread of Life, I pray thee,
let me gladly here obey thee;
never to my hurt invited,
be thy love with love requited:
from this banquet let me measure,
Lord, how vast and deep its treasure;
through the gifts thou here dost give
   me,
as thy guest in heaven receive me.

154 George Ratcliffe Woodward (1848-1934)

1. Ding dong, merrily on high!
In heaven the bells are ringing;
ding dong, verily the sky
is riven with angel singing.

Gloria, hosanna in excelsis!
Gloria, hosanna in excelsis!

2. E'en so here below, below,
let steeple bells be swungen,
and io, io, io,
by priest and people sungen.

3. Pray you, dutifully prime
your matin chime, ye ringers;
may you beautifully rhyme
your evetime song, ye singers.

155 J. B. de Santeuil (1630-1697)
trans. Isaac Williams (1802-1865) alt.

1. Disposer supreme,
and Judge of the earth,
thou choosest for thine
the meek and the poor;
to frail earthen vessels,
and things of no worth,
entrusting thy riches
which ay shall endure.

2. Those vessels are frail,
though full of thy light,
and many, once made,
are broken and gone;
thence brightly appeareth
thy truth in its might,
as through the clouds riven
the lightnings have shone.

3. Like clouds are they borne
to do thy great will,
and swift as the winds
about the world go:
the Word with his wisdom
their spirits doth fill;
they thunder, they lighten,
the waters o'erflow.

4. Their sound goeth forth,
'Christ Jesus the Lord!'
then Satan doth fear,
his citadels fall;
as when the dread trumpets
went forth at thy word,
and one long blast shattered
the Canaanites' wall.

5. O loud be their cry,
   and stirring their sound,
   to rouse us, O Lord,
   from slumber of sin:
   the lights thou hast kindled
   in darkness around,
   O may they awaken
   our spirits within.

6. All honour and praise,
   dominion and might,
   to God, Three in One,
   eternally be,
   who round us hath shed
   his own marvellous light,
   and called us from darkness
   his glory to see.

156 Gerard Markland (b. 1953), based on Isaiah 43:1-4
© 1978 Kevin Mayhew Ltd

Do not be afraid, for I have redeemed
you.
I have called you by your name;
you are mine.

1. When you walk through the waters,
   I'll be with you.
   You will never sink beneath the waves.

2. When the fire is burning all around
   you,
   you will never be consumed by the
   flames.

3. When the fear of loneliness is looming,
   then remember I am at your side.

4. When you dwell in the exile of the
   stranger,
   remember you are precious in my eyes.

5. You are mine, O my child, I am your
   Father,
   and I love you with a perfect love.

157 Bangor Antiphoner (c.690)
trans. John Mason Neale (1818-1866)

1. Draw nigh and take the body of the
   Lord,
   and drink the holy blood for you
   outpoured.

2. Saved by that body and that holy
   blood,
   with souls refreshed, we render
   thanks to God.

3. Salvation's giver, Christ, the only Son,
   by his dear cross and blood the vict'ry
   won.

4. Offered was he for greatest and for
   least,
   himself the victim, and himself the
   priest.

5. Approach ye then with faithful hearts
   sincere,
   and take the pledges of salvation here.

158 Aurelius Clemens Prudentius (348-c. 413)
trans. Edward Caswall (1814-1878) alt.

1. Earth has many a noble city;
   Beth'lem, thou dost all excel:
   out of thee the Lord from heaven
   came to rule his Israel.

2. Fairer than the sun at morning
   was the star that told his birth,
   to the world its God announcing,
   seen in fleshly form on earth.

3. Eastern sages at his cradle
   make oblations rich and rare;
   see them give in deep devotion
   gold and frankincense and myrrh.

Continued overleaf

4. Sacred gifts of mystic meaning:
   incense doth their God disclose,
   gold the King of kings proclaimeth,
   myrrh his sepulchre foreshows.

5. Jesu, whom the Gentiles worshipped
   at thy glad Epiphany,
   unto thee with God the Father
   and the Spirit glory be.

159   Taizé Community, based on Scripture
© Ateliers et Presses de Taizé

Eat this bread, drink this cup,
come to him and never be hungry.
Eat this bread, drink this cup,
trust in him and you will not thirst.

1. Christ is the Bread of Life,
   the true bread sent from the Father.

2. Your ancestors ate manna in the
      desert,
   but this is the bread come down
      from heaven.

3. Eat his flesh, and drink his blood,
   and Christ will raise you up on the
      last day.

4. Anyone who eats this bread
   will live for ever.

5. If we believe and eat this bread
   we will have eternal life.

160   William Whiting (1825-1878) alt.

1. Eternal Father, strong to save,
   whose arm doth bind the restless wave,
   who bidd'st the mighty ocean deep
   its own appointed limits keep:
   O hear us when we cry to thee
   for those in peril on the sea.

2. O Saviour, whose almighty word
   the winds and waves submissive heard,
   who walkedst on the foaming deep,
   and calm, amid its rage, didst sleep:
   O hear us when we cry to thee
   for those in peril on the sea.

3. O sacred Spirit, who didst brood
   upon the waters dark and rude,
   and bid their angry tumult cease,
   and give, for wild confusion, peace:
   O hear us when we cry to thee
   for those in peril on the sea.

4. O Trinity of love and power,
   our brethren shield in danger's hour.
   From rock and tempest, fire and foe,
   protect them whereso'er they go,
   and ever let there rise to thee
   glad hymns of praise from land and sea.

161   Robert Dobbie (1901-1995)

1. Eternal God, we consecrate
   these children to your care,
   to you their talents dedicate,
   for they your image bear.

2. To them our solemn pledge we give
   their lives by prayer to shield.
   May they in truth and honour live,
   and to your guidance yield.

3. Your Spirit's power on them bestow,
   from sin their hearts preserve;
   in Christ their master may they grow,
   and him for ever serve.

4. So may the waters of this rite
   become a means of grace,
   and these your children show the light
   that shone in Jesus' face.

162

John White Chadwick (1840-1904) alt.

1. Eternal Ruler of the ceaseless round
of circling planets singing on their way;
guide of the nations from the night
profound
into the glory of the perfect day;
rule in our hearts, that we may ever be
guided and strengthened and upheld
by thee.

2. We are of thee, the children of thy
love,
by virtue of thy well-belovèd Son;
descend, O Holy Spirit, like a dove,
into our hearts, that we may be as one:
as one with thee, to whom we ever
tend;
as one with him, our Brother and our
Friend.

3. We would be one in hatred of all
wrong,
one in our love of all things sweet and
fair,
one with the joy that breaketh into
song,
one with the grief that trembles into
prayer,
one in the power that makes thy
children free
to follow truth, and thus to follow
thee.

4. O clothe us with thy heavenly
armour, Lord,
thy trusty shield, thy sword of love
divine;
our inspiration be thy constant word;
we ask no victories that are not thine:
give or withhold, let pain or pleasure
be;
enough to know that we are serving
thee.

163

Stuart Garrard (b. 1963)
© 1995 Thankyou Music

Every minute of every day
I get my life from you.
In every possible kind of way
your life comes bursting through.
You're the one I depend upon,
the source of my life,
you're the only one.
I didn't know living could be such fun,
it's eternal life and it's just begun.

164

Traditional

Exaudi nos, Domine,
dona nobis pacem tuam.

*Translation: Hear us, O Lord,
give us your peace.*

165

Brian Doerksen (b. 1965)
© 1989 Vineyard Songs, Canada
Administered by CopyCare

Faithful One, so unchanging,
Ageless One, you're my rock of peace.
Lord of all, I depend on you,
I call out to you again and again,
I call out to you again and again.

You are my rock in times of trouble,
you lift me up when I fall down.
All through the storm your love is the
anchor,
my hope is in you alone.

166
Thomas Benson Pollock (1836-1896)

1. Faithful Shepherd, feed me
in the pastures green;
faithful Shepherd, lead me
where thy steps are seen.

2. Hold me fast, and guide me
in the narrow way;
so, with thee beside me,
I shall never stray.

3. Daily bring me nearer
to the heavenly shore;
may my faith grow clearer,
may I love thee more.

4. Hallow every pleasure,
every gift and pain;
be thyself my treasure,
though none else I gain.

5. Day by day prepare me
as thou seest best,
then let angels bear me
to thy promised rest.

167
Timothy Dudley-Smith (b. 1926)
based on Luke 2:29-32
© Timothy Dudley-Smith

1. Faithful vigil ended,
watching, waiting cease;
Master, grant your servant
his discharge in peace.

2. All the Spirit promised,
all the Father willed,
now these eyes behold it
perfectly fulfilled.

3. This your great deliv'rance
sets your people free;
Christ their light uplifted
all the nations see.

4. Christ, your people's glory!
watching, doubting cease;
grant to us your servants
our discharge in peace.

168
Ian Smale (b. 1949)
© 1984 Thankyou Music

Father God,
I wonder how I managed to exist
without the knowledge of your
    parenthood
and your loving care.
But now I am your child,
I am adopted in your family
and I can never be alone,
'cause, Father God, you're there
    beside me.

I will sing your praises,
I will sing your praises,
I will sing your praises,
for evermore.
(Repeat)

169
Maria Willis (1824-1908)

1. Father, hear the prayer we offer:
not for ease that prayer shall be,
but for strength that we may ever
live our lives courageously.

2. Not for ever in green pastures
do we ask our way to be;
but the steep and rugged pathway
may we tread rejoicingly.

3. Not for ever by still waters
would we idly rest and stay;
but would smite the living fountains
from the rocks along our way.

4. Be our strength in hours of weakness,
in our wand'rings be our guide;
through endeavour, failure, danger,
Father, be thou at our side.

170 Jenny Hewer (b. 1945)
© 1975 Thankyou Music

1. Father, I place into your hands
   the things I cannot do.
   Father, I place into your hands
   the things that I've been through.
   Father, I place into your hands
   the way that I should go,
   for I know I always can trust you.

2. Father, I place into your hands
   my friends and family.
   Father, I place into your hands
   the things that trouble me.
   Father I place into your hands
   the person I would be,
   for I know I always can trust you.

3. Father, we love to see your face,
   we love to hear your voice.
   Father, we love to sing your praise
   and in your name rejoice.
   Father, we love to walk with you
   and in your presence rest,
   for we know we always can trust you.

4. Father, I want to be with you
   and do the things you do.
   Father, I want to speak the words
   that you are speaking too.
   Father, I want to love the ones
   that you will draw to you,
   for I know that I am one with you.

171 Bob Fitts
© 1985 Scripture in Song/Integrity Music/
CopyCare

Father in heaven, how we love you,
we lift your name in all the earth.
May your kingdom be established in
   our praises
as your people declare your holy works.
Blessèd be the Lord God Almighty,
who was and is and is to come.
Blessèd be the Lord God Almighty,
who reigns for evermore.

172 Stewart Cross (1928-1989)
© Mrs M. Cross.

1. Father, Lord of all creation,
   ground of Being, Life and Love;
   height and depth beyond description
   only life in you can prove:
   you are mortal life's dependence:
   thought, speech, sight are ours by
      grace;
   yours is every hour's existence,
   sovereign Lord of time and space.

2. Jesus Christ, the Man for Others,
   we, your people, make our prayer:
   help us love – as sisters, brothers –
   all whose burdens we can share.
   Where your name binds us together
   you, Lord Christ, will surely be;
   where no selfishness can sever
   there your love the world may see.

3. Holy Spirit, rushing, burning
   wind and flame of Pentecost,
   fire our hearts afresh with yearning
   to regain what we have lost.
   May your love unite our action,
   nevermore to speak alone:
   God, in us abolish faction,
   God, through us your love make
      known.

173 Latin (c. 10th century)
trans. Alfred E. Alston (1862-1927)

1. Father most holy,
   merciful and loving,
   Jesu, Redeemer,
   ever to be worshipped,
   life-giving Spirit,
   Comforter most gracious,
   God everlasting.

Continued overleaf

2. Three in a wondrous
Unity unbroken,
One perfect Godhead,
love that never faileth,
light of the angels,
succour of the needy,
hope of all living.

3. All thy creation
serveth its Creator,
thee every creature
praiseth without ceasing;
we too would sing thee
psalms of true devotion:
hear, we beseech thee.

4. Lord God Almighty,
unto thee be glory,
One in Three Persons,
over all exalted.
Thine, as is meet,
be honour, praise and blessing
now and for ever.

174 Edward Cooper (1770-1833)

1. Father of heaven, whose love profound
a ransom for our souls hath found,
before thy throne we sinners bend,
to us thy pard'ning love extend.

2. Almighty Son, incarnate Word,
our Prophet, Priest, Redeemer, Lord,
before thy throne we sinners bend,
to us thy saving grace extend.

3. Eternal Spirit, by whose breath
the soul is raised from sin and death,
before thy throne we sinners bend,
to us thy quick'ning power extend.

4. Thrice Holy! Father, Spirit, Son;
mysterious Godhead, Three in One,
before thy throne we sinners bend,
grace, pardon, life, to us extend.

175 Philip Doddridge (1702-1751)

1. Father of peace, and God of love.
We own thy power to save;
that power by which our Shepherd
rose
victorious o'er the grave.

2. We triumph in that Shepherd's name,
still watchful for our good;
who brought th'eternal cov'nant
down,
and sealed it with his blood.

3. So may thy Spirit seal my soul,
and mould it to thy will;
that my fond heart no more may stray,
but keep thy promise still.

4. Still may we gain superior strength,
and press with vigour on;
till full perfection crown our hopes,
and fix us near thy throne.

176 Terrye Coelho (b. 1952)
© 1976 CCCM Music/Maranatha! Music
Administered by CopyCare

1. Father, we adore you,
lay our lives before you.
How we love you!

2. Jesus, we adore you . . .

3. Spirit, we adore you . . .

177

Donna Adkins (b. 1940)
© 1976 CCCM Music/Maranatha! Music
Administered by CopyCare

1. Father, we love you,
   we worship and adore you,
   glorify your name in all the earth.
   Glorify your name, glorify your name,
   glorify your name in all the earth.

2. Jesus, we love you . . .

3. Spirit, we love you . . .

178

From the *Didache* (first century)
trans. F. Bland Tucker (1895-1984)
© Church Publishing Inc.

1. Father, we thank thee who hast planted
   thy holy name within our hearts.
   Knowledge and faith and life immortal
   Jesus thy Son to us imparts.

2. Thou, Lord, didst make all for thy
      pleasure,
   didst give us food for all our days,
   giving in Christ the bread eternal;
   thine is the power, be thine the praise.

3. Watch o'er thy Church, O Lord, in
      mercy,
   save it from evil, guard it still,
   perfect it in thy love, unite it,
   cleansed and conformed unto thy will.

4. As grain, once scattered on the hillsides,
   was in this broken bread made one,
   so from all lands thy church be
      gathered
   into thy kingdom by thy Son.

179

Robin Mann (b. 1949)
© 1986 Kevin Mayhew Ltd

*Father welcomes all his children
to his fam'ly through his Son.
Father giving his salvation,
life for ever has been won.*

1. Little children, come to me,
   for my kingdom is of these.
   Love and new life have I to give,
   pardon for your sin.

2. In the water, in the word,
   in his promise, be assured:
   all who believe and are baptised
   shall be born again.

3. Let us daily die to sin;
   let us daily rise with him –
   walk in the love of Christ our Lord,
   live in the peace of God.

180

Fred Kaan (b. 1929)
© 1968, 1996 Stainer & Bell Ltd

1. Father, who in Jesus found us,
   God, whose love is all around us,
   who to freedom new unbound us,
   keep our hearts with joy aflame.

2. For the sacramental breaking,
   for the honour of partaking,
   for your life our lives remaking,
   young and old, we praise your name.

3. From the service of this table
   lead us to a life more stable,
   for our witness make us able;
   blessings on our work we claim.

4. Through our calling closely knitted,
   daily to your praise committed,
   for a life of service fitted,
   let us now your love proclaim.

181
John Samuel Bewley Monsell (1811-1875) alt.

1. Fight the good fight with all thy might;
   Christ is thy strength, and Christ thy
   right;
   lay hold on life, and it shall be
   thy joy and crown eternally.

2. Run the straight race through God's
   good grace,
   lift up thine eyes and seek his face;
   life with its way before us lies;
   Christ is the path, and Christ the prize.

3. Cast care aside, lean on thy guide;
   his boundless mercy will provide;
   trust, and thy trusting soul shall prove
   Christ is its life, and Christ its love.

4. Faint not nor fear, his arms are near;
   he changeth not, and thou art dear;
   only believe, and thou shalt see
   that Christ is all in all to thee.

5. So shalt thou, Lord, receive from me
   the praise and glory due;
   and so shall I begin on earth
   the song for ever new.

6. So shall each fear, each fret, each care,
   be turnèd into song;
   and every winding of the way
   the echo shall prolong.

7. So shall no part of day or night
   unblest or common be;
   but all my life, in every step,
   be fellowship with thee.

182
Horatius Bonar (1808-1889)

1. Fill thou my life, O Lord my God,
   in every part with praise,
   that my whole being may proclaim
   thy being and thy ways.

2. Not for the lip of praise alone,
   nor e'en the praising heart,
   I ask, but for a life made up
   of praise in every part.

3. Praise in the common things of life,
   its goings out and in;
   praise in each duty and each deed,
   however small and mean.

4. Fill every part of me with praise:
   let all my being speak
   of thee and of thy love, O Lord,
   poor though I be and weak.

183
Timothy Dudley-Smith (b. 1926)
© Timothy Dudley-Smith

1. Fill your hearts with joy and gladness,
   sing and praise your God and mine!
   Great the Lord in love and wisdom,
   might and majesty divine!
   He who framed the starry heavens
   knows and names them as they shine!
   Fill your hearts with joy and gladness,
   sing and praise your God and mine!

2. Praise the Lord, his people, praise him!
   Wounded souls his comfort know;
   those who fear him find his mercies,
   peace for pain and joy for woe;
   humble hearts are high exalted,
   human pride and power laid low.
   Praise the Lord, his people, praise him!
   Wounded souls his comfort know.

3. Praise the Lord for times and seasons,
   cloud and sunshine, wind and rain;
   spring to melt the snows of winter
   till the waters flow again;
   grass upon the mountain pastures,
   golden valleys thick with grain.
   Praise the Lord for times and seasons,
   cloud and sunshine, wind and rain.

4. Fill your hearts with joy and gladness,
peace and plenty crown your days;
love his laws, declare his judgements,
walk in all his words and ways;
he the Lord and we his children:
praise the Lord, all people, praise!
Fill your hearts with joy and gladness,
peace and plenty crown your days!

184 John Raphael Peacey (1896-1971)
By kind permission of the Revd M. J. Hancock.

1. Filled with the Spirit's power,
with one accord
the infant Church
confessed its risen Lord.
O Holy Spirit,
in the Church today
no less your power
of fellowship display.

2. Now with the mind of Christ
set us on fire,
that unity
may be our great desire.
Give joy and peace;
give faith to hear your call,
and readiness
in each to work for all.

3. Widen our love, good Spirit,
to embrace
in your strong care
the people of each race.
Like wind and fire
with life among us move,
till we are known as Christ's,
and Christians prove.

185 Unknown
trans. John Mason Neale (1818-1866) alt.

1. Finished the strife of battle now,
gloriously crowned the victor's brow;
sing with gladness, banish sadness:
Alleluia, alleluia!

2. After the death that him befell,
Jesus Christ has harrowed hell;
songs of praising we are raising:
Alleluia, alleluia!

3. On the third morning he arose,
shining with vict'ry o'er his foes;
earth is singing, heaven is ringing:
Alleluia, alleluia!

4. Lord, by your wounds on you we call,
you, by your death, have freed us all;
may our living be thanksgiving:
Alleluia, alleluia!

186 John Henry Newman (1801-1890) alt.

1. Firmly I believe and truly
God is Three and God is One;
and I next acknowledge duly
manhood taken by the Son.

2. And I trust and hope most fully
in the Saviour crucified;
and each thought and deed unruly
do to death as he has died.

3. Simply to his grace and wholly
light and life and strength belong,
and I love supremely, solely,
him the holy, him the strong.

4. And I hold in veneration,
for the love of him alone,
holy Church as his creation,
and her teachings as his own.

Continued overleaf

5. Adoration ay be given,
   with and through th'angelic host,
   to the God of earth and heaven,
   Father, Son and Holy Ghost.

   When the tune 'Alton' is used the
   following last line is added:
   Amen. Father, Son and Holy Ghost.

187 Susan Sayers (b. 1946)
© 1986 Kevin Mayhew Ltd

1. Fishes of the ocean and the birds of
   the air,
   they all declare the wonderful works
   of God
   who has created everything,
   everywhere;
   let the whole earth sing of his love!

2. Apples in the orchard and the corn in
   the field,
   the plants all yield their fruit in due
   season,
   so the generosity of God is revealed;
   let the whole earth sing of his love!

3. Energy and colour from the sun with
   its light,
   the moon by night; the patterns of
   the stars
   all winking in the darkness on a
   frosty cold night;
   let the whole earth sing of his love!

4. Muddy hippopotamus and dainty
   gazelle,
   the mice as well, are all of his making,
   furry ones and hairy ones and some
   with a shell;
   let the whole earth sing of his love!

5. All that we can hear and everything
   we can see,
   including me, we all of us spring
   from God
   who cares for everybody unendingly;
   let the whole earth sing of his love!

188 Ian Smale (b. 1949)
© 1985 Thankyou Music

5 0 0 0 + hungry folk,
5 0 0 0 + hungry folk,
5 0 0 0 + hungry folk
came 4 2 listen 2 Jesus.

The 6 x 2 said 0 0 0,
the 6 x 2 said 0 0 0,
the 6 x 2 said 0 0 0,
where can I get some food from?

Just 1 had 1 2 3 4 5,
just 1 had 1 2 3 4 5,
just 1 had 1 2 3 4 5
loaves and 1 2 fishes.

When Jesus blessed the 5 + 2,
when Jesus blessed the 5 + 2,
when Jesus blessed the 5 + 2
they were increased many x over.

5 0 0 0 + 8 it up,
5 0 0 0 + 8 it up,
5 0 0 0 + 8 it up,
with 1 2 3 4 5 6 7 8 9 10 11 12
basketfuls left over.

189 Michael Cockett (b. 1938)
© 1978 Kevin Mayhew Ltd

Follow me, follow me,
leave your home and family,
leave your fishing nets and boats upon
   the shore.
Leave the seed you have sown,
leave the crops that you've grown,
leave the people you have known and
follow me.

1. The foxes have their holes
   and the swallows have their nests,
   but the Son of Man
   has no place to lie down.
   I do not offer comfort,
   I do not offer wealth,
   but in me will all happiness be found.

2. If you would follow me,
   you must leave old ways behind.
   You must take my cross and
   follow on my path.
   You may be far from loved ones,
   you may be far from home,
   but my Father will welcome you at last.

3. Although I go away
   you will never be alone,
   for the Spirit will be
   there to comfort you.
   Though all of you may scatter,
   each follow his own path,
   still the Spirit of love will lead you
   home.

190
William Walsham How (1823-1897)
adapted by Michael Forster (b. 1946)
© 2000 Kevin Mayhew Ltd

1. For all the saints who from their
   labours rest,
   who thee by faith before the world
   confessed,
   thy name, O Jesus, be for ever blest:
   Alleluia!

2. Thou wast their rock, their refuge
   and their might,
   thou, Lord, the vision ever in their
   sight,
   thou in the darkness drear their one
   true light.
   Alleluia!

3. O may thy servants, faithful, true
   and bold,
   strive for thy kingdom as the saints
   of old,
   and win with them the glorious
   crown of gold:
   Alleluia!

4. O blest communion, fellowship divine!
   We feebly struggle, they in glory
   shine,
   yet all are one in thee, for all are thine:
   Alleluia!

*5. And when the road is steep, the
   journey long,
   steals on the ear the distant welcome
   song,
   and hope is bright again, and faith is
   strong:
   Alleluia!

*6. The golden evening brightens in the
   west,
   soon, soon to faithful pilgrims
   cometh rest:
   sweet is the calm of Paradise the blest:
   Alleluia!

*7. But lo! There breaks a yet more
   glorious day;
   the saints triumphant rise in bright
   array:
   the King of glory passes on his way:
   Alleluia!

*8. From earth's wide bounds, from
   ocean's farthest coast,
   through gates of pearl streams in the
   countless host,
   singing to Father, Son and Holy Ghost.
   Alleluia!

191 Richard Mant (1776-1848)

1. For all thy saints, O Lord,
   who strove in thee to live,
   who followed thee, obeyed, adored,
   our grateful hymn receive.

2. For all thy saints, O Lord,
   who strove in thee to die,
   and found in thee a full reward,
   accept our thankful cry.

3. Thine earthly members fit
   to join thy saints above,
   in one communion ever knit,
   one fellowship of love.

4. Jesu, thy name we bless,
   and humbly pray that we
   may follow them in holiness,
   who lived and died for thee.

5. All might, all praise, be thine,
   Father, co-equal Son,
   and Spirit, bond of love divine,
   while endless ages run.

2. Apostles, prophets, martyrs,
   who served you here on earth,
   now reign with you in heaven,
   singing your praise and worth.
   With them, and all whose witness
   is known to you alone,
   we share our earthly journey
   towards your heavenly throne.

3. We praise you, God our Father,
   we worship Christ, your Son,
   we glorify your Spirit,
   forever three, yet one.
   On earth we see you dimly,
   in heaven face to face;
   and then with all who've served you,
   we'll praise you, God of grace.

Verse 2 may be replaced with an
appropriate stanza from the following:

25th January
Conversion of Paul
Blinded by light from heaven
which blazed down from above,
fired by the glorious vision
Paul chose your way of love.
So Lord, like Paul, convert us,
transform our night to day;
empower us with your Spirit,
and guide us in your way.

192

Verses 1-3: Horatio Bolton Nelson (1823-1913), adapted by Stuart Thomas (b. 1954)
All other verses: Stuart Thomas, except 'Holy Innocents': Susan Sayers (b. 1946)
© Kevin Mayhew Ltd

1. For all your saints still active,
   for those whose work is done;
   for saints with you in glory whose
      earthly race is run.
   You rose as King and Sovereign,
   that they the crown might wear,
   reserved for those who humbly
   your earthly pathway share.

19th March
Joseph of Nazareth
We praise you, Lord, for Joseph,
true carer for your Son;
Jesus he did take to Egypt
till Herod's rage was done.
A carpenter by training,
he made for Christ a home;
through Joseph's care and nurture
our Father's love is known.

14th May

Matthias

To take the place of Judas,
disciples sought God's will;
the lot fell to Matthias
that needed space to fill.
We follow his example
with you, Lord, as our friend;
may we, with you beside us,
continue to the end.

11th June

Barnabas

For Barnabas we praise you,
who journeyed far with Paul;
encouraging and hopeful,
your love he shared with all;
in ministry and caring
may we bring hope and cheer,
to banish doubt and darkness,
and drive away all fear.

24th June

Birth of John the Baptist

Give thanks for John the Baptist,
forerunner of the Word,
who went ahead preparing
the way for Christ our Lord.
Greatest among the prophets,
he saw in Christ the One
whom God had sent to save us,
Jesus, his only Son.

29th June

Peter

For Peter, Lord, we praise you,
eager and unafraid;
though three times he denied you,
on him your charge you laid.
Lord, make us faithful pastors,
to feed your flock with care;
to tend them with devotion,
their burden gladly share.

3rd July

Thomas

For Thomas we now thank you,
who wanted you to prove
that you indeed were risen,
the Lord of life and love.
In all our human searching,
inspire us with your grace,
and even when we're doubting,
help us to see your face.

22nd July

Mary Magdalene

We praise you now for Mary,
whose life was changed and turned
by you, her friend and master;
for you she longed and yearned.
In tears, she sensed you call her
and as your voice she heard,
the woman once rejected
saw first the Risen Lord.

25th July

James

We praise you for the witness
of James, the one who died
in telling of his Saviour,
Jesus the Crucified.
Lord, help us not to treasure
our worldly goods or fame,
but may we, trials enduring,
bring glory to your name.

24th August

Bartholomew

Bartholomew the apostle,
least known among your friends,
remained a faithful foll'wer
and served you to the end.
His deeds may not be noted,
but he to Christ stayed true;
may we too seek your glory,
and only honour you.

Continued overleaf

21st September

Matthew

Matthew the tax-collector,
left all his worldly gain,
to rise and follow Jesus;
he tells us: 'Do the same!'
The good news of our Saviour
his gospel words declare;
may we forsake what's passing,
his risen life to share.

18th October

Luke

For Luke, the faithful doctor,
we thank you; for he shows
the healing Christ, who reaches
to share our pains and woes.
Stretch out your hand to save us,
to cleanse us deep within,
and make us whole to serve you,
to heal this world of sin.

28th October

Simon and Jude

For Jude and Simon, praise, Lord,
who walked the pilgrim way;
the call of Christ compelled them
to serve him, come what may.
Like them, with hearts enlivened,
may we that hope retain,
and walk the rugged pathway
eternal life to gain.

30th November

Andrew

We thank you, Lord, for Andrew,
who, answering your call,
went straight to tell his brother
he'd met the Lord of All.
At once he left his fishing,
and home beside the sea.
May we take up your challenge:
'Get up! Come, follow me!'

26th December

Stephen

For Stephen, true and righteous,
we praise you, Lord, and bless;
he stood to challenge evil,
and your great name confess.
Like him, may we be willing
your Lordship to proclaim;
that, faced with opposition,
we may uphold your Name.

27th December

John the Evangelist

John, your beloved disciple,
wrote down all that he knew
of Christ, our Lord and Saviour,
that we might know him too.
We praise you for his record
of peace and love and grace;
through Christ we see the Father,
and meet him in this place.

28th December

Holy Innocents

With aching hearts we honour
those infants killed in hate
by Herod's jealous fury
faced with a Prince so great.
Such innocents as martyrs
unnerve us with their pain;
yet safe in Jesus' keeping
they shall not die again.

193

Dave Richards (b. 1947)
© *1977 Thankyou Music*

For I'm building a people of power
and I'm making a people of praise,
that will move through this land by
    my Spirit,
and will glorify my precious name.

Build your Church, Lord,
make us strong, Lord,
join our hearts, Lord,
through your Son.
Make us one, Lord, in your body,
in the kingdom of your Son.

194 John Raphael Peacey (1896-1971)
© By kind permission of the Revd M. J. Hancock

1. For Mary, mother of our Lord,
God's holy name be praised,
who first the Son of God adored,
as on her child she gazed.

2. The angel Gabriel brought the word
she should Christ's mother be;
Our Lady, handmaid of the Lord,
made answer willingly.

3. The heavenly call she thus obeyed,
and so God's will was done;
the second Eve love's answer made
which our redemption won.

4. She gave her body for God's shrine,
her heart to piercing pain,
and knew the cost of love divine
when Jesus Christ was slain.

5. Dear Mary, from your lowliness
and home in Galilee,
there comes a joy and holiness
to every family.

6. Hail, Mary, you are full of grace,
above all women blest;
and blest your Son, whom your
  embrace
in birth and death confessed.

195 Folliot Sandford Pierpoint (1835-1917)

1. For the beauty of the earth,
for the beauty of the skies,
for the love which from our birth
over and around us lies:

*Lord of all, to thee we raise
this our sacrifice of praise.*

2. For the beauty of each hour
of the day and of the night,
hill and vale and tree and flower,
sun and moon and stars of light:

3. For the joy of human love,
brother, sister, parent, child,
friends on earth, and friends above,
pleasures pure and undefiled:

4. For each perfect gift of thine,
to our race so freely given,
graces human and divine,
flowers of earth and buds of heaven:

5. For thy Church which evermore
lifteth holy hands above,
offering up on every shore
her pure sacrifice of love:

196 Nick Fawcett (b. 1957)
© 2004 Kevin Mayhew Ltd

1. For the days when you feel near,
for the times when all is clear;
when your presence seems so real,
that it colours all we feel:
for the blessing of such days,
Lord, accept our grateful praise.

2. For the times when you feel far,
when we wonder where you are;
when we call and call again,
but our prayers appear in vain –
when it seems you just don't care,
Lord, assure us you're still there.

Continued overleaf

3. For the truth that day by day
   you are present, come what may:
   when we see you, when we don't,
   when we trust you, when we won't.
   For the peace such love imparts,
   Lord, we come with grateful hearts.

197 Fred Pratt Green (1903-2000)
© 1970 Stainer & Bell Ltd

1. For the fruits of his creation,
   thanks be to God;
   for his gifts to every nation,
   thanks be to God;
   for the ploughing, sowing, reaping,
   silent growth while we are sleeping,
   future needs in earth's safekeeping,
   thanks be to God.

2. In the just reward of labour,
   God's will is done;
   in the help we give our neighbour,
   God's will is done;
   in our world-wide task of caring
   for the hungry and despairing,
   in the harvests we are sharing,
   God's will is done.

3. For the harvests of his Spirit,
   thanks be to God;
   for the good we all inherit,
   thanks be to God;
   for the wonders that astound us,
   for the truths that still confound us,
   most of all, that love has found us,
   thanks be to God.

198 Fred Kaan (b. 1929)
© 1968 Stainer & Bell Ltd

1. For the healing of the nations,
   Lord, we pray with one accord;
   for a just and equal sharing
   of the things that earth affords.
   To a life of love in action
   help us rise and pledge our word.

2. Lead us, Father, into freedom,
   from despair your world release;
   that, redeemed from war and hatred,
   all may come and go in peace.
   Show us how through care and goodness
   fear will die and hope increase.

3. All that kills abundant living,
   let it from the earth be banned;
   pride of status, race or schooling
   dogmas that obscure your plan.
   In our common quest for justice
   may we hallow life's brief span.

4. You, creator-God, have written
   your great name on humankind;
   for our growing in your likeness
   bring the life of Christ to mind;
   that by our response and service
   earth its destiny may find.

199 Rosamond E. Herklots (1905-1987) alt.
© Oxford University Press

1. 'Forgive our sins as we forgive',
   you taught us, Lord, to pray;
   but you alone can grant us grace
   to live the words we say.

2. How can your pardon reach and bless
   the unforgiving heart
   that broods on wrongs, and will not let
   old bitterness depart?

3. In blazing light your Cross reveals
   the truth we dimly knew:
   what trivial debts are owed to us,
   how great our debt to you!

4. Lord, cleanse the depths within our
      souls,
   and bid resentment cease.
   Then, bound to all in bonds of love,
   our lives will spread your peace.

200 James Quinn (b. 1919)
© 1969 Geoffrey Chapman, an imprint
of Continuum Int. Publishing Group
Used by permission

1. Forth in the peace of Christ we go;
   Christ to the world with joy we bring;
   Christ in our minds, Christ on our
      lips,
   Christ in our hearts, the world's true
      King.

2. King of our hearts, Christ makes us
      kings;
   kingship with him his servants gain;
   with Christ, the Servant-Lord of all,
   Christ's world we serve to share
      Christ's reign.

3. Priests of the world, Christ sends us
      forth
   this world of time to consecrate,
   our world of sin by grace to heal,
   Christ's world in Christ to re-create.

4. Prophets of Christ, we hear his Word:
   he claims our minds to search his ways;
   he claims our lips to speak his truth;
   he claims our hearts to sing his praise.

5. We are his Church, he makes us one:
   here is one hearth for all to find;
   here is one flock, one Shepherd-King;
   here is one faith, one heart, one mind.

201 Charles Wesley (1707-1788) alt.

1. Forth in thy name, O Lord, I go,
   my daily labour to pursue;
   thee, only thee, resolved to know,
   in all I think or speak or do.

2. The task thy wisdom hath assigned
   O let me cheerfully fulfil;
   in all my works thy presence find,
   and prove thy good and perfect will.

3. Thee may I set at my right hand,
   whose eyes my inmost substance see,
   and labour on at thy command,
   and offer all my works to thee.

4. Give me to bear thy easy yoke,
   and every moment watch and pray,
   and still to things eternal look,
   and hasten to thy glorious day.

5. For thee delightfully employ
   whate'er thy bounteous grace hath
      given,
   and run my course with even joy,
   and closely walk with thee to heaven.

202 George Hunt Smyttan (1822-1870)
adapted by Michael Forster (b. 1946)
© 1999 Kevin Mayhew Ltd

1. Forty days and forty nights
   you were fasting in the wild;
   forty days and forty nights,
   tempted still, yet unbeguiled.

2. Sunbeams scorching all the day,
   chilly dew-drops nightly shed,
   prowling beasts about your way,
   stones your pillow, earth your bed.

3. Let us your endurance share,
   and from earthly greed abstain,
   with you vigilant in prayer,
   with you strong to suffer pain.

Continued overleaf

4. Then if evil on us press,
   flesh or spirit to assail,
   Victor in the wilderness,
   help us not to swerve or fail.

5. So shall peace divine be ours;
   holy gladness, pure and true:
   come to us, angelic powers,
   such as ministered to you.

6. Keep, O keep us, Saviour dear,
   ever constant by your side,
   that with you we may appear
   at th'eternal Eastertide.

203 Isaac Watts (1674-1748)
based on Psalm 117

1. From all that dwell below the skies
   let the Creator's praise arise:
   let the Redeemer's name be sung
   through every land by every tongue.

2. Eternal are thy mercies, Lord;
   eternal truth attends thy word:
   thy praise shall sound from shore to
        shore,
   till suns shall rise and set no more.

204 Liturgy of St James
trans. Charles William Humphreys
(1840-1921)

1. From glory to glory advancing,
   we praise thee, O Lord;
   thy name with the Father and Spirit
   be ever adored.
   From strength unto strength we go
        forward
   on Sion's highway,
   to appear before God
   in the city of infinite day.

2. Thanksgiving and glory and worship
   and blessing and love,
   one heart and one song have the saints
   upon earth and above.
   Evermore, O Lord, to thy servants
   thy presence be nigh;
   ever fit us by service on earth
   for thy service on high.

205 Graham Kendrick (b. 1950)
© 1983 Thankyou Music

1. From heaven you came, helpless babe,
   entered our world, your glory veiled;
   not to be served but to serve,
   and give your life that we might live.

   This is our God, the Servant King,
   he calls us now to follow him,
   to bring our lives as a daily offering
   of worship to the Servant King.

2. There in the garden of tears,
   my heavy load he chose to bear;
   his heart with sorrow was torn.
   'Yet not my will but yours,' he said.

3. Come see his hands and his feet,
   the scars that speak of sacrifice,
   hands that flung stars into space,
   to cruel nails surrendered.

4. So let us learn how to serve,
   and in our lives enthrone him;
   each other's needs to prefer,
   for it is Christ we're serving.

206 Michael Forster (b. 1946), based on the *Didache*
© 1992 Kevin Mayhew Ltd

1. From many grains, once scattered far
        and wide,
   each one alone, to grow as best it may,
   now safely gathered in and unified,
   one single loaf we offer here today.

So may your Church, in every time
  and place,
be in this meal united by your grace.

2. From many grapes, once living on
     the vine,
  now crushed and broken under
     human feet,
  we offer here this single cup of wine:
  the sign of love, unbroken and
     complete.
  So may we stand among the crucified,
  and live the risen life of him who died.

3. From many places gathered, we are
     here,
  each with a gift that we alone can
     bring.
  O Spirit of the living God, draw near,
  make whole by grace our broken
     offering.
  O crush the pride that bids us stand
     alone;
  let flow the love that makes our
     spirits one.

207 Godfrey Thring (1823-1903) alt.

1. From the eastern mountains
  pressing on they come,
  wise men in their wisdom,
  to his humble home;
  stirred by deep devotion,
  hasting from afar,
  ever journeying onward,
  guided by a star.

2. There their Lord and Saviour
  meek and lowly lay,
  wondrous light that led them
  onward on their way,

ever now to lighten
nations from afar,
as they journey homeward
by that guiding star.

3. Thou who in a manger
  once hast lowly lain,
  who dost now in glory
  o'er all kingdoms reign,
  guide your scattered people
  homeward from afar,
  young and old together,
  by thy guiding star.

4. Gather in the outcasts,
  all who've gone astray;
  throw thy radiance o'er them,
  guide them on their way:
  those who never knew thee,
  those who've wandered far,
  guide them by the brightness
  of thy guiding star.

5. Until every nation,
  whether bond or free,
  'neath thy starlit banner,
  Jesus, follow thee
  o'er the distant mountains
  to that heavenly home,
  where nor sin nor sorrow
  evermore shall come.

208 John L. Bell (b. 1949) and Graham Maule (b. 1958) © 1989, 1996 WGRG, Iona Community

1. From the falter of breath,
  through the silence of death,
  to the wonder that's breaking beyond;
  God has woven a way,
  unapparent by day,
  for all those of whom heaven is fond.

Continued overleaf

2. From frustration and pain,
   through hope hard to sustain,
   to the wholeness here promised,
   there known;
   Christ has gone where we fear
   and has vowed to be near
   on the journey we make on our own.

3. From the dimming of light,
   through the darkness of night,
   to the glory of goodness above;
   God the Spirit is sent
   to ensure heaven's intent
   is embraced and completed in love.

4. From today till we die
   through all questioning why,
   to the place from which time and
   tide flow;
   angels tread on our dreams
   and magnificent themes
   of heaven's promise are echoed below.

210
Graham Kendrick (b. 1950)
© 1988 Make Way Music

1. From the sun's rising unto the sun's
   setting,
   Jesus our Lord shall be great in the
   earth;
   and all earth's kingdoms shall be his
   dominion,
   all of creation shall sing of his worth.

   *Let every heart, every voice, every
   tongue join with spirits ablaze;
   one in his love, we will circle the world
   with the song of his praise.
   O, let all his people rejoice,
   and let all the earth hear his voice!*

2. To every tongue, tribe and nation he
   sends us,
   to make disciples, to teach and baptise.
   For all authority to him is given;
   now as his witnesses we shall arise.

3. Come, let us join with the Church
   from all nations,
   cross every border, throw wide every
   door;
   workers with him as he gathers his
   harvest,
   till earth's far corners our Saviour
   adore.

209
Paul S. Deming
© 1976 Integrity's Hosanna! Music/
Sovereign Music UK

From the rising of the sun to the
   going down of the same,
the Lord's name is to be praised. *(x2)*
Praise ye the Lord,
praise him all ye servants of the Lord,
   praise the name of the Lord.
Blessèd be the name of the Lord from
   this time forth
and for evermore.

211
Michael Forster (b. 1946)
© 1994 Kevin Mayhew Ltd

1. From the very depths of darkness
   springs a bright and living light;
   out of falsehood and deceit
   a greater truth is brought to sight;
   in the halls of death, defiant,
   life is dancing with delight!
   The Lord is risen indeed!

Christ is risen! Hallelujah! (x3)
The Lord is risen indeed!

*2. Jesus meets us at the dawning
of the resurrection day;
speaks our name with love, and gently
says that here we may not stay:
'Do not cling to me, but go to
all the fearful ones and say,
"The Lord is risen indeed!" '

*3. So proclaim it in the high-rise,
in the hostel let it ring;
make it known in Cardboard City,
let the homeless rise and sing:
'He is Lord of life abundant,
and he changes everything;
the Lord is risen indeed!'

4. In the heartlands of oppression,
sound the cry of liberty;
where the poor are crucified,
behold the Lord of Calvary;
from the fear of death and dying,
Christ has set his people free;
the Lord is risen indeed!

5. To the tyrant, tell the gospel
of a love that can't be known
in a guarded palace-tomb,
condemned to live and die alone:
'Take the risk of love and freedom;
Christ has rolled away the stone!
The Lord is risen indeed!'

6. When our spirits are entombed
in mortal prejudice and pride;
when the gates of hell itself
are firmly bolted from inside;
at the bidding of his Spirit,
we may fling them open wide;
the Lord is risen indeed!

212 Charles Kingsley (1819-1875)

1. From thee all skill and science flow,
all pity, care, and love,
all calm and courage, faith and hope:
O pour them from above.

2. Impart them, Lord, to each and all,
as each and all shall need,
to rise, like incense, each to thee,
in noble thought and deed.

3. And hasten, Lord, that perfect day
when pain and death shall cease,
and thy just rule shall fill the earth
with health and light and peace.

213 Jean Holloway (b. 1939)
© 1993 Kevin Mayhew Ltd

Gather around, for the table is spread,
welcome the food and rest!
Wide is our circle, with Christ at the
head,
he is the honoured guest.
Learn of his love, grow in his grace,
pray for the peace he gives;
here at this meal, here in this place,
know that his Spirit lives!
Once he was known in the breaking
of bread,
shared with a chosen few;
multitudes gathered
and by him were fed,
so will he feed us too.

214 Christine McCann (b. 1951)
© 1978 Kevin Mayhew Ltd

1. Gifts of bread and wine, gifts we've
offered,
fruits of labour, fruits of love, taken,
offered, sanctified, blessed and broken;
words of one who died;

Continued overleaf

'Take my body, take my saving blood.'
Gifts of bread and wine: Christ our Lord.

2. Christ our Saviour, living presence
    here,
    as he promised while on earth:
    'I am with you for all time,
    I am with you in this bread and wine.'

3. To the Father, with the Spirit,
    one in union with the Son,
    for God's people, joined in prayer,
    faith is strengthened by the food we
        share.

215 Traditional

1. Give me joy in my heart, keep me
    praising,
    give me joy in my heart, I pray.
    Give me joy in my heart, keep me
    praising,
    keep me praising till the end of day.

    Sing hosanna! Sing hosanna!
    Sing hosanna to the King of kings!
    Sing hosanna! Sing hosanna!
    Sing hosanna to the King!

2. Give me peace in my heart,
    keep me resting . . .

3. Give me love in my heart,
    keep me serving . . .

4. Give me light in my heart,
    keep me shining . . .

216 Estelle White (b. 1925)
© 1976 Kevin Mayhew Ltd

1. Give me peace, O Lord, I pray,
    in my work and in my play;
    and inside my heart and mind,
    Lord, give me peace.

2. Give peace to the world, I pray,
    let all quarrels cease today.
    May we spread your light and love:
    Lord, give us peace.

217 Martin E. Leckebusch (b. 1962)
© 2000 Kevin Mayhew Ltd

1. Give thanks for those whose faith is
    firm
    when all around seems bleak:
    on God's good promise they rely,
    so while they live and when they die
    how forcefully they speak –
    the strong who once were weak!

2. Give thanks for those whose hope is
    clear,
    beyond mere mortal sight:
    who seek the city God has planned,
    the true, eternal promised land,
    and steer towards that light,
    a beacon ever bright.

3. Give thanks for those whose love is
    pure,
    a sparkling, precious stone:
    they show by what they say and do
    an inward beauty, warm and true,
    for God's concerns they own –
    his love through them is known.

4. Give thanks for saints of ages past
    and saints alive today:
    though often by this world despised,
    their hearts by God are richly prized –
    give thanks that we may say
    we share their pilgrim way.

218 Chris Tomlin (b. 1972)
© 2000 worshiptogether.com songs/Six Steps Music

1. Give thanks to the Lord,
   our God and King:
   his love endures for ever.
   For he is good, he is above all things:
   his love endures for ever.
   Sing praise, sing praise.

2. With a mighty hand
   and outstretched arm:
   his love endures for ever.
   For the life that's been reborn:
   his love endures for ever.
   Sing praise, sing praise,
   sing praise, sing praise.

   For ever, God is faithful,
   for ever God is strong.
   For ever God is with us,
   for ever, for ever.

3. From the rising to the setting sun:
   his love endures for ever.
   By the grace of God, we will carry on:
   his love endures for ever.
   Sing praise, sing praise,
   sing praise, sing praise.

219 Henry Smith
© 1978 Integrity's Hosanna! Music/
Sovereign Music UK

Give thanks with a grateful heart,
give thanks to the Holy One,
give thanks because he's given
Jesus Christ, his Son.
And now let the weak say, 'I am strong',
let the poor say, 'I am rich',
because of what the Lord has done for
us.
And now let the weak say, 'I am strong',
let the poor say, 'I am rich',
because of what the Lord has done for
us.

220 Isaac Watts (1674-1748), based on Psalm 136 alt.

1. Give to our God immortal praise;
   mercy and truth are all his ways:
   wonders of grace to God belong,
   repeat his mercies in your song.

2. Give to the Lord of lords renown,
   the King of kings with glory crown:
   his mercies ever shall endure
   when earthly powers are known no
   more.

3. He sent his Son with power to save
   from guilt and darkness and the grave:
   wonders of grace to God belong,
   repeat his mercies in your song.

4. Through earthly life he guides our feet,
   and leads us to his heavenly seat:
   his mercies ever shall endure
   when earthly powers are known no
   more.

221 Isaac Watts (1674-1748) alt.

1. Give us the wings of faith to rise
   within the veil, and see
   the saints above, how great their joys,
   how bright their glories be.

2. Once they were mourning here below,
   their couch was wet with tears;
   they wrestled hard, as we do now,
   with sins and doubts and fears.

3. We ask them whence their vict'ry
   came:
   they, with united breath,
   ascribe the conquest to the Lamb,
   their triumph to his death.

Continued overleaf

4. They marked the footsteps that he
   trod,
   his zeal inspired their breast,
   and, foll'wing their incarnate God,
   they reached the promised rest.

5. Our glorious Leader claims our praise
   for his own pattern giv'n;
   while the great cloud of witnesses
   show the same path to heaven.

222 Mike Anderson (b. 1956),
adapted from the Liturgy
© 1999 Kevin Mayhew Ltd

Gloria, gloria, in excelsis Deo.
Gloria, gloria, in excelsis Deo.

1. Lord God, heavenly King,
   peace you bring to us;
   we worship you, we give you thanks,
   we sing our song of praise.

2. Jesus, Saviour of all, Lord God,
   Lamb of God,
   you take away our sins, O Lord,
   have mercy on us all.

3. At the Father's right hand, Lord,
   receive our prayer,
   for you alone are the Holy One,
   and you alone are Lord.

4. Glory, Father and Son, glory,
   Holy Spirit,
   to you we raise our hands up high,
   we glorify your name.

223 John Newton (1725-1807)
based on Isaiah 33:20-21 alt.

1. Glorious things of thee are spoken,
   Zion, city of our God;
   he whose word cannot be broken
   formed thee for his own abode.

On the Rock of Ages founded,
what can shake thy sure repose?
With salvation's walls surrounded,
thou may'st smile at all thy foes.

2. See, the streams of living waters,
   springing from eternal love,
   well supply thy sons and daughters,
   and all fear of want remove.
   Who can faint while such a river
   ever flows and thirsts assuage?
   Grace which, like the Lord, the giver,
   never fails from age to age.

3. Round each habitation hov'ring,
   see the cloud and fire appear
   for a glory and a cov'ring,
   showing that the Lord is near.
   Thus they march, the pillar leading,
   light by night and shade by day;
   daily on the manna feeding
   which he gives them when they pray.

4. Saviour, if of Zion's city
   I through grace a member am,
   let the world deride or pity,
   I will glory in thy name.
   Fading is the worldling's pleasure,
   boasted pomp and empty show;
   solid joys and lasting treasure
   none but Zion's children know.

224 'Viva, viva, Gesù', 18th century
trans. Edward Caswall (1814-1878) alt.

1. Glory be to Jesus
   who, in bitter pains,
   poured for me the lifeblood
   from his sacred veins.

2. Grace and life eternal
   in that blood I find:
   blest be his compassion,
   infinitely kind.

3. Blest, through endless ages,
   be the precious stream
   which, from endless torment,
   did the world redeem.

4. There the fainting spirit
   drinks of life her fill;
   there, as in a fountain,
   laves herself at will.

5. Abel's blood for vengeance
   pleaded to the skies,
   but the blood of Jesus
   for our pardon cries.

6. Oft as it is sprinkled
   on our guilty hearts
   Satan in confusion
   terror-struck departs.

7. Oft as earth exulting
   wafts its praise on high
   angel hosts rejoicing,
   make their glad reply.

8. Lift, then, all your voices,
   swell the mighty flood;
   louder still and louder,
   praise the precious blood.

225 Charles Wesley (1707-1788)

1. Glory, love, and praise, and honour
   for our food, now bestowed,
   render we the Donor.
   Bounteous God, we now confess
      thee;
   God, who thus blessest us,
   meet it is to bless thee.

2. Thankful for our every blessing,
   let us sing Christ the Spring,
   never, never ceasing.
   Source of all our gifts and graces
   Christ we own; Christ alone
   calls for all our praises.

3. He dispels our sin and sadness,
   life imparts, cheers our hearts,
   fills with food and gladness.
   Who himself for all hath given,
   us he feeds, us he leads
   to a feast in heaven.

226 Traditional Peruvian
© 1976 Kevin Mayhew Ltd

1. Glory to God, glory to God,
   glory to the Father.
   Glory to God, glory to God,
   glory to the Father.
   To him be glory for ever.
   To him be glory for ever.
   Alleluia, amen.
   Alleluia, amen,
   alleluia, amen,
   alleluia, amen.

2. Glory to God, glory to God,
   Son of the Father.
   Glory to God, glory to God,
   Son of the Father.
   To him be glory for ever.
   To him be glory for ever.
   Alleluia, amen.
   Alleluia, amen,
   alleluia, amen,
   alleluia, amen.

Continued overleaf

3. Glory to God, glory to God,
   glory to the Spirit.
   Glory to God, glory to God,
   glory to the Spirit.
   To him be glory for ever.
   To him be glory for ever.
   Alleluia, amen.
   Alleluia, amen,
   alleluia, amen,
   alleluia, amen.

227 John E. Bowers (b. 1923)
© John E. Bowers

1. 'Glory to God!' all heaven with joy is
   ringing;
   angels proclaim the gospel of Christ's
   birth,
   'Glory to God!', and still their song is
   bringing
   good news of God incarnate here on
   earth.

2. Lowly in wonder shepherds kneel
   before him,
   no gift to bring save love of heart and
   mind:
   come like those shepherds, sing his
   praise, adore him,
   a babe so weak, yet Lord of
   humankind.

3. Humble, yet regal, wise men kneel
   before him,
   gold, incense, myrrh, their gifts to
   Christ they bring:
   come like those wise men, sing his
   praise, adore him
   a babe so poor and modest, yet a King.

4. Though now no crib or cradle is
   concealing
   Jesus our Lord in that far-distant
   shrine,
   Christ at each eucharist is still
   revealing
   his very self in forms of bread and
   wine.

228 John L. Bell (b. 1949) and Graham Maule
(b. 1958) based on Psalm 148
© 1993 WGRG, Iona Community

1. Glory to God above!
   Heavens declare his love;
   praise him, you angels,
   praise him all you high and heavenly
   host.
   Worship him, sun and moon;
   stars complement their tune;
   grounded in God's good purpose,
   let his grace become your boast.

   O sing hallelujah
   and praise God for evermore.

2. Glory to God below
   let depths of ocean show;
   lightning and hail, snow,
   wind and cloud perform at his
   command!
   Let every mountain range,
   forest and grove and grange,
   creatures of earth and air and sea
   praise God in every land.

3. 'Glory to God!' now sing
   commoner, queen and king;
   women and men of
   every age unite to praise the Lord.
   Worship God's holy name
   and let your lives proclaim
   God's saving power extends to those
   who love and serve his word.

229 Thomas Ken (1637-1710)

1. Glory to thee, my God, this night
for all the blessings of the light;
keep me, O keep me, King of kings,
beneath thine own almighty wings.

2. Forgive me, Lord, for thy dear Son,
the ill that I this day have done,
that with the world, myself and thee,
I, ere I sleep, at peace may be.

3. Teach me to live, that I may dread
the grave as little as my bed;
teach me to die, that so I may
rise glorious at the aweful day.

4. O may my soul on thee repose,
and with sweet sleep mine eyelids close;
sleep that may me more vig'rous
make
to serve my God when I awake.

5. Praise God, from whom all blessings
flow;
praise him, all creatures here below;
praise him above, ye heavenly host;
praise Father, Son and Holy Ghost.

230 H. C. A. Gaunt (1902-1983)
© Oxford University Press

1. Glory to thee, O God,
for all thy saints in light,
who nobly strove and conquered
in the well-fought fight.
Their praises sing,
who life outpoured
by fire and sword for Christ their King.

2. Thanks be to thee, O Lord,
for saints thy Spirit stirred
in humble paths to live thy life and
speak thy word.

Unnumbered they,
whose candles shine
to lead our footsteps after thine.

3. Lord God of truth and love,
'thy kingdom come', we pray;
give us thy grace to know thy truth
and walk thy way:
that here on earth
thy will be done,
till saints in earth and heaven are one.

231 Michael Forster (b. 1946)
© 1998 Kevin Mayhew Ltd

1. Go back, go back to Galilee,
go with the one who died,
and witness there to risen life
among the crucified.
Where human folk are living still
in fear of worldly power,
their Christ, with wounds still open,
stands and shares their finest hour.

2. Go back, go back to Galilee,
Christ meets us on the way,
and calls us all to follow truth
where evil still holds sway.
There in the face of hate and fear,
the Spirit gives us breath;
his song is life and liberty
which puts an end to death.

3. 'Go back, go back to Galilee,'
the centuries repeat,
'where evil, faced with deathless hope,
still struggles in defeat.'
So when we find the empty tomb
a safer place to be,
the angel prompts us yet again,
'Go back to Galilee.'

232 James Edward Seddon (1915-1983)
© *The representatives of the late James Edward Seddon/ Jubilate Hymns. Used by permission*

1. Go forth and tell!
O Church of God, awake!
God's saving news
to all the nations take:
proclaim Christ Jesus,
Saviour, Lord and King,
that all the world
his worthy praise may sing.

2. Go forth and tell!
God's love embraces all;
he will in grace
respond to all who call;
how shall they call
if they have never heard
the gracious invitation
of his word?

3. Go forth and tell!
where still the darkness lies;
in wealth or want,
the sinner surely dies:
give us, O Lord,
concern of heart and mind,
a love like yours
which cares for all mankind.

4. Go forth and tell!
the doors are open wide:
share God's good gifts –
let no one be denied;
live out your life
as Christ your Lord shall choose,
your ransomed powers
for his sole glory use.

5. Go forth and tell!
O Church of God, arise!
Go in the strength
which Christ your Lord supplies;
go till all nations
his great name adore
and serve him, Lord and King,
for evermore.

233 Traditional

Go, tell it on the mountain,
over the hills and everywhere.
Go, tell it on the mountain
that Jesus Christ is born.

1. While shepherds kept their watching
o'er wand'ring flocks by night,
behold, from out of heaven,
there shone a holy light.

2. And lo, when they had seen it,
they all bowed down and prayed;
they travelled on together
to where the babe was laid.

3. When I was a seeker,
I sought both night and day:
I asked my Lord to help me
and he showed me the way.

4. He made me a watchman
upon the city wall,
and, if I am a Christian,
I am the least of all.

234 Susan Sayers (b. 1946)
© *1986 Kevin Mayhew Ltd*

1. Go wand'ring in the sun,
let it warm you through.
That's how warm and comforting
God's love can be for you.

2. Just watch a feather fall,
lay it on your cheek.
Jesus is as gentle
with the frightened and the weak.

3. Enjoy the drops of rain,
   sparkling as they fall.
   Jesus is as gen'rous
   with his blessings to us all.

4. Well, can you hold the sea,
   make a living flower?
   Neither can we understand
   the greatness of his power.

5. Yet run against the wind –
   very soon you'll see –
   just as strong and real
   is Jesus' love for you and me.

2. God be with you till we meet again;
   and when doubts and fears oppress
      you,
   may his holy peace possess you;
   God be with you till we meet again.

3. God be with you till we meet again;
   in distress his grace sustain you;
   in success from pride restrain you;
   God be with you till we meet again.

4. God be with you till we meet again;
   may he go through life beside you,
   and through death in safety guide you;
   God be with you till we meet again.

235 *Book of Hours* (1514)

God be in my head,
and in my understanding;
God be in mine eyes,
and in my looking;
God be in my mouth,
and in my speaking;
God be in my heart,
and in my thinking;
God be at mine end,
and at my departing.

237

Carol Owens (b. 1931)
© 1972 Bud John Songs/EMI Christian Music
Publishing. Administered by Kevin Mayhew Ltd

1. God forgave my sin in Jesus' name.
   I've been born again in Jesus' name.
   And in Jesus' name I come to you
   to share his love as he told me to.

   He said: 'Freely, freely you have received;
   freely, freely give.
   Go in my name, and because you believe,
   others will know that I live.'

236

Donald Hughes (1911-1967)
Based on J. E. Rankin (1828-1904)
© Paul Hughes

1. God be with you till we meet again;
   may he through the days direct you;
   may he in life's storms protect you;
   God be with you till we meet again.

   Till we meet! Till we meet!
   Till we meet at Jesus' feet;
   till we meet! Till we meet!
   God be with you till we meet again!

2. All power is given in Jesus' name,
   in earth and heaven in Jesus' name.
   And in Jesus' name I come to you
   to share his power as he told me to.

3. God gives us life in Jesus' name,
   he lives in us in Jesus' name.
   And in Jesus' name I come to you
   to share his peace as he told me to.

238

George Wallace Briggs (1875-1959) alt.
© 1953, renewal 1981 Hymn Society of America/
Hope Publishing Co. Administered by CopyCare

1. God has spoken – by the prophets,
spoken the unchanging Word,
each from age to age proclaiming
God, the one, the righteous Lord.
'Mid the world's despair and turmoil
one firm anchor holding fast:
God eternal reigns forever,
God the first, and God the last.

2. God has spoken – by Christ Jesus,
Christ, the everlasting Son,
brightness of the Father's glory,
with the Father ever one;
spoken by the Word incarnate,
God of God, ere time was born,
light of light, to earth descending,
Christ, as God in human form.

3. God is speaking – by the Spirit,
speaking to our hearts again,
in the age-long word declaring
God's own message, now as then.
Through the rise and fall of nations
one sure faith yet standing fast;
God abides, the Word unchanging,
God the first, and God the last.

239

John L. Bell (b. 1949) and Graham Maule
(b. 1958)
© 1989 WGRG, Iona Community

1. God, in the planning and purpose of
life,
hallowed the union of husband and
wife:
this we embody where love is
displayed,
rings are presented and promises made.

2. Jesus was found, at a similar feast,
taking the roles of both waiter and
priest,
turning the worldly towards the
divine,
tears into laughter and water to wine.

3. Therefore we pray that his Spirit
preside
over the wedding of bridegroom and
bride,
fulfilling all that they've hoped will
come true,
lighting with love all they dream of
and do.

4. Praise then the Maker, the Spirit, the
Son,
source of the love through which two
are made one.
God's is the glory, the goodness and
grace
seen in this marriage and known in
this place.

240

Alan J. Price
© 1994 Daybreak Music Ltd

God is good, God is great,
he's the one who did create
everything that there is by his power.
God is good, God is great,
he's the one who did create
everything that there is by his power.

1. Thank you, Lord, for the things I can
see,
thank you, thank you, Lord.
Thank you, Lord, for the sounds I
can hear,
thank you, thank you, Lord.

2. Thank you, Lord, for my family,
   thank you, thank you, Lord.
   Thank you, Lord, for all my friends,
   thank you, thank you, Lord.

3. Thank you, Lord, for the birds in
   the sky,
   thank you, thank you, Lord.
   Thank you, Lord, for the ants on the
   ground,
   thank you, thank you, Lord.

4. Thank you, Lord, for your love to me,
   thank you, thank you, Lord.
   Thank you, Lord, that you're always
   near,
   thank you, thank you, Lord.

241 Fred Pratt Green (1903-2000)
    © 1979 Stainer & Bell Ltd

1. God is here! As we his people
   meet to offer praise and prayer,
   may we find in fuller measure
   what it is in Christ we share.
   Here, as in the world around us,
   all our varied skills and arts
   wait the coming of his Spirit
   into open minds and hearts.

2. Here are symbols to remind us
   of our lifelong need of grace;
   here are table, font and pulpit;
   here the cross has central place.
   Here in honesty of preaching,
   here in silence, as in speech,
   here in newness and renewal,
   God the Spirit comes to each.

3. Here our children find a welcome
   in the Shepherd's flock and fold;
   here as bread and wine are taken,
   Christ sustains us, as of old;

here the servants of the Servant
seek in worship to explore
what it means in daily living
to believe and to adore.

4. Lord of all, of Church and Kingdom,
   in an age of change and doubt,
   keep us faithful to the gospel,
   help us work your purpose out.
   here, in this day's dedication,
   all we have to give, receive:
   we, who cannot live without you,
   we adore you! We believe!

242 Percy Dearmer (1867-1936) alt.

1. God is love: his the care,
   tending each, everywhere.
   God is love, all is there!
   Jesus came to show him,
   that we all might know him!

   Sing aloud, loud, loud!
   Sing aloud, loud, loud!
   God is good! God is truth!
   God is beauty! Praise him!

2. None can see God above;
   we can share life and love;
   thus may we Godward move,
   seek him in creation,
   holding every nation.

3. Jesus lived on the earth,
   hope and life brought to birth
   and affirmed human worth,
   for he came to save us
   by the truth he gave us.

4. To our Lord praise we sing,
   light and life, friend and King,
   coming down, love to bring,
   pattern for our duty,
   showing God in beauty.

243

Timothy Rees (1874-1939) alt.
© Geoffrey Chapman, an imprint of Continuum
International Publishing Group.
Used by permission

1. God is love: let heaven adore him;
God is love: let earth rejoice;
let creation sing before him,
and exalt him with one voice.
He who laid the earth's foundation,
he who spread the heavens above,
he who breathes through all creation,
he is love, eternal Love.

2. God is love: and he enfoldeth
all the world in one embrace;
with unfailing grasp he holdeth
every child of every race.
And when human hearts are breaking
under sorrow's iron rod,
then they find that self-same aching
deep within the heart of God.

3. God is love: and though with blindness
sin afflicts the human soul,
God's eternal loving-kindness
guides and heals and makes us whole.
Sin and death and hell shall never
o'er us final triumph gain;
God is love, so love for ever
o'er the universe must reign.

2. That Word of Life, before all things
in primal darkness spoken,
became for us the Word made flesh
for our redemption broken.
His glory set aside,
for us he lived and died,
obedient to the death,
renewed in life and breath,
to endless glory woken!

3. That Breath of God, who brooded first
upon the new creation,
who lit with light the Virgin's womb
to bear the world's salvation;
that Dove whose shadow graced
th'anointed Saviour's face,
now challenges us all
to recognise the call
to hope and liberation.

4. O great Creator, Spirit, Word,
the well-spring of creation,
our Alpha and our Omega,
our hope and our salvation;
to Father, Spirit, Son,
the Three for ever One,
and One for ever Three,
mysterious Trinity,
be praise and adoration.

244

Michael Forster (b. 1946)
© 1996 Kevin Mayhew Ltd

1. God is our strength from days of old,
the hope of every nation;
whose power conceived the universe
and set the earth's foundation.
Though hidden from our sight
in uncreated light,
his presence yet is known,
his wondrous purpose shown,
resplendent in creation!

245

Nick Fawcett (b. 1957)
© 2004 Kevin Mayhew Ltd

1. God is the giver of love,
holding us all in his arms,
filling our hearts and feeding our souls,
grace flowing down from above.

2. God is the giver of light,
shining on me and on you,
yearning to help and craving to guide,
bringing an end to the night.

3. God is the giver of joy,
   aching to fill us with cheer,
   he makes us glad and brings us delight,
   bliss that no ill can destroy.

4. God is the giver of peace,
   striving to make his world whole,
   hungry to heal and thirsty to mend,
   working that hatred might cease.

5. God is the giver of all,
   eager to bless us each day,
   hands open wide, he longs to impart
   gifts to enrich and enthral.

246 Arthur Campbell Ainger (1841-1919)
adapted by Michael Forster (b. 1946)
This version © 1996 Kevin Mayhew Ltd

1. God is working his purpose out
   as year succeeds to year.
   God is working his purpose out,
   and the time is drawing near.
   Nearer and nearer draws the time,
   the time that shall surely be,
   when the earth shall be filled
   with the glory of God
   as the waters cover the sea.

*2. From the east to the utmost west
   wherever foot has trod,
   through the mouths of his messengers
   echoes forth the voice of God:
   'Listen to me, ye continents,
   ye islands, give ear to me,
   that the earth shall be filled
   with the glory of God
   as the waters cover the sea.'

3. How can we do the work of God,
   how prosper and increase
   harmony in the human race,
   and the reign of perfect peace?

What can we do to urge the time,
the time that shall surely be,
when the earth shall be filled
with the glory of God
as the waters cover the sea?

*4. March we forth in the strength of
   God,
   his banner is unfurled;
   let the light of the gospel shine
   in the darkness of the world:
   strengthen the weary, heal the sick
   and set every captive free,
   that the earth shall be filled
   with the glory of God
   as the waters cover the sea.

5. All our efforts are nothing worth
   unless God bless the deed;
   vain our hopes for the harvest tide
   till he brings to life the seed.
   Yet ever nearer draws the time,
   the time that shall surely be,
   when the earth shall be filled
   with the glory of God
   as the waters cover the sea.

247 William Cowper (1731-1800)

1. God moves in a mysterious way
   his wonders to perform;
   he plants his footsteps in the sea,
   and rides upon the storm.

2. Deep in unfathomable mines
   of never-failing skill,
   he treasures up his bright designs,
   and works his sovereign will.

3. Ye fearful saints, fresh courage take;
   the clouds ye so much dread
   are big with mercy, and shall break
   in blessings on your head.

Continued overleaf

4. Judge not the Lord by feeble sense,
but trust him for his grace;
behind a frowning providence
he hides a shining face.

5. His purposes will ripen fast,
unfolding every hour;
the bud may have a bitter taste,
but sweet will be the flower.

6. Blind unbelief is sure to err,
and scan his work in vain;
God is his own interpreter,
and he will make it plain.

248 Harry Emerson Fosdick (1878-1969) alt.
© *The Estate of the late H. E. Fosdick*
Used by permission of Dr Elinor Fosdick Downs

1. God of grace and God of glory,
on thy people pour thy power;
now fulfil thy Church's story;
bring her bud to glorious flower.
Grant us wisdom, grant us courage,
for the facing of this hour.

2. Lo, the hosts of evil round us
scorn thy Christ, assail his ways;
from the fears that long have bound us
free our hearts to faith and praise.
Grant us wisdom, grant us courage,
for the living of these days.

3. Cure thy children's warring madness,
bend our pride to thy control;
shame our wanton selfish gladness,
rich in goods and poor in soul.
Grant us wisdom, grant us courage,
lest we miss thy kingdom's goal.

4. Set our feet on lofty places,
gird our lives that they may be
armoured with all Christlike graces
as we set your people free.
Grant us wisdom, grant us courage,
lest we fail the world or thee.

249 Nick Fawcett (b. 1957)
© *1997 Kevin Mayhew Ltd*

1. God of life, God of love,
all around we glimpse your greatness,
here on earth and far above.
We would worship all our days
even though no words can ever
give to you sufficient praise.

2. God of life, God of truth,
we rejoice that you are with us,
never distant or aloof.
Like a father, you are there,
reaching out your arms to hold us,
speaking words that show you care.

3. God of life, God of grace,
you have walked this earth before us,
giving truth a human face.
Knowing sorrow, knowing pain,
you were beaten, bruised and broken,
but in triumph rose again.

4. God of life, God of love –
felt as wind and tongues of fire
yet as gentle as a dove –
every moment, every hour,
you are working deep within us
through your sovereign selfless power.

5. God of life, God on high,
we can barely grasp your goodness,
language fails us when we try.
As a father, through your Son,
by the Spirit you are with us,
somehow three, yet also one.

250 Jean Holloway (b. 1939)
© *1999 Kevin Mayhew Ltd*

1. God of love, you freely give us
blessings more than we deserve;
be our light in times of darkness,
be our strength when fears unnerve.

In this age when proof convinces,
help us see where wisdom lies;
more enduring than persuasion
is your truth which never dies.

2. Son incarnate, yours the presence
which can heal an aching heart;
over death you reign triumphant,
you alone new life impart.
From your birth so long awaited,
to the cross on Calvary,
you will serve as our example,
let us, Lord, your servants be.

3. Holy Spirit, inspiration
day by day, yet mystery;
with the Son and the Creator
you form mystic unity.
Draw us into your communion,
with the love that sets us free;
bind our hearts to you for ever,
holy, blessèd Trinity.

251 Henry Francis Lyte (1793-1847)
based on Psalm 67, alt.

1. God of mercy, God of grace,
show the brightness of thy face;
shine upon us, Saviour, shine,
fill thy Church with light divine;
and thy saving health extend
unto earth's remotest end.

2. Let the people praise thee, Lord;
be by all that live adored;
let the nations shout and sing
glory to their Saviour King;
at thy feet their tribute pay,
and thy holy will obey.

3. Let the people praise thee, Lord;
earth shall then her fruits afford;
God to us his blessing give,
we to God devoted live;
all below, and all above,
one in joy and light and love.

252 Michael Forster (b. 1946)
© 1993 Kevin Mayhew Ltd

1. God of the Passover,
Author and Lord of salvation,
gladly we gather to bring
you our hearts' adoration;
ransomed and free,
called and commissioned to be
signs of your love for creation.

2. Here we remember that ev'ning
of wonder enthralling,
myst'ry of passion divine,
and betrayal appalling.
Breaking the bread,
'This is my body,' he said,
'do this, my passion recalling.'

3. God of the Eucharist,
humbly we gather before you
and, at your table,
for pardon and grace we implore you.
Under the cross,
counting as profit our loss,
safe in its shade, we adore you.

253 Stephen Eric Smyth
© Stephen Eric Smyth

1. God, our Creator, hear us sing in
praise.
God, always tender, God who knows
our ways.
God, always present, God who really
cares.
We offer thanks for all the love you
share.
We sing in praise for the great gifts
you give:
all of creation, everything that lives,
glories of nature, our own time on
earth,
sending your Son among us proves
our worth.

Continued overleaf

Loud is our praise as we sing of you,
one with people of faith, ancient and
new.
Bless us afresh with your grace, we pray.
Help us witness your love today.

2. Thanks for the blessings of the talents,
   skills,
   fam'lies and friendships by which
   lives are filled.
   Thanks for the graces, gifts you
   spread so wide:
   those that the world sees and those
   deep inside.
   Even in hard times we can praise
   your name.
   You're always with us, loving just the
   same.
   Sickness or sorrow, loneliness or doubt,
   help us remember your hand reaches
   out.

3. Gathered together, sister, brothers all,
   baptised in Jesus, faithful to your call.
   We are one fam'ly, may your will be
   done
   and, for all people, may your
   Kingdom come.
   'God who is love', you are our Father
   true;
   Jesus, our brother, fully human too;
   Spirit, your presence, with us every
   day;
   love is your essence, love our truest
   way.

4. God, our Creator, hear us sing in
   praise.
   God, always tender, God who knows
   our ways.
   God, always present, God who really
   cares.
   We offer thanks for all the love you
   share.

We sing in praise for the great gifts
   you give:
all of creation, everything that lives,
glories of nature, our own time on
   earth,
sending your Son among us proves
   our worth.

254 Traditional English, alt.

1. God rest you merry, gentlefolk,
   let nothing you dismay,
   for Jesus Christ our Saviour
   was born on Christmas Day,
   to save us all from Satan's power
   when we were gone astray:

   O tidings of comfort and joy,
   comfort and joy,
   O tidings of comfort and joy.

2. In Bethlehem, in Jewry,
   this blessèd babe was born,
   and laid within a manger,
   upon this blessèd morn;
   at which his mother Mary
   did nothing take in scorn:

3. From God, our heavenly Father,
   a blessèd angel came,
   and unto certain shepherds
   brought tidings of the same,
   how that in Bethlehem was born
   the Son of God by name:

4. 'Fear not,' then said the angel,
   'let nothing you affright,
   this day is born a Saviour,
   of virtue, power and might;
   by him the world is overcome
   and Satan put to flight.'

5. The shepherds at those tidings
   rejoicèd much in mind,
   and left their flocks a-feeding,
   in tempest, storm and wind,
   and went to Bethlehem straightway
   this blessèd babe to find:

6. But when to Bethlehem they came,
   whereat this infant lay,
   they found him in a manger,
   where oxen feed on hay;
   his mother Mary kneeling,
   unto the Lord did pray:

7. Now to the Lord sing praises,
   all you within this place,
   and with true love and fellowship
   each other now embrace;
   this holy tide of Christmas
   all others doth deface:

255 vs. 1 & 2 unknown (17th century)
    v. 3 William E. Hickson (1803-1870) alt.

1. God save our gracious Queen,
   long live our noble Queen,
   God save the Queen.
   Send her victorious,
   happy and glorious,
   long to reign over us:
   God save the Queen.

2. Thy choicest gifts in store
   on her be pleased to pour,
   long may she reign:
   may she defend our laws,
   and ever give us cause
   to sing with heart and voice
   God save the Queen!

3. Not on this land alone,
   but be God's mercies known
   on every shore.

Lord, make the nations see
that all humanity
should form one family
the wide world o'er.

256 v. 1 Reginald Heber (1783-1826)
    v. 2 Richard Whately (1787-1863)

1. God that madest earth and heaven,
   darkness and light;
   who the day for toil hast given,
   for rest the night;
   may thine angel-guards defend us,
   slumber sweet thy mercy send us,
   holy dreams and hopes attend us,
   this live-long night.

2. Guard us waking, guard us sleeping,
   and, when we die,
   may we in thy mighty keeping
   all peaceful lie:
   when the last dread call shall wake us,
   do not thou our God forsake us,
   but to reign in glory take us
   with thee on high.

257 Basil E. Bridge (b. 1927)
    © Basil E. Bridge. Used by permission

1. God the Father, name we treasure,
   each new generation draws
   from the past that you have given
   for the future that is yours;
   may these children, in your keeping,
   love your ways, obey your laws.

2. Christ, the name that Christians
      carry,
   Christ, who from the Father came,
   calling us to share your sonship,
   for these children grace we claim;
   may they be your true disciples,
   yours in deed as well as name.

Continued overleaf

3. Holy Spirit, from the Father
   on the friends of Jesus poured,
   may our children share those graces
   promised to them in the word,
   and their gifts find rich fulfilment,
   dedicated to our Lord.

4. As we now with high thanksgiving
   their triumphant names record,
   grant that we, like them, believing
   in the promise of thy word,
   may, like them, in all good living
   praise and magnify the Lord!

258

John L. Bell (b. 1949) and
Graham Maule (b. 1958)
© 1979 WGRG, Iona Community

God to enfold you,
Christ to uphold you,
Spirit to keep you in heaven's sight;
so may God grace you,
heal and embrace you,
lead you through darkness
into the light.

259

C. A. Alington (1872-1955)
© Hymns Ancient & Modern Ltd

1. God, whose city's sure foundation
   stands upon his holy hill,
   by his mighty inspiration
   chose of old and chooseth still
   men and women from each nation
   his good pleasure to fulfil.

2. Here before us through the ages,
   while the Christian years went by,
   saints, confessors, martyrs, sages,
   strong to live and strong to die,
   wrote their names upon the pages
   of God's blessèd company.

3. Some there were like lamps of
      learning
   shining in a faithless night,
   some on fire with love, and burning
   with a flaming zeal for right,
   some by simple goodness turning
   souls from darkness unto light.

260

John Arlott (1914-1991) alt.
© The Estate of the late L. T. J. Arlott

1. God, whose farm is all creation,
   take the gratitude we give;
   take the finest of our harvest,
   crops we grow that all may live.

2. Take our ploughing, seeding, reaping,
   hopes and fears of sun and rain,
   all our thinking, planning, waiting,
   ripened in this fruit and grain.

3. All our labour, all our watching,
   all our calendar of care,
   in these crops of your creation,
   take, O God: they are our prayer.

261

Ian D. Craig
© 1993 Daybreak Music Ltd

1. God's love is deeper than the deepest
      ocean,
   God's love is wider than the widest sea,
   God's love is higher than the highest
      mountain,
   deeper, wider, higher is God's love to
      me.

2. God's grace is deeper than the deepest
      ocean,
   God's grace is wider than the widest
      sea,
   God's grace is higher than the highest
      mountain,
   deeper, wider, higher is God's grace to
      me.

3. God's joy is deeper than the deepest
   ocean,
   God's joy is wider than the widest sea,
   God's joy is higher than the highest
   mountain,
   deeper, wider, higher is God's joy to
   me.

4. God's peace is deeper than the
   deepest ocean,
   God's peace is wider than the widest
   sea,
   God's peace is higher than the highest
   mountain,
   deeper, wider, higher is God's peace
   to me.

   Deeper, wider, higher,
   deeper, wider, higher,
   deeper, wider, higher is God to me.

262 Alan Dale (1902-1979) and Hubert J. Richards
© 1982 Kevin Mayhew Ltd

1. God's Spirit is in my heart.
   He has called me and set me apart.
   This is what I have to do,
   what I have to do.

   He sent me to give the Good News to
   the poor,
   tell pris'ners that they are pris'ners no
   more,
   tell blind people that they can see,
   and set the downtrodden free,
   and go tell everyone the news
   that the kingdom of God has come,
   and go tell everyone the news that God's
   kingdom has come.

2. Just as the Father sent me,
   so I'm sending you out to be
   my witnesses throughout the world,
   the whole of the world.

3. Don't carry a load in your pack,
   you don't need two shirts on your
   back.
   A workman can earn his own keep,
   can earn his own keep.

4. Don't worry what you have to say,
   don't worry because on that day
   God's Spirit will speak in your heart,
   will speak in your heart.

263 Michael Forster (b. 1946)
© 1999 Kevin Mayhew Ltd

1. Going home, moving on,
   through God's open door;
   hush, my soul, have no fear,
   Christ has gone before.
   Parting hurts, love protests,
   pain is not denied;
   yet, in Christ, life and hope
   span the great divide.
   Going home, moving on,
   through God's open door;
   hush, my soul, have no fear,
   Christ has gone before,
   Christ has gone before.

2. No more guilt, no more fear,
   all the past is healed:
   broken dreams now restored,
   perfect grace revealed.
   Christ has died, Christ is ris'n,
   Christ will come again:
   death destroyed, life restored,
   love alone shall reign.
   Going home, moving on,
   through God's open door;
   hush, my soul, have no fear,
   Christ has gone before,
   Christ has gone before.

264

Michael Forster (b. 1946)
© 1993 Kevin Mayhew Ltd

1. Goliath was big and Goliath was
   strong,
   his sword was sharp and his spear was
   long;
   he bragged and boasted but he was
   wrong:
   biggest isn't always best!

   Biggest isn't always best!
   Biggest isn't always best!
   God told David, 'Don't be afraid,
   biggest isn't always best!'

2. A shepherd boy had a stone and sling;
   he won the battle and pleased the
   King!
   Then all the people began to sing:
   'Biggest isn't always best!'

3. So creatures made in a smaller size,
   like tiny sparrows and butterflies,
   are greater than we may realise:
   biggest isn't always best!

265

John Mason Neale (1818-1866) alt.

1. Good Christians all, rejoice
   with heart and soul and voice!
   Give ye heed to what we say:
   News! News! Jesus Christ is born
   today;
   ox and ass before him bow,
   and he is in the manger now:
   Christ is born today, Christ is born
   today!

2. Good Christians all, rejoice
   with heart and soul and voice!
   Now ye hear of endless bliss:
   Joy! Joy! Jesus Christ was born for this.

He hath opened heaven's door,
and we are blest for evermore:
Christ was born for this,
Christ was born for this.

3. Good Christians all, rejoice
   with heart and soul and voice!
   Now ye need not fear the grave:
   Peace! Peace! Jesus Christ was born to
   save;
   calls you one, and calls you all,
   to gain his everlasting hall:
   Christ was born to save,
   Christ was born to save.

266

Cyril Argentine Alington (1872-1955) alt.
© Hymns Ancient & Modern

1. Good Christians all, rejoice and sing.
   Now is the triumph of our King.
   To all the world glad news we bring:
   Alleluia!

2. The Lord of Life is ris'n for ay:
   bring flowers of song to strew his way;
   let humankind rejoice and say:
   Alleluia!

3. Praise we in songs of victory
   that Love, that Life, which cannot die
   and sing with hearts uplifted high:
   Alleluia!

4. Thy name we bless, O risen Lord,
   and sing today with one accord
   the life laid down, the life restored:
   Alleluia!

267
John Mason Neale (1818-1866) alt.

1. Good King Wenceslas looked out
   on the feast of Stephen,
   when the snow lay round about,
   deep, and crisp, and even;
   brightly shone the moon that night,
   though the frost was cruel,
   when a poor man came in sight,
   gath'ring winter fuel.

2. 'Hither, page, and stand by me,
   if thou know'st it, telling,
   yonder peasant, who is he,
   where and what his dwelling?'
   'Sire, he lives a good league hence,
   underneath the mountain,
   right against the forest fence,
   by Saint Agnes' fountain.'

3. 'Bring me flesh, and bring me wine,
   bring me pine logs hither:
   thou and I will see him dine,
   when we bring him thither.'
   Page and monarch, forth they went,
   forth they went together;
   through the rude wind's wild lament,
   and the bitter weather.

4. 'Sire, the night is darker now,
   and the wind blows stronger;
   fails my heart, I know not how;
   I can go no longer.'
   'Mark my footsteps good, my page;
   tread thou in them boldly:
   thou shalt find the winter's rage
   freeze thy blood less coldly.'

5. In his master's steps he trod,
   where the snow lay dinted;
   heat was in the very sod
   which the Saint had printed.
   Therefore, Christians all, be sure,
   wealth or rank possessing,
   ye who now will bless the poor,
   shall yourselves find blessing.

268
Christopher Wordsworth (1807-1885)

1. Gracious Spirit, Holy Ghost,
   taught by thee, we covet most
   of thy gifts at Pentecost,
   holy, heavenly love.

2. Love is kind, and suffers long,
   love is meek, and thinks no wrong,
   love than death itself more strong;
   therefore give us love.

3. Prophecy will fade away,
   melting in the light of day;
   love will ever with us stay;
   therefore give us love.

4. Faith will vanish into sight;
   hope be emptied in delight;
   love in heaven will shine more bright;
   therefore give us love.

5. Faith and hope and love we see
   joining hand in hand agree;
   but the greatest of the three,
   and the best, is love.

6. From the overshadowing
   of thy gold and silver wing
   shed on us, who to thee sing,
   holy, heavenly love.

269
Jean Holloway (b. 1939)
© 1998 Kevin Mayhew Ltd

1. Grant us the courage, gracious God,
   to change the things we can,
   pursuing justice, spreading hope
   that Jesus Christ began.

2. Give us serenity to bear
   the things we cannot change;
   acceptance of the things we find
   mysterious or strange.

Continued overleaf

3. We ask for wisdom to discern
the changes we can make;
and pray for your sustaining love
through risks we choose to take.

4. Encourage all who love your church
to try the bold and new;
forsaking safe, familiar ways
for greater trust in you.

5. Your Holy Spirit leads the way
to change we dream not of –
through fear of the unknown, and on
to costly deeds of love.

Suffer and serve till all are fed,
and show how grandly love intends
to work till all creation sings,
to fill all worlds, to crown all things.

5. Great God, in Christ you set us free
your life to live, your joy to share.
Give us your Spirit's liberty
to turn from guilt and dull despair
and offer all that faith can do
while love is making all things new.

270 Brian Wren (b. 1936)
© 1975, 1995 Stainer & Bell Ltd

1. Great God, your love has called us here
as we, by love, for love were made.
Your living likeness still we bear,
though marred, dishonoured,
disobeyed.
We come, with all our heart and mind
your call to hear, your love to find.

2. We come with self-inflicted pains
of broken trust and chosen wrong,
half-free, half-bound by inner chains,
by social forces swept along,
by powers and systems close confined
yet seeking hope for humankind.

3. Great God, in Christ you call our name
and then receive us as your own,
not through some merit, right or claim
but by your gracious love alone.
We strain to glimpse your mercy-seat
and find you kneeling at our feet.

4. Then take the towel, and break the
bread,
and humble us, and call us friends.

271 Noel Richards (b. 1955) and Gerald Coates
© 1992 Thankyou Music

1. Great is the darkness that covers the
earth,
oppression, injustice and pain.
Nations are slipping in hopeless despair,
though many have come in your
name.
Watching while sanity dies,
touched by the madness and lies.

Come, Lord Jesus, come, Lord Jesus,
pour out your Spirit, we pray.
Come, Lord Jesus, come, Lord Jesus,
pour out your Spirit on us today.

2. May now your church rise with
power and love,
this glorious gospel proclaim.
In every nation salvation will come
to those who believe in your name.
Help us bring light to this world
that we might speed your return.

3. Great celebrations on that final day
when out of the heavens you come.
Darkness will vanish, all sorrow will
end,
and rulers will bow at your throne.
Our great commission complete,
then face to face we shall meet.

272

Steve McEwan
© 1985 Body Songs. Administered by CopyCare

1. Great is the Lord and most worthy of
   praise,
   the city of our God, the holy place,
   the joy of the whole earth.
   Great is the Lord, in whom we have
   the victory.
   He aids us against the enemy,
   we bow down on our knees.

2. And, Lord, we want to lift your name
   on high,
   and, Lord, we want to thank you
   for the works you've done in our lives;
   and, Lord, we trust in your unfailing
   love,
   for you alone are God eternal,
   throughout earth and heaven above.

2. Summer and winter,
   and springtime and harvest,
   sun, moon and stars
   in their courses above,
   join with all nature
   in manifold witness
   to thy great faithfulness,
   mercy and love.

3. Pardon for sin
   and a peace that endureth,
   thine own dear presence
   to cheer and to guide;
   strength for today
   and bright hope for tomorrow,
   blessings all mine,
   with ten thousand beside!

273

Thomas Obadiah Chisholm (1866-1960)
© 1923, renewal 1951 Hope Publishing Co.
Administered by CopyCare

1. Great is thy faithfulness,
   O God, my Father,
   there is no shadow
   of turning with thee;
   thou changest not,
   thy compassions, they fail not;
   as thou hast been
   thou for ever wilt be.

   Great is thy faithfulness!
   Great is thy faithfulness!
   Morning by morning
   new mercies I see;
   all I have needed
   thy hand hath provided,
   great is thy faithfulness,
   Lord, unto me!

274

John Newton (1725-1807)

1. Great Shepherd of thy people, hear,
   thy presence now display;
   as thou hast given a place for prayer,
   so give us hearts to pray.

2. Within these walls let holy peace
   and love and concord dwell;
   here give the troubled conscience ease,
   the wounded spirit heal.

3. May we in faith receive thy word,
   in faith present our prayers,
   and in the presence of our Lord
   unburden all our cares.

4. The hearing ear, the seeing eye,
   the contrite heart, bestow;
   and shine upon us from on high,
   that we in grace may grow.

275 William Williams (1717-1791)
trans. Peter Williams (1727-1796) and others

1. Guide me, O thou great Redeemer,
   pilgrim through this barren land;
   I am weak, but thou art mighty,
   hold me with thy powerful hand:
   Bread of Heaven, Bread of Heaven,
   feed me till I want no more,
   feed me till I want no more.

2. Open now the crystal fountain,
   whence the healing stream doth flow;
   let the fire and cloudy pillar
   lead me all my journey through;
   strong deliverer, strong deliverer,
   be thou still my strength and shield,
   be thou still my strength and shield.

3. When I tread the verge of Jordan,
   bid my anxious fears subside;
   death of death, and hell's destruction,
   land me safe on Canaan's side;
   songs of praises, songs of praises,
   I will ever give to thee,
   I will ever give to thee.

276 Greek (3rd century or earlier)
trans. John Keble (1792-1866)

1. Hail, gladdening Light,
   of his pure glory poured
   from th'immortal Father,
   heavenly, blest,
   holiest of holies,
   Jesus Christ our Lord.

2. Now we are come
   to the sun's hour of rest,
   the lights of evening
   round us shine,
   we hymn the Father,
   Son and Holy Spirit divine.

3. Worthiest art thou at all times
   to be sung with undefilèd tongue,
   Son of our God,
   giver of life, alone:
   therefore in all the world thy glories,
   Lord, they own.

277 Charles Wesley (1707-1788)
Thomas Cotterill (1779-1823) and others, alt.

1. Hail the day that sees him rise,
   alleluia!
   to his throne above the skies;
   alleluia!
   Christ the Lamb, for sinners giv'n,
   alleluia!
   enters now the highest heaven!
   alleluia!

2. There for him high triumph waits;
   lift your heads, eternal gates!
   He hath conquered death and sin;
   take the King of Glory in!

*3. Circled round with angel-powers,
   their triumphant Lord and ours;
   wide unfold the radiant scene,
   take the King of Glory in!

*4. Lo, the heaven its Lord receives,
   yet he loves the earth he leaves;
   though returning to his throne,
   calls the human race his own.

*5. See, he lifts his hands above;
   see, he shows the prints of love;
   hark, his gracious lips bestow
   blessings on his Church below.

*6. Still for us he intercedes,
   his prevailing death he pleads;
   near himself prepares our place,
   he the first-fruits of our race.

7. Lord, though parted from our sight,
   far above the starry height,
   grant our hearts may thither rise,
   seeking thee above the skies.

8. Ever upward let us move,
   wafted on the wings of love;
   looking when our Lord shall come,
   longing, sighing after home.

4. Worship, honour, power and blessing,
   thou art worthy to receive;
   loudest praises, without ceasing,
   it is right for us to give:
   help, ye bright angelic spirits!
   bring your sweetest, noblest lays;
   help to sing our Saviour's merits,
   help to chant Immanuel's praise.

278 John Bakewell (1721-1819) alt.

1. Hail, thou once despisèd Jesus,
   hail, thou Galilean King!
   Thou didst suffer to release us;
   thou didst free salvation bring.
   Hail, thou universal Saviour,
   bearer of our sin and shame;
   by thy merits we find favour;
   life is given through thy name.

2. Paschal Lamb, by God appointed,
   all our sins on thee were laid;
   by almighty love anointed,
   thou hast full atonement made.
   All thy people are forgiven
   through the virtue of thy blood;
   opened is the gate of heaven,
   we are reconciled to God.

3. Jesus, hail! enthroned in glory,
   there for ever to abide;
   all the heavenly hosts adore thee,
   seated at thy Father's side:
   there for sinners thou art pleading,
   there thou dost our place prepare;
   ever for us interceding,
   till in glory we appear.

279 John Ellerton (1826-1893)

1. Hail to the Lord who comes,
   comes to his temple gate,
   not with his angel host,
   not in his kingly state:
   no shouts proclaim him nigh,
   no crowds his coming wait.

2. But borne upon the throne
   of Mary's gentle breast,
   watched by her duteous love,
   in her fond arms at rest;
   thus to his Father's house,
   he comes, the heavenly guest.

3. There Joseph at her side
   in rev'rent wonder stands;
   and, filled with holy joy,
   old Simeon in his hands
   takes up the promised child,
   the glory of all lands.

4. O Light of all the earth,
   thy children wait for thee:
   come to thy temples here,
   that we, from sin set free,
   before thy Father's face
   may all presented be.

280
Paraphrase of Psalm 72 by James Montgomery (1771-1854)

1. Hail to the Lord's anointed,
   great David's greater son!
   Hail, in the time appointed,
   his reign on earth begun!
   He comes to break oppression,
   to set the captive free;
   to take away transgression,
   and rule in equity.

2. He comes with succour speedy
   to those who suffer wrong;
   to help the poor and needy,
   and bid the weak be strong;
   to give them songs for sighing,
   their darkness turn to light,
   whose souls, condemned and dying,
   were precious in his sight.

3. He shall come down like showers
   upon the fruitful earth,
   and love, joy, hope, like flowers,
   spring in his path to birth:
   before him on the mountains
   shall peace the herald go;
   and righteousness in fountains
   from hill to valley flow.

4. Kings shall fall down before him,
   and gold and incense bring;
   all nations shall adore him,
   his praise all people sing;
   to him shall prayer unceasing
   and daily vows ascend;
   his kingdom still increasing,
   a kingdom without end.

5. O'er every foe victorious,
   he on his throne shall rest,
   from age to age more glorious,
   all-blessing and all-blest;
   the tide of time shall never
   his covenant remove;
   his name shall stand for ever;
   that name to us is love.

281
Latin (14th century)
trans. Henry N. Oxenham (1829-1888)

1. Hail, true body, born of Mary,
   by a wondrous virgin-birth.
   Thou who on the cross wast offered
   to redeem the sons of earth;

2. Thou whose side became a fountain
   pouring forth thy precious blood,
   give us now; and at our dying,
   thine own self to be our food.

3. O sweetest Jesu,
   O gracious Jesu,
   O Jesu, blessèd Mary's Son.

282
From the Liturgy

Halle, halle, hallelujah!
Halle, halle, hallelujah!
Halle, halle, hallelujah!
Hallelujah, hallelujah!

283
Unknown

Hallelu, hallelu, hallelu, hallelujah;
we'll praise the Lord! *(Repeat)*
We'll praise the Lord, hallelujah! *(x3)*
We'll praise the Lord!

284
Adam Fox (1883-1977)
based on the Liturgy of Malabar
© *Hymns Ancient & Modern Ltd*

1. Hands that have been handling,
   holy things and high,
   still, Lord in thy service
   bless and fortify.

2. Ears which heard the message
of the words of life,
keep thou closed and guarded
from the noise of strife.

3. Eyes whose contemplation
looked upon thy love,
let them gaze expectant
on the world above.

4. 'Holy, holy, holy,'
thee our lips confessed:
on those lips for ever
let no falsehood rest.

5. Feet which trod the pavement
round about God's board,
let them walk in glory
where God's light is poured.

6. Bodies that have tasted
of the living bread,
be they recreated
in their living Head.

7. Be we all one Body,
all our members one,
measured by the stature
of God's full-grown Son.

285 Robert Bridges (1844-1930)
based on 'O quam juvat',
Charles Coffin (1676-1749) alt.

1. Happy are they, they that love God,
whose hearts have Christ confessed,
who by his cross have found their life,
and 'neath his yoke their rest.

2. Glad is the praise, sweet are the songs,
when they together sing;
and strong the prayers that bow the ear
of heaven's eternal King.

3. Christ to their homes giveth his peace,
and makes their loves his own:
but ah, what tares the evil one
hath in his garden sown!

4. Sad were our lot, evil this earth,
did not its sorrows prove
the path whereby the sheep may find
the fold of Jesus' love.

5. Then shall they know, they that love
him,
how hope is wrought through pain;
their fellowship, through death itself,
unbroken will remain.

286 'Vox clara ecce intonat', (6th century)
trans. Edward Caswall (1814-1878)

1. Hark! a herald voice is calling:
'Christ is nigh!' it seems to say;
'Cast away the dreams of darkness,
O ye children of the day!'

2. Startled at the solemn warning,
let the earth-bound soul arise;
Christ, her sun, all sloth dispelling,
shines upon the morning skies.

3. Lo, the Lamb, so long expected,
comes with pardon down from
heav'n;
let us haste, with tears of sorrow,
one and all to be forgiv'n.

4. So when next he comes with glory,
wrapping all the earth in fear,
may he then, as our defender,
on the clouds of heav'n appear.

5. Honour, glory, virtue, merit,
to the Father and the Son,
with the co-eternal Spirit,
while unending ages run.

287 William Cowper (1731-1800)
based on John 21:16

1. Hark, my soul, it is the Lord;
'tis thy Saviour, hear his word;
Jesus speaks, and speaks to thee,
'Say, poor sinner, lov'st thou me?

2. 'I delivered thee when bound,
and, when wounded, healed thy
wound;
sought thee wand'ring, set thee right,
turned thy darkness into light.

3. 'Can a woman's tender care
cease towards the child she bare?
Yes, she may forgetful be,
yet will I remember thee.

4. 'Mine is an unchanging love,
higher than the heights above,
deeper than the depths beneath,
free and faithful, strong as death.

5. 'Thou shalt see my glory soon,
when the work of grace is done;
partner of my throne shalt be:
say, poor sinner, lov'st thou me?'

6. Lord, it is my chief complaint
that my love is weak and faint;
yet I love thee, and adore;
O for grace to love thee more!

288 Philip Doddridge (1702-1751)
based on Luke 4:18-19

1. Hark, the glad sound! the Saviour
comes,
the Saviour promised long:
let every heart prepare a throne,
and every voice a song.

2. He comes, the pris'ners to release
in Satan's bondage held;
the gates of brass before him burst,
the iron fetters yield.

3. He comes, the broken heart to bind,
the bleeding soul to cure,
and with the treasures of his grace
to bless the humble poor.

4. Our glad hosannas, Prince of Peace,
thy welcome shall proclaim;
and heaven's eternal arches ring
with thy belovèd name.

289 Charles Wesley (1707-1788), George
Whitefield (1714-1770), Martin Madan
(1726-1790) and others, alt.

1. Hark, the herald-angels sing
glory to the new-born King;
peace on earth and mercy mild,
God and sinners reconciled:
joyful, all ye nations rise,
join the triumph of the skies,
with th'angelic host proclaim,
'Christ is born in Bethlehem.'

Hark, the herald-angels sing
glory to the new-born King.

2. Christ, by highest heaven adored,
Christ, the everlasting Lord,
late in time behold him come,
offspring of a virgin's womb!
Veiled in flesh the Godhead see,
hail, th'incarnate Deity!
Pleased as man with us to dwell,
Jesus, our Emmanuel.

3. Hail, the heav'n-born Prince of Peace!
   Hail, the Sun of Righteousness!
   Light and life to all he brings,
   ris'n with healing in his wings;
   mild he lays his glory by,
   born that we no more may die,
   born to raise us from the earth,
   born to give us second birth.

290 Bryn Austin Rees (1911-1983)
© *Alexander Scott*

1. Have faith in God, my heart,
   trust and be unafraid;
   God will fulfil in every part
   each promise he has made.

2. Have faith in God, my mind,
   though oft thy light burns low;
   God's mercy holds a wiser plan
   than thou canst fully know.

3. Have faith in God, my soul,
   his Cross for ever stands;
   and neither life nor death can pluck
   his children from his hands.

4. Lord Jesus, make me whole;
   grant me no resting-place,
   until I rest, heart, mind and soul,
   the captive of thy grace.

291 Christian Strover (b. 1932)
© *Christian Strover/Jubilate Hymns*
Used by permission.

1. Have you heard the raindrops
   drumming on the rooftops?
   Have you heard the raindrops
   dripping on the ground?
   Have you heard the raindrops
   splashing in the streams
   and running to the rivers all around?

There's water, water of life,
Jesus gives us the water of life;
there's water, water of life,
Jesus gives us the water of life.

2. There's a busy worker
   digging in the desert,
   digging with a spade that
   flashes in the sun;
   soon there will be water
   rising in the well-shaft,
   spilling from the bucket as it comes.

3. Nobody can live
   who hasn't any water,
   when the land is dry,
   then nothing much grows;
   Jesus gives us life if we drink
   the living water,
   sing it so that everybody knows.

292 Gerald Coates, Noel Richards (b. 1955) and
Tricia Richards. © *1993 Thankyou Music*

He has risen, he has risen,
he has risen, Jesus is alive.

1. When the life flowed from his body,
   seemed like Jesus' mission failed.
   But his sacrifice accomplished,
   vict'ry over sin and hell.

2. In the grave God did not leave him,
   for his body to decay;
   raised to life, the great awakening,
   Satan's power he overcame.

3. If there were no resurrection,
   we ourselves could not be raised;
   but the Son of God is living,
   so our hope is not in vain.

4. When the Lord rides out of heaven,
   mighty angels at his side,
   they will sound the final trumpet,
   from the grave we shall arise.

Continued overleaf

5. He has given life immortal,
   we shall see him face to face;
   through eternity we'll praise him,
   Christ the champion of our faith.

   He has risen, he has risen,
   he has risen, Jesus is alive.

Twila Paris (b. 1958).
© 1985 Straightway Music/Mountain
Spring/EMI Christian Music Publishing.
Administered by Kevin Mayhew Ltd

293

He is exalted,
the King is exalted on high;
I will praise him.
He is exalted,
for ever exalted
and I will praise his name!
He is the Lord;
for ever his truth shall reign.
Heaven and earth rejoice
in his holy name.
He is exalted,
the King is exalted on high.

294 Unknown

1. He is Lord, he is Lord.
   He is risen from the dead and he is
   Lord.
   Every knee shall bow, every tongue
   confess
   that Jesus Christ is Lord.

2. He is King, he is King.
   He is risen from the dead and he is
   King.
   Every knee shall bow, every tongue
   confess
   that Jesus Christ is King.

3. He is love, he is love.
   He is risen from the dead and he is
   love.
   Every knee shall bow, every tongue
   confess
   that Jesus Christ is love.

295 Kevin Prosch
© 1991 Mercy/Vineyard Publishing

1. He is the Lord, and he reigns on high;
   he is the Lord.
   Spoke into the darkness, created the
   light.
   He is the Lord.
   Who is like unto him, never-ending
   in days;
   he is the Lord.
   And he comes in power when we call
   on his name.
   He is the Lord.

   Show your power,
   O Lord our God,
   show your power,
   O Lord our God, our God.

2. Your gospel, O Lord, is the hope for
   our nation;
   you are the Lord.
   It's the power of God for our
   salvation.
   You are the Lord.
   We ask not for riches, but look to the
   cross;
   you are the Lord.
   And for our inheritance give us the
   lost.
   You are the Lord.

   Send your power,
   O Lord our God,
   send your power,
   O Lord our God, our God.

296

Michael Forster (b. 1946)
© 1993 Kevin Mayhew Ltd

1. Heaven is open wide,
   and Christ in glory stands,
   with all authority endowed
   and set at God's right hand.
   Above the world of noise
   extends his reign of peace,
   and all the blood of martyrs calls
   our angry ways to cease.

2. Heaven is open wide,
   and perfect love we see
   in God's eternal self revealed:
   the blessèd Trinity.
   Christ for the Church has prayed,
   that we may all be one,
   and share the triune grace whereby
   creation was begun.

3. Heaven is open wide,
   and Christ in glory stands:
   the Source and End, the First and Last,
   with justice in his hands.
   Let all the thirsty come
   where life is flowing free,
   and Christ, in splendour yet unknown,
   our morning star will be.

297

John L. Bell (b. 1949) and Graham Maule (b. 1958)
© 1987 WGRG, Iona Community

1. Heaven shall not wait
   for the poor to lose their patience,
   the scorned to smile,
   the despised to find a friend:
   Jesus is Lord,
   he has championed the unwanted;
   in him injustice
   confronts its timely end.

2. Heaven shall not wait
   for the rich to share their fortunes,
   the proud to fall,
   the élite to tend the least:
   Jesus is Lord;
   he has shown the masters' priv'lege –
   to kneel and wash
   servants' feet before they feast.

3. Heaven shall not wait
   for the dawn of great ideas,
   thoughts of compassion
   divorced from cries of pain:
   Jesus is Lord;
   he has married word and action;
   his cross and company
   make his purpose plain.

4. Heaven shall not wait
   for our legalised obedience,
   defined by statute,
   to strict conventions bound:
   Jesus is Lord;
   he has hallmarked true allegiance –
   goodness appears
   where his grace is sought and found.

5. Heaven shall not wait
   for triumphant hallelujahs,
   when earth has passed
   and we reach another shore:
   Jesus is Lord
   in our present imperfection;
   his power and love
   are for now and then for evermore.

298

William Watkins Reid (b. 1923), alt.
© 1952, renewal 1987 by the Hymn Society of America / Hope Publishing Co

1. Help us, O Lord, to learn
   the truths your word imparts,
   to study that your laws may be
   inscribed upon our hearts.

Continued overleaf

2. Help us, O Lord, to live
   that faith which we proclaim,
   that all our thoughts and words and
     deeds
   may glorify your name.

3. Help us, O Lord, to teach
   the beauty of your ways,
   that all who seek may find the Christ,
   and make a life of praise.

299 Charles Wesley (1707-1788) alt.

1. Help us to help each other, Lord,
   each other's cross to bear;
   let each a helping hand afford,
   and feel each other's care.

2. Up into thee, our living head,
   let us in all things grow,
   and by thy sacrifice be led
   the fruits of love to show.

3. Drawn by the magnet of thy love
   let all our hearts agree;
   and ever t'wards each other move,
   and ever move t'wards thee.

4. This is the bond of perfectness,
   thy spotless charity.
   O let us still we pray, possess
   the mind that was in thee.

300 *Celtic Daily Prayer*, Northumbria Community
© Copyright Control

Here am I, Lord,
I've come to do your will;
here am I, Lord,
in your presence I am still.

301 Chris Bowater (b. 1947)
© 1981 Sovereign Lifestyle Music Ltd

Here I am, wholly available.
As for me, I will serve the Lord.
Here I am, wholly available.
As for me, I will serve the Lord.

1. The fields are white unto harvest,
   but O, the lab'rers are so few,
   so, Lord, I give myself to help the
     reaping,
   to gather precious souls unto you.

2. The time is right in the nation
   for works of power and authority;
   God's looking for a people who are
     willing
   to be counted in his glorious victory.

3. As salt are we ready to savour,
   in darkness are we ready to be light?
   God's seeking out a very special
     people
   to manifest his truth and his might.

302 Marty Haugen (b. 1950)
© 1982 GIA Publications Inc.

1. Here in this place new light is
     streaming,
   now is the darkness vanished away,
   see in this space our fears and our
     dreamings,
   brought here to you in the light of
     this day.
   Gather us in – the lost and forsaken,
   gather us in – the blind and the lame;
   call to us now, and we shall awaken,
   we shall arise at the sound of our
     name.

2. We are the young – our lives are a
   myst'ry,
   we are the old – who yearn for your
   face,
   we have been sung throughout all of
   hist'ry,
   called to be light to the whole human
   race.
   Gather us in – the rich and the
   haughty,
   gather us in – the proud and the
   strong;
   give us a heart so meek and so lowly,
   give us the courage to enter the song.

3. Here we will take the wine and the
   water,
   here we will take the bread of new
   birth,
   here you shall call your sons and your
   daughters,
   call us anew to be salt for the earth.
   Give us to drink the wine of
   compassion,
   give us to eat the bread that is you;
   nourish us well, and teach us to fashion
   lives that are holy and hearts that are
   true.

4. Not in the dark of buildings confining,
   not in some heaven, light-years away,
   but here in this place the new light is
   shining,
   now is the Kingdom, and now is the
   day.
   Gather us in and hold us for ever,
   gather us in and make us your own;
   gather us in – all peoples together,
   fire of love in our flesh and our bone.

303 Graham Kendrick (b. 1950)
© *1992 Make Way Music*

1. Here is bread, here is wine,
   Christ is with us, he is with us.
   Break the bread, taste the wine,
   Christ is with us here.

   In this bread there is healing,
   in this cup is life for ever.
   In this moment, by the Spirit,
   Christ is with us here.

2. Here is grace, here is peace,
   Christ is with us, he is with us;
   know his grace, find his peace,
   feast on Jesus here.

3. Here we are, joined in one,
   Christ is with us, he is with us;
   we'll proclaim, till he comes,
   Jesus crucified.

304 Horatius Bonar (1808-1889) alt.

1. Here, O my Lord, I see you face to
   face;
   here faith would touch and handle
   things unseen;
   here grasp with firmer hand th'eternal
   grace,
   and all my weariness upon you lean.

2. Here would I feed upon the bread of
   God;
   here drink with you the royal wine of
   heav'n;
   here would I lay aside each earthly
   load;
   here taste afresh the calm of sin
   forgiv'n.

Continued overleaf

3. I have no help but you; nor do I need
   another arm save yours to lean upon:
   it is enough, my Lord, enough
   indeed,
   my strength is in your might, your
   might alone.

305 Timothy Dudley-Smith (b. 1926)
© *Timothy Dudley-Smith*

1. Here on the threshold of a new
   beginning,
   by grace forgiven, now we leave
   behind
   our long-repented selfishness and
   sinning,
   and all our blessings call again to
   mind:
   Christ to redeem us, ransom and
   restore us,
   the love that holds us in a Saviour's
   care,
   faith strong to welcome all that lies
   before us,
   our unknown future, knowing God
   is there.

2. May we, your children, feel with
   Christ's compassion
   an earth disordered, hungry and in
   pain;
   then, at your calling, find the will to
   fashion
   new ways where freedom, truth and
   justice reign;
   where wars are ended, ancient wrongs
   are righted,
   and nations value human life and
   worth;
   where in the darkness lamps of hope
   are lighted
   and Christ is honoured over all the
   earth.

3. So may your wisdom shine from
   scripture's pages
   to mould and make us stones with
   which to build
   God's holy temple, through eternal
   ages,
   one church united, strong and Spirit-
   filled;
   heirs to the fullness of your new
   creation
   in faith we follow, pledged to be your
   own;
   yours is the future, ours the
   celebration,
   for Christ is risen! God is on the
   throne!

306 Traditional

1. He's got the whole world in his hand.
   (x4)

2. He's got you and me, brother . . .

3. He's got you and me, sister . . .

4. He's got the little tiny baby . . .

5. He's got everybody here . . .

307 Charles Edward Oakley (1832-1865) adapted

1. Hills of the north, rejoice,
   echoing songs arise,
   hail with united voice
   him who made earth and skies:
   he comes in righteousness and love,
   he brings salvation from above.

2. Isles of the southern seas
   sing to the list'ning earth,
   carry on every breeze
   hope of a world's new birth:
   in Christ shall all be made anew,
   his word is sure, his promise true.

3. Lands of the east, arise,
   he is your brightest morn,
   greet him with joyous eyes,
   praise shall his path adorn:
   the God whom you have longed to
      know
   in Christ draws near, and calls you
      now.

4. Shores of the utmost west,
   lands of the setting sun,
   welcome the heavenly guest
   in whom the dawn has come:
   he brings a never-ending light
   who triumphed o'er our darkest night.

5. Shout, as you journey on,
   songs be in every mouth,
   lo, from the north they come,
   from east and west and south:
   in Jesus all shall find their rest,
   in him the longing earth be blest.

Jimmy Owens (b. 1930)
© 1972 Bud John Songs/EMI Christian Music
Publishing

308

1. Holy, holy, holy, holy.
   Holy, holy, holy Lord God almighty;
   and we lift our hearts before you
   as a token of our love,
   holy, holy, holy, holy.

2. Gracious Father, gracious Father,
   we are glad to be your children,
      gracious Father;
   and we lift our heads before you
   as a token of our love,
   gracious Father, gracious Father.

3. Risen Jesus, risen Jesus,
   we are glad you have redeemed us,
      risen Jesus;
   and we lift our hands before you
   as a token of our love,
   risen Jesus, risen Jesus.

4. Holy Spirit, Holy Spirit,
   come and fill our hearts anew,
      Holy Spirit;
   and we lift our voice before you
   as a token of our love,
   Holy Spirit, Holy Spirit.

5. Hallelujah, hallelujah,
   hallelujah, hallelujah, hallelujah;
   and we lift our hearts before you
   as a token of our love,
   hallelujah, hallelujah.

309 Unknown

1. Holy, holy, holy is the Lord,
   holy is the Lord God almighty.
   Holy, holy, holy is the Lord,
   holy is the Lord God almighty:
   who was, and is, and is to come;
   holy, holy, holy is the Lord.

2. Jesus, Jesus, Jesus is the Lord,
   Jesus is the Lord God almighty:
      (Repeat)
   who was, and is, and is to come;
   Jesus, Jesus, Jesus is the Lord.

3. Worthy, worthy, worthy is the Lord,
   worthy is the Lord God almighty:
      (Repeat)
   who was, and is and is to come;
   worthy, worth, worthy is the Lord.

Continued overleaf

4. Glory, glory, glory to the Lord,
   glory to the Lord God almighty:
   (Repeat)
   who was, and is, and is to come;
   glory, glory, glory to the Lord.

310 Reginald Heber (1783-1826)

1. Holy, holy, holy!
   Lord God almighty!
   Early in the morning
   our song shall rise to thee;
   holy, holy, holy!
   Merciful and mighty!
   God in three persons,
   blessèd Trinity!

*2. Holy, holy, holy!
   All the saints adore thee,
   casting down their golden crowns
   around the glassy sea;
   cherubim and seraphim
   falling down before thee,
   which wert, and art,
   and evermore shall be.

3. Holy, holy, holy!
   Though the darkness hide thee,
   though the sinful mortal eye
   thy glory may not see,
   only thou art holy,
   there is none beside thee,
   perfect in power,
   in love, and purity.

4. Holy, holy, holy!
   Lord God almighty!
   All thy works shall praise thy name,
   in earth and sky and sea;
   holy, holy, holy!
   Merciful and mighty!
   God in three persons,
   blessèd Trinity!

311 Brian Foley (b. 1919)
© 1971 Faber Music Ltd

1. Holy Spirit, come, confirm us
   in the truth that Christ makes known;
   we have faith and understanding
   through your promised light alone.

2. Holy Spirit, come, console us,
   come as Advocate to plead;
   loving Spirit from the Father,
   grant in Christ the help we need.

3. Holy Spirit, come, renew us,
   come yourself to make us live;
   holy through your loving presence,
   holy through the gifts you give.

4. Holy Spirit, come, possess us,
   you the love of Three in One,
   Holy Spirit of the Father,
   Holy Spirit of the Son.

312 Samuel Longfellow (1819-1892)

1. Holy Spirit, truth divine,
   dawn upon this soul of mine:
   voice of God, and inward light,
   wake my spirit, clear my sight.

2. Holy Spirit, love divine,
   glow within this heart of mine:
   kindle every high desire,
   purify me with your fire.

3. Holy Spirit, power divine,
   fill and nerve this will of mine:
   boldly may I always live,
   bravely serve and gladly give.

4. Holy Spirit, law divine,
   reign within this soul of mine:
   be my law, and I shall be
   firmly bound, for ever free.

5. Holy Spirit, peace divine,
   still this restless heart of mine:
   speak to calm this tossing sea,
   grant me your tranquillity.

6. Holy Spirit, joy divine,
   gladden now this heart of mine:
   in the desert ways I sing –
   spring, O living water, spring!

313 Martin E. Leckebusch (b. 1962)
© 1999 Kevin Mayhew Ltd

1. Holy Spirit, will you be
   one who intercedes for me?
   When I wonder what to pray,
   how to phrase the words I say.
   Come in might and majesty –
   help me in my frailty.

2. Holy Spirit, will you be
   one who intercedes through me?
   When I lack the words to tell
   what my feelings say too well
   speak through every sigh and groan
   making my emotions known.

3. Holy Spirit, will you be
   one who intercedes with me?
   Come, and search my heart and mind,
   my desires and motives find;
   take my deepest thoughts and cares,
   turn them into fervent prayers.

4. Holy Spirit, you will be
   one who intercedes for me!
   You alone can understand
   what the mind of God has planned –
   and within his will you lead
   all for whom you intercede.

314 Carl Tuttle (b. 1953)
© 1985 Firmpaths Music
Administered by CopyCare

1. Hosanna, hosanna,
   hosanna in the highest! *(Repeat)*

   Lord, we lift up your name,
   with hearts full of praise;
   be exalted, O Lord, my God!
   Hosanna in the highest!

2. Glory, glory, glory
   to the King of kings! *(Repeat)*

315 Isaac Watts (1674-1748)
based on Isaiah 52:7-10; Matthew 13:16-17

1. How beauteous are their feet,
   who stand on Zion's hill,
   who bring salvation on their tongues
   and words of peace reveal!

2. How happy are our ears
   that hear this happy sound,
   which kings and prophets waited for,
   and sought, but never found!

3. How blessèd are our eyes
   that see this heavenly light,
   prophets and kings desired it long,
   but died without the sight!

4. The Lord makes bare his arm
   through all the earth abroad:
   let every nation now behold
   their Saviour and their God.

316 Isaac Watts (1674-1748) and others

1. How bright these glorious spirits
      shine!
   What rapture they display!
   How came they to the blissful seats
   of everlasting day?

Continued overleaf

2. Lo! these are they from suff'rings great
who came to realms of light,
and in the blood of Christ have washed
those robes that shine so bright.

3. Now with triumphal palms they stand
before the throne on high,
and serve the God they love amidst
the glories of the sky.

4. Hunger and thirst are felt no more,
nor sun with scorching ray:
God is their sun, whose cheering beams
diffuse eternal day.

5. The Lamb, who dwells amid the throne,
shall o'er them still preside,
feed them with nourishment divine,
and all their footsteps guide.

6. In pastures green he'll lead his flock
where living streams appear;
and God the Lord from every eye
shall wipe off every tear.

2. Behold the man upon a cross,
my sin upon his shoulders;
ashamed, I hear my mocking voice
call out among the scoffers.
It was my sin that held him there
until it was accomplished;
his dying breath has brought me life –
I know that it is finished.

3. I will not boast in anything,
no gifts, no power, no wisdom;
but I will boast in Jesus Christ,
his death and resurrection.
Why should I gain from his reward?
I cannot give an answer,
but this I know with all my heart,
his wounds have paid my ransom.

318 Joseph Hart (1712-1768)

1. How good is the God we adore!
Our faithful, unchangeable friend:
his love is as great as his power
and knows neither measure nor end.

2. For Christ is the first and the last;
his Spirit will guide us safe home;
we'll praise him for all that is past
and trust him for all that's to come.

317 Stuart Townend (b. 1963)
© 1995 Thankyou Music

1. How deep the Father's love for us,
how vast beyond all measure,
that he should give his only Son
to make a wretch his treasure.
How great the pain of searing loss,
the Father turns his face away,
as wounds which mar the Chosen One
bring many sons to glory.

319
v. 1 Leonard E. Smith Jnr (b. 1942)
based on Isaiah 52:7-10, vs. 2-4 unknown.
*© 1974 New Jerusalem Music. Administered in
Europe by Kingsway Music*

1. How lovely on the mountains
are the feet of him
who brings good news, good news,
announcing peace,
proclaiming news of happiness:
our God reigns, our God reigns.

Our God reigns. (x4)

2. You watchmen, lift your voices
joyfully as one,
shout for your King, your King!
See eye to eye,
the Lord restoring Zion:
our God reigns, our God reigns.

3. Wasteplaces of Jerusalem,
break forth with joy!
We are redeemed, redeemed.
The Lord has saved
and comforted his people:
our God reigns, our God reigns.

4. Ends of the earth, see
the salvation of our God!
Jesus is Lord, is Lord!
Before the nations,
he has bared his holy arm:
our God reigns, our God reigns!

320 John Mason (c. 1645-1694)

1. How shall I sing that majesty
which angels do admire?
Let dust in dust and silence lie;
sing, sing, ye heav'nly choir.
Thousands of thousands stand around
thy throne, O God most high;
ten thousand times ten thousand
sound
thy praise; but who am I?

2. Thy brightness unto them appears,
whilst I thy footsteps trace;
a sound of God comes to my ears,
but they behold thy face.
They sing because thou art their Sun;
Lord, send a beam on me;
for where heav'n is but once begun
there alleluias be.

3. How great a being, Lord, is thine,
which doth all beings keep!
Thy knowledge is the only line
to sound so vast a deep.
Thou art a sea without a shore,
a sun without a sphere;
thy time is now and evermore,
thy place is everywhere.

321 John Newton (1725-1807)

1. How sweet the name of Jesus sounds
in a believer's ear!
It soothes our sorrows, heals our
wounds,
and drives away our fear.

2. It makes the wounded spirit whole,
and calms the troubled breast;
'tis manna to the hungry soul,
and to the weary, rest.

3. Dear name! the rock on which I build,
my shield and hiding-place,
my never-failing treas'ry filled
with boundless stores of grace.

4. Jesus! my shepherd, brother, friend,
my prophet, priest, and king,
my Lord, my life, my way, my end,
accept the praise I bring.

5. Weak is the effort of my heart,
and cold my warmest thought;
but when I see thee as thou art,
I'll praise thee as I ought.

6. Till then I would thy love proclaim
with every fleeting breath;
and may the music of thy name
refresh my soul in death.

322
Dave Bilbrough
© 1983 Thankyou Music

I am a new creation,
no more in condemnation,
here in the grace of God I stand.

My heart is overflowing,
my love just keeps on growing,
here in the grace of God I stand.

And I will praise you, Lord,
yes, I will praise you, Lord,
and I will sing of all that you have
    done.

A joy that knows no limit,
a lightness in my spirit,
here in the grace of God I stand.

323
Suzanne Toolan (b. 1927)
© 1966, 1970, 1986, 1993 GIA Publications Inc.

1. I am the bread of life.
   You who come to me shall not hunger;
   and who believe in me shall not thirst.
   No one can come to me unless the
       Father beckons.

   And I will raise you up,
   and I will raise you up,
   and I will raise you up on the last day.

2. The bread that I will give is my flesh
       for the life of the world,
   and if you eat of this bread,
   you shall live for ever,
   you shall live for ever.

3. Unless you eat of the flesh of the Son
       of Man,
   and drink of his blood,
   and drink of his blood,
   you shall not have life within you.

4. I am the resurrection, I am the life.
   If you believe in me, even though
       you die, you shall live for ever.

5. Yes, Lord, I believe that you are the
       Christ,
   the Son of God,
   who has come into the world.

324
Frances Ridley Havergal (1836-1879)

1. I am trusting thee, Lord Jesus,
   trusting only thee;
   trusting thee for full salvation,
   great and free.

2. I am trusting thee for pardon,
   at thy feet I bow;
   for thy grace and tender mercy,
   trusting now.

3. I am trusting thee for cleansing
   in the crimson flood;
   trusting thee to make me holy
   by thy blood.

4. I am trusting thee to guide me;
   thou alone shalt lead,
   every day and hour supplying
   all my need.

5. I am trusting thee for power,
   thine can never fail;
   words which thou thyself shalt give me
   must prevail.

6. I am trusting thee, Lord Jesus;
   never let me fall;
   I am trusting thee for ever,
   and for all.

325
Marc Nelson
© 1987 Mercy/Vineyard Music Publishing
Administered by CopyCare

1. I believe in Jesus;
   I believe he is the Son of God.
   I believe he died and rose again.

I believe he paid for us all.
And I believe he's here now
standing in our midst;
here with the power to heal now,
and the grace to forgive.

2. I believe in you, Lord;
   I believe you are the Son of God.
   I believe you died and rose again.
   I believe you paid for us all.
   And I believe you're here now
   standing in our midst;
   here with the power to heal now,
   and the grace to forgive.

326
Ascribed to St Patrick (372-466),
trans. Cecil Frances Alexander (1818-1895) alt.

1. I bind unto myself today
   the strong name of the Trinity,
   by invocation of the same,
   the Three in One, and One in Three.

2. I bind unto myself today
   the virtues of the starlit heav'n,
   the glorious sun's life-giving ray
   the whiteness of the moon at even,
   the flashing of the lightning free,
   the whirling wind's tempestuous
      shocks,
   the stable earth, the deep salt sea
   around the old eternal rocks.

3. I bind unto myself today
   the power of God to hold and lead,
   his eye to watch, his might to stay,
   his ear to hearken to my need;
   the wisdom of my God to teach,
   his hand to guide, his shield to ward,
   the word of God to give me speech,
   his heav'nly host to be my guard.

PART TWO

4. Christ be with me, Christ within me,
   Christ behind me, Christ before me,
   Christ beside me, Christ to win me,
   Christ to comfort and restore me;
   Christ beneath me, Christ above me,
   Christ in quiet, Christ in danger,
   Christ in hearts of all that love me,
   Christ in mouth of friend and stranger.

DOXOLOGY

5. I bind unto myself the name,
   the strong name of the Trinity,
   by invocation of the same,
   the Three in One, and One in Three,
   of whom all nature hath creation,
   eternal Father, Spirit, Word.
   Praise to the Lord of my salvation:
   salvation is of Christ the Lord.
   Amen.

327
William Young Fullerton (1857-1932) alt.

1. I cannot tell
   how he whom angels worship
   should stoop to love
   the peoples of the earth,
   or why as shepherd
   he should seek the wand'rer
   with his mysterious promise
   of new birth.
   But this I know,
   that he was born of Mary,
   when Bethl'em's manger
   was his only home,
   and that he lived at
   Nazareth and laboured,
   and so the Saviour,
   Saviour of the world, is come.

Continued overleaf

2. I cannot tell
  how silently he suffered,
  as with his peace
  he graced this place of tears,
  or how his heart
  upon the cross was broken,
  the crown of pain
  to three and thirty years.
  But this I know,
  he heals the broken-hearted,
  and stays our sin,
  and calms our lurking fear,
  and lifts the burden
  from the heavy laden,
  for yet the Saviour,
  Saviour of the world, is here.

3. I cannot tell
  how he will win the nations,
  how he will claim
  his earthly heritage,
  how satisfy
  the needs and aspirations
  of east and west,
  of sinner and of sage.
  But this I know,
  all flesh shall see his glory,
  and he shall reap
  the harvest he has sown,
  and some glad day
  his sun shall shine in splendour
  when he the Saviour,
  Saviour of the world, is known.

4. I cannot tell
  how all the lands shall worship,
  when, at his bidding,
  every storm is stilled,
  or who can say
  how great the jubilation
  when every heart
  with perfect love is filled.

But this I know,
the skies will thrill with rapture,
and myriad, myriad
human voices sing,
and earth to heav'n,
and heav'n to earth, will answer:
'At last the Saviour,
Saviour of the world, is King!'

328

Brian A. Wren (b. 1936)
© 1971, 1995 Stainer & Bell Ltd

1. I come with joy, a child of God,
  forgiven, loved and free,
  the life of Jesus to recall,
  in love laid down for me.

2. I come with Christians far and near
  to find, as all are fed,
  the new community of love
  in Christ's communion bread.

3. As Christ breaks bread, and bids us
      share,
  each proud division ends.
  The love that made us, makes us one,
  and strangers now are friends.

4. The Spirit of the risen Christ,
  unseen, but ever near,
  is in such friendship better known,
  alive among us here.

5. Together met, together bound
  by all that God has done,
  we'll go with joy, to give the world
  the love that makes us one.

329
Sydney Carter (1915-2004)
© 1963 Stainer & Bell Ltd

1. I danced in the morning when the
   world was begun,
   and I danced in the moon and the
   stars and the sun,
   and I came down from heaven and I
   danced on the earth,
   at Bethlehem I had my birth.

   Dance then, wherever you may be,
   I am the Lord of the Dance, said he,
   and I'll lead you all, wherever you may
   be,
   and I'll lead you all in the dance, said he.

2. I danced for the scribe and the
   Pharisee,
   but they would not dance and they
   wouldn't follow me.
   I danced for the fishermen, for James
   and John –
   they came with me and the dance
   went on.

3. I danced on the Sabbath and I cured
   the lame;
   the holy people said it was a shame.
   They whipped and they stripped and
   they hung me on high,
   and they left me there on a cross to die.

4. I danced on a Friday when the sky
   turned black –
   it's hard to dance with the devil on
   your back.
   They buried my body, and they
   thought I'd gone,
   but I am the dance, and I still go on.

5. They cut me down and I leapt up
   high;
   I am the life that'll never, never die;
   I'll live in you if you'll live in me –
   I am the Lord of the Dance, said he.

330
Estelle White (b. 1925)
© 1978 Kevin Mayhew Ltd

1. I give my hands to do your work
   and, Jesus Lord, I give them willingly.
   I give my feet to go your way
   and every step I shall take cheerfully.

   O, the joy of the Lord is my strength,
   my strength!
   O, the joy of the Lord is my help, my
   help!
   For the power of his Spirit is in my soul
   and the joy of the Lord is my strength.

2. I give my eyes to see the world
   and everyone, in just the way you do.
   I give my tongue to speak your words,
   to spread your name and freedom-
   giving truth.

3. I give my mind in every way
   so that each thought I have will come
   from you.
   I give my spirit to you, Lord,
   and every day my prayer will spring
   anew.

4. I give my heart that you may love
   in me your Father and the human race.
   I give myself that you may grow
   in me and make my life a song of
   praise.

331
Carl Tuttle (b. 1953)
© 1982 Firmpaths Music

1. I give you all the honour
   and praise that's due your name,
   for you are the King of Glory,
   the Creator of all things.

   And I worship you,
   I give my life to you,
   I fall down on my knees.
   Yes, I worship you,
   I give my life to you,
   I fall down on my knees.

Continued overleaf

2. As your Spirit moves upon me now,
   you meet my deepest need,
   and I lift my hands up to your throne,
   your mercy I've received.
   And I worship you,
   I give my life to you,
   I fall down on my knees.
   Yes, I worship you,
   I give my life to you,
   I fall down on my knees.

3. You have broken chains that bound me,
   you've set this captive free,
   I will lift my voice to praise your name
   for all eternity.

332
Michael Forster (b. 1946)
based on the Good Friday 'Reproaches'.
© 1996 Kevin Mayhew Ltd

1. I give you love, and how do you repay?
   When you were slaves I strove to set
   you free;
   I led you out from under Pharaoh's
   yoke,
   but you led out your Christ to Calvary.
   My people, tell me, what is my offence?
   What have I done to harm you?
   Answer me!

2. For forty years I was your constant
   guide,
   I fed you with my manna from on
   high.
   I led you out to live in hope and peace,
   but you led out my only Son to die.

3. With cloud and fire I marked the
   desert way,
   I heard your cries of rage and calmed
   your fear.
   I opened up the sea and led you
   through,
   but you have opened Christ with nail
   and spear.

4. When in distress you cried to me for
   food,
   I sent you quails in answer to your call,
   and saving water from the desert rock,
   but to my Son you offered bitter gall.

5. I gave you joy when you were in
   despair,
   with songs of hope, I set your hearts
   on fire;
   crowned you with grace, the people
   of my choice,
   but you have crowned my Christ
   with thorny briar.

6. When you were weak, exploited and
   oppressed,
   I heard your cry and listened to your
   plea.
   I raised you up to honour and renown,
   but you have raised me on a shameful
   tree.

333
Susan Sayers (b. 1946)
© 1986 Kevin Mayhew Ltd

1. I have a friend who is deeper than
   the ocean,
   I have a friend who is wider than the
   sky,
   I have a friend who always
   understands me,
   whether I'm happy or ready to cry.

2. If I am lost he will search until he
   finds me,
   if I am scared he will help me to be
   brave.
   All I've to do is turn to him and ask
   him.
   I know he'll honour the promise he
   gave.

3. 'Don't be afraid,' Jesus said, 'for I am
    with you.
    Don't be afraid,' Jesus said, 'for I am
    here.
    Now and for ever, anywhere you travel,
    I shall be with you, I'll always be near.'

335 Laurie Klein (b. 1950)
© 1978 House of Mercy Music/Maranatha!
Music. Administered by CopyCare

I love you, Lord,
and I lift my voice to worship you,
O my soul rejoice.
Take joy, my King, in what you hear.
May it ⎱ be a sweet, sweet sound in
Let me ⎰ your ear.

334 Horatius Bonar (1808-1889)

1. I heard the voice of Jesus say,
   'Come unto me and rest;
   lay down, thou weary one, lay down
   thy head upon my breast.'
   I came to Jesus as I was,
   so weary, worn and sad;
   I found in him a resting-place,
   and he has made me glad.

2. I heard the voice of Jesus say,
   'Behold, I freely give
   the living water, thirsty one;
   stoop down and drink and live.'
   I came to Jesus, and I drank
   of that life-giving stream;
   my thirst was quenched, my soul
       revived,
   and now I live in him.

3. I heard the voice of Jesus say,
   'I am this dark world's light;
   look unto me, thy morn shall rise,
   and all thy day be bright.'
   I looked to Jesus, and I found
   in him my star, my sun;
   and in that light of life I'll walk
   till trav'lling days are done.

336 Annie Sherwood Hawks (1835-1918)

1. I need thee every hour,
   most gracious Lord;
   no tender voice like thine
   can peace afford.

   I need thee, O I need thee!
   every hour I need thee;
   O bless me now,
   my Saviour! I come to thee.

2. I need thee every hour;
   stay thou near by;
   temptations lose their power
   when thou art nigh.

3. I need thee every hour,
   in joy or pain;
   come quickly and abide,
   or life is vain.

4. I need thee every hour;
   teach me thy will,
   and thy rich promises
   in me fulfil.

5. I need thee every hour,
   most Holy One;
   O make me thine indeed,
   thou blessèd Son!

337 Dan Schutte (b. 1947)
based on Isaiah 6
© 1981 Daniel L. Schutte and New Dawn Music

1. I, the Lord of sea and sky,
   I have heard my people cry.
   All who dwell in dark and sin
   my hand will save.
   I who made the stars of night,
   I will make their darkness bright.
   Who will bear my light to them?
   Whom shall I send?

   Here I am, Lord. Is it I, Lord?
   I have heard you calling in the night.
   I will go, Lord, if you lead me.
   I will hold your people in my heart.

2. I, the Lord of snow and rain,
   I have borne my people's pain.
   I have wept for love of them.
   They turn away.
   I will break their hearts of stone,
   give them hearts for love alone.
   I will speak my word to them.
   Whom shall I send?

3. I, the Lord of wind and flame,
   I will tend the poor and lame.
   I will set a feast for them.
   My hand will save.
   Finest bread I will provide
   till their hearts be satisfied.
   I will give my life to them.
   Whom shall I send?

338 John Glynn (b. 1948)
© 1976 Kevin Mayhew Ltd

1. I watch the sunrise lighting the sky,
   casting its shadows near.
   And on this morning, bright though
     it be,
   I feel those shadows near me.

But you are always close to me,
following all my ways.
May I be always close to you,
following all your ways, Lord.

2. I watch the sunlight shine through
     the clouds,
   warming the earth below.
   And at the mid-day, life seems to say:
   'I feel your brightness near me.'
   For you are always . . .

3. I watch the sunset fading away,
   lighting the clouds with sleep.
   And as the evening closes its eyes,
   I feel your presence near me.
   For you are always . . .

4. I watch the moonlight guarding the
     night,
   waiting till morning comes.
   The air is silent, earth is at rest –
   only your peace is near me.
   Yes, you are always . . .

339 Matt Redman
© 1994 Thankyou Music

1. I will offer up my life
   in spirit and truth,
   pouring out the oil of love
   as my worship to you.
   In surrender I must give
   my every part;
   Lord, receive the sacrifice
   of a broken heart.

   Jesus, what can I give,
   what can I bring
   to so faithful a friend,
   to so loving a King?
   Saviour, what can be said,
   what can be sung
   as a praise of your name
   for the things you have done?

O my words could not tell,
not even in part,
of the debt of love that is owed
by this thankful heart.

2. You deserve my every breath
for you've paid the great cost;
giving up your life to death,
even death on a cross.
You took all my shame away,
there defeated my sin,
opened up the gates of heav'n,
and have beckoned me in.

341 David Ruis
© 1993 Shade Tree Music/Maranatha! Music

1. I will worship (I will worship)
with all of my heart (with all of my
heart);
I will praise you (I will praise you)
with all of my strength (all my
strength).
I will seek you (I will seek you)
all of my days (all of my days);
I will follow (I will follow)
all of your ways (all your ways).

I will give you all my worship,
I will give you all my praise;
you alone I long to worship,
you alone are worthy of my praise.

2. I will bow down (I will bow down),
hail you as king (hail you as king);
I will serve you (I will serve you),
give you everything (everything).
I will lift up (I will lift up)
my eyes to your throne (my eyes to
your throne);
I will trust you (I will trust you),
trust you alone (trust in you alone).

340 Francis Harold Rowley (1854-1952)
© HarperCollins Religious.

1. I will sing the wondrous story
of the Christ who died for me,
how he left the realms of glory
for the cross on Calvary.
Yes, I'll sing the wondrous story
of the Christ who died for me –
sing it with his saints in glory,
gathered by the crystal sea.

2. I was lost but Jesus found me,
found the sheep that went astray,
raised me up and gently led me
back into the narrow way.
Days of darkness still may meet me,
sorrow's path I oft may tread;
but his presence still is with me,
by his guiding hand I'm led.

3. He will keep me till the river
rolls its waters at my feet:
then he'll bear me safely over,
made by grace for glory meet.
Yes, I'll sing the wondrous story
of the Christ who died for me –
sing it with his saints in glory,
gathered by the crystal sea.

342 Brian Howard (b. 1930)
© 1975 Mission Hills Music.
Administered by CopyCare

1. If I were a butterfly,
I'd thank you, Lord, for giving me
wings,
and if I were a robin in a tree,
I'd thank you, Lord, that I could sing,
and if I were a fish in the sea,
I'd wiggle my tail and I'd giggle with
glee,
but I just thank you, Father,
for making me 'me'.

Continued overleaf

For you gave me a heart,
and you gave me a smile,
you gave me Jesus
and you made me your child,
and I just thank you, Father,
for making me 'me'.

2. If I were an elephant,
   I'd thank you, Lord, by raising my
      trunk,
   and if I were a kangaroo,
   you know I'd hop right up to you,
   and if I were an octopus,
   I'd thank you, Lord, for my fine looks,
   but I just thank you, Father,
   for making me 'me'.

3. If I were a wiggly worm,
   I'd thank you, Lord, that I could
      squirm,
   and if I were a billy goat,
   I'd thank you, Lord, for my strong
      throat,
   and if I were a fuzzy wuzzy bear,
   I'd thank you, Lord, for my fuzzy
      wuzzy hair,
   but I just thank you, Father,
   for making me 'me'.

The story of love he came to tell us,
bound in the making of the world.
We are the pages still unwritten:
let the story be told.

2. If we try to avoid
   inconvenient giving,
   or if love is destroyed
   by our failure to serve,
   then let the wide, unflinching,
      selfless giving
   of the God who walked this earth
   nourish our roots until we fruit
   in the joy of the Lord.

3. If we start to object
   to the path we are given
   and decide to select
   other ways of our own,
   then let the full acceptance,
      firm obedience
   of the God who walked this earth
   nourish our roots until we fruit
   in the joy of the Lord.

343 Susan Sayers (b. 1946)
© 1984 Kevin Mayhew Ltd

1. If we only seek peace
   when it's to our advantage,
   if we fail to release
   the down-trodden and poor,
   then let the gen'rous, caring,
      boundless sharing
   of the God who walked this earth
   nourish our roots until we fruit
   in the joy of the Lord.

344 Traditional
© 1991 WGRG, Iona Community

If you believe and I believe
and we together pray,
the Holy Spirit shall come down
and set God's people free,
and set God's people free,
and set God's people free,
the Holy Spirit shall come down
and set God's people free.

345

Rob Hayward
© 1985 Thankyou Music

I'm accepted, I'm forgiven,
I am fathered by the true and living
  God.
I'm accepted, no condemnation,
I am loved by the true and living
  God.
There's no guilt or fear as I draw near
to the Saviour and Creator of the
  world.
There is joy and peace as I release
my worship to you, O Lord.

346

Michael Forster (b. 1946)
© 1993 Kevin Mayhew Ltd

1. I'm black, I'm white, I'm short, I'm tall,
   I'm all the human race.
   I'm young, I'm old, I'm large, I'm small,
   and Jesus knows my face.

   The love of God is free to everyone,
   free to everyone, free to everyone.
   The love of God is free, oh yes!
   That's what the gospel says.

2. I'm rich, I'm poor, I'm pleased, I'm sad,
   I'm everyone you see.
   I'm quick, I'm slow, I'm good, I'm bad,
   I know that God loves me.

3. So tall and thin, and short and wide,
   and any shade of face,
   I'm one of those for whom Christ died,
   part of the human race.

347

Isaac Watts (1674-1748)

1. I'm not ashamed to own my Lord,
   or to defend his cause;
   maintain the honour of his word,
   the glory of his cross.

2. Jesus, my God, I know his name;
   his name is all my trust;
   nor will he put my soul to shame,
   nor let my hope be lost.

3. Firm as his throne his promise stands;
   and he can well secure
   what I've committed to his hands,
   till the decisive hour.

4. Then will he own my worthless name
   before his Father's face;
   and in the new Jerusalem
   appoint my soul a place.

348

Graham Kendrick (b. 1950)
© 1986 Thankyou Music

I'm special because God has loved me,
for he gave the best thing that he had
  to save me;
his own Son, Jesus,
crucified to take the blame,
for all the bad things I have done.
Thank you, Jesus,
thank you, Lord,
for loving me so much.
I know I don't deserve anything;
help me feel your love right now
to know deep in my heart
that I'm your special friend.

349

Walter Chalmers Smith (1824-1908)
based on 1 Timothy 1:17

1. Immortal, invisible,
   God only wise,
   in light inaccessible hid
   from our eyes,
   most blessèd, most glorious,
   the Ancient of Days,
   almighty, victorious,
   thy great name we praise.

Continued overleaf

2. Unresting, unhasting,
   and silent as light,
   nor wanting, nor wasting,
   thou rulest in might;
   thy justice like mountains
   high soaring above
   thy clouds which are fountains
   of goodness and love.

3. To all life thou givest,
   to both great and small;
   in all life thou livest,
   the true life of all;
   we blossom and flourish
   as leaves on the tree,
   and wither and perish;
   but naught changeth thee.

4. Great Father of glory,
   pure Father of light,
   thine angels adore thee,
   all veiling their sight;
   all laud we would render,
   O help us to see
   'tis only the splendour
   of light hideth thee.

350 John Greenleaf Whittier (1807-1892)

1. Immortal love, for ever full,
   for ever flowing free,
   for ever shared, for ever whole,
   a never-ebbing sea.

2. Our outward lips confess the name
   all other names above;
   love only knoweth whence it came
   and comprehendeth love.

3. O warm, sweet, tender, even yet
   a present help is he;
   and faith has still its Olivet,
   and love its Galilee.

4. The healing of his seamless dress
   is by our beds of pain;
   we touch him in life's throng and press,
   and we are whole again.

5. Through him the first fond prayers
      are said
   our lips of childhood frame;
   the last low whispers of our dead
   are burdened with his name.

6. Alone, O love ineffable,
   thy saving name is giv'n;
   to turn aside from thee is hell,
   to walk with thee is heav'n.

351 Kevin Nichols (b. 1929)
© 1976 Kevin Mayhew Ltd

1. In bread we bring you, Lord, our
      bodies' labour.
   In wine we offer you our spirits' grief.
   We do not ask you, Lord, who is my
      neighbour,
   but stand united now, one in belief.
   O we have gladly heard your Word,
      your holy Word,
   and now in answer, Lord, our gifts we
      bring.
   Our selfish hearts make true, our
      failing faith renew,
   our lives belong to you, our Lord and
      King.

2. The bread we offer you is blessed and
      broken,
   and it becomes for us our spirits' food.
   Over the cup we bring your Word is
      spoken;
   make it your gift to us, your healing
      blood.

Take all that daily toil plants in our
    hearts' poor soil,
take all we start and spoil, each
    hopeful dream,
the chances we have missed, the
    graces we resist,
Lord, in thy Eucharist, take and
    redeem.

4. No guilt in life, no fear in death,
    this is the power of Christ in me;
    from life's first cry to final breath,
    Jesus commands my destiny.
    No power of hell, no scheme of man,
    can ever pluck me from his hand;
    till he returns or calls me home,
    here in the power of Christ I'll stand!

352 Stuart Townend (b. 1963) and Keith Getty
© 2001 Thankyou Music

1. In Christ alone my hope is found,
    he is my light, my strength, my song;
    this cornerstone, this solid ground,
    firm through the fiercest drought and
        storm.
    What heights of love, what depths of
        peace,
    when fears are stilled, when strivings
        cease!
    My comforter, my all in all,
    here in the love of Christ I stand.

2. In Christ alone! – who took on flesh,
    fullness of God in helpless babe!
    This gift of love and righteousness,
    scorned by the ones he came to save:
    till on that cross as Jesus died,
    the wrath of God was satisfied –
    for every sin on him was laid;
    here in the death of Christ I live.

3. There in the ground his body lay,
    light of the world by darkness slain:
    then bursting forth in glorious day
    up from the grave he rose again!
    And as he stands in victory
    sin's curse has lost its grip on me,
    for I am his and he is mine –
    bought with the precious blood of
        Christ.

353 John Oxenham (1852-1941) alt.
© Desmond Dunkerley

1. In Christ there is no east or west,
    in him no south or north,
    but one great fellowship of love
    throughout the whole wide earth.

2. In him shall true hearts everywhere
    their high communion find;
    his service is the golden cord,
    close binding humankind.

3. Join hands, united in the faith,
    whate'er your race may be;
    who serve my Father as their own
    are surely kin to me.

4. In Christ now meet both east and
        west,
    in him meet south and north;
    all Christlike souls are one in him,
    throughout the whole wide earth.

354 Frances Ridley Havergal (1836-1879)

1. In full and glad surrender,
    I give myself to thee,
    thine utterly and only,
    and evermore to be.

Continued overleaf

2. O Son of God, who lov'st me,
   I will be thine alone;
   and all I have and am, Lord,
   shall henceforth be thine own!

3. Reign over me, Lord Jesus,
   O make my heart thy throne;
   it shall be thine, dear Saviour,
   it shall be thine alone.

4. O come and reign, Lord Jesus,
   rule over everything!
   And keep me always loyal
   and true to thee, my King.

My hope I cannot measure,
my path to life is free,
my Saviour has my treasure,
and he will walk with me.

355 Anna Laetitia Waring (1820-1910) based on Psalm 23

1. In heavenly love abiding,
   no change my heart shall fear;
   and safe is such confiding,
   for nothing changes here.
   The storm may roar without me,
   my heart may low be laid,
   but God is round about me,
   and can I be dismayed?

2. Wherever he may guide me,
   no want shall turn me back;
   my Shepherd is beside me,
   and nothing shall I lack.
   His wisdom ever waketh,
   his sight is never dim,
   he knows the way he taketh,
   and I will walk with him.

3. Green pastures are before me,
   which yet I have not seen;
   bright skies will soon be o'er me,
   where the dark clouds have been.

356 William Henry Draper (1855-1933) alt.

1. In our day of thanksgiving
   one psalm let us offer
   for the saints who before us
   have found their reward;
   when the shadow of death
   fell upon them, we sorrowed,
   but now we rejoice
   that they rest in the Lord.

2. In the morning of life,
   and at noon, and at even,
   he called them away
   from our worship below;
   but not till his love,
   at the font and the altar,
   supplied them with grace
   for the way they should go.

3. These stones that have echoed
   their praises are holy,
   and dear is the ground
   where their feet have once trod;
   yet here they confessed
   they were strangers and pilgrims,
   and still they were seeking
   the city of God.

4. Sing praise, then, for all who
   here sought and here found him,
   whose journey is ended,
   whose perils are past:
   they believed in the light;
   and its glory is round them,
   where the clouds of earth's sorrow
   are lifted at last.

357
Christina Georgina Rossetti (1830-1894)

1. In the bleak mid-winter
frosty wind made moan,
earth stood hard as iron,
water like a stone;
snow had fallen, snow on snow,
snow on snow,
in the bleak mid-winter, long ago.

2. Our God, heav'n cannot hold him
nor earth sustain;
heav'n and earth shall flee away
when he comes to reign.
In the bleak mid-winter
a stable-place sufficed
the Lord God almighty, Jesus Christ.

3. Enough for him, whom cherubim
worship night and day,
a breastful of milk,
and a mangerful of hay:
enough for him, whom angels
fall down before,
the ox and ass and camel which adore.

4. Angels and archangels
may have gathered there,
cherubim and seraphim
thronged the air;
but only his mother
in her maiden bliss
worshipped the belovèd with a kiss.

5. What can I give him,
poor as I am?
If I were a shepherd
I would bring a lamb;
if I were a wise man
I would do my part,
yet what I can I give him:
give my heart.

358
John Bowring (1792-1872)
based on Galatians 6:14

1. In the Cross of Christ I glory,
tow'ring o'er the wrecks of time;
all the light of sacred story
gathers round its head sublime.

2. When the woes of life o'ertake me,
hopes deceive, and fears annoy,
never shall the Cross forsake me;
Lo! it glows with peace and joy.

3. When the sun of bliss is beaming
light and love upon my way,
from the Cross the radiance streaming
adds more lustre to the day.

4. Bane and blessing, pain and pleasure,
by the Cross are sanctified;
peace is there that knows no measure,
joys that through all time abide.

359
Martin E. Leckebusch (b. 1962)
© 1999 Kevin Mayhew Ltd

1. In the garden Mary lingers,
broken and forlorn,
then an unexpected greeting
names her in the dawn:
so she meets her risen Saviour
on the resurrection morn.

2. Evening journey: two disciples,
grieving for the dead,
find a stranger walks beside them,
cheers their hearts instead –
finally they recognise him
as he breaks and shares the bread.

3. Ten distraught, confused apostles
hide away in fear;
rumours that the grave is empty
they are shocked to hear –
yet when Jesus stands among them
dread and sorrow disappear.

Continued overleaf

4. Fishermen who toiled for nothing
   on the lake all night
   hear the sound of Jesus' welcome
   in the morning light:
   in the friendship shared at breakfast
   old mistakes are lost to sight.

5. Every day a fresh beginning –
   newness, come what may!
   In the most unlikely places
   Jesus reigns today;
   from the past to new horizons
   Christ our Saviour leads the way.

360

Taizé Community
© Ateliers et Presses de Taizé

In the Lord I'll be ever thankful,
in the Lord, I will rejoice!
Look to God, do not be afraid;
lift up your voices: the Lord is near,
lift up your voices: the Lord is near.

361

Margaret Rizza (b. 1929)
© 1998 Kevin Mayhew Ltd

In the Lord is my joy and salvation,
he gives light to all his creation.
In the Lord is my joy and salvation,
he gives peace and true consolation.
In the Lord is my salvation.
In the Lord is my salvation.

362

John L. Bell (b. 1949) and Graham Maule
(b. 1958).
© 1987, 1997 WGRG, Iona Community

1. Inspired by love and anger,
   disturbed by endless pain,
   aware of God's own bias,
   we ask him once again:
   'How long must some folk suffer?
   How long can few folk mind?
   How long dare vain self-int'rest
   turn prayer and pity blind?'

2. From those for ever victims
   of heartless human greed,
   their cruel plight composes
   a litany of need:
   'Where are the fruits of justice?
   Where are the signs of peace?
   When is the day when pris'ners
   and dreams find their release?'

3. From those for ever shackled
   to what their wealth can buy,
   the fear of lost advantage
   provokes the bitter cry:
   'Don't query our position!
   Don't criticise our wealth!
   Don't mention those exploited
   by politics and stealth!'

4. To God, who through the prophets
   proclaimed a diff'rent age,
   we offer earth's indiff'rence,
   its agony and rage:
   'When will the wronged be righted?
   When will the kingdom come?
   When will the world be gen'rous
   to all instead of some?'

5. God asks: 'Who will go for me?
   Who will extend my reach?
   And who, when few will listen,
   will prophesy and preach?
   And who, when few bid welcome,
   will offer all they know?
   And who, when few dare follow,
   will walk the road I show?'

6. Amused in someone's kitchen,
   asleep in someone's boat,
   attuned to what the ancients
   exposed, proclaimed and wrote,
   a Saviour without safety,
   a tradesman without tools
   has come to tip the balance
   with fishermen and fools.

363

Edmund Hamilton Sears (1810-1876) alt.

1. It came upon the midnight clear,
   that glorious song of old,
   from angels bending near the earth
   to touch their harps of gold:
   'Peace on the earth, goodwill to all,
   from heav'n's all-gracious King!'
   The world in solemn stillness lay
   to hear the angels sing.

2. Still through the cloven skies they
      come,
   with peaceful wings unfurled;
   and still their heav'nly music floats
   o'er all the weary world:
   above its sad and lowly plains
   they bend on hov'ring wing;
   and ever o'er its Babel-sounds
   the blessèd angels sing.

3. Yet with the woes of sin and strife
   the world has suffered long;
   beneath the angel-strain have rolled
   two thousand years of wrong;
   and warring humankind hears not
   the love-song which they bring;
   O hush the noise of mortal strife,
   and hear the angels sing!

4. And ye, beneath life's crushing load,
   whose forms are bending low,
   who toil along the climbing way
   with painful steps and slow:
   look now! for glad and golden hours
   come swiftly on the wing;
   O rest beside the weary road,
   and hear the angels sing.

5. For lo, the days are hast'ning on,
   by prophets seen of old,
   when with the ever-circling years
   comes round the age of gold;
   when peace shall over all the earth
   its ancient splendours fling,
   and all the world give back the song
   which now the angels sing.

364

William Walsham How (1823-1897)

1. It is a thing most wonderful,
   almost too wonderful to be,
   that God's own Son should come
      from heav'n,
   and die to save a child like me.

2. And yet I know that it is true:
   he chose a poor and humble lot,
   and wept and toiled, and mourned
      and died,
   for love of those who loved him not.

3. I cannot tell how he could love
   a child so weak and full of sin;
   his love must be most wonderful,
   if he could die my love to win.

4. I sometimes think about the cross,
   and shut my eyes, and try to see
   the cruel nails and crown of thorns,
   and Jesus crucified for me.

5. But even could I see him die,
   I could but see a little part
   of that great love which, like a fire,
   is always burning in his heart.

6. It is most wonderful to know
   his love for me so free and sure;
   but 'tis more wonderful to see
   my love for him so faint and poor.

7. And yet I want to love thee, Lord;
   O light the flame within my heart,
   and I will love thee more and more,
   until I see thee as thou art.

365 Spiritual

It's me, it's me, it's me, O Lord,
standing in the need of prayer. (Repeat)

1. Not my brother or my sister,
   but it's me, O Lord,
   standing in the need of prayer.
   (Repeat)

2. Not my mother or my father . . .

3. Not the stranger or my neighbour . . .

366
Basil E. Bridge (b. 1927)
© *1990 Oxford University Press*
from New Songs of Praise 5

1. It's rounded like an orange,
   this earth on which we stand;
   and we praise the God who holds it
   in the hollow of his hand.

   So Father, we would thank you
   for all that you have done,
   and for all that you have given us
   through the coming of your Son.

2. A candle, burning brightly,
   can cheer the darkest night,
   and these candles tell how Jesus
   came to bring a dark world light.

3. The ribbon round the orange
   reminds us of the cost;
   how the Shepherd, strong and gentle,
   gave his life to save the lost.

4. Four seasons with their harvest
   supply the food we need,
   and the Spirit gives a harvest
   that can make us rich indeed.

5. We come with our Christingles
   to tell of Jesus' birth,
   and we praise the God who blessed us
   by his coming to this earth.

367
Latin (17th century)
trans. Henry Williams Baker (1821-1877)

1. Jesu, grant me this, I pray,
   ever in thy heart to stay;
   let me evermore abide
   hidden in thy wounded side.

2. If the world or Satan lay
   tempting snares about my way,
   I am safe when I abide
   in thy heart and wounded side.

3. If the flesh, more dang'rous still,
   tempt my soul to deeds of ill,
   naught I fear when I abide
   in thy heart and wounded side.

4. Death will come one day to me;
   Jesu, cast me not from thee:
   dying let me still abide
   in thy heart and wounded side.

368
Tom S. Colvin (b. 1925) based on a song from
North Ghana
© *1969 Hope Publishing. Administered by CopyCare*

Jesu, Jesu,
fill us with your love,
show us how to serve
the neighbours we have from you.

1. Kneels at the feet of his friends,
   silently washes their feet,
   Master who acts as a slave to them.

2. Neighbours are wealthy and poor,
   varied in colour and race,
   neighbours are near us and far away.

3. These are the ones we should serve,
   these are the ones we should love,
   all these are neighbours to us and you.

4. Loving puts us on our knees,
   silently washing their feet,
   this is the way we should live with you.

369

Charles Wesley (1707-1788) alt.

1. Jesu, lover of my soul,
   let me to thy bosom fly,
   while the gath'ring waters roll,
   while the tempest still is high:
   hide me, O my Saviour, hide,
   till the storm of life is past;
   safe into the haven guide,
   O receive my soul at last.

2. Other refuge have I none,
   hangs my helpless soul on thee;
   leave, ah, leave me not alone,
   still support and comfort me.
   All my trust on thee is stayed,
   all my help from thee I bring;
   cover my defenceless head
   with the shadow of thy wing.

3. Plenteous grace with thee is found,
   grace to cleanse from every sin;
   let the healing streams abound,
   make and keep me pure within.
   Thou of life the fountain art,
   freely let me take of thee,
   spring thou up within my heart,
   rise to all eternity.

370

Latin, 8th century
trans. John Chandler (1806-1876)

1. Jesu, our hope, our heart's desire,
   thy work of grace we sing;
   Redeemer of the world art thou,
   its maker and its King.

2. How vast the mercy and the love
   which laid our sins on thee,
   and led thee to a cruel death,
   to set thy people free!

3. But now the bonds of death are burst,
   the ransom has been paid;
   and thou art on thy Father's throne,
   in glorious robes arrayed.

4. O may thy mighty love prevail
   our sinful souls to spare;
   O may we stand around thy throne,
   and see thy glory there.

5. Jesu, our only joy be thou,
   as thou our prize wilt be;
   in thee be all our glory now
   and through eternity.

6. All praise to thee who art gone up
   triumphantly to heav'n;
   all praise to God the Father's name,
   and Holy Ghost be giv'n.

371

From the Swahili
trans. Edmund S. Palmer (1856-1931)

1. Jesu, Son of Mary,
   fount of life alone,
   here we hail thee present
   on thine altar-throne.
   Humbly we adore thee,
   Lord of endless might,
   in the mystic symbols
   veiled from earthly sight.

2. Think, O Lord, in mercy
   on the souls of those
   who, in faith gone from us,
   now in death repose.
   Here 'mid stress and conflict
   toils can never cease;
   there, the warfare ended,
   bid them rest in peace.

Continued overleaf

3. Often were they wounded
   in the deadly strife;
   heal them, good Physician,
   with the balm of life.
   Every taint of evil,
   frailty and decay,
   good and gracious Saviour,
   cleanse and purge away.

4. Rest eternal grant them,
   after weary fight;
   shed on them the radiance
   of thy heavenly light.
   Lead them onward, upward,
   to the holy place,
   where thy saints made perfect
   gaze upon thy face.

372 Patrick Matsikenyiri
© Copyright Control

Jesu tawa pano;
Jesu tawa pano;
Jesu tawa pano;
tawa pano, mu zita renyu.

Jesus, we are here, (x3)
Jesus, we are here for you.

373 St Bernard of Clairvaux (1091-1153)
trans. Edward Caswall (1814-1878) alt.

1. Jesu, the very thought of thee
   with sweetness fills the breast;
   but sweeter far thy face to see,
   and in thy presence rest.

2. No voice can sing, no heart can frame,
   nor can the mem'ry find,
   a sweeter sound than Jesu's name,
   the Saviour of mankind.

3. O hope of every contrite heart,
   O joy of all the meek,
   to those who ask how kind thou art,
   how good to those who seek!

4. But what to those who find? Ah, this
   nor tongue nor pen can show;
   the love of Jesus, what it is
   his true disciples know.

5. Jesu, our only joy be thou,
   as thou our prize wilt be;
   in thee be all our glory now,
   and through eternity.

374 'Jesu, dulcis memoria' (12th century)
trans. Ray Palmer (1808-1887) alt.

1. Jesu, thou joy of loving hearts,
   thou fount of life, thou perfect grace;
   from the best bliss that earth imparts
   we turn unfilled to seek thy face.

2. Thy truth unchanged hath ever stood;
   thou savest those that on thee call;
   to them that seek thee thou art good,
   to them that find thee, all in all.

3. We taste thee, O thou living bread,
   and long to feast upon thee still;
   we drink of thee, the fountain-head,
   and thirst our souls from thee to fill.

4. Our restless spirits yearn for thee,
   where'er our changeful lot is cast,
   glad when thy gracious smile we see,
   blest when our faith is holding fast.

5. O Jesu, ever with us stay;
   make all our moments calm and
      bright;
   chase the dark night of sin away;
   shed o'er the world thy holy light.

375 Jennifer Atkinson and Robin Mark (b. 1955)
© 1991 Authentic Publishing

1. Jesus, all for Jesus;
   all I am and have and ever hope to be.
   (Repeat)

2. All of my ambitions, hopes and plans,
   I surrender these into your hands.
   (Repeat)

   For it's only in your will that I am free.
   For it's only in your will that I am free.

376 Michael Frye
© 1999 Vineyard Songs (UK/Eire)
Administered by CopyCare

1. Jesus, be the centre,
   be my source, be my light,
   Jesus.

2. Jesus, be the centre,
   be my hope, be my song,
   Jesus.

   Be the fire in my heart,
   be the wind in these sails,
   be the reason that I live,
   Jesus, Jesus.

3. Jesus, be my vision,
   be my path, be my guide,
   Jesus.

377 Susan Warner (1819-1885)

1. Jesus bids us shine
   with a pure, clear light,
   like a little candle
   burning in the night.
   In this world is darkness:
   so we must shine,
   you in your small corner,
   and I in mine.

2. Jesus bids us shine,
   first of all for him;
   well he sees and knows it,
   if our light grows dim.
   He looks down from heaven
   to see us shine,
   you in your small corner,
   and I in mine.

3. Jesus bids us shine,
   then, for all around;
   many kinds of darkness
   in the world abound
   sin, and want and sorrow;
   so we must shine,
   you in your small corner,
   and I in mine.

378 John L. Bell (b. 1949) and
Graham Maule (b. 1958)
© 1989, 1998 WGRG, Iona Community

1. Jesus calls us here to meet him
   as, through word and song and prayer,
   we affirm God's promised presence
   where his people live and care.
   Praise the God who keeps his promise;
   praise the Son who calls us friends;
   praise the Spirit who, among us,
   to our hopes and fears attends.

2. Jesus calls us to confess him
   Word of Life and Lord of all,
   sharer of our flesh and frailness
   saving all who fail or fall.
   Tell his holy human story;
   tell his tales that all may hear;
   tell the world that Christ in glory
   came to earth to meet us here.

Continued overleaf

3. Jesus calls us to each other:
   vastly diff'rent though we are;
   race and colour, class and gender
   neither limit nor debar.
   Join the hand of friend and stranger,
   join the hands of age and youth;
   join the faithful and the doubter
   in their common search for truth.

4. Jesus calls us to his table
   rooted firm in time and space,
   where the church in earth and heaven
   finds a common meeting place.
   Share the bread and wine, his body;
   share the love of which we sing;
   share the feast for saints and sinners
   hosted by our Lord and King.

379 Cecil Frances Alexander (1818-1895)

1. Jesus calls us: o'er the tumult
   of our life's wild, restless sea;
   day by day his sweet voice soundeth,
   saying, 'Christian, follow me.'

2. As of old Saint Andrew heard it
   by the Galilean lake,
   turned from home and toil and
     kindred,
   leaving all for his dear sake.

3. Jesus calls us from the worship
   of the vain world's golden store,
   from each idol that would keep us,
   saying, 'Christian, love me more.'

4. In our joys and in our sorrows,
   days of toil and hours of ease,
   still he calls, in cares and pleasures,
   that we love him more than these.

5. Jesus call us: by thy mercies,
   Saviour, make us hear thy call,
   give our hearts to thine obedience,
   serve and love thee best of all.

380 Matt Redman

1. Jesus Christ, I think upon your
     sacrifice;
   you became nothing, poured out to
     death.
   Many times I've wondered at your
     gift of life,
   and I'm in that place once again,
   I'm in that place once again.

   And once again I look upon
   the cross where you died,
   I'm humbled by your mercy
   and I'm broken inside.
   Once again I thank you,
   once again I pour out my life.

2. Now you are exalted to the highest
     place,
   King of the heavens, where one day
     I'll bow.
   But for now I marvel at this saving
     grace,
   and I'm full of praise once again,
   I'm full of praise once again.

   Thank you for the cross, thank you
     for the cross,
   thank you for the cross, my friend.
   Thank you for the cross, thank you
     for the cross,
   thank you for the cross, my friend.

381
v. 1: 'Surrexit hodie' (14th century) trans. anon.
as in *Lyra Davidica* (1708)
vs. 2-3 from J. Arnold's *Compleat Psalmodist*
(1749)

1. Jesus Christ is ris'n today, alleluia!
   our triumphant holy day, alleluia!
   who did once, upon the cross, alleluia!
   suffer to redeem our loss, alleluia!

2. Hymns of praise then let us sing,
   alleluia!
   unto Christ, our heav'nly King,
   alleluia!
   who endured the cross and grave,
   alleluia!
   sinners to redeem and save, alleluia!

3. But the pains that he endured, alleluia!
   our salvation have procured; alleluia!
   now above the sky he's King, alleluia!
   where the angels ever sing, alleluia!

John L. Bell (b. 1949) and Graham Maule
(b. 1958)
382 © 1988 WGRG, Iona Community.
Used by permission from 'Enemy of Apathy'

1. Jesus Christ is waiting,
   waiting in the streets:
   no one is his neighbour,
   all alone he eats.
   Listen, Lord Jesus,
   I am lonely too;
   make me, friend or stranger,
   fit to wait on you.

2. Jesus Christ is raging,
   raging in the streets,
   where injustice spirals
   and real hope retreats.
   Listen, Lord Jesus,
   I am angry too;
   in the Kingdom's causes
   let me rage with you.

3. Jesus Christ is healing,
   healing in the streets
   curing those who suffer,
   touching those he greets.
   Listen, Lord Jesus,
   I have pity too;
   let my care be active,
   healing, just like you.

4. Jesus Christ is dancing,
   dancing in the streets,
   where each sign of hatred
   he, with love, defeats.
   Listen, Lord Jesus,
   I should triumph too;
   where good conquers evil,
   let me dance with you.

5. Jesus Christ is calling,
   calling in the streets,
   'Who will join my journey?
   I will guide their feet.'
   Listen, Lord Jesus,
   let my fears be few;
   walk one step before me,
   I will follow you.

383 Percy Dearmer (1867-1936)
after John Mason Neale (1818-1866) alt.

1. Jesus, good above all other,
   gentle child of gentle mother,
   in a stable born our brother,
   give us grace to persevere.

2. Jesus, cradled in a manger,
   for us facing every danger,
   living as a homeless stranger,
   make we thee our King most dear.

3. Jesus, for thy people dying,
   risen Master, death defying,
   Lord in heav'n thy grace supplying,
   keep us to thy presence near.

4. Jesus, who our sorrows bearest,
   all our thoughts and hopes thou
      sharest,
   thou to us the truth declarest;
   help us all thy truth to hear.

Continued overleaf

5. Lord, in all our doings guide us;
   pride and hate shall ne'er divide us;
   we'll go on with thee beside us,
   and with joy we'll persevere.

384 Patrick Appleford (b. 1924)
© Josef Weinberger Ltd

1. Jesus, humble was your birth
   when you came from heaven to earth;
   every day in all we do,
   make us humble, Lord, like you.

2. Jesus, strong to help and heal,
   showing that your love is real;
   every day in all we do,
   make us strong and kind like you.

3. Jesus, when you were betrayed,
   still you trusted God and prayed;
   every day in all we do,
   help us trust and pray like you.

4. Jesus, risen from the dead,
   with us always, as you said;
   every day in all we do,
   help us live and love like you.

385 Gill Hutchinson
© 1992 Sea Dream Music

Jesus is greater than the greatest heroes,
Jesus is closer than the closest friends.
He came from heaven and he died to
   save us,
to show us love that never ends.
(Repeat)

Son of God, and the Lord of glory,
he's the light, follow in his way.
He's the truth that we can believe in,
and he's the life, he's living today.
(Repeat)

386 Wendy Churchill
© 1981 Authentic Publishing

1. Jesus is King and I will extol him,
   give him the glory and honour his
      name.
   He reigns on high, enthroned in the
      heavens,
   Word of the Father, exalted for us.

2. We come to him, our Priest and
      Apostle,
   clothed in his glory and bearing his
      name,
   laying our lives with gladness before
      him;
   filled with his Spirit we worship the
      King.

3. O Holy One, our hearts do adore you;
   thrilled with your goodness we give
      you our praise.
   Angels in light with worship
      surround him,
   Jesus, our Saviour, for ever the same.

387 David J. Mansell (b. 1936)
© 1982 Authentic Publishing

1. Jesus is Lord!
   Creation's voice proclaims it,
   for by his power each tree and flower
   was planned and made.
   Jesus is Lord!
   The universe declares it;
   sun, moon and stars in heaven cry:
   Jesus is Lord!

   Jesus is Lord! Jesus is Lord!
   Praise him with alleluias,
   for Jesus is Lord!

2. Jesus is Lord!
Yet from his throne eternal
in flesh he came to die in pain
on Calv'ry's tree.
Jesus is Lord!
From him all life proceeding,
yet gave his life as ransom
thus setting us free.

3. Jesus is Lord!
O'er sin the mighty conqu'ror,
from death he rose and all his foes
shall own his name.
Jesus is Lord!
God sends his Holy Spirit
to show by works of power
that Jesus is Lord.

388 Philip Lawson Johnston
© 1991 Thankyou Music

1. Jesus is the name we honour;
Jesus is the name we praise.
Majestic Name above all other names,
the highest heaven and earth proclaim
that Jesus is our God.

We will glorify,
we will lift him high,
we will give him honour and praise.
We will glorify,
we will lift him high,
we will give him honour and praise.

2. Jesus is the name we worship;
Jesus is the name we trust.
He is the King above all other kings,
let all creation stand and sing
that Jesus is our God.

3. Jesus is the Father's splendour;
Jesus is the Father's joy.
He will return to reign in majesty,
and every eye at last will see
that Jesus is our God.

389 John Barnett
© 1988 Mercy/Vineyard Publishing
Administered by CopyCare

Jesus, Jesus,
holy and anointed One, Jesus.
Jesus, Jesus,
risen and exalted One, Jesus.

Your name is like honey on my lips,
your Spirit like water to my soul.
Your word is a lamp unto my feet.
Jesus, I love you, I love you.

390 Christian Fürchtegott Gellert (1715-1769)
trans. Frances Elizabeth Cox (1812-1897) alt.

1. Jesus lives! thy terrors now
can no more, O death, appal us;
Jesus lives! by this we know
thou, O grave, canst not enthral us.
Alleluia.

2. Jesus lives! henceforth is death
but the gate of life immortal:
this shall calm our trembling breath,
when we pass its gloomy portal.
Alleluia.

3. Jesus lives! for us he died;
then, alone to Jesus living,
pure in heart may we abide,
glory to our Saviour giving.
Alleluia.

4. Jesus lives! our hearts know well
naught from us his love shall sever;
life nor death nor powers of hell
tear us from his keeping ever.
Alleluia.

5. Jesus lives! to him the throne
over all the world is given:
may we go where he is gone,
rest and reign with him in heaven.
Alleluia.

391
Charles Wesley (1707-1788)

1. Jesus, Lord, we look to thee,
   let us in thy name agree;
   show thyself the Prince of Peace;
   bid all strife for ever cease.

2. Make us of one heart and mind,
   courteous, merciful and kind,
   lowly, meek in thought and word,
   altogether like our Lord.

3. Let us for each other care,
   each the other's burden bear;
   to thy Church the pattern give,
   show how true believers live.

4. Free from anger and from pride,
   let us thus in God abide;
   all the depths of love express,
   all the heights of holiness.

392
Basil E. Bridge (b. 1927)
© Basil E. Bridge. Used by permission

1. Jesus, Lord, we pray,
   be our guest today;
   gospel story has recorded
   how your glory was afforded
   to a wedding day;
   be our guest we pray.

2. Lord of love and life,
   blessing man and wife,
   as they stand, their need confessing,
   may your hand take theirs in blessing;
   you will share their life;
   bless this man and wife.

3. Lord of hope and faith,
   faithful unto death,
   let the ring serve as a token
   of a love sincere, unbroken,
   love more strong than death,
   Lord of hope and faith.

393
H. W. Rattle
© Scripture Union

Jesus' love is very wonderful,
Jesus' love is very wonderful,
Jesus' love is very wonderful,
oh wonderful love!
So high you can't get over it,
so low you can't get under it,
so wide you can't get round it,
oh wonderful love!

394
Paul Oakley
© 1995 Thankyou Music

Jesus, lover of my soul,
all-consuming fire is in your gaze.
Jesus, I want you to know
I will follow you all my days.
For no one else in history is like you,
and history itself belongs to you.
Alpha and Omega, you have loved me,
and I will share eternity with you.

It's all about you, Jesus,
and all this is for you,
for your glory and your fame.
It's not about me,
as if you should do things my way;
you alone are God,
and I surrender to your ways.

395
Nadia Hearn (b. 1944)
© 1974 Scripture in Song, a division of Intergrity Music/CopyCare

Jesus, Name above all names,
beautiful Saviour, glorious Lord,
Emmanuel, God is with us,
blessèd Redeemer, living Word.

396 Timothy Dudley-Smith (b. 1926)
© *Timothy Dudley-Smith*

1. Jesus, Prince and Saviour,
   Lord of life who died,
   Christ, the friend of sinners,
   mocked and crucified;
   for a world's salvation
   he his body gave,
   lay at last death's victim
   lifeless in the grave.

   Lord of life triumphant,
   risen now to reign!
   King of endless ages,
   Jesus lives again!

2. In his power and Godhead
   every vict'ry won,
   pain and passion ended,
   all his purpose done:
   Christ the Lord is risen!
   sighs and sorrows past,
   death's dark night is over,
   morning comes at last!

3. Resurrection morning,
   sinners' bondage freed!
   Christ the Lord is risen,
   he is ris'n indeed!
   Jesus, Prince and Saviour,
   Lord of life who died,
   Christ the King of glory
   now is glorified!

397 Graham Kendrick (b. 1950)
© *1986 Thankyou Music*

1. Jesus put this song into our hearts, *(x2)*
   it's a song of joy no one can take away.
   Jesus put this song into our hearts.

2. Jesus taught us how to live in
   harmony, *(x2)*
   diff'rent faces, diff'rent races, he
   made us one.
   Jesus taught us how to live
   in harmony.

3. Jesus turned our sorrow into dancing,
   (x2)
   changed our tears of sadness into
   rivers of joy.
   Jesus turned our sorrow into a dance.

398 Taizé Community, based on Scripture
© *Ateliers et Presses de Taizé*

Jesus, remember me
when you come into your kingdom.

399 Isaac Watts (1674-1748) alt.

1. Jesus shall reign where'er the sun
   does his successive journeys run;
   his kingdom stretch from shore to
   shore,
   till moons shall wax and wane no
   more.

2. People and realms of every tongue
   dwell on his love with sweetest song,
   and infant voices shall proclaim
   their early blessings on his name.

3. Blessings abound where'er he reigns:
   the pris'ners leap to lose their chains;
   the weary find eternal rest,
   and all the humble poor are blest.

4. To him shall endless prayer be made,
   and praises throng to crown his head;
   his name like incense shall arise
   with every morning sacrifice.

Continued overleaf

5. Let every creature rise and bring
   peculiar honours to our King;
   angels descend with songs again,
   and earth repeat the loud amen.

400

Chris Bowater (b. 1947)
© 1988 Sovereign Lifestyle Music Ltd

Jesus shall take the highest honour,
Jesus shall take the highest praise;
let all earth join heaven in exalting
the Name which is above all other
names.
Let's bow the knee in humble
adoration,
for at his name every knee must bow.
Let every tongue confess
he is Christ, God's only Son,
Sovereign Lord, we give you glory now.

For all honour and blessing and power
belongs to you, belongs to you.
All honour and blessing and power
belongs to you, belongs to you,
Lord Jesus Christ, Son of the living God.

401

Graham Kendrick (b. 1950)
© 1977 Thankyou Music

1. Jesus, stand among us
   at the meeting of our lives,
   be our sweet agreement
   at the meeting of our eyes.

   O Jesus, we love you,
   so we gather here,
   join our hearts in unity
   and take away our fear.

2. So to you we're gathering
   out of each and every land,
   Christ the love between us
   at the joining of our hands.

Optional verse for Holy Communion

3. Jesus stand among us
   at the breaking of the bread;
   join us as one body
   as we worship you, our Head.

402

William Pennefather (1816-1873)

1. Jesus, stand among us
   in thy risen power;
   let this time of worship
   be a hallowed hour.

2. Breathe the Holy Spirit
   into every heart;
   bid the fears and sorrows
   from each soul depart.

3. Thus with quickened footsteps
   we'll pursue our way,
   watching for the dawning
   of eternal day.

403

Unknown
trans. Dermott Monahan (1906-1957)
© The Trustees for Methodist Church Purposes

1. Jesus the Lord said: 'I am the Bread,
   the Bread of Life for mankind am I.
   The Bread of Life for mankind am I,
   the Bread of Life for mankind am I.'
   Jesus the Lord said: 'I am the Bread,
   The Bread of Life for mankind am I.'

2. Jesus the Lord said: 'I am the Door,
   the Way and the Door for the poor
   am I.
   The Way and the Door for the poor
   am I,
   the Way and the Door for the poor
   am I.'
   Jesus the Lord said: 'I am the Door,
   the Way and the Door for the poor
   am I.'

3. Jesus the Lord said: 'I am the Light,
   the one true Light of the world am I.
   The one true Light of the world am I,
   the one true Light of the world am I.'
   Jesus the Lord said: 'I am the Light,
   the one true Light of the world am I.'

4. Jesus the Lord said: 'I am the Shepherd,
   the one good Shepherd of the sheep
   am I.
   The one good Shepherd of the sheep
   am I,
   the one good Shepherd of the sheep
   am I.'
   Jesus the Lord said: 'I am the Shepherd,
   the one good Shepherd of the sheep
   am I.'

5. Jesus the Lord said: 'I am the Life,
   the Resurrection and the Life am I.
   The Resurrection and the Life am I,
   the Resurrection and the Life am I.'
   Jesus the Lord said: 'I am the Life,
   the Resurrection and the Life am I'.

404   Charles Wesley (1707-1788)

1. Jesus, the name high over all,
   in hell, or earth, or sky:
   angels and mortals prostrate fall,
   and devils fear and fly.

2. Jesus, the name to sinners dear,
   the name to sinners giv'n;
   it scatters all their guilty fear,
   it turns their hell to heav'n.

3. Jesus, the pris'ner's fetters breaks,
   and bruises Satan's head;
   power into strengthless souls he speaks,
   and life into the dead.

4. O, that the world might taste and see
   the riches of his grace!
   The arms of love that compass me,
   hold all the human race.

5. His only righteousness I show,
   his saving grace proclaim:
   'tis all my business here below
   to cry: 'Behold the Lamb!'

6. Happy, if with my latest breath
   I may but gasp his name:
   preach him to all, and cry in death:
   'Behold, behold the Lamb!'

405   John Gibson

Jesus, we celebrate your victory;
Jesus, we revel in your love.
Jesus, we rejoice you've set us free;
Jesus, your death has brought us life.

1. It was for freedom that Christ has set
   us free,
   no longer to be subject to a yoke of
   slavery;
   so we're rejoicing in God's victory,
   our hearts responding to his love.

2. His Spirit in us releases us from fear,
   the way to him is open, with
   boldness we draw near.
   And in his presence our problems
   disappear;
   our hearts responding to his love.

406

Martin E. Leckebusch (b. 1962)
© 1999 Kevin Mayhew Ltd

1. Jesus, we have heard your Spirit
saying we belong to you,
showing us our need for mercy,
focusing our hopes anew;
you have won our hearts' devotion,
now we feel your guiding hand:
where you lead us, we will follow
on the paths your love has planned.

2. As a chosen, pilgrim people
we are learning day by day
what it means to be disciples,
to believe and to obey.
Word and table show your purpose;
hearts and lives we gladly bring –
where you lead us, we will follow,
suffering Saviour, risen King.

3. How we yearn that every people
should exalt your matchless name,
yet so often this world's systems
countermand your regal claim.
If we stand for truth and justice
we, like you, may suffer loss;
where you lead us, we will follow –
give us grace to bear our cross.

4. So we journey on together,
keen to make our calling sure;
through our joys, our fears, our crises,
may our faith be made mature.
Jesus, hope of hearts and nations,
sovereign Lord of time and space,
where you lead us, we will follow
till we see you face to face.

407

William Cowper (1731-1800)

1. Jesus, where'er thy people meet,
there they behold thy mercy-seat;
where'er they seek thee thou art found,
and every place is hallowed ground.

2. For thou, within no walls confined,
inhabitest the humble mind;
such ever bring thee when they come,
and, going, take thee to their home.

3. Dear Shepherd of thy chosen few,
thy former mercies here renew;
here to our waiting hearts proclaim
the sweetness of thy saving name.

4. Here may we prove the power of
prayer
to strengthen faith and sweeten care,
to teach our faint desires to rise,
and bring all heav'n before our eyes.

5. Lord, we are few, but thou art near;
nor short thine arm, nor deaf thine ear;
O rend the heav'ns, come quickly
down,
and make a thousand hearts thine
own.

408

Michael Forster (b. 1946)
© 1997 Kevin Mayhew Ltd

1. Join the song of praise and protest,
all the nations of the earth:
God, who loves the poor and humble,
sings of dignity and worth.
Those the world has long rejected
take at last their rightful place,
sharing in the song of Mary,
filled with unexpected grace!

2. God has rocked the earth's
foundations,
turned its values upside-down:
strength is overcome by weakness
and the humble wear the crown.
Now the power of God in action
undermines the nations' pride,
lifts the poor and feeds the hungry,
pushing rich and proud aside.

3. Join the song of praise and protest
as the voiceless find a voice,
as the powerless rise triumphant
and the broken hearts rejoice.
Now the God of all creation
rights the long-accepted wrongs;
let the voices of the nations
swell the liberation song.

409 Isaac Watts (1674-1748),
based on Psalm 98, alt.

1. Joy to the world! The Lord is come;
let earth receive her King;
let every heart prepare him room,
and heaven and nature sing,
and heaven and nature sing,
and heaven and heaven and nature
sing.

2. Joy to the earth! The Saviour reigns;
let us our songs employ;
while fields and floods, rocks, hills
and plains
repeat the sounding joy,
repeat the sounding joy,
repeat, repeat the sounding joy.

3. He rules the world with truth and
grace,
and makes the nations prove
the glories of his righteousness,
and wonders of his love,
and wonders of his love,
and wonders, and wonders of his love.

410 Fred Dunn (1907-1979)
© 1977 Thankyou Music

Jubilate, everybody,
serve the Lord in all your ways and
come before his presence singing;
enter now his courts with praise.

For the Lord our God is gracious,
and his mercy everlasting.
Jubilate, jubilate, jubilate, Deo!

411 Henry Scott Holland (1847-1918) alt.

1. Judge eternal, throned in splendour,
Lord of lords and King of kings,
with thy living fire of judgement
purge this realm of bitter things:
solace all its wide dominion
with the healing of thy wings.

2. Still the weary folk are pining
for the hour that brings release:
and the city's crowded clangour
cries aloud for sin to cease;
and the homesteads and the
woodlands
plead in silence for their peace.

3. Crown, O God, thine own endeavour;
cleave our darkness with thy sword;
feed thy people's hungry spirits
with the richness of thy word:
cleanse the body of this nation
through the glory of the Lord.

412 Traditional

1. Just a closer walk with thee,
grant it, Jesus, if you please;
daily walking close to thee,
let it be, dear Lord, let it be.

2. Through the day of toil that's near,
if I fall, dear Lord, who cares?
Who with me my burden shares?
None but thee, dear Lord, none but
thee.

Continued overleaf

3. When my feeble life is o'er,
time for me will be no more.
Guide me gently, safely on
to the shore, dear Lord, to the shore.

413 Charlotte Elliott (1789-1871)

1. Just as I am, without one plea
but that thy blood was shed for me,
and that thou bidst me come to thee,
O Lamb of God, I come.

2. Just as I am, though tossed about
with many a conflict, many a doubt,
fightings and fears within, without,
O Lamb of God, I come.

3. Just as I am, poor, wretched, blind;
sight, riches, healing of the mind,
yea, all I need, in thee to find,
O Lamb of God, I come.

4. Just as I am, thou wilt receive,
wilt welcome, pardon, cleanse, relieve:
because thy promise I believe,
O Lamb of God, I come.

5. Just as I am, thy love unknown
has broken every barrier down,
now to be thine, yea, thine alone,
O Lamb of God, I come.

6. Just as I am, of that free love
the breadth, length, depth and height
   to prove,
here for a season, then above,
O Lamb of God, I come.

414 Traditional

Keep watch with me,
pray with me and do not be afraid;
keep watch with me,
pray with me and do not be afraid;

keep watch with me,
pray with me and do not be afraid;
keep watch with me,
pray with me and do not be afraid;
keep watch with me,
pray with me,
do not be afraid.

415 John L. Bell (b. 1949) and Graham Maule (b. 1958)
© 1987 WGRG, Iona Community

Kindle a flame to lighten the dark
and take all fear away.

416 George Herbert (1593-1633)

1. King of glory, King of peace,
I will love thee;
and, that love may never cease,
I will move thee.
Thou hast granted my appeal,
thou hast heard me;
thou didst note my ardent zeal,
thou hast spared me.

2. Wherefore with my utmost art,
I will sing thee,
and the cream of all my heart
I will bring thee.
Though my sins against me cried,
thou didst clear me,
and alone, when they replied,
thou didst hear me.

3. Sev'n whole days, not one in sev'n,
I will praise thee;
in my heart, though not in heav'n,
I can raise thee.
Small it is, in this poor sort
to enrol thee:
e'en eternity's too short
to extol thee.

417

Naomi Batya and Sophie Conty.
© 1980 Maranatha! Music
Administered by CopyCare

King of kings and Lord of lords,
glory, hallelujah.
King of kings and Lord of lords,
glory, hallelujah.
Jesus, Prince of Peace,
glory, hallelujah.
Jesus, Prince of Peace,
glory, hallelujah.

418

Jarrod Cooper
© 1996 Sovereign Lifestyle Music

1. King of kings, majesty,
   God of heaven living in me,
   gentle Saviour, closest friend,
   strong deliv'rer, beginning and end,
   all within me falls at your throne.

   Your majesty, I can but bow,
   I lay my all before you now.
   In royal robes I don't deserve
   I live to serve your majesty.

2. Earth and heaven worship you,
   love eternal, faithful and true,
   who bought the nations, ransomed
   souls,
   brought this sinner near to your
   throne;
   all within me cries out in praise.

419 Spiritual

1. Kum ba yah, my Lord,
   kum ba yah, *(x3)*
   O Lord, kum ba yah.

2. Someone's crying, Lord,
   kum ba yah, *(x3)*
   O Lord, kum ba yah.

3. Someone's singing, Lord,
   kum ba yah, *(x3)*
   O Lord, kum ba yah.

4. Someone's praying, Lord,
   kum ba yah, *(x3)*
   O Lord, kum ba yah.

420

Taizé Community, based on Scripture
© Ateliers et Presses de Taizé

Laudate Dominum,
laudate Dominum,
omnes gentes, alleluia. (Repeat)

or

Sing praise and bless the Lord,
sing praise and bless the Lord,
peoples, nations, alleluia. (Repeat)

1. Praise the Lord, all you nations,
   praise God all you peoples.
   Alleluia.
   Strong is God's love and mercy,
   always faithful for ever. Alleluia.

2. Alleluia, alleluia.
   Let everything living give praise to
   the Lord.
   Alleluia, alleluia.
   Let everything living give praise to
   the Lord.

421 John Henry Newman (1801-1890)

1. Lead, kindly light,
   amid th'encircling gloom,
   lead thou me on;
   the night is dark,
   and I am far from home;
   lead thou me on.
   Keep thou my feet;
   I do not ask to see
   the distant scene;
   one step enough for me.

Continued overleaf

2. I was not ever thus,
   nor prayed that thou
   shouldst lead me on;
   I loved to choose
   and see my path; but now
   lead thou me on.
   I loved the garish day,
   and, spite of fears,
   pride ruled my will:
   remember not past years.

3. So long thy power
   hath blest me, sure it still
   will lead me on,
   o'er moor and fen,
   o'er crag and torrent, till
   the night is gone;
   and with the morn
   those angel faces smile,
   which I have loved long since,
   and lost awhile.

422 James Edmeston (1791-1867)

1. Lead us, heavenly Father, lead us
   o'er the world's tempestuous sea;
   guard us, guide us, keep us, feed us,
   for we have no help but thee;
   yet possessing every blessing
   if our God our Father be.

2. Saviour, breathe forgiveness o'er us,
   all our weakness thou dost know,
   thou didst tread this earth before us,
   thou didst feel its keenest woe;
   lone and dreary, faint and weary,
   through the desert thou didst go.

3. Spirit of our God, descending,
   fill our hearts with heavenly joy,
   love with every passion blending,
   pleasure that can never cloy;
   thus provided, pardoned, guided,
   nothing can our peace destroy.

423 Graham Kendrick (b. 1950)
© 1983 Thankyou Music

1. Led like a lamb to the slaughter,
   in silence and shame,
   there on your back you carried a world
   of violence and pain.
   Bleeding, dying, bleeding, dying.

   You're alive, you're alive,
   you have risen!
   Alleluia! And the power
   and the glory is given,
   alleluia! Jesus to you.

2. At break of dawn, poor Mary,
   still weeping she came,
   when through her grief she heard
   your voice
   now speaking her name.
   Mary, Master, Mary, Master.

3. At the right hand of the Father
   now seated on high
   you have begun your eternal reign
   of justice and joy.
   Glory, glory, glory, glory.

424 Liturgy of St James
trans. G. Moultrie (1829-1885)

1. Let all mortal flesh keep silence
   and with fear and trembling stand;
   ponder nothing earthly-minded,
   for with blessing in his hand
   Christ our God on earth descendeth,
   our full homage to demand.

2. King of kings, yet born of Mary,
   as of old on earth he stood,
   Lord of lords, in human vesture,
   in the body and the blood.
   He will give to all the faithful
   his own self for heavenly food.

3. Rank on rank the host of heaven
   spreads its vanguard on the way,
   as the Light of light descendeth
   from the realms of endless day,
   that the powers of hell may vanish
   as the darkness clears away.

4. At his feet the six-winged seraph;
   cherubim, with sleepless eye,
   veil their faces to the Presence,
   as with ceaseless voice they cry,
   alleluia, alleluia,
   alleluia, Lord most high.

425 George Herbert (1593-1633)

1. Let all the world in every corner sing,
   my God and King!
   The heavens are not too high,
   his praise may thither fly;
   the earth is not too low,
   his praises there may grow.
   Let all the world in every corner sing,
   my God and King!

2. Let all the world in every corner sing,
   my God and King!
   The Church with psalms must shout,
   no door can keep them out;
   but, above all, the heart
   must bear the longest part.
   Let all the world in every corner sing,
   my God and King!

426 Matt Redman
© 1977 Thankyou Music

Let everything that, everything that,
everything that has breath, praise the
Lord.
Let everything that, everything that,
everything that has breath, praise the
Lord.

1. Praise you in the morning,
   praise you in the evening,
   praise you when I'm young and when
   I'm old.
   Praise you when I'm laughing,
   praise you when I'm grieving,
   praise you every season of the soul.
   If we could see how much you're worth,
   your power, your might, your endless
   love,
   then surely we would never cease to
   praise.

2. Praise you in the heavens,
   joining with the angels,
   praising you for ever and a day.
   Praise you on the earth now,
   joining with creation,
   calling all the nations to your praise.
   If they could see how much you're
   worth,
   your power, your might, your endless
   love,
   then surely we would never cease to
   praise.

Let everything that, everything that,
everything that has breath, praise the
Lord.
Let everything that, everything that,
everything that has breath, praise the
Lord.

427 Martin E. Leckebusch (b. 1962)
© 1999 Kevin Mayhew Ltd

1. Let love be found among us –
   the gift of God it is,
   the hallmark of his children,
   the sign that we are his.
   We claim that God has called us –
   no idle boast or fraud
   if love directs our actions
   and proves we know the Lord!

Continued overleaf

2. The reason God has loved us
   is simply sovereign choice –
   our love is but an echo
   to his resounding voice:
   for God is love, and showed it
   by giving us his Son:
   through him our past is pardoned –
   a new life has begun.

3. How deeply God has loved us,
   accepting us as friends –
   so let us show each other
   this love which never ends:
   for though we cannot find him
   with sight or touch or sound,
   yet God himself is present
   where love is truly found.

428 Charles Wesley (1707-1788) and others, alt.

1. Let saints on earth in concert sing
   with those whose work is done;
   for all the servants of our King
   in heaven and earth are one.

2. One family, we dwell in him,
   one Church, above, beneath;
   though now divided by the stream,
   the narrow stream of death.

3. The people of the living God,
   to his command we bow:
   part of the host have crossed the flood,
   and part are crossing now.

4. E'en now to their eternal home
   there pass some spirits blest;
   while others to the margin come,
   waiting their call to rest.

5. Jesu, be thou our constant guide;
   then, when the word is giv'n,
   bid Jordan's narrow stream divide,
   and bring us safe to heaven.

429 Susan Sayers (b. 1946)
© 1984 Kevin Mayhew Ltd

1. Let the mountains dance and sing!
   Let the trees all sway and swing!
   All creation praise its King! Alleluia!

2. Let the water sing its song!
   And the powerful wind so strong
   whistle as it blows along! Alleluia!

3. Let the blossom all break out
   in a huge unspoken shout,
   just to show that God's about!
   Alleluia!

430 Dave Bilbrough
© 1979 Thankyou Music

Let there be love shared among us,
let there be love in our eyes.
May now your love sweep this nation;
cause us, O Lord, to arise.
Give us a fresh understanding,
brotherly love that is real.
Let there be love shared among us,
let there be love.

431 Unknown

1. Let us break bread together
   on our knees.
   Let us break bread together
   on our knees.
   When I fall on my knees
   with my face to the rising sun,
   O Lord, have mercy on me.

2. Let us share wine together
   on our knees.
   Let us share wine together
   on our knees.
   When I fall on my knees
   with my face to the rising sun,
   O Lord, have mercy on me.

3. Let us praise God together
   on our knees.
   Let us praise God together
   on our knees.
   When I fall on my knees
   with my face to the rising sun,
   O Lord, have mercy on me.

432 Marty Haugen (b. 1952)
© 1994 GIA Publications Inc.

1. Let us build a house where love can
   dwell
   and all can safely live,
   a place where saints and children tell
   how hearts learn to forgive.
   Built of hopes and dreams and visions,
   rock of faith and vault of grace;
   here the love of Christ shall end
   divisions:

   all are welcome, all are welcome,
   all are welcome in this place.

2. Let us build a house where prophets
   speak,
   and words are strong and true,
   where all God's children dare to seek
   to dream God's reign anew.
   Here the cross shall stand as witness
   and symbol of God's grace;
   here as one we claim the faith of Jesus:

3. Let us build a house where love is
   found
   in water, wine and wheat:
   a banquet hall on holy ground,
   where peace and justice meet.
   Here the love of God, through Jesus,
   is revealed in time and space;
   as we share in Christ the feast that
   frees us:

4. Let us build a house where hands will
   reach
   beyond the wood and stone
   to heal and strengthen, serve and teach,
   and live the Word they've known.
   Here the outcast and the stranger
   bear the image of God's face;
   let us bring an end to fear and danger:

5. Let us build a house where all are
   named,
   their songs and visions heard
   and loved and treasured, taught and
   claimed
   as words within the Word.
   Built of tears and cries and laughter,
   prayers of faith and songs of grace,
   let this house proclaim from floor to
   rafter:

433 James Edward Seddon (1915-1983)
© The representatives of the late James Edward
Seddon/ Jubilate Hymns. Used by permission

1. Let us praise God together, let us
   praise;
   let us praise God together all our days.
   He is faithful in all his ways,
   he is worthy of all our praise,
   his name be exalted on high.

2. Let us seek God together, let us pray;
   let us seek his forgiveness as we pray.
   He will cleanse us from all our sin,
   he will help us the fight to win,
   his name be exalted on high.

3. Let us serve God together, him obey;
   let our lives show his goodness
   through each day.
   Christ the Lord is the world's true
   light,
   let us serve him with all our might,
   his name be exalted on high.

434 Fred Kaan (b. 1929)
© 1975 Stainer & Bell Ltd

1. Let us talents and tongues employ,
   reaching out with a shout of joy:
   bread is broken, the wine is poured,
   Christ is spoken and seen and heard.

   Jesus lives again,
   earth can breathe again,
   pass the word around:
   loaves abound!

2. Christ is able to make us one,
   at his table he sets the tone,
   teaching people to live to bless,
   love in word and in deed express.

3. Jesus calls us in, sends us out
   bearing fruit in a world of doubt,
   gives us love to tell, bread to share:
   God-Immanuel everywhere!

435 John Milton (1608-1674),
based on Psalm 136

1. Let us, with a gladsome mind,
   praise the Lord, for he is kind;

   for his mercies ay endure,
   ever faithful, ever sure.

2. Let us blaze his name abroad,
   for of gods he is the God;

3, He, with all-commanding might,
   filled the new-made world with light;

4. He the golden-tressèd sun
   caused all day his course to run;

5. And the moon to shine at night,
   'mid her starry sisters bright;

6. All things living he doth feed,
   his full hand supplies their need;

7. Let us, with a gladsome mind,
   praise the Lord, for he is kind;

436 Michael Forster (b. 1946)
© 1993 Kevin Mayhew Ltd

1. Life for the poor was hard and tough,
   Jesus said, 'That's not good enough;
   life should be great and here's the sign:
   I'll turn the water into wine.'

   Jesus turned the water into wine, (x3)
   and the people saw that life was good.

2. Life is a thing to be enjoyed,
   not to be wasted or destroyed.
   Laughter is part of God's design;
   let's turn the water into wine!

3. Go to the lonely and the sad,
   give them the news to make them
   glad,
   helping the light of hope to shine,
   turning the water into wine!

437 George William Kitchin (1827-1912) and
Michael Robert Newbolt (1874-1956) alt.
© Hymns Ancient & Modern Ltd

Lift high the Cross,
the love of Christ proclaim
till all the world adore his sacred name!

1. Come, Christians,
   follow where our Saviour trod,
   o'er death victorious,
   Christ the Son of God.

2. Led on their way by this
   triumphant sign,
   the hosts of God in joyful
   praise combine:

*3. Each new disciple
   of the Crucified
   is called to bear the seal
   of him who died:

*4. Saved by the Cross
   whereon their Lord was slain,
   now Adam's children
   their lost home regain:

5. From north and south,
   from east and west they raise
   in growing harmony
   their song of praise:

*6. O Lord, once lifted
   on the glorious tree,
   as thou hast promised,
   draw us unto thee:

7. Let every race
   and every language tell
   of him who saves
   from fear of death and hell:

*8. From farthest regions,
   let them homage bring,
   and on his Cross
   adore their Saviour King:

*9. Set up thy throne,
   that earth's despair may cease
   beneath the shadow
   of its healing peace:

10. For thy blest Cross
   which doth for all atone,
   creation's praises rise
   before thy throne:

11. So let the world
   proclaim with one accord
   the praises of our
   ever-living Lord.

438 Georg Weissel (1590-1635)
trans. Catherine Winkworth (1827-1878)

1. Lift up your heads, you mighty gates,
   behold, the King of Glory waits,
   the King of kings is drawing near,
   the Saviour of the world is here.

2. O blest the land, the city blest
   where Christ the ruler is confessed.
   O happy hearts and happy homes
   to whom this King in triumph comes.

3. Fling wide the portals of your heart,
   make it a temple set apart
   from earthly use for heaven's employ,
   adorned with prayer and love and joy.

4. Come, Saviour, come, with us abide;
   our hearts to thee we open wide:
   thy Holy Spirit guide us on,
   until our glorious goal is won.

439 Henry Montagu Butler (1833-1918) alt.

1. 'Lift up your hearts!'
   We lift them, Lord, to thee;
   here at thy feet
   none other may we see:
   'Lift up your hearts!'
   E'en so, with one accord,
   we lift them up,
   we lift them to the Lord.

2. Above the swamps
   of subterfuge and shame,
   the deeds, the thoughts,
   that honour may not name,
   the halting tongue
   that dares not tell the whole,
   O Lord of truth,
   lift every human soul.

3. Lift every gift
   that thou thyself hast giv'n:
   low lies the best
   till lifted up to heav'n;
   low lie the pounding heart,
   the teeming brain,
   till, sent from God,
   they mount to God again.

Continued overleaf

4. Then, as the trumpet-call,
   in after years,
   'Lift up your hearts!'
   rings pealing in our ears,
   still shall those hearts respond,
   with full accord,
   'We lift them up,
   we lift them to the Lord.'

440
Nick Fawcett (b. 1957)
© 2004 Kevin Mayhew Ltd

1. Lift up your voice, give thanks with
   songs of praise,
   sing to our God, your hymns of
   worship raise;
   tell of his grace, so wonderful and free,
   his mercy reaching out to you and me.

2. Lift up your voice, give thanks with
   songs of love,
   sing of the Saviour sent from God
   above;
   tell of the one who, at the Father's call,
   through gracious service showed his
   care for all.

3. Lift up your voice, give thanks with
   songs of joy,
   sing of a love that nothing can destroy;
   tell of the friend, who died that we
   might live,
   who offers hope that no one else can
   give.

4. Lift up your voice, give thanks with
   songs of trust,
   sing of the God who lifts hope from
   the dust;
   tell of the Christ, who, just as he had
   said,
   defeated evil, rising from the dead.

5. Lift up your voice, give thanks with
   songs of awe,
   sing to the Lord who lives for
   evermore;
   tell of the king whose glory fills the sky,
   the Lord of lords who reigns
   enthroned on high.

441
Tim Hughes
© 2000 Thankyou Music

1. Light of the world,
   you stepped down into darkness,
   opened my eyes, let me see
   beauty that made this heart adore you,
   hope of a life spent with you.

   So here I am to worship,
   here I am to bow down,
   here I am to say that you're my God.
   And you're altogether lovely,
   altogether worthy,
   altogether wonderful to me.

2. King of all days,
   oh so highly exalted,
   glorious in heaven above;
   humbly you came to the earth you
   created,
   all for love's sake became poor.

   And I'll never know how much it cost
   to see my sin upon that cross.
   And I'll never know how much it cost
   to see my sin upon that cross.

442
Ascribed to Thomas à Kempis (c. 1379-1471)
trans. John Mason Neale (1818-1866)

1. Light's abode, celestial Salem,
   vision whence true peace doth spring,
   brighter than the heart can fancy,
   mansion of the highest King;
   O how glorious are the praises
   which of thee the prophets sing!

2. There for ever and for ever
alleluia is outpoured;
for unending, for unbroken
is the feast-day of the Lord;
all is pure and all is holy
that within thy walls is stored.

3. There no cloud or passing vapour
dims the brightness of the air;
endless noon-day, glorious noon-day,
from the Sun of suns is there;
there no night brings rest from labour,
for unknown are toil and care.

4. O how glorious and resplendent,
fragile body, shalt thou be,
when endued with so much beauty,
full of health and strong and free,
full of vigour, full of pleasure
that shall last eternally.

5. Now with gladness, now with courage,
bear the burden on thee laid,
that hereafter these thy labours
may with endless gifts be paid;
and in everlasting glory
thou with brightness be arrayed.

6. Laud and honour to the Father,
laud and honour to the Son,
laud and honour to the Spirit,
ever Three and ever One,
consubstantial, co-eternal,
while unending ages run.

443   Latin, 4th century
trans. John Mason Neale (1818-1866)

1. Light's glitt'ring morn bedecks the sky;
heav'n thunders forth its victor-cry:
alleluia, alleluia,
the glad earth shouts her triumph high,
and groaning hell makes wild reply:

alleluia, alleluia, alleluia, alleluia,
alleluia.

2. While he, the King, the mighty King,
despoiling death of all its sting,
alleluia, alleluia,
and trampling down the pow'rs of
night,
brings forth his ransomed saints to
light:

3. His tomb of late the threefold guard
of watch and stone and seal had barred;
alleluia, alleluia,
but now, in pomp and triumph high,
he comes from death to victory:

4. The pains of hell are loosed at last,
the days of mourning now are past;
alleluia, alleluia,
an angel robed in light hath said,
'The Lord is risen from the dead':

PART TWO

5. O bitter the apostles' pain
for their dear Lord so lately slain,
alleluia, alleluia,
by rebel servants doomed to die
a death of cruel agony:

6. With gentle voice the angel gave
the women tidings at the grave:
alleluia, alleluia,
'Fear not, your Master shall ye see;
he goes before to Galilee':

7. Then, hast'ning on their eager way
the joyful tidings to convey,
alleluia, alleluia,
their Lord they met, their living Lord,
and falling at his feet adored:

8. His faithful followers with speed
to Galilee forthwith proceed,
alleluia, alleluia,
that there once more they may
behold
the Lord's dear face, as he foretold;

Continued overleaf

alleluia, alleluia, alleluia, alleluia,
alleluia.

PART THREE

9. That Eastertide with joy was bright,
the sun shone out with fairer light,
alleluia, alleluia,
when, to their longing eyes restored,
the glad apostles saw their Lord:

10. He bade them see his hands, his side,
where yet the glorious wounds abide;
alleluia, alleluia,
the tokens true which made it plain
their Lord indeed was ris'n again:

11. Jesu, the King of gentleness,
do thou thyself our hearts possess,
alleluia, alleluia,
that we may give thee all our days
the tribute of our grateful praise:

DOXOLOGY

12. O Lord of all, with us abide
in this our joyful Eastertide;
alleluia, alleluia,
from every weapon death can wield
thine own redeemed for ever shield:

13. All praise be thine, O risen Lord,
from death to endless life restored;
alleluia, alleluia,
all praise to God the Father be
and Holy Ghost eternally:

444 Graham Kendrick (b. 1950)
© 1988 Make Way Music

1. Like a candle flame,
flick'ring small
in our darkness,
uncreated light
shines through infant eyes.

God is with us,
alleluia,
come to save us,
alleluia,
alleluia!

2. Stars and angels sing,
yet the earth
sleeps in shadows;
can this tiny spark
set a world on fire?

3. Yet his light shall shine
from our lives,
spirit blazing,
as we touch the flame
of his holy fire.

445 Michael Perry (1942-1996)
© Mrs B. Perry/Jubilate Hymns

1. Like a mighty river flowing,
like a flower in beauty growing,
far beyond all human knowing
is the perfect peace of God.

2. Like the hills serene and even,
like the coursing clouds of heaven,
like the heart that's been forgiven
is the perfect peace of God.

3. Like the summer breezes playing,
like the tall trees softly swaying,
like the lips of silent praying
is the perfect peace of God.

4. Like the morning sun ascended,
like the scents of evening blended,
like a friendship never ended
is the perfect peace of God.

5. Like the azure ocean swelling,
like the jewel all-excelling,
far beyond our human telling
is the perfect peace of God.

446

Aniceto Nazareth
© 1984 Kevin Mayhew Ltd

Listen, let your heart keep seeking;
listen to his constant speaking;
listen to the Spirit calling you.
Listen to his inspiration;
listen to his invitation;
listen to the Spirit calling you.

1. He's in the sound of the thunder,
in the whisper of the breeze.
He's in the might of the whirlwind,
in the roaring of the seas.

2. He's in the laughter of children,
in the patter of the rain.
Hear him in cries of the suffering,
in their moaning and their pain.

3. He's in the noise of the city,
in the singing of the birds.
And in the night-time the stillness
helps you listen to his word.

447

Eric Boswell (b. 1959)
© 1959 Warner/Chappell Music Ltd
Used by permission of Faber Music Ltd

1. Little donkey, little donkey,
on the dusty road,
got to keep on plodding onwards
with your precious load.
Been a long time, little donkey,
through the winter's night;
don't give up now, little donkey,
Bethlehem's in sight.

Ring out those bells tonight,
Bethlehem, Bethlehem,
follow that star tonight,
Bethlehem, Bethlehem.
Little donkey, little donkey,
had a heavy day,
little donkey, carry Mary safely on her
way.

2. Little donkey, little donkey,
journey's end is near.
There are wise men, waiting for a
sign to bring them here.
Do not falter, little donkey,
there's a star ahead;
it will guide you, little donkey,
to a cattle shed.

448

Traditional Czech carol
trans. Percy Dearmer (1867-1936)
Alternative version of text © 1999 Kevin Mayhew Ltd

1. Little Jesus, sweetly sleep, do not stir;
we will lend a coat of fur;
we will rock you, rock you, rock you,
we will rock you, rock you, rock you;
see the fur to keep you warm,
snugly round your tiny form.

2. Mary's little baby sleep, sweetly sleep,
sleep in comfort, slumber deep;
we will rock you, rock you, rock you,
we will rock you, rock you, rock you;
we will serve you all we can,
darling, darling little man.

Alternative words:

Christopher Massey (b. 1956)
© 1999 Kevin Mayhew Ltd

1. Little Jesus, sleep away, in the hay,
while we worship, watch and pray.
We will gather at the manger,
worship this amazing stranger:
little Jesus born on earth,
sign of grace and human worth.

2. Little Jesus, sleep away, while you may;
pain is for another day.
While you sleep, we will not wake you,
when you cry we'll not forsake you.
Little Jesus, sleep away,
we will worship you today.

449 Charles Wesley (1707-1788), John Cennick (1718-1755) and Martin Madan (1728-1790) alt.

1. Lo, he comes with clouds descending,
   once for mortal sinners slain;
   thousand thousand saints attending
   swell the triumph of his train.
   Alleluia! Alleluia! Alleluia!
   Christ appears on earth to reign.

2. Every eye shall now behold him
   robed in dreadful majesty;
   we who set at naught and sold him,
   pierced and nailed him to the tree,
   deeply grieving, deeply grieving,
      deeply grieving,
   shall the true Messiah see.

3. Those dear tokens of his passion
   still his dazzling body bears,
   cause of endless exultation
   to his ransomed worshippers:
   with what rapture, with what rapture,
      with what rapture
   gaze we on those glorious scars!

4. Yea, amen, let all adore thee,
   high on thine eternal throne;
   Saviour, take the power and glory,
   claim the kingdom for thine own.
   Alleluia! Alleluia! Alleluia!
   Thou shalt reign, and thou alone.

450 Rowland Hill (1744-1833) and others

1. Lo, round the throne, a glorious
      band,
   the saints in countless myriads stand,
   of every tongue redeemed to God,
   arrayed in garments washed in blood.

2. Through tribulation great they came;
   they bore the cross, despised the
      shame;
   from all their labours now they rest,
   in God's eternal glory blest.

3. They see their Saviour face to face,
   and sing the triumphs of his grace;
   him day and night they ceaseless
      praise,
   to him the loud thanksgiving raise:

4. 'Worthy the Lamb, for sinners slain,
   through endless years to live and
      reign;
   thou hast redeemed us by thy blood,
   and made us kings and priests to
      God.'

5. O may we tread the sacred road
   that saints and holy martyrs trod;
   wage to the end the glorious strife,
   and win, like them, a crown of life.

451 Fred Pratt Green (1903-2000)
         © 1971 Stainer & Bell Ltd

1. Long ago, prophets knew
   Christ would come, born a Jew,
   come to make all things new,
   bear his people's burden,
   freely love and pardon.

   Ring, bells, ring, ring, ring!
   Sing, choirs, sing, sing, sing!
   When he comes, when he comes,
   who will make him welcome?

2. God in time, God in man,
   this is God's timeless plan:
   God will come, as a man,
   born himself of woman,
   God divinely human.

3. Mary hail! Though afraid,
   she believed, she obeyed.
   In her womb, God is laid:
   till the time expected,
   nurtured and protected.

4. Journey ends! Where afar
   Bethlem shines, like a star,
   stable door stands ajar.
   Unborn Son of Mary,
   Saviour, do not tarry!

   Ring, bells, ring, ring, ring!
   Sing, choirs, sing, sing, sing!
   Jesus comes! Jesus comes!
   We will make him welcome!

452 Bernadette Farrell (b. 1957)
© 1993 Bernadette Farrell

1. Longing for light, we wait in darkness.
   Longing for truth, we turn to you.
   Make us your own, your holy people,
   light for the world to see.

   Christ, be our light!
   Shine in our hearts,
   shine through the darkness.
   Christ, be our light!
   Shine in your church
   gathered today.

2. Longing for peace, our world is
      troubled.
   Longing for hope, many despair.
   Your word alone has power to save us.
   Make us your living voice.

3. Longing for food, many are hungry.
   Longing for water, many still thirst.
   Make us your bread, broken for others,
   shared until all are fed.

4. Longing for shelter, many are homeless.
   Longing for warmth, many are cold.
   Make us your building, sheltering
      others,
   walls made of living stone.

5. Many the gifts, many the people,
   many the hearts that yearn to belong.
   Let us be servants to one another,
   making your kingdom come.

453 George Hugh Bourne (1840-1925)

1. Lord, enthroned in heav'nly
      splendour,
   first begotten from the dead,
   thou alone, our strong defender,
   liftest up thy people's head.
   Alleluia, alleluia,
   Jesu, true and living bread.

2. Here our humblest homage pay we,
   here in loving rev'rence bow;
   here for faith's discernment pray we,
   lest we fail to know thee now.
   Alleluia, alleluia,
   thou art here, we ask not how.

3. Though the lowliest form doth veil
      thee
   as of old in Bethlehem,
   here as there thine angels hail thee,
   Branch and Flower of Jesse's Stem.
   Alleluia, alleluia,
   we in worship join with them.

4. Paschal Lamb, thine off'ring, finished
   once for all when thou wast slain,
   in its fullness undiminished
   shall for evermore remain.
   Alleluia, alleluia,
   cleansing souls from every stain.

5. Life-imparting heav'nly manna,
   stricken rock with streaming side,
   heaven and earth with loud hosanna
   worship thee, the Lamb who died.
   Alleluia, alleluia,
   ris'n, ascended, glorified!

454 Timothy Dudley-Smith (b. 1926)
© *Timothy Dudley-Smith*

1. Lord, for the years
   your love has kept and guided,
   urged and inspired us,
   cheered us on our way,
   sought us and saved us,
   pardoned and provided,
   Lord of the years,
   we bring our thanks today.

2. Lord, for that word,
   the word of life which fires us,
   speaks to our hearts
   and sets our souls ablaze,
   teaches and trains,
   rebukes us and inspires us,
   Lord of the word,
   receive your people's praise.

3. Lord, for our land,
   in this our generation,
   spirits oppressed by pleasure,
   wealth and care:
   for young and old,
   for commonwealth and nation,
   Lord of our land,
   be pleased to hear our prayer.

4. Lord, for our world;
   when we disown and doubt him,
   loveless in strength,
   and comfortless in pain;
   hungry and helpless,
   lost indeed without him:
   Lord of the world,
   we pray that Christ may reign.

5. Lord, for ourselves;
   in living power remake us,
   self on the cross
   and Christ upon the throne;
   past put behind us,
   for the future take us,
   Lord of our lives,
   to live for Christ alone.

455 From Ghana, traditional

Lord, have mercy.
Lord, have mercy.
Lord, have mercy.
Lord, have mercy on us.

Kyrie eleison.
Kyrie eleison.
Kyrie eleison.
Kyrie eleison.

456 From Russia, traditional

Lord, have mercy.
Lord, have mercy.
Lord, have mercy.

Kyrie eleison.
Kyrie eleison.
Kyrie eleison.

457 Robert Critchley and Dawn Critchley
© *1989 Thankyou Music*

1. Lord, I come before your throne of
     grace;
   I find rest in your presence,
   and fullness of joy.
   In worship and wonder I behold your
     face,
   singing, 'What a faithful God have I.'

   What a faithful God have I,
   what a faithful God;
   what a faithful God have I,
   faithful in every way.

2. Lord of mercy, you have heard my cry;
   through the storm you're the beacon,
   my song in the night.
   In the shelter of your wings, hear my
     heart's reply,
   singing, 'What a faithful God have I.'

3. Lord all sov'reign, granting peace
   from heav'n,
   let me comfort those who suffer
   with the comfort you have giv'n.
   I will tell of your great love for as
   long as I live,
   singing, 'What a faithful God have I.'

458 Geoff Bullock (b. 1955)
© 1992 Word/Maranatha! Music
Administered by CopyCare

1. Lord, I come to you,
   let my heart be changed, renewed,
   flowing from the grace
   that I found in you.
   And, Lord, I've come to know
   the weaknesses I see in me
   will be stripped away
   by the power of your love.

   Hold me close,
   let your love surround me,
   bring me near,
   draw me to your side;
   and as I wait,
   I'll rise up like an eagle,
   and I will soar with you;
   your Spirit leads me on
   in the power of your love.

2. Lord, unveil my eyes,
   let me see you face to face,
   the knowledge of your love
   as you live in me.
   Lord, renew my mind
   as your will unfolds in my life,
   in living every day
   in the power of your love.

459 Isaac Watts (1674-1748)
from Psalm 119

1. Lord, I have made thy word my
   choice,
   my lasting heritage:
   there shall my noblest powers rejoice,
   my warmest thoughts engage.

2. I'll read the hist'ries of thy love,
   and keep thy laws in sight,
   while through the promises I rove
   with ever-fresh delight.

3. 'Tis a broad land of wealth unknown,
   where springs of life arise,
   seeds of immortal bliss are sown,
   and hidden glory lies.

460 Nick Fawcett (b. 1957)
© 2004 Kevin Mayhew Ltd

1. Lord, I lift
   my hands to you in prayer,
   my mind in turmoil,
   heart overwhelmed by care.

2. Come to me;
   and let me still your soul.
   No need to fret now;
   love waits to make you whole.

3. Lord, I come;
   your word has been fulfilled.
   Your peace flows freely;
   storms deep within are stilled.

461 Rick Founds
© 1989 Maranatha! Praise Inc.
Administered by CopyCare

Lord, I lift your name on high;
Lord, I love to sing your praises.
I'm so glad you're in my life;
I'm so glad you came to save us.
(Repeat)

Continued overleaf

You came from heaven to earth
to show the way,
from the earth to the cross,
my debt to pay,
from the cross to the grave,
from the grave to the sky,
Lord, I lift your name on high.

462 Richard Baxter (1615-1691)

1. Lord, it belongs not to my care
   whether I die or live:
   to love and serve thee is my share,
   and this thy grace must give.

2. Christ leads me through no darker
      rooms
   than he went through before;
   he that into God's kingdom comes
   must enter by this door.

3. Come, Lord, when grace hath made
      me meet
   thy blessèd face to see;
   for if thy work on earth be sweet,
   what will thy glory be!

4. Then shall I end my sad complaints
   and weary, sinful days,
   and join with the triumphant saints
   and sing my Saviour's praise.

5. My knowledge of that life is small,
   the eye of faith is dim;
   but 'tis enough that Christ knows all,
   and I shall be with him.

463 Patrick Appleford (b. 1925)
© 1960 Josef Weinberger Ltd

1. Lord Jesus Christ, you have come to us,
   you are one with us, Mary's Son.
   Cleansing our souls from all their sin,
   pouring your love and goodness in,
   Jesus, our love for you we sing,
   living Lord.

2. Lord Jesus Christ, now and every day
   teach us how to pray, Son of God.
   You have commanded us to do
   this in remembrance, Lord, of you.
   Into our lives your power breaks
      through,
   living Lord.

3. Lord Jesus Christ, you have come to us,
   born as one of us, Mary's Son.
   Led out to die on Calvary,
   risen from death to set us free,
   living Lord Jesus, help us see
   you are Lord.

4. Lord Jesus Christ, I would come to
      you,
   live my life for you, Son of God.
   All your commands I know are true,
   your many gifts will make me new,
   into my life your power breaks
      through,
   living Lord.

464 German, anon.
trans. Catherine Winkworth (1827-1878)

1. Lord Jesus Christ, be present now,
   and let your Holy Spirit bow
   all hearts in love and fear today
   to hear the truth and keep your way.

2. Open our lips to sing your praise,
   our hearts in true devotion raise,
   strengthen our faith, increase our light,
   that we may know your name aright.

465 'Mnōeo Christe' by Bishop Synesius (375-430)
trans. Allen William Chatfield (1808-1896)

1. Lord Jesus, think on me,
   and purge away my sin;
   from earth-born passions set me free,
   and make me pure within.

2. Lord Jesus, think on me,
   with care and woe opprest;
   let me thy loving servant be
   and taste thy promised rest.

3. Lord Jesus, think on me
   amid the battle's strife;
   in all my pain and misery
   be thou my health and life.

4. Lord Jesus, think on me,
   nor let me go astray;
   through darkness and perplexity
   point thou the heavenly way.

5. Lord Jesus, think on me,
   when flows the tempest high:
   when on doth rush the enemy,
   O Saviour, be thou nigh.

6. Lord Jesus, think on me,
   that, when the flood is past,
   I may th'eternal brightness see,
   and share thy joy at last.

466 Oliver Wendell Holmes (1809-1894)

1. Lord of all being, throned afar,
   thy glory flames from sun and star;
   centre and soul of ev'ry sphere,
   yet to each loving heart how near.

2. Sun of our life, thy quickening ray
   sheds on our path the glow of day;
   Star of our hope, thy softened light
   cheers the long watches of the night.

3. Lord of all life, below, above,
   whose light is truth, whose warmth is
      love,
   before thy ever-blazing throne
   we ask no lustre of our own.

4. Grant us thy truth to make us free,
   and kindling hearts that burn for
      thee,
   till all thy living altars claim
   one holy light, one heavenly flame.

467 Jan Struther (1901-1953)
© Oxford University Press

1. Lord of all hopefulness,
   Lord of all joy,
   whose trust, ever childlike,
   no cares could destroy,
   be there at our waking,
   and give us, we pray,
   your bliss in our hearts, Lord,
   at the break of the day.

2. Lord of all eagerness,
   Lord of all faith,
   whose strong hands were skilled
   at the plane and the lathe,
   be there at our labours,
   and give us, we pray,
   your strength in our hearts, Lord,
   at the noon of the day.

Continued overleaf

3. Lord of all kindliness,
Lord of all grace,
your hands swift to welcome,
your arms to embrace,
be there at our homing,
and give us, we pray,
your love in our hearts, Lord,
at the eve of the day.

4. Lord of all gentleness,
Lord of all calm,
whose voice is contentment,
whose presence is balm,
be there at our sleeping,
and give us, we pray,
your peace in our hearts, Lord,
at the end of the day.

468 Timothy Dudley-Smith (b. 1926)
© *Timothy Dudley-Smith*

1. Lord of all life and power
at whose creative word
in nature's first primeval hour
our formless being stirred,
you made the light to shine,
O shine on us, we pray,
renew with light and life divine
your Church in this our day.

2. Lord of the fertile earth
who caused the world to be,
whose life alone can bring to birth
the fruits of land and sea,
teach us to use aright
and share the gifts you give,
to tend the earth as in your sight
that all the world may live.

3. Lord of the cross and grave
who died and lives again,
who came in love to seek and save
and then to rise and reign,
we share, as once you shared,
in mortal birth and breath,
and ours the risen life that dared
to vanquish sin and death.

4. Lord of the wind and flame,
the promised Spirit's sign,
possess our hearts in Jesus' name,
come down, O Love divine!
Help us in Christ to grow,
from sin and self to cease,
and daily in our lives to show
your love and joy and peace.

5. Lord of the passing years
whose changeless purpose stands,
our lives and loves, our hopes and fears,
we place within your hands;
we bring you but your own,
forgiven, loved and free,
to follow Christ, and Christ alone,
through all the days to be.

469 Cyril A. Alington (1872-1955)
© *Lady Fiona Mynors. Used by permission*

1. Lord of all, to whom alone
all our heart's desires are known,
when we stand before thy throne,
Jesus, hear and save.

2. Son of Man, before whose eyes
every secret open lies,
at thy great and last assize,
Jesus, hear and save.

3. Son of God, whose angel host
(thou hast said) rejoiceth most
o'er the sinner who was lost,
Jesus, hear and save.

4. Saviour, who didst not condemn
those who touched thy garment's
hem,
mercy show to us and them:
Jesus, hear and save.

5. Lord, the way to sinners shown,
Lord, the truth by sinners known,
love incarnate on the throne,
Jesus, hear and save.

470 Cyril A. Alington (1872-1955)
© Hymns Ancient & Modern Ltd

1. Lord of beauty, thine the splendour
shown in earth and sky and sea,
burning sun and moonlight tender,
hill and river, flower and tree:
lest we fail our praise to render
touch our eyes that they may see.

2. Lord of wisdom, whom obeying
mighty waters ebb and flow,
while unhasting, undelaying,
planets on their courses go:
in thy laws thyself displaying,
teach our minds thyself to know.

3. Lord of life, alone sustaining
all below and all above,
Lord of love, by whose ordaining
sun and stars sublimely move:
in our earthly spirits reigning,
lift our hearts that we may love.

4. Lord of beauty, bid us own thee,
Lord of truth, our footsteps guide,
till as Love our hearts enthrone thee,
and, with vision purified,
Lord of all, when all have known thee,
thou in all art glorified.

471 Jack C. Winslow (1882-1974) alt.
© Mrs J. Tyrrell

1. Lord of creation, to you be all praise!
Most mighty your working, most
wondrous your ways!
Your glory and might are beyond us
to tell,
and yet in the heart of the humble
you dwell.

2. Lord of all power, I give you my will,
in joyful obedience your tasks to fulfil.
Your bondage is freedom; your
service is song;
and, held in your keeping, my
weakness is strong.

3. Lord of all wisdom, I give you my
mind,
rich truth that surpasses my knowledge
to find;
what eye has not seen and what ear
has not heard
is taught by your Spirit and shines
from your word.

4. Lord of all bounty, I give you my heart;
I praise and adore you for all you
impart,
your love to inspire me, your counsel
to guide,
your presence to shield me, whatever
betide.

5. Lord of all being, I give you my all;
if e'er I disown you, I stumble and fall;
but, led in your service your word to
obey,
I'll walk in your freedom to the end
of the way.

472 Hubert Richards (b. 1921)
© 1991 Kevin Mayhew Ltd

Lord of creation,
may your will be done.

Lord of creation,
may your will be done.

473 Catherine Walker (b. 1958)
© Catherine Walker. Used by permission

Lord of life, I come to you;
Lord of all, my Saviour be;
Lord of love, come bless us
with the light of your love.

474 Jack C. Winslow (1882-1974)
© Mrs J. Tyrrell. Used by permission

1. Lord of lords and King eternal,
   down the years in wondrous ways
   you have blessed our land and
      guided,
   leading us through darkest days.
   For your rich and faithful mercies,
   Lord, accept our thankful praise.

2. Speak to us and every nation,
   bid our jarring discords cease;
   to the starving and the homeless
   bid us bring a full release;
   and on all this earth's sore turmoil
   breathe the healing of your peace.

3. Love that binds us all together
   be upon the Church outpoured;
   shame our pride and quell our
      factions,
   smite them with your Spirit's sword;
   till the world, our love beholding,
   claims your power and calls you
      Lord.

4. Brace the wills of all your people
   who in every land and race
   know the secrets of your kingdom,
   share the treasures of your grace;
   till the summons of your Spirit
   wakes new life in every place.

5. Saviour, by your mighty Passion
   once you turned sheer loss to gain,
   wresting in your risen glory
   victory from your cross and pain;
   now O Saviour, dead and risen,
   in us triumph, live, and reign.

475 Albert F. Bayly (1901-1984)
© Oxford University Press. Used by permission

1. Lord of the boundless curves of space
   and time's deep mystery,
   to your creative might
   we trace all nature's energy.

2. Your mind conceived the galaxy,
   each atom's secret planned,
   and every age of history
   your purpose, Lord, has spanned.

3. Your Spirit gave the living cell
   its hidden, vital force:
   the instincts which all life impel
   derive from you, their source.

4. Science explores your reason's ways,
   and faith can this impart:
   that in the face of Christ our gaze
   looks deep within your heart.

5. Christ is your wisdom's perfect word,
   your mercy's crowning deed:
   and in his love our hearts have heard
   your strong compassion plead.

6. Give us to know your truth; but more,
   the strength to do your will;
   until the love our souls adore
   shall all our being fill.

476 Ian D. Craig
© 1993 Daybreak Music Ltd

1. Lord of the future, Lord of the past,
   Lord of our lives, we adore you.
   Lord of forever, Lord of our hearts,
   we give all praise to you.

2. Lord of tomorrow, Lord of today,
   Lord over all, you are worthy.
   Lord of creation, Lord of all truth,
   we give all praise to you.

477 Isaac Watts (1674-1748)
based on Psalm 84

1. Lord of the worlds above
   how pleasant and how fair
   the dwellings of thy love,
   thy earthly temples, are!
   To thine abode
   my heart aspires,
   with warm desires
   to see my God.

2. O happy souls that pray
   where God appoints to hear!
   O happy ones that pay
   their constant service there!
   They praise thee still;
   and happy they
   that love the way
   to Sion's hill.

3. They go from strength to strength
   through this dark vale of tears,
   till each arrives at length,
   till each in heaven appears:
   O glorious seat!
   when God our King
   shall thither bring
   our willing feet.

478 James Montgomery (1771-1854) alt.
This version © 1996 Kevin Mayhew Ltd

1. Lord, teach us how to pray aright
   with rev'rence and with fear;
   though fallen sinners in thy sight,
   we may, we must, draw near.

2. Our spirits fail through lack of prayer:
   O grant us power to pray;
   and, when to meet thee we prepare,
   Lord, meet us by the way.

3. God of all grace, we bring to thee
   a broken, contrite heart;
   give what thine eye delights to see,
   truth in the inward part;

4. Faith in the only sacrifice
   that can for sin atone,
   to cast our hopes, to fix our eyes,
   on Christ, on Christ alone.

5. Patience to watch and wait and weep,
   though mercy long delay;
   courage our fainting souls to keep,
   and trust in thee alway.

6. Give these, and then thy will be done;
   thus, strengthened with all might,
   we, through thy Spirit and thy Son,
   shall pray, and pray aright.

479 Graham Kendrick (b. 1950)
© 1987 Make Way Music

1. Lord, the light of your love is shining,
   in the midst of the darkness, shining;
   Jesus, Light of the World,
      shine upon us,
   set us free by the truth you now bring
   us.
   Shine on me, shine on me.

Continued overleaf

Shine, Jesus, shine,
fill this land with the Father's glory;
blaze, Spirit, blaze,
set our hearts on fire.
Flow, river, flow,
flood the nations with grace and mercy;
send forth your word, Lord,
and let there be light.

2. Lord, I come to your awesome
   presence,
   from the shadows into your radiance;
   by the blood I may enter your
   brightness,
   search me, try me, consume all my
   darkness.
   Shine on me, shine on me.

3. As we gaze on your kingly brightness,
   so our faces display your likeness,
   ever changing from glory to glory;
   mirrored here may our lives tell your
   story.
   Shine on me, shine on me.

480
Nick Fawcett (b. 1957)
© 2004 Kevin Mayhew Ltd

1. Lord, there are times when I have to
   ask, 'Why?' –
   times when catastrophe gives faith
   the lie.
   Innocents suffer and evil holds sway,
   grant me some answers, Lord, teach
   me your way.

2. Lord, there are times when I have to
   ask, 'Where?' –
   times when it seems that you simply
   don't care.
   Though I call out, you seem distant,
   aloof,
   grant me some answers, Lord, show
   me some proof.

3. Lord, there are times when I have to
   ask, 'What?' –
   times when your love is not easy to
   spot.
   What is life's purpose and what of me
   here?
   Grant me some answers, Lord, make
   your will clear.

4. Lord, there are times when I have to
   ask, 'How?' –
   times when what's preached doesn't
   square with life now.
   Wrestling with doubt I ask, 'How can
   this be?'
   Grant me some answers, Lord, help
   me to see.

5. Lord, there are times when the
   questions run fast –
   times when I fear that my faith may
   not last.
   Help me, support me, Lord, help me
   get through.
   Lead me through darkness till light
   shines anew.

481
Henry Williams Baker (1821-1877)

1. Lord, thy word abideth,
   and our footsteps guideth;
   who its truth believeth
   light and joy receiveth.

2. When our foes are near us,
   then thy word doth cheer us,
   word of consolation,
   message of salvation.

3. When the storms are o'er us,
   and dark clouds before us,
   then its light directeth,
   and our way protecteth.

4. Who can tell the pleasure,
   who recount the treasure,
   by thy word imparted
   to the simple-hearted?

5. Word of mercy, giving
   succour to the living;
   word of life, supplying
   comfort to the dying.

6. O that we, discerning
   its most holy learning,
   Lord, may love and fear thee,
   evermore be near thee.

482 Nick Fawcett (b. 1957)
© 2004 Kevin Mayhew Ltd

1. Lord, today your voice is calling,
   lifting thoughts to things above;
   life is wonderful, enthralling,
   touched by your unfailing love.
   Suddenly I see the beauty
   often hidden from my gaze,
   so I come, not out of duty,
   but with glad and grateful praise.

2. Lord, I sometimes fail to value
   all your blessings as I should.
   Slow to make the time to thank you,
   blind to so much that is good.
   Days are lived in such a hurry
   there's no time to stop and stare,
   joy is crushed by weight of worry,
   happiness obscured by care.

3. Lord, today I come rejoicing,
   vowed to waste your gifts no more;
   bringing praise and gladly voicing
   what I should have voiced before.
   Pouring out my adoration,
   scarcely knowing where to start,
   with a song of exultation,
   Lord, I thank you from the heart.

483 Jean Holloway (b. 1939)
© 1995 Kevin Mayhew Ltd

1. Lord, we come to ask your healing,
   teach us of love;
   all unspoken shame revealing,
   teach us of love.
   Take our selfish thoughts and actions,
   petty feuds, divisive factions,
   hear us now to you appealing,
   teach us of love.

2. Soothe away our pain and sorrow,
   hold us in love;
   grace we cannot buy or borrow,
   hold us in love.
   Though we see but dark and danger,
   though we spurn both friend and
   stranger,
   though we often dread tomorrow,
   hold us in love.

3. When the bread is raised and broken,
   fill us with love;
   words of consecration spoken,
   fill us with love.
   As our grateful prayers continue,
   make the faith that we have in you
   more than just an empty token,
   fill us with love.

4. Help us live for one another,
   bind us in love;
   stranger, neighbour, father, mother –
   bind us in love.
   All are equal at your table,
   through your Spirit make us able
   to embrace as sister, brother,
   bind us in love.

484
Martin E. Leckebusch (b. 1962)
© 1999 Kevin Mayhew Ltd

1. Lord, we thank you for the promise
   seen in every human birth:
   you have planned each new
     beginning;
   who could hope for greater worth?
   Hear our prayer for those we cherish;
   claim our children as your own:
   in the fertile ground of childhood
   may eternal seed be sown.

2. Lord, we thank you for the vigour
   burning in the years of youth:
   strength to face tomorrow's challenge,
   zest for life and zeal for truth.
   In the choice of friends and partners,
   when ideas and values form,
   may the message of your kingdom
   be the guide, the goal, the norm.

3. Lord, we thank you for the harvest
   of the settled, middle years:
   times when work and home can
     prosper,
   when life's richest fruit appears;
   but when illness, stress and hardship
   fill so many days with dread,
   may your love renew the vision
   of a clearer road ahead.

4. Lord, we thank you for the beauty
   of a heart at last mature:
   crowned with peace and rich in
     wisdom,
   well-respected and secure;
   but to those who face the twilight
   frail, bewildered, lacking friends,
   Lord, confirm your gracious offer:
   perfect life which never ends.

485
Martin E. Leckebusch (b. 1962)
© 2004 Kevin Mayhew Ltd

1. Lord, we turn to you for mercy:
   may our prayerful words express
   something of our heartfelt sorrow
   for the sins we now confess.

2. We have trusted far too often
   in our human strength and skill;
   we have proudly disregarded
   what we knew to be your will.

3. Yet by your immense compassion
   you invite, accept, restore,
   leading us to greater wholeness
   than we ever knew before.

4. Your forgiveness lifts our burdens,
   setting heart and spirit free
   to fulfil our true potential,
   all that we were meant to be.

5. For you teach a way of wisdom
   we may clearly understand:
   walking with the God of mercy
   step by step, and hand in hand.

486
Susan Sayers (b. 1946)
© 1984 Kevin Mayhew Ltd

1. Lord, when I turn my back on you
   the fears and darkness grow.
   I need you, oh, I need you, Lord,
   to show me where to go.

2. With you beside me, Lord, I find
   the evils that I face
   become instead a joyfulness,
   a fountain of your grace.

3. So shape me to your purpose, Lord,
   and tell me what to do;
   and if I start to turn away,
   then turn me back to you.

4. And when the world is over, Lord,
   or over just for me,
   there is nowhere but with you, Lord,
   that I would rather be.

487 Nick Fawcett (b. 1957)
© 2004 Kevin Mayhew Ltd

1. Lord, you call us to a journey,
   to a never-ending quest;
   always seeking new horizons,
   always reaching for the best.

2. Young or old, it makes no diff'rence,
   still the journey's just begun,
   keep on looking in the distance,
   never dream the race is run.

3. Let the search for truth continue,
   may its flame for ever burn –
   what we know is only partial,
   there is more we need to learn.

4. Do not fear what seems to challenge,
   do not cling to what is dead.
   Let the voice of God disturb you –
   by the way of Christ be led.

5. Faith must always be evolving,
   if it is to stay alive –
   not viewed as some destination,
   where one day we must arrive.

6. Lord, you call us to a journey,
   always taking one step more.
   Help us then to keep believing
   that you hold the best in store.

488 Nick Fawcett (b. 1957)
© 2004 Kevin Mayhew Ltd

1. Lord, you created a world rich in
   splendour,
   touched with a beauty no words can
   express.
   Able to move us to outbursts of
   wonder,
   so much to thrill us and so much to
   bless.

2. Mountains and moorlands rise up to
   the heavens,
   rivers and streams tumble down to
   the sea,
   gifts that amaze in profusion
   surround us,
   each a reflection of your majesty.

3. Promise of springtime and harvest of
   autumn,
   cold winter mornings and warm
   summer days,
   season by season brings new joys to
   greet us,
   reason to thank you and reason to
   praise.

4. Deep in the forest, remote in the
   desert,
   down in the ocean or high in the air;
   life in abundance is everywhere
   round us,
   proof of your power and sign of your
   care.

5. Lord, you have given a world rich in
   splendour,
   touched with a beauty that fills us
   with awe;
   hear now our praises, we bring you
   our worship,
   with all creation we kneel and adore.

489

Martin Smith
© 1992 Thankyou Music

Lord, you have my heart,
and I will search for yours;
Jesus, take my life and lead me on.
Lord, you have my heart,
and I will search for yours;
let me be to you a sacrifice.

And I will praise you, Lord
(I will praise you, Lord).
And I will sing of love come down
(I will sing of love come down).
And as you show your face
(show your face),
we'll see your glory here.

490

Christina Georgina Rossetti (1830-1894)

1. Love came down at Christmas,
   Love all lovely, Love divine;
   Love was born at Christmas,
   star and angels gave the sign.

2. Worship we the Godhead,
   Love incarnate, Love divine;
   worship we our Jesus:
   but wherewith for sacred sign?

3. Love shall be our token,
   love be yours and love be mine,
   love to God and all men,
   love for plea and gift and sign.

491

Charles Wesley (1707-1788) alt.

1. Love divine, all loves excelling,
   joy of heaven, to earth come down,
   fix in us thy humble dwelling,
   all thy faithful mercies crown.

2. Jesu, thou art all compassion,
   pure unbounded love thou art;
   visit us with thy salvation,
   enter every trembling heart.

3. Breathe, O breathe thy loving Spirit
   into every troubled breast;
   let us all in thee inherit,
   let us find thy promised rest.

4. Take away the love of sinning,
   Alpha and Omega be;
   end of faith, as its beginning,
   set our hearts at liberty.

5. Come, almighty to deliver,
   let us all thy grace receive;
   suddenly return, and never,
   never more thy temples leave.

6. Thee we would be always blessing,
   serve thee as thy hosts above;
   pray, and praise thee without ceasing,
   glory in thy perfect love.

7. Finish then thy new creation,
   pure and spotless let us be;
   let us see thy great salvation
   perfectly restored in thee.

8. Changed from glory into glory,
   till in heaven we take our place,
   till we cast our crowns before thee,
   lost in wonder, love, and praise.

492

Luke Connaughton (1917-1979) alt.
© McCrimmon Publishing Co. Ltd

1. Love is his word, love is his way,
   feasting with all, fasting alone,
   living and dying, rising again,
   love, only love, is his way.

   *Richer than gold is the love of my Lord:
   better than splendour and wealth.*

2. Love is his way, love is his mark,
sharing his last Passover feast,
Christ at the table, host to the twelve,
love, only love, is his mark.

3. Love is his mark, love is his sign,
bread for our strength, wine for our
joy,
'This is my body, this is my blood.'
Love, only love, is his sign.

4. Love is his sign, love is his news,
'Do this,' he said, 'lest you forget
all my deep sorrow, all my dear blood.'
Love, only love, is his news.

5. Love is his news, love is his name,
we are his own, chosen and called,
family, brethren, cousins and kin.
Love, only love, is his name.

6. Love is his name, love is his law,
hear his command, all who are his,
'Love one another, I have loved you.'
Love, only love, is his law.

7. Love is his law, love is his word:
love of the Lord, Father and Word,
love of the Spirit, God ever one,
love, only love, is his word.

493 Pamela Hayes
© 1998 Kevin Mayhew Ltd

1. Lovely in your littleness,
longing for our lowliness,
longing for our lowliness,
searching for our meekness:
Jesus is our joy, Jesus is our joy.

2. Peace within our powerlessness,
hope within our helplessness,
hope within our helplessness,
love within our loneliness:
Jesus is our joy, Jesus is our joy.

3. Held in Mary's tenderness,
tiny hands are raised to bless,
tiny hands are raised to bless,
touching us with God's caress:
Jesus is our joy, Jesus is our joy.

4. Joy, then, in God's graciousness,
peace comes with gentleness,
peace comes with gentleness,
filling hearts with gladness:
Jesus is our joy, Jesus is our joy.

494 Charles Wesley (1707-1788)

1. Love's redeeming work is done;
fought the fight, the battle won:
lo, our Sun's eclipse is o'er,
lo, he sets in blood no more.

2. Vain the stone, the watch, the seal;
Christ has burst the gates of hell;
death in vain forbids his rise;
Christ has opened paradise.

3. Lives again our glorious King;
where, O death, is now thy sting?
Dying once, he all doth save;
where thy victory, O grave?

4. Soar we now where Christ has led,
foll'wing our exalted Head;
made like him, like him we rise;
ours the cross, the grave, the skies.

5. Hail the Lord of earth and heav'n!
praise to thee by both be giv'n;
thee we greet triumphant now;
hail, the Resurrection thou!

495 Jane Elizabeth Leeson (1809-1881)

1. Loving Shepherd of thy sheep,
   keep me, Lord, in safety keep;
   nothing can thy power withstand,
   none can pluck me from thy hand.

2. Loving Shepherd, thou didst give
   thine own life that I might live;
   may I love thee day by day,
   gladly thy sweet will obey.

3. Loving Shepherd, ever near,
   teach me still thy voice to hear;
   suffer not my steps to stray
   from the straight and narrow way.

4. Where thou leadest may I go,
   walking in thy steps below;
   then, before thy Father's throne,
   Jesu, claim me for thine own.

496 Robert Lowry (1826-1899)

1. Low in the grave he lay,
   Jesus, my Saviour;
   waiting the coming day,
   Jesus, my Lord.

   Up from the grave he arose,
   with a mighty triumph o'er his foes;
   he arose a victor
   from the dark domain,
   and he lives for ever
   with his saints to reign.
   He arose! He arose!
   Hallelujah! Christ arose!

2. Vainly they watch his bed,
   Jesus, my Saviour;
   vainly they seal the dead,
   Jesus, my Lord.

3. Death cannot keep its prey,
   Jesus, my Saviour;
   he tore the bars away,
   Jesus, my Lord.

497 Based on Luke 1:46

Magnificat, magnificat,
anima mea Dominum. *(Repeat)*

Translation: My soul praises and
magnifies the Lord.

498 Jack W. Hayford (b. 1934)
© 1976 Rocksmith Music Inc.

Majesty, worship his majesty;
unto Jesus be glory, honour and praise.
Majesty, kingdom, authority
flow from his throne unto his own:
his anthem raise.
So exalt, lift up on high the name of
   Jesus;
magnify, come glorify
Christ Jesus the King.
Majesty, worship his majesty,
Jesus who died, now glorified,
King of all kings.

499 Sebastian Temple (1928-1997)
based on the Prayer of St Francis
© 1967 OCP Publications

1. Make me a channel of your peace.
   Where there is hatred, let me bring
      your love.
   Where there is injury, your pardon,
      Lord;
   and where there's doubt, true faith in
      you.

O, Master, grant that I may never seek
so much to be consoled as to console,
to be understood as to understand,
to be loved as to love with all my soul.

2. Make me a channel of your peace.
   Where there's despair in life, let me
   bring hope.
   Where there is darkness, only light,
   and where there's sadness, ever joy.

3. Make me a channel of your peace.
   It is in pardoning that we are
   pardoned,
   in giving of ourselves that we receive,
   and in dying that we're born to
   eternal life.

500 Graham Kendrick (b. 1950)
© 1986 Thankyou Music

1. Make way, make way, for Christ the
   King
   in splendour arrives;
   fling wide the gates and welcome him
   into your lives.

   Make way (make way),
   make way (make way),
   for the King of kings
   (for the King of kings);
   make way (make way),
   make way (make way),
   and let his kingdom in!

2. He comes the broken hearts to heal,
   the pris'ners to free;
   the deaf shall hear, the lame shall
   dance,
   the blind shall see.

3. And those who mourn with heavy
   hearts,
   who weep and sigh,
   with laughter, joy and royal crown
   he'll beautify.

4. We call you now to worship him
   as Lord of all,
   to have no gods before him,
   their thrones must fall.

501 Michael Forster (b. 1946)
© 1996 Kevin Mayhew Ltd

1. Mary, blessèd grieving mother,
   waiting by the cross of shame,
   through your patient, prayerful vigil,
   kindle hope's eternal flame;
   crying in the pains of earth,
   singing of redemption's birth.

2. Where the crosses of the nations
   darken still the noonday skies,
   see the sad madonna weeping
   through a million mothers' eyes.
   Holy Mary, full of grace,
   all our tears with yours embrace.

3. Standing with the suff'ring Saviour,
   still oppressed by hate and fear,
   where the gentle still are murdered
   and protesters disappear:
   mother of the crucified,
   call his people to your side!

4. Holy mother, watching, waiting,
   for the saving of the earth;
   in the loneliness of dying,
   speak of hope and human worth,
   there for all the world to see,
   lifted up at Calvary!

502 West Indian Spiritual, alt.
© 1999, 2004 Kevin Mayhew Ltd

1. Mary had a baby, yes, Lord,
   Mary had a baby, yes, my Lord,
   Mary had a baby, yes, Lord,
   the people came to Bethlehem
   to see her son.

2. What did she name him, yes, Lord?
   (x3)

3. Mary named him Jesus, yes, Lord, *(x3)*

4. Where was he born, yes, Lord? *(x3)*

5. Born in a stable, yes, Lord, *(x3)*

6. Where did she lay him, yes, Lord? *(x3)*

7. Laid him in a manger, yes, Lord, *(x3)*

2. May the glory of Jesus fill his church.
   (May the glory of Jesus fill his church.)
   May the glory of Jesus fill his church.
   (Radiant glory of Jesus),
   shining from our faces
   as we gaze in adoration.

3. May the beauty of Jesus fill my life.
   (May the beauty of Jesus fill my life.)
   May the beauty of Jesus fill my life.
   (Perfect beauty of Jesus),
   fill my thoughts, my words, my deeds;
   may I give in adoration.
   Fill my thoughts, my words, my deeds;
   may I give in adoration.

503 Cliff Barrows (b. 1923)
© 1982 Cliff Barrows. Used by permission

May God's blessing surround you
   *each day
as you trust him and walk in his way.
May his presence within guard and
   keep you from sin,
go in peace, go in joy, go in love.

* *Alternative - tonight*

505 John Newton (1725-1807)
based on 2 Corinthians 13:14

1. May the grace of Christ our Saviour,
   and the Father's boundless love,
   with the Holy Spirit's favour,
   rest upon us from above.

2. Thus may we abide in union
   with each other and the Lord,
   and possess, in sweet communion,
   joys which earth cannot afford.

504 Graham Kendrick (b. 1950)
© 1986 Thankyou Music

1. May the fragrance of Jesus fill this
   place.
   (May the fragrance of Jesus fill this
   place.)
   May the fragrance of Jesus fill this
   place.
   (Lovely fragrance of Jesus),
   rising from the sacrifice
   of lives laid down in adoration.

506 Kate Barclay Wilkinson (1859-1928)

1. May the mind of Christ my Saviour
   live in me from day to day,
   by his love and power controlling
   all I do and say.

2. May the word of God dwell richly
   in my heart from hour to hour,
   so that I may triumph only
   in his saving power.

3. May the peace of God my Father
rule my life in everything,
that I may be calm to comfort
sick and sorrowing.

4. May the love of Jesus fill me,
as the waters fill the sea;
him exalting, self abasing,
this is victory.

5. May I run the race before me,
strong and brave to face the foe,
looking only unto Jesus,
as I onward go.

507 Graham Kendrick (b. 1950)
© 1986 Thankyou Music

1. Meekness and majesty,
manhood and deity,
in perfect harmony, the Man who is
God.
Lord of eternity dwells in humanity,
kneels in humility and washes our feet.

O what a mystery, meekness and majesty.
Bow down and worship for this is your
God,
this is your God.

2. Father's pure radiance,
perfect in innocence,
yet learns obedience to death on a cross.
Suff'ring to give us life,
conqu'ring through sacrifice,
and as they crucify prays: 'Father
forgive.'

3. Wisdom unsearchable,
God the invisible,
love indestructible in frailty appears.
Lord of infinity, stooping so tenderly,
lifts our humanity
to the heights of his throne.

508 Martin Smith
© 1995 Curious? Music UK

1. Men of faith, rise up and sing
of the great and glorious King.
You are strong when you feel weak,
in your brokenness complete.

Shout to the north and the south,
sing to the east and the west.
Jesus is Saviour to all,
Lord of heaven and earth.

2. Rise up, women of the truth,
stand and sing to broken hearts.
Who can know the healing power,
of our awesome King of love?

We've been through fire,
we've been through rain,
we've been refined by the power of
his name.
We've fallen deeper in love with you,
you've burned the truth on our lips.

3. Rise up, church with broken wings,
fill this place with songs again
of our God who reigns on high,
by his grace again we'll fly.

509 William Hubert Vanstone (1923-1999)
© Mrs I. Shore. Used by permission

1. Morning glory, starlit sky,
leaves in spring-time, swallows' flight,
autumn gales, tremendous seas,
sounds and scents of summer night;

2. Soaring music, towering words,
art's perfection, scholar's truth,
joy supreme of human love,
memory's treasure, grace of youth;

3. Open, Lord, are these, thy gifts,
gifts of love to mind and sense;
hidden is love's agony,
love's endeavour, love's expense.

Continued overleaf

4. Love that gives, gives evermore,
   gives with zeal, with eager hands,
   spares not, keeps not, all outpours,
   ventures all, its all expends.

5. Drained is love in making full;
   bound in setting others free;
   poor in making many rich;
   weak in giving power to be.

6. Therefore he who thee reveals
   hangs, O Father, on that Tree
   helpless; and the nails and thorns
   tell of what thy love must be.

7. Thou art God, no monarch thou,
   throned in easy state to reign;
   thou art God, whose arms of love
   aching, spent, the world sustain.

510 Eleanor Farjeon (1881-1965)
© *David Higham Associates. Used by permission from* The Children's Bells, *Oxford University Press*

1. Morning has broken like the first
   morning,
   blackbird has spoken like the first
   bird.
   Praise for the singing! Praise for the
   morning!
   Praise for them, springing fresh from
   the Word!

2. Sweet the rain's new fall, sunlit from
   heaven,
   like the first dew-fall on the first grass.
   Praise for the sweetness of the wet
   garden,
   sprung in completeness where his feet
   pass.

3. Mine is the sunlight! Mine is the
   morning
   born of the one light Eden saw play!
   Praise with elation, praise every
   morning,
   God's re-creation of the new day!

511 Estelle White (b. 1925)
© *McCrimmon Publishing Co. Ltd*

1. 'Moses, I know you're the man,'
   the Lord said.
   'You're going to work out my plan,'
   the Lord said.
   'Lead all the Israelites out of slavery,
   and I shall make them a wandering
   race
   called the people of God.'

   So every day we're on our way,
   for we're a travelling, wandering race
   called the people of God.

2. 'Don't get too set in your ways,'
   the Lord said.
   'Each step is only a phase,'
   the Lord said.
   'I'll go before you and I shall be a sign
   to guide my travelling, wandering race.
   You're the people of God.'

3. 'No matter what you may do,'
   the Lord said,
   'I shall be faithful and true,'
   the Lord said.
   'My love will strengthen you as you
   go along,
   for you're my travelling, wandering
   race.
   You're the people of God.'

4. 'Look at the birds in the air,'
   the Lord said.
   'They fly unhampered by care,'
   the Lord said.
   'You will move easier if you're
   travelling light,
   for you're a wandering, vagabond
   race.'
   You're the people of God.'

5. 'Foxes have places to go,'
   the Lord said,
   'but I've no home here below,'
   the Lord said.
   'So if you want to be with me all your
   days,
   keep up the moving and travelling on.
   You're the people of God.'

512 Ray Palmer (1808-1887)

1. My faith looks up to thee,
   thou Lamb of Calvary,
   Saviour divine!
   Now hear me while I pray,
   take all my guilt away,
   O let me from this day
   be wholly thine.

2. May thy rich grace impart
   strength to my fainting heart,
   my zeal inspire.
   As thou hast died for me,
   O may my love to thee
   pure, warm and changeless be,
   a living fire.

3. While life's dark maze I tread,
   and griefs around me spread,
   be thou my guide;
   bid darkness turn to day,
   wipe sorrow's tears away,
   nor let me ever stray
   from thee aside.

4. When ends life's transient dream,
   when death's cold sullen stream
   shall o'er me roll,
   blest Saviour, then in love,
   fear and distrust remove;
   O bear me safe above,
   a ransomed soul.

513 Henry Williams Baker (1821-1877)

1. My Father, for another night
   of quiet sleep and rest,
   for all the joy of morning light,
   thy holy name be blest.

2. Now with the new-born day I give
   myself anew to thee,
   that as thou willest I may live,
   and what thou willest be.

3. Whate'er I do, things great or small,
   whate'er I speak or frame,
   thy glory may I seek in all,
   do all in Jesus' name.

4. My Father, for his sake, I pray,
   thy child accept and bless;
   and lead me by thy grace today
   in paths of righteousness.

514 Matthew Bridges (1800-1894)

1. My God, accept my heart this day,
   and make it always thine,
   that I from thee no more may stray,
   no more from thee decline.

2. Before the cross of him who died,
   behold, I prostrate fall;
   let every sin be crucified,
   and Christ be all in all.

3. Anoint me with thy heav'nly grace,
   and seal me for thine own;
   that I may see thy glorious face,
   and worship near thy throne.

4. Let every thought and work and word
   to thee be ever giv'n:
   then life shall be thy service, Lord,
   and death the gate of heav'n.

Continued overleaf

5. All glory to the Father be,
   all glory to the Son,
   all glory, Holy Ghost, to thee,
   while endless ages run.

515 Philip Doddridge (1702-1751), alt.
v. 3 Michael Forster (b. 1946)
© 1996 Kevin Mayhew Ltd

1. My God, and is thy table spread,
   and does thy cup with love o'erflow?
   Thither be all thy children led,
   and let them all thy sweetness know.

2. Hail, sacred feast, which Jesus makes!
   Rich banquet of his flesh and blood!
   Thrice happy all, who here partake
   that sacred stream, that heav'nly
   food.

3. What wondrous love! What perfect
   grace,
   for Jesus, our exalted host,
   invites us to this special place
   who offer least and need the most.

4. O let thy table honoured be,
   and furnished well with joyful guests;
   and may each soul salvation see,
   that here its sacred pledges tastes.

516 Frederick William Faber (1814-1863)
This version © Jubilate Hymns. Used by permission

1. My God, how wonderful you are,
   your majesty how bright;
   how beautiful your mercy-seat,
   in depths of burning light!

2. Creator from eternal years
   and everlasting Lord,
   by holy angels day and night
   unceasingly adored!

3. How wonderful, how beautiful
   the sight of you must be –
   your endless wisdom, boundless power,
   and awesome purity!

4. O how I fear you, living God,
   with deepest, tend'rest fears,
   and worship you with trembling hope
   and penitential tears!

5. But I may love you too, O Lord,
   though you are all-divine,
   for you have stooped to ask of me
   this feeble love of mine.

6. Father of Jesus, love's reward,
   great King upon your throne,
   what joy to see you as you are
   and know as I am known!

517 17th century Latin
trans. Edward Caswall (1814-1878)

1. My God, I love thee; not because
   I hope for heav'n thereby,
   nor yet because who love thee not
   are lost eternally.

2. Thou, O my Jesus, thou didst me
   upon the cross embrace;
   for me didst bear the nails and spear,
   and manifold disgrace.

3. And griefs and torments numberless,
   and sweat of agony;
   yea, death itself – and all for me
   who was thine enemy.

4. Then why, O blessèd Jesu Christ,
   should I not love thee well?
   Not for the sake of winning heav'n,
   nor of escaping hell.

5. Not from the hope of gaining aught,
   not seeking a reward;
   but as thyself hast lovèd me,
   O ever-loving Lord.

6. So would I love thee, dearest Lord,
   and in thy praise will sing;
   solely because thou art my God,
   and my most loving King.

518 Robin Mark (b. 1955)
© 1996 Daybreak Music Ltd

1. My heart will sing to you
   because of your great love,
   a love so rich, so pure,
   a love beyond compare;
   the wilderness, the barren place,
   become a blessing
   in the warmth of your embrace.

2. When earthly wisdom dims
   the light of knowing you,
   or if my search for understanding
   clouds your way,
   to you I fly, my hiding-place,
   where revelation
   is beholding face to face.

   May my heart sing your praise for ever,
   may my voice lift your name, my God;
   may my soul know no other treasure
   than your love, than your love.

519 Darlene Zschech (b. 1965)
© 1993 Darlene Zschech/Hillsong Publishing/
Kingsway Music

1. My Jesus, my Saviour,
   Lord, there is none like you.
   All of my days I want to praise
   the wonders of your mighty love.

2. My comfort, my shelter,
   tower of refuge and strength,
   let every breath, all that I am,
   never cease to worship you.

Shout to the Lord,
all the earth, let us sing
power and majesty,
praise to the King.
Mountains bow down
and the seas will roar
at the sound of your name.
I sing for joy
at the work of your hands.
For ever I'll love you,
for ever I'll stand.
Nothing compares to the promise
I have in you.

520 Graham Kendrick (b. 1950)
© 1989 Make Way Music

1. My Lord, what love is this,
   that pays so dearly,
   that I, the guilty one,
   may go free!

   Amazing love, O what sacrifice,
   the Son of God, given for me.
   My debt he pays, and my death he dies,
   that I might live,
   that I might live.

2. And so they watched him die,
   despised, rejected;
   but O, the blood he shed
   flowed for me!

3. And now this love of Christ
   shall flow like rivers;
   come, wash your guilt away,
   live again!

521 Samuel Crossman (c. 1624-1684) alt.

1. My song is love unknown,
   my Saviour's love to me,
   love to the loveless shown,
   that they might lovely be.
   O who am I, that for my sake,
   my Lord should take frail flesh and die?

2. He came from his blest throne,
   salvation to bestow;
   but men refused, and none
   the longed-for Christ would know.
   But O, my friend, my friend indeed,
   who at my need his life did spend!

3. Sometimes they strew his way,
   and his sweet praises sing:
   resounding all the day
   hosannas to their King:
   then 'Crucify!' is all their breath,
   and for his death they thirst and cry.

4. Why, what hath my Lord done?
   What makes this rage and spite?
   He made the lame to run,
   he gave the blind their sight.
   Sweet injuries! Yet they at these
   themselves displease,
       and 'gainst him rise.

5. They rise, and needs will have
   my dear Lord made away;
   a murderer they save,
   the Prince of Life they slay.
   Yet cheerful he to suff'ring goes,
   that he his foes from thence might free.

6. Here might I stay and sing,
   no story so divine;
   never was love, dear King,
   never was grief like thine.
   This is my friend in whose sweet praise
   I all my days could gladly spend.

522 John Byrom (1692-1763)

1. My spirit longs for thee
   within my troubled breast,
   though I unworthy be
   of so divine a guest.

2. Of so divine a guest
   unworthy though I be,
   yet has my heart no rest
   unless it come from thee.

3. Unless it come from thee,
   in vain I look around;
   in all that I can see
   no rest is to be found.

4. No rest is to be found
   but in thy blessèd love:
   O let my wish be crowned,
   and send it from above!

523 St Teresa of Avila (1545-1582)
© Ateliers et Presses de Taizé

Nada te turbe,
nada te espante.
Quien a Dios tiene nada le falta.
Nada te turbe,
nada te espante.
Solo Dios basta.

or

Nothing can trouble,
nothing can frighten.
Those who seek God shall never go
    wanting.
Nothing can trouble,
nothing can frighten.
God alone fills us.

524

Timothy Dudley-Smith (b. 1926)
© *Timothy Dudley-Smith*

1. Name of all majesty,
   fathomless mystery,
   King of the ages
   by angels adored;
   power and authority,
   splendour and dignity,
   bow to his mastery,
   Jesus is Lord!

2. Child of our destiny,
   God from eternity,
   love of the Father
   on sinners outpoured;
   see now what God has done
   sending his only Son,
   Christ the belovèd One,
   Jesus is Lord!

3. Saviour of Calvary,
   costliest victory,
   darkness defeated
   and Eden restored;
   born as a man to die,
   nailed to a cross on high,
   cold in the grave to lie,
   Jesus is Lord!

4. Source of all sovereignty,
   light, immortality,
   life everlasting
   and heaven assured;
   so with the ransomed, we
   praise him eternally,
   Christ in his majesty,
   Jesus is Lord!

525

Sarah Flower Adams (1805-1848)

1. Nearer, my God, to thee,
   nearer to thee!
   E'en though it be a cross
   that raiseth me:
   still all my song would be,
   'Nearer, my God, to thee,
   nearer to thee.'

2. Though, like the wanderer,
   the sun gone down,
   darkness be over me,
   my rest a stone;
   yet in my dreams I'd be
   nearer, my God, to thee,
   nearer to thee!

3. There let the way appear,
   steps unto heav'n;
   all that thou sendest me
   in mercy giv'n:
   angels to beckon me
   nearer, my God, to thee,
   nearer to thee!

4. Then, with my waking thoughts
   bright with thy praise,
   out of my stony griefs
   Bethel I'll raise;
   so by my woes to be
   nearer, my God, to thee,
   nearer to thee!

5. Or if on joyful wing
   cleaving the sky,
   sun, moon and stars forgot,
   upwards I fly,
   still all my song shall be,
   'Nearer, my God, to thee,
   nearer to thee.'

526

John Keble (1792-1866)
based on Lamentations 3:23

1. New every morning is the love
   our wak'ning and uprising prove;
   through sleep and darkness safely
      brought,
   restored to life and power and thought.

2. New mercies, each returning day,
   hover around us while we pray;
   new perils past, new sins forgiv'n,
   new thoughts of God, new hopes of
      heav'n.

3. If on our daily course our mind
   be set to hallow all we find,
   new treasures still, of countless price,
   God will provide for sacrifice.

4. Old friends, old scenes, will lovelier
      be,
   as more of heav'n in each we see;
   some soft'ning gleam of love and
      prayer
   shall dawn on every cross and care.

5. The trivial round, the common task,
   will furnish all we need to ask,
   room to deny ourselves, a road
   to bring us daily nearer God.

6. Only, O Lord, in thy dear love
   fit us for perfect rest above;
   and help us, this and every day,
   to live more nearly as we pray.

527

Erik Routley (1917-1982)
© 1974 Hope Publishing Co. Administered by
CopyCare

1. New songs of celebration render
   to him who has great wonders done.
   Love sits enthroned in ageless
      splendour:
   come and adore the mighty one.

He has made known his great salvation
which all his friends with joy confess:
he has revealed to every nation
his everlasting righteousness.

2. Joyfully, heartily resounding,
   let every instrument and voice
   peal out the praise of grace
      abounding,
   calling the whole world to rejoice.
   Trumpets and organs, set in motion
   such sounds as make the heavens ring;
   all things that live in earth and ocean,
   make music for your mighty King.

3. Rivers and seas and torrents roaring,
   honour the Lord with wild acclaim;
   mountains and stones look up
      adoring
   and find a voice to praise his name.
   Righteous, commanding, ever
      glorious,
   praises be his that never cease:
   just is our God, whose truth victorious
   establishes the world in peace.

528

George B. Caird (1917-1984)
© G. B. Caird Memorial Trust

1. Not far beyond the sea,
   nor high above the heavens,
   but very nigh thy voice, O God, is
      heard.
   For each new step of faith we take
   thou hast more truth and light to break
   forth from thy holy word.

2. Rooted and grounded in thy love,
   with saints on earth and saints above
   we join in full accord,
   to grasp the breadth, length, depth
      and height,
   the crucified and risen might
   of Christ, th'incarnate word.

3. Help us to press toward that mark,
and, though our vision now is dark,
to live by what we see.
So, when we see thee face to face,
thy truth and light our dwelling-place
for evermore shall be.

529 George Wallace Briggs (1875-1959) alt.
© Oxford University Press

1. Now is eternal life,
if ris'n with Christ we stand,
in him to life reborn,
and held within his hand;
no more we fear death's ancient dread,
in Christ arisen from the dead.

2. The human mind so long
brooded o'er life's brief span;
was it, O God, for naught,
for naught that life began?
Thou art our hope, our vital breath;
shall hope undying end in death?

3. And God, the living God,
stooped down to share our state;
by death destroying death,
Christ opened wide life's gate.
He lives, who died; he reigns on high;
who lives in him shall never die.

4. Unfathomed love divine,
reign thou within my heart;
from thee nor depth nor height,
nor life nor death can part;
my life is hid in God with thee,
now and through all eternity.

5. Thee will I love and serve
now in time's passing day;
thy hand shall hold me fast
when time is done away,
in God's unknown eternal spheres
to serve him through eternal years.

530 Fred Kaan (b. 1929)
© 1968 Stainer & Bell Ltd

1. Now let us from this table rise,
renewed in body, mind and soul;
with Christ we die and rise again,
his selfless love has made us whole.

2. With minds alert, upheld by grace,
to spread the Word in speech and deed,
we follow in the steps of Christ,
at one with all in hope and need.

3. To fill each human house with love,
it is the sacrament of care;
the work that Christ began to do
we humbly pledge ourselves to share.

4. Then grant us grace, Companion-God,
to choose again the pilgrim way,
and help us to accept with joy
the challenge of tomorrow's day.

531 St Thomas Aquinas (1227-1274)
trans. John Mason Neale (1818-1866),
Edward Caswall (1814-1878) and others

1. Now, my tongue, the myst'ry telling
of the glorious body sing,
and the blood, all price excelling,
which the Gentiles' Lord and King,
in a virgin's womb once dwelling,
shed for this world's ransoming.

2. Giv'n for us, for us descending
of a virgin to proceed,
he, with us in converse blending,
scattered here the gospel seed,
till his sojourn drew to ending,
which he closed with wondrous deed.

3. At the last great supper lying,
circled by his chosen band,
meekly with the law complying,
first he finished its command.
Then, immortal food supplying,
gave himself with his own hand.

Continued overleaf

4. Word made flesh, by word he maketh
very bread his flesh to be;
we, in wine, Christ's blood partaketh,
and if senses fail to see,
faith alone the true heart waketh,
to behold the mystery.

PART TWO

5. Therefore we, before him bending,
this great sacrament revere:
types and shadows have their ending,
for the newer rite is here;
faith, our outward sense befriending,
makes our inward vision clear.

6. Glory let us give and blessing
to the Father and the Son,
honour, might and praise addressing,
while eternal ages run;
ever too his love confessing,
who, from both, with both is one.
(Amen.)

532 'Nun danket alle Gott' Martin Rinkart (1586-1649)
trans. Catherine Winkworth (1827-1878)

1. Now thank we all our God,
with hearts and hands and voices,
who wondrous things hath done,
in whom his world rejoices;
who from our mother's arms
hath blessed us on our way
with countless gifts of love,
and still is ours today.

2. O may this bounteous God
through all our life be near us,
with ever joyful hearts
and blessèd peace to cheer us;
and keep us in his grace,
and guide us when perplexed,
and free us from all ills
in this world and the next.

3. All praise and thanks to God
the Father now be given,
the Son and him who reigns
with them in highest heaven,
the one eternal God,
whom earth and heaven adore;
for thus it was, is now,
and shall be evermore.

533 John Macleod Campbell Crum (1872-1958) alt.
© 1928 Oxford University Press

1. Now the green blade riseth
from the buried grain,
wheat that in the dark earth
many days has lain;
Love lives again,
that with the dead has been:
Love is come again,
like wheat that springeth green.

2. In the grave they laid him,
Love by hatred slain,
thinking that never
he would wake again,
laid in the earth
like grain that sleeps unseen:
Love is come again,
like wheat that springeth green.

3. Forth he came at Easter,
like the risen grain,
he that for three days
in the grave had lain;
quick from the dead,
my risen Lord is seen:
Love is come again,
like wheat that springeth green.

4. When our hearts are wintry,
grieving or in pain,
thy touch can call us
back to life again;

fields of our hearts,
that dead and bare have been:
Love is come again,
like wheat that springeth green.

534 Attributed to John Francis Wade (1711-1786)
trans. Frederick Oakeley (1802-1880)

1. O come, all ye faithful,
joyful and triumphant,
O come ye, O come ye to Bethlehem;
come and behold him,
born the king of angels:

O come, let us adore him,
O come, let us adore him,
O come, let us adore him,
Christ the Lord.

2. God of God,
Light of Light,
lo, he abhors not the Virgin's womb;
very God, begotten not created:

*3. See how the shepherds,
summoned to his cradle,
leaving their flocks, draw nigh with
lowly fear;
we too will thither bend our joyful
footsteps:

*4. Lo, star-led chieftains,
Magi, Christ adoring,
offer him incense, gold and myrrh;
we to the Christ-child bring our
hearts' oblations:

*5. Child, for us sinners
poor and in the manger,
fain we embrace thee, with love and
awe;
who would not love thee, loving us
so dearly?

6. Sing, choirs of angels,
sing in exultation,
sing, all ye citizens of heaven above;
glory to God in the highest:

7. Yea, Lord, we greet thee,
born this happy morning,
Jesu, to thee be glory giv'n;
Word of the Father, now in flesh
appearing:

535 From the *Great O Antiphons* (12th-13th
century) trans. John Mason Neale (1818-1866)

1. O come, O come, Emmanuel,
and ransom captive Israel,
that mourns in lonely exile here,
until the Son of God appear.

Rejoice, rejoice!
Emmanuel shall come to thee,
O Israel.

2. O come, thou rod of Jesse, free
thine own from Satan's tyranny;
from depths of hell thy people save,
and give them vict'ry o'er the grave.

3. O come, thou dayspring, come and
cheer
our spirits by thine advent here;
disperse the gloomy clouds of night,
and death's dark shadows put to flight.

4. O come, thou key of David, come
and open wide our heavenly home;
make safe the way that leads on high,
and close the path to misery.

5. O come, O come, thou Lord of might,
who to thy tribes on Sinai's height
in ancient times didst give the Law,
in cloud and majesty and awe.

536
Chrysogonus Waddell, based on Isaiah 40
© *Chrysogonus Waddell*

1. O comfort my people
and calm all their fear,
and tell them the time of
salvation draws near.
O tell them I come
to remove all their shame.
Then they will forever
give praise to my name.

2. Proclaim to the cities
of Judah my word;
that 'gentle yet strong
is the hand of the Lord.
I rescue the captives,
my people defend,
and bring them to justice
and joy without end.'

3. 'All mountains and hills
shall become as a plain,
for vanished are mourning
and hunger and pain.
And never again shall
these war against you.
Behold I come quickly
to make all things new.'

537
Robert Balgarnie Young Scott (1899-1987)
© *Emmanuel College Toronto*

1. O day of God, draw nigh
in beauty and in power,
come with thy timeless judgement now
to match our present hour.

2. Bring to our troubled minds,
uncertain and afraid,
the quiet of a steadfast faith,
calm of a call obeyed.

3. Bring justice to our land,
that all may dwell secure,
and finely build for days to come
foundations that endure.

4. Bring to our world of strife
thy sovereign word of peace,
that war may haunt the earth no more
and desolation cease,

5. O day of God, draw nigh;
as at creation's birth
let there be light again, and set
thy judgements in the earth.

538
Henry Ernest Hardy
(Father Andrew SDC) (1869-1946)
© *Copyright Mowbray/Cassell plc*

1. O dearest Lord, thy sacred head
with thorns was pierced for me;
O pour thy blessing on my head
that I may think for thee.

2. O dearest Lord, thy sacred hands
with nails were pierced for me;
O shed thy blessing on my hands
that they may work for thee.

3. O dearest Lord, thy sacred feet
with nails were pierced for me;
O pour thy blessing on my feet
that they may follow thee.

4. O dearest Lord, thy sacred heart
with spear was pierced for me;
O pour thy Spirit in my heart
that I may live for thee.

539 William Cowper (1731-1800)

1. O for a closer walk with God,
a calm and heav'nly frame;
a light to shine upon the road
that leads me to the Lamb.

2. What peaceful hours I once enjoyed,
how sweet their mem'ry still!
But they have left an aching void
the world can never fill.

3. The dearest idol I have known,
   whate'er that idol be,
   help me to tear it from thy throne,
   and worship only thee.

4. So shall my walk be close with God,
   calm and serene my frame;
   so purer light shall mark the road
   that leads me to the Lamb.

540 Charles Wesley (1707-1788)

1. O for a heart to praise my God,
   a heart from sin set free;
   a heart that's sprinkled with the blood
   so freely shed for me.

2. A heart resigned, submissive, meek,
   my great Redeemer's throne;
   where only Christ is heard to speak,
   where Jesus reigns alone.

3. A humble, lowly, contrite heart,
   believing, true and clean,
   which neither life nor death can part
   from him that dwells within.

4. A heart in every thought renewed,
   and full of love divine;
   perfect and right and pure and good –
   a copy, Lord, of thine.

5. Thy nature, gracious Lord, impart,
   come quickly from above;
   write thy new name upon my heart,
   thy new best name of love.

541 Charles Wesley (1707-1788)

Tune 1 – 'Selby'

1. O for a thousand tongues to sing
   my dear Redeemer's praise,
   the glories of my God and King,
   the triumphs of his grace!

2. Jesus! the name that charms our fears,
   that bids our sorrows cease;
   'tis music in the sinner's ears,
   'tis life and health and peace.

3. He breaks the pow'r of cancelled sin,
   he sets the pris'ner free;
   his blood can make the foulest clean;
   his blood availed for me.

4. He speaks; and, list'ning to his voice,
   new life the dead receive;
   the mournful broken hearts rejoice,
   the humble poor believe.

5. Hear him, ye deaf; his praise, ye dumb,
   your loosened tongues employ;
   ye blind, behold your Saviour come;
   and leap, ye lame, for joy!

6. My gracious Master and my God,
   assist me to proclaim
   and spread through all the earth abroad
   the honours of thy name.

Tune 2 – 'Lyngham'

1. O for a thousand tongues to sing
   my dear Redeemer's praise,
   my dear Redeemer's praise,
   the glories of my God and King,
   the triumphs of his grace,
   the triumphs of his grace,
   the triumphs of his grace!

2. Jesus! the name that charms our fears,
   that bids our sorrows cease,
   that bids our sorrows cease;
   'tis music in the sinner's ears,
   'tis life and health and peace. *(x3)*

3. He breaks the power of cancelled sin,
   he sets the pris'ner free,
   he sets the pris'ner free;
   his blood can make the foulest clean;
   his blood availed for me. *(x3)*

Continued overleaf

4. He speaks; and, list'ning to his voice,
   new life the dead receive,
   new life the dead receive;
   the mournful broken hearts rejoice,
   the humble poor believe. *(x3)*

5. Hear him, ye deaf; his praise, ye dumb,
   your loosened tongues employ,
   your loosened tongues employ;
   ye blind, behold your Saviour come;
   and leap, ye lame, for joy! *(x3)*

6. My gracious Master and my God,
   assist me to proclaim,
   assist me to proclaim
   and spread through all the earth abroad
   the honours of thy name. *(x3)*

542 Graham Kendrick (b. 1950)
© 1991 Make Way Music

O give thanks to the Lord,
for his love will never end.
O give thanks to the Lord,
for his love it never will end.
(Repeat)

1. Sing to him, sing your praise to him,
   tell the world of all he has done.
   Fill the nations with celebrations
   to welcome him as he comes.

2. Give him thanks for the fruitful earth,
   for the sun, the seasons, the rain.
   For the joys of his good creation,
   the life and breath he sustains.

3. Let the heavens rejoice before him,
   the earth and all it contains.
   All creation in jubilation,
   join in the shout, 'The Lord reigns!'

4. Let the hearts of those who seek him
   be happy now in his love.
   Let their faces look up and gaze
   at his gracious smile from above.

543 Joanne Pond
© 1980 Thankyou Music

O give thanks to the Lord,
all you his people,
O give thanks to the Lord,
for he is good.
Let us praise, let us thank,
let us celebrate and dance,
O give thanks to the Lord,
for he is good.

544 Michael Perry (1942-1996)
© Mrs B. Perry/Jubilate Hymns. Used by permission

1. O God beyond all praising,
   we worship you today,
   and sing the love amazing
   that songs cannot repay;
   for we can only wonder
   at every gift you send,
   at blessings without number
   and mercies without end:
   we lift our hearts before you
   and wait upon your word,
   we honour and adore you,
   our great and mighty Lord.

2. Then hear, O gracious Saviour,
   accept the love we bring,
   that we who know your favour
   may serve you as our King;
   and whether our tomorrows
   be filled with good or ill,
   we'll triumph through our sorrows
   and rise to bless you still:
   to marvel at your beauty
   and glory in your ways,
   and make a joyful duty
   our sacrifice of praise.

545 Philip Doddridge (1702-1751) and John Logan (1748-1788) alt.

1. O God of Bethel, by whose hand
   thy people still are fed,
   who through this earthly pilgrimage
   has all our forebears led.

2. Our vows, our prayers, we now present
   before thy throne of grace;
   God of our forebears, be the God
   of their succeeding race.

3. Through each mysterious path of life
   be thou our constant guide;
   give us each day our daily bread,
   and raiment fit provide.

4. O spread thy cov'ring wings around,
   till all our journeys cease,
   and at our Father's loved abode
   our souls arrive in peace.

546 Gilbert Keith Chesterton (1874-1936)
© Oxford University Press

1. O God of earth and altar,
   bow down and hear our cry,
   our earthly rulers falter,
   our people drift and die;
   the walls of gold entomb us,
   the swords of scorn divide,
   take not thy thunder from us,
   but take away our pride.

2. From all that terror teaches,
   from lies of tongue and pen,
   from all the easy speeches
   that comfort cruel men,
   from sale and profanation
   of honour and the sword,
   from sleep and from damnation,
   deliver us, good Lord!

3. Tie in a living tether
   the prince and priest and thrall,
   bind all our lives together,
   smite us and save us all;
   in ire and exultation
   aflame with faith and free,
   lift up a living nation,
   a single sword to thee.

547 Isaac Watts (1674-1748) alt.

1. O God, our help in ages past,
   our hope for years to come,
   our shelter from the stormy blast,
   and our eternal home.

2. Beneath the shadow of thy throne,
   thy saints have dwelt secure;
   sufficient is thine arm alone,
   and our defence is sure.

3. Before the hills in order stood,
   or earth received her frame,
   from everlasting thou art God,
   to endless years the same.

4. A thousand ages in thy sight
   are like an evening gone;
   short as the watch that ends the night
   before the rising sun.

5. Time, like an ever-rolling stream,
   will bear us all away;
   we fade and vanish, as a dream
   dies at the op'ning day.

6. O God, our help in ages past,
   our hope for years to come,
   be thou our guard while troubles last,
   and our eternal home.

548

Edward Osler (1798-1863)

1. O God, unseen yet ever near,
   thy presence may we feel;
   and, thus inspired with holy fear,
   before thine altar kneel.

2. Here may thy faithful people know
   the blessings of thy love,
   the streams that through the desert
     flow,
   the manna from above.

3. We come, obedient to thy word,
   to feast on heavenly food;
   our meat the body of the Lord,
   our drink his precious blood.

4. Thus may we all thy word obey,
   for we, O God, are thine;
   and go rejoicing on our way,
   renewed with strength divine.

549

Bernadette Farrell (b. 1957)
© 1992 Bernadette Farrell

1. O God, you search me and you know
     me.
   All my thoughts lie open to your gaze.
   When I walk or lie down you are
     before me:
   ever the maker and keeper of my days.

2. You know my resting and my rising.
   You discern my purpose from afar.
   And with love everlasting you besiege
     me:
   in every moment of life and death,
     you are.

3. Before a word is on my tongue, Lord,
   you have known its meaning through
     and through.
   You are with me, beyond my
     understanding:
   God of my present, my past and
     future too.

4. Although your Spirit is upon me,
   still I search for shelter from your light.
   There is nowhere on earth I can
     escape you:
   even the darkness is radiant in your
     sight.

5. For you created me and shaped me,
   gave me life within my mother's
     womb.
   For the wonder of who I am, I praise
     you:
   safe in your hands, all creation is
     made new.

550

John Mason Neale (1818-1866) alt.
verse 6 © 1996 Kevin Mayhew Ltd

1. O happy band of pilgrims,
   if onward ye will tread,
   with Jesus as your fellow,
   to Jesus as your head.

2. The cross that Jesus carried
   he carried as your due:
   the crown that Jesus weareth
   he weareth it for you.

3. The faith by which ye see him,
   the hope in which ye yearn,
   the love that through all troubles
   to him alone will turn.

4. What are they but forerunners
   to lead you to his sight,
   the longed-for distant dawning
   of uncreated light?

5. The trials that beset you,
   the sorrows ye endure,
   are known to Christ your Saviour,
   whose perfect grace will cure.

6. O happy band of pilgrims,
   let fear not dim your eyes,
   remember, your afflictions
   shall lead to such a prize!

551 Philip Doddridge (1702-1751) alt.

1. O happy day! that fixed my choice
   on thee, my Saviour and my God!
   Well may this glowing heart rejoice,
   and tell its raptures all abroad.

   O happy day! O happy day!
   When Jesus washed my sins away,
   he taught me how to watch and pray,
   and live rejoicing every day;
   O happy day! O happy day!
   When Jesus washed my sins away.

2. 'Tis done, the work of grace is done!
   I am my Lord's, and he is mine!
   He drew me, and I followed on,
   glad to confess the voice divine.

3. Now rest, my long-divided heart,
   fixed on this blissful centre, rest;
   nor ever from thy Lord depart,
   with him of every good possessed.

4. High heaven, that heard the solemn
   vow,
   that vow renewed shall daily hear;
   till in life's latest hour I bow,
   and bless in death a bond so dear.

552 Graham Kendrick (b. 1950)
© 1991 Make Way Music

O, heaven is in my heart.
O, heaven is in my heart.
(Repeat)

1. Leader The kingdom of our God is
            here,
   All   **heaven is in my heart.**
   Leader The presence of his majesty,
   All   **heaven is in my heart.**
   Leader And in his presence joy
            abounds,
   All   **heaven is in my heart.**
   Leader The light of holiness
            surrounds,
   All   **heaven is in my heart.**

2. Leader His precious life on me he
            spent,
   All   **heaven is in my heart.**
   Leader To give me life without an
            end,
   All   **heaven is in my heart.**
   Leader In Christ is all my confidence,
   All   **heaven is in my heart.**
   Leader The hope of my inheritance,
   All   **heaven is in my heart.**

3. Leader We are a temple for his
            throne,
   All   **heaven is in my heart.**
   Leader And Christ is the foundation
            stone,
   All   **heaven is in my heart.**
   Leader He will return to take us
            home,
   All   **heaven is in my heart.**
   Leader The Spirit and the Bride say,
            'Come!',
   All   **heaven is in my heart.**

553 Michael Forster (b. 1946)
© 2004 Kevin Mayhew Ltd

1. O holy, heavenly kingdom
   God's faithful long to see,
   where peace and wholeness prosper
   and every heart is free,
   where justice flows like fountains
   and praises never cease,
   come, make your home among us,
   and give this world your peace.

2. Among us and around us,
   yet veiled from mortal sight,
   the vision of the prophets
   and God's proclaimed delight;
   where tears find consolation,
   and open wounds are healed,
   where eyes and ears are opened,
   the kingdom is revealed.

3. O call us to your table,
   invite us to the feast,
   where Christ will bring together
   the greatest and the least,
   where grace will flow among us
   like rich, abundant wine,
   and those the world rejected
   will feast on love divine.

4. By grace alone united,
   we join the heavenly throng;
   with countless saints and martyrs,
   we sing the kingdom's song.
   'O holy, holy, holy!'
   the universe resounds
   with praise and adoration
   and endless grace abounds.

554 Charles Coffin (1676-1749)
trans. John Chandler (1808-1876) alt.

1. O Holy Spirit, Lord of grace,
   eternal fount of love,
   inflame, we pray, our inmost hearts
   with fire from heaven above.

2. As thou dost join with holiest bonds
   the Father and the Son,
   so fill thy saints with mutual love
   and link their hearts in one.

3. To God the Father, God the Son
   and God the Holy Ghost,
   be praise eternal from the earth,
   and from the angel-host.

555 Traditional

O, how good is the Lord! (x3)
I never will forget what he has done for
me.

1. He gives us salvation,
   how good is the Lord. *(x3)*
   I never will forget
   what he has done for me.

2. He gives us his Spirit . . .

3. He gives us his healing . . .

4. He gives us his body . . .

5. He gives us his freedom . . .

6. He gives us each other . . .

7. He gives us his glory . . .

556 John Ernest Bode (1816-1874)

1. O Jesus, I have promised
   to serve thee to the end;
   be thou for ever near me,
   my Master and my friend:
   I shall not fear the battle
   if thou art by my side,
   nor wander from the pathway
   if thou wilt be my guide.

*2. O let me feel thee near me;
the world is ever near;
I see the sights that dazzle,
the tempting sounds I hear;
my foes are ever near me,
around me and within;
but, Jesus, draw thou nearer,
and shield my soul from sin.

*3. O let me hear thee speaking
in accents clear and still,
above the storms of passion,
the murmurs of self-will;
O speak to reassure me,
to hasten or control;
O speak and make me listen,
thou guardian of my soul.

4. O Jesus, thou hast promised,
to all who follow thee,
that where thou art in glory
there shall thy servant be;
and, Jesus, I have promised
to serve thee to the end:
O give me grace to follow,
my Master and my friend.

5. O let me see thy foot-marks,
and in them plant mine own;
my hope to follow duly
is in thy strength alone:
O guide me, call me, draw me,
uphold me to the end;
and then in heaven receive me,
my Saviour and my friend.

557 Greek hymn (8th century)
trans. John Brownlie (1857-1925)

1. O King enthroned on high,
thou Comforter divine,
blest Spirit of all truth, be nigh
and make us thine.

2. Thou art the source of life,
thou art our treasure-store;
give us thy peace, and end our strife
for evermore.

3. Descend, O heavenly Dove,
abide with us alway;
and in the fullness of thy love
cleanse us, we pray.

558 John Wimber (1934-1997)
© 1979 Mercy/Vineyard Publishing
Administered by CopyCare

1. O let the Son of God enfold you
with his Spirit and his love,
let him fill your heart and satisfy your
soul.
O let him have the things that hold
you,
and his Spirit like a dove
will descend upon your life and make
you whole.

*Jesus, O Jesus,
come and fill your lambs.
Jesus, O Jesus,
come and fill your lambs.*

2. O come and sing this song with
gladness
as your hearts are filled with joy,
lift your hands in sweet surrender to
his name.
O give him all your tears and sadness,
give him all your years of pain,
and you'll enter into life in Jesus' name.

559 Phillips Brooks (1835-1893) alt.

1. O little town of Bethlehem,
   how still we see thee lie!
   Above thy deep and dreamless sleep
   the silent stars go by.
   Yet in thy dark streets shineth
   the everlasting light;
   the hopes and fears of all the years
   are met in thee tonight.

2. O morning stars, together
   proclaim the holy birth,
   and praises sing to God the King,
   and peace to all the earth.
   For Christ is born of Mary;
   and, gathered all above,
   while mortals sleep, the angels keep
   their watch of wond'ring love;

3. How silently, how silently,
   the wondrous gift is giv'n!
   So God imparts to human hearts
   the blessings of his heav'n.
   No ear may hear his coming;
   but in this world of sin,
   where meek souls will receive him still,
   the dear Christ enters in.

4. O holy child of Bethlehem,
   descend to us, we pray;
   cast out our sin, and enter in,
   be born in us today.
   We hear the Christmas angels
   the great glad tidings tell:
   O come to us, abide with us,
   our Lord Emmanuel.

560 Patrick Appleford (b. 1925)
© 1965 Josef Weinberger Ltd

1. O Lord, all the world belongs to you,
   and you are always making all things
   new.

What is wrong you forgive,
and the new life you give
is what's turning the world upside
down.

2. The world's only loving to its friends,
   but you have brought us love that
   never ends;
   loving enemies too,
   and this loving with you
   is what's turning the world upside
   down.

3. This world lives divided and apart.
   You draw us all together and we start,
   in your body, to see
   that in a fellowship we
   can be turning the world upside
   down.

4. The world wants the wealth to live
   in state,
   but you show us a new way to be
   great:
   like a servant you came,
   and if we do the same,
   we'll be turning the world upside
   down.

5. O Lord, all the world belongs to you,
   and you are always making all
   things new.
   Send your Spirit on all
   in your Church, whom you call
   to be turning the world upside down.

561 Taizé Community
© Ateliers et Presses de Taizé

O Lord, hear my prayer,
O Lord, hear my prayer:
when I call answer me.
O Lord, hear my prayer,
O Lord, hear my prayer.
Come and listen to me.

562

Psalm 101 (102) adapted by Margaret Rizza (b. 1929)
© 2002 Kevin Mayhew Ltd

O Lord, listen to my prayer,
my prayer as I call to you;
O Lord, listen to my prayer,
my prayer as I call to you.
Repeat

563

Stuart K. Hine (1899-1989)
© 1953 Stuart K. Hine/The Stuart Hine Trust
Published by Kingsway Music

1. O Lord my God!
   When I in awesome wonder
   consider all the works
   thy hand hath made;
   I see the stars,
   I hear the mighty thunder,
   thy power throughout
   the universe displayed:

   Then sings my soul,
   my Saviour God, to thee,
   how great thou art! How great thou art!
   Then sings my soul,
   my Saviour God, to thee,
   how great thou art! How great thou art!

2. When through the woods
   and forest glades I wander
   and hear the birds sing
   sweetly in the trees;
   when I look down
   from lofty mountain grandeur,
   and hear the brook,
   and feel the gentle breeze:

3. And when I think that God,
   his Son not sparing,
   sent him to die –
   I scarce can take it in:
   that on the Cross,
   my burden gladly bearing,
   he bled and died
   to take away my sin:

4. When Christ shall come
   with shout of acclamation
   and take me home –
   what joy shall fill my heart!
   Then shall I bow
   in humble adoration,
   and there proclaim,
   my God, how great thou art!

564

From Psalm 131
© The Grail (England) from 'The Psalms. The Grail Translations'

O Lord, my heart is not proud,
nor haughty my eyes.
I have not gone after things too great,
nor marvels beyond me.
Truly I have set my soul in silence
   and peace;
at rest, as a child in its mother's arms,
so is my soul.

565

Albert F. Bayly (1901-1984)
© Oxford University Press. Used by permission

1. O Lord of every shining constellation
   that wheels in splendour through the
      midnight sky,
   grant us your Spirit's true illumination
   to read the secrets of our work on high.

2. You, Lord, have made the atom's
      hidden forces,
   your laws its mighty energies fulfil;
   teach us, to whom you give such rich
      resources,
   in all we use, to serve your holy will.

Continued overleaf

3. O Life, awaking life in cell and tissue,
   from flower to bird, from beast to
      brain of man;
   help us to trace, from birth to final
      issue,
   the sure unfolding of your age-long
      plan.

4. You, Lord, have stamped your image
      on your creatures,
   and, though they mar that image,
      love them still;
   lift up our eyes to Christ, that in his
      features
   we may discern the beauty of your will.

5. Great Lord of nature, shaping and
      renewing,
   you made us more than nature's sons
      to be;
   you help us tread, with grace our
      souls enduing,
   the road to life and immortality.

566 Christopher Wordsworth (1807-1885)

1. O Lord of heav'n and earth and sea,
   to thee all praise and glory be.
   How shall we show our love to thee
   who givest all?

2. The golden sunshine, vernal air,
   sweet flowers and fruit, thy love declare;
   when harvests ripen, thou art there,
   who givest all.

3. For peaceful homes, and healthful days,
   for all the blessings earth displays,
   we owe thee thankfulness and praise,
   who givest all.

4. Thou didst not spare thine only Son,
   but gav'st him for a world undone,
   and freely with that blessèd one
   thou givest all.

5. Thou giv'st the Holy Spirit's dow'r,
   Spirit of life and love and pow'r,
   and dost his sev'nfold graces show'r
   upon us all.

6. For souls redeemed, for sins forgiv'n,
   for means of grace and hopes of
      heav'n,
   Father, what can to thee be giv'n,
   who givest all?

7. To thee, from whom we all derive
   our life, our gifts, our power to give:
   O may we ever with thee live,
   who givest all.

567 Nick Fawcett (b. 1957)
© 2004 Kevin Mayhew Ltd

1. O Lord, we want to praise you,
   your holy name confess,
   your mighty deeds acknowledge,
   your awesome love express.
   We want to give you worship,
   to lift your name on high,
   yet somehow words are lacking
   however hard we try.

2. O Lord, we want to praise you,
   through all we say and do,
   to so live out the gospel
   that all may know it's true.
   We want to bring you glory,
   to help your kingdom grow,
   yet though we strive to serve you,
   it rarely seems to show.

3. O Lord, we want to praise you,
   to celebrate your love,
   to thank you for the blessings
   you pour down from above.
   We want to bring you honour
   respond with all our hearts,
   yet sacrifice is costly –
   we rarely even start.

4. O Lord, we come to praise you,
   poor though our words may be;
   although our faults are many
   we come, still, joyfully.
   For though we often fail you
   and know you but in part,
   you look beneath the surface
   and see what's in the heart.

568
Graham Kendrick (b. 1950)
© 1986 Thankyou Music

O Lord, your tenderness,
melting all my bitterness,
O Lord, I receive your love.
O Lord, your loveliness,
changing all my ugliness,
O Lord, I receive your love.
O Lord, I receive your love,
O Lord, I receive your love.

569
Charles Wesley (1707-1788)

1. O love divine, how sweet thou art!
   When shall I find my longing heart
   all taken up by thee?
   I thirst, I faint, I die to prove
   the greatness of redeeming love,
   the love of Christ to me.

2. Stronger his love than death or hell;
   its riches are unsearchable:
   the first-born sons of light
   desire in vain its depth to see;
   they cannot reach the mystery,
   the length and breadth and height.

3. God only knows the love of God;
   O that it now were shed abroad
   in this poor stony heart!
   For love I sigh, for love I pine;
   this only portion, Lord, be mine,
   be mine this better part.

4. For ever would I take my seat
   with Mary at the Master's feet:
   be this my happy choice;
   my only care, delight, and bliss,
   my joy, my heaven on earth, be this,
   to hear the Bridegroom's voice!

5. Thy only love do I require,
   nothing on earth beneath desire,
   nothing in heaven above:
   let earth and heaven, and all things
     go,
   give me thine only love to know,
   give me thine only love.

570
Benjamin Webb (1819-1885) alt
from Thomas à Kempis (c. 1379-1471)

1. O love, how deep, how broad, how
     high!
   It fills the heart with ecstasy,
   that God, the Son of God,
   should take our mortal form for
     mortals' sake.

2. He sent no angel to our race
   of higher or of lower place,
   but wore the robe of human frame
   himself, and to this lost world came.

3. For us he was baptised and bore
   his holy fast, and hungered sore;
   for us temptations sharp he knew;
   for us the tempter overthrew.

4. For us to wicked powers betrayed,
   scourged, mocked, in purple robe
     arrayed,
   he bore the shameful cross and death;
   for us at length gave up his breath.

5. For us he rose from death again,
   for us he went on high to reign,
   for us he sent his Spirit here
   to guide, to strengthen and to cheer.

Continued overleaf

6. To him whose boundless love has won
   salvation for us through his Son,
   to God the Father glory be,
   both now and through eternity.

571 George Matheson (1842-1906)

1. O Love that wilt not let me go,
   I rest my weary soul in thee;
   I give thee back the life I owe,
   that in thine ocean depths its flow
   may richer, fuller be.

2. O Light that follow'st all my way,
   I yield my flick'ring torch to thee;
   my heart restores its borrowed ray,
   that in thy sunshine's blaze its day
   may brighter, fairer be.

3. O Joy that seekest me through pain,
   I cannot close my heart to thee;
   I trace the rainbow through the rain,
   and feel the promise is not vain
   that morn shall tearless be.

4. O Cross that liftest up my head,
   I dare not ask to fly from thee:
   I lay in dust life's glory dead,
   and from the ground there blossoms
     red
   life that shall endless be.

572 William Walsham How (1823-1897)

1. O my Saviour, lifted
   from the earth for me,
   draw me, in thy mercy,
   nearer unto thee.

2. Lift my earth-bound longings,
   fix them, Lord, above;
   draw me with the magnet
   of thy mighty love.

3. Lord, thine arms are stretching
   ever far and wide,
   to enfold thy children
   to thy loving side.

4. And I come, O Jesus:
   dare I turn away?
   No, thy love hath conquered,
   and I come today.

5. Bringing all my burdens,
   sorrow, sin and care;
   at thy feet I lay them,
   and I leave them there.

573 Dorothy Francis Gurney (1858-1932)

1. O perfect love,
   all human thought transcending,
   lowly we kneel
   in prayer before thy throne,
   that theirs may be
   the love which knows no ending,
   whom thou for evermore
   dost join in one.

2. O perfect life,
   be thou their full assurance
   of tender charity
   and steadfast faith,
   of patient hope
   and quiet, brave endurance,
   with childlike trust that fears
   not pain nor death.

3. Grant them the joy
   which brightens earthly sorrow,
   grant them the peace
   which calms all earthly strife;
   and to life's day
   the glorious unknown morrow
   that dawns upon
   eternal love and life.

574 Henry Williams Baker (1821-1877)
based on Psalms 148 and 150, alt.

1. O praise ye the Lord!
   praise him in the height;
   rejoice in his word, ye angels of light;
   ye heavens, adore him,
   by whom ye were made,
   and worship before him,
   in brightness arrayed.

2. O praise ye the Lord!
   praise him upon earth,
   in tuneful accord, all you of new birth;
   praise him who hath brought you
   his grace from above,
   praise him who hath taught you
   to sing of his love.

3. O praise ye the Lord!
   all things that give sound;
   each jubilant chord re-echo around;
   loud organs his glory
   forth tell in deep tone,
   and, sweet harp, the story
   of what he hath done.

4. O praise ye the Lord!
   thanksgiving and song
   to him be outpoured all ages along:
   for love in creation,
   for heaven restored,
   for grace of salvation,
   O praise ye the Lord!

575 Ralph Wright (b. 1938)
© GIA Publications Inc.

1. O raise your eyes on high and see,
   there stands our sovereign Lord;
   his glory is this day revealed,
   his word a two-edged sword.

2. We glimpse the splendour and the
      power
   of him who conquered death,
   the Christ in whom the universe
   knows God's creating breath.

3. Of every creed and nation King,
   in him all strife is stilled;
   the promise made to Abraham
   in him has been fulfilled.

4. The prophets stand and with great joy
   give witness as they gaze;
   the Father with a sign has sealed
   our trust, our hope, our praise.

576 Paul Gerhardt (1607-1676)
based on 'Salve caput cruentatum'
trans. Henry Williams Baker (1821-1877)

1. O sacred head, surrounded
   by crown of piercing thorn!
   O bleeding head, so wounded,
   so shamed and put to scorn!
   Death's pallid hue comes o'er thee,
   the glow of life decays;
   yet angel-hosts adore thee,
   and tremble as they gaze.

2. Thy comeliness and vigour
   is withered up and gone,
   and in thy wasted figure
   I see death drawing on.
   O agony and dying!
   O love to sinners free!
   Jesu, all grace supplying,
   turn thou thy face on me.

3. In this thy bitter passion,
   good Shepherd, think of me
   with thy most sweet compassion,
   unworthy though I be:
   beneath thy cross abiding
   for ever would I rest,
   in thy dear love confiding,
   and with thy presence blest.

577

St Ambrose (c. 340-397)
trans. John Ellerton (1826-1893)
and Fenton John Anthony Hort (1828-1892)

1. O strength and stay upholding all
   creation,
   who ever dost thyself unmoved abide,
   yet day by day the light in due
   gradation
   from hour to hour through all its
   changes guide.

2. Grant to life's day a calm unclouded
   ending,
   an eve untouched by shadows of decay,
   the brightness of a holy death-bed
   blending
   with dawning glories of th'eternal day.

3. Hear us, O Father, gracious and
   forgiving,
   through Jesus Christ thy co-eternal
   Word,
   who with the Holy Ghost by all
   things living
   now and to endless ages art adored.

578

Estelle White (b. 1925)
© McCrimmon Publishing Co. Ltd

1. O, the love of my Lord is the essence
   of all that I love here on earth.
   All the beauty I see he has given to me,
   and his giving is gentle as silence.

2. Every day, every hour, every moment
   have been blessed by the strength of
   his love.
   At the turn of each tide he is there at
   my side,
   and his touch is as gentle as silence.

3. There've been times when I've turned
   from his presence,
   and I've walked other paths, other ways;
   but I've called on his name in the
   dark of my shame,
   and his mercy was gentle as silence.

579

William Harry Turton (1856-1938),
based on John 17
© Copyright Control

1. O thou, who at thy Eucharist didst
   pray
   that all thy Church might be for ever
   one,
   grant us at every eucharist to say,
   with longing heart and soul, 'Thy
   will be done.'
   O may we all one bread, one body be,
   through this blest sacrament of unity.

2. For all thy Church, O Lord, we
   intercede;
   make thou our sad divisions soon to
   cease;
   draw us the nearer each to each, we
   plead,
   by drawing all to thee, O Prince of
   Peace:
   thus may we all one bread, one body
   be,
   through this blest sacrament of unity.

3. We pray thee too for wand'rers from
   thy fold;
   O bring them back, good Shepherd
   of the sheep,
   back to the faith which saints
   believed of old,
   back to the Church which still that
   faith doth keep;
   soon may we all one bread, one body
   be,
   through this blest sacrament of unity.

4. So, Lord, at length when sacraments
shall cease,
may we be one with all thy Church
above,
one with thy saints in one unbroken
peace,
one with thy saints in one
unbounded love;
more blessèd still, in peace and love
to be
one with the Trinity in unity.

2. O when they crown him
Lord of all . . .

3. O when all knees bow at his
name . . .

4. O when they sing the Saviour's
praise . . .

5. O when the saints go marching in . . .

580
Charles Wesley (1707-1788)
based on Leviticus 6:13

1. O thou who camest from above
the fire celestial to impart,
kindle a flame of sacred love
on the mean altar of my heart.

2. There let it for thy glory burn
with inextinguishable blaze,
and trembling to its source return
in humble prayer and fervent praise.

3. Jesus, confirm my heart's desire
to work and speak and think for thee;
still let me guard the holy fire
and still stir up the gift in me.

4. Ready for all thy perfect will,
my acts of faith and love repeat,
till death thy endless mercies seal,
and make the sacrifice complete.

581 Traditional

1. O when the saints go marching in,
O when the saints go marching in,
I want to be in that number
when the saints go marching in.

582
Robert Grant (1779-1838),
based on Psalm 104

1. O worship the King
all glorious above;
O gratefully sing
his power and his love:
our shield and defender,
the Ancient of Days,
pavilioned in splendour,
and girded with praise.

2. O tell of his might,
O sing of his grace,
whose robe is the light,
whose canopy space;
his chariots of wrath
the deep thunder-clouds form,
and dark is his path
on the wings of the storm.

3. This earth, with its store
of wonders untold,
almighty, thy power
hath founded of old:
hath stablished it fast
by a changeless decree,
and round it hath cast,
like a mantle, the sea.

Continued overleaf

4. Thy bountiful care
what tongue can recite?
It breathes in the air,
it shines in the light;
it streams from the hills,
it descends to the plain,
and sweetly distils
in the dew and the rain.

5. Frail children of dust,
and feeble as frail,
in thee do we trust,
nor find thee to fail;
thy mercies how tender,
how firm to the end!
Our maker, defender,
redeemer, and friend.

6. O measureless might,
ineffable love,
while angels delight
to hymn thee above,
thy humbler creation,
though feeble their lays,
with true adoration
shall sing to thy praise.

583 John Samuel Bewley Monsell (1811-1875)

1. O worship the Lord
in the beauty of holiness;
bow down before him,
his glory proclaim;
with gold of obedience
and incense of lowliness,
kneel and adore him:
the Lord is his name.

2. Low at his feet lay
thy burden of carefulness:
high on his heart
he will bear it for thee,
comfort thy sorrows,
and answer thy prayerfulness,
guiding thy steps
as may best for thee be.

3. Fear not to enter
his courts in the slenderness
of the poor wealth
thou wouldst reckon as thine:
truth in its beauty,
and love in its tenderness,
these are the off'rings
to lay on his shrine.

4. These, though we bring them
in trembling and fearfulness,
he will accept
for the name that is dear;
mornings of joy give
for evenings of tearfulness,
trust for our trembling
and hope for our fear.

584 'Corde natus ex parentis' by
Aurelius Clemens Prudentius (348-413)
trans. John Mason Neale (1818-1866) alt.

1. Of the Father's love begotten,
ere the worlds began to be,
he is Alpha and Omega,
he the source, the ending he,
of the things that are, and have been,
and that future years shall see,
evermore and evermore.

2. At his word they were created;
he commanded; it was done:
heaven and earth and depths of ocean
in their threefold order one;
all that grows beneath the shining
of the light of moon and sun,
evermore and evermore.

*3. O that birth for ever blessèd,
when the Virgin, full of grace,
by the Holy Ghost conceiving,
bore the Saviour of our race,
and the babe, the world's Redeemer,
first revealed his sacred face,
evermore and evermore.

*4. O ye heights of heaven, adore him;
angel hosts, his praises sing;
powers, dominions, bow before him,
and extol our God and King:
let no tongue on earth be silent,
every voice in concert ring,
evermore and evermore.

*5. This is he whom seers and sages
sang of old with one accord;
whom the writings of the prophets
promised in their faithful word;
now he shines, the long-expected;
let our songs declare his worth,
evermore and evermore.

6. Christ, to thee, with God the Father,
and, O Holy Ghost, to thee,
hymn and chant and high
thanksgiving,
and unwearied praises be;
honour, glory, and dominion,
and eternal victory,
evermore and evermore.

585 Henry Kirke White (1785-1806) and others

1. Oft in danger, oft in woe,
onward, Christians, onward go;
bear the toil, endure the strife,
strengthened with the bread of life.

2. Onward through the desert night,
keeping faith and vision bright;
face the challenge of the hour
trusting in your Saviour's power.

3. Let not sorrow dim your eye,
soon shall every tear be dry;
let not fears your course impede,
great your strength if great your need.

4. Let your drooping hearts be glad;
march in faith and honour clad;
march, nor think the journey long,
march to hope's eternal song.

5. Onward then, undaunted, move;
more than faithful God will prove;
though the raging waters flow,
Christian pilgrims, onward go.

586 Kathy Galloway
© *Kathy Galloway*

1. Oh, the life of the world is a joy and
a treasure,
unfolding in beauty the green-
growing tree,
the changing of seasons in mountain
and valley,
the stars and the bright restless sea.

2. Oh, the life of the world is a fountain
of goodness
overflowing in labour and passion
and pain,
in the sound of the city and the
silence of wisdom,
in the birth of a child once again.

3. Oh, the life of the world is the source
of our healing.
It rises in laughter and wells up in song;
it springs from the care of the poor
and the broken
and refreshes where justice is strong.

Continued overleaf

4. So give thanks for the life and give
   love to the maker,
   and rejoice in the gift of the bright
   risen Son,
   and walk in the peace and the power
   of the Spirit
   till the days of our living are done.

587 George Bennard (1873-1958)
© The Rodeheaver Co. Administered by CopyCare

1. On a hill far away
   stood an old rugged cross,
   the emblem of suffering and shame;
   and I loved that old cross
   where the dearest and best
   for a world of lost sinners was slain.

   So I'll cherish the old rugged cross,
   till my trophies at last I lay down;
   I will cling to the old rugged cross
   and exchange it some day for a crown.

2. O that old rugged cross,
   so despised by the world,
   has a wondrous attraction for me:
   for the dear Lamb of God
   left his glory above
   to bear it to dark Calvary.

3. In the old rugged cross,
   stained with blood so divine,
   a wondrous beauty I see.
   For t'was on that old cross
   Jesus suffered and died
   to pardon and sanctify me.

4. To the old rugged cross
   I will ever be true,
   its shame and reproach gladly bear.
   Then he'll call me some day
   to my home far away;
   there his glory for ever I'll share.

588 Traditional English carol, alt.

1. On Christmas night all Christians
   sing,
   to hear the news the angels bring,
   on Christmas night all Christians
   sing,
   to hear the news the angels bring,
   news of great joy, news of great mirth,
   news of our merciful King's birth.

2. Then why should we on earth be so
   sad,
   since our Redeemer made us glad,
   then why should we on earth be so
   sad,
   since our Redeemer made us glad,
   when from our sin he set us free,
   all for to gain our liberty?

3. When sin departs before his grace,
   then life and health come in its place,
   when sin departs before his grace,
   then life and health come in its place,
   angels and earth with joy may sing,
   all for to see the new-born King.

4. All out of darkness we have light,
   which made the angels sing this night:
   all out of darkness we have light,
   which made the angels sing this night:
   'Glory to God and peace to men,
   now and for evermore. Amen.'

589 Charles Coffin (1676-1749)
trans. John Chandler (1806-1876) alt.

1. On Jordan's bank the Baptist's cry
   announces that the Lord is nigh;
   awake, and hearken, for he brings
   glad tidings of the King of kings.

2. Then cleansed be every breast from sin;
   make straight the way for God within;
   prepare we in our hearts a home,
   where such a mighty guest may come.

3. For thou art our salvation, Lord,
   our refuge and our great reward;
   without thy grace we waste away,
   like flowers that wither and decay.

4. To heal the sick stretch out thine hand,
   and bid the fallen sinner stand;
   shine forth and let thy light restore
   earth's own true loveliness once more.

5. All praise, eternal Son, to thee
   whose advent doth thy people free,
   whom with the Father we adore
   and Holy Ghost for evermore.

590 T. C. Hunter Clare (1910-1984)
© Copyright Control

1. On the day of Pentecost,
   when the twelve assembled,
   came on them the Holy Ghost
   in fire that tongues resembled,
   in fire that tongues resembled.

2. In the power of God he came,
   as the Lord had told them,
   in his blessèd, holy name
   with wisdom to uphold them,
   with wisdom to uphold them.

3. In the Spirit then they stood
   to proclaim Christ dying,
   and that he for all our good
   doth live, true strength supplying,
   doth live, true strength supplying.

4. Still the might by which we live
   from our God descendeth;
   still his Spirit Christ doth give,
   who guideth and defendeth,
   who guideth and defendeth.

5. Praise, O praise our heavenly King
   for his grace toward us;
   gladly now his glory sing,
   who doth his power afford us,
   who doth his power afford us.

591 Traditional

On the holy cross I see
Jesus' hands nailed fast for me;
on the holy cross I see
Jesus' feet nailed fast for me.
Loving Jesus, let me be
still and quiet, close to thee;
learning all thy love for me,
giving all my love to thee.

592 Cecil Frances Alexander (1818-1895) alt.
This version © 1996 Kevin Mayhew Ltd

1. Once in royal David's city
   stood a lowly cattle shed,
   where a mother laid her baby
   in a manger for his bed:
   Mary was that mother mild,
   Jesus Christ her little child.

2. He came down to earth from heaven,
   who is God and Lord of all,
   and his shelter was a stable,
   and his cradle was a stall;
   with the needy, poor and lowly,
   lived on earth our Saviour holy.

3. For he is our childhood's pattern,
   day by day like us he grew;
   he was little, weak and helpless,
   tears and smiles like us he knew;
   and he feeleth for our sadness,
   and he shareth in our gladness.

Continued overleaf

4. And our eyes at last shall see him
through his own redeeming love,
for that child so dear and gentle
is our Lord in heaven above;
and he leads his children on
to the place where he is gone.

593 William Bright (1824-1901)

1. Once, only once, and once for all,
his precious life he gave;
before the Cross our spirits fall,
and own it strong to save.

2. 'One off'ring, single and complete,'
with lips and heart we say;
but what he never can repeat
he shows forth day by day.

3. For, as the priest of Aaron's line
within the holiest stood,
and sprinkled all the mercy-shrine
with sacrificial blood;

4. So he who once atonement wrought,
our Priest of endless power,
presents himself for those he bought
in that dark noontide hour.

5. And so we show thy death, O Lord,
till thou again appear;
and feel, when we approach thy board,
we have an altar here.

6. All glory to the Father be,
all glory to the Son,
all glory, Holy Ghost, to thee,
while endless ages run.

594 Paraphrase of Ephesians 4:11-16
John L. Bell (b. 1949)
© 1997, 2002 WGRG, Iona Community

1. One is the body and one is the Head,
one is the Spirit by whom we are led;
one God and Father, ⸺
one faith and one call for all.

2. Christ who ascended to heaven above
is the same Jesus whose nature is love,
who once descended
to bring to this earth new birth.

3. Gifts have been given well suited to
each;
some to be prophets, to pastor or
preach,
some, through the Gospel,
to challenge, convert and teach.

4. Called to his service are women and
men
so that his body might ever again
witness through worship,
through deed and through word
to Christ our Lord.

595 Sydney Carter (1915-2004)
© 1971, 1997 Stainer & Bell Ltd

1. One more step along the world I go,
one more step along the world I go.
From the old things to the new
keep me travelling along with you.

And it's from the old
I travel to the new,
keep me travelling
along with you.

2. Round the corners of the world I turn,
more and more about the world I learn.
All the new things that I see
you'll be looking at along with me.

3. As I travel through the bad and good,
   keep me travelling the way I should.
   Where I see no way to go,
   you'll be telling me the way, I know.

4. Give me courage when the world is
      rough,
   keep me loving though the world is
      tough.
   Leap and sing in all I do,
   keep me travelling along with you.

5. You are older than the world can be,
   you are younger than the life in me.
   Ever old and ever new,
   keep me travelling along with you.

596 Graham Kendrick (b. 1950)
      © 1981 Thankyou Music

1. One shall tell another,
   and he shall tell his friend,
   husbands, wives and children
   shall come following on.
   From house to house in families
   shall more be gathered in,
   and lights will shine in every street,
   so warm and welcoming.

   Come on in and taste the new wine,
   the wine of the kingdom,
   the wine of the kingdom of God.
   Here is healing and forgiveness,
   the wine of the kingdom,
   the wine of the kingdom of God.

2. Compassion of the Father
   is ready now to flow,
   through acts of love and mercy
   we must let it show.
   He turns now from his anger
   to show a smiling face,
   and longs that all should stand beneath
   the fountain of his grace.

3. He longs to do much more than
   our faith has yet allowed,
   to thrill us and surprise us
   with his sovereign power.
   Where darkness has been darkest
   the brightest light will shine;
   his invitation comes to us,
   it's yours and it is mine.

597 Martin E. Leckebusch (b. 1962)
      © 1999 Kevin Mayhew Ltd

1. One whose heart is hard as steel
   joins the others for a meal;
   time for Judas now to choose:
   light or darkness, win or lose?
   Has it really come to this?
   Cold betrayal with a kiss!

2. Simon Peter speaks for all,
   swears that he will never fall.
   Near the fire, the pressure grows –
   three denials – cockerel crows –
   wounded love in Jesus' eyes;
   Peter hides away, and cries.

3. Sent to Caiaphas the priest
   to be judged before the feast:
   wildest accusations fly –
   'By our law this man should die!' –
   yet that law was his, which they
   claim to cherish and obey.

4. 'What is truth? Are you a king?'
   Pilate's troubled questioning;
   then before the mob he stands,
   calls for water, cleans his hands;
   still they clamour, 'Crucify!' –
   he condemns their king to die.

Continued overleaf

5. Christ is tried – yet so are we,
   by his humble dignity:
   pain and love upon his face
   meet to show the way of grace:
   all our judgement there he bore;
   we are pardoned evermore.

598 Gerrit Gustafson
© 1990 Integrity's Hosanna! Music/Sovereign
Music UK

Only by grace can we enter,
only by grace can we stand;
not by our human endeavour,
but by the blood of the Lamb.

Into your presence you call us,
you call us to come.
Into your presence you draw us,
and now by your grace we come,
now by your grace we come.

Lord, if you mark our transgressions,
who would stand?
Thanks to your grace we are cleansed
by the blood of the Lamb.
(*Repeat*)

599 Michael Forster (b. 1946)
© 1996 Kevin Mayhew Ltd

1. Onward, Christian pilgrims,
   Christ will be our light;
   see, the heavenly vision
   breaks upon our sight!
   Out of death's enslavement
   Christ has set us free,
   on then to salvation,
   hope and liberty.

   Onward, Christian pilgrims,
   Christ will be our light;
   see, the heavenly vision
   breaks upon our sight!

2. Onward, Christian pilgrims,
   up the rocky way,
   where the dying Saviour
   bids us watch and pray.
   Through the darkened valley
   walk with those who mourn,
   share the pain and anger,
   share the promised dawn!

3. Onward, Christian pilgrims,
   in the early dawn;
   death's great seal is broken,
   life and hope reborn!
   Faith in resurrection
   strengthens pilgrims' hearts,
   every load is lightened,
   every fear departs.

4. Onward, Christian pilgrims,
   hearts and voices raise,
   till the whole creation
   echoes perfect praise;
   swords are turned to ploughshares,
   pride and envy cease,
   truth embraces justice,
   hope resolves in peace.

600 Robert Cull (b. 1949)
© 1976 CCCM Music/Maranatha! Music
Administered by CopyCare

Open our eyes, Lord,
we want to see Jesus,
to reach out and touch him
and say that we love him;
open our ears, Lord,
and help us to listen;
O, open our eyes, Lord,
we want to see Jesus!

601

Paul Baloche (b. 1962)
© 1997 Integrity's Hosanna! Music

Open the eyes of my heart, Lord,
open the eyes of my heart;
I want to see you, I want to see you.
Open the eyes of my heart, Lord,
open the eyes of my heart;
I want to see you, I want to see you.

To see you high and lifted up,
shining in the light of your glory.
Pour out your power and love;
as we sing holy, holy, holy.

Holy, holy, holy,
holy, holy, holy,
holy, holy, holy,
I want to see you.

602

Harriet Auber (1773-1862)

1. Our blest Redeemer, ere he breathed
   his tender last farewell,
   a Guide, a Comforter, bequeathed
   with us to dwell.

2. He came in tongues of living flame,
   to teach, convince, subdue;
   all-powerful as the wind he came,
   as viewless too.

3. He came sweet influence to impart,
   a gracious, willing guest,
   while he can find one humble heart
   wherein to rest.

4. And his that gentle voice we hear,
   soft as the breath of ev'n,
   that checks each fault, that calms
       each fear,
   and speaks of heav'n.

5. And every virtue we possess,
   and every vict'ry won,
   and every thought of holiness,
   are his alone.

6. Spirit of purity and grace,
   our weakness, pitying, see:
   O make our hearts thy dwelling-place,
   and worthier thee.

603

Traditional Caribbean,
based on Matthew 6:9-13 and Luke 11:2-4

1. Our Father, who art in heaven,
   hallowed be thy name.
   Thy kingdom come, thy will be done,
   hallowed be thy name. (x2)

2. On earth as it is in heaven,
   hallowed be thy name.
   Give us this day our daily bread,
   hallowed be thy name. (x2)

3. Forgive us our trespasses,
   hallowed be thy name.
   as we forgive those who trespass
       against us.
   hallowed be thy name. (x2)

4. Lead us not into temptation,
   hallowed be thy name.
   but deliver us from all that is evil.
   hallowed be thy name. (x2)

5. For thine is the kingdom,
   the power, and the glory,
   hallowed be thy name.
   for ever, and for ever and ever.
   hallowed be thy name. (x2)

6. Amen, amen, it shall be so.
   hallowed be thy name.
   Amen, amen, it shall be so.
   hallowed be thy name. (x2)

604

Our Father (Julian Wiener – b. 1965)
based on Matthew 6:9-13 and Luke 11:2-4
© 1984, 1999 Kevin Mayhew Ltd

Our Father, who art in heaven,
hallowed be thy name;
thy kingdom come;
thy will be done on earth as it is in
  heaven.
Give us this day our daily bread;
and forgive us our trespasses
as we forgive those who trespass
  against us;
and lead us not into temptation,
but deliver us from all that is evil.

Doxology
For the kingdom,
the power and the glory are yours,
now and for ever. Amen.

605

Timothy Dudley-Smith (b. 1926)
© Timothy Dudley-Smith

1. Our Father God in heaven
   on whom our world depends,
   to you let praise be given
   for families and friends;
   for parents, sisters, brothers,
   a home where love belongs,
   but on this day for mothers
   we bring our thankful songs.

2. What wealth of God's bestowing
   for all the world to share!
   What strength of heart outgoing
   to children everywhere!
   Our deepest joys and sorrows
   a mother's path must trace,
   and earth's unknown tomorrows
   are held in her embrace.

3. How well we know the story
   that tells of Jesus' birth,
   the Lord of heaven's glory
   become a child of earth;

a helpless infant sleeping,
yet King of realms above,
who finds in Mary's keeping
the warmth of human love.

4. Our Father God in heaven,
   to you we lift our prayer,
   that every child be given
   such tenderness and care,
   where life is all for others,
   where love your love displays:
   for God's good gift of mothers
   let earth unite in praise!

606

Jo Hemming and Nigel Hemming
© 2001 Vineyard Song (UK/Eire)
Administered by CopyCare

Our God is a great big God,
our God is a great big God,
our God is a great big God
and he holds us in his hands.
(Repeat)

He's higher than a skyscraper
and he's deeper than a submarine.
He's wider than the universe
and beyond my wildest dreams.
And he's known me and he's loved me
since before the world began.
How wonderful to be a part
of God's amazing plan.

Our God is a great big God,
our God is a great big God,
our God is a great big God
and he holds us in his hands.
Our God is a great big God,
our God is a great big God,
our God is a great big God
and he holds us in his hands.
And he holds us in his hands.

607
Ruth Harms Calkin
© *Ruth Harms Calkin*

Our God is so great,
so strong and so mighty,
there's nothing that he cannot do.
(Repeat)

The rivers are his,
the mountains are his,
the stars are his handiwork too.
Our God is so great,
so strong and so mighty,
there's nothing that he cannot do.

608
v. 1 unknown
vs. 2-5 Sandra Joan Billington (b. 1946)
© *1976, 1996 Kevin Mayhew Ltd*

1. Our God loves us,
   his love will never end.
   He rests within our hearts
   for our God loves us.

2. His gentle hand
   he stretches over us.
   Though storm-clouds threaten the day,
   he will set us free.

3. He comes to us
   in sharing bread and wine.
   He brings us life that will reach
   past the end of time.

4. Our God loves us,
   his faithful love endures,
   and we will live like his child
   held in love secure.

5. The joys of love
   as off'rings now we bring.
   The pains of love will be lost
   in the praise we sing.

609
Brenton Brown (b. 1973)
© *1998 Vineyard Songs (UK/Eire)*

1. Over all the earth, you reign on high,
   every mountain stream, every sunset
   sky.
   But my one request, Lord, my only
   aim
   is that you'd reign in me again.

   Lord, reign in me, reign in your power
   over all my dreams, in my darkest hour.
   You are the Lord of all I am,
   so won't you reign in me again.

2. Over every thought, over every word,
   may my life reflect the beauty of my
   Lord;
   'cause you mean more to me than
   any earthly thing,
   so won't you reign in me again.

610
Ruth Brown
© *Oxford University Press*

Over the earth is a mat of green,
over the green is dew,
over the dew are the arching trees,
over the trees the blue.
Across the blue are scudding clouds,
over the clouds the sun,
over it all is the love of God,
blessing us every one.

611
Martin Smith
© *1994 Curious? Music UK*

Over the mountains and the sea
your river runs with love for me,
and I will open up my heart
and let the Healer set me free.
I'm happy to be in the truth,
and I will daily lift my hands,
for I will always sing of
when your love came down.

Continued overleaf

I could sing of your love for ever,
I could sing of your love for ever,
I could sing of your love for ever,
I could sing of your love for ever.

Oh, I feel like dancing,
it's foolishness, I know;
but when the world has seen the light,
they will dance with joy
like we're dancing now.

612 Noel Richards (b. 1955)
© 1994 Thankyou Music

1. Overwhelmed by love,
   deeper than oceans, high as the
      heavens.
   Ever-living God,
   your love has rescued me.

2. All my sin was laid
   on your dear Son, your precious One.
   All my debt he paid,
   great is your love for me.

   No one could ever earn your love,
   your grace and mercy is free.
   Lord, these words are true,
   so is my love for you.

613 vs. 1-4 unknown, v. 5 the Editors
v. 5 © 1999 Kevin Mayhew Ltd

1. Peace is flowing like a river,
   flowing out through you and me,
   spreading out into the desert,
   setting all the captives free.

   (This refrain is not always sung.)

   Let it flow through me,
   let it flow through me,
   let the mighty peace of God
   flow out through me. (Repeat)

2. Love is flowing like a river,
   flowing out through you and me,
   spreading out into the desert,
   setting all the captives free.

3. Joy is flowing like a river,
   flowing out through you and me,
   spreading out into the desert,
   setting all the captives free.

4. Hope is flowing like a river,
   flowing out through you and me,
   spreading out into the desert,
   setting all the captives free.

5. Christ brings peace to all creation,
   flowing out through you and me,
   love, joy, hope and true salvation,
   setting all the captives free.

614 Edward Henry Bickersteth (1825-1906)

1. Peace, perfect peace,
   in this dark world of sin?
   The blood of Jesus
   whispers peace within.

2. Peace, perfect peace,
   by thronging duties pressed?
   To do the will of Jesus,
   this is rest.

3. Peace, perfect peace,
   with sorrows surging round?
   In Jesus' presence
   naught but calm is found.

4. Peace, perfect peace,
   with loved ones far away?
   In Jesus' keeping
   we are safe, and they.

5. Peace, perfect peace,
   our future all unknown?
   Jesus we know,
   and he is on the throne.

6. Peace, perfect peace,
   death shad'wing us and ours?
   Jesus has vanquished death
   and all its powers.

7. It is enough: earth's struggles
   soon shall cease,
   and Jesus call us
   to heaven's perfect peace.

615 Kevin Mayhew (b. 1942)
© 1976 Kevin Mayhew Ltd

1. Peace, perfect peace,
   is the gift of Christ our Lord.
   Peace, perfect peace,
   is the gift of Christ our Lord.
   Thus, says the Lord,
   will the world know my friends.
   Peace, perfect peace,
   is the gift of Christ our Lord.

2. Love, perfect love . . .

3. Faith, perfect faith . . .

4. Hope, perfect hope . . .

5. Joy, perfect joy . . .

616 Graham Kendrick (b. 1950)
© 1988 Make Way Music

Peace to you.
We bless you now
in the name of the Lord.
Peace to you.
We bless you now
in the name of the Prince of Peace.
Peace to you.

617 Albert F. Bayly (1901-1984) alt.
© Oxford University Press

1. Praise and thanksgiving, Father,
   we offer,
   for all things living you have made
   good;
   harvest of sown fields, fruits of the
   orchard,
   hay from the mown fields, blossom
   and wood.

2. Lord, bless the labour we bring to
   serve you,
   that with our neighbour we may be
   fed.
   Sowing or tilling, we would work
   with you;
   harvesting, milling, for daily bread.

3. Father, providing food for your
   children,
   your wisdom guiding teaches us share
   one with another, so that, rejoicing,
   sister and brother may know your
   care.

4. Then will your blessing reach every
   people;
   each one confessing your gracious
   hand:
   where you are reigning no one will
   hunger,
   your love sustaining fruitful the land.

618 Thomas Ken (1637-1710)

Praise God, from whom all blessings
flow,
praise him, all creatures here below,
praise him above ye heavenly host,
praise Father, Son and Holy Ghost.

619

Andy Piercy (b. 1951) and Dave Clifton (b. 1955). Based on the Doxology
© 1993 IQ Music Ltd

Praise God from whom all blessings
flow,
praise him, all creatures here below.
Praise him above, you heavenly host,
praise Father, Son and Holy Ghost.
(Repeat)

Give glory to the Father, give glory to
the Son,
give glory to the Spirit while endless
ages run.
'Worthy the Lamb,' all heaven cries,
'to be exalted thus.'
'Worthy the Lamb,' our hearts reply,
'for he was slain for us.'

Praise God from whom all blessings
flow,
praise him all creatures here below.
Praise him above, you heavenly host,
praise Father, Son and Holy Ghost.
(Repeat)

Praise God from whom all blessings
flow,
praise God from whom all blessings
flow.
(Repeat)

Praise God from whom all blessings
flow,
praise him all creatures here below.
Praise him above, you heavenly host,
praise Father, Son and Holy Ghost.
(Repeat)

Praise Father, Son and Holy Ghost.
Praise Father, Son and Holy Ghost.

620

John Kennett, based on Psalm 150
© 1981 Thankyou Music

Praise him on the trumpet,
the psalt'ry and harp;
praise him on the timbrel and the
dance;
praise him with stringed instruments
too;
praise him on the loud cymbals,
praise him on the loud cymbals;
let everything that has breath praise
the Lord!

Hallelujah, praise the Lord;
hallelujah, praise the Lord:
let everything that has breath
praise the Lord!
Hallelujah, praise the Lord;
hallelujah, praise the Lord:
let everything that has breath
praise the Lord!

621

Percy Dearmer (1867-1936)
based on Carey Bonner (1859-1938)

1. Praise him, praise him,
all his children praise him!
He is love, he is love.
Praise him, praise him,
all his children praise him!
He is love, he is love.

2. Thank him, thank him,
all his children thank him!
He is love, he is love.
Thank him, thank him,
all his children thank him!
He is love, he is love.

3. Love him, love him,
all his children love him!
He is love, he is love.
Love him, love him,
all his children love him!
He is love, he is love.

4. Crown him, crown him,
   all his children crown him!
   He is love, he is love.
   Crown him, crown him,
   all his children crown him!
   He is love, he is love.

622 Unknown

1. Praise him, praise him,
   praise him in the morning,
   praise him in the noontime.
   Praise him, praise him,
   praise him when the sun goes down.

2. Love him, love him, . . .

3. Trust him, trust him, . . .

4. Serve him, serve him, . . .

5. Jesus, Jesus, . . .

623 Henry Francis Lyte (1793-1847), based on Psalm 103

1. Praise, my soul, the King of heaven!
   To his feet thy tribute bring;
   ransomed, healed, restored, forgiven,
   who like me his praise should sing?
   Praise him! Praise him!
   Praise him! Praise him!
   Praise the everlasting King!

2. Praise him for his grace and favour
   to our fathers in distress;
   praise him still the same as ever,
   slow to chide and swift to bless.
   Praise him! Praise him!
   Praise him! Praise him!
   Glorious in his faithfulness!

3. Father-like, he tends and spares us;
   well our feeble frame he knows;
   in his hands he gently bears us,
   rescues us from all our foes.
   Praise him! Praise him!
   Praise him! Praise him!
   Widely as his mercy flows!

4. Angels, help us to adore him;
   ye behold him face to face;
   sun and moon, bow down before him,
   dwellers all in time and space.
   Praise him! Praise him!
   Praise him! Praise him!
   Praise with us the God of grace!

624 Henry Williams Baker (1821-1877)

1. Praise, O praise our God and King;
   hymns of adoration sing:

   for his mercies still endure
   ever faithful, ever sure.

2. Praise him that he made the sun
   day by day his course to run:

3. And the silver moon by night,
   shining with her gentle light:

4. Praise him that he gave the rain
   to mature the swelling grain:

5. And hath bid the fruitful field
   crops of precious increase yield:

6. Praise him for our harvest-store;
   he hath filled the garner-floor:

7. And for richer food than this,
   pledge of everlasting bliss:

8. Glory to our bounteous King;
   glory let creation sing:
   glory to the Father, Son
   and blest Spirit, Three in One.

625

vs. 1 and 2 from *Foundling Hospital Collection* (1796)
v. 3 Edward Osler (1798-1863)

1. Praise the Lord, ye heavens, adore
   him!
   Praise him, angels, in the height;
   sun and moon, rejoice before him,
   praise him, all ye stars and light.
   Praise the Lord, for he hath spoken;
   worlds his mighty voice obeyed:
   laws, which never shall be broken,
   for their guidance he hath made.

2. Praise the Lord, for he is glorious:
   never shall his promise fail.
   God hath made his saints victorious;
   sin and death shall not prevail.
   Praise the God of our salvation,
   hosts on high, his power proclaim;
   heaven and earth and all creation,
   laud and magnify his name!

3. Worship, honour, glory, blessing,
   Lord, we offer to thy name;
   young and old, thy praise expressing,
   join their Saviour to proclaim.
   As the saints in heaven adore thee,
   we would bow before thy throne;
   as thine angels serve before thee,
   so on earth thy will be done.

626

Michael Forster (b. 1946)
© 1999 Kevin Mayhew Ltd

1. Praise to God for saints and martyrs,
   inspiration to us all;
   in the presence of our Saviour,
   their example we recall:
   lives of holy contemplation,
   sacrifice or simple love,
   witnesses to truth and justice,
   honoured here and crowned above.

2. How we long to share their story,
   faithful in response to grace,
   signs of God's eternal presence
   in the realm of time and space.
   Now, their pilgrimage completed,
   cross of Christ their only boast,
   they unite their own rejoicing
   with the great angelic host.

3. Saints and martyrs, now in glory,
   robed before your Saviour's face,
   let us join your intercession
   for God's holy human race.
   Let us join with you in singing
   Mary's liberation song,
   till a just and free creation
   sings, with the angelic throng:

4. Praise and honour to the Father,
   adoration to the Son,
   with the all-embracing Spirit
   wholly Three and holy One.
   All the universe, united
   in complete diversity,
   sings as one your endless praises,
   ever blessèd Trinity!

627

John Henry Newman (1801-1890)

1. Praise to the Holiest in the height,
   and in the depth be praise:
   in all his words most wonderful,
   most sure in all his ways.

2. O loving wisdom of our God!
   when all was sin and shame,
   a second Adam to the fight,
   and to the rescue came.

3. O wisest love! that flesh and blood,
   which did in Adam fail,
   should strive afresh against the foe,
   should strive and should prevail.

4. And that a higher gift than grace
should flesh and blood refine,
God's presence and his very self,
and essence all-divine.

5. And in the garden secretly,
and on the cross on high,
should teach his brethren, and inspire
to suffer and to die.

6. Praise to the Holiest in the height,
and in the depth be praise;
in all his words most wonderful,
most sure in all his ways.

628 Joachim Neander (1650-1680)
trans. Catherine Winkworth (1827-1878)

1. Praise to the Lord,
the Almighty, the King of creation!
O my soul, praise him,
for he is thy health and salvation.
All ye who hear,
now to his temple draw near;
joining in glad adoration.

2. Praise to the Lord,
who o'er all things so wondrously
reigneth,
shieldeth thee gently from harm,
or when fainting sustaineth:
hast thou not seen
how thy heart's wishes have been
granted in what he ordaineth?

3. Praise to the Lord,
who doth prosper thy work and
defend thee,
surely his goodness and mercy
shall daily attend thee:
ponder anew
what the Almighty can do,
if to the end he befriend thee.

4. Praise to the Lord,
O let all that is in us adore him!
All that hath life and breath,
come now with praises before him.
Let the 'Amen'
sound from his people again,
gladly for ay we adore him.

629 S. N. Sedgewick (1872-1941)
© Copyright Control

1. Praise we now the word of grace;
may our hearts its truth embrace:
from its pages may we hear
Christ our teacher, speaking clear.

2. May the gospel of the Lord
everywhere be spread abroad,
that the world around may own
Christ as King, and Christ alone.

630 Nick Fawcett (b. 1957)
© 1999 Kevin Mayhew Ltd

1. Proclaim, proclaim the story,
proclaim the one who came that he
might die!
Make known to all his glory,
lift up his name on high!

2. Lift up, lift up your voices,
for Christ is risen, risen from the tomb!
All heaven and earth rejoices:
his light shines through the gloom.

3. Sing out, sing out hosanna!
Rejoice and honour Christ the King
of kings!
Lift high his royal banner,
lift up your voice and sing.

4. He reigns, he reigns triumphant –
come kneel in homage, worship and
adore.
Rejoice with hearts exultant:
he rules for evermore.

631 Brian Doerksen (b. 1965)
© 1990 Mercy/Vineyard Publishing

1. Purify my heart,
   let me be as gold and precious silver.
   Purify my heart,
   let me be as gold, pure gold.

   Refiner's fire,
   my heart's one desire
   is to be holy,
   set apart for you, Lord.
   I choose to be holy,
   set apart for you, my master,
   ready to do your will.

2. Purify my heart,
   cleanse me from within and make me
      holy.
   Purify my heart,
   cleanse me from my sin, deep within.

632 Susan Sayers (b. 1946)
© 1986 Kevin Mayhew Ltd

Push, little seed,
push, push, little seed,
till your head pops out of the ground.
This is the air,
and now you are there
you can have a good look round.
You'll see God's sky,
you'll see God's sun,
you'll feel his raindrops one by one,
as you grow, grow, grow, grow,
grow to be wheat for bread.
So push, little seed,
push, push, little seed,
that the world may be fed.

633 Fred Kaan (b. 1929)
© 1989 Stainer & Bell Ltd

1. Put peace into each other's hands
   and like a treasure hold it,
   protect it like a candle-flame,
   with tenderness enfold it.

2. Put peace into each other's hands
   with loving expectation;
   be gentle in your words and ways,
   in touch with God's creation.

3. Put peace into each other's hands
   like bread we break for sharing;
   look people warmly in the eye:
   our life is meant for caring.

4. As at communion, shape your hands
   into a waiting cradle;
   the gift of Christ receive, revere,
   united round the table.

5. Put Christ into each other's hands,
   he is love's deepest measure;
   in love make peace, give peace a
      chance,
   and share it like a treasure.

634 Paul Gerhardt (1607-1676)
trans. John Wesley (1703-1791) and others

1. Put thou thy trust in God,
   in duty's path go on;
   walk in his strength with faith and
      hope,
   so shall thy work be done.

2. Commit thy ways to him,
   thy works into his hands,
   and rest on his unchanging word,
   who heaven and earth commands.

3. Though years on years roll on,
his cov'nant shall endure;
though clouds and darkness hide his
path,
the promised grace is sure.

4. Give to the winds thy fears;
hope, and be undismayed:
God hears thy sighs and counts thy
tears;
God shall lift up thy head.

5. Through waves and clouds and storms
his power will clear thy way:
wait thou his time; the darkest night
shall end in brightest day.

6. Leave to his sov'reign sway
to choose and to command;
so shalt thou, wond'ring, own his way,
how wise, how strong his hand.

635 Fred Pratt Green (1903-2000)
© 1973, 1980 Stainer & Bell Ltd

1. Rejoice in God's saints, today and all
days!
A world without saints forgets how to
praise.
Their faith in acquiring the habit of
prayer,
their depth of adoring, Lord, help us
to share.

2. Some march with events to turn
them God's way;
some need to withdraw, the better to
pray;
some carry the gospel through fire
and through flood:
our world is their parish: their
purpose is God.

3. Rejoice in those saints, unpraised and
unknown,
who bear someone's cross or shoulder
their own:
they shame our complaining, our
comforts, our cares:
what patience in caring, what
courage, is theirs!

4. Rejoice in God's saints, today and all
days!
A world without saints forgets how to
praise.
In loving, in living, they prove it is
true:
the way of self-giving, Lord, leads us
to you.

636 Unknown
Based on Philippians 4:4

Rejoice in the Lord always and again
I say rejoice. *(Repeat)*
Rejoice, rejoice and again I say
rejoice. *(Repeat)*

637 Robert Bridges (1844-1930)

1. Rejoice, O land, in God thy might;
his will obey, him serve aright;
for thee the saints uplift their voice:
fear not, O land, in God rejoice.

2. Glad shalt thou be, with blessing
crowned,
with joy and peace thou shalt abound;
yea, love with thee shall make his
home
until thou see God's kingdom come.

3. He shall forgive thy sins untold:
remember thou his love of old;
walk in his way, his word adore,
and keep his truth for evermore.

638
Charles Wesley (1707-1788)

1. Rejoice, the Lord is King!
   Your Lord and King adore;
   mortals, give thanks and sing,
   and triumph evermore.

   Lift up your heart, lift up your voice;
   rejoice, again I say, rejoice.

2. Jesus the Saviour reigns,
   the God of truth and love;
   when he had purged our stains,
   he took his seat above.

3. His kingdom cannot fail;
   he rules o'er earth and heav'n;
   the keys of death and hell
   are to our Jesus giv'n.

4. He sits at God's right hand
   till all his foes submit,
   and bow to his command,
   and fall beneath his feet.

639
Graham Kendrick (b. 1950)
and Chris Rolinson (b. 1958)
© 1981 Thankyou Music

1. Restore, O Lord,
   the honour of your name,
   in works of sov'reign power
   come shake the earth again,
   that all may see,
   and come with rev'rent fear
   to the living God,
   whose kingdom shall outlast the years.

2. Restore, O Lord,
   in all the earth your fame,
   and in our time revive
   the church that bears your name.
   And in your anger,
   Lord, remember mercy,
   O living God,
   whose mercy shall outlast the years.

3. Bend us, O Lord,
   where we are hard and cold,
   in your refiner's fire:
   come purify the gold.
   Though suff'ring comes
   and evil crouches near,
   still our living God
   is reigning, he is reigning here.

4. Restore, O Lord,
   the honour of your name,
   in works of sov'reign power
   come shake the earth again,
   that all may see,
   and come with rev'rent fear
   to the living God,
   whose kingdom shall outlast the years.

640
Henry Hart Milman (1791-1868) alt.

1. Ride on, ride on in majesty!
   Hark, all the tribes hosanna cry;
   thy humble beast pursues his road
   with palms and scattered garments
       strowed.

2. Ride on, ride on in majesty!
   In lowly pomp ride on to die;
   O Christ, thy triumphs now begin
   o'er captive death and conquered sin.

3. Ride on, ride on in majesty!
   The wingèd squadrons of the sky
   look down with sad and wond'ring
       eyes
   to see th'approaching sacrifice.

4. Ride on, ride on in majesty!
   Thy last and fiercest strife is nigh;
   the Father, on his sapphire throne,
   awaits his own appointed Son.

5. Ride on, ride on in majesty!
   In lowly pomp ride on to die;
   bow thy meek head to mortal pain,
   then take, O God, thy power, and
      reign.

641 H. C. A. Gaunt (1902-1983)

1. Rise and hear! The Lord is speaking,
   as the gospel words unfold;
   we, in all our age-long seeking,
   find no firmer truth to hold.

2. Word of goodness, truth, and beauty,
   heard by simple folk and wise,
   word of freedom, word of duty,
   word of life beyond our eyes.

3. Word of God's forgiveness granted
   to the wild or guilty soul,
   word of love that works undaunted,
   changes, heals, and makes us whole.

4. Speak to us, O Lord, believing,
   as we hear, the sower sows;
   may our hearts, your word receiving,
   be the good ground where it grows.

642 Unknown, based on Genesis 6:4

Rise and shine,
and give God his glory, glory, (x3)
children of the Lord.

1. The Lord said to Noah,
   'There's gonna be a floody, floody.'
   Lord said to Noah,
   'There's gonna be a floody, floody.
   Get those children out of the muddy,
      muddy,
   children of the Lord.'

2. So Noah, he built him,
   he built him an arky, arky,
   Noah, he built him,
   he built him an arky, arky,
   built it out of hickory barky, barky,
   children of the Lord.

3. The animals, they came on,
   they came on, by twosies, twosies,
   animals, they came on, they came on,
   by twosies, twosies,
   elephants and kangaroosies, roosies,
   children of the Lord.

4. It rained and poured
   for forty daysies, daysies,
   rained and poured
   for forty daysies, daysies,
   nearly drove those animals
      crazies, crazies,
   children of the Lord.

5. The sun came out
   and dried up the landy, landy,
   sun came out
   and dried up the landy, landy,
   everything was fine and dandy, dandy,
   children of the Lord.

6. If you get to heaven
   before I do-sies, do-sies,
   you get to heaven
   before I do-sies, do-sies,
   tell those angels I'm comin'
      too-sies, too-sies,
   children of the Lord.

643 Augustus Montague Toplady (1740-1778) alt.

1. Rock of ages, cleft for me,
   let me hide myself in thee;
   let the water and the blood,
   from thy riven side which flowed,
   be of sin the double cure:
   cleanse me from its guilt and power.

Continued overleaf

2. Not the labours of my hands
can fulfil thy law's demands;
could my zeal no respite know,
could my tears for ever flow,
all for sin could not atone:
thou must save, and thou alone.

3. Nothing in my hands I bring,
simply to thy cross I cling;
naked, come to thee for dress;
helpless, look to thee for grace;
tainted, to the fountain fly;
wash me, Saviour, or I die.

4. While I draw this fleeting breath,
when mine eyelids close in death,
when I soar through tracts unknown,
see thee on thy judgement throne;
Rock of ages, cleft for me,
let me hide myself in thee.

644 William Romanis (1824-1899)

1. Round me falls the night;
Saviour, be my light;
through the hours in darkness
    shrouded
let me see thy face unclouded;
let thy glory shine
in this heart of mine.

2. Earthly work is done,
earthly sounds are none;
rest in sleep and silence seeking,
let me hear thee softly speaking;
in my spirit's ear
whisper, 'I am near.'

3. Blessèd, heavenly light,
shining through earth's night;
voice, that oft of love hast told me,
arms, so strong to clasp and hold me;
thou thy watch wilt keep,
Saviour, o'er my sleep.

645 Timothy Dudley-Smith (b. 1926)
© *Timothy Dudley-Smith*

1. Saint Luke, beloved physician,
with honour now recall,
who served his Master's mission,
who ministered to Paul;
whose skill to distant ages
bequeathed a gift unpriced,
a gospel in whose pages
we see the face of Christ.

2. He tells for us the stories
of Jesus here on earth,
the unsung pains and glories
that marked the church's birth;
the Spirit's power in preaching,
the contrite sinner freed,
the grace and mercy reaching
our deepest human need.

3. For all who work our healing
we lift our hearts in prayer,
the love of God revealing
in science, skill and care:
his gifts be still imparted
to those who make us whole,
like Luke the tender-hearted,
physician of the soul.

646 Adrian Howard and Pat Turner
© *1985 Restoration Music Ltd*

1. Salvation belongs to our God,
who sits on the throne,
and to the Lamb.
Praise and glory, wisdom and thanks,
honour and power and strength.

Be to our God for ever and ever,
be to our God for ever and ever,
be to our God for ever and ever. Amen.

2. And we, the redeemed, shall be strong
   in purpose and unity,
   declaring aloud,
   praise and glory, wisdom and thanks,
   honour and power and strength.

647 <small>Unknown</small>

1. Sanctus, sanctus, sanctus,
   I lift my voice in worship;
   I'll sing your praise for all my days,
   holy, holy Lord.

2. Sanctus, sanctus, sanctus,
   I lift my soul in gladness;
   I'll celebrate your love so great,
   holy, holy Lord.

3. Sanctus, sanctus, sanctus,
   I lift my eyes in wonder;
   I glimpse your grace in every place,
   holy, holy Lord.

4. Sanctus, sanctus, sanctus,
   I lift my gifts in homage;
   I'll honour you in all I do,
   holy, holy Lord.

5. Sanctus, sanctus, sanctus,
   I lift my life in worship;
   I will adore you evermore,
   holy, holy Lord.

648 <small>John Ellerton (1826-1893)</small>

1. Saviour, again
   to thy dear name we raise
   with one accord
   our parting hymn of praise;
   we stand to bless thee
   ere our worship cease;
   then, lowly kneeling,
   wait thy word of peace.

2. Grant us thy peace
   upon our homeward way;
   with thee began,
   with thee shall end, the day:
   guard thou the lips from sin,
   the hearts from shame,
   that in this house
   have called upon thy name.

3. Grant us thy peace,
   Lord, through the coming night;
   turn thou for us
   its darkness into light;
   from harm and danger
   keep thy children free,
   for dark and light
   are both alike to thee.

4. Grant us thy peace
   throughout our earthly life,
   our balm in sorrow,
   and our stay in strife;
   then, when thy voice
   shall bid our conflict cease,
   call us, O Lord,
   to thine eternal peace.

649 <small>Edward Caswall (1814-1878)</small>

1. See, amid the winter's snow,
   born for us on earth below,
   see, the tender Lamb appears,
   promised from eternal years.

   Hail, thou ever-blessèd morn,
   hail, redemption's happy dawn!
   Sing through all Jerusalem,
   Christ is born in Bethlehem.

2. Lo, within a manger lies
   he who built the starry skies;
   he, who, throned in heights sublime,
   sits amid the cherubim.

Continued overleaf

3. Say, you holy shepherds, say,
   what your joyful news today?
   Wherefore have you left your sheep
   on the lonely mountain steep?

   Hail, thou ever-blessèd morn,
   hail, redemption's happy dawn!
   Sing through all Jerusalem,
   Christ is born in Bethlehem.

4. 'As we watched at dead of night,
   there appeared a wondrous light;
   angels, singing peace on earth,
   told us of the Saviour's birth.'

5. Sacred infant, all divine,
   what a tender love was thine,
   thus to come from highest bliss,
   down to such a world as this!

6. Virgin mother, Mary, blest,
   by the joys that fill thy breast,
   pray for us, that we may prove
   worthy of the Saviour's love.

650   Michael Perry (1942-1996)
© 1965 Mrs B. Perry/Jubilate Hymns
Used by permission

1. See him lying on a bed of straw:
   a draughty stable with an open door.
   Mary cradling the babe she bore:
   the Prince of Glory is his name.

   O now carry me to Bethlehem
   to see the Lord of love again:
   just as poor as was the stable then,
   the Prince of Glory when he came!

2. Star of silver, sweep across the skies,
   show where Jesus in the manger lies;
   shepherds, swiftly from your stupor rise
   to see the Saviour of the world!

3. Angels, sing again the song you sang,
   sing the glory of God's gracious plan;
   sing that Beth'lem's little baby can
   be the Saviour of us all.

4. Mine are riches, from your poverty;
   from your innocence, eternity;
   mine, forgiveness by your death for me,
   child of sorrow for my joy.

651   Michael Forster (b. 1946)
© 1993 Kevin Mayhew Ltd

1. See the holy table,
   spread for our healing;
   hear the invitation
   to share in bread and wine.
   Catch the scent of goodness,
   taste and touch salvation;
   all mortal senses
   tell of love divine!

2. As the bread is broken,
   Christ is remembered;
   as the wine is flowing,
   his passion we recall;
   as redemption's story
   opens up before us,
   hope is triumphant,
   Christ is all in all.

3. Tell again the story,
   wonder of wonders:
   Christ, by grace eternal,
   transforms the simplest food!
   Sign of hope and glory,
   life in all its fullness,
   God's whole creation
   ransomed and renewed!

652

v. 1 Karen Lafferty (b. 1948), vs. 2 and 3
unknown, based on Matthew 6:33, 7:7
© 1972 CCCM Music/Maranatha! Music
Administered by CopyCare

1. Seek ye first the kingdom of God,
   and his righteousness,
   and all these things shall be added
      unto you;
   allelu, alleluia.

   Alleluia, alleluia,
   alleluia, allelu, alleluia.

2. You shall not live by bread alone,
   but by every word
   that proceeds from the mouth of God;
   allelu, alleluia.

3. Ask and it shall be given unto you,
   seek and ye shall find;
   knock, and it shall be opened unto
      you;
   allelu, alleluia.

653

Michael Forster (b. 1946)
based on Psalm 104
© 1997 Kevin Mayhew Ltd

Send forth your Spirit, Lord,
renew the face of the earth. (Repeat)

1. Bless the Lord, O my soul,
   O Lord God, how great you are;
   you are clothed in honour and glory,
   you set the world on its foundations.

2. Lord, how great are your works,
   in wisdom you made them all;
   all the earth is full of your creatures,
   your hand always open to feed them.

3. May your wisdom endure,
   rejoice in your works, O Lord.
   I will sing for ever and ever,
   in praise of my God and my King.

654

John L. Bell (b. 1949) and
Graham Maule (b. 1958)
© 1988 WGRG, Iona Community

1. She sits like a bird, brooding on the
      waters,
   hov'ring on the chaos of the world's
      first day;
   she sighs and she sings, mothering
      creation,
   waiting to give birth to all the Word
      will say.

2. She wings over earth, resting where
      she wishes,
   lighting close at hand or soaring
      through the skies;
   she nests in the womb, welcoming
      each wonder,
   nourishing potential hidden to our
      eyes.

3. She dances in fire, startling her
      spectators,
   waking tongues of ecstasy where
      dumbness reigned;
   she weans and inspires all whose
      hearts are open,
   nor can she be captured, silenced or
      restrained.

4. For she is the Spirit, one with God in
      essence,
   gifted by the Saviour in eternal love;
   she is the key opening the scriptures,
   enemy of apathy and heavenly dove.

655

Charles Wesley (1707-1788)
based on Genesis 32:24-30

1. Shepherd divine, our wants relieve
   in this our evil day;
   to all thy tempted foll'wers give
   the power to watch and pray.

Continued overleaf

2. Long as our fiery trials last,
   long as the cross we bear,
   O let our souls on thee be cast
   in never-ceasing prayer.

3. The Spirit's interceding grace
   give us in faith to claim;
   to wrestle till we see thy face,
   and know thy hidden name.

4. Till thou thy perfect love impart,
   till thou thyself bestow,
   be this the cry of every heart,
   'I will not let thee go.'

5. I will not let thee go, unless
   thou tell thy name to me;
   with all thy great salvation bless,
   and make me more like thee.

6. Then let me on the mountain-top
   behold thy shining face;
   where faith in sight is swallowed up,
   and prayer in endless praise.

656 David Fellingham (b. 1945)
    © 1988 Thankyou Music

Shout for joy and sing your praises to
   the King,
lift your voice and let your hallelujahs
   ring;
come before his throne to worship
   and adore,
enter joyfully now the presence of the
   Lord.

You are my Creator, you are my
   Deliv'rer,
you are my Redeemer, you are Lord,
and you are my Healer.
You are my Provider,
you are now my Shepherd, and my
   Guide,
Jesus, Lord and King, I worship you.

657 Martin E. Leckebusch (b. 1962)
    © 1999 Kevin Mayhew Ltd

1. Show me how to stand for justice:
   how to work for what is right,
   how to challenge false assumptions,
   how to walk within the light.
   May I learn to share more freely
   in a world so full of greed,
   showing your immense compassion
   by the life I choose to lead.

2. Teach my heart to treasure mercy,
   whether given or received –
   for my need has not diminished
   since the day I first believed:
   let me seek no satisfaction
   boasting of what I have done,
   but rejoice that I am pardoned
   and accepted in your Son.

3. Gladly I embrace a lifestyle
   modelled on your living word,
   in humility submitting
   to the truth which I have heard.
   Make me conscious of your presence
   every day in all I do;
   by your Spirit's gracious prompting
   may I learn to walk with you.

658 Joseph Mohr (1792-1848)
    trans. John Freeman Young (1820-1885)

1. Silent night, holy night.
   All is calm, all is bright,
   round yon virgin mother and child;
   holy infant, so tender and mild,
   sleep in heavenly peace,
   sleep in heavenly peace.

2. Silent night, holy night.
   Shepherds quake at the sight,
   glories stream from heaven afar,
   heavenly hosts sing alleluia:
   Christ, the Saviour is born,
   Christ, the Saviour is born.

3. Silent night, holy night.
   Son of God, love's pure light,
   radiant beams from thy holy face,
   with the dawn of redeeming grace:
   Jesus, Lord, at thy birth,
   Jesus, Lord, at thy birth.

659
v. 1 Pamela Hayes
v. 2 Margaret Rizza (b. 1929)
© 1998 Kevin Mayhew Ltd

Silent, surrendered, calm and still,
open to the word of God.
Heart humbled to his will,
offered is the servant of God.

*Come, Holy Spirit, bring us light,
teach us, heal us, give us life.
Come, Lord, O let our hearts
flow with love and all that is true.

* for use at Pentecost

660
Mike Anderson (b. 1956)
© 1999 Kevin Mayhew Ltd

Sing it in the valleys,
shout it from the mountain tops,
Jesus came to save us,
and his saving never stops.
He is King of kings,
and new life he brings,
sing it in the valleys,
shout it from the mountain tops,
oh, shout it from the mountain tops.

1. Jesus, you are by my side,
   you take all my fears.
   If I only come to you,
   you will heal the pain of years.

2. You have not deserted me,
   though I go astray.
   Jesus, take me in your arms,
   help me walk with you today.

3. Jesus, you are living now,
   Jesus, I believe.
   Jesus, take me, heart and soul,
   yours alone I want to be.

661
Sabine Baring-Gould (1834-1924)

1. Sing lullaby!
   Lullaby baby, now reclining,
   sing lullaby!
   Hush, do not wake the infant king.
   Angels are watching,
   stars are shining
   over the place where he is lying:
   sing lullaby!

2. Sing lullaby!
   Lullaby baby, now a-sleeping,
   sing lullaby!
   Hush, do not wake the infant king.
   Soon will come sorrow
   with the morning,
   soon will come bitter grief and
      weeping:
   sing lullaby!

3. Sing lullaby!
   Lullaby baby, now a-dozing,
   sing lullaby!
   Hush, do not wake the infant king.
   Soon comes the cross,
   the nails, the piercing,
   then in the grave at last reposing:
   sing lullaby!

Continued overleaf

4. Sing lullaby!
   Lullaby! is the babe awaking?
   Sing lullaby.
   Hush, do not stir the infant king.
   Dreaming of Easter,
   gladsome morning,
   conquering death, its bondage
      breaking:
   sing lullaby!

662 Venantius Fortunatus (c. 530-609)
trans. John Mason Neale (1818-1866)

1. Sing, my tongue, the glorious battle,
   sing the last the dread affray;
   o'er the Cross, the victor's trophy,
   sound the high triumphal lay;
   how, the pains of death enduring,
   earth's Redeemer won the day.

2. When at length th'appointed fullness
   of the sacred time was come,
   he was sent, the world's creator,
   from the Father's heavenly home,
   and was found in human fashion,
   offspring of the Virgin's womb.

3. Now the thirty years are ended
   which on earth he willed to see,
   willingly he meets his Passion,
   born to set his people free;
   on the cross the Lamb is lifted,
   there the sacrifice to be.

4. There the nails and spear he suffers,
   vinegar and gall and reed;
   from his sacred body piercèd
   blood and water both proceed:
   precious flood, which all creation
   from the stain of sin hath freed.

PART TWO
5. Faithful Cross, above all other,
   one and only noble tree!
   None in foliage, none in blossom,
   none in fruit thy peer may be;
   sweetest wood and sweetest iron,
   sweetest weight is hung on thee!

6. Bend, O lofty tree, thy branches,
   thy too rigid sinews bend;
   and awhile the stubborn hardness,
   which thy birth bestowed, suspend;
   and the limbs of heaven's high
      monarch
   gently on thine arms extend.

7. Thou alone wast counted worthy
   this world's ransom to sustain,
   that by thee a wrecked creation
   might its ark and haven gain,
   with the sacred blood anointed
   of the Lamb that hath been slain.

8. Praise and honour to the Father,
   praise and honour to the Son,
   praise and honour to the Spirit,
   ever Three and ever One,
   One in might and One in glory,
   while eternal ages run.
   (Amen.)

663 Ernest Sands (b. 1922)
© 1981 Ernest Sands

1. Sing of the Lord's goodness, Father of
   all wisdom,
   come to him and bless his name.
   Mercy he has shown us, his love is for
   ever,
   faithful to the end of days.

   Come then, all you nations,
   sing of your Lord's goodness,
   melodies of praise and thanks to God.

Ring out the Lord's glory,
praise him with your music,
worship him and bless his name.

2. Power he has wielded, honour is his
   garment,
   risen from the snares of death.
   His word he has spoken, one bread
   he has broken,
   new life he now gives to all.

3. Courage in our darkness, comfort in
   our sorrow,
   Spirit of our God most high;
   solace for the weary, pardon for the
   sinner,
   splendour of the living God.

4. Praise him with your singing, praise
   him with the trumpet,
   praise God with the lute and harp;
   praise him with the cymbals, praise
   him with your dancing,
   praise God till the end of days.

664

Johann Jakob Schütz (1640-1690)
trans. Frances Elizabeth Cox (1812-1897)

1 Sing praise to God who reigns above,
  the God of all creation,
  the God of power, the God of love,
  the God of our Salvation;
  with healing balm my soul he fills,
  and every faithless murmur stills:
  to God all praise and glory!

2. The Lord is never far away,
   but, through all grief distressing,
   an ever-present help and stay,
   our peace and joy and blessing;
   as with a mother's tender hand
   he leads his own, his chosen band;
   to God all praise and glory!

3. Thus all my gladsome way along
   I sing aloud my praises,
   that all may hear the grateful song
   my voice unwearied raises,
   be joyful in the Lord, my heart;
   both soul and body bear your part:
   to God all praise and glory!

665

Francesca Leftley (b. 1955), based on the 'Gloria'
© 1978 Kevin Mayhew Ltd

1. Sing to God a song of glory,
   peace he brings to all on earth.
   Worship we the King of heaven;
   praise and bless his holy name.

Glory, glory, sing his glory.
Glory to our God on high.

2. Sing to Christ, the Father's loved one,
   Jesus, Lord and Lamb of God:
   hear our prayer, O Lord, have mercy,
   you who bear the sins of all.

3. Sing to Christ, the Lord and Saviour,
   seated there at God's right hand:
   hear our prayer, O Lord, have mercy,
   you alone the Holy One.

4. Glory sing to God the Father,
   glory to his only Son,
   glory to the Holy Spirit,
   glory to the Three in One.

666

George Bourne Timms (1910-1997)
© Oxford University Press.
Used by permission

1. Sing we of the blessèd Mother
   who received the angel's word,
   and obedient to his summons
   bore in love the infant Lord;
   sing we of the joys of Mary
   at whose breast that child was fed,
   who is Son of God eternal
   and the everlasting Bread.

Continued overleaf

2. Sing we, too, of Mary's sorrows,
   of the sword that pierced her through,
   when beneath the cross of Jesus
   she his weight of suff'ring knew,
   looked upon her Son and Saviour
   reigning high on Calv'ry's tree,
   saw the price of our redemption
   paid to set the sinner free.

3. Sing again the joys of Mary
   when she saw the risen Lord,
   and, in prayer with Christ's apostles,
   waited on his promised word:
   from on high the blazing glory
   of the Spirit's presence came,
   heavenly breath of God's own being,
   manifest through wind and flame.

4. Sing the greatest joy of Mary
   when on earth her work was done,
   and the Lord of all creation
   brought her to his heavenly home:
   virgin mother, Mary blessèd,
   raised on high and crowned with grace,
   may your Son, the world's redeemer,
   grant us all to see his face.

2 As thou, Lord, hast lived for others,
   so may we for others live;
   freely have thy gifts been granted,
   freely may thy servants give:
   thine the gold and thine the silver,
   thine the wealth of land and sea,
   we but stewards of thy bounty,
   held in solemn trust for thee.

3. Come, O Christ, and reign among
   us,
   King of love, and Prince of peace;
   hush the storm of strife and passion,
   bid its cruel discords cease;
   by thy patient years of toiling,
   by thy silent hours of pain,
   quench our fevered thirst of pleasure,
   shame our selfish greed of gain.

4. Son of God, eternal Saviour,
   source of life and truth and grace,
   Son of Man, whose birth incarnate
   hallows all our human race,
   thou who prayedest, thou who willest,
   that thy people should be one,
   grant, O grant our hope's fruition:
   here on earth thy will be done.

667 S. C. Lowry (1855-1932)

1. Son of God, eternal Saviour,
   source of life and truth and grace,
   Son of Man, whose birth incarnate
   hallows all our human race,
   thou, our Head, who, throned in
   glory,
   for thine own dost ever plead,
   fill us with thy love and pity;
   heal our wrongs, and help our need.

668 James Montgomery (1771-1854) alt.

1. Songs of praise the angels sang,
   heaven with alleluias rang,
   when creation was begun,
   when God spake and it was done.

2. Songs of praise awoke the morn
   when the Prince of Peace was born;
   songs of praise arose when he
   captive led captivity.

3. Heaven and earth must pass away,
   songs of praise shall crown that day;
   God will make new heavens and
     earth,
   songs of praise shall hail their birth.

4. And shall we alone be dumb
   till that glorious kingdom come?
   No, the Church delights to raise
   psalms and hymns and songs of praise.

5. Saints below, with heart and voice,
   still in songs of praise rejoice;
   learning here, by faith and love,
   songs of praise to sing above.

6. Hymns of glory, songs of praise,
   Father, unto thee we raise;
   Jesu, glory unto thee,
   ever with the Spirit be.

669 Christopher Wordsworth (1807-1885)

1. Songs of thankfulness and praise,
   Jesus, Lord, to thee we raise,
   manifested by the star
   to the sages from afar;
   branch of royal David's stem,
   in thy birth at Bethlehem;
   anthems be to thee addressed:
   God in man made manifest.

2. Manifest at Jordan's stream,
   prophet, priest and King supreme,
   and at Cana wedding-guest,
   in thy Godhead manifest,
   manifest in power divine,
   changing water into wine;
   anthems be to thee addressed:
   God in man made manifest.

3. Manifest in making whole,
   palsied limbs and fainting soul,
   manifest in valiant fight,
   quelling all the devil's might,
   manifest in gracious will,
   ever bringing good from ill;
   anthems be to thee addressed:
   God in man made manifest.

4. Sun and moon shall darkened be,
   stars shall fall, the heavens shall flee;
   Christ will then like lightning shine,
   all will see his glorious sign.
   All will then the trumpet hear,
   all will see the judge appear;
   thou by all wilt be confessed:
   God in man made manifest.

5. Grant us grace to see thee, Lord,
   mirrored in thy holy word;
   may we imitate thee now,
   and be pure, as pure art thou;
   that we like to thee may be
   at thy great Epiphany,
   and may praise thee, ever blest,
   God in man made manifest.

670 'Anima Christi' ascribed to John XXII (1249-1334) trans. unknown

1. Soul of my Saviour,
   sanctify my breast;
   Body of Christ,
   be thou my saving guest;
   Blood of my Saviour,
   bathe me in thy tide,
   wash me with water
   flowing from thy side.

Continued overleaf

2. Strength and protection
   may thy passion be;
   O blessèd Jesus,
   hear and answer me;
   deep in thy wounds, Lord,
   hide and shelter me;
   so shall I never,
   never part from thee.

3. Guard and defend me
   from the foe malign;
   in death's dread moments
   make me only thine;
   call me, and bid me
   come to thee on high,
   when I may praise thee
   with thy saints for aye.

671 Andrew Reed (1787-1862)

1. Spirit divine, attend our prayers
   and make this house your home;
   descend with all your gracious powers:
   O come, great Spirit, come!

2. Come as the light: to us reveal
   our emptiness and woe,
   and lead us in those paths of life
   where all the righteous go.

3. Come as the fire; and purge our hearts
   like sacrificial flame;
   let our whole life an off'ring be
   to our Redeemer's name.

4. Come as the dove; and spread your
   wings,
   the wings of peaceful love;
   and let your church on earth become
   blest as the church above.

5. Come as the wind, with rushing sound
   and pentecostal grace,
   that all of woman born may see
   the glory of your face.

6. Spirit divine, attend our prayers;
   make this lost world your home;
   descend with all your gracious powers;
   O come, great Spirit, come!

672 Helen Kennedy
© St Mungo Music

1. Spirit of God, come dwell within me.
   Open my heart, O come set me free,
   fill me with love for Jesus, my Lord,
   O fill me with living water.

   Jesus is living, Jesus is here.
   Jesus, my Lord, come closer to me.
   Jesus, our Saviour dying for me,
   and rising to save his people.

2. Lord, how I thirst, O Lord, I am weak.
   Lord, come to me, you alone do I seek.
   Lord, you are life, and love and hope,
   O fill me with living water.

3. Lord, I am blind. O Lord, I can't see.
   Stretch out your hand, O Lord,
   comfort me.
   Lead me your way in light and in truth,
   O fill me with living water.

673 Sean Bowman
© 2004 Kevin Mayhew Ltd

1. Spirit of God, our light amid the
   darkness,
   shine on your people, fill our hearts
   anew;
   show us your glory, fill your whole
   creation,
   Light of the world, we bring our lives
   to you.

2. Spirit of hope, our joy and consolation,
share in our gladness, lift us when we
fall,
grant us the strength to be a steadfast
witness,
filled with your strength to bring new
hope to all.

3. Spirit of love, our source of true
compassion,
grant us your peace and fill us with
new life,
come, fill our hearts with your great
love unbounded,
fill all the world with love which ends
all strife.

4. Spirit of truth, our shield and our
defender,
be our sure fortress, fill us with your
might,
grant us your wisdom, be our
inspiration,
filled with your truth, your glory and
your light.

675

Daniel Iverson (1890-1972)
© 1963 Birdwing Music/EMI Christian Music
Publishing. Administered by Kevin Mayhew Ltd

1. Spirit of the living God,
fall afresh on me.
Spirit of the living God,
fall afresh on me.
Melt me, mould me, fill me, use me.
Spirit of the living God,
fall afresh on me.

2. Spirit of the living God,
fall afresh on us.
Spirit of the living God,
fall afresh on us.
Melt us, mould us, fill us, use us.
Spirit of the living God,
fall afresh on us.

*When appropriate a third verse may be
added, singing 'on them', for example,
before Confirmation, or at a service for
the sick.*

674

Paul Armstrong
© 1984 Restoration Music Ltd
Sovereign Music UK

Spirit of the living God,
fall afresh on me;
Spirit of the living God,
fall afresh on me;
fill me anew, fill me anew;
Spirit of the Lord,
fall afresh on me.

676 James Montgomery (1771-1854)

1. Stand up and bless the Lord,
ye people of his choice;
stand up and bless the Lord your God
with heart and soul and voice.

2. Though high above all praise,
above all blessing high,
who would not fear his holy name,
and laud and magnify?

3. O for the living flame
from his own altar brought,
to touch our lips, our mind inspire,
and wing to heaven our thought.

Continued overleaf

4. God is our strength and song,
   and his salvation ours;
   then be his love in Christ proclaimed
   with all our ransomed powers.

5. Stand up and bless the Lord,
   the Lord your God adore;
   stand up and bless his glorious name
   henceforth for evermore.

677 Jean Holloway (b. 1939)
    © 1996 Kevin Mayhew Ltd

1. Stand up, stand up for Jesus,
   stand up before his cross,
   an instrument of torture
   inflicting pain and loss;
   transformed by his obedience
   to God's redeeming plan,
   the cross was overpowered
   by Christ, both God and man.

2. Stand up, stand up for Jesus,
   be counted as his own;
   his gospel of forgiveness
   he cannot spread alone.
   The love which draws us to him,
   he calls us out to share;
   he calls us to the margins
   to be his presence there.

3. Stand up, stand up for Jesus,
   in faith and hope be strong,
   stand firm for right and justice,
   opposed to sin and wrong.
   Give comfort to the wounded,
   and care for those in pain,
   for Christ, in those who suffer,
   is crucified again.

4. Stand up, stand up for Jesus,
   who reigns as King of kings,
   be ready for the challenge
   of faith his kingship brings.
   He will not force obedience,
   he gives to each the choice
   to turn from all that's holy,
   or in his love rejoice.

5. Stand up, stand up for Jesus,
   give courage to the weak,
   be unashamed to praise him,
   be bold his name to speak.
   Confront the cross unflinching,
   Christ's love has set us free;
   he conquered death for ever
   and lives eternally.

678 Based on Matthew 26:36-42
    © Ateliers et Presses de Taizé

Stay with me, remain here with me,
watch and pray, watch and pray.

1. Stay here and keep watch with me.
   Watch and pray, watch and pray!

2. Watch and pray not to give way to
   temptation.

3. The Spirit is eager, but the flesh is weak.

4. My heart is nearly broken with
   sorrow.
   Remain here with me, stay awake
   and pray.

5. Father, if it is possible let this cup
   pass me by.

6. Father, if this cannot pass me by
   without my drinking it,
   your will be done.

   Stay with me, remain here with me,
   watch and pray, watch and pray.

679 Spiritual

Steal away, steal away,
steal away to Jesus.
Steal away, steal away home,
I ain't got long to stay here.

1. My Lord, he calls me;
   he calls me by the thunder;
   the trumpet sounds within-a my soul;
   I ain't got long to stay here.

2. Green trees are bending,
   the sinner stands a-trembling;
   the trumpet sounds within-a my soul;
   I ain't got long to stay here.

680 Syriac Liturgy, perhaps by Ephraim the Syrian (c. 306-373), trans. Charles William Humphreys (1840-1921) and Percy Dearmer (1867-1936)

1. Strengthen for service, Lord, the hands
   that holy things have taken;
   let ears that now have heard thy songs
   to clamour never waken.

2. Lord, may the tongues which 'Holy'
      sang
   keep free from all deceiving;
   the eyes which saw thy love be bright,
   thy blessèd hope perceiving.

3. The feet that tread thy holy courts
   from light do thou not banish;
   the bodies by thy Body fed
   with thy new life replenish.

681 Graham Kendrick (b. 1950) © 1988 Make Way Music

1. Such love, pure as the whitest snow;
   such love weeps for the shame I know;
   such love, paying the debt I owe;
   O Jesus, such love.

2. Such love, stilling my restlessness;
   such love, filling my emptiness;
   such love, showing me holiness;
   O Jesus, such love.

3. Such love springs from eternity;
   such love, streaming through history;
   such love, fountain of life to me;
   O Jesus, such love.

682 John Keble (1792-1866)

1. Sun of my soul, thou Saviour dear,
   it is not night if thou be near:
   O may no earth-born cloud arise
   to hide thee from thy servant's eyes.

2. When the soft dews of kindly sleep
   my wearied eyelids gently steep,
   be my last thought, how sweet to rest
   for ever on my Saviour's breast.

3. Abide with me from morn till eve,
   for without thee I cannot live;
   abide with me when night is nigh,
   for without thee I dare not die.

4. Watch by the sick; enrich the poor
   with blessings from thy boundless store;
   be every mourner's sleep tonight
   like infant's slumbers, pure and light.

683 From Daniel 3 © Ateliers et Presses de Taizé

Surrexit Christus, alleluia!
Cantate Domino, alleluia!

Translation: Christ is risen.
      Sing to the Lord.

1. All you heavens, bless the Lord.
   Stars of the heavens, bless the Lord.

Continued overleaf

2. Sun and moon, bless the Lord.
   And you, night and day, bless the Lord.

   Surrexit Christus, alleluia!
   Cantate Domino, alleluia!
   Translation: Christ is risen.
   Sing to the Lord.

3. Frost and cold, bless the Lord.
   Ice and snow, bless the Lord.

4. Fire and heat, bless the Lord.
   And you, light and darkness,
   bless the Lord.

5. Spirits and souls of the just,
   bless the Lord.
   Saints and the humble-hearted,
   bless the Lord.

684 Francis Stanfield (1835-1914) alt.

1. Sweet sacrament divine,
   hid in thy earthly home,
   lo, round thy lowly shrine,
   with suppliant hearts we come;
   Jesus, to thee our voice we raise,
   in songs of love and heartfelt praise,
   sweet sacrament divine,
   sweet sacrament divine.

2. Sweet sacrament of peace,
   dear home of every heart,
   where restless yearnings cease,
   and sorrows all depart,
   there in thine ear all trustfully
   we tell our tale of misery,
   sweet sacrament of peace,
   sweet sacrament of peace.

3. Sweet sacrament of rest,
   Ark from the ocean's roar,
   within thy shelter blest
   soon may we reach the shore;
   save us, for still the tempest raves;
   save, lest we sink beneath the waves,
   sweet sacrament of rest,
   sweet sacrament of rest.

4. Sweet sacrament divine,
   earth's light and jubilee,
   in thy far depths doth shine
   thy Godhead's majesty;
   sweet light, so shine on us, we pray,
   that earthly joys may fade away,
   sweet sacrament divine,
   sweet sacrament divine.

685 Francesca Leftley (b. 1955)
© 1984 Kevin Mayhew Ltd

1. Take me, Lord, use my life
   in the way you wish to do.
   Fill me, Lord, touch my heart
   till it always thinks of you.
   Take me now, as I am,
   this is all I can offer.

   Here today I, the clay,
   will be moulded by my Lord.

2. Lord, I pray that each day
   I will listen to your will.
   Many times I have failed
   but I know you love me still.
   Teach me now, guide me, Lord,
   keep me close to you always.

3. I am weak, fill me now
   with your strength and set me free.
   Make me whole, fashion me
   so that you will live in me.
   Hold me now in your hands,
   form me now with your Spirit.

686

vs. 1 and 3 Margaret Rizza (b. 1929)
v. 2 unknown
© 1998 Kevin Mayhew Ltd

1. Take my hands, Lord,
to share in your labours,
take my eyes, Lord, to see your needs,
let me hear the voice of lonely people,
let my love, Lord, bring riches to the
poor.

2. Give me someone to feed when I'm
hungry,
when I'm thirsty give water for
their thirst.
When I stand in need of tenderness,
give me someone to hold who longs
for love.

3. Keep my heart ever open to others,
may my time, Lord, be spent with
those in need;
may I tend to those who need
your care.
Take my life, Lord, and make it
truly yours,
take my life, Lord, and make it truly
yours.

687

Frances Ridley Havergal (1836-1879)

1. Take my life, and let it be
consecrated, Lord, to thee;
take my moments and my days,
let them flow in ceaseless praise.

2. Take my hands, and let them move
at the impulse of thy love;
take my feet, and let them be
swift and beautiful for thee.

3. Take my voice, and let me sing
always, only, for my King;
take my lips, and let them be
filled with messages from thee.

4. Take my silver and my gold;
not a mite would I withhold;
take my intellect, and use
every power as thou shalt choose.

5. Take my will, and make it thine:
it shall be no longer mine;
take my heart: it is thine own;
it shall be thy royal throne.

6. Take my love; my Lord, I pour
at thy feet its treasure-store;
take myself, and I will be
ever, only, all for thee.

688

John L. Bell (b. 1949) and Graham Maule
(b. 1958)
© 1988 WGRG, Iona Community

1. Take this moment, sign and space;
take my friends around;
here among us make the place
where your love is found.

2. Take the time to call my name,
take the time to mend
who I am and what I've been,
all I've failed to tend.

3. Take the tiredness of my days,
take my past regret,
letting your forgiveness touch
all I can't forget.

4. Take the little child in me,
scared of growing old;
help him (her) here to find his (her)
worth
made in Christ's own mould.

5. Take my talents, take my skills,
take what's yet to be;
let my life be yours, and yet,
let it still be me.

689 Charles William Everest (1814-1877)
based on Mark 8, alt.

1. Take up thy cross, the Saviour said,
   if thou wouldst my disciple be;
   deny thyself, the world forsake,
   and humbly follow after me.

2. Take up thy cross – let not its weight
   fill thy weak spirit with alarm:
   his strength shall bear thy spirit up,
   and brace thy heart, and nerve thine
   arm.

3. Take up thy cross, nor heed the shame,
   nor let thy foolish pride rebel:
   thy Lord for thee the Cross endured,
   to save thy soul from death and hell.

4. Take up thy cross then in his strength,
   and calmly every danger brave;
   'twill guide thee to a better home,
   and lead to vict'ry o'er the grave.

5. Take up thy cross, and follow Christ,
   nor think till death to lay it down;
   for only those who bear the cross
   may hope to wear the glorious crown.

6. To thee, great Lord, the One in Three,
   all praise for evermore ascend:
   O grant us in our home to see
   the heavenly life that knows no end.

690 George Herbert (1593-1633)

1. Teach me, my God and King,
   in all things thee to see;
   and what I do in anything
   to do it as for thee.

2. A man that looks on glass,
   on it may stay his eye;
   or, if he pleaseth, through it pass,
   and then the heaven espy.

3. All may of thee partake;
   nothing can be so mean
   which, with this tincture, 'For thy sake',
   will not grow bright and clean.

4. A servant with this clause
   makes drudgery divine;
   who sweeps a room, as for thy laws,
   makes that the action fine.

5. This is the famous stone
   that turneth all to gold;
   for that which God doth touch and
   own
   cannot for less be told.

691 Graham Kendrick (b. 1950) and Steve
Thompson
© 1993 Make Way Music

Teach me to dance
to the beat of your heart,
teach me to move
in the power of your Spirit,
teach me to walk
in the light of your presence,
teach me to dance
to the beat of your heart.
Teach me to love
with your heart of compassion,
teach me to trust
in the word of your promise,
teach me to hope
in the day of your coming,
teach me to dance
to the beat of your heart.

1. You wrote the rhythm of life,
   created heaven and earth,
   in you is joy without measure.
   So, like a child in your sight,
   I dance to see your delight,
   for I was made for your pleasure,
   pleasure.

2. Let all my movements express
a heart that loves to say 'yes',
a will that leaps to obey you.
Let all my energy blaze
to see the joy in your face;
let my whole being praise you, praise
you.

692 Timothy Dudley-Smith (b. 1926) based on
Luke 1:46-55
© Timothy Dudley-Smith

1. Tell out, my soul, the greatness of the
Lord!
Unnumbered blessings, give my spirit
voice;
tender to me the promise of his word;
in God my Saviour shall my heart
rejoice.

2. Tell out, my soul, the greatness of
his Name!
Make known his might, the deeds his
arm has done;
his mercy sure, from age to age the
same;
his holy Name, the Lord, the Mighty
One.

3. Tell out, my soul, the greatness of
his might!
Powers and dominions lay their
glory by.
Proud hearts and stubborn wills are
put to flight,
the hungry fed, the humble
lifted high.

4. Tell out, my soul, the glories of his
word!
Firm is his promise, and his mercy
sure.
Tell out, my soul, the greatness of
the Lord
to children's children and for
evermore!

693 Martin Smith
© Copyright 1993 Curious? Music UK

1. Thank you for saving me;
what can I say?
You are my everything,
I will sing your praise.
You shed your blood for me;
what can I say?
You took my sin and shame,
a sinner called by name.

Great is the Lord.
Great is the Lord.
For we know your truth has set us free;
you've set your hope in me.

(Last time:
Thank you for saving me;
what can I say?)

2. Mercy and grace are mine,
forgiven is my sin;
Jesus, my only hope,
the Saviour of the world.
'Great is the Lord,' we cry;
God, let your kingdom come.
Your word has let me see,
thank you for saving me.

694 Susan Sayers (b. 1946)
© 1986 Kevin Mayhew Ltd

1. Thank you for the summer morning,
misting into heat;
thank you for the diamonds
of dew beneath my feet;
thank you for the silver
where a snail has wandered by;
oh, we praise the name
of him who made
the earth and sea and sky.

Continued overleaf

2. Thank you for the yellow fields
   of corn like waving hair;
   thank you for the red surprise
   of poppies here and there;
   thank you for the blue of
   an electric dragonfly;
   oh, we praise the name
   of him who made
   the earth and sea and sky.

3. Thank you for the splintered light
   among the brooding trees;
   thank you for the leaves that rustle
   in a sudden breeze;
   thank you for the branches
   and the fun of climbing high;
   oh, we praise the name
   of him who made
   the earth and sea and sky.

4. Thank you for the ev'ning
   as the light begins to fade;
   clouds so red and purple
   that the setting sun has made;
   thank you for the shadows
   as the owls come gliding by;
   oh, we praise the name
   of him who made
   the earth and sea and sky.

695 Diane Davis Andrew
adapted by Geoffrey Marshall-Taylor (b. 1943)
© 1971 Celebration

1. Thank you, Lord, for this new day,
   (x3)
   right where we are.
   Alleluia, praise the Lord, (x3)
   right where we are.

2. Thank you, Lord, for food to eat, *(x3)*
   right where we are.

3. Thank you, Lord, for clothes to wear,
   (x3)
   right where we are.

4. Thank you, Lord, for all your gifts,
   (x3)
   right where we are.

696 Stephen Dean
© 1994 Stephen Dean
Published by OCP Publications

1. Thanks be to God whose love has
   gathered us today;
   thanks be to God who helps and
   guides us on our way.
   Thanks be to God who gives us voice
   that we may thank him:

   Deo gratias, Deo gratias,
   thanks be to God most high.

2. Thanks be to God for all the gifts of
   life and light;
   thanks be to God whose care protects
   us, day and night;
   thanks be to God who keeps in mind
   us who forget him:

3. Thanks be to God who knows our
   secret joys and fears;
   thanks be to God who when we call
   him, always hears;
   thanks be to God our rock and
   strength, ever sustaining:

4. Thanks be to God who never turns
   his face away;
   thanks be to God who heals and
   pardons all who stray;
   thanks be to God who welcomes us
   into the Kingdom:

5. Thanks be to God who made our
   world and all we see;
   thanks be to God who gave his Son
   to set us free;
   thanks be to God whose Spirit brings
   warmth and rejoicing:

697

Jean Holloway (b. 1939)
© 1994 Kevin Mayhew Ltd

Thanks for the fellowship found at
  this meal,
thanks for a day refreshed;
thanks to the Lord for his presence
  we feel,
thanks for the food he blessed.
Joyfully sing praise to the Lord,
praise to the risen Son,
alleluia, ever adored,
pray that his will be done.
As he was known in the breaking
  of bread,
now is he known again,
and by his hand have the hungry
  been fed,
thanks be to Christ. Amen!

698

R. T. Brooks (1918-1985)
© 1954, renewal 1982 Hope Publishing Co.
Administered by CopyCare

1. Thanks to God whose word was
     spoken
   in the deed that made the earth:
   his the voice that called a nation,
   his the fires that tired its worth.
   God has spoken, God has spoken:
   praise him for his open word!

2. Thanks to God whose Word incarnate
   heights and depths of life did share;
   deeds and words and death and rising
   grace in human form declare.
   God has spoken, God has spoken:
   praise him for his open word!

3. Thanks to God whose word was
     written
   in the Bible's sacred page,
   record of the revelation
   showing God to every age.
   God has spoken, God has spoken:
   praise him for his open word!

4. Thanks to God whose word is
     published
   in the tongues of every race;
   see its glory undiminished
   by the change of time of place.
   God has spoken, God has spoken:
   praise him for his open word!

5. Thanks to God whose word is
     answered
   by the Spirit's voice within;
   here we drink of joy unmeasured,
   life redeemed from death and sin.
   God is speaking, God is speaking:
   praise him for his open word!

699

Charles Coffin (1676-1749)
trans. John Chandler (1806-1876) alt.

1. The advent of our King
   our prayers must now employ,
   and we must hymns of welcome sing
   in strains of holy joy.

2. The everlasting Son
   incarnate deigns to be;
   himself a servant's form puts on,
   to set his servants free.

3. Daughter of Sion, rise
   to meet thy lowly King;
   nor let thy faithless heart despise
   the peace he comes to bring.

4. As Judge, on clouds of light,
   he soon will come again,
   and his true members all unite
   with him in heaven to reign.

5. All glory to the Son
   who comes to set us free,
   with Father, Spirit, ever One,
   through all eternity.

700
Sabine Baring-Gould (1843-1924), based on 'Birjina gaztettobat zegoen'

1. The angel Gabriel from heaven came,
   his wings as drifted snow, his eyes
      as flame.
   'All hail,' said he, 'thou lowly maiden,
      Mary,
   most highly favoured lady.' Gloria!

2. 'For known a blessèd Mother thou
      shalt be.
   All generations laud and honour thee.
   Thy Son shall be Emmanuel, by
      seers foretold,
   most highly favoured lady.' Gloria!

3. Then gentle Mary meekly bowed
      her head.
   'To me be as it pleaseth God,' she
      said.
   'My soul shall laud and magnify his
      holy name.'
   Most highly favoured lady! Gloria!

4. Of her, Emmanuel, the Christ,
      was born
   in Bethlehem, all on a Christmas morn;
   and Christian folk throughout the
      world will ever say:
   'Most highly favoured lady.' Gloria!

701
Lionel Muirhead (1845-1925) alt.

1. The Church of God a kingdom is,
   where Christ in power doth reign;
   where spirits yearn till, seen in bliss,
   their Lord shall come again.

2. Glad companies of saints possess
   this Church below, above;
   and God's perpetual calm doth bless
   their paradise of love.

3. An altar stands within the shrine
   whereon, once sacrificed,
   is set, immaculate, divine,
   the Lamb of God, the Christ.

4. There rich and poor, from countless
      lands,
   praise Christ on mystic rood;
   there nations reach forth holy hands
   to take God's holy food.

5. There pure life-giving streams o'erflow
   the sower's garden-ground;
   and faith and hope fair blossoms show,
   and fruits of love abound.

6. O King, O Christ, this endless grace
   to all your people bring,
   to see the vision of your face
   in joy, O Christ, our King.

702
Samuel John Stone (1839-1900)

1. The Church's one foundation
   is Jesus Christ, her Lord;
   she is his new creation,
   by water and the word;
   from heaven he came and sought her
   to be his holy bride,
   with his own blood he bought her,
   and for her life he died.

2. Elect from every nation,
   yet one o'er all the earth,
   her charter of salvation,
   one Lord, one faith, one birth;
   one holy name she blesses,
   partakes one holy food,
   and to one hope she presses,
   with every grace endued.

3. 'Mid toil and tribulation,
and tumult of her war,
she waits the consummation
of peace for evermore;
till with the vision glorious
her longing eyes are blest,
and the great Church victorious
shall be the Church at rest.

4. Yet she on earth hath union
with God the Three in One,
and mystic sweet communion
with those whose rest is won:
O happy ones and holy!
Lord, give us grace that we
like them, the meek and lowly,
on high may dwell with thee.

703 St John of Damascus (c. 750)
trans. John Mason Neale (1818-1866)

1. The day of resurrection!
Earth, tell it out abroad;
the passover of gladness,
the passover of God!
From death to life eternal,
from earth unto the sky,
our Christ hath brought us over
with hymns of victory.

2. Our hearts be pure from evil,
that we may see aright
the Lord in rays eternal
of resurrection-light;
and list'ning to his accents,
may hear so calm and plain
his own 'All hail' and, hearing,
may raise the victor strain.

3. Now let the heavens be joyful,
and earth her song begin,
the round world keep high triumph,
and all that is therein;
let all things, seen and unseen,
their notes of gladness blend,
for Christ the Lord hath risen,
our joy that hath no end.

704 John Ellerton (1826-1893)

1. The day thou gavest, Lord, is ended:
the darkness falls at thy behest;
to thee our morning hymns ascended;
thy praise shall sanctify our rest.

2. We thank thee that thy Church
unsleeping,
while earth rolls onward into light,
through all the world her watch is
keeping,
and rests not now by day or night.

3. As o'er each continent and island
the dawn leads on another day,
the voice of prayer is never silent,
nor dies the strain of praise away.

4. The sun that bids us rest is waking
our brethren 'neath the western sky,
and hour by hour fresh lips are
making
thy wondrous doings heard on high.

5. So be it, Lord; thy throne shall never,
like earth's proud empires, pass away;
thy kingdom stands, and grows for
ever,
till all thy creatures own thy sway.

705

From William Sandys' *Christmas Carols, Ancient and Modern* (1833) alt.

1. The first Nowell the angel did say
   was to certain poor shepherds in
      fields as they lay:
   in fields where they lay keeping
      their sheep,
   on a cold winter's night that was
      so deep.

   Nowell, Nowell, Nowell, Nowell,
   born is the King of Israel!

2. They lookèd up and saw a star,
   shining in the east, beyond them far,
   and to the earth it gave great light,
   and so it continued both day and night.

3. And by the light of that same star,
   three wise men came from country far;
   to seek for a king was their intent,
   and to follow the star wherever it went.

4. This star drew nigh to the north-west,
   o'er Bethlehem it took its rest,
   and there it did both stop and stay
   right over the place where Jesus lay.

5. Then entered in those wise men three,
   full rev'rently upon their knee,
   and offered there in his presence,
   their gold and myrrh and frankincense.

6. Then let us all with one accord
   sing praises to our heavenly Lord,
   who with the Father we adore
   and Spirit blest for evermore.

706

Thomas Olivers (1725-1799) based on the Hebrew *Yigdal* alt.

1. The God of Abraham praise,
   who reigns enthroned above,
   Ancient of everlasting Days,
   and God of love:
   Jehovah, great I AM,
   by earth and heaven confessed;
   we bow and bless the sacred name,
   for ever blest.

2. The God of Abraham praise,
   at whose supreme command
   from earth we rise, and seek the joys
   at his right hand:
   we all on earth forsake,
   its wisdom, fame and power;
   and him our only portion make,
   our shield and tower.

3. The God of Abraham praise,
   whose all-sufficient grace
   shall guide us all our happy days,
   in all our ways:
   he is our faithful friend;
   he is our gracious God;
   and he will save us to the end,
   through Jesus' blood.

4. He by himself has sworn –
   we on his oath depend –
   we shall, on eagles' wings upborne,
   to heaven ascend:
   we shall behold his face,
   we shall his power adore,
   and sing the wonders of his grace
   for evermore.

5. The whole triumphant host
   give thanks to God on high:
   'Hail, Father, Son and Holy Ghost!'
   they ever cry:
   Hail, Abraham's God and ours!
   We join the heavenly throng,
   and celebrate with all our powers
   in endless song.

707

George Herbert (1593-1633)
based on Psalm 23

1. The God of love my shepherd is,
   and he that doth me feed;
   while he is mine and I am his,
   what can I want or need?

2. He leads me to the tender grass,
   where I both feed and rest;
   then to the streams that gently pass:
   in both I have the best.

3. Or if I stray, he doth convert,
   and bring my mind in frame,
   and all this not for my desert,
   but for his holy name.

4. Yea, in death's shady black abode
   well may I walk, nor fear;
   for thou art with me, and thy rod
   to guide, thy staff to bear.

5. Surely thy sweet and wondrous love
   shall measure all my days;
   and, as it never shall remove,
   so neither shall my praise.

708

Venantius Fortunatus (530-600)
trans. John Mason Neale (1818-1866)

1. The God whom earth and sea and
      sky
   adore and laud and magnify,
   whose might they own, whose praise
      they tell,
   in Mary's body deigned to dwell.

2. O mother blest, the chosen shrine
   wherein the architect divine,
   whose hand contains the earth and sky,
   vouchsafed in hidden guise to lie:

3. Blest in the message Gabriel brought;
   blest in the work the Spirit wrought;
   most blest, to bring to human birth
   the long-desired of all the earth.

4. O Lord, the virgin-born, to thee
   eternal praise and glory be,
   whom with the Father we adore
   and Holy Ghost for evermore.

709

Martin E. Leckebusch (b. 1962)
© 2004 Kevin Mayhew Ltd

1. The gracious invitation stands
   for any who will come;
   the Father runs with open arms
   to children heading home –
   and all who trudge with weary feet
   along life's dusty road
   receive at last a welcome chance
   to lose their heavy load.

2. No longer need we clothe our lives
   in garments soiled and torn
   when Christ gives robes of
      righteousness
   for what was old and worn:
   to those bereft of dignity
   and yearning to be whole,
   forgiveness brings the healing power
   which liberates the soul.

3. When all that busy lives produce
   is dry futility,
   we find in Christ the living source
   of full reality;
   and if, within our hearts, the truth
   is what we long to hear,
   the whisper of the Spirit comes
   as music to the ear.

4. Whoever looks for nourishment
   will find the table spread:
   the finest riches heaven holds,
   foretold in wine and bread.
   The banquet is for everyone,
   the greatest and the least:
   for all are called as honoured guests
   to come and join the feast!

710
From *Epistle to Diognetus* (c.150)
trans. Frances Bland Tucker (1895-1984)
© *Church Publishing Inc.*

1. The great Creator of the worlds,
   the sov'reign God of heav'n,
   his holy and immortal truth
   to all on earth has giv'n.

2. He sent no angel of his host
   to bear his mighty word,
   but him through whom the worlds
      were made,
   the everlasting Lord.

3. He sent him not in wrath and power,
   but grace and peace to bring;
   in kindness, as a king might send
   his son, himself a king.

4. He sent him down as sending God;
   in flesh to us he came;
   as one with us he dwelt with us,
   and bore a human name.

5. He came as Saviour to his own,
   the way of love he trod;
   he came to win us by goodwill,
   for force is not of God.

6. Not to oppress, but summon all
   their truest life to find,
   in love God sent his Son to save,
   not to condemn mankind.

711 Thomas Kelly (1769-1855)

1. The head that once was crowned
      with thorns
   is crowned with glory now:
   a royal diadem adorns
   the mighty victor's brow.

2. The highest place that heav'n affords
   is his, is his by right.
   The King of kings and Lord of lords,
   and heav'n's eternal light.

3. The joy of all who dwell above,
   the joy of all below,
   to whom he manifests his love,
   and grants his name to know.

4. To them the cross, with all its shame,
   with all its grace is giv'n;
   their name an everlasting name,
   their joy the joy of heav'n.

5. They suffer with their Lord below,
   they reign with him above,
   their profit and their joy to know
   the myst'ry of his love.

6. The cross he bore is life and health,
   though shame and death to him;
   his people's hope, his people's wealth,
   their everlasting theme.

712
Isaac Watts (1674-1748)
based on Psalm 19

1. The heav'ns declare thy glory, Lord;
   in every star thy wisdom shines;
   but when our eyes behold thy word,
   we read thy name in fairer lines.

2. The rolling sun, the changing light,
   and nights and days, thy power confess;
   but the blest volume thou hast writ
   reveals thy justice and thy grace.

3. Sun, moon, and stars convey thy
      praise
   round the whole earth, and never
      stand;
   so, when thy truth began its race,
   it touched and glanced on every land.

4. Nor shall thy spreading gospel rest
   till through the world thy truth has
   run;
   till Christ has all the nations blest
   that see the light or feel the sun.

5. Great Sun of Righteousness, arise;
   bless the dark world with heav'nly
   light;
   thy gospel makes the simple wise,
   thy laws are pure, thy judgements right.

6. Thy noblest wonders here we view,
   its souls renewed and sins forgiv'n:
   Lord, cleanse my sins, my soul renew,
   and make thy word my guide to
   heav'n.

713 Traditional

1. The holly and the ivy,
   when they are both full grown,
   of all the trees that are in the wood
   the holly bears the crown.

   The rising of the sun
   and the running of the deer,
   the playing of the merry organ,
   sweet singing in the choir.

2. The holly bears a blossom,
   white as the lily flower,
   and Mary bore sweet Jesus Christ
   to be our sweet Saviour.

3. The holly bears a berry,
   as red as any blood,
   and Mary bore sweet Jesus Christ
   to do poor sinners good.

4. The holly bears a prickle,
   as sharp as any thorn,
   and Mary bore sweet Jesus Christ
   on Christmas day in the morn.

5. The holly bears a bark,
   as bitter as any gall,
   and Mary bore sweet Jesus Christ
   for to redeem us all.

6. The holly and the ivy,
   when they are both full grown,
   of all the trees that are in the wood
   the holly bears the crown.

714 Graham Kendrick (b. 1950)
© *1981 Thankyou Music*

1. The King is among us,
   his Spirit is here,
   let's draw near and worship,
   let songs fill the air.

2. He looks down upon us,
   delight in his face,
   enjoying his children's love,
   enthralled by our praise.

3. For each child is special,
   accepted and loved,
   a love gift from Jesus
   to his Father above.

4. And now he is giving
   his gifts to us all,
   for no one is worthless
   and each one is called.

5. The Spirit's anointing
   on all flesh comes down,
   and we shall be channels
   for works like his own.

6. We come now believing
   your promise of power,
   for we are your people
   and this is your hour.

7. The King is among us,
   his Spirit is here,
   let's draw near and worship,
   let songs fill the air.

715 Henry Williams Baker (1821-1877), based on Psalm 23

1. The King of love my shepherd is,
   whose goodness faileth never;
   I nothing lack if I am his
   and he is mine for ever.

2. Where streams of living water flow
   my ransomed soul he leadeth,
   and where the verdant pastures grow
   with food celestial feedeth.

3. Perverse and foolish oft I strayed,
   but yet in love he sought me,
   and on his shoulder gently laid,
   and home, rejoicing, brought me.

4. In death's dark vale I fear no ill
   with thee, dear Lord, beside me;
   thy rod and staff my comfort still,
   thy cross before to guide me.

5. Thou spread'st a table in my sight,
   thy unction grace bestoweth:
   and O what transport of delight
   from thy pure chalice floweth!

6. And so through all the length of days
   thy goodness faileth never;
   good Shepherd, may I sing thy praise
   within thy house for ever.

716 Robert Willis (b. 1947)
© The Very Revd Robert Willis

1. 'The kingdom is upon you!'
   the voice of Jesus cries,
   fulfilling with its message
   the wisdom of the wise;
   it lightens with fresh insight
   the striving human mind,
   creating new dimensions
   of faith for all to find.

2. 'God's kingdom is upon you!'
   the message sounds today,
   it summons every pilgrim
   to take the questing way,
   with eyes intent on Jesus,
   our leader and our friend,
   who trod faith's road before us,
   and trod it to the end.

3. The kingdom is upon us!
   Stirred by the Spirit's breath,
   we glory in its freedom
   from emptiness and death;
   we celebrate its purpose,
   its mission and its goal,
   alive with the conviction
   that Christ can make us whole.

717 Mike Anderson (b. 1956), based on Matthew 5:3-10
© 1999 Kevin Mayhew Ltd

The kingdom of heaven,
the kingdom of heaven is yours.
A new world in Jesus
a new world in Jesus is yours.

1. Blessèd are you in sorrow and grief,
   for you shall all be consoled;
   blessèd are you, the gentle of heart,
   you shall inherit the earth.

2. Blessèd are you who hunger for right,
   for you shall be satisfied;
   blessèd are you the merciful ones,
   for you shall be pardoned too.

3. Blessèd are you whose hearts are pure,
   your eyes shall gaze on the Lord;
   blessèd are you who strive after peace,
   the Lord will call you his own.

4. Blessèd are you who suffer for right,
   the heavenly kingdom is yours;
   blessèd are you who suffer for me,
   for you shall reap your reward.

718 Josiah Conder (1789-1855)

1. The Lord is King! lift up thy voice,
   O earth, and all ye heav'ns, rejoice;
   from world to world the joy shall ring,
   'The Lord omnipotent is King!'

2. The Lord is King! who then shall dare
   resist his will, distrust his care,
   or murmer at his wise decrees,
   or doubt his royal promises?

3. He reigns! ye saints, exalt your strains;
   your God is King, your Father reigns;
   and he is at the Father's side,
   the man of love, the crucified.

*4. Alike pervaded by his eye
   all parts of his dominion lie:
   this world of ours and worlds unseen,
   and thin the boundary between!

5. One Lord one empire all secures;
   he reigns, and life and death are yours;
   through earth and heav'n one song
      shall ring,
   'The Lord omnipotent is King!'

719 Based on Psalm 27
© Ateliers et Presses de Taizé

The Lord is my light,
my light and salvation:
in God I trust,
in God I trust.

720 Taizé Community
© Ateliers et Presses de Taizé

The Lord is my song, the Lord is
   my praise:
all my hope comes from God.
The Lord is my song, the Lord is
   my praise:
God, the well-spring of life.

721 Thomas Kelly (1769-1855)

1. The Lord is ris'n indeed:
   now is his work performed;
   now is the mighty captive freed,
   and death's strong castle stormed.

2. The Lord is ris'n indeed:
   then hell has lost his prey;
   with him is ris'n the ransomed seed
   to reign in endless day.

3. The Lord is ris'n indeed:
   he lives, to die no more;
   he lives, the sinner's cause to plead,
   whose curse and shame he bore.

4. The Lord is ris'n indeed:
   attending angels, hear!
   up to the courts of heav'n with speed
   the joyful tidings bear.

5. Then take your golden lyres
   and strike each cheerful chord;
   join, all ye bright celestial choirs,
   to sing our risen Lord.

722 John Milton (1608-1674)
based on Psalms 82, 85 and 86

1. The Lord will come and not be slow,
   his footsteps cannot err;
   before him righteousness shall go,
   his royal harbinger.

2. Truth from the earth, like to a flower,
   shall bud and blossom then;
   and justice, from her heav'nly bower,
   look down on mortal men.

3. Rise, God, judge thou the earth in
      might,
   this wicked earth redress;
   for thou art he who shalt by right
   the nations all possess.

Continued overleaf

4. The nations all whom thou hast made
shall come, and all shall frame
to bow them low before thee, Lord,
and glorify thy name.

5. For great thou art, and wonders great
by thy strong hand are done;
thou in thy everlasting seat
remainest God alone.

723 Psalm 23 from *The Scottish Psalter* (1650)

1. The Lord's my shepherd, I'll not want.
He makes me down to lie
in pastures green.
He leadeth me the quiet waters by.

2. My soul he doth restore again,
and me to walk doth make
within the paths of righteousness,
e'en for his own name's sake.

3. Yea, though I walk in death's dark vale,
yet will I fear no ill.
For thou art with me, and thy rod
and staff me comfort still.

4. My table thou hast furnishèd
in presence of my foes,
my head thou dost with oil anoint,
and my cup overflows.

5. Goodness and mercy all my life
shall surely follow me.
And in God's house for evermore
my dwelling-place shall be.

724 Stuart Townend (b. 1963)
based on Psalm 23
© 1996 Thankyou Music

1. The Lord's my shepherd, I'll not want;
he makes me lie in pastures green,
he leads me by the still, still waters,
his goodness restores my soul.

And I will trust in you alone,
and I will trust in you alone,
for your endless mercy follows me,
your goodness will lead me home.

2. He guides my ways in righteousness,
and he anoints my head with oil;
and my cup – it overflows with joy,
I feast on his pure delights.

3. And though I walk the darkest path –
I will not fear the evil one,
for you are with me, and your rod
and staff
are the comfort I need to know.

725 Susan Sayers (b. 1946)
© 1996 Kevin Mayhew Ltd

1. The love we share, the love we come
to celebrate,
so rich and full, so healing and so
strong,
comes from the love of God our
loving Father
within whose care we all of us belong.
A love which breathed creation into
being,
a love which hears our deepest hopes
and dreams;
a love which now within this marriage-
making
alights on bride and groom to bless
and make them one.

2. Through future years, may they hold
bright the memory
of all the joys on this their wedding
day.
And as their love grows stronger yet
and deeper
their rings express much more than
words can say.

They speak of love that never has an ending,
of love that shines, encircles in embrace,
of love whose heart is always free and open;
our human love reflects the beauty of God's grace.

5. His righteous government and power,
shall over all extend;
on judgement and on justice based,
his reign shall have no end.

6. Lord Jesus, reign in us, we pray,
and make us thine alone,
who with the Father ever art
and Holy Spirit one.

726 Guatemalan
trans. Christine Carson
© WGRG, Iona Community

The peace of the earth be with you,
the peace of the heavens too;
the peace of the rivers be with you,
the peace of the oceans too.
Deep peace falling over you.
God's peace growing in you.

728 John E. Bowers (b. 1923)
© John E. Bowers

1. The prophets spoke in days of old
to those of stubborn will.
Their message lives and is retold
where hearts are stubborn still.

2. And Jesus told his hearers then
of love, of joy, of peace.
His message lives, he speaks again,
and sinners find release.

3. Shall we not hear that message, Lord,
to lead us on the way?
Come, Christ, make plain your saving word,
and speak to us today.

727 John Morrison (1750-1798)
based on Isaiah 9:2-7

1. The people that in darkness sat
a glorious light have seen;
the light has shined on them who long
in shades of death have been.

2. To hail thee, Sun of Righteousness,
the gath'ring nations come;
the joy as when the reapers bear
their harvest treasures home.

3. For unto us a child is born,
to us a Son is giv'n,
and on his shoulder ever rests,
all power in earth and heav'n.

4. His name shall be the Prince of Peace
the everlasting Lord,
the Wonderful, the Counsellor,
the God by all adored.

729 Venantius Fortunatus (530-609)
trans. John Mason Neale (1818-1866) and others

1. The royal banners forward go,
the cross shines forth in mystic glow;
where he in flesh, our flesh who made,
our sentence bore, our ransom paid.

2. There whilst he hung, his sacred side
by soldier's spear was opened wide,
to cleanse us in the precious flood
of water mingled with his blood.

Continued overleaf

3. Fulfilled is now what David told
   in true prophetic song of old,
   how God the sinner's king should be;
   for God is reigning from the tree.

4. O tree of glory, tree most fair,
   ordained those holy limbs to bear,
   how bright in purple robe it stood,
   the purple of a Saviour's blood!

5. To thee, eternal Three in One,
   let homage meet by all be done,
   as by the cross thou dost restore,
   so rule and guide us evermore. Amen.

730 Michael Forster (b. 1946)
based on Isaiah 35
© 1993 Kevin Mayhew Ltd

1. The Saviour will come,
   resplendent in joy;
   the lame and the sick
   new strength will enjoy.
   The desert, rejoicing,
   shall burst into flower,
   the deaf and the speechless
   will sing in that hour!

2. The Saviour will come,
   like rain on the earth,
   to harvest at last
   his crop of great worth.
   In patience await him,
   with firmness of mind;
   both mercy and judgement
   his people will find.

3. The Saviour will come,
   his truth we shall see:
   where lepers are cleansed
   and captives set free.
   No finely clad princeling
   in palace of gold,
   but Christ with his people,
   O wonder untold!

731 Basil E. Bridge (b. 1927)
© Basil E. Bridge

1. The Son of God proclaim,
   the Lord of time and space;
   the God who bade the light break forth
   now shines in Jesus' face.

2. He, God's creative word,
   the Church's Lord and head,
   here bids us gather as his friends
   and share his wine and bread.

3. The Lord of life and death
   with wond'ring praise we sing;
   we break the bread at his command
   and name him God and King.

4. We take this cup in hope;
   for he, who gladly bore
   the shameful cross, is ris'n again
   and reigns for evermore.

732 Damian Lundy (1944-1997)
© 1978, 1993 Kevin Mayhew Ltd

1. The Spirit lives to set us free,
   walk, walk in the light.
   He binds us all in unity,
   walk, walk in the light.

   Walk in the light, (x3)
   walk in the light of the Lord.

2. Jesus promised life to all,
   walk, walk in the light.
   The dead were wakened by his call,
   walk, walk in the light.

3. He died in pain on Calvary,
   walk, walk in the light,
   to save the lost like you and me,
   walk, walk in the light.

4. We know his death was not the end,
   walk, walk in the light.
   He gave his Spirit to be our friend,
   walk, walk in the light.

5. By Jesus' love our wounds are healed,
   walk, walk in the light.
   The Father's kindness is revealed,
   walk, walk in the light.

6. The Spirit lives in you and me,
   walk, walk in the light.
   His light will shine for all to see,
   walk, walk in the light.

733
Latin hymn (17th century)
trans. Francis Pott (1832-1909)

1. The strife is o'er, the battle done;
   now is the Victor's triumph won;
   O let the song of praise be sung:
   Alleluia, alleluia, alleluia.

2. Death's mightiest powers have done
        their worst,
   and Jesus hath his foes dispersed;
   let shouts of praise and joy outburst:
   Alleluia, alleluia, alleluia.

3. On the third morn he rose again
   glorious in majesty to reign;
   O let us swell the joyful strain:
   Alleluia, alleluia, alleluia.

4. Lord, by the stripes which wounded
        thee
   from death's dread sting thy servants
        free,
   that we may live, and sing to thee:
   Alleluia, alleluia, alleluia.

734
Traditional West Indian

1. The Virgin Mary had a baby boy,
   the Virgin Mary had a baby boy,
   the Virgin Mary had a baby boy,
   and they said that his name was Jesus.

   He came from the glory,
   he came from the glorious kingdom.
   He came from the glory,
   he came from the glorious kingdom.
   O yes, believer. O yes, believer.
   He came from the glory,
   he came from the glorious kingdom.

2. The angels sang when the baby was
        born, (x3)
   and proclaimed him the Saviour Jesus.

3. The wise men saw where the baby
        was born, (x3)
   and they saw that his name was Jesus.

735
Unknown

1. The wise man built his house
   upon the rock, *(x3)*
   and the rain came tumbling down.
   And the rain came down
   and the floods came up,
   the rain came down
   and the floods came up, } *(x2)*
   and the house on the rock stood firm.

2. The foolish man built his house
   upon the sand, *(x3)*
   and the rain came tumbling down.
   And the rain came down
   and the floods came up,
   the rain came down
   and the floods came up, } *(x2)*
   and the house on the sand fell flat.

736

Michael Forster (b. 1946)
© 1997 Kevin Mayhew Ltd

The world is full of smelly feet,
weary from the dusty street.
The world is full of smelly feet,
we'll wash them for each other.

1. Jesus said to his disciples,
   'Wash those weary toes!
   Do it in a cheerful fashion,
   never hold your nose!'

2. People on a dusty journey
   need a place to rest;
   Jesus says, 'You say you love me,
   this will be the test!'

3. We're his friends, we recognise him
   in the folk we meet;
   smart or scruffy, we'll still love him,
   wash his smelly feet!

3. Fountain of goodness,
   Jesus, Lord and God,
   cleanse us, unclean,
   with thy most cleansing blood;
   increase our faith and love,
   that we may know
   the hope and peace
   which from thy presence flow.

4. O Christ, whom now
   beneath a veil we see,
   may what we thirst for
   soon our portion be:
   to gaze on thee unveiled,
   and see thy face,
   the vision of thy glory
   and thy grace.

737

Thomas Aquinas (1227-1274)
trans. James Russell Woodford (1820-1885) alt.

1. Thee we adore,
   O hidden Saviour, thee
   who in thy sacrament
   art pleased to be;
   both flesh and spirit
   in thy presence fail,
   yet here thy presence
   we devoutly hail.

2. O blest memorial
   of our dying Lord,
   who living bread
   to all doth here afford;
   O may our souls
   for ever feed on thee,
   and thou, O Christ,
   for ever precious be.

738

John Gowans (b. 1934)
© Salvationist Publishing & Supplies
Administered by CopyCare

1. There are hundreds of sparrows,
   thousands, millions,
   they're two a penny, far too many
   there must be;
   there are hundreds and thousands,
   millions of sparrows,
   but God knows every one, and God
   knows me.

2. There are hundreds of flowers,
   thousands, millions,
   and flowers fair the meadows wear
   for all to see;
   there are hundreds and thousands,
   millions of flowers,
   but God knows every one, and God
   knows me.

3. There are hundreds of planets,
    thousands, millions,
    way out in space each has a place by
    God's decree;
    there are hundreds and thousands,
    millions of planets,
    but God knows every one, and God
    knows me.

4. There are hundreds of children,
    thousands, millions,
    and yet their names are written on
    God's memory;
    there are hundreds and thousands,
    millions of children,
    but God knows every one, and God
    knows me.

739
Erik Routley (1917-1982)
based on the Hungarian of Kiràly Imre von
Pécselyi (c. 1590-c. 1641)
© *Hinshaw Music Inc.*

1. There in God's garden stands the
    tree of wisdom
    whose leaves hold forth the healing
    of the nations:
    tree of all knowledge, tree of all
    compassion,
    tree of all beauty.

2. Its name is Jesus, name that says
    'Our Saviour':
    there on its branches see the scars of
    suff'ring:
    see where the tendrils of our human
    selfhood
    feed on his lifeblood.

3. Thorns not its own are tangled in its
    foliage;
    our greed has starved it, our despite
    has choked it;
    yet, look, it lives! Its grief has not
    destroyed it,
    nor fire consumed it.

4. See how its branches reach to us in
    welcome;
    hear what the voice says, 'Come to
    me, ye weary:
    give me your sickness, give me all
    your sorrow:
    I will give blessing.'

5. All heav'n is singing, 'Thanks to
    Christ whose Passion
    offers in mercy healing, strength and
    pardon:
    peoples and nations, take it, take it,
    freely.'
    Amen, my Master.

740 Cecil Frances Alexander (1818-1895) alt.

1. There is a green hill far away,
    outside a city wall,
    where the dear Lord was crucified
    who died to save us all.

2. We may not know, we cannot tell
    what pains he had to bear,
    but we believe it was for us
    he hung and suffered there.

3. He died that we might be forgiv'n,
    he died to make us good;
    that we might go at last to heav'n,
    saved by his precious blood.

4. There was no other good enough
    to pay the price of sin;
    he only could unlock the gate
    of heav'n, and let us in.

5. O, dearly, dearly has he loved,
    and we must love him too,
    and trust in his redeeming blood,
    and try his works to do.

741

Isaac Watts (1674-1748)

1. There is a land of pure delight,
   where saints immortal reign;
   infinite day excludes the night,
   and pleasures banish pain.

2. There everlasting spring abides,
   and never-with'ring flowers;
   death, like a narrow sea, divides
   that heav'nly land from ours.

3. Sweet fields beyond the swelling flood
   stand dressed in living green;
   so to the Jews old Canaan stood,
   while Jordan rolled between.

4. But tim'rous mortals start and shrink
   to cross the narrow sea,
   and linger shiv'ring on the brink,
   and fear to launch away.

5. O could we make our doubts remove,
   those gloomy doubts that rise,
   and see the Canaan that we love
   with unbeclouded eyes;

6. Could we but climb where Moses
      stood,
   and view the landscape o'er,
   not Jordan's stream, nor death's cold
      flood,
   should fright us from the shore!

742

Anne Quigley
© 1992 Anne Quigley
Published by GIA Publications

There is a longing in our hearts,
O Lord, for you to reveal youself to us.
There is a longing in our hearts for love
we only find in you, our God.

1. For justice, for freedom, for mercy:
   hear our prayer.
   In sorrow, in grief:
   be near, hear our prayer, O God.

2. For wisdom, for courage, for comfort:
   hear our prayer.
   In weakness, in fear:
   be near, hear our prayer, O God.

3. For healing, for wholeness, for new life:
   hear our prayer.
   In sickness, in death:
   be near, hear our prayer, O God.

4. Lord save us, take pity,
   light in our darkness.
   We call you, we wait:
   be near, hear our prayer, O God.

743

Melody Green (b. 1946), based on Scripture
© 1982 Ears To Hear Music/Birdwing Music/
BMG Songs Inc/EMI Christian Music Publishing
Administered by Kevin Mayhew Ltd

1. There is a Redeemer,
   Jesus, God's own Son,
   precious Lamb of God, Messiah,
   Holy One.

   Thank you, O my Father,
   for giving us your Son,
   and leaving your Spirit
   till the work on earth is done.

2. Jesus, my Redeemer,
   name above all names,
   precious Lamb of God, Messiah,
   O for sinners slain.

3. When I stand in glory,
   I will see his face,
   and there I'll serve my King for ever,
   in that holy place.

744
Paul Oakley
© 1995 Thankyou Music

1. There's a place where the streets shine
with the glory of the Lamb.
There's a way, we can go there,
we can live there beyond time.

Because of you, because of you,
because of your love,
because of your blood.

2. No more pain, no more sadness,
no more suff'ring, no more tears.
No more sin, no more sickness,
no injustice, no more death.

Because of you . . .

All our sins are washed away,
and we can live for ever,
now we have this hope,
because of you.
O, we'll see you face to face,
and we will dance together
in the city of our God,
because of you.

3. There is joy everlasting,
there is gladness, there is peace.
There is wine everflowing,
there's a wedding, there's a feast.

Because of you . . .

All our sins are washed away . . .

745
E. R. (Tedd) Smith
© 1973 Hope Publishing
Administered by CopyCare

1. There's a quiet understanding
when we're gathered in the Spirit:
it's a promise that he gives us
when we gather in his name.
There's a love we feel in Jesus,
there's a manna that he feeds us:
it's a promise that he gives us
when we gather in his name.

2. And we know when we're together,
sharing love and understanding,
that our brothers and our sisters
feel the oneness that he brings.
Thank you, thank you, thank you,
Jesus,
for the way you love and feed us,
for the many ways you lead us,
thank you, thank you, Lord.

746
Brian A. Wren (b. 1936)
© 1969, 1995 Stainer & Bell Ltd

1. There's a spirit in the air,
telling Christians everywhere:
'Praise the love that Christ revealed,
living, working, in our world!'

2. Lose your shyness, find your tongue,
tell the world what God has done:
God in Christ has come to stay.
Live tomorrow's life today!

3. When believers break the bread,
when a hungry child is fed,
praise the love that Christ revealed,
living, working, in our world.

4. Still the Spirit gives us light,
seeing wrong and setting right:
God in Christ has come to stay.
Live tomorrow's life today!

5. When a stranger's not alone,
where the homeless find a home,
praise the love that Christ revealed,
living, working, in our world.

6. May his Spirit fill our praise,
guide our thoughts and change our
ways.
God in Christ has come to stay.
Live tomorrow's life today!

7. There's a Spirit in the air,
   calling people everywhere:
   praise the love that Christ revealed,
   living, working, in our world.

747 Frederick William Faber (1814-1863) alt.

1. There's a wideness in God's mercy,
   like the wideness of the sea;
   there's a kindness in his justice,
   which is more than liberty.

2. There is no place where earth's sorrows
   are more felt than up in heav'n;
   there is no place where earth's failings
   have such kindly judgement giv'n.

3. For the love of God is broader
   than the scope of human mind,
   and the heart of the Eternal
   is most wonderfully kind.

4. But we make his love too narrow
   by false limits of our own;
   and we magnify his strictness
   with a zeal he will not own.

5. There is plentiful redemption
   in the blood that has been shed;
   there is joy for all the members
   in the sorrows of the Head.

6. If our love were but more simple,
   we should take him at his word;
   and our lives would be all gladness
   in the joy of Christ our Lord.

748 Robin Mark (b. 1955)
© 1996 Daybreak Music Ltd

1. These are the days of Elijah,
   declaring the word of the Lord;
   and these are the days of your
       servant, Moses,
   righteousness being restored.
   And though these are days of great
       trial,
   of famine and darkness and sword,
   still we are the voice in the desert
       crying,
   'Prepare ye the way of the Lord.'

   Behold, he comes riding on the clouds,
   shining like the sun at the trumpet call;
   lift your voice, it's the year of jubilee,
   out of Zion's hill salvation comes.

2. These are the days of Ezekiel,
   the dry bones becoming as flesh;
   and these are the days of your
       servant, David,
   rebuilding a temple of praise.
   These are the days of the harvest,
   the fields are as white in the world,
   and we are the labourers in your
       vineyard,
   declaring the word of the Lord.

749 Susan Sayers (b. 1946)
© 2004 Kevin Mayhew Ltd

1. These vows of love are taken,
   as rings of love received,
   we witness here among us a mystery
       believed:
   that in God's holy presence a
       marriage has begun
   and these your precious children have
       now become as one.

For the things of earth and heaven
draw closer as we pray,
and in heav'n the angels celebrate
with us on earth today.

2. For all our many blessings we offer
thanks and praise,
for gifts of love and fellowship our
thankful hearts we raise.
God's hand has held us safely and
brought us to this day,
God has guided and protected and
taught us on the way.
For the love we learn on earth is the
love we'll find in heav'n
and the human love we celebrate is
love that God has giv'n.

750 Edward Hayes Plumptre (1821-1891) alt.

1. Thine arm, O Lord, in days of old
was strong to heal and save;
it triumphed o'er disease and death,
o'er darkness and the grave:
to thee they went, the blind, the
dumb,
the palsied and the lame,
the outcasts with their grievances,
the sick with fevered frame.

2. And lo, thy touch brought life and
health,
gave speech and strength and sight;
and youth renewed and frenzy calmed
owned thee, the Lord of light:
and now, O Lord, be near to bless,
almighty as before,
in crowded street, by restless couch,
as by that ancient shore.

3. Be thou our great deliv'rer still,
thou Lord of life and death;
restore and quicken, soothe and bless,
with thine almighty breath:
to hands that work, and eyes that see,
give wisdom's heav'nly lore,
that whole and sick, and weak and
strong,
may praise thee evermore.

751 'À toi la gloire' by Edmond Louis Budry (1854-1932) trans. Richard Birch Hoyle (1875-1939)
© *Copyright Control*

1. Thine be the glory,
risen, conqu'ring Son,
endless is the vict'ry
thou o'er death hast won;
angels in bright raiment
rolled the stone away,
kept the folded grave-clothes
where thy body lay.

Thine be the glory,
risen, conqu'ring Son,
endless is the vict'ry
thou o'er death hast won.

2. Lo! Jesus meets us,
risen from the tomb;
lovingly he greets us,
scatters fear and gloom.
Let the Church with gladness
hymns of triumph sing,
for her Lord now liveth;
death hath lost its sting.

3. No more we doubt thee,
glorious Prince of Life!
Life is naught without thee:
aid us in our strife.
Make us more than conqu'rors
through thy deathless love.
Bring us safe through Jordan
to thy home above.

752
Mary Fawler Maude (1819-1913) alt.

1. Thine for ever! God of love,
   hear us from thy throne above;
   thine for ever may we be
   here and in eternity.

2. Thine for ever! Lord of life,
   shield us through our earthly strife;
   thou the life, the truth, the way,
   guide us to the realms of day.

3. Thine for ever! O how blest
   they who find in thee their rest!
   Saviour, guardian, heav'nly friend,
   O defend us to the end.

4. Thine for ever! Shepherd, keep
   us thy frail and trembling sheep;
   safe within thy tender care,
   let us all thy goodness share.

5. Thine for ever! thou our guide,
   all our wants by thee supplied,
   all our sins by thee forgiv'n,
   lead us, Lord, from earth to heav'n.

753
Doreen Newport (1927-2004)
© 1969, 1973 Stainer & Bell Ltd

1. Think of a world without any flowers,
   think of a world without any trees,
   think of a sky without any sunshine,
   think of the air without any breeze.
   We thank you, Lord, for flowers and
     trees and sunshine,
   we thank you, Lord, and praise your
     holy name.

2. Think of a world without any animals,
   think of a field without any herd,
   think of a stream without any fishes,
   think of a dawn without any bird.
   We thank you, Lord, for all your
     living creatures,
   we thank you, Lord, and praise your
     holy name.

3. Think of a world without any people,
   think of a street with no one living
     there,
   think of a town without any houses,
   no one to love and nobody to care.
   We thank you, Lord, for families and
     friendships,
   we thank you, Lord, and praise your
     holy name.

754
James Quinn (b. 1919), from 8th-century Irish
© Continuum International Publishing Group Ltd

1. This day God gives me strength of
     high heaven,
   sun and moon shining, flame in my
     hearth;
   flashing of lightning, wind in its
     swiftness,
   deeps of the ocean, firmness of earth.

2. This day God sends me strength as
     my steersman,
   might to uphold me, wisdom as guide.
   Your eyes are watchful, your ears are
     list'ning,
   your lips are speaking, friend at my
     side.

3. God's way is my way, God's shield is
     round me,
   God's host defends me, saving from ill;
   angels of heaven, drive from me always
   all that would harm me, stand by me
     still.

4. Rising, I thank you, mighty and
   strong one,
   King of creation, giver of rest,
   firmly confessing threeness of Persons,
   oneness of Godhead, Trinity blest.

Lord, I give you my heart,
I give you my soul;
I live for you alone.
Every breath that I take,
every moment I'm awake,
Lord, have your way in me.

755

vs. 1 and 2 Jimmy Owens (b. 1930)
© 1978 Bud John Songs/EMI Christian Music
Publishing. Administered by Kevin Mayhew Ltd
vs. 3-5 Damian Lundy (1944-1997)
© Kevin Mayhew Ltd

1. This is my body, broken for you,
   bringing you wholeness,
     making you free.
   Take it and eat it, and when you do,
   do it in love for me.

2. This is my blood, poured out for you,
   bringing forgiveness, making you free.
   Take it and drink it, and when you do,
   do it in love for me.

3. Back to my Father soon I shall go.
   Do not forget me; then you will see
   I am still with you, and you will know
   you're very close to me.

4. Filled with my Spirit, how you will
     grow!
   You are my branches; I am the tree.
   If you are faithful, others will know
   you are alive in me.

5. Love one another; I have loved you,
   and I have shown you how to be free;
   serve one another, and when you do,
   do it in love for me.

757

James Quinn (b. 1919)
© Continuum International Publishing Group Ltd

1. This is my will, my one command,
   that love should dwell among you all.
   This is my will that you should love
   as I have shown that I love you.

2. No greater love can be than this:
   to choose to die to save one's friends.
   You are my friends if you obey
   all I command that you should do.

3. I call you now no longer slaves;
   no slave knows all his master does.
   I call you friends, for all I hear
   my Father say, you hear from me.

4. You chose not me, but I chose you,
   that you should go and bear much
     fruit.
   I called you out that you in me
   should bear much fruit that will abide.

5. All that you ask my Father dear
   for my name's sake you shall receive.
   This is my will, my one command,
   that love should dwell in each, in all.

756

Reuben Morgan
© 1995 Reuben Morgan/Hillsongs Australia

This is my desire, to honour you.
Lord, with all my heart,
I worship you.
All I have within me I give you praise.
All that I adore is in you.

758

Marie Barnett
© 1995 Mercy/Vineyard Publishing

This is the air I breathe,
this is the air I breathe;
your holy presence living in me.

Continued overleaf

This is my daily bread,
this is my daily bread;
your very word spoken to me.

And I, I'm desp'rate for you.
And I, I'm lost without you.

759 Les Garrett (b. 1944)
© 1967 Scripture in Song/Integrity Music/
Sovereign Music UK

1. This is the day, this is the day
that the Lord has made,
that the Lord has made;
we will rejoice, we will rejoice
and be glad in it, and be glad in it.
This is the day that the Lord has made;
we will rejoice and be glad in it.
This is the day, this is the day
that the Lord has made.

2. This is the day, this is the day
when he rose again,
when he rose again;
we will rejoice, we will rejoice
and be glad in it, and be glad in it.
This is the day when he rose again;
we will rejoice and be glad in it.
This is the day, this is the day
when he rose again.

3. This is the day, this is the day
when the Spirit came,
when the Spirit came;
we will rejoice, we will rejoice
and be glad in it, and be glad in it.
This is the day when the Spirit came;
we will rejoice and be glad in it.
This is the day, this is the day
when the Spirit came.

760 Isaac Watts (1674-1748)

1. This is the day the Lord has made,
he calls the hours his own:
let heav'n rejoice, let earth be glad,
and praise surround his throne.

2. Today he rose and left the dead,
and Satan's empire fell;
today the saints his triumphs spread,
and all his wonders tell.

3. Hosanna to th'anointed King,
to David's holy Son!
Make haste to help us, Lord, and bring
salvation from thy throne.

4. Blest be the Lord: let us proclaim
his messages of grace;
who comes, in God his Father's name,
to save our sinful race.

5. Hosanna in the highest strains
the Church on earth can raise;
the highest heav'ns in which he reigns
shall give him nobler praise.

761 George Ratcliffe Woodward (1848-1934)

1. This joyful Eastertide,
away with sin and sorrow.
My love, the Crucified,
hath sprung to life this morrow.

Had Christ, that once was slain,
ne'er burst his three-day prison,
our faith had been in vain:
but now hath Christ arisen,
arisen, arisen, arisen.

2. My flesh in hope shall rest,
and for a season slumber;
till trump from east to west
shall wake the dead in number.

3. Death's flood hath lost its chill,
   since Jesus crossed the river:
   lover of souls, from ill
   my passing soul deliver.

762 Traditional

This little light of mine,
I'm gonna let it shine, } x3
let it shine, let it shine, let it shine.

1. The light that shines is the light of love,
   lights the darkness from above,
   it shines on me and it shines on you,
   and shows what the power of love
   can do.
   I'm gonna shine my light both far
   and near,
   I'm gonna shine my light both bright
   and clear.
   Where there's a dark corner in this
   land,
   I'm gonna let my little light shine.

2. On Monday he gave me the gift of
   love,
   Tuesday peace came from above.
   On Wednesday he told me to have
   more faith,
   on Thursday he gave me a little more
   grace.
   On Friday he told me to watch and
   pray,
   on Saturday he told me just what to
   say,
   on Sunday he gave me the power
   divine
   to let my little light shine.

763 Susan Sayers (b. 1946)
© 1991 Kevin Mayhew Ltd

This world you have made
is a beautiful place:
it tells the power of your love.
We rejoice in the beauty
of your world,
from the seas
to the heavens above.

1. The morning whispers of purity;
   the evening of your peace;
   the thunder booms your exuberance
   in the awesome power you release.

2. The tenderness of a new-born child;
   the gentleness of the rain;
   simplicity in a single cell;
   and complexity in a brain.

3. Your stillness rests in a silent pool;
   infinity drifts in space;
   your grandeur straddles the mountain
   tops;
   and we see your face in each face.

764 William Walsham How (1823-1897)

1. Thou art the Christ, O Lord,
   the Son of God most high:
   for ever be adored that name
   in earth and sky,
   in which, though mortal strength
   may fail,
   the saints of God at last prevail.

2. O surely he was blest
   with blessedness unpriced,
   who, taught of God, confessed
   the Godhead in the Christ;
   for of thy church, Lord, thou didst
   own
   thy saint a true foundation-stone.

Continued overleaf

3. Thrice fallen, thrice restored,
   the bitter lesson learnt,
   that heart for thee, O Lord,
   with triple ardour burnt.
   The cross he took he laid not down
   until he grasped the martyr's crown.

4. O bright triumphant faith,
   O courage void of fears,
   O love most strong in death,
   O penitential tears!
   By these, Lord, keep us lest we fall,
   and make us go where thou shalt call.

765
George Washington Doane (1799-1859)
based on John 14

1. Thou art the Way: by thee alone
   from sin and death we flee;
   and all who would the Father seek
   must seek him, Lord, by thee.

2. Thou art the Truth: thy word alone
   true wisdom can impart;
   thou only canst inform the mind
   and purify the heart.

3. Thou art the Life: the rending tomb
   proclaims thy conqu'ring arm;
   and those who put their trust in thee
   nor death nor hell shall harm.

4. Thou art the Way, the Truth, the Life:
   grant us that Way to know,
   that Truth to keep, that Life to win,
   whose joys eternal flow.

766
Emily Elizabeth Steele Elliott (1836-1897)
based on Luke 2:7
adapted by Michael Forster (b. 1946)
This version © 1996 Kevin Mayhew Ltd

1. Thou didst leave thy throne
   and thy kingly crown
   when thou camest to earth for me,

but in Bethlehem's home
was there found no room
for thy holy nativity.

O come to my heart, Lord Jesus,
there is room in my heart for thee.

2. Heaven's arches rang
   when the angels sang
   and proclaimed thee of royal degree,
   but in lowliest birth
   didst thou come to earth
   and in deepest humility.

3. Though the fox found rest,
   and the bird its nest
   in the shade of the cedar tree,
   yet the world found no bed
   for the Saviour's head
   in the desert of Galilee.

4. Though thou camest, Lord,
   with the living word
   that should set all thy people free,
   yet with treachery, scorn
   and a crown of thorn
   did they bear thee to Calvary.

5. When the heavens shall ring
   and the angels sing
   at thy coming to victory,
   let thy voice call me home,
   saying 'Heaven has room,
   there is room at my side for thee.'

767
John Marriott (1780-1825) alt.

1. Thou, whose almighty word
   chaos and darkness heard,
   and took their flight;
   hear us, we humbly pray,
   and where the gospel day
   sheds not its glorious ray,
   let there be light.

2. Thou, who didst come to bring
on thy redeeming wing,
healing and sight,
health to the sick in mind,
sight to the inly blind,
O now to humankind
let there be light.

3. Spirit of truth and love,
life-giving, holy Dove,
speed forth thy flight;
move on the water's face,
bearing the lamp of grace,
and in earth's darkest place
let there be light.

4. Holy and blessèd Three,
glorious Trinity,
Wisdom, Love, Might;
boundless as ocean's tide
rolling in fullest pride,
through the earth far and wide
let there be light.

768 Timothy Dudley-Smith (b. 1926)
© Timothy Dudley-Smith

1. Though pilgrim strangers here below,
we ask, as through the world we go,
to plant a flower, to pluck a weed,
to serve unsought a neighbour's need:
and to our children leave behind
a better world for humankind.

2. A friendlier world be theirs, we pray,
through lessons learned by us today;
where all shall cherish, all shall share,
the earth which God created fair:
where fear, disease and famine cease,
and peoples learn to live in peace.

3. O Prince of peace, whose reign on
earth
brings freedom, light and hope to
birth,
may we and all who name your Name
the love of God in Christ proclaim:
in Christ, by whom are sins forgiv'n,
the Life, the Truth, the Way to heav'n.

769 Psalm 34 in *New Version* (Tate and Brady, 1696)

1. Through all the changing scenes of life,
in trouble and in joy,
the praises of my God shall still
my heart and tongue employ.

2. O magnify the Lord with me,
with me exalt his name;
when in distress to him I called,
he to my rescue came.

3. The hosts of God encamp around
the dwellings of the just;
deliv'rance he affords to all
who on his succour trust.

4. O make but trial of his love:
experience will decide
how blest are they, and only they,
who in his truth confide.

5. Fear him, ye saints, and you will then
have nothing else to fear;
make you his service your delight,
your wants shall be his care.

6. To Father, Son and Holy Ghost,
the God whom we adore,
be glory as it was, is now,
and shall be evermore.

770 Bernhardt Severin Ingemann (1789-1862)
trans. Sabine Baring-Gould (1834-1924) alt.

1. Through the night of doubt and
   sorrow
   onward goes the pilgrim band,
   singing songs of expectation,
   marching to the promised land.
   Clear before us, through the darkness,
   gleams and burns the guiding light;
   so we march in hope united,
   stepping fearless through the night.

2. One the light of God's own presence
   o'er his ransomed people shed,
   chasing far the gloom and terror,
   bright'ning all the path we tread.
   One the object of our journey,
   one the faith which never tires,
   one the earnest looking forward,
   one the hope our God inspires.

3. One the strain that lips of thousands
   lift as from the heart of one:
   one the conflict, one the peril,
   one the march in God begun.
   One the gladness of rejoicing
   on the far eternal shore,
   where the one almighty Father
   reigns in love for evermore.

4. Onward, therefore, fellow pilgrims,
   onward with the Cross our aid;
   bear its shame and fight its battle,
   till we rest beneath its shade.
   Soon shall come the great awaking,
   soon the rending of the tomb;
   then the scatt'ring of all shadows,
   and the end of toil and gloom.

771 Traditional South African
© 1990 Wild Goose Publications, Iona Community

1. *Thuma mina. Thuma mina,*
   thuma mina, thuma mina Somandla.

2. Send me, Jesus, send me, Jesus,
   send me, Jesus, send me, Lord.

3. Lead me, . . .

4. Fill me, Lord . . .

5. Thuma mina . . .

772 Edward Hayes Plumptre (1821-1891) alt.

1. Thy hand, O God, has guided
   thy flock, from age to age;
   the wondrous tale is written,
   full clear, on every page;
   our forebears owned thy goodness,
   and we their deeds record;
   and both of this bear witness:
   one Church, one Faith, one Lord.

2. Thy heralds brought glad tidings
   to greatest, as to least;
   they bade them rise, and hasten
   to share the great King's feast;
   and this was all their teaching,
   in every deed and word,
   to all alike proclaiming:
   one Church, one Faith, one Lord.

3. When shadows thick were falling,
   and all seemed sunk in night,
   thou, Lord, didst send thy servants,
   thy chosen sons of light.
   On them and on thy people
   thy plenteous grace was poured,
   and this was still their message:
   one Church, one Faith, one Lord.

4. Through many a day of darkness,
   through many a scene of strife,
   the faithful few fought bravely
   to guard the nation's life.
   Their gospel of redemption,
   sin pardoned, hope restored,
   was all in this enfolded:
   one Church, one Faith, one Lord.

5. And we, shall we be faithless?
   Shall hearts fail, hands hang down?
   Shall we evade the conflict,
   and cast away our crown?
   Not so: in God's deep counsels
   some better thing is stored:
   we will maintain, unflinching,
   one Church, one Faith, one Lord.

6. Thy mercy will not fail us,
   nor leave thy work undone;
   with thy right hand to help us,
   the vict'ry shall be won;
   and then by all creation,
   thy name shall be adored.
   And this shall be their anthem:
   One Church, one Faith, one Lord.

773 Frederick Lucian Hosmer (1840-1929)

1. Thy kingdom come! on bended knee
   the passing ages pray;
   and faithful souls have yearned to see
   on earth that kingdom's day.

2. But the slow watches of the night
   not less to God belong;
   and for the everlasting right
   the silent stars are strong.

3. And lo, already on the hills
   the flags of dawn appear;
   gird up your loins, ye prophet souls,
   proclaim the day is near.

4. The day in whose clear-shining light
   all wrong shall stand revealed,
   when justice shall be throned in might,
   and every hurt be healed.

5. When knowledge, hand in hand with
   peace,
   shall walk the earth abroad:
   the day of perfect righteousness,
   the promised day of God.

774 Lewis Hensley (1824-1905) alt.

1. Thy kingdom come, O God,
   thy rule, O Christ, begin;
   break with thine iron rod
   the tyrannies of sin.

2. Where is thy reign of peace
   and purity and love?
   When shall all hatred cease,
   as in the realms above?

3. When comes the promised time
   that war shall be no more,
   and lust, oppression, crime
   shall flee thy face before?

4. We pray thee, Lord, arise,
   and come in thy great might;
   revive our longing eyes,
   which languish for thy sight.

5. Some scorn thy sacred name,
   and wolves devour thy fold;
   by many deeds of shame
   we learn that love grows cold.

6. O'er lands both near and far
   thick darkness broodeth yet:
   arise, O morning star,
   arise, and never set.

775
J. Armitage Robinson (1858-1933)

1. 'Tis good, Lord, to be here,
thy glory fills the night;
thy face and garments, like the sun,
shine with unborrowed light.

2. 'Tis good, Lord, to be here,
thy beauty to behold,
where Moses and Elijah stand,
thy messengers of old.

3. Fulfiller of the past,
promise of things to be,
we hail thy body glorified,
and our redemption see.

4. Before we taste of death,
we see thy kingdom come;
we fain would hold the vision bright,
and make this hill our home.

5. 'Tis good, Lord, to be here,
yet we may not remain;
but since thou bidst us leave the
   mount,
come with us to the plain.

776
Noel Richards (b. 1955)
© 1991 Thankyou Music

1. To be in your presence,
to sit at your feet,
where your love surrounds me
and makes me complete.

This is my desire, O Lord,
this is my desire,
this is my desire, O Lord,
this is my desire.

2. To rest in your presence,
not rushing away,
to cherish each moment,
here I would stay.

777
Frances Jane van Alstyne
(Fanny J. Crosby) (1820-1915)

1. To God be the glory!
great things he hath done;
so loved he the world
that he gave us his Son;
who yielded his life
an atonement for sin,
and opened the life-gate
that all may go in.

Praise the Lord, praise the Lord!
let the earth hear his voice;
praise the Lord, praise the Lord!
let the people rejoice:
O come to the Father,
through Jesus the Son,
and give him the glory;
great things he hath done!

2. O perfect redemption,
the purchase of blood!
to every believer
the promise of God;
the vilest offender
who truly believes,
that moment from Jesus
a pardon receives.

3. Great things he hath taught us,
great things he hath done,
and great our rejoicing
through Jesus the Son;
but purer, and higher,
and greater will be
our wonder, our rapture,
when Jesus we see.

778 Fred Pratt Green (1903-2000)
© 1973 Stainer & Bell Ltd

1. To mock your reign, O dearest Lord,
they made a crown of thorns;
set you with taunts along that road
from which no one returns.
They could not know, as we do now,
how glorious is that crown:
that thorns would flower upon your
brow,
your sorrows heal our own.

2. In mock acclaim, O gracious Lord,
they snatched a purple cloak,
your passion turned, for all they cared,
into a soldier's joke.
They could not know, as we do now,
that, though we merit blame,
you will your robe of mercy throw
around our naked shame.

3. A sceptred reed, O patient Lord,
they thrust into your hand,
and acted out their grim charade
to its appointed end.
They could not know, as we do now,
though empires rise and fall,
your kingdom shall not cease to grow
till love embraces all.

ear and heart delighting well;
name of sweetness passing measure,
saving us from sin and hell.

*3. 'Tis the name for adoration,
name for songs of victory;
name for holy meditation
in the vale of misery;
name for joyful veneration
by the citizens on high.

*4. 'Tis the name that whoso preacheth
speaks like music to the ear;
who in prayer this name beseecheth
sweetest comfort findeth near;
who its perfect wisdom reacheth
heav'nly joy possesseth here.

5. Jesus is the name exalted
over every other name;
in this name, whene'er assaulted,
we can put our foes to shame:
strength to them who else had halted,
eyes to blind, and feet to lame.

6. Therefore we in love adoring
this most blessèd name revere,
holy Jesus, thee imploring
so to write it in us here,
that hereafter, heav'nward soaring,
we may sing with angels there.

779 'Gloriosi Salvatoris' (15th century)
trans. John Mason Neale (1818-1866) alt.

1. To the name of our salvation
laud and honour let us pay,
which for many a generation
hid in God's foreknowledge lay,
but with holy exultation
we may sing aloud today.

2. Jesus is the name we treasure,
name beyond what words can tell;
name of gladness, name of pleasure,

780 William Chatterton Dix (1837-1898) alt.

1. To thee, O Lord, our hearts we raise
in hymns of adoration;
to thee bring sacrifice of praise
with shouts of exultation:
bright robes of gold the fields adorn,
the hills with joy are ringing,
the valleys stand so thick with corn
that even they are singing.

Continued overleaf

2. And now, on this our festal day,
   thy bounteous hand confessing,
   upon thine altar, Lord, we lay
   the first-fruits of thy blessing:
   by thee our souls are truly fed
   with gifts of grace supernal;
   thou who dost give us earthly bread,
   give us the bread eternal.

3. We bear the burden of the day,
   and often toil seems dreary;
   but labour ends with sunset ray,
   and rest comes for the weary:
   may we, the angel-reaping o'er,
   stand at the last accepted,
   Christ's golden sheaves for evermore
   to garners bright elected.

4. O blessèd is that land of God,
   where saints abide for ever;
   where golden fields spread far and
       broad,
   where flows the crystal river:
   the strains of all its holy throng
   with ours today are blending;
   thrice blessèd is that harvest-song
   which never hath an ending.

781 Taizé Community
© *Ateliers et Presses de Taizé*

Ubi caritas et amor.
Ubi caritas Deus ibi est.

Translation: Where there is charity
           and love, there is God.

1. Your love, O Jesus Christ,
   has gathered us together.

2. May your love, O Jesus Christ,
   be foremost in our lives.

3. Let us love one another
   as God has loved us.

4. Let us be one in love together
   in the one bread of Christ.

5. The love of God in Jesus Christ
   bears eternal joy.

6. The love of God in Jesus Christ
   will never have an end.

782 'Puer nobis nascitur' (15th century)
trans. Percy Dearmer (1867-1936) alt.

1. Unto us a boy is born!
   King of all creation;
   came he to a world forlorn,
   the Lord of every nation,
   the Lord of every nation.

2. Cradled in a stall was he,
   watched by cows and asses;
   but the very beasts could see
   that he the world surpasses,
   that he the world surpasses.

3. Then the fearful Herod cried,
   'Power is mine in Jewry!'
   So the blameless children died
   the victims of his fury,
   the victims of his fury.

4. Now may Mary's Son, who came
   long ago to love us,
   lead us all with hearts aflame
   unto the joys above us,
   unto the joys above us.

5. Omega and Alpha he!
   Let the organ thunder,
   while the choir with peals of glee
   shall rend the air asunder,
   shall rend the air asunder.

783
Stephen Langton (1160-1228)

Veni, lumen cordium.
Veni, Sancte Spiritus.

Translation: Come, light of our hearts.
Come, Holy Spirit, come.

784
Reginald Heber (1783-1826)

1. Virgin-born, we bow before thee:
   blessèd was the womb that bore thee;
   Mary, maid and mother mild,
   blessèd was she in her child.

2. Blessèd was the breast that fed thee;
   blessèd was the hand that led thee;
   blessèd was the parent's eye
   that watched thy slumb'ring infancy.

3. Blessèd she by all creation,
   who brought forth the world's
        salvation,
   blessèd they, for ever blest,
   who love thee most and serve thee best.

4. Virgin-born, we bow before thee:
   blessèd was the womb that bore thee;
   Mary, maid and mother mild,
   blessèd was she in her child.

785
Taizé Community, based on Scripture
© Ateliers et Presses de Taizé

Wait for the Lord, whose day is near.
Wait for the Lord: keep watch take heart!

1. Prepare the way for the Lord.
   Make a straight path for God.
   Prepare the way for the Lord.

2. Rejoice in the Lord always:
      God is at hand.
   Joy and gladness for all who seek the
      Lord.

3. The glory of the Lord shall be revealed.
   All the earth will see the Lord.

4. I waited for the Lord.
   God heard my cry.

5. Our eyes are fixed on the Lord our
      God.

6. Seek first the kingdom of God.
   Seek and you shall find.

7. O Lord show us your way.
   Guide us in your truth.

786
Philipp Nicolai (1556-1608)
trans. Francis Crawford Burkitt (1864-1935) alt.

1. Wake, O wake! with tidings thrilling
   the watchmen all
   the air are filling:
   arise, Jerusalem, arise!
   Midnight strikes! no more delaying,
   'The hour has come!'
   we hear them saying.
   Where are ye all, ye maidens wise?
   The Bridegroom comes in sight,
   raise high your torches bright!
   Alleluia!
   The wedding song
   swells loud and strong:
   go forth and join the festal throng.

Continued overleaf

2. Sion hears the watchmen shouting,
   her heart leaps up
   with joy undoubting,
   she stands and waits with eager eyes;
   see her Friend from heav'n
      descending,
   adorned with truth
   and grace unending!
   her light burns clear, her star doth rise.
   Now come, thou precious Crown,
   Lord Jesu, God's own son!
   Hosanna!
   Let us prepare
   to follow there,
   where in thy supper we may share.

3. Every soul in thee rejoices;
   from earthly and
   angelic voices
   be glory giv'n to thee alone!
   Now the gates of pearl receive us,
   thy presence never more
   shall leave us,
   we stand with angels round thy throne.
   Earth cannot give below
   the bliss thou dost bestow.
   Alleluia!
   Grant us to raise,
   to length of days,
   the triumph-chorus of thy praise.

787 Michael Forster (b. 1946)
© 1993 Kevin Mayhew Ltd

1. Waken, O sleeper, wake and rise,
   salvation's day is near,
   and let the dawn of light and truth
   dispel the night of fear.

2. Let us prepare to face the day
   of judgement and of grace,
   to live as people of the light,
   and perfect truth embrace.

3. Watch then and pray, we cannot know
   the moment or the hour,
   when Christ, unheralded, will come
   with life-renewing power.

4. Then shall the nations gather round
   as futile conflicts cease,
   and re-invest the means of war
   in justice, truth and peace.

788 Estelle White (b. 1925)
© 1976 Kevin Mayhew Ltd

Walk with me, O my Lord,
through the darkest night and brightest
   day.
Be at my side, O Lord,
hold my hand and guide me on my way.

1. Sometimes the road seems long,
   my energy is spent.
   Then, Lord, I think of you
   and I am given strength.

2. Stones often bar my path
   and there are times I fall,
   but you are always there
   to help me when I call.

3. Just as you calmed the wind
   and walked upon the sea,
   conquer, my living Lord,
   the storms that threaten me.

4. Help me to pierce the mists
   that cloud my heart and mind,
   so that I shall not fear
   the steepest mountain-side.

5. As once you healed the lame
   and gave sight to the blind,
   help me when I'm downcast
   to hold my head up high.

789

Traditional South African
v. 1 trans. Anders Nyberg (b. 1955);
vs. 2 and 3 trans. Andrew Maries (b. 1949)
v. 1 © 1990 Wild Goose Publications, Iona
Community, vs. 2 and 3 Sovereign Music UK

1. We are marching in the light of God.
   (x4)
   We are marching,
   Oo-ooh! We are marching in the
   light of God. *(Repeat)*

2. We are living in the love of God . . .

3. We are moving in the power of
   God . . .

790

Graham Kendrick (b. 1950)
© 1986 Thankyou Music

1. We believe in God the Father,
   maker of the universe,
   and in Christ, his Son our Saviour,
   come to us by virgin birth.
   We believe he died to save us,
   bore our sins, was crucified;
   then from death he rose victorious,
   ascended to the Father's side.

   Jesus, Lord of all, Lord of all; (x4)
   name above all names,
   name above all names!

2. We believe he sends his Spirit
   on his Church with gifts of power;
   God, his word of truth affirming,
   sends us to the nations now.
   He will come again in glory,
   judge the living and the dead:
   every knee shall bow before him,
   then must every tongue confess.

791

Viola Grafstrom
© 1996 Thankyou Music

We bow down and confess
you are Lord in this place.
We bow down and confess
you are Lord in this place.
You are all I need;
it's your face I seek.
In the presence of your light
we bow down, we bow down.

792

The Iona Community
© 1989 WGRG/Iona Community

1. We cannot measure how you heal
   or answer every sufferer's prayer,
   yet we believe your grace responds
   where faith and doubt unite to care.
   Your hands, though bloodied on the
   cross,
   survive to hold and heal and warn,
   to carry all through death to life
   and cradle children yet unborn.

2. The pain that will not go away,
   the guilt that clings from things long
   past,
   the fear of what the future holds,
   are present as if meant to last.
   But present too is love which tends
   the hurt we never hoped to find,
   the private agonies inside,
   the memories that haunt the mind.

3. So some have come who need your
   help
   and some have come to make amends,
   as hands which shaped and saved the
   world
   are present in the touch of friends.
   Lord, let your Spirit meet us here
   to mend the body, mind and soul,
   to disentangle peace from pain
   and make your broken people whole.

793

Susan Mee (b. 1946)
© 1995 Kevin Mayhew Ltd

1. We eat the plants that grow from the
    seed,
   but it's God who gives the harvest.
   Cures can be made from herbs and
       from weeds,
   but it's God who gives the harvest.
   Everything beneath the sun,
   all the things we claim we've done,
   all are part of God's creation:
   we can meet people's needs
   with things we grow from seed,
   but it's God who gives the harvest.

2. We find the iron and turn it into steel,
   but it's God who gives the harvest.
   We pull the levers, we turn the wheels,
   but it's God who gives the harvest.
   Everything we say we've made,
   plastic bags to metal spades,
   all are part of God's creation:
   we can make lots of things
   from microchips to springs,
   but it's God who gives the harvest.

794

Susan Sayers (b. 1946)
© 2004 Kevin Mayhew Ltd

1. We gather here, we gather now,
   drawn by the love we know and share.
   We come to celebrate in our joy
   the union of this bridal pair.
   To them our hearts reach out with love,
   on them the light of heav'n above
   shines down in grace abundant and
       free
   to bless them both eternally.

2. And we who join to wish them well,
   offer them both our love and prayer
   that they may walk in fullness of life
   the journey they have come to share.

That they may know if storms come
    near
that they have friends and fam'ly here
for we commit ourselves to pray
and love and cherish them each day.

795

Isaac Watts (1674-1748)

1. We give immortal praise
   to God the Father's love
   for all our comforts here
   and better hopes above:
   he sent his own
   eternal Son,
   to die for sins
   that we had done.

2. To God the Son belongs
   immortal glory too,
   who bought us with his blood
   from everlasting woe:
   and now he lives,
   and now he reigns,
   and sees the fruit
   of all his pains.

3. To God the Spirit's name
   immortal worship give,
   whose new-creating power
   makes the dead sinner live:
   his work completes
   the great design,
   and fills the soul
   with joy divine.

4. To God the Trinity
   be endless honours done,
   the undivided Three,
   and the mysterious One:
   where reason fails
   with all her powers,
   there faith prevails,
   and love adores.

796
Richard Godfrey Parsons (1882-1948)
© Copyright Control

1. We hail thy presence glorious,
   O Christ our great High Priest,
   o'er sin and death victorious,
   at thy thanksgiving feast:
   as thou art interceding
   for us in heav'n above,
   thy Church on earth is pleading
   thy perfect work of love.

2. Through thee in every nation
   thine own their hearts upraise,
   off'ring one pure oblation,
   one sacrifice of praise:
   with thee in blest communion
   the living and the dead
   are joined in closest union,
   one Body with one Head.

3. O living bread from heaven,
   Jesu, our Saviour good,
   who thine own self hast given
   to be our souls' true food;
   for us thy body broken
   hung on the cross of shame:
   this bread its hallowed token
   we break in thy dear name.

4. O stream of love unending,
   poured from the one true vine,
   with our weak nature blending
   the strength of life divine;
   our thankful faith confessing
   in thy life-blood outpoured,
   we drink this cup of blessing
   and praise thy name, O Lord.

5. May we, thy word believing,
   thee through thy gifts receive,
   that, thou within us living,
   we all to God may live;
   draw us from earth to heaven
   till sin and sorrow cease,
   forgiving and forgiven,
   in love and joy and peace.

797
Michael Forster (b. 1946)
based on the speech by Martin Luther King Jr.
© 1997 Kevin Mayhew Ltd

1. We have a dream:
   this nation will arise,
   and truly live
   according to its creed,
   that all are equal
   in their maker's eyes,
   and none shall suffer
   through another's greed.

2. We have a dream
   that one day we shall see
   a world of justice,
   truth and equity,
   where sons of slaves
   and daughters of the free
   will share the banquet
   of community.

*3. We have a dream
   of deserts brought to flower
   once made infertile
   by oppression's heat,
   when love and truth
   shall end oppressive power,
   and streams of righteousness
   and justice meet.

*4. We have a dream:
   our children shall be free
   from judgements based on
   colour or on race;
   free to become
   whatever they may be,
   of their own choosing
   in the light of grace.

5. We have a dream
   that truth will overcome
   the fear and anger
   of our present day;

Continued overleaf

that black and white
will share a common home,
and hand in hand
will walk the pilgrim way.

6. We have a dream:
each valley will be raised,
and every mountain,
every hill brought down;
then shall creation
echo perfect praise,
and share God's glory
under freedom's crown!

798 Edward Joseph Burns (b. 1938)
© *The Revd Edward J. Burns*

1. We have a gospel to proclaim,
good news for all throughout the earth;
the gospel of a Saviour's name:
we sing his glory, tell his worth.

2. Tell of his birth at Bethlehem,
not in a royal house or hall,
but in a stable dark and dim,
the Word made flesh, a light for all.

3. Tell of his death at Calvary,
hated by those he came to save;
in lonely suff'ring on the cross:
for all he loved, his life he gave.

4. Tell of that glorious Easter morn,
empty the tomb, for he was free;
he broke the power of death and hell
that we might share his victory.

5. Tell of his reign at God's right hand,
by all creation glorified.
He sends his Spirit on his Church
to live for him, the Lamb who died.

6. Now we rejoice to name him King:
Jesus is Lord of all the earth.
This gospel-message we proclaim:
we sing his glory, tell his worth.

799 Fred Kaan (b. 1929)
© *1968 Stainer & Bell Ltd*

1. We have a King who rides a donkey,
(x3)
and his name is Jesus.

Jesus the King is risen, (x3)
early in the morning.

2. Trees are waving a royal welcome *(x3)*
for the King called Jesus.

3. We have a King who cares for people
(x3)
and his name is Jesus.

4. A loaf and a cup upon the table, *(x3)*
bread-and-wine is Jesus.

5. We have a King with a bowl and
towel, *(x3)*
Servant-King is Jesus.

6. What shall we do with our life this
morning? *(x3)*
Give it up in service!

Verse 4 is suitable for Communion.

800 William Bullock (1798-1874) and
Henry Williams Baker (1821-1877)

1. We love the place, O God,
wherein thine honour dwells;
the joy of thine abode
all earthly joy excels.

2. It is the house of prayer,
wherein thy servants meet;
and thou, O Lord, art there
thy chosen flock to greet.

3. We love the sacred font;
for there the holy Dove
to pour is ever wont
his blessing from above.

4. We love thine altar, Lord;
   O what on earth so dear?
   For there, in faith adored,
   we find thy presence near.

5. We love the word of life,
   the word that tells of peace,
   of comfort in the strife,
   and joys that never cease.

6. We love to sing below
   for mercies freely giv'n;
   but O, we long to know
   the triumph-song of heav'n.

7. Lord Jesus, give us grace
   on earth to love thee more,
   in heav'n to see thy face,
   and with thy saints adore.

801 Matthias Claudius (1740-1815)
trans. Jane Montgomery Campbell
(1817-1878) alt.

1. We plough the fields and scatter
   the good seed on the land,
   but it is fed and watered
   by God's almighty hand:
   he sends the snow in winter,
   the warmth to swell the grain,
   the breezes and the sunshine,
   and soft, refreshing rain.

   All good gifts around us
   are sent from heaven above;
   then thank the Lord, O thank the Lord,
   for all his love.

2. He only is the maker
   of all things near and far;
   he paints the wayside flower,
   he lights the evening star;
   he fills the earth with beauty,
   by him the birds are fed;
   much more to us, his children,
   he gives our daily bread.

3. We thank thee then, O Father,
   for all things bright and good:
   the seed-time and the harvest,
   our life, our health, our food.
   Accept the gifts we offer
   for all thy love imparts,
   and, what thou most desirest,
   our humble, thankful hearts.

802 Judith Beatrice O'Neill (b. 1930)
© *Judith Beatrice O'Neill*

1. We praise you, Lord, for Jesus Christ
   who died and rose again;
   he lives to break the power of sin,
   and over death to reign.

2. We praise you that this child now
   shares
   the freedom Christ can give,
   has died to sin with Christ, and now
   with Christ is raised to live.

3. We praise you, Lord, that now this
   child
   is grafted to the vine,
   is made a member of your house
   and bears the cross as sign.

4. We praise you, Lord, for Jesus Christ;
   he loves this child we bring:
   he frees, forgives, and heals us all,
   he gives and reigns as King.

803 Vincent Stuckey Stratton Coles (1845-1929)

1. We pray thee, heavenly Father,
   to hear us in thy love,
   and pour upon thy children
   the unction from above;
   that so in love abiding,
   from all defilement free,
   we may in pureness offer
   our Eucharist to thee.

Continued overleaf

2. Be thou our guide and helper,
   O Jesus Christ, we pray;
   so may we well approach thee,
   if thou wilt be the Way:
   thou, very Truth, hast promised
   to help us in our strife,
   food of the weary pilgrim,
   eternal source of life.

3. And thou, creator Spirit,
   look on us, we are thine;
   renew in us thy graces,
   upon our darkness shine;
   that, with thy benediction
   upon our souls outpoured,
   we may receive in gladness
   the body of the Lord.

4. O Trinity of Persons,
   O Unity most high,
   on thee alone relying
   thy servants would draw nigh:
   unworthy in our weakness,
   on thee our hope is stayed,
   and blessed by thy forgiveness
   we will not be afraid.

804 Thomas Kelly (1769-1855) alt.

1. We sing the praise of him who died,
   of him who died upon the cross;
   the sinner's hope, though all deride,
   will turn to gain this bitter loss.

2. Inscribed upon the cross we see
   in shining letters, 'God is love';
   he bears our sins upon the tree;
   he brings us mercy from above.

3. The cross! it takes our guilt away:
   it holds the fainting spirit up;
   it cheers with hope the gloomy day,
   and sweetens every bitter cup.

4. It makes the coward spirit brave
   to face the darkness of the night;
   it takes the terror from the grave,
   and gilds the bed of death with light.

5. The balm of life, the cure of woe,
   the measure and the pledge of love,
   the sinner's refuge here below,
   the angels' theme in heaven above.

805 John Henry Hopkins (1820-1891), alt.

1. We three kings of Orient are;
   bearing gifts we traverse afar;
   field and fountain, moor and
       mountain,
   following yonder star.

   O star of wonder, star of night,
   star with royal beauty bright,
   westward leading, still proceeding,
   guide us to thy perfect light.

2. Born a King on Bethlehem plain,
   gold I bring, to crown him again,
   King for ever, ceasing never,
   over us all to reign.

3. Frankincense to offer have I,
   incense owns a Deity nigh,
   prayer and praising, gladly raising,
   worship him, God most high.

4. Myrrh is mine, its bitter perfume
   breathes a life of gathering gloom;
   sorrowing, sighing, bleeding, dying,
   sealed in the stone-cold tomb.

5. Glorious now behold him arise,
   King and God and sacrifice;
   alleluia, alleluia,
   earth to heaven replies.

806 Fred Kaan (b. 1929)
© 1967, 1991, 1997 Stainer & Bell Ltd

1. We turn to you, O God of every
   nation,
   giver of good and origin of life;
   your love is at the heart of all creation,
   your hurt is people's pain in war and
   death.

2. We turn to you, that we may be
   forgiven
   for crucifying Christ on earth again.
   We know that we have never wholly
   striven,
   to share with all the promise of your
   reign.

3. Free every heart from haughty self-
   reliance,
   our ways of thought inspire with
   simple grace;
   break down among us barriers of
   defiance,
   speak to the soul of all the human race.

4. On all who rise on earth for right
   relations,
   we pray the light of love from hour to
   hour.
   Grant wisdom to the leaders of the
   nations,
   the gift of carefulness to those in
   power.

5. Teach us, good Lord, to serve the
   need of others,
   help us to give and not to count the
   cost.
   Unite us all to live as sisters, brothers,
   defeat our Babel with your Pentecost!

807 Doug Horley (b. 1953)
© 1993 Thankyou Music

We want to see Jesus lifted high,
a banner that flies across this land,
that all men might see the truth
and know he is the way to heaven.
(Repeat)

We want to see, we want to see,
we want to see Jesus lifted high.
We want to see, we want to see,
we want to see Jesus lifted high.

Step by step we're moving forward,
little by little taking ground,
every prayer a powerful weapon,
strongholds come tumbling down
and down, and down, and down.

808 John L. Bell (b. 1949) and Graham Maule
(b. 1958)
© 1989 WGRG, Iona Community

1. We will lay our burden down,
   we will lay our burden down,
   we will lay our burden down
   in the hands of the risen Lord.

2. We will light the flame of love,
   we will light the flame of love,
   we will light the flame of love,
   as the hands of the risen Lord.

3. We will show both hurt and hope,
   we will show both hurt and hope,
   we will show both hurt and hope,
   like the hands of the risen Lord.

4. We will walk the path of peace,
   we will walk the path of peace,
   we will walk the path of peace,
   hand in hand with the risen Lord.

809 Graham Kendrick (b. 1950)
© 1989 Make Way Music

1. We'll walk the land with hearts on fire;
and every step will be a prayer.
Hope is rising, new day dawning;
sound of singing fills the air.

2. Two thousand years, and still the flame
is burning bright across the land.
Hearts are waiting, longing, aching,
for awakening once again.

Let the flame burn brighter
in the heart of the darkness,
turning night to glorious day.
Let the song grow louder,
as our love grows stronger;
let it shine! Let it shine!

3. We'll walk for truth, speak out for love;
in Jesus' name we shall be strong,
to lift the fallen, to save the children,
to fill the nation with your song.

810 Spiritual, alt.

1. Were you there
when they crucified my Lord?
(Repeat)
O, sometimes it causes me to
tremble, tremble, tremble.
Were you there
when they crucified my Lord?

2. Were you there
when they nailed him to a tree? . . .

3. Were you there
when they pierced him in the side? . . .

4. Were you there
when they laid him in the tomb? . . .

5. Were you there
when he rose to glorious life? . . .

811 Joseph Medlicott Scriven (1819-1886)

1. What a friend we have in Jesus,
all our sins and griefs to bear!
What a privilege to carry
everything to him in prayer!
O what peace we often forfeit,
O what needless pain we bear,
all because we do not carry
everything to God in prayer!

2. Have we trials and temptations?
Is there trouble anywhere?
We should never be discouraged:
take it to the Lord in prayer!
Can we find a friend so faithful,
who will all our sorrows share?
Jesus knows our every weakness –
take it to the Lord in prayer!

3. Are we weak and heavy-laden,
cumbered with a load of care?
Jesus only is our refuge,
take it to the Lord in prayer!
Do thy friends despise, forsake thee?
Take it to the Lord in prayer!
In his arms he'll take and shield thee,
thou wilt find a solace there.

812 William Chatterton Dix (1837-1898) alt.

1. What child is this who, laid to rest,
on Mary's lap is sleeping?
Whom angels greet with anthems
sweet,
while shepherds watch are keeping?
This, this is Christ the King,
whom shepherds guard and angels
sing:
come, greet the infant Lord,
the babe, the Son of Mary!

2. Why lies he in such mean estate,
where ox and ass are feeding?
Good Christians, fear: for sinners here
the silent Word is pleading.
Nails, spear, shall pierce him through,
the cross be borne for me, for you;
hail, hail the Word made flesh,
the babe, the Son of Mary!

3. So bring him incense, gold and myrrh,
come rich and poor, to own him.
The King of kings salvation brings,
let loving hearts enthrone him.
Raise, raise the song on high,
the Virgin sings her lullaby:
joy, joy for Christ is born,
the babe the Son of Mary!

813 Joseph Addison (1672-1719) alt.

1. When all thy mercies, O my God,
my rising soul surveys,
transported with the view, I'm lost
in wonder, love and praise.

2. Unnumbered comforts to my soul
thy tender care bestowed,
before my infant heart conceived
from whom those comforts flowed.

3. When in such slippery paths I ran
in childhood's careless days,
thine arm unseen conveyed me safe,
to walk in adult ways.

4. When worn with sickness oft hast thou
with health renewed my face;
and when in sins and sorrows sunk,
revived my soul with grace.

5. Ten thousand thousand precious gifts
my daily thanks employ,
and not the least a cheerful heart
which tastes those gifts with joy.

6. Through every period of my life
thy goodness I'll pursue,
and after death in distant worlds
the glorious theme renew.

7. Through all eternity to thee
a joyful song I'll raise;
for O! eternity's too short
to utter all thy praise.

814 John L. Bell (b. 1949) and Graham Maule (b. 1958)
© 1987, 2002 WGRG, Iona Community.

1. When God Almighty came to earth,
he took the pain of Jesus' birth,
he took the flight of refugee,
and whispered: 'Humbly follow me.'

2. When God Almighty went to work,
carpenter's sweat he did not shirk,
profit and loss he did not flee,
but whispered: 'Humbly follow me.'

3. When God Almighty walked the
street,
the critic's curse he had to meet,
the cynic's smile he had to see,
and whispered: 'Humbly follow me.'

4. When God Almighty met the folk,
of peace and truth he gladly spoke
to set the slave and tyrant free,
and whispered: 'Humbly follow me.'

5. When God Almighty took his place
to save the fallen, human race,
he took it boldly on a tree,
and whispered: 'Humbly follow me.'

6. When God Almighty comes again,
he'll meet us incognito as then;
and though no words may voice his
plea,
he'll whisper: 'Are you following me?'

815
Paul Booth
© 1977 Stainer & Bell Ltd

1. When God made the garden of
   creation,
   he filled it full of his love;
   when God made the garden of
   creation,
   he saw that it was good.
   There's room for you, and room for
   me,
   and room for everyone:
   for God is a Father who loves his
   children,
   and gives them a place in the sun.
   When God made the garden of
   creation,
   he filled it full of his love.

2. When God made the hamper of
   creation,
   he filled it full of his love;
   when God made the hamper of
   creation,
   he saw that it was good.
   There's food for you, and food for me,
   and food for everyone:
   but often we're greedy, and waste
   God's bounty,
   so some don't get any at all.
   When God made the hamper of
   creation,
   he filled it full of his love.

3. When God made the family of
   creation,
   he made it out of his love;
   when God made the family of
   creation,
   he saw that it was good.
   There's love for you, and love for me,
   and love for everyone:
   but sometimes we're selfish, ignore
   our neighbours,
   and seek our own place in the sun.
   When God made the family of
   creation,
   he made it out of his love.

4. When God made us stewards of
   creation
   he made us his vision to share;
   when God made us stewards of
   creation
   our burdens he wanted to bear.
   He cares for you,
   he cares for me,
   he cares for all in need;
   for God is a Father who loves his
   children
   no matter what colour or creed.
   When God made us stewards of
   creation
   he gave us his vision to share.

816
John Keble (1792-1866)

1. When God of old came down from
   heav'n,
   in power and wrath he came;
   before his feet the clouds were riv'n,
   half darkness and half flame.

2. But when he came the second time,
   he came in power and love;
   softer than gale at morning prime
   hovered his holy Dove.

3. The fires, that rushed on Sinai down
   in sudden torrents dread,
   now gently light, a glorious crown,
   on every sainted head.

4. And as on Israel's awestruck ear
   the voice exceeding loud,
   the trump that angels quake to hear,
   thrilled from the deep, dark cloud;

5. So, when the Spirit of our God
   came down his flock to find,
   a voice from heav'n was heard
      abroad,
   a rushing, mighty wind.

6. It fills the church of God; it fills
   the sinful world around;
   only in stubborn hearts and wills
   no place for it is found.

7. Come, Lord, come wisdom, love,
      and power,
   open our ears to hear;
   let us not miss th'accepted hour:
   save, Lord, by love or fear.

817 Keri Jones and David Matthew
© 1978 Authentic Publishing
Administered by CopyCare

When I feel the touch
of your hand upon my life,
it causes me to sing a song
that I love you, Lord.
So from deep within
my spirit singeth unto thee,
you are my King,
you are my God,
and I love you, Lord.

818 Wayne and Cathy Perrin
© 1980 Integrity's Hosanna! Music/Sovereign
Music UK

When I look into your holiness,
when I gaze into your loveliness,
when all things that surround
become shadows in the light of you;
when I've found the joy
of reaching your heart,
when my will becomes
enthralled in your love,

when all things that surround
become shadows in the light of you:
I worship you, I worship you,
the reason I live is to worship you.
I worship you, I worship you,
the reason I live is to worship you.

819 Sydney Carter (1915-2004)
© 1965 Stainer & Bell Ltd

1. When I needed a neighbour,
   were you there, were you there?
   When I needed a neighbour,
   were you there?

And the creed and the colour
and the name won't matter,
were you there?

2. I was hungry and thirsty,
   were you there, were you there?
   I was hungry and thirsty,
   were you there?

3. I was cold, I was naked,
   were you there, were you there?
   I was cold, I was naked,
   were you there?

4. When I needed a shelter,
   were you there, were you there?
   When I needed a shelter,
   were you there?

5. When I needed a healer,
   were you there, were you there?
   When I needed a healer,
   were you there?

6. Wherever you travel,
   I'll be there, I'll be there,
   wherever you travel,
   I'll be there.

820 Isaac Watts (1674-1748)

1. When I survey the wondrous cross
on which the Prince of Glory died,
my richest gain I count but loss,
and pour contempt on all my pride.

2. Forbid it, Lord, that I should boast,
save in the death of Christ, my God:
all the vain things that charm me most,
I sacrifice them to his blood.

3. See from his head, his hands, his feet,
sorrow and love flow mingling down:
did e'er such love and sorrow meet,
or thorns compose so rich a crown?

4. Were the whole realm of nature mine,
that were an off'ring far too small;
love so amazing, so divine,
demands my soul, my life, my all.

821 Fred Pratt Green (1903-2000)
© 1980 Stainer & Bell Ltd

1. When Jesus came to Jordan
to be baptised by John,
he did not come for pardon,
but as his Father's Son.
He came to share repentance
with all who mourn their sins,
to speak the vital sentence
with which good news begins.

2. He came to share temptation,
our utmost woe and loss;
for us and our salvation
to die upon the cross.
So when the Dove descended
on him, the Son of Man,
the hidden years had ended,
the age of grace began.

3. Come, Holy Spirit, aid us
to keep the vows we make,
this very day invade us,
and every bondage break.
Come, give our lives direction,
the gift we covet most;
to share the resurrection
that leads to Pentecost.

822 German (19th century)
trans. Edward Caswall (1814-1878)

1. When morning gilds the skies,
my heart awaking cries,
may Jesus Christ be praised.
Alike at work and prayer
to Jesus I repair;
may Jesus Christ be praised.

2. The night becomes as day,
when from the heart we say:
may Jesus Christ be praised.
The powers of darkness fear,
when this sweet chant they hear:
may Jesus Christ be praised.

3. In heaven's eternal bliss
the loveliest strain is this:
may Jesus Christ be praised.
Let air, and sea, and sky
from depth to height reply:
may Jesus Christ be praised.

4. Be this, while life is mine,
my canticle divine:
may Jesus Christ be praised.
Be this th'eternal song
through all the ages on:
may Jesus Christ be praised.

823

Matt Redman
© 1997 Thankyou Music

1. When the music fades,
all is stripped away,
and I simply come.
Longing just to bring
something that's of worth,
that will bless your heart.

I'll bring you more than a song,
for a song in itself
is not what you have required.
You search much deeper within,
through the way things appear;
you're looking into my heart.

I'm coming back to the heart of worship,
and it's all about you,
all about you, Jesus.
I'm sorry, Lord,
for the thing I've made it,
when it's all about you,
all about you, Jesus.

2. King of endless worth,
no one could express
how much you deserve.
Though I'm weak and poor
all I have is yours,
every single breath.

I'll bring you . . .

824 Unknown

1. When the Spirit of the Lord
is within my heart } (x2)
I will sing as David sang.
I will sing, I will sing,
I will sing as David sang. } (x2)

2. When the Spirit of the Lord
is within my heart
I will clap as David clapped . . .

3. When the Spirit of the Lord
is within my heart
I will dance as David danced . . .

4. When the Spirit of the Lord
is within my heart
I will praise as David praised . . .

825 Christopher Smart (1722-1771)

1. Where is this stupendous stranger?
prophets, shepherds, kings, advise:
lead me to my Master's manger,
show me where my Saviour lies.

2. O most mighty, O most holy,
far beyond the seraph's thought!
Art thou then so mean and lowly
as unheeded prophets taught?

3. O the magnitude of meekness,
worth from worth immortal sprung!
O the strength of infant weakness,
if eternal is so young!

4. God all-bounteous, all-creative,
whom no ills from good dissuade,
is incarnate, and a native
of the very world he made.

826 William Jervois (1852-1905)

1. Wherefore, O Father, we thy humble
servants
here bring before thee Christ thy
well-belovèd,
all-perfect off'ring, sacrifice immortal,
spotless oblation.

Continued overleaf

2. See now thy children, making intercession
through him our Saviour, Son of God incarnate,
for all thy people, living and departed,
pleading before thee.

827 Nahum Tate (1652-1715)

1. While shepherds watched their flocks by night,
all seated on the ground,
the angel of the Lord came down,
and glory shone around.

2. 'Fear not,' said he, (for mighty dread had seized their troubled mind)
'glad tidings of great joy I bring
to you and all mankind.

3. To you in David's town this day
is born of David's line
a Saviour, who is Christ the Lord;
and this shall be the sign:

4. The heavenly babe you there shall find
to human view displayed,
all meanly wrapped in swathing bands,
and in a manger laid.'

5. Thus spake the seraph, and forthwith appeared a shining throng
of angels praising God, who thus
addressed their joyful song:

6. 'All glory be to God on high,
and on the earth be peace,
goodwill henceforth from heaven to all
begin and never cease.'

828 Heinrich Schenck (1656-1727) trans. Frances Elizabeth Cox (1812-1897)

1. Who are these like stars appearing,
these, before God's throne who stand?
Each a golden crown is wearing:
who are all this glorious band?
Alleluia, hark, they sing,
praising loud their heavenly King.

2. Who are these in dazzling brightness,
clothed in God's own righteousness,
these, whose robes of purest whiteness
shall their lustre still possess,
still untouched by time's rude hand?
Whence came all this glorious band?

3. These are they who have contended
for their Saviour's honour long,
wrestling on till life was ended,
following not the sinful throng;
these, who well the fight sustained,
triumph by the Lamb have gained.

4. These are they whose hearts were riven,
sore with woe and anguish tried,
who in prayer full oft have striven
with the God they glorified;
now, their painful conflict o'er,
God has bid them weep no more.

5. These, th'Almighty contemplating,
did as priests before him stand,
soul and body always waiting
day and night at his command:
now in God's most holy place
blest they stand before his face.

829 Graham Kendrick (b. 1950) © 1988 Make Way Music

1. Who can sound the depths of sorrow
in the Father heart of God,
for the children we've rejected,
for the lives so deeply scarred?

And each light that we've extinguished
has brought darkness to our land:
upon our nation, upon our nation
have mercy, Lord.

2. We have scorned the truth you gave us,
we have bowed to other lords.
We have sacrificed the children
on the altar of our gods.
O let truth again shine on us,
let your holy fear descend:
upon our nation, upon our nation
have mercy, Lord.

(Men)
3. Who can stand before your anger?
Who can face your piercing eyes?
For you love the weak and helpless,
and you hear the victims' cries.

(All)
Yes, you are a God of justice,
and your judgement surely comes:
upon our nation, upon our nation
have mercy, Lord.

(Women)
4. Who will stand against the violence?
Who will comfort those who mourn?
In an age of cruel rejection,
who will build for love a home?

(All)
Come and shake us into action,
come and melt our hearts of stone:
upon your people, upon your people
have mercy, Lord.

5. Who can sound the depths of mercy
in the Father heart of God?
For there is a Man of sorrows
who for sinners shed his blood.
He can heal the wounds of nations,
he can wash the guilty clean:
because of Jesus, because of Jesus
have mercy, Lord.

830
Paul Oakley
© 1995 Thankyou Music

Who is there like you,
and who else would give their life for
me,
even suffering in my place?
And who could repay you?
All of creation looks to you,
and you provide for all you have made.

So I'm lifting up my hands,
lifting up my voice,
lifting up your name,
and in your grace I rest,
for your love has come to me
and set me free.
And I'm trusting in your word,
trusting in your cross,
trusting in your blood
and all your faithfulness.
For your power at work in me
is changing me.

831
Paul Booth
© Paul Booth. Administered by CopyCare

1. Who put the colours in the rainbow?
Who put the salt into the sea?
Who put the cold into the snowflake?
Who made you and me?
Who put the hump upon the camel?
Who put the neck on the giraffe?
Who put the tail upon the monkey?
Who made hyenas laugh?
Who made whales and snails and
quails?
Who made hogs and dogs and frogs?
Who made bats and cats and rats?
Who made everything?

Continued overleaf

2. Who put the gold into the sunshine?
   Who put the sparkle in the stars?
   Who put the silver in the moonlight?
   Who made Earth and Mars?
   Who put the scent into the roses?
   Who taught the honey-bee to dance?
   Who put the tree inside the acorn?
   It surely can't be chance!
   Who made seas and leaves and trees?
   Who made snow and winds that blow?
   Who made streams and rivers flow?
   God made all of these!

833 C. Austin Miles (1868-1946)
© The Rodeheaver Co.
Administered by CopyCare

Wide, wide as the ocean,
high as the heavens above;
deep, deep as the deepest sea
is my Saviour's love.
I, though so unworthy,
still am a child of his care,
for his word teaches me that
his love reaches me everywhere.

832 John L. Bell (b. 1949) and Graham Maule
(b.1958) *© 1987, 2002 WGRG, Iona Community*

1. Who would think that what was
        needed
   to transform and save the earth
   might not be a plan or army,
   proud in purpose, proved in worth?
   Who would think, despite derision,
   that a child might lead the way?
   God surprises earth with heaven,
   coming here on Christmas Day.

2. Shepherds watch and wise men
        wonder,
   monarchs scorn and angels sing;
   such a place as none would reckon
   hosts a holy, helpless thing.
   Stable beasts and by-passed strangers
   watch a baby laid in hay:
   God surprises earth with heaven,
   coming here on Christmas Day.

3. Centuries of skill and science
   span the past from which we move,
   yet experience questions whether,
   with such progress, we improve.
   While the human lot we ponder,
   lest our hopes and humour fray,
   God surprises earth with heaven,
   coming here on Christmas Day.

834 John L. Bell (b. 1949) and Graham Maule
(b. 1958)
© 1987 WGRG, Iona Community

1. Will you come and follow me
   if I but call your name?
   Will you go where you don't know,
   and never be the same?
   Will you let my love be shown,
   will you let my name be known,
   will you let my life be grown
   in you, and you in me?

2. Will you leave yourself behind
   if I but call your name?
   Will you care for cruel and kind,
   and never be the same?
   Will you risk the hostile stare
   should your life attract or scare,
   will you let me answer prayer
   in you, and you in me?

3. Will you let the blinded see
   if I but call your name?
   Will you set the pris'ners free,
   and never be the same?
   Will you kiss the leper clean
   and do such as this unseen,
   and admit to what I mean
   in you, and you in me?

4. Will you love the 'you' you hide
   if I but call your name?
   Will you quell the fear inside,
   and never be the same?
   Will you use the faith you've found
   to reshape the world around
   through my sight and touch and
      sound
   in you, and you in me?

5. Lord, your summons echoes true
   when you but call my name.
   Let me turn and follow you,
   and never be the same.
   In your company I'll go
   where your love and footsteps show.
   Thus I'll move and live and grow
   in you, and you in me.

835 Priscilla Jane Owens (1829-1899)

1. Will your anchor hold
   in the storms of life,
   when the clouds unfold
   their wings of strife?
   When the strong tides lift,
   and the cables strain,
   will your anchor drift,
   or firm remain?

   We have an anchor
   that keeps the soul
   steadfast and sure
   while the billows roll;
   fastened to the rock
   which cannot move,
   grounded firm and deep
   in the Saviour's love!

2. Will your anchor hold
   in the straits of fear,
   when the breakers roar
   and the reef is near?
   While the surges rage,
   and the wild winds blow,
   shall the angry waves
   then your bark o'erflow?

3. Will your anchor hold
   in the floods of death,
   when the waters cold
   chill your latest breath?
   On the rising tide
   you can never fail,
   while your anchor holds
   within the veil.

4. Will your eyes behold
   through the morning light,
   the city of gold
   and the harbour bright?
   Will you anchor safe
   by the heav'nly shore,
   when life's storms are past
   for evermore?

836 Isaac Watts (1674-1748)
based on Hebrews 4:15-16; 5:7

1. With joy we meditate the grace
   of our High Priest above;
   his heart is made of tenderness,
   and ever yearns with love.

2. Touched with a sympathy within,
   he knows our feeble frame;
   he knows what sore temptations mean
   for he has felt the same.

3. He in the days of feeble flesh
   poured out his cries and tears;
   and, in his measure, feels afresh
   what every member bears.

Continued overleaf

4. He'll never quench the smoking flax,
   but raise it to a flame;
   the bruisèd reed he never breaks,
   nor scorns the meanest name.

5. Then let our humble faith address
   his mercy and his power:
   we shall obtain deliv'ring grace
   in every needful hour.

837 Taizé Community
© Ateliers et Presses de Taizé

Within our darkest night,
you kindle the fire that never dies
   away,
that never dies away. *(Repeat)*

838 Tim Hughes
© 2002 Thankyou Music

1. Wonderful, so wonderful is your
      unfailing love;
   your cross has spoken mercy over me.
   No eye has seen, no ear has heard,
      no heart could fully know
   how glorious, how beautiful you are.

   Beautiful one, I love you,
   beautiful one, I adore,
   beautiful one, my soul must sing.

2. Powerful, so powerful, your glory fills
      the skies,
   your mighty works displayed for all
      to see.
   The beauty of your majesty awakes
      my heart to sing
   how marvellous, how wonderful you
      are.

   Beautiful one, I love you,
   beautiful one, I adore,
   beautiful one, my soul must sing.
   (Repeat)

You opened my eyes to your wonders
   anew,
you captured my heart with this love,
'cause nothing on earth is as beautiful
   as you.
(Repeat)

Beautiful one . . .

My soul, my soul must sing,
my soul, my soul must sing,
my soul, my soul must sing,
beautiful one.
(Repeat)

Beautiful one . . .

839 'Chorus novae Jerusalem' by St Fulbert of Chartres
(c. 1028), trans. Robert Campbell (1814-1868)

1. Ye choirs of new Jerusalem,
   your sweetest notes employ,
   the Paschal victory to hymn
   in strains of holy joy.

2. For Judah's Lion burst his chains,
   and crushed the serpent's head;
   and brought with him,
   from death's domain,
   the long-imprisoned dead.

3. From hell's devouring jaws the prey
   alone our leader bore;
   his ransomed hosts pursue their way
   where he hath gone before.

4. Triumphant in his glory now
   his sceptre ruleth all;
   earth, heav'n and hell before him bow
   and at his footstool fall.

5. While joyful thus his praise we sing,
   his mercy we implore,
   into his palace bright to bring,
   and keep us evermore.

6. All glory to the Father be,
all glory to the Son,
all glory, Holy Ghost, to thee,
while endless ages run.

840 Richard Baxter (1615-1691) and John Hampden Gurney (1802-1862)

1. Ye holy angels bright,
who wait at God's right hand,
or through the realms of light
fly at your Lord's command,
assist our song,
for else the theme
too high doth seem
for mortal tongue.

2. Ye blessèd souls at rest,
who ran this earthly race,
and now, from sin released,
behold the Saviour's face,
God's praises sound,
as in his sight
with sweet delight
ye do abound.

3. Ye saints, who toil below,
adore your heav'nly King,
and onward as ye go
some joyful anthem sing;
take what he gives
and praise him still,
through good or ill,
who ever lives.

4. My soul, bear thou thy part,
triumph in God above:
and with a well-tuned heart
sing thou the songs of love;
let all thy days
till life shall end,
whate'er he send,
be filled with praise.

841 Charles Wesley (1707-1788)

1. Ye servants of God,
your Master proclaim,
and publish abroad
his wonderful name;
the name all victorious
of Jesus extol:
his kingdom is glorious,
and rules over all.

2. God ruleth on high,
almighty to save;
and still he is nigh:
his presence we have:
the great congregation
his triumph shall sing,
ascribing salvation
to Jesus our King.

3. Salvation to God
who sits on the throne!
let all cry aloud,
and honour the Son.
The praises of Jesus
the angels proclaim,
fall down on their faces,
and worship the Lamb.

4. Then let us adore,
and give him his right:
all glory and power,
all wisdom and might,
and honour and blessing,
with angels above,
and thanks never-ceasing,
and infinite love.

842 Philip Doddridge (1702-1751) alt.

1. Ye servants of the Lord,
   each for his coming wait,
   observant of his heav'nly word,
   and watchful at his gate.

2. Let all your lamps be bright,
   and trim the golden flame;
   gird up your loins as in his sight,
   for awesome is his name.

3. Watch! 'tis your Lord's command,
   and while we speak, he's near;
   mark the first signal of his hand,
   and ready all appear.

4. O happy servants they,
   in such a posture found,
   who share their Saviour's triumph day,
   with joy and honour crowned.

5. Christ shall the banquet spread
   with his own royal hand,
   and raise each faithful servant's head
   amid th'angelic band.

843 Cyril Argentine Alington (1872-1955)
© Hymns Ancient & Modern Ltd

1. Ye that know the Lord is gracious,
   ye for whom a cornerstone
   stands, of God elect and precious,
   laid that ye may build thereon,
   see that on that sure foundation
   ye a living temple raise,
   towers that may tell forth salvation,
   walls that may re-echo praise.

2. Living stones, by God appointed
   each to his allotted place,
   kings and priests, by God anointed,
   shall ye not declare his grace?
   Ye, a royal generation,
   tell the tidings of your birth,
   tidings of a new creation
   to an old and weary earth.

3. Tell the praise of him who called you
   out of darkness into light,
   broke the fetters that enthralled you,
   gave you freedom, peace and sight:
   tell the tale of sins forgiven,
   strength renewed and hope restored,
   till the earth, in tune with heaven,
   praise and magnify the Lord.

844 Athelstan Riley (1858-1945) alt.
© Oxford University Press

1. Ye watchers and ye holy ones,
   bright seraphs, cherubim and thrones,
   raise the glad strain, alleluia!
   Cry out, dominions, princedoms,
     powers,
   virtues, archangels, angels' choirs,

   Alleluia, alleluia, alleluia,
   alleluia, alleluia!

2. O higher than the cherubim,
   more glorious than the seraphim,
   lead their praises, alleluia.
   O Mary, bearer of the Word,
   most gracious, magnify the Lord:

3. Respond, ye souls in endless rest,
   ye patriarchs and prophets blest,
   alleluia, alleluia.
   Ye holy twelve, ye martyrs strong,
   all saints triumphant, raise the song:

4. O friends, in gladness let us sing,
   supernal anthems echoing,
   alleluia, alleluia.
   To God the Father, God the Son
   and God the Spirit, Three in One:

845
Vincent Stuckey Stratton Coles (1845-1929)

1. Ye who own the faith of Jesus
sing the wonders that were done,
when the love of God the Father
o'er our sin the vict'ry won,
when he made the Virgin Mary
mother of his only Son.

Hail Mary, hail Mary,
hail Mary, full of grace.

2. Blessèd were the chosen people
out of whom the Lord did come,
blessèd was the land of promise
fashioned for his earthly home;
but more blessèd was the mother,
she who bore him in her womb.

3. Wherefore let all faithful people
tell the honour of her name,
let the Church in her foreshadowed
part in her thanksgiving claim;
what Christ's mother sang in gladness
let Christ's people sing the same.

*4. Let us weave our supplications,
she with us and we with her,
for advancement of the faithful,
for each faithful worshipper,
for the doubting, for the sinful,
for each heedless wanderer.

*5. May the mother's intercessions
on our homes a blessing win,
that the children all be prospered,
strong and fair and pure within,
following our Lord's own footsteps,
firm in faith and free from sin.

*6. For the sick and for the agèd,
for our dear ones far away,
for the hearts that mourn in secret,
all who need our prayers today,
for the faithful gone before us,
may the Holy Virgin pray.

7. Praise, O Mary, praise the Father,
praise thy Saviour and thy Son,
praise the everlasting Spirit,
who hath made thee ark and throne;
o'er all creatures high exalted,
lowly praise the Three in One.

846
Unknown

Yesterday, today, for ever,
Jesus is the same;
all may change, but Jesus never,
glory to his name!
Glory to his name! Glory to his name!
All may change, but Jesus never,
glory to his name!

847
Mark Altrogge
© 1987 People of Destiny International
Administered by CopyCare

You are beautiful beyond description,
too marvellous for words,
too wonderful for comprehension,
like nothing ever seen or heard.
Who can grasp your infinite wisdom?
Who can fathom the depth of your
love?
You are beautiful beyond description,
majesty, enthroned above.

And I stand, I stand in awe of you.
I stand, I stand in awe of you.
Holy God, to whom all praise is due,
I stand in awe of you.

848
Margaret Rizza (b. 1929)
© 1998 Kevin Mayhew Ltd

You are the centre, you are my life,
you are the centre, O Lord, of my life.
Come, Lord, and heal me, Lord of
my life,
come, Lord, and teach me, Lord of
my life.
You are the centre, Lord, of my life.
Give me your Spirit and teach me
your ways,
give me your peace, Lord, and set me
free.*
You are the centre, Lord, of my life.

Second time:
You are the centre, you are my life,
you are the centre, O Lord, of my life.

849
Mavis Ford and Julie Sharp
*© 1978 Authentic Publishing
Administered by CopyCare*

You are the King of Glory,
you are the Prince of Peace,
you are the Lord of heaven and earth,
you're the Son of righteousness.
Angels bow down before you,
worship and adore, for
you have the words of eternal life,
you are Jesus Christ the Lord.
Hosanna to the Son of David!
Hosanna to the King of kings!
Glory in the highest heaven,
for Jesus the Messiah reigns.

850
Noel Richards (b. 1955)
© 1985 Thankyou Music

You laid aside your majesty,
gave up everything for me,
suffered at the hands of those you
had created.
You took all my guilt and shame,
when you died and rose again;
now today you reign,
in heaven and earth exalted.
I really want to worship you, my Lord,
you have won my heart and I am yours
for ever and ever;
I will love you.
You are the only one who died for me,
gave your life to set me free,
so I lift my voice to you in adoration.

851
Edmund R. Morgan (1888-1979), based on
Revelation 1:12-16
© Hymns Ancient & Modern Ltd

1. You, living Christ, our eyes behold,
   amid your Church appearing,
   all girt about your breast with gold
   and bright apparel wearing;
   your countenance is burning bright,
   a sun resplendent in its might;
   Lord Christ, we see your glory.

2. Your glorious feet have sought and
   found
   your own of every nation;
   with everlasting voice you sound
   the call of our salvation;
   your eyes of flame still search and know
   the whole outspreading realm below:
   Lord Christ, we see your glory.

3. O risen Christ, today alive,
   amid your Church abiding,
   who now your blood and body give,
   new life and strength providing,
   we join in heavenly company
   to sing your praise triumphantly,
   for we have seen your glory.

852 David Adam (b. 1936)
    © SPCK

1. You, Lord, are in this place.
   Your presence fills it;
   your presence is peace.

2. You, Lord, are in my heart.
   Your presence fills it;
   your presence is peace.

3. You, Lord, are in my mind.
   Your presence fills it;
   your presence is peace.

4. You, Lord, are in my life.
   Your presence fills it;
   your presence is peace.

853 Steffi Geiser Rubin and Stuart Dauermann
    (b. 1944)
    © 1975 Lillenas Publishing Co.
    Administered by CopyCare

You shall go out with joy
and be led forth with peace,
and the mountains and the hills
shall break forth before you.
There'll be shouts of joy
and the trees of the field shall clap,
shall clap their hands.
And the trees of the field
shall clap their hands,
and the trees of the field
shall clap their hands,
and the trees of the field
shall clap their hands,
and you'll go out with joy.

854 Martin E. Leckebusch (b. 1962)
    © 1999 Kevin Mayhew Ltd

1. You stood there on the shore-line
   and waited in the dawn
   to share with your disciples
   the newness of the morn;
   be with us now, Lord Jesus,
   and make your presence known;
   in resurrection power
   declare today your own.

2. When hours of tiring labour
   had brought them scant reward,
   in your immense provision
   they recognised their Lord;
   when drudgery seems endless,
   demeaning all our skill,
   let this be our contentment:
   to know and do your will.

3. On bread and fish they feasted
   around a charcoal fire:
   that resurrection breakfast
   was all they could desire!
   Like them, may we discover
   the joy which never ends
   when you, the King of glory,
   count us among your friends.

4. Where Simon Peter languished
   in guilt and burning shame,
   you spoke of restoration,
   and not of endless blame;
   where sin and failure haunt us,
   remind us what is true:
   that we are now forgiven
   and called to follow you.

855   Brian Doerksen (b. 1965) and Brenton Brown
© 2000 Vineyard Songs (UK/Eire)

1. Your love is amazing, steady and
   unchanging,
   your love is a mountain, firm beneath
   my feet.
   Your love is a myst'ry, how you gently
   lift me,
   when I am surrounded, your love
   carries me.

   Hallelujah, hallelujah, hallelujah,
   your love makes me sing.
   Hallelujah, hallelujah, hallelujah,
   your love makes me sing.

2. Your love is surprising, I can feel it
   rising,
   all the joy that's growing deep inside
   of me.
   Every time I see you, all your
   goodness shines through,
   I can feel this God-song, rising up in
   me.

   Hallelujah . . .

   Yes, you make me sing.
   Lord, you make me sing, sing, sing.
   How you make me sing.

   Hallelujah . . .

1. You made the heavens,
   the earth and sea;
   your power is awesome,
   and you still love me.

2. Your ways are righteous,
   your laws are just,
   love is your promise,
   and in you I trust.

3. Your love is healing,
   your love endures;
   my life is changed, Lord,
   now I know I'm yours.

857   Unknown

Zacchaeus was a very little man,
and a very little man was he.
He climbed up into a sycamore tree,
for the Saviour he wanted to see.
And when the Saviour passed that way,
he looked into the tree and said,
'Now Zacchaeus, you come down,
for I'm coming to your house for tea.'

856   Mike Anderson (b. 1956)
© 1999 Kevin Mayhew Ltd

Your love's greater (greater),
greater than the greatest mountain,
your love's deeper (deeper),
deeper than the deepest sea;
a love that never dies,
a love that reaches deep inside,
more wondrous than all the universe.

858   Sue McClellan (b. 1951), John Paculabo
(b. 1946) and Keith Ryecroft
© 1972 Thankyou Music

Zip bam boo, zama lama la boo,
there's freedom in Jesus Christ. (Repeat)
Though we hung him on a cross
till he died in pain,
three days later he's alive again.
Zip bam boo, zama lama la boo,
there's freedom in Jesus Christ.

1. This Jesus was a working man
   who shouted 'Yes' to life,
   but didn't choose to settle down,
   or take himself a wife.
   To live for God he made his task,
   'Who is this man?' the people ask.
   Zip bam boo, zama lama la boo,
   there's freedom in Jesus Christ.

2. He'd come to share good news from
       God
   and show that he is Lord.
   He made folk whole who trusted him
   and took him at his word.
   He fought oppression, loved the poor,
   gave the people hope once more.
   Zip bam boo, zama lama la boo,
   there's freedom in Jesus Christ.

3. 'He's mad! He claims to be God's Son
   and give new life to men!
   Let's kill this Christ, once and for all,
   no trouble from him then!'
   'It's death then, Jesus, the cross for
       you!'
   Said, 'Man, that's what I came to do!'
   Zip bam boo, zama lama la boo,
   there's freedom in Jesus Christ.

INDEXES

Index of Authors and Sources of Text

Scriptural Index

Index of Uses

Index of Hymns for the Lectionary

All-Age Index

Index of First Lines and Titles

Index of Authors and Sources of Text

'À toi la gloire' 751
'Ad regias Agni dapes' 51
Adam, David 92, 852
Adams, Sarah Flower 525
Addison, Joseph 813
Adkins, Donna 177
Ainger, Arthur Campbell 246
Ainger, Geoffrey 81
Alexander, Cecil Frances 26, 94, 326, 379, 592, 740
Alford, Henry 144
Alington, Cyril Argentine 259, 266, 469, 470, 843
Alston, Alfred E. 173
Alstott, Owen 30
Alstyne, Frances Jane van 75, 777
Altrogge, Mark 847
Anderson, Mike 222, 660, 717, 856
Andrew, Diane Davis 695
Andrew S. D. C., Father 538
'Anima Christi', John XXII 670
Appleford, Patrick 384, 463, 560
Aquinas, Thomas 737
Arlott, John 260
Armstrong, Paul 674
Arnold, J. 381
Atkinson, Jennifer 375
Auber, Harriet 602

Baker, Henry Williams 367, 481, 513, 574, 576, 624, 715, 800
Bakewell, John 278
Baloche, Paul 7, 601
Bancroft, Charitie L. 70
'Bangor Antiphoner' (c.690) 157
Bankhead, Dave 135
Baring-Gould, Sabine 661, 700, 770
Barnett, John 389
Barnett, Marie 758
Barrows, Cliff 503
Batya, Naomi 417
Baxter, Richard 462, 840
Bayly, Albert F. 475, 565, 617
Bell, G. K. A. 99
Bell, John L 82, 110, 113, 151, 208, 228, 239, 258, 297, 362, 378, 382, 415, 594, 654, 688, 808, 814, 832, 834
Bennard, George 587
Bickersteth, Edward Henry 614
Bilbrough, Dave 5, 13, 322, 430
Billington, Sandra Joan 608
'Birjina gaztettobat zegoen' 700
Blake, William 37
Boberg, Karl 563
Bode, John Ernest 553, 556
Bonar, Horatius 182, 304, 334
Bonner, Carey 621
'Book of Hours' (1514) 235
Booth, Paul 815, 831
Borthwick, Jane L. 63
Boswell, Eric 447

Bourne, George Hugh 453
Bowater, Chris 301, 400
Bowers, John E. 108, 109, 227, 728
Bowman, Sean 673
Bowring, John 358
Bridge, Basil E. 257, 366, 392, 731
Bridges, Matthew 150, 514
Bridges, Robert 9, 19, 285, 637
Briggs, George Wallace 137, 238, 529
Bright, William 38, 593
Brooks, Phillips 559
Brooks, R. T. 698
Brown, Brenton 609, 855
Brown, Ruth 610
Browne, S. 122
Brownlie, John 557
Budry, Edmond Louis 751
Bullock, Geoff 458
Bullock, William 800
Bunyan, John 27
Burkitt, Francis Crawford 786
Burns, Edward Joseph 798
Butler, Henry Montagu 439
Byrne, Mary 66
Byrom, John 107, 522

Caird, George B. 528
Calkin, Ruth Harms 607
Campbell, Jane Montgomery 801
Campbell, Robert 51, 839
'Cantico di Frate Sole',
    St Francis of Assisi 10
Carson, Christine 726
Carter, Sydney 329, 595, 819
Caswall, Edward 28, 50, 139, 158, 224, 286, 373, 517, 531, 649, 822
Cennick, John 449
Chadwick, John White 162
Chandler, John 97, 370, 554, 589, 699
Chapman, Morris 60
Chatfield, Allen William 465
Chesterton, Gilbert Keith 546
Chisholm, Thomas Obadiah 273
'Chorus novæ Jerusalem',
    St Fulbert of Chartres 839
'Christmas Carols, Ancient and
    Modern', William Sandys
    (1833) 705
Churchill, Wendy 386
Clare, T. C. Hunter 590
Claudius, Matthias 801
Clephane, Elizabeth 72
Clifton, Dave 619
Coates, Gerald 271, 292
Cockett, Michael 25, 189
Coelho, Terrye 176
Coffin, Charles 285, 554, 589, 699
Coles, Vincent Stuckey Stratton 803, 845
Collinson, Valerie 117
Colvin, Tom S. 368

'Compleat Psalmodist',
    J. Arnold (1749) 381
Conder, Josiah 83, 718
Connaughton, Luke 492
Conty, Sophie 417
Cook, Vikki 70
Cooper, Edward 174
Cooper, Jarrod 418
'Corde natus ex parentis', Aurelius
    Clemens Prudentius 584
Cosin, John 124
Cotterill, Thomas 277
Cowper, William 247, 287, 407, 539
Cox, Frances Elizabeth 390, 664, 828
Craig, Ian D. 261, 476
Critchley, Dawn 457
Critchley, Robert 457
Crosby, Fanny J. 75, 777
Cross, Stewart 172
Crossman, Samuel 521
Crum, John Macleod Campbell 533
Cull, Robert 600

Dale, Alan 262
Daniels, John 45
Dauermann, Stuart 853
Day, John 21
Dean, Stephen 696
Dearmer, Percy 1, 27, 44, 242, 383, 448, 621, 680, 782
Deming, Paul S. 209
'Didache' (1st century) 178, 206
'Discendi, amor santo', Bianco da
    Siena 120
Dix, William Chatterton 33, 46, 780, 812
Doane, George Washington 765
Dobbie, Robert 161
Doddridge, Philip 175, 288, 515, 545, 551, 842
Doerksen, Brian 132, 165, 631, 855
Draper, William Henry 10, 356
Dudley-Smith, Timothy 167, 183, 305, 396, 454, 468, 524, 605, 645, 692, 768
Dunn, Fred 410

Edmeston, James 422
Ellerton, John 279, 577, 648, 704
Elliot, Emily Elizabeth Steele 766
Elliott, Charlotte 413
Ephraim the Syrian 680
'Epistle to Diognetus' (c.150) 710
Evans, David J. 62
Everest, Charles William 689

Faber, Frederick William 516, 747
Farjeon, Eleanor 510
Farrell, Bernadette 452, 549
Fawcett, Nick 116, 196, 245, 249, 440, 460, 480, 482, 487, 488, 567, 630

Fellingham, David 656
Fishel, Donald 31
Fitts, Bob 171
Foley, Brian 311
Ford, Mavis 849
Forster, Michael 14, 50, 59, 85,
121, 124, 125, 190, 202, 206, 211,
231, 244, 246, 252, 263, 264, 296,
332, 346, 408, 436, 501, 515, 553,
599, 626, 651, 653, 730, 736, 766,
787, 797
Fortunatus, Venantius 662, 708, 729
Fosdick, Harry Emerson 248
'Foundling Hospital Collection'
(1796) 625
Founds, Rick 461
Fox, Adam 284
Franck, Johann 153
Frye, Michael 376
Fullerton, William Young 327

Galloway, Kathy 586
Garrard, Stuart 163
Garrett, Les 759
Gaunt, Howard Charles Adie 130,
230, 641
Gellert, Christian Fürchtegott 390
Gerhardt, Paul 576, 634
German (19th century) 822
Getty, Keith 352
Gibson, John 405
Gillard, Richard 91
Gillman, Bob 73
'Gloria, laus et honor',
St Theodulph of Orleans 12
'Gloriosi Salvatoris'
(15th century) 779
Glynn, John 338
Good Friday 'Reproaches' 332
Gowans, John 738
Grafstrom, Viola 791
Grant, Robert 582
'Great O Antiphons' 535
Greek (3rd century or earlier) 276
Greek hymn (8th century) 557
Green, Fred Pratt 35, 100, 197, 241,
451, 635, 778, 743, 821
Groves, Alexander 86
Gurney, Dorothy Frances 573
Gurney, John Hampden 840
Gustafson, Gerrit 598

Hall, William John 79
Hardy, Henry Ernest 538
Hart, Joseph 318
Harvill, Jamie 78
Hatch, Edwin 87
Haugen, Marty 133, 302, 432
Havergal, Frances Ridley 324, 354,
687
Hawks, Annie Sherwood 336
Hayes, Pamela 493, 659
Hayford, Jack W. 498
Hayward, Rob 345

Hearn, Naida 395
Heber, Reginald 84, 89, 256,
310, 784
Hebrew 'Yigdal' 706
Heerman, J. 9
Hemming, Jo 606
Hemming, Nigel 606
Hensley, Lewis 774
Herbert, George 131, 416, 425, 690,
707
Herklots, Rosamond, E. 199
Hewer, Jenny 170
Hickson, William E. 255
Hill, Rowland 450
Hine, Stuart K. 563
Holland, Henry Scott 411
Holloway, Jean 213, 250, 269, 483,
677, 697
Holmes, Oliver Wendell 466
Hopkins, John Henry 805
Horley, Doug 807
Hort, Fenton John Anthony 577
Hosmer, Frederick Lucian 773
How, William Walsham 190, 364,
572, 764
Howard, Adrian 646
Howard, Brian 342
Hoyle, Richard Birch 751
Hughes, Donald Wynn 147, 236
Hughes, Tim 441, 838
Hull, Eleanor 66
Humphreys, Charles William 204, 680
Hupton, Job 142
Hutchinson, Gill 385

Idle, Christopher 119
Ingemann, Berhardt Severin 770
Iona Community 792
Irish (8th century) 754
Iverson, Daniel 675

Jervois, William 826
'Jesu dulcis memoria'
(12th century) 374
John XXII 670
Johnson, Samuel 111
Johnston, Philip Lawson 388
Jones, Keri 817
Jones, Richard G. 115

Kaan, Fred 180, 198, 434, 530, 633,
799, 806
Keble, John 79, 276, 526, 682, 816
Kelly, Thomas 711, 721, 804
Kempis, Thomas à 442, 570
Ken, Thomas 57, 229, 618
Kendrick, Graham 16, 54, 67, 118,
136, 205, 210, 303, 348, 397, 401,
423, 444, 479, 500, 504, 507, 520,
542, 552, 568, 596, 616, 639, 681,
691, 714, 790, 809, 829
Kennedy, Helen 672
Kennett, John 620
Kethe, William 21
King Jnr, Martin Luther 797

King, Mary Lou 48
Kingsley, Charles 212
Kirkbride-Barthow, Mary 48
Kirkpatrick, William James 59
Kitchin, George William 437
Klein, Laurie 335

Lafferty, Karen 652
Langton, Stephen 139, 783
Lathbury, Mary Artemisia 86
Latin (17th century) 367
Latin (8th century) 370
Latin hymn (17th century) 733
Latin meditation (11th century) 9
LeBlanc, Lenny 7
Leckebusch, Martin E. 53, 138, 141,
146, 217, 313, 359, 406, 427, 484,
485, 597, 657, 709, 854
Leeson, Jane Elizabeth 495
Leftley, Francesca 665, 685
Littledale, Richard F. 120
Liturgy of Malabar 284
Liturgy of St James 204, 424
Logan, John 545
Longfellow, Samuel 312
Lowry, Robert 496
Lowry, Somerset Corry 3, 667
'Lucis Creator Optime' 80
Lundy, Damian 29, 732, 755
Lunt, Janet 90
'Lyra Davidica' (1708) 381
Lyte, Henry Francis 6, 251, 623

McCann, Christine 214
McClellan, Sue 114, 858
McEwan, Steve 272
Madan, Martin 289, 449
Mann, Robin 179
Mansell, David J. 387
Mant, Richard 88, 191
Maries, Andrew 789
Mark, Robin 375, 518, 748
Markland, Gerard 156
Marriott, John 767
Marshall-Taylor, Geoffrey 695
Mason, John 320
Massey, Christopher 448
Matheson, George 571
Matsikenyiri, Patrick 372
Matthew, David 817
Maude, Mary Fawler 752
Maule, Graham 82, 110, 113, 151,
208, 228, 239, 258, 297, 362, 378,
382, 415, 654, 688, 808, 814, 832,
834
Maurus, Rabanus 101, 124
Mayhew, Kevin 615
Mee, Susan 793
'Meine Hoffnung stehet feste',
Joachim Neander 19
Miles, C. Austin 833
Milman, Henry Hart 640
Milton, John 435, 722
'Mnõeo Christe', Bishop Synesius 465
Mohr, Joseph 658

Monahan, Dermott 403
Monsell, John Samuel Bewley 181, 583
Montgomery, James 39, 280, 478, 668, 676
Morgan, Edmund R. 851
Morgan, Patricia 135
Morgan, Reuben 756
Morrison, John 727
Moultrie, G. 424
Muirhead, Lionel 701

Nazareth, Aniceto 4, 446
Neale, John Mason 2, 12, 69, 77, 96, 142, 143, 148, 157, 185, 265, 267, 383, 442, 443, 531, 535, 550, 584, 662, 703, 708, 729, 779
Neander, Joachim 19, 628
Nelson, Horatio Bolton 192
Nelson, Marc 325
'New Version', Tate and Brady (1696) 42, 769
Newbolt, Michael Robert 437
Newman, John Henry 186, 421, 627
Newport, Doreen 753
Newton, John 34, 223, 274, 321, 505
Nichols, Kevin 351
Nicolai, Philipp 786
Noel, Caroline Maria 52
North Ghanaian song 368
Northumbria Community 300
'Nun danket alle Gott' 532
Nyberg, Anders 789
Nystrom, Martin 43

'O quam juvat' 285
'O Støre Gud', Karl Boberg 563
Oakeley, Frederick 534
Oakley, Charles Edward 307
Oakley, Paul 394, 744, 830
Olivers, Thomas 706
O'Neill, Judith Beatrice 802
Osler, Edward 548, 625
Owens, Carol 237
Owens, Jimmy 112, 308, 755
Owens, Priscilla Jane 835
Oxenham, Henry N. 281
Oxenham, John 353

Paculabo, John 114, 858
Palmer, Edmund S. 371
Palmer, Ray 374, 512
Paris, Twila 293
Parsons, Richard Godfrey 796
Peacey, John Raphael 56, 184, 194,
Pécselyi, Kiràly Imre von 739
Pennefather, William 402
Perrin, Cathy 818
Perrin, Wayne 818
Perronet, Edward 14
Perry, Michael 445, 544, 650
Pestel, Thomas 71
Phillips, C. S. 101
Piercy, Andy 619
Pierpoint, Folliot Sandford 195
Plumptre, Edward Hayes 750, 772

Pollock, Thomas Benson 166
Pond, Joanne 543
Pott, Francis 40, 733
Price, Alan J. 64, 240
Prosch, Kevin 295
Prudentius, Aurelius Clemens 158, 584
'Psalms and Hymns', William John Hall (1836) 79
'Psalter', John Day (1562) 21
'Puer nobis nascitur' (15th century) 782

Quigley, Anne 742
'Quincunque centum quæritis' (18th century) 28
Quinn, James 200, 754, 757

Rankin, J.E. 236
Rattle, H. W. 393
Redman, Beth 76
Redman, Matt 76, 339, 380, 426, 823
Reed, Andrew 671
Rees, Bryn Austin 290
Rees, John 34
Rees, Timothy 98, 243
Reid, William Watkins 298
Richards, Dave 193
Richards, Hubert J. 262, 472
Richards, Noel 271, 292, 612, 776, 850
Richards, Tricia 15, 292
Riley, Athelstan 844
Rinkart, Martin 532
Rizza, Margaret 361, 562, 659, 686, 848
Robinson, J. Armitage 775
Rolinson, Chris 639
Romanis, William 644
Rossetti, Christina Georgina 357, 490
Routley, Erik 527, 739
Rowley, Francis Harold 340
Rubin, Steffi Geiser 853
Ruis, David 341
Ryecroft, Keith 114, 858

Sadler, Gary 78
St Ambrose 577
St Bernard of Clairvaux 373
St Francis of Assisi 10, 499
St Fulbert of Chartres 839
St Germanus 2
St John of Damascus 143, 703
St Patrick 94, 326
St Teresa of Avila 523
St Theodulph of Orleans 12
St Thomas Aquinas 531
'Salve caput cruentatum' 576
Sands, Ernest 663
Sandys, William 705
Santeuil, J., B. de 155
Saward, Michael 103
Sayers, Susan 187, 192, 234, 333, 343, 429, 486, 632, 694, 725, 749, 763, 794

Schenck, Heinrich 828
Schlegel, Katherina von 63
Schutte, Dan 337
Schütz, Johann Jakob 664
Scott, Robert Balgarnie Young 537
Scriven, Joseph Medlicott 811
Sears, Edmund Hamilton 363
Seddon, James Edward 232, 433
Sedgewick, S. N. 629
Siena, Bianco da 120
Simpson, Ray 149
Smale, Ian 168, 188
Smart, Christopher 825
Smith Jnr, Leonard E. 319
Smith, E. R. (Tedd) 745
Smith, Henry 219
Smith, Martin 489, 508, 611, 693
Smith, Walter Chalmers 349
Smythe, Stephen Eric 253
Smyttan, George Hunt 202
Sparrow-Simpson, William John 11
Spiritual 365, 419, 679, 810
'Stabat Mater', Jacopone da Todi 50
Stanfield, Francis 684
Stone, Samuel John 702
Strover, Christian 291
Struther, Jan 467
Surrexit hodie (14th century) 381
Synesius, Bishop 465
Syriac Liturgy, perhaps by Ephraim the Syrian 680

Taizé Community 8, 74, 159, 360, 398, 420, 561, 720, 781, 785, 837
Tate and Brady 42, 769
Tate, Nahum 827
'Te lucis ante terminum' 69
Temple, Sebastian 24, 499
'The Scottish Psalter' (1650) 723
Thomas, Stuart 192
Thompson, Colin P. 106
Thompson, Steve 691
Thring, Godfrey 207
Timms, George Bourne 666
Todi, Jacopone da 50
Tomlin, Chris 218
Toolan, Suzanne 323
Toplady, Augustus Montague 643
Townend, Stuart 18, 317, 352, 724
Traditional 17, 164, 215, 233, 306, 344, 412, 414, 455, 456, 555, 581, 591, 713, 762
Traditional Caribbean 603
Traditional Czech carol 448
Traditional English 254
Traditional English carol 588
Traditional Peruvian 226
Traditional South African 771, 789
Traditional West Indian 734
Tucker, F. Bland 23, 104, 178, 710
Turner, Pat 646
Turner, Roy 20
Turton, William Harry 579
Tuttle, Carl 314, 331
Twells, Henry 49

'Urbs beata Jerusalem'
  (c. 7th century) 96

Vanstone, W. H. 509
'Viva, viva, Gesù' (18th century) 224
'Vox clara ecce intonat'
  (6th century) 286

Waddell, Chrysogonus 536
Wade, John Francis 534
Walker, Catherine 473
Waring, Anna Laetitia 355
Warner, Susan 377
Watts, Isaac 58, 68, 127, 203, 220,
221, 315, 316, 347, 399, 409, 459,
477, 547, 712, 741, 760, 795, 820,
836
Webb, Benjamin 570
Weisse, Michael 102

Weissel, Georg 438
Welsey, Charles 22, 36, 55, 105, 123,
128, 129, 134, 140, 201, 225, 277,
289, 299, 369, 391, 404, 428, 449,
491, 494, 540, 541, 569, 580, 638,
655, 841
Wesley, John 634
West Indian Spiritual 502
West, Peter 48
Whately, Richard 256
White, Estelle 216, 330, 511,
578, 788
White, Henry Kirke 585
Whitefield, George 289
Whiting, William 160
Whittier, John Greenleaf 152, 350
Wilkinson, Kate Barclay 506
Williams, Isaac 65, 155
Williams, Peter 275

Williams, William 275
Willis, Maria 169
Willis, Robert 716
Wimber, John 558
Winkworth, Catherine 102, 153, 438,
464, 532, 628
Winslow, Jack C. 471, 474
Wolcott, Samuel 95
Woodford, James Russell 737
Woodward, George Ratcliffe 154, 761
Wordsworth, Christopher 32, 268,
566, 669
Wren, Brian A. 270, 328, 746
Wright, Ralph 575

Young, John Freeman 658

Zschech, Darlene 519

Scriptural Index

GENESIS

1	Creator of the earth and skies	147
	Fishes of the ocean	187
	Lord of the boundless curves	475
	She sits like a bird (*Enemy of apathy*)	654
	Thanks to God whose word was spoken	698
1:1	I bind unto myself today	326
	Lord of creation, to you be all praise!	471
	Teach me to dance	691
	Who put the colours in the rainbow?	831
1:1-4	Blest Creator of the light	80
	Come, Holy Ghost, our hearts inspire	123
	Eternal Father, strong to save	160
	God is our strength from days of old	244
	Lord, the light of your love	479
	Thou, whose almighty word	767
1:1-5	Lord of all life and power	468
	Of the Father's love begotten	584
1:1-31	Songs of praise the angels sang	668
1:2-3	All over the world	20
1:3	He is the Lord	295
1:6-10	Creator of the earth and skies	147
1:26	For the healing of the nations	198
	Great God, your love has called us	270
1:27	Dance and sing	151
1:28	Lord of all life and power	468
1-2	When God made the garden of creation	815
2:7	Before Jehovah's aweful throne	68
	Breathe on me, Breath of God	87
	Now is eternal life	529
2:15	God, whose farm is all creation	260
2:19-20	If I were a butterfly	342
3:14-15	Ye choirs of new Jerusalem	839
3:15	Jesus, the name high over all	404
4:7	Restore, O Lord	639
4:10	Glory be to Jesus	224
5:1-3	Eternal God, we consecrate	161
6:4	Rise and shine	642
6:13-8:18	Rise and shine	642
8:22	Glory, love, and praise, and honour	225
	Great is thy faithfulness	273
	We plough the fields and scatter	801
9	O Love that wilt not let me go	571
11:1-4	Creator of the earth and skies	147
11:9	It came upon the midnight clear	363
22:12	O Lord, my God (*How great thou art*)	563
22:14	Shout for joy and sing	656
22:16	Beneath the cross of Jesus	72
	Blessèd assurance	75
	Nearer, my God, to thee	525
	The God of Abraham praise	706
28:10-19	As Jacob with travel was weary one day	41
32:22-23	Come, O thou traveller unknown	134
49:24	Rock of ages	643

EXODUS

2:1-11	Our Father God in heaven	605
3:5	Be still, for the presence of the Lord	62
	Jesus, where'er thy people meet	407
3:6	The God of Abraham praise	706
3:10-11	Moses, I know you're the man	511

Exodus

3:14	The God of Abraham praise	706
3:15	The head that once was crowned with	
	thorns	711
12:11	The day of resurrection	703
12:13	At the Lamb's high feast we sing	51
12:21	At the Lamb's high feast we sing	51
13:17-14:31	Come, faithful pilgrims all	121
13:21	Glorious things of thee are spoken	223
	Guide me, O thou great Redeemer	275
	Through the night of doubt and sorrow	770
13-17	I give you love	332
14:28	At the Lamb's high feast we sing	51
	Come, ye faithful, raise the strain	143
15:2	The Lord is my song	720
15:26	Shout for joy and sing	656
16	At the Lamb's high feast we sing	51
16:4	At the Lamb's high feast we sing	51
	Glorious things of thee are spoken	223
	Guide me, O thou great Redeemer	275
17:6	Father, most holy, merciful and loving	173
19:1-25	O come, O come, Emmanuel	535
20:3	Make way, make way	500
25:17	My God, how wonderful you are	516
25-40	Great God, your love has called us	270
32:29	Take my life, and let it be	687
33:22	Rock of ages	643
34:6	Praise, my soul, the King of heaven	623

LEVITICUS

6:13	O thou who camest from above	580
16:2-15	Once, only once, and once for all	593
19:15	Beauty for brokenness (*God of the poor*)	67
25:9-10	These are the days (*Days of Elijah*)	748

NUMBERS

6:24	May God's blessing surround you	503
6:24-26	God to enfold you	258
14:18	Praise, my soul, the King of heaven	623
14:21	Hail, gladdening Light	276
20:8-11	Father, most holy, merciful and loving	173
	Lord, enthroned in heavenly splendour	453
23:10	God be in my head	235

DEUTERONOMY

5:7	Make way, make way	500
8:3	Seek ye first	652
10:8	Stand up and bless the Lord	676
10:17	Alleluia, sing to Jesus	33
	To thee, O Lord, our hearts we raise	780
26:1-11	God, whose farm is all creation	260
29:10-15	Stand up and bless the Lord	676
30:19-20	Lord of life	473
31:8	Lord, we thank you for the promise	484
32:3-4	Ascribe greatness	48
33:27	Fight the good fight	181

JOSHUA

1:9	Be bold, be strong	60
3:7	Guide me, O thou great Redeemer	275

Joshua

3:14-17	Thine be the glory	751
	This joyful Eastertide	761
3:16	Let saints on earth in concert sing	428
6:20	Disposer supreme	155
14:10-12	Lord, we thank you for the promise	484
24:15	Here I am	301

1 SAMUEL

1:21-28	Our Father God in heaven	605
1:28	Eternal God, we consecrate	161
7:12	Here on the threshold of a new beginning	305
16:7	Holy Spirit, will you be (One who intercedes)	313
17:4-50	Goliath was big and Goliath was strong	264

2 SAMUEL

6:14	Teach me to dance	691
	When the Spirit of the Lord	824
7:16	Rejoice, the Lord is King	638
	The day thou gavest, Lord, is ended	704
11:1-15	Creator of the earth and skies	147
14:17	God be with you till we meet again	236
22:2	For all the saints	190
23:5	Put thou thy trust in God	634

1 KINGS

1:34	God save our gracious Queen	255
8:1-11	Blessèd city, heavenly Salem	77
8:22-30	Blessèd city, heavenly Salem	77
8:27	In the bleak mid-winter	357
8:30-40	Christ is made the sure foundation	96
8:30-53	Great Shepherd of thy people	274
8:41-43	Blessèd city, heavenly Salem	77
19:9-18	Dear Lord and Father of mankind	152
19:12	Listen, let your heart keep seeking	446

2 KINGS

6:17	Open the eyes of my heart	601
19:15	Above all powers, above all kings	7

1 CHRONICLES

28:9	Holy Spirit, will you be (One who intercedes)	313
	Jesus, the name high over all	404

2 CHRONICLES

1:10	Grant us the courage, gracious God	269
6:18	Deck thyself, my soul, with gladness	153
15:4	Jesus, the name high over all	404
20:12	I will worship	341
36:23	Come and see the shining hope	119

NEHEMIAH

8:10	O Love that wilt not let me go	571
9:5	Stand up and bless the Lord	676

JOB

1:21	Blessèd be your name	76
3:1-11	Lord of beauty, thine the splendour	470
3:11-26	Lord, there are times	480
7:1-4	Lord, there are times	480

Job

13:15	O God beyond all praising	544
21:22-26	Lord, there are times	480
29:16	Come, thou Holy Spirit, come	139
38:4	Who put the colours in the rainbow?	831
38:7	Songs of praise the angels sang	668
38:7-11	Angels from the realms of glory	39
	Eternal Father, strong to save	160
	O little town of Bethlehem	559
42:3	It is a thing most wonderful	364

PSALMS

2:1-2	God of grace and God of glory	248
	My song is love unknown	521
2:6	As Jacob with travel was weary one day	41
2:8	I cannot tell	327
2:9	Thy kingdom come, O God	774
3:3	As the deer pants for the water	43
3:5-6	Lord, we thank you for the promise	484
4:1	O Lord, hear my prayer	561
4:8	This joyful Eastertide	761
5:3	When morning gilds the skies	822
5:7	It's me, O Lord	365
6:6	Give us the wings of faith	221
7:17	Thanks be to God	696
8	God, our Creator	253
8:1	Let all the world in every corner sing	425
	Lord of beauty, thine the splendour	470
8:1-9	O Lord, my God (How great thou art)	563
8:2	Jesus shall reign	399
8:3	Fill your hearts with joy and gladness	183
8:4	O God beyond all praising	544
8:5	Be thou my guardian and my guide	65
9:1-2	O Lord, we want to praise you	567
9:10	Lord Jesus Christ, be present	464
10:14	Abide with me	6
12	Who can sound the depths of sorrow	829
15	God be in my head	235
16:5	Amazing grace	34
	Be thou my vision	66
	The God of Abraham praise	706
16:9	This joyful Eastertide	761
16:9-11	He has risen	292
16:11	All my days (Beautiful Saviour)	18
	For the days when you feel near	196
	O, heaven is in my heart	552
17:8	He's got the whole world in his hand	306
	O God of Bethel, by whose hand	545
18:2	Faithful One, so unchanging	165
	For all the saints	190
	Rock of ages	643
	Shout for joy and sing	656
18:5	Be thou my guardian and my guide	65
18:11	Put thou thy trust in God	634
18:33	God of grace and God of glory	248
19	From all that dwell below the skies	203
	The heavens declare thy glory, Lord	712
19:1	All heaven declares	15
	Wonderful, so wonderful (Beautiful one)	838
19:1-4	Creation sings!	146
19:1-6	God of life, God of love	249
	Lord of beauty, thine the splendour	470
	Lord of the boundless curves	475
19:4	I love you, Lord, and I lift my voice	335
19:5	Creator of the starry height	148

Psalms

19:7-14	God be in my head	235
19:8	Your love's greater	856
19:10	As the deer pants for the water	43
21:6	For the days when you feel near	196
22:1-2	For the days when you feel near	196
	Lord, there are times	480
22:3	Father in heaven, how we love you	
	(*Blessed be the Lord God Almighty*)	171
22:19	For the days when you feel near	196
23	Nada te turbe (*Nothing can trouble*)	523
	The Lord's my shepherd	723
	The Lord's my shepherd	724
23:1	Great Shepherd of thy people	274
23:1-3	How bright these glorious spirits shine!	316
23:1-6	Abide with me	6
	Faithful Shepherd, feed me	166
	Father, most holy, merciful and loving	173
	Forth in the peace of Christ we go	200
	In heavenly love abiding	355
	The God of love my shepherd is	707
	The King of love my shepherd is	715
23:3	Spirit divine, attend our prayers	671
23:4	God be in my head	235
23:6	At this time of giving	54
24:1	God, whose farm is all creation	260
24:3-6	God be in my head	235
24:7	King of glory, King of peace	416
	Make way, make way	500
24:7-10	For all the saints	190
	Hail the day that sees him rise	277
25:2	Be still and know that I am God	61
26:8	We love the place, O God	800
27:1	Abide with me	6
	Be bold, be strong	60
	God is our strength from days of old	244
	In the Lord is my joy	361
	The Lord is my light	719
27:4	To be in your presence (*My desire*)	776
27:6	Put thou thy trust in God	634
27:8	Lord, you have my heart	489
	Spirit of God (*Mallaig Sprinkling Song*)	672
28:7	Guide me, O thou great Redeemer	275
	Thanks be to God	696
28:7-8	I give my hands	330
29:1	To God be the glory!	777
29:2	When I look into your holiness	818
31:1	Jesu, lover of my soul	369
31:2-3	For all the saints	190
31:3	Abide with me	6
	For all the saints	190
	We pray thee, heavenly Father	803
31:5	Father, I place into your hands	170
31:14	Be still and know that I am God	61
32:8	Lord of all being	466
33:9	Of the Father's love begotten	584
33:12	Lord, for the years	454
33:20	O God, our help in ages past	547
34	In the Lord I'll be ever thankful	360
34:1	Let everything that has breath	426
34:1-3	God, whose city's sure foundation	259
34:1-22	Through all the changing scenes of life	769
34:8	Christians lift your hearts and voices	109
	Jesus, the name high over all	404
34:18	Jesus Christ (*Once again*)	380

36:6	Immortal, invisible, God only wise	349
36:7	O God of Bethel, by whose hand	545
	Wonderful, so wonderful (*Beautiful one*)	838
36:7-8	All my days (*Beautiful Saviour*)	18
36:9	Jesu, lover of my soul	369
37:25	Lord, we thank you for the promise	484
38:4	God is good, God is great	240
40:1	Good King Wenceslas	267
40:1-2	God, our Creator	253
40:2	God of grace and God of glory	248
	Jesu, lover of my soul	369
	Spirit of God (*Mallaig Sprinkling Song*)	672
40:11-17	Lord Jesus, think on me	465
42:1-2	There is a longing	742
42:1-11	All my hope on God is founded	19
	As pants the hart for cooling streams	42
	As the deer pants for the water	43
42:5	Lord of life	473
42:7	Overwhelmed by love	612
42:8	Lord of life	473
42:11	Lord of life	473
43:5	Lord of life	473
44:3	How beauteous are their feet	315
	Thy hand, O God, has guided	772
44:4	Let all the world in every corner sing	425
45:2-8	Jesu, our hope, our heart's desire	370
45:6	Hail to the Lord's anointed	280
	The day thou gavest, Lord, is ended	704
46:1	Immortal, invisible, God only wise	349
	O God, our help in ages past	547
46:1-11	Glorious things of thee are spoken	223
46:2	Abide with me	6
46:10	Be still and know that I am God	61
	Be still, for the presence of the Lord	62
	Be still, my soul	63
47	The Lord is King!	718
47:1-9	He is exalted	293
48:1-14	Glorious things of thee are spoken	223
	Great is the Lord and most worthy	
	of praise	272
48:3	O God, our help in ages past	547
48:10	Let all the world in every corner sing	425
	Thy hand, O God, has guided	772
48:12-13	Lord, we thank you for the promise	484
48:14	Abide with me	6
51	Lord, have mercy (*Ghana*)	455
	Lord, have mercy (*Russian*)	456
51:2	My Lord, what love is this	
	(*Amazing love*)	520
51:6	Lord, teach us how to pray aright	478
51:6-10	Lord Jesus, think on me	465
51:7	I will offer up my life	339
51:10	All you who seek a comfort sure	28
51:10-17	Great Shepherd of thy people	274
51:16-17	When the music fades	
	(*The heart of worship*)	823
51:17	Jesus Christ (*Once again*)	380
	Lord, teach us how to pray aright	478
	O for a heart to praise my God	540
52:8	I am trusting thee, Lord Jesus	324
55:1-2	All creatures of our God and King	10
	O Lord, hear my prayer	561
55:16-17	I watch the sunrise (*Close to you*)	338
55:17	Praise him, praise him, praise him	622

56:3	Be still and know that I am God	61
56:3-4	Have faith in God, my heart	290
57:1	Jesu, lover of my soul	369
57:8	Crown him with many crowns	150
57:9	O Lord, we want to praise you	567
57:10	Great is thy faithfulness	273
59:16	Over the mountains and the sea	
	(*I could sing of your love for ever*)	611
61:3	The God of Abraham praise	706
62:2	For all the saints	190
63:1	Spirit of God (*Mallaig Sprinkling Song*)	672
63:3-4	O Lord, we want to praise you	567
65	Fill your hearts with joy and gladness	183
65:1	Come, ye faithful, raise the anthem	142
65:6-13	Lord, you created	488
65:7	Eternal Father, strong to save	160
65:8	I watch the sunrise (*Close to you*)	338
65:9-13	God, whose farm is all creation	260
65:13	To thee, O Lord, our hearts we raise	780
66:1-3	My Jesus, my Saviour	519
67	God, whose farm is all creation	260
67:1-7	God of mercy, God of grace	251
68:4	God moves in a mysterious way	247
68:5-6	Our Father God in heaven	605
68:18	Songs of praise the angels sang	668
68:33	God moves in a mysterious way	247
69	O give thanks (Kendrick)	542
71:1	I am trusting thee, Lord Jesus	324
	I'm not ashamed to own my Lord	347
	We pray thee, heavenly Father	803
71:3	For all the saints	190
71:16	Jesus, the name high over all	404
71:18	Lord, we thank you for the promise	484
72:1-19	Hail to the Lord's anointed	280
	Jesus shall reign	399
72:5	Christ, the fair glory of the holy angels	101
	From all that dwell below the skies	203
72:6	The Saviour will come, resplendent	
	in joy	730
72:7	It came upon the midnight clear	363
72:8	Christ, the fair glory of the holy angels	101
	From all that dwell below the skies	203
72:11	From the eastern mountains	207
72:17-19	From the eastern mountains	207
72:19	Christ, the fair glory of the holy angels	101
73:1	O, how good is the Lord	555
73:1-3	Lord, there are times	480
73:15-17	For the days when you feel near	196
73:21-26	For the days when you feel near	196
73:24	Abide with me	6
	Lord of all being	466
	Lord of creation, to you be all praise!	471
78:4	Lord, we thank you for the promise	484
78:15	Father, most holy, merciful and loving	173
78:20	Blessèd be your name	76
78:24	There's a quiet understanding	745
78:24-25	Alleluia, sing to Jesus	33
	Bread is blessed and broken	82
	Bread of heaven, on thee we feed	83
	Guide me, O thou great Redeemer	275
	My God, and is thy table spread	515
81:16	I, the Lord of sea and sky	
	(*Here I am, Lord*)	337
82	Who can sound the depths of sorrow	829

84:2	Alleluia, alleluia, give thanks to the	
	risen Lord	31
84:7	From glory to glory advancing	204
85:1-4	Lord of lords and King eternal	474
85:8-13	Fill your hearts with joy and gladness	183
	We love the place, O God	800
85:8-14	Onward, Christian pilgrims	599
	We have a dream	797
85:10	Thy kingdom come	773
86:9	Angels from the realms of glory	39
	Help us, O Lord, to learn	298
86:13	Great is thy faithfulness	273
86:15	Praise, my soul, the King of heaven	623
87:1-3	City of God, how broad and far	111
	Glorious things of thee are spoken	223
	God, whose city's sure foundation	259
	Light's abode, celestial Salem	442
88:9	Oft in danger, oft in woe	585
88:14	For the days when you feel near	196
89:1	Over the mountains and the sea	
	(*I could sing of your love for ever*)	611
89:13	Thine arm, O Lord, in days of old	750
89:14-15	We have a dream	797
89:15	The Spirit lives to set us free	732
89:28-29	I'm not ashamed to own my Lord	347
89:46-48	Lord, there are times	480
90	O God, our help in ages past	547
90:1-2	Lord of all life and power	468
	Lord of the boundless curves	475
	Lord, we thank you for the promise	484
90:12	Creator of the earth and skies	147
91:2	All my hope on God is founded	19
	For all the saints	190
91:4	Glory to thee, my God, this night	229
	Jesu, lover of my soul	369
	O God of Bethel, by whose hand	545
91:6	Beneath the cross of Jesus	72
91:11	God that madest earth and heaven	256
92:4	My Jesus, my Saviour	519
92:5	O Lord, my God (*How great thou art*)	563
93:1	How lovely on the mountains	319
95	Let all the world in every corner sing	425
95:2	Come into his presence	126
	Guide me, O thou great Redeemer	275
	Songs of praise the angels sang	668
95:3-5	Our God is so great	607
95:5	He's got the whole world in his hand	306
95:6	Deck thyself, my soul, with gladness	153
95:6-7	I will worship	341
95:7	He's got the whole world in his hand	306
	Light of the world (*Here I am to worship*)	441
96	Let all the world in every corner sing	425
96:1	My Jesus, my Saviour	519
96:2-3	Alleluia, alleluia, give thanks to the	
	risen Lord	31
96:4	Thank you for saving me	693
96:7	My Jesus, my Saviour	519
	To God be the glory!	777
96:8	Come into his presence	126
96:11-13	O give thanks (Kendrick)	542
97:1	God is love: let heaven adore him	243
	God is working his purpose out	246
	Here on the threshold of a new	
	beginning	305

	Rejoice, the Lord is King	638
97:2	Put thou thy trust in God	634
97:5	My Jesus, my Saviour	519
97:9	Above all powers, above all kings	7
97:12	Lord, today your voice is calling	482
98	O give thanks (Kendrick)	542
98:1-9	Joy to the world!	409
98:4	My Jesus, my Saviour	519
	Shout for joy and sing	656
98:8	A great and mighty wonder	2
100	Before Jehovah's aweful throne	68
	Let all the world in every corner sing	425
100:1-5	All people that on earth do dwell	21
	Jubilate, everybody	410
100:4	Christians, lift up your hearts	108
	Shout for joy and sing	656
100:5	From all that dwell below the skies	203
	O give thanks (Kendrick)	542
	Praise, O praise our God and King	624
	Your love's greater	856
101:1	Over the mountains and the sea	
	(*I could sing of your love for ever*)	611
102:19	Praise to the Holiest	627
102:25	God is love: let heaven adore him	243
	God is our strength from days of old	244
102:27	O God, our help in ages past	547
103	Bless the Lord, my soul	74
	Lord, today your voice is calling	482
	O, how good is the Lord	555
103:1	I will worship	314
103:1-2	Lord, today your voice is calling	482
103:1-4	Bless the Lord, my soul	74
103:3	Be still and know that I am God	61
103:8	Praise, my soul, the King of heaven	623
103:11	Great is thy faithfulness	273
103:20	Angel-voices ever singing	40
103:20-22	Let everything that has breath	426
104	Lord of beauty, thine the splendour	470
	O worship the King	582
	Send forth your Spirit, Lord	653
104:1-30	Lord, you created	488
104:9	Eternal Father, strong to save	160
104:12	If I were a butterfly	342
104:14	Fill your hearts with joy and gladness	183
104:24-25	If I were a butterfly	342
104:30	Breathe on me, Breath of God	87
	Lord of all life and power	468
	You are the centre	848
104:31	Angel-voices ever singing	40
104:33	Let everything that has breath	426
104:33-34	Hallelu, hallelu	283
105	Come, faithful pilgrims all	121
105:40	Bread is blessed and broken	82
	Guide me, O thou great Redeemer	275
	My God, and is thy table spread	515
105:41	Father, most holy, merciful and loving	173
	Peace is flowing like a river	613
106:1-2	Hallelu, hallelu	283
107:9	Thanks for the fellowship	697
107:10	Jesus, the name high over all	404
107:23-32	Lead us, heavenly Father, lead us	422
108:6	There is a longing	742
110:1	Father of heaven, whose love profound	174
	Rejoice, the Lord is King	638

	Ye choirs of new Jerusalem	839
110:4	Father of heaven, whose love profound	174
112:7	I am trusting thee, Lord Jesus	324
113	Hallelu, hallelu	283
113:1-3	From all that dwell below the skies	203
	From the rising of the sun	209
113:1-6	Let all the world in every corner sing	425
113:3	Give thanks to the Lord (*For ever*)	218
116:17	All my hope on God is founded	19
117	From all that dwell below the skies	203
	Hallelu, hallelu	283
	Laudate Dominum	420
	Your love's greater	856
117:1-2	Great is thy faithfulness	273
	Laudate Dominum	420
118:1	Confitemini Domino	145
118:1-2	Blessèd city, heavenly Salem	77
118:6	Abide with me	6
118:14	In the Lord is my joy	361
	Stand up and bless the Lord	676
118:19-24	This is the day	759
118:19-29	Blessèd city, heavenly Salem	77
118:21	Thanks be to God	696
118:22	Christ is made the sure foundation	96
118:24	This is the day the Lord has made	760
118:25-26	Holy, holy, holy is the Lord	309
	Hosanna, hosanna	314
	There is a longing	742
118:26	This is the day the Lord has made	760
119:15	Help us, O Lord, to learn	298
119:25	Jesus, the name high over all	404
119:45	Lord of creation, to you be all praise!	471
119:57	Amazing grace	34
119:105	Lord of all being	466
119:114	How sweet the name of Jesus sounds	321
119:160	From all that dwell below the skies	203
121:1-8	God that madest earth and heaven	256
121:3	All my hope on God is founded	19
121:5-6	I watch the sunrise (*Close to you*)	338
122:1	Christians, lift up your hearts	108
123:1	I will worship	341
123:2	Wait for the Lord	785
124:8	O God, our help in ages past	547
125:1	I am trusting thee, Lord Jesus	324
126:6	Come, ye faithful, raise the strain	143
	Jesus put this song	397
128:1-4	Jesus, Lord, we pray	392
129:8	Peace to you	616
130	Lord, there are times	480
130:3	Only by grace	598
130:6	I watch the sunrise (*Close to you*)	338
130:7	There's a wideness in God's mercy	747
131	O Lord, my heart is not proud	564
134	Now thank we all our God	532
135:1-3	Hallelu, hallelu	283
136	All my hope on God is founded	19
	Give to our God immortal praise	220
	Let us, with a gladsome mind	435
136:1	O give thanks (Kendrick)	542
	O give thanks (Pond)	543
136:1-4	Give thanks to the Lord (*For ever*)	218
136:12	Give thanks to the Lord (*For ever*)	218
	Thine arm, O Lord, in days of old	750
139	O God, you search me	549

Psalms

	Our God is a great big God	606
	She sits like a bird (*Enemy of apathy*)	654
139:6	You are beautiful (*I stand in awe*)	847
139:9-10	He's got the whole world in his hand	306
139:14-16	Lord, we thank you for the promise	484
139:23	Lord, the light of your love	479
140:4	Be thou my guardian and my guide	65
141:2	Hail, gladdening Light	276
143:6	Spirit of God (*Mallaig Sprinkling Song*)	672
143:8	Be still and know that I am God	61
144:12	God the Father, name we treasure	257
144:15	God the Father, name we treasure	257
145:1-3	Lord, today your voice is calling	482
145:4-6	God of life, God of love	249
145:8	Praise, my soul, the King of heaven	623
145:17	Let us praise God together	433
145:21	Let everything that has breath	426
146:1-2	Hallelu, hallelu	283
146:7	Jesus, the name high over all	404
	Thanks for the fellowship	697
146:10	Come, ye faithful, raise the anthem	142
147:2	From the eastern mountains	207
147:3	I cannot tell	327
147:4-18	Fill your hearts with joy and gladness	183
147:12	Come, ye faithful, raise the anthem	142
147:16	We plough the fields and scatter	801
147:18	Breathe on me, Breath of God	87
	Lord, the light of your love	479
148	Fishes of the ocean	187
	Glory to God above	228
	God, our Creator	253
	Lord, you created	488
	New songs of celebration render	527
	O praise ye the Lord!	574
	Our God is so great	607
	Praise the Lord, ye heavens, adore him	625
	When morning gilds the skies	822
148:1	Gloria (Anderson)	222
148:1-2	Let everything that has breath	426
148:2	Angel-voices ever singing	40
	Ye holy angels bright	840
148:3	Praise, my soul, the King of heaven	623
148:11-12	Let everything that has breath	426
148:13	Let us praise God together	433
149	All praise to our redeeming Lord	22
	New songs of celebration render	527
149:1-2	Of the Father's love begotten	584
149:2	Come, ye faithful, raise the anthem	142
150	Dance and sing	151
	Hallelu, hallelu	283
	New songs of celebration render	527
	O praise ye the Lord!	574
	Praise him on the trumpet	620
	Sing of the Lord's goodness	663
150:1	Come into his presence	126
150:6	Let everything that has breath	426
	Praise to the Lord, the Almighty	628

PROVERBS

2:20	Spirit divine, attend our prayers	671
3:5	I am trusting thee, Lord Jesus	324
3:26	Blessèd city, heavenly Salem	77
9:2	Author of life divine	55
9:5	Broken for me	90

Proverbs

	Gather around, for the table is spread	213
	My God, and is thy table spread	515
14:34	Lord, for the years	454

SONG OF SOLOMON

1:3	May the fragrance of Jesus fill this place	504
2:8-13	Christian people, raise your song	106
5:16	Light of the world (*Here I am to worship*)	441
6:4	Stand up, stand up for Jesus	677
8:6	At the name of Jesus	52
	Hark, my soul, it is the Lord	287
	Jesus, Lord, we pray	392

ISAIAH

1:3	What child is this	812
2:4-5	Onward, Christian pilgrims	599
	Waken, O sleeper, wake and rise	787
	We are marching	789
2:11	Blessing and honour (*Ancient of Days*)	78
2:17	Blessing and honour (*Ancient of Days*)	78
6:1	Open the eyes of my heart	601
6:1-3	Bright the vision that delighted	88
	Holy, holy, holy	308
	Immortal, invisible, God only wise	349
	Let all mortal flesh keep silence	424
	Lord, the light of your love	479
	Ye watchers and ye holy ones	844
6:1-8	Thuma mina	771
6:2-3	Crown him with many crowns	150
	Holy, holy, holy is the Lord	309
	Holy, holy, holy! Lord God almighty	310
6:3	Christ, the fair glory of the holy angels	101
	Open the eyes of my heart	601
6:5-7	Stand up and bless the Lord	676
6:8	Here I am	301
6:8-9	I, the Lord of sea and sky (*Here I am, Lord*)	337
	Inspired by love and anger	362
7:4	Fight the good fight	181
7:14	Come and join the celebration	117
	Hail, thou once despisèd Jesus	278
	Hark, the herald-angels sing	289
	Jesus, Name above all names	395
	O come, O come, Emmanuel	535
9	The people that in darkness sat	727
9:1-2	Lord, the light of your love	479
9:2	Longing for light (*Christ, be our light*)	452
9:2-7	Thy kingdom come, O God	774
9:5-6	Crown him with many crowns	150
	Hark, the herald-angels sing	289
	O thou who camest from above	580
	Unto us a boy is born	782
	You are the King of Glory (*Hosanna to the Son of David*)	849
9:6	All my days (*Beautiful Saviour*)	18
	God is working his purpose out	246
	Hark, the glad sound!	288
	King of glory, King of peace	416
	King of kings and Lord of lords	417
	Peace to you	616
	Rejoice, the Lord is King	638
	Songs of praise the angels sang	668
11:1-2	Come, Holy Ghost, our souls inspire	124
	Come, Holy Spirit, come	125

Isaiah

	Come, thou Holy Spirit, come	139
	Lord, enthroned in heavenly splendour	453
	O come, O come, Emmanuel	535
11:1-9	All over the world	20
	God is working his purpose out	246
	May the mind of Christ my Saviour	506
	Who would think that what was needed (*God's surprise*)	832
11:9	From thee all skill and science flow	212
11:10	Crown him with many crowns	150
12:2-3	The Lord is my song	720
12:2-6	I give my hands	330
14:12	Christ, whose glory fills the skies	105
16:1	See, amid the winter's snow	649
22:2	O come, O come, Emmanuel	535
25:4	God is our strength from days of old	244
25:6-8	Glory, love, and praise, and honour	225
25:8	How bright these glorious spirits shine!	316
30:21	I am trusting thee, Lord Jesus	324
	Lord Jesus, think on me	465
31:1	Blessèd be your name	76
31:6	Blessèd be your name	76
33:20-21	Glorious things of thee are spoken	223
35	The Saviour will come, resplendent in joy	730
35:10	From thee all skill and science flow	212
36:25-26	All over the world	20
40:1	All you who seek a comfort sure	28
	Lord, thy word abideth	481
40:1-11	Do not be afraid	156
	O comfort my people	536
40:4-5	Wait for the Lord	785
	We have a dream	797
40:5	I cannot tell	327
40:7-8	Immortal, invisible, God only wise	349
40:7-9	Lord, thy word abideth	481
	On Jordan's bank the Baptist's cry	589
40:9	Go, tell it on the mountain	233
40:11	Great Shepherd of thy people	274
	Praise, my soul, the King of heaven	623
40:12	It's rounded like an orange	366
40:26	Fill your hearts with joy and gladness	183
40:31	Lord, I come to you	458
	The God of Abraham praise	706
42:7	Jesus, the name high over all	404
42:23	Let the mountains dance and sing	429
43:1-4	Do not be afraid	156
43:11	All for Jesus! All for Jesus!	11
44:24	Shout for joy and sing	656
45:12	He's got the whole world in his hand	306
45:21	How beauteous are their feet	315
45:23	Blessing and honour (*Ancient of Days*)	78
46:4	God be with you till we meet again	236
48:18	Peace is flowing like a river	613
49:6	From the eastern mountains	207
49:10	How bright these glorious spirits shine!	316
49:13	Let the mountains dance and sing	429
49:15	Hark, my soul, it is the Lord	287
49:16	Come, O thou traveller unknown	134
52:3	From heaven you came	205
53	How lovely on the mountains	319
53:1-12	Christ triumphant	103
53:3	Come, see the Lord	138
	My Lord, what love is this (*Amazing love*)	520

Isaiah

53:3-5	Come, wounded healer	141
	God of life, God of love	249
53:4	Above all powers, above all kings	7
53:4-5	How deep the Father's love for us	317
53:4-7	Ah, holy Jesu, how hast thou offended	9
	Come and see	118
	Led like a lamb	423
	The strife is o'er, the battle done	733
	What a friend we have in Jesus	811
53:5	You laid aside your majesty (*I really want to worship you*)	850
53:6	Before Jehovah's aweful throne	68
	Overwhelmed by love	61
53:8	At the cross she keeps her station	50
53:12	Bread of heaven, on thee we feed	83
	Jesus Christ (*Once again*)	380
55	The gracious invitation	709
55:1	Songs of praise the angels sang	668
55:1-2	Christ is the heavenly food	98
55:3	Put thou thy trust in God	634
55:7	Thanks be to God	696
55:12	You shall go out with joy	853
56:5	The head that once was crowned with thorns	711
56:6-7	In Christ there is no east or west	353
57:15	Deck thyself, my soul, with gladness	153
	Jesus, the name high over all	404
58:6-7	Come, faithful pilgrims all	121
58:7	Praise and thanksgiving	617
59:19	Lord Jesus, think on me	465
61:1-2	Here on the threshold of a new beginning	305
61:1-3	Come, Holy Ghost, our souls inspire	124
	God is working his purpose out	246
	Hail to the Lord's anointed	280
	Hark, the glad sound!	288
	I cannot tell	327
	I give you all the honour (*I worship you*)	331
	Inspired by love and anger	362
	Lord, for the years	454
	Make way, make way	500
	O for a thousand tongues to sing	541
61:3	The gracious invitation	709
62:11	The advent of our King	699
64:1	Jesus, where'er thy people meet	407
64:4	Lord of creation, to you be all praise!	471
64:8	Take me, Lord	685
65:17-25	Though pilgrim strangers here below	768
65:19	Great is the darkness (*Come, Lord Jesus*)	271
66:1	Alleluia, Sing to Jesus	33

JEREMIAH

1:5	Now thank we all our God	532
9:23-24	How deep the Father's love for us	317
14:7-10	Father of heaven, whose love profound	174
14:8	God is our strength from days of old	244
14:19-22	Father of heaven, whose love profound	174
17:13	God is our strength from days of old	244
31:3	Your love's greater	856
51:46	Fight the good fight	181

LAMENTATIONS

3:23	New every morning is the love	526
3:25	Jesus, the name high over all	404

Lamentations

3:40-41	Lift up your hearts!	439
3:41	Christians lift your hearts and voices	109

EZEKIEL

1:26	Come, ye faithful, raise the anthem	142
	Ride on, ride on in majesty	640
3:16	Go, tell it on the mountain	233
10:1	Ye watchers and ye holy ones	844
11:23	Love divine, all loves excelling	491
33:7	Go, tell it on the mountain	233
36:25-26	I, the Lord of sea and sky	
	(*Here I am, Lord*)	337
36:26	All you who seek a comfort sure	28
37	Breathe on me, Breath of God	87
47:12	For the healing of the nations	198

DANIEL

2:22	God moves in a mysterious way	247
2:44	Blessing and honour (*Ancient of Days*)	78
3:28	Adoramus te, Domine	8
4:13	Ye watchers and ye holy ones	844
7:9	Come, ye faithful, raise the anthem	142
	Crown him with many crowns	150
	O worship the King	582
	The God of Abraham praise	706
7:9-14	Blessing and honour (*Ancient of Days*)	78
7:9-22	Immortal, invisible, God only wise	349
7:10	Angel-voices ever singing	40
	Come, let us join our cheerful songs	127
9:21	Christ, the fair glory of the holy angels	101
12:1-3	Christ, the fair glory of the holy angels	101

HOSEA

12:3-5	Come, O thou traveller unknown	134
13:4	All for Jesus! All for Jesus!	11
14	Lord, we turn to you for mercy	
	(*God of mercy*)	485
14:4	Christ, the fair glory of the holy angels	101
	I'm black, I'm white, I'm tall, I'm short	346
	It is a thing most wonderful	364

JOEL

2:21	Rejoice, O land, in God thy might	637
2:28	All over the world	20
	The King is among us	714
2:29	Great is the darkness (*Come, Lord Jesus*)	271

AMOS

5:24	Alleluia! Alleluia!	
	(*Alleluia! Raise the Gospel*)	30
	Peace is flowing like a river	613

OBADIAH

21	Come and see the shining hope	119

MICAH

4:3	Onward, Christian pilgrims	599
4:3-4	Waken, O sleeper, wake and rise	787
4:6	Here in this place (*Gather us in*)	302
5:1	Earth has many a noble city	158
6:3-5	I give you love	332

HABAKKUK

2:14	All over the world	20
3:2	Restore, O Lord	639

ZEPHANIAH

1:7	Let all mortal flesh keep silence	424
3:17	I'm black, I'm white, I'm tall, I'm short	346
3:19	Here in this place (*Gather us in*)	302

HAGGAI

2:6	Restore, O Lord	639
2:7	Angels from the realms of glory	39
	Come, thou long-expected Jesus	140

ZECHARIAH

2:13	Let all mortal flesh keep silence	424
8:4-5	Lord, we thank you for the promise	484
13:9	Purify my heart	631

MALACHI

1:11	From all that dwell below the skies	203
	From the sun's rising	210
2:6	God be in my head	235
3:1	Angels from the realms of glory	39
	Hail to the Lord who comes	279
3:3	Purify my heart	631
	Restore, O Lord	639
3:6	Abide with me	6
	Great is thy faithfulness	273
4:2	Christ, whose glory fills the skies	105
	Go wandering in the sun	234
	Hark, the herald-angels sing	289
	Judge eternal, throned in splendour	411
	O come, O come, Emmanuel	535
	You are the King of Glory	
	(*Hosanna to the Son of David*)	849

MATTHEW

1:16-20	Jesus calls us: o'er the tumult	379
1:16-25	Come and join the celebration	117
1:21	Hail, thou once despisèd Jesus	278
	Hark, the herald-angels sing	289
	Jesu, our hope, our heart's desire	370
	Jesus, Name above all names	395
	Jesus, the name high over all	404
	Let us talents and tongues employ	434
	Like a candle flame	444
	Morning has broken	510
	O little town of Bethlehem	559
	The angel Gabriel from heaven came	700
	The Virgin Mary had a baby boy	734
1:23	Hail, true body	281
2:1-2	Cloth for the cradle	113
	Long ago, prophets knew	451
2:1-12	Angels from the realms of glory	39
	A great and mighty wonder	2
	As with gladness men of old	46
	Brightest and best	89
	Come and join the celebration	117
	Crown him with many crowns	150
	Earth has many a noble city	158
	From the eastern mountains	207
	Glory to God!	227
	In the bleak mid-winter	357

	O come, all ye faithful	534
	See him lying on a bed of straw	650
	The first Nowell	705
	The Virgin Mary had a baby boy	734
	We three kings of Orient are	805
	What child is this	812
	Who would think that what was needed	
	(*God's surprise*)	832
2:2	Adoramus te, Domine	8
2:6	Earth has many a noble city	158
2:9-10	Little donkey	447
2:11	At this time of giving	54
	Cloth for the cradle	113
	O worship the Lord in the beauty	
	of holiness	583
2:13-18	Unto us a boy is born	782
3:1-3	Come on and celebrate	135
3:1-12	On Jordan's bank the Baptist's cry	589
3:11	All over the world	20
	Christ, when for us you were baptized	104
	Come, Holy Spirit, come	125
3:13-17	Christ, when for us you were baptized	104
	Father welcomes all his children	179
3:16	Eternal Ruler of the ceaseless round	162
	O King enthroned on high	557
	O let the Son of God enfold you	558
	Spirit divine, attend our prayers	671
4:1-11	At even, ere the sun was set	49
	Lead us, heavenly Father, lead us	422
	Love is his word	492
	O love, how deep, how broad, how high	570
4:4	Seek ye first	652
4:16	God is our strength from days of old	244
4:16-17	Lord, the light of your love	479
4:17-25	Jesus Christ is waiting	382
4:18-20	Follow me	189
4:18-22	Dear Lord and Father of mankind	152
	Jesus calls us: o'er the tumult	379
	O happy day	551
	When God almighty came to earth	814
4:21	I danced in the morning	
	(*Lord of the Dance*)	329
5:1-12	Alleluia! Alleluia! (*Alleluia!*	
	Raise the Gospel)	30
5:3-4	The Church's one foundation	702
5:3-12	The kingdom of heaven	717
5:4	All you who seek a comfort sure	28
5:5	Fill your hearts with joy and gladness	183
	Make way, make way	500
5:8	Blest are the pure in heart	79
	God be in my head	235
5:12	For all the saints	190
	For all thy saints, O Lord	191
5:13-14	Here I am	301
5:13-16	Here in this place (*Gather us in*)	302
5:14-16	Here on the threshold of a new	
	beginning	305
	Like a candle flame	444
	The Spirit lives to set us free	732
5:16	Be the centre of my life	64
	Christ is the world's Light	100
	Come, faithful pilgrims all	121
	Jesus bids us shine	377
	This little light of mine	762

5:41	Brother, sister, let me serve you	91
5:44	O Lord, all the world belongs to you	560
6:9-13	A brighter dawn is breaking	1
	For the fruits of his creation	197
	Forgive our sins as we forgive	199
	God forgave my sin (*Freely, freely*)	237
	Make me a channel of your peace	499
	O God of Bethel, by whose hand	545
	O thou, who at thy Eucharist didst pray	579
	Our Father (Caribbean)	603
	Our Father (Wiener)	604
	Thy kingdom come	773
	Thy kingdom come, O God	774
	We plough the fields and scatter	801
6:10	Here on the threshold of a new	
	beginning	305
	Jesus, all for Jesus	375
	Lord, for the years	454
	Lord of creation, may your will be done	472
	Lord of creation, to you be all praise!	471
	Thank you for saving me	693
6:11	Lord, we thank you for the promise	484
	This is the air I breathe	758
6:16-18	O Lord, we want to praise you	567
6:20	Blest Creator of the light	80
6:26	Moses, I know you're the man	511
6:28-29	There are hundreds of sparrows	
	(*God knows me*)	738
6:31-33	Lord, for the years	454
6:33	Lord, we thank you for the promise	484
	Seek ye first	652
7:7	Come, all who look to Christ today	115
	Seek ye first	652
7:10	Glory to thee, O God	230
	Thanks for the fellowship	697
7:11	Praise and thanksgiving	617
	We plough the fields and scatter	801
7:13	A new commandment	4
	And now, O Father, mindful of the love	38
	Faithful Shepherd, feed me	166
	I will sing the wondrous story	340
	Loving Shepherd of thy sheep	495
7:14	As with gladness men of old	46
7:24-27	The wise man	735
8:2	Will you come and follow me	834
8:10-11	In Christ there is no east or west	353
8:11	Glory, love, and praise, and honour	225
	The Spirit lives to set us free	732
8:16	At even, ere the sun was set	49
8:17	What a friend we have in Jesus	811
8:20	Follow me	189
	Moses, I know you're the man	511
	Thou didst leave thy throne	766
8:23-27	Eternal Father, strong to save	160
	I cannot tell	327
	Inspired by love and anger	362
	Sweet sacrament divine	684
8:26	Be still, my soul	63
	Calm me, Lord	92
	Holy Spirit, truth divine	312
8:28	Jesus, the name high over all	404
9:9	Follow me	189
	Jesus Christ is waiting	382
	When God almighty came to earth	814

	Will you come and follow me	834
9:17	One shall tell another (*New Wine*)	596
9:20-22	Lord of all, to whom alone	469
9:21	Immortal love, for ever full	350
9:27	Spirit of God (*Mallaig Sprinkling Song*)	672
9:37	Here I am	301
9:38	From the sun's rising	210
10:5-15	Lord, you call us to a journey	487
10:8	God forgave my sin (*Freely, freely*)	237
	Jesus, the name high over all	404
10:8-9	God's Spirit is in my heart	
	(*Go, tell everyone*)	262
	If you believe and I believe	344
10:24-39	Christ for the world we sing!	95
10:29-31	There are hundreds of sparrows	
	(*God knows me*)	738
10:37-39	Jesus, we have heard your Spirit	406
10:38	Follow me	189
	Lift high the Cross	437
	Take up thy cross, the Saviour said	689
	When God almighty came to earth	814
11:5	Jesus, the name high over all	404
	My song is love unknown	521
11:16-19	Jesus Christ is waiting	382
11:17	I danced in the morning	
	(*Lord of the Dance*)	329
11:19	Alleluia, sing to Jesus	33
	Love is his word	492
11:28	Christ for the world we sing!	95
	Lord, I lift my hands to you in prayer	460
11:28-29	Here in this place (*Gather us in*)	302
	Lord Jesus, think on me	465
11:28-30	All you who seek a comfort sure	28
	Come, wounded healer	141
	Forth in thy name, O Lord, I go	201
	Happy are they, they that love God	285
	I cannot tell	327
	I heard the voice of Jesus say	334
	Love divine, all loves excelling	491
11:29	Have faith in God, my heart	290
12:18	Beauty for brokenness (*God of the poor*)	67
12:21	Come, thou long-expected Jesus	140
12:29	Christ the Lord is risen again	102
12:50	In Christ there is no east or west	353
13:4-9	Now, my tongue, the mystery telling	531
	We plough the fields and scatter	801
13:16-17	How beauteous are their feet	315
13:23	Come, Lord, to our souls	130
13:24-33	Happy are they, they that love God	285
13:25	Come, ye thankful people, come	144
13:31-34	O Lord, we want to praise you	567
13:39	Alleluia, alleluia, hearts to heaven	
	and voices raise	32
13:41	At the name of Jesus	52
	Come, ye thankful people, come	144
13:44-46	O Lord, we want to praise you	567
13:52	Come, Lord, to our souls	130
13:55	Inspired by love and anger	362
	Lord of all hopefulness	467
14:5	Father, Lord of all creation	172
14:13-21	Gather around, for the table is spread	213
14:19	Break thou the bread	86
14:22-23	Eternal Father, strong to save	160
14:36	Jesus Christ is waiting	382
15:21-28	In Christ there is no east or west	353
15:30-31	My song is love unknown	521
	Thine arm, O Lord, in days of old	750
15:32-39	Gather around, for the table is spread	213
15:36	Break thou the bread	86
16:16	I believe in Jesus	325
16:18-19	Firmly I believe and truly	186
16:24	Follow me	189
	Take up thy cross, the Saviour said	689
16:24-28	Jesus, we have heard your Spirit	406
17:8	Lift up your hearts!	439
18:1-4	Jesus, humble was your birth	384
18:10	How shall I sing that majesty	320
18:12	Amazing grace	34
	Hark, my soul, it is the Lord	287
	I will sing the wondrous story	340
	The King of love my shepherd is	715
18:20	Jesus calls us here to meet him	378
	There's a quiet understanding	745
19:3-5	These vows of love are taken	749
19:14	Father welcomes all his children	179
	God is here! As we his people	241
20:23	At the cross she keeps her station	50
20:28	From heaven you came	205
	Hail, true body	281
	Jesus is Lord! Creation's voice	
	proclaims it	387
20:30	Lord, have mercy (Ghana)	455
	Lord, have mercy (Russian)	456
21:1-11	All glory, laud and honour	12
	Clap your hands, all you people	112
	Lift up your heads	438
	We have a King who rides a donkey	799
21:5	The advent of our King	699
21:8-9	Give me joy in my heart	215
	Hark, the glad sound!	288
	Holy, holy, holy is the Lord	309
	Hosanna, hosanna	314
	Lord, enthroned in heavenly splendour	453
	My song is love unknown	521
	Ride on, ride on in majesty	640
	This is the day the Lord has made	760
	Wake, O wake! with tidings thrilling	786
	You are the King of Glory	
	(*Hosanna to the Son of David*)	849
21:12-16	Jesus Christ is waiting	382
21:33-46	Blessèd city, heavenly Salem	77
22:1-4	Come, risen Lord	137
22:1-10	Thy hand, O God, has guided	772
22:1-14	Christians lift your hearts and voices	109
	Come, now, the table's spread	133
22:34-40	Firmly I believe and truly	186
22:45	Hail to the Lord's anointed	280
23:11	O Lord, all the world belongs to you	560
24:12	Lift up your hearts!	439
24:30	Hark! A thrilling voice is calling	286
	Led like a lamb	423
24:30-31	Lo, he comes with clouds descending	449
	O Lord, my God (*How great thou art*)	563
	This joyful Eastertide	761
24:35	God of love	250
24:42-44	Come, thou long-expected Jesus	140
	Waken, O sleeper, wake and rise	787
	Ye servants of the Lord	842

Matthew

25:1-13	Give me joy in my heart	215
	Wake, O wake! with tidings thrilling	786
	Will you come and follow me	834
25:9	Give me peace, O Lord, I pray	216
25:21	As Jacob with travel was weary one day	41
	Lord Jesus, think on me	465
25:31	At the name of Jesus	52
25:31-46	When I needed a neighbour	819
25:34	As Jacob with travel was weary one day	41
25:34-40	Take my hands, Lord	686
26:15	Christ is the world's Light	100
26:20-25	One whose heart is hard as steel	597
26:26	There's a spirit in the air	746
26:26-28	At the cross she keeps her station	50
	Broken for me	90
	Come, risen Lord	137
	Glory to God!	227
	Love is his word	492
26:26-29	At this table we remember	53
	Gifts of bread and wine	21
	God of the Passover	252
	This is my body (*In love for me*)	755
26:26-30	As the disciples	44
26:29	Glory, love, and praise, and honour	225
26:31-35	One whose heart is hard as steel	597
26:36-46	From heaven you came	205
26:39	Lord of creation, may your will be done	472
26:41	Be thou my guardian and my guide	65
	Forth in thy name, O Lord, I go	201
	Onward, Christian pilgrims	599
26:47-50	One whose heart is hard as steel	597
26:57-75	One whose heart is hard as steel	597
27:11-26	One whose heart is hard as steel	597
27:22	My song is love unknown	521
27:26	My song is love unknown	521
27:29	Come and see	118
	O dearest Lord, thy sacred head	538
	O sacred head, surrounded	576
	The head that once was crowned with thorns	711
27:32-61	Were you there when they crucified my Lord?	810
27:39-44	How deep the Father's love for us	317
27:39-46	Ah, holy Jesu, how hast thou offended	9
	A man there lived in Galilee	3
27:66	Love's redeeming work is done	494
	Low in the grave he lay	496
28:1-7	All in an Easter garden	17
28:1-10	A brighter dawn is breaking	1
	From the very depths of darkness	211
	Go back, go back to Galilee	231
	Thine be the glory	751
28.6	He has risen	292
28:7	Jesus Christ is risen today	381
28:9	Adoramus te, Domine	8
	Christian people, raise your song	106
	The day of resurrection	703
28:18-19	A man there lived in Galilee	3
	God forgave my sin (*Freely, freely*)	237
28:19	Great is the darkness (*Come, Lord Jesus*)	271
28:19-20	From the sun's rising	210
	Gifts of bread and wine	214
	God the Father, name we treasure	257
28:20	Alleluia, sing to Jesus	33

Matthew

	Firmly I believe and truly	186
	Lord of all being	466

MARK

1:1-4	Wait for the Lord	785
1:1-8	On Jordan's bank the Baptist's cry	589
1:1-11	Christ, when for us you were baptized	104
1:8	All over the world	20
1:9-11	Father welcomes all his children	179
1:9-13	O love, how deep, how broad, how high	570
1:10	Come, Holy Ghost, our souls inspire	124
	Come, Holy Spirit, come	125
	Eternal Ruler of the ceaseless round	162
	O King enthroned on high	557
	O let the Son of God enfold you	558
	Spirit divine, attend our prayers	671
1:12	At even, ere the sun was set	49
	Lead us, heavenly Father, lead us	422
	Love is his word	492
1:14	Christ, when for us you were baptized	104
1:15	Here in this place (*Gather us in*)	302
1:16-20	Dear Lord and Father of mankind	152
	O happy day	551
	When God almighty came to earth	814
	Will you come and follow me	834
1:17	Follow me	189
	Jesus Christ is waiting	382
1:21-28	Firmly I believe and truly	186
	Jesus Christ is waiting	382
1:21-34	Jesus, humble was your birth	384
1:24	There is a Redeemer	743
1:32	At even, ere the sun was set	49
1:32-34	Christ for the world we sing!	95
1:40	Will you come and follow me	834
1:40-45	From thee all skill and science flow	212
1:41	Lord of the boundless curves	475
2:5	God forgave my sin (*Freely, freely*)	237
2:14	Follow me	189
	When God almighty came to earth	814
	Will you come and follow me	834
2:22	One shall tell another (*New Wine*)	596
3:27	Christ the Lord is risen again	102
3:28	Immortal love, for ever full	350
3:31-35	In Christ there is no east or west	353
4:3-9	Now, my tongue, the mystery telling	531
	We plough the fields and scatter	801
4:9	Hands that have been handling	284
	Lord Jesus Christ, be present	464
4:11	Lord of lords and King eternal	474
4:20	Hands that have been handling	284
4:26-29	Come, ye thankful people, come	144
	For the fruits of his creation	197
	Now the green blade riseth	533
4:35-41	Be still, my soul	63
	Eternal Father, strong to save	160
	I cannot tell	327
	Inspired by love and anger	362
	Sweet sacrament divine	684
4:39	Calm me, Lord	92
	Holy Spirit, truth divine	312
4:40	Have faith in God, my heart	290
5:12	Jesus, the name high over all	404
5:24-34	Lord of all, to whom alone	469
5:34	Christ is the heavenly food	98

Mark

6:3	Hail, true body	281
	Inspired by love and anger	362
	Jesu, Son of Mary	371
	Lord of all hopefulness	467
6:7-11	Lord, you call us to a journey	487
6:30-44	5000 + hungry folk	188
	Gather around, for the table is spread	213
6:41	Break thou the bread	86
6:45-52	Eternal Father, strong to save	160
7:37	All things bright and beautiful	26
8:1-10	Gather around, for the table is spread	213
8:23	Spirit of God (*Mallaig Sprinkling Song*)	672
8:25	Lord of beauty, thine the splendour	470
8:34	Follow me	189
	Lift high the Cross	437
	Lo round the throne, a glorious band	450
	Take up thy cross, the Saviour said	689
8:34-38	Jesus, we have heard your Spirit	406
8:38	At the name of Jesus	52
9:24	Christ, whose glory fills the skies	105
	I believe in Jesus	325
9:41	For all the saints	190
10:6-9	These vows of love are taken	749
10:14	Father welcomes all his children	179
	Jesus Christ is waiting	382
10:18	God is good, God is great	240
10:35-45	Father of heaven, whose love profound	174
10:39	At the cross she keeps her station	50
10:45	Come, wounded healer	141
	From heaven you came	205
	God of love	250
	Hail to the Lord who comes	279
	How deep the Father's love for us	317
	Jesu, our hope, our heart's desire	370
	Jesus is Lord! Creation's voice proclaims it	387
11:1-10	We have a King who rides a donkey	799
11:1-11	All glory, laud and honour	12
11:8-10	Hark, the glad sound!	288
	Hosanna, hosanna	314
	Lord, enthroned in heavenly splendour	453
	My song is love unknown	521
	Ride on, ride on in majesty	640
	Wake, O wake! with tidings thrilling	786
	You are the King of Glory (*Hosanna to the Son of David*)	849
11:8-19	Give me joy in my heart	215
11:9	Clap your hands, all you people	112
	This is the day the Lord has made	760
11:9-10	Holy, holy, holy is the Lord	309
	Holy, holy, holy	308
11:22	Have faith in God, my heart	290
12:29	I will worship	341
12:37	Cloth for the cradle	113
	Hail to the Lord's anointed	280
13:11	God be in my head	235
13:25-26	Lo, he comes with clouds descending	449
	O Lord, my God (*How great thou art*)	563
13:26	Led like a lamb	423
13:33	Waken, O sleeper, wake and rise	787
13:37	Ye servants of God	841
14:10	Christ is the world's Light	100
14:10-11	Jesus, humble was your birth	384
14:12-16	Christians lift your hearts and voices	109

14:15	An upper room did our Lord prepare	35
14:17-21	Jesus, humble was your birth	384
14:22	There's a spirit in the air	746
14:22-24	Broken for me	90
	Christians lift your hearts and voices	109
	Come, risen Lord	137
14:22-25	At this table we remember	53
	Gifts of bread and wine	21
	God of the Passover	252
	Love is his word	492
	This is my body (*In love for me*)	755
14:22-26	As the disciples	44
14:27-31	One whose heart is hard as steel	597
14:32-42	From heaven you came	205
14:32-49	Jesus, humble was your birth	384
14:34-36	Lord of creation, may your will be done	472
	Lord of creation, to you be all praise!	471
14:38	Be thou my guardian and my guide	65
	Forth in thy name, O Lord, I go	201
	Onward, Christian pilgrims	599
14:43-45	One whose heart is hard as steel	597
14:53-72	One whose heart is hard as steel	597
15:1-15	One whose heart is hard as steel	597
15:13	My song is love unknown	521
15:15-17	At the cross she keeps her station	50
	My song is love unknown	521
	O dearest Lord, thy sacred head	538
	O sacred head, surrounded	576
15:16-34	How deep the Father's love for us	317
15:17-20	Come and see	118
	The head that once was crowned with thorns	711
15:21-47	Were you there when they crucified my Lord?	810
15:33-34	How deep the Father's love for us	317
15:46	Above all powers, above all kings	7
16:1-6	All in an Easter garden	17
16:1-8	From the very depths of darkness	211
	Thine be the glory	751
16:4	Love's redeeming work is done	494
16:6	He has risen	292
	Jesus Christ is risen today	381
16:15	Alleluia, alleluia, give thanks to the risen Lord	31

LUKE

1-2	The angel Gabriel from heaven came	700
1:1-4	Saint Luke, beloved physician	645
1:9	Wait for the Lord	785
1:19	Christ, the fair glory of the holy angels	101
1:26	Christ, the fair glory of the holy angels	101
1:26-38	For Mary, mother of our Lord	194
	Long ago, prophets knew	451
	Mary, blessed grieving mother	501
	Of the Father's love begotten	584
	The Virgin Mary had a baby boy	734
	Ye who own the faith of Jesus	845
1:31	Jesus, the name high over all	404
1:33	Blessing and honour (*Ancient of Days*)	78
	Crown him with many crowns	150
	Rejoice, the Lord is King	638
	The day thou gavest, Lord, is ended	704
1:35	God is our strength from days of old	244
	There is a Redeemer	743

Luke

1:39-47	Come and join the celebration	117
1:46	Christ is the King!	99
	Magnificat	497
1:46-55	Join the song of praise and protest	
	(*Magnificat*)	408
	Tell out, my soul	692
	Ye who own the faith of Jesus	845
1:51-52	Fill your hearts with joy and gladness	183
1:53	Thanks for the fellowship	697
1:75	Come and see the shining hope	119
1:78	Christ, whose glory fills the skies	105
2:1-7	Mary had a baby	502
	Once in royal David's city	592
2:1-20	Come and join the celebration	117
	Crown him with many crowns	150
	God rest you merry, gentlefolk	254
	See, amid the winter's snow	649
	See him lying on a bed of straw	650
	Silent night	658
	What child is this	812
2:4	Little donkey	447
2:5-7	Once in royal David's city	592
2:6-7	Jesus, humble was your birth	384
2:6-20	Cloth for the cradle	113
2:7	Away in a manger	59
	Born in the night, Mary's child	81
	Brightest and best	89
	From the eastern mountains	207
	I cannot tell	327
	Jesus, good above all other	383
	Little Jesus, sweetly sleep	448
	Long ago, prophets knew	451
	Thou didst leave thy throne	766
	Unto us a boy is born	782
	We have a gospel to proclaim	798
	Who would think that what was needed	
	(*God's surprise*)	832
2:7-35	For Mary, mother of our Lord	194
2:8-14	A great and mighty wonder	2
	Angels from the realms of glory	39
	Behold, the great Creator	71
	Go, tell it on the mountain	233
	The Virgin Mary had a baby boy	734
2:8-20	In the bleak mid-winter	357
	Lift up your voice	440
	O come, all ye faithful	534
	Our Father God in heaven	605
	The first Nowell	705
	While shepherds watched	827
2:11	Lift up your heads	438
	My Jesus, my Saviour	519
2:13-14	Ding dong, merrily on high!	154
	It came upon the midnight clear	363
	Like a candle flame	444
	O little town of Bethlehem	559
2:13-20	Glory to God!	227
2:14	Alleluia, alleluia, hearts to heaven	
	and voices raise	32
	Angels from the realms of glory	39
	Christ is the world's Light	100
	Come, faithful pilgrims all	121
	Come into his presence	126
	Ding dong, merrily on high!	154
	Gloria (Anderson)	222

Luke

	Glory to God (Peruvian Gloria)	226
	Hark, the herald-angels sing	289
2:21	Jesus, the name high over all	404
2:22-40	Hail to the Lord who comes	279
2:25	Come, thou long-expected Jesus	140
2:29-32	Faithful vigil ended	167
2:32	From the eastern mountains	207
2:35	At the cross she keeps her station	50
	Sing we of the blessèd Mother	666
3:1-4	Wait for the Lord	785
3:1-18	On Jordan's bank the Baptist's cry	589
3:2-14	Cloth for the cradle	113
3:7-18	Christ, when for us you were baptized	104
3:11	Praise and thanksgiving	617
3:15-17	Come, gracious Spirit, heavenly Dove	122
3:16	All over the world	20
3:21-22	Christ, when for us you were baptized	104
	Come, gracious Spirit, heavenly Dove	122
	Father welcomes all his children	179
3:22	Come, Holy Ghost, our souls inspire	124
	Come, Holy Spirit, come	125
	Eternal Ruler of the ceaseless round	162
	God is our strength from days of old	244
	O King enthroned on high	557
	O let the Son of God enfold you	558
	Spirit divine, attend our prayers	671
4:1-13	At even, ere the sun was set	49
	Forty days and forty nights	202
	Lead us, heavenly Father, lead us	422
	Love is his word	492
	O love, how deep, how broad, how high	570
4:4	Seek ye first	652
4:8-21	Christ's is the world (*A touching place*)	110
4:16-21	Lift up your voice	440
4:18	God is working his purpose out	246
	God's Spirit is in my heart	
	(*Go, tell everyone*)	262
	Hail to the Lord's anointed	280
	I give you all the honour (*I worship you*)	331
	Jesus, the name high over all	404
	Make way, make way	500
	O for a thousand tongues to sing	541
	Will you come and follow me	834
4:18-19	Hark, the glad sound!	288
	Here on the threshold of a new	
	beginning	305
	Lord, for the years	454
4:34	Be still, my soul	63
	There is a Redeemer	743
4:36	I believe in Jesus	325
4:39	Jesus Christ is waiting	382
4:40	At even, ere the sun was set	49
5:1-11	O happy day	551
5:11-12	Dear Lord and Father of mankind	152
	Will you come and follow me	834
5:17	I believe in Jesus	325
5:27	Follow me	189
	When God almighty came to earth	814
	Will you come and follow me	834
5:37	One shall tell another (*New Wine*)	596
6:20-23	The kingdom of heaven	717
6:21	Make way, make way	500
6:24-26	Alleluia! Alleluia! (*Alleluia!*	
	Raise the Gospel)	30

Luke

6:27	O Lord, all the world belongs to you	560
6:35	For all the saints	190
6:47-49	The wise man	735
7:12-15	Our Father God in heaven	605
7:16	Father, Lord of all creation	172
7:21	Jesus, the name high over all	404
7:22	My song is love unknown	521
	Thine arm, O Lord, in days of old	750
	Thou, whose almighty word	767
7:34	Alleluia, sing to Jesus	33
	Jesus, Prince and Saviour	396
7:37	I danced in the morning	
	(*Lord of the Dance*)	329
7:38	I will offer up my life	339
7:43	Love is his word	492
7:48	God forgave my sin (*Freely, freely*)	237
8:4-5	Colours of day (*Light up the fire*)	114
8:5-8	Now, my tongue, the mystery telling	531
	We have a gospel to proclaim	798
8:12	Born in the night, Mary's child	81
8:16	Christ is the King!	99
8:19-21	In Christ there is no east or west	353
8:22-25	Be still, my soul	63
	Calm me, Lord	92
	Eternal Father, strong to save	160
	I cannot tell	327
	Inspired by love and anger	362
	Sweet sacrament divine	684
8:24	Holy Spirit, truth divine	312
8:26-39	Lord Jesus, think on me	465
8:43-48	Lord of all, to whom alone	469
8:44	Immortal love, for ever full	350
9:6	Saint Luke, beloved physician	645
9:10-17	5000 + hungry folk	188
	Gather around, for the table is spread	213
9:11	Saint Luke, beloved physician	645
9:16	Break thou the bread	86
9:23	Follow me	189
	Lift high the Cross	437
	Take up thy cross, the Saviour said	689
9:23-27	Jesus, we have heard your Spirit	406
9:26	At the name of Jesus	52
9:48	Let us build a house (*All are welcome*)	432
9:58	Jesus Christ is waiting	382
	Thou didst leave thy throne	766
	When God almighty came to earth	814
9:58-59	Follow me	189
	Moses, I know you're the man	511
	Will you come and follow me	834
10:1-12	Lord, you call us to a journey	487
10:2	From the sun's rising	210
	Here I am	301
10:4	Moses, I know you're the man	511
10:6	God forgave my sin (*Freely, freely*)	237
10:9	Here in this place (*Gather us in*)	302
10:23-24	How beauteous are their feet	315
10:25-29	In bread we bring you, Lord	351
10:34	Hark, my soul, it is the Lord	287
	When I needed a neighbour	819
10:36	Jesu, Jesu, fill us with your love	368
10:39	To be in your presence (*My desire*)	776
11:1	Lord Jesus Christ (*Living Lord*)	463
	Lord, teach us how to pray aright	478
11:2	Thank you for saving me	693

Luke

11:2-4	God forgave my sin (*Freely, freely*)	237
	Make me a channel of your peace	499
	O God of Bethel, by whose hand	545
	Our Father (Caribbean)	603
	Our Father (Wiener)	604
	Thy kingdom come	773
	Thy kingdom come, O God	774
	We plough the fields and scatter	801
11:3	Praise and thanksgiving	617
11:9	Come, all who look to Christ today	115
	Jesus, the name high over all	404
11:13	Come, gracious Spirit, heavenly Dove	122
11:22	Christ the Lord is risen again	102
11:33	Christ is the King!	99
11:42	Beauty for brokenness (*God of the poor*)	67
12:13	Clap your hands, all you people	112
12:24	Moses, I know you're the man	511
12:27-28	There are hundreds of sparrows	
	(*God knows me*)	738
12:31	Wait for the Lord	785
12:35	Ye servants of the Lord	842
12:35-36	Christ is the King!	99
12:4	Moses, I know you're the man	511
12:6-7	There are hundreds of sparrows	
	(*God knows me*)	738
12:40	Come, thou long-expected Jesus	140
12:49	Colours of day (*Light up the fire*)	114
13:1-5	Creator of the earth and skies	147
13:10-17	I danced in the morning	
	(*Lord of the Dance*)	329
13:24	As with gladness men of old	46
	Faithful Shepherd, feed me	166
	I will sing the wondrous story	340
	Loving Shepherd of thy sheep	495
14:7-14	Jesus, humble was your birth	384
14:12-24	I, the Lord of sea and sky	
	(*Here I am, Lord*)	337
14:13	Thine arm, O Lord, in days of old	750
14:15-24	The gracious invitation	709
14:16-24	Thy hand, O Lord, has guided	772
14:21	From the eastern mountains	207
	Here in this place (*Gather us in*)	302
14:23	From the eastern mountains	207
15:1-10	Father of heaven, whose love profound	174
15:2	Let us build a house (*All are welcome*)	432
15:3	I will sing the wondrous story	340
15:3-7	I have a friend	333
15:4-6	Amazing grace	34
	Hark, my soul, it is the Lord	287
	The King of love my shepherd is	715
15:11-24	Christ's is the world (*A touching place*)	110
15:11-32	God of life, God of love	249
	The gracious invitation	709
15:20	Lord, I come to you	458
15:24	Christ the Lord is risen again	102
17:5	Lord Jesus Christ, be present	464
17:5-6	Have faith in God, my heart	290
17:5-10	Firmly I believe and truly	186
17:13	Lord, have mercy (Ghana)	455
	Lord, have mercy (Russian)	456
17:20-21	O, heaven is in my heart	552
18:9-14	Lift up your hearts!	439
18:16	Father welcomes all his children	179
	God is here! As we his people	241

Luke

18:19	God is good, God is great	240
19:1-5	Zacchaeus was a very little man	857
19:10	Lord of all life and power	468
	The Spirit lives to set us free	732
19:28-38	All glory, laud and honour	12
	My song is love unknown	521
19:37-38	Clap your hands, all you people	112
	Ride on, ride on in majesty	640
	You are the King of Glory	
	(*Hosanna to the Son of David*)	849
19:38	Gloria (Anderson)	222
	Holy, holy, holy	308
	Holy, holy, holy is the Lord	309
20:21	God's Spirit is in my heart	
	(*Go, tell everyone*)	262
20:27-38	Christian people, raise your song	106
20:44	Hail to the Lord's anointed	280
21:27	Led like a lamb	423
21:28	Colours of day (*Light up the fire*)	114
21:33	Songs of praise the angels sang	668
21:36	Forth in thy name, O Lord, I go	201
	Lord of all, to whom alone	469
	Onward, Christian pilgrims	599
	Waken, O sleeper, wake and rise	787
22:3-6	Christ is the world's Light	100
	Ye servants of the Lord	842
22:12	An upper room did our Lord prepare	35
	Come, risen Lord	137
22:14-20	At this table we remember	53
22:19	Christians lift your hearts and voices	109
	There's a spirit in the air	746
22:19-20	Amazing grace	34
	Broken for me	90
	Come, risen Lord	137
	Gifts of bread and wine	214
	God of the Passover	252
	Here in this place (*Gather us in*)	302
	Lord Jesus Christ (*Living Lord*)	463
	Love is his word	492
	Thee we adore, O hidden Saviour, thee	737
	This is my body (*In love for me*)	755
22:26	O Lord, all the world belongs to you	560
22:30	As your family, Lord, see us here	47
22:31-34	One whose heart is hard as steel	597
22:39-44	Stay with me	678
22:40-46	From heaven you came	205
22:47-62	One whose heart is hard as steel	597
22:54-62	Lord of all being	466
22:60-61	At even, ere the sun was set	49
	O sacred head, surrounded	576
22:63	Come and see	118
23:1-5	One whose heart is hard as steel	597
23:4	God forgave my sin (*Freely, freely*)	237
23:13-25	One whose heart is hard as steel	597
23:21	My song is love unknown	521
23:26-55	Were you there when they crucified my Lord?	810
23:33-34	All you who seek a comfort sure	28
23:34	Come and see	118
23:42-43	Jesus, remember me	398
23:43	Lord it belongs not to my care	462
24:1-8	From the very depths of darkness	211
	Thine be the glory	751
24:2	Love's redeeming work is done	494

Luke

24:6	He has risen	292
	Jesus Christ is risen today	381
24:9	Abide with me	6
24:13-32	In the garden Mary lingers	359
24:13-35	Come, risen Lord	137
	Thanks for the fellowship	697
24:28-34	As the disciples	44
	Colours of day (*Light up the fire*)	114
24:30	Break the bread and pour the wine	85
24:30-32	Break thou the bread	86
24:32	Come, Lord, to our souls	130
24:34	Alleluia, alleluia, give thanks to the risen Lord	31
24:35	Break the bread and pour the wine	85
	Christians, lift up your hearts	108
	Gather around, for the table is spread	213
	Jesus, stand among us	401
24:36-43	As we are gathered	45
24:45	Come, Lord, to our souls	130
24:47	Colours of day (*Light up the fire*)	114
24:49-52	Be still, for the presence of the Lord	62

JOHN

1:1	Come, see the Lord	138
	Father of heaven, whose love profound	174
	I bind unto myself today	326
	Lord, for the years	454
1:1-4	Christ, the fair glory of the holy angels	101
1:1-5	Cloth for the cradle	113
	Lord of all life and power	468
1:1-14	At the name of Jesus	52
	Come, see the Lord	138
	Jesus calls us here to meet him	378
	Of the Father's love begotten	584
1:1-18	Christ for the world we sing!	95
	Long ago, prophets knew	451
1:3	Come, let us with our Lord arise	129
	Light of the world (*Here I am to worship*)	441
1:4	God has spoken – by the prophets	238
	Hail, gladdening Light	276
1:4-5	Like a candle flame	444
1:6	On Jordan's bank the Baptist's cry	589
1:9	Hail, gladdening Light	276
	Jesus the Lord said: 'I am the Bread'	403
	Like a candle flame	444
1:9-10	Lead, kindly light	421
1:10	My song is love unknown	521
1:11	Ah, holy Jesu, how hast thou offended	9
	Light of the world (*Here I am to worship*)	441
1:12	I am trusting thee, Lord Jesus	324
1:14	A great and mighty wonder	2
	Be thou my vision	66
	Christ triumphant	103
	Christians, awake!	107
	Come, ye faithful, raise the anthem	142
	Crown him with many crowns	150
	Earth has many a noble city	158
	Father, Lord of all creation	172
	Father of heaven, whose love profound	174
	Give us the wings of faith	221
	Glory to God!	227
	God is our strength from days of old	244
	Hail, gladdening Light	276
	Hark, the herald-angels sing	289

John

	I bind unto myself today	326
	It's rounded like an orange	366
	Jesus, Name above all names	395
	Lord of all, to whom alone	469
	My song is love unknown	521
	Now, my tongue, the mystery telling	531
	O come, all ye faithful	534
	Thanks to God whose word was spoken	698
	The advent of our King	699
	We have a gospel to proclaim	798
	What child is this	812
1:15	On Jordan's bank the Baptist's cry	589
1:16	Deck thyself, my soul, with gladness	153
1:29	And did those feet in ancient time	37
	Christ the Lord is risen again	102
	Come and see the shining hope	119
	Hail the day that sees him rise	277
	Hail, thou once despisèd Jesus	278
	How bright these glorious spirits shine!	316
	Jesus, the name high over all	404
	Just as I am, without one plea	413
	Lo round the throne, a glorious band	450
	My faith looks up to thee	512
	On a hill far away	587
	There is a Redeemer	743
1:29-42	Christ, when for us you were baptized	104
1:32	Eternal Ruler of the ceaseless round	162
	O King enthroned on high	557
	O let the Son of God enfold you	558
	Spirit divine, attend our prayers	671
1:35-39	Dear Lord and Father of mankind	152
1:37	O happy day	551
1:43	Follow me	189
	Will you come and follow me	834
1:51	As Jacob with travel was weary one day	41
	Blessèd assurance	752:
2:1-11	God, in the planning	239
	Jesus, Lord, we pray	392
	Life for the poor was hard and tough	436
2:15	Jesus Christ is waiting	382
3:3	Give thanks to the Lord (*For ever*)	218
	God forgave my sin (*Freely, freely*)	237
	Hark, the herald-angels sing	289
	I cannot tell	327
3:8	Breathe on me, Breath of God	87
	God of love	250
3:14	O my Saviour, lifted from the earth	572
	We want to see Jesus lifted high	807
3:16	Father of heaven, whose love profound	174
	From heaven you came	205
	I'm special	348
	Lord of all life and power	468
	Name of all majesty	524
	To God be the glory!	777
3:17	Come, let us with our Lord arise	129
3:36	Now is eternal life	529
4:10	Spirit of God (*Mallaig Sprinkling Song*)	672
4:10-15	Have you heard the raindrops	291
4:14	Holy Spirit, truth divine	312
	I heard the voice of Jesus say	334
	Jesu, lover of my soul	369
4:23-24	Lord Jesus Christ, be present	464
4:24	I will offer up my life	339

John

4:34	Christ, when for us you were baptized	104
4:35	Here I am	301
4:38	From the sun's rising	210
4:42	I cannot tell	327
	Jesu, our hope, our heart's desire	370
	Jesu, the very thought of thee	373
	Lift up your heads	438
	My Jesus, my Saviour	519
	Of the Father's love begotten	584
5:1-9	Have faith in God, my heart	290
5:3	Thou, whose almighty word	767
5:9	I danced in the morning (*Lord of the Dance*)	329
5:24	Now is eternal life	529
5:28	O for a thousand tongues to sing	541
	The Spirit lives to set us free	732
5:35	God, whose city's sure foundation	259
6:1-15	5000 + hungry folk	188
	Gather around, for the table is spread	213
6:16-21	Eternal Father, strong to save	160
6:24-35	Jesus the Lord said: 'I am the Bread'	403
6:28	God is working his purpose out	246
6:30-35	At this table we remember	53
6:31	Bread is blessed and broken	82
	My God, and is thy table spread	515
6:31-32	Guide me, O thou great Redeemer	275
6:32-58	Eat this bread	159
6:33	At this table we remember	53
	Break thou the bread	86
	Here, O my Lord	304
6:35	Draw nigh and take the body	157
6:35-44	I am the bread of life	323
6:48	Break thou the bread	86
	Oft in danger, oft in woe	585
	Sing we of the blessèd Mother	666
	To thee, O Lord, our hearts we raise	780
6:48-51	Jesus the Lord said: 'I am the Bread'	403
6:50	Bread is blessed and broken	82
6:50-52	I danced in the morning (*Lord of the Dance*)	329
6:51	Christians lift your hearts and voices	109
	Hands that have been handling	284
6:51-55	Bread of heaven, on thee we feed	83
	Christ is the heavenly food	98
	Jesu, thou joy of loving hearts	374
	Lord, enthroned in heavenly splendour	453
	Thee we adore, O hidden Saviour, thee	737
	We hail thy presence glorious	796
6:53-54	Hail, true body	281
6:56-59	Jesus the Lord said: 'I am the Bread'	403
6:58	This is the air I breathe	758
6:63	Come, Lord, to our souls	130
6:67-68	You are the King of Glory (*Hosanna to the Son of David*)	849
6:68	Bread of the world in mercy broken	84
	Creator of the earth and skies	147
	Jesus, lover of my soul (*It's all about you*)	394
	My Jesus, my Saviour	519
6:69	Be still, for the presence of the Lord	62
	There is a Redeemer	743
7:37-38	Breathe on me, Breath of God	87
	Have you heard the raindrops	291
7:38	Lord, enthroned in heavenly splendour	453
	Spirit of God (*Mallaig Sprinkling Song*)	672

John

8:1-11	Christ's is the world (*A touching place*)	110
8:12	Christ is the world's Light	100
	Christ, whose glory fills the skies	105
	Colours of day (*Light up the fire*)	114
	Come, my Way, my Truth, my Life	131
	For all the saints	190
	Hail, gladdening Light	276
	Hail to the Lord who comes	279
	Here on the threshold of a new beginning	305
	I heard the voice of Jesus say	334
	Jesus, be the centre	376
	Jesus the Lord said: 'I am the Bread'	403
	Lead, kindly light	421
	Light of the world (*Here I am to worship*)	441
	Lord, the light of your love	479
	O Love that wilt not let me go	571
	Onward, Christian pilgrims	599
	Round me falls the night	644
	The Lord is my light	719
	The Spirit lives to set us free	732
	Thou, whose almighty word	767
8:32	Eternal Ruler of the ceaseless round	162
	God is love: his the care	242
	Lord, the light of your love	479
	Thou didst leave thy throne	766
8:36	Onward, Christian pilgrims	599
	Thanks be to God	696
9:1-41	Amazing grace	34
9:5	Hail to the Lord who comes	279
	Jesus the Lord said: 'I am the Bread'	403
9:25	Light of the world (*Here I am to worship*)	441
9:35-41	Come, Lord, to our souls	130
9:38	I believe in Jesus	325
10:1-11	Jesus the Lord said: 'I am the Bread'	403
10:3	Here in this place (*Gather us in*)	302
10:9	Lord it belongs not to my care	462
10:10	For the healing of the nations	198
	The gracious invitation	709
10:11-16	Ah, holy Jesu, how hast thou offended	9
	All for Jesus! All for Jesus!	11
	Father of peace, and God of love	175
	Happy are they, they that love God	285
	How sweet the name of Jesus sounds	321
	I cannot tell	327
	Jesus, where'er thy people meet	407
	O sacred head, surrounded	576
	O thou, who at thy Eucharist didst pray	579
	Thine for ever! God of love	752
10:11-18	Loving Shepherd of thy sheep	495
10:14-15	It's rounded like an orange	366
10:27-29	Lord, we thank you for the promise	484
10:28	Loving Shepherd of thy sheep	495
11	Jesus, the name high over all	404
11:1-45	Jesus the Lord said: 'I am the Bread'	403
11:25-27	Breathe on me, Breath of God	87
	I am the bread of life	323
	I danced in the morning (*Lord of the Dance*)	329
	Love's redeeming work is done	494
	Now is eternal life	529
11:27	I believe in Jesus	325
11:34-36	It is a thing most wonderful	364
11:43	The Spirit lives to set us free	732

John

11:52	Ubi caritas	781
12:12-15	All glory, laud and honour	12
	You are the King of Glory (*Hosanna to the Son of David*)	849
12:13	Give me joy in my heart	215
	Hark, the glad sound!	288
	Holy, holy, holy	308
	Holy, holy, holy is the Lord	309
	Hosanna, hosanna	314
	Lord, enthroned in heavenly splendour	453
	My song is love unknown	521
	Ride on, ride on in majesty	640
	This is the day the Lord has made	760
	Wake, O wake! with tidings thrilling	786
12:14-15	We have a King who rides a donkey	799
12:15	The advent of our King	699
12:21	Open our eyes, Lord	600
12:26	O Jesus, I have promised	556
12:27	At even, ere the sun was set	49
12:28	Father, we love you (*Glorify your name*)	177
12:31-32	Lift high the Cross	437
12:32	Alleluia! Alleluia! (*Alleluia! Raise the Gospel*)	30
12:35	The Spirit lives to set us free	732
12:46	Creator of the earth and skies	147
	Jesus the Lord said: 'I am the Bread'	403
	Longing for light (*Christ, be our light*)	452
12:50	Creator of the earth and skies	147
13:1	An upper room did our Lord prepare	35
13:1-15	The world is full of smelly feet	736
	You laid aside your majesty (*I really want to worship you*)	850
13:4	Great God, your love has called us	270
13:4-11	An upper room did our Lord prepare	35
	Have you heard the raindrops	291
13:5	Jesu, Jesu, fill us with your love	368
13:14-17	Jesus, humble was your birth	384
13:18-30	One whose heart is hard as steel	597
13:33	This is my will	757
13:34	Give me joy in my heart	215
13:34-35	A new commandment	4
	Love is his word	492
	Peace, perfect peace, is the gift	615
	This is my body (*In love for me*)	755
	Ubi caritas	781
13:35	Give thanks for those	217
13:36-38	One whose heart is hard as steel	597
14	Take up thy cross, the Saviour said	689
14:1	Have faith in God, my heart	290
	I believe in Jesus	325
14:2	As Jacob with travel was weary one day	41
	Hail the day that sees him rise	277
	Hail, thou once despisèd Jesus	278
14:3	O Jesus, I have promised	556
14:6	All my days (*Beautiful Saviour*)	18
	Come, my Way, my Truth, my Life	131
	Fight the good fight	181
	How sweet the name of Jesus sounds	321
	Jesus the Lord said: 'I am the Bread'	403
	Lord it belongs not to my care	462
	Lord of all, to whom alone	469
	One more step along the world I go	595
	The gracious invitation	709
	Thine for ever! God of love	752

John

	Thou art the Way: by thee alone	765
	Though pilgrim strangers here below	768
	We pray thee, heavenly Father	803
	We want to see Jesus lifted high	807
14:6-7	Christ is the world's Light	100
14:8-27	Come, gracious Spirit, heavenly Dove	122
14:16	The Spirit lives to set us free	732
14:18	Alleluia, sing to Jesus	33
	Follow me	189
14:23-28	This is my body (*In love for me*)	755
14:25-27	God forgave my sin (*Freely, freely*)	237
	O Lord, all the world belongs to you	560
14:26	Come, thou Holy Spirit, come	139
	Holy Spirit, come, confirm us	311
	Lord of all being	466
	Lord of creation, to you be all praise!	471
	O King enthroned on high	557
	Praise him, praise him, all his children	621
14:27	Exaudi nos, Domine	164
	Give me joy in my heart	215
	Give me peace, O Lord, I pray	216
	Like a mighty river flowing	445
	Peace, perfect peace, is the gift	615
	Put peace into each other's hands	633
	Saviour, again to thy dear name we raise	648
15:1-9	This is my body (*In love for me*)	755
15:1-17	A new commandment	4
	We hail thy presence glorious	796
15:4	If we only seek peace	343
15:4-5	Abide with me	6
15:5	Jesus the Lord said: 'I am the Bread'	403
15:7	I danced in the morning	
	(*Lord of the Dance*)	329
15:8	Let us talents and tongues employ	434
15:11	An upper room did our Lord prepare	35
	Deck thyself, my soul, with gladness	153
15:12	This is my body (*In love for me*)	755
15:13-17	This is my will	757
15:15	Great God, your love has called us	270
	King of kings, majesty	418
15:15-16	Jesus calls us: o'er the tumult	379
15:16	If we only seek peace	343
15:26	O King enthroned on high	557
	Our blest Redeemer, ere he breathed	602
15:26-27	Come, gracious Spirit, heavenly Dove	122
16:4-15	Come, gracious Spirit, heavenly Dove	122
16:7	Our blest Redeemer, ere he breathed	602
16:13	Grant us the courage, gracious God	269
16:20	Come, ye faithful, raise the strain	143
	Jesus put this song	397
16:22	In the Cross of Christ I glory	358
16:24	An upper room did our Lord prepare	35
	Give me joy in my heart	215
16:28	God the Father, name we treasure	257
16:32	Follow me	189
16:33	One more step along the world I go	595
17:1-11	Christ is the King!	99
17:8	Come, Lord, to our souls	130
17:11	O thou, who at thy Eucharist didst pray	579
17:17	From all that dwell below the skies	203
	Help us, O Lord, to learn	298
17:20-23	Lord of lords and King eternal	474
17:21	As we are gathered	45
	Christ is the heavenly food	98

John

	Forth in the peace of Christ we go	200
	God forgave my sin (*Freely, freely*)	237
	O thou, who at thy Eucharist didst pray	579
17:24	Jesu, our hope, our heart's desire	370
	Lord it belongs not to my care	462
	O Jesus, I have promised	556
17:26	Will you come and follow me	834
18	It is a thing most wonderful	364
18:11	Praise to the Holiest	627
18:33-37	Lord of the boundless curves	475
18:37	God is love: his the care	242
18:40	My song is love unknown	521
19:1	Come, Lord, to our souls	130
19:2	At the cross she keeps her station	50
	The head that once was crowned	
	with thorns	711
	Come and see	118
	O dearest Lord, thy sacred head	538
	O sacred head, surrounded	576
19:5	Come, Lord, to our souls	130
19:6	My song is love unknown	521
19:14-22	You laid aside your majesty	
	(*I really want to worship you*)	850
19:16-18	Come, Lord, to our souls	130
19:17-42	Were you there when they crucified	
	my Lord?	810
19:20	There is a green hill far away	740
19:25	Mary, blessed grieving mother	501
	O sacred head, surrounded	576
	Sing we of the blessèd Mother	666
19:25-27	Our Father God in heaven	605
19:30	At the cross she keeps her station	50
	How deep the Father's love for us	317
19:34	At the cross she keeps her station	50
	At the Lamb's high feast we sing	51
	Glory be to Jesus	224
	Hail, true body	281
	Jesu, grant me this, I pray	367
	Lord, enthroned in heavenly splendour	453
	O dearest Lord, thy sacred head	538
	Rock of ages	643
	Sing, my tongue, the glorious battle	662
	Soul of my Saviour	670
	What child is this	812
20:1-18	From the very depths of darkness	211
	Led like a lamb	423
	Love's redeeming work is done	494
	Thine be the glory	751
20:11	Jesus, stand among us	401
	Jesus, stand among us in thy risen power	402
20:11-22	In the garden Mary lingers	359
20:19	Saviour, again to thy dear name we raise	648
	The day of resurrection	703
	Thine be the glory	751
20:19-31	As we are gathered	45
20:20	Come, see the Lord	138
20:21	An upper room did our Lord prepare	35
20:21-22	Breathe on me, Breath of God	87
	God's Spirit is in my heart	
	(*Go, tell everyone*)	262
	O Lord, all the world belongs to you	560
20:26	The peace of the earth be with you	726
20:26-28	Come, wounded healer	141
20:26-29	Crown him with many crowns	150

John

	From heaven you came	205
	Jesu, grant me this, I pray	367
	Jesus, where'er thy people meet	407
	My God, I love thee	517
	O dearest Lord, thy sacred head	538
	We will lay our burden down	808
20:27-28	Hail the day that sees him rise	277
	There is a green hill far away	740
20:31	Jesus, the name high over all	404
21	You stood there on the shoreline (*Resurrection breakfast*)	854
21:15-17	Father, we adore you	176
21:16	Hark, my soul, it is the Lord	287
21:19	Follow me	189
	In the garden Mary lingers	359
	Will you come and follow me	834

ACTS

1:4-5	All over the world	20
1:6-11	Alleluia, sing to Jesus	33
	Hail the day that sees him rise	277
1:8	Be still, for the presence of the Lord	62
	God forgave my sin (*Freely, freely*)	237
1:11	At the name of Jesus	52
	Once in royal David's city	592
	The advent of our King	699
1:12-14	As the disciples	44
1:14	Christ for the world we sing!	95
1:14-26	Sing we of the blessèd Mother	666
1:24	Holy Spirit, will you be (*One who intercedes*)	313
	Our Father God in heaven	605
	Lord of all, to whom alone	469
2	Christians, lift up your hearts	108
	She sits like a bird (*Enemy of apathy*)	654
2:1-4	Come down, O Love divine	120
	Come, Holy Ghost, our souls inspire	124
	Come, Holy Spirit, come	125
	Father, hear the prayer we offer	169
	Filled with the Spirit's power	184
	Lord of all life and power	468
	Lord, the light of your love	479
	O Holy Spirit, Lord of grace	554
	Our blest Redeemer, ere he breathed	602
	Sing we of the blessèd Mother	666
	Spirit of the living God (Iverson)	675
2:1-11	God of life, God of love	249
2:2-3	Spirit divine, attend our prayers	671
2:3	Christ, when for us you were baptized	104
2:5-47	Filled with the Spirit's power	184
2:15	Now the green blade riseth	533
2:17	The King is among us	714
2:18	All over the world	20
	Great is the darkness (*Come, Lord Jesus*)	271
2:21	Jesu, thou joy of loving hearts	374
2:23	To the name of our salvation	779
2:23-24	Alleluia, Alleluia, give thanks to the risen Lord	31
2:24	At the Lamb's high feast we sing	51
	Come, ye faithful, raise the strain	143
	Jesu, our hope, our heart's desire	370
	Low in the grave he lay	496
	We have a gospel to proclaim	798
2:27	He has risen	292

Acts

2:31	Come, see the Lord	138
2:33	God the Father, name we treasure	257
	Jesus Christ (*Once again*)	380
	Led like a lamb	423
2:34	Rejoice, the Lord is King	638
2:38-39	God the Father, name we treasure	257
2:42-47	As the disciples	44
2:44-45	From thee all skill and science flow	212
2:44-46	Break the bread and pour the wine	85
2:46	Lord, today your voice is calling	482
3:8	O for a thousand tongues to sing	541
3:14	Ah, holy Jesu, how hast thou offended	9
3:15	Author of life divine	55
	Christ, the fair glory of the holy angels	101
	Come, let us with our Lord arise	129
	From the very depths of darkness	211
	Good Christians all, rejoice and sing	266
	Jesus, Prince and Saviour	396
	My song is love unknown	521
	Thine be the glory	751
3:16	Jesus, the name high over all	404
	Saint Luke, beloved physician	645
3:22	Father of heaven, whose love profound	174
4:2	O for a thousand tongues to sing	541
4:11	Christ is made the sure foundation	96
4:12	All hail the power of Jesus' name	14
	Hail, thou once despisèd Jesus	278
	Jesus, Name above all names	395
	Jesus, the name high over all	404
	To the name of our salvation	779
4:24	Come, let us with our Lord arise	129
4:31	There's a quiet understanding	745
4:31-33	As the disciples	44
4:32	Break the bread and pour the wine	85
7:48-49	Alleluia, sing to Jesus	33
	Praise to the Holiest	627
10:38	Thou, whose almighty word	767
10:42	The advent of our King	699
12:7	And can it be	36
13:32-33	Have faith in God, my heart	290
13:47	Hail to the Lord who comes	279
14:15	Lord of beauty, thine the splendour	470
16:13-15	Come, Lord, to our souls	130
17:6	O Lord, all the world belongs to you	560
17:11	Come, Lord, to our souls	130
17:16-18	Colours of day (*Light up the fire*)	114
17:23-28	Proclaim, proclaim the story	630
17:24-31	Lord of the boundless curves	475
18:9-10	Colours of day (*Light up the fire*)	114
20:7-12	As the disciples	44
20:29	Thy kingdom come, O God	774
22:16	My Lord, what love is this (*Amazing love*)	520
26:17-18	Colours of day (*Light up the fire*)	114
26:18	God, whose city's sure foundation	259
27:23	Eternal God, we consecrate	161

ROMANS

1:16	He is the Lord	295
1:20	Creation sings!	146
4:5	Christ triumphant	103
4:20-21	Give thanks for those	217
	God, whose city's sure foundation	259
5:1	Christians, lift up your hearts	108
5:1-2	I am a new creation	322

Romans

	I'm accepted, I'm forgiven	345
5:5	Holy, holy, holy	308
5:6	Abide with me	6
5:7-8	I'm special	348
5:8	Come on and celebrate	135
	There's a spirit in the air	746
5:9	Glory be to Jesus	224
5:10	From heaven you came	205
	Hark, the herald-angels sing	289
	My God, I love thee	517
5:14	Now, my tongue, the mystery telling	531
6:3	Christians, lift up your hearts	108
6:4	Christians, lift up your hearts	108
6:4-8	Alleluia, alleluia, give thanks to the risen Lord	31
6:5-11	Lift up your voice	440
6:6-14	Firmly I believe and truly	186
6:8	Now let us from this table rise	530
	The Lord is risen indeed	721
6:9	I danced in the morning (Lord of the Dance)	329
6:10	In Christ alone	352
6:11	Bread of the world in mercy broken	84
6:11-18	Life of all power	468
6:13	Hands that have been handling	284
6:18	Onward, Christian pilgrims	599
6:19	Hands that have been handling	284
7:15-20	O Lord, we want to praise you	567
8:1	And can it be	36
	I am a new creation	322
	I'm accepted, I'm forgiven	345
8:1-3	The Spirit lives to set us free	732
8:1-11	Father of heaven, whose love profound	174
8:2	Come and celebrate	116
8:9	Spirit of God (Mallaig Sprinkling Song)	672
	The Spirit lives to set us free	732
8:11	We give immortal praise	795
8:14	Come, gracious Spirit, heavenly Dove	122
8:14-17	From the falter of breath	208
	Jesus, we have heard your Spirit	406
8:15	Abba, Father, let me be	5
	Alleluia (x 8)	29
8:15-16	God the Father, name we treasure	257
8:16	If I were a butterfly	342
	Thanks to God whose word was spoken	698
8:17	Here on the threshold of a new beginning	305
8:19-22	Creation sings!	146
8:26-27	God of life, God of love	249
	Holy Spirit, will you be (One who intercedes)	313
8:26-39	Hail the day that sees him rise	277
8:29	Hail to the Lord who comes	279
8:31-39	Jesus lives! thy terrors now	390
	Now is eternal life	529
	You are beautiful (I stand in awe)	847
8:32	O Lord, my God (How great thou art)	563
8:34	And now, O Father, mindful of the love	38
8:35-38	God of life, God of love	249
8:37	Thine be the glory	751
8:38	O for a heart to praise my God	540
8:38-39	O Love that wilt not let me go	571
	We give immortal praise	795
8:39	Such love	681

Romans

	There's a spirit in the air	746
10:9	Alleluia (x 8)	29
10:9-10	I believe in Jesus	325
10:12	Christians lift your hearts and voices	109
10:12-13	Lord of all, to whom alone	469
10:14	Go forth and tell	232
10:14-15	How beauteous are their feet	315
11:6	Only by grace	598
11:33-36	You are beautiful (I stand in awe)	847
12:1	All that I am	24
	Father, we adore you	176
	I give my hands	330
	Jesu, tawa pano	372
	Lord, you have my heart	489
	Teach me to dance	691
12:1-2	Lord, for the years	454
	Take my life, and let it be	687
	Take this moment	688
12:2	Hands that have been handling	284
	Lord, I come to you	458
12:5	Hands that have been handling	284
12:6	God the Father, name we treasure	257
12:9	Jesus, Lord, we pray	392
12:11	God, whose city's sure foundation	259
12:12	As your family, Lord, see us here	47
12:15	Brother, sister, let me serve you	91
13:11-12	Here in this place (Gather us in)	302
15:12	O come, O come, Emmanuel	535
15:13	Christ is the heavenly food	98
	Come and celebrate	116
	Come, all who look to Christ today	115
	Fill thou my life, O Lord my God	182
	God of love	250
15:33	The peace of the earth be with you	726

1 CORINTHIANS

1:10-16	Lord of lords and King eternal	474
1:10-18	Christ is the King!	99
1:12	Lord, we come to ask your healing	483
1:18-31	Come, wounded healer	141
	Firmly I believe and truly	186
1:24	Lord of the boundless curves	475
1:25	God of love	250
1:25-27	Be thou my vision	66
1:28	Disposer supreme	155
2:9	Lord of creation, to you be all praise!	471
	Wonderful, so wonderful (Beautiful one)	838
2:9-10	Lord of all being	466
2:10-12	Holy Spirit, will you be (One who intercedes)	313
3:6	We plough the fields and scatter	801
3:9	Come, ye thankful people, come	144
3:10-11	Blessèd city, heavenly Salem	77
3:11	Christ is made the sure foundation	96
	O, heaven is in my heart	552
	The Church's one foundation	702
3:16	Spirit of God (Mallaig Sprinkling Song)	672
	The Spirit lives to set us free	732
3:16-23	Blessèd city, heavenly Salem	77
5:7	Christ the Lord is risen again	102
	Hail, thou once despisèd Jesus	278
	Lord, enthroned in heavenly splendour	453
5:7-8	At the Lamb's high feast we sing	51
	Deck thyself, my soul, with gladness	153

1 Corinthians

5:17	Christian people, raise your song	106
6:16-17	These vows of love are taken	749
6:19-20	Lift up your heads	438
6:20	Bind us together, Lord	73
	Blessèd assurance	75
	The Church's one foundation	702
	We give immortal praise	795
7:22	Christ, when for us you were baptized	104
	Lord of creation, to you be all praise!	471
7:23	There is a green hill far away	740
8:3	My God, how wonderful you are	516
8:11	I'm black, I'm white, I'm tall, I'm short	346
9:10-11	God, whose farm is all creation	260
9:24	Fight the good fight	181
	Forth in thy name, O Lord, I go	201
	Jesus, the name high over all	404
	May the mind of Christ my Saviour	506
9:24-27	Fight the good fight	181
10:1-4	Christ is the heavenly food	98
10:4	Rock of ages	643
10:16-17	As the disciples	44
	Christ is the heavenly food	98
	Come, risen Lord	137
	Deck thyself, my soul, with gladness	153
	From many grains	206
	O thou, who at thy Eucharist didst pray	579
	Ubi caritas	781
	We hail thy presence glorious	796
10:17	Hands that have been handling	284
10:21	Jesus, all for Jesus	375
10:24	From heaven you came	205
10:31	God be in my head	235
11:17-34	As the disciples	44
11:23-25	Amazing grace	34
	Christians, lift up your hearts	108
	Gifts of bread and wine	214
	God of the Passover	252
	Lord Jesus Christ (*Living Lord*)	463
	Love is his word	492
	Thee we adore, O hidden Saviour, thee	737
	This is my body (*In love for me*)	755
11:23-26	Father, who in Jesus found us	180
	Here is bread	303
	I come with joy	328
11:23-29	At this table we remember	53
11:24-27	Christians lift your hearts and voices	109
11:25	Come, let us use the grace divine	128
11:26	Come, let us with our Lord arise	129
	Once, only once, and once for all	593
11:26-29	At this table we remember	53
12:3	Come into his presence	126
	Father, Lord of all creation	172
	Father of heaven, whose love profound	174
	Heaven shall not wait	297
	Lord Jesus Christ (*Living Lord*)	463
12:4-6	At this time of giving	54
12:7	Come, all who look to Christ today	115
12:8-9	God has spoken – by the prophets	238
12:9	From thee all skill and science flow	212
	Lord of creation, to you be all praise!	471
12:11	From thee all skill and science flow	212
12:12	Bind us together, Lord	73
12:12-13	Come, risen Lord	137
12:13	Christ, when for us you were baptized	104

1 Corinthians

12:12-31	Christ is the King!	99
	Jesus, Lord, we look to thee	391
12:27	O Lord, all the world belongs to you	560
12:27-31	One is the body	594
13	The love we share	725
13:1-13	Gracious Spirit, Holy Ghost	268
	O perfect love	573
13:4-8	A new commandment	4
13:7	Father, I place into your hands	170
13:9	Lord, you call us to a journey	487
13:11-12	It is a thing most wonderful	364
13:12	Come, O thou traveller unknown	134
	He has risen	292
	Here, O my Lord	304
	Lo round the throne, a glorious band	450
	Lord it belongs not to my care	462
	Lord, you call us to a journey	487
	Loving Shepherd of thy sheep	495
	The God of Abraham praise	706
13:12-13	Ubi caritas	781
13:13	Jesus, Lord, we pray	392
14:15	Jesus, be the centre	376
15:2	God is love: let heaven adore him	243
15:3	Alleluia, alleluia, give thanks to the risen Lord	31
15:3-4	Jesus Christ is risen today	381
	Lord, I lift your name on high	461
	Lord of all life and power	468
15:4-7	Now the green blade riseth	533
15:13-20	He has risen	292
15:14	This joyful Eastertide	761
15:20	Alleluia, alleluia, hearts to heaven and voices raise	32
	Blessèd assurance	75
	Hail the day that sees him rise	277
15:20-28	Lift up your voice	440
15:26-28	Going home, moving on	263
15:45	Praise to the Holiest	627
15:49	Eternal God, we consecrate	161
15:51-57	He has risen	292
15:52	Lift up your hearts!	439
	This joyful Eastertide	761
15:54-57	Jesus lives! thy terrors now	390
	Lift high the Cross	437
	Lord of lords and King eternal	474
15:55	Christ the Lord is risen again	102
	Love's redeeming work is done	494
15:55-57	Abide with me	6
	Bind us together, Lord	73
	Thine be the glory	751
15:56-57	Jesus, we celebrate your victory	405
16:13	Grant us the courage, gracious God	269

2 CORINTHIANS

1:3-4	All you who seek a comfort sure	28
1:22	Father of peace, and God of love	175
2:14	May the fragrance of Jesus fill this place	504
3:16	Author of life divine	55
	Spirit of God (*Mallaig Sprinkling Song*)	672
3:17	Christ, when for us you were baptized	104
3:17-18	Lord, the light of your love	479
	Love divine, all loves excelling	491
3:18	For the healing of the nations	198
	Here, O my Lord	304

2 Corinthians

	May the fragrance of Jesus fill this place	504
4:5	Jesus, all for Jesus	375
4:6	Eternal God, we consecrate	161
	It is a thing most wonderful	364
	Kindle a flame	415
	Lord, the light of your love	479
4:7	Disposer supreme	155
5:7	Give thanks for those	217
	Men of faith	508
5:7-8	O God, our help in ages past	547
5:16-21	In Christ there is no east or west	353
5:17	Hands that have been handling	284
	I am a new creation	322
	Long ago, prophets knew	451
	Love divine, all loves excelling	491
	The Church's one foundation	702
5:19	There's a spirit in the air	746
5:21	Come and see	118
6:1	Come, now is the time to worship	132
6:7	Lord, today your voice is calling	482
6:10	Give thanks with a grateful heart	219
6:18	Here in this place (*Gather us in*)	302
7:4	All you who seek a comfort sure	28
8-9	Light of the world (*Here I am to worship*)	441
8:9	Come, wounded healer	141
	Name of all majesty	524
9:7-9	All that I am	24
9:8	Now thank we all our God	532
9:10-11	Glory, love, and praise, and honour	225
9:15	At this time of giving	54
10:4	We want to see Jesus lifted high	807
10:5	Over all the earth	609
12:9-10	Come, O thou traveller unknown	134
	Lord of all being	466
12:10	Give thanks with a grateful heart	219
	Men of faith	508
13:13	May the grace of Christ our Saviour	505
13:14	Father of heaven, whose love profound	174
	For all thy saints, O Lord	191
	God of love	250

GALATIANS

1:15-16	God, whose city's sure foundation	259
2:19-20	Come on and celebrate	135
	From heaven you came	205
2:20	All you who seek a comfort sure	28
	Alleluia, alleluia, give thanks to the risen Lord	31
	I am trusting thee, Lord Jesus	324
	I bind unto myself today	326
	I'm black, I'm white, I'm tall, I'm short	346
	In full and glad surrender	354
	It is a thing most wonderful	364
	My faith looks up to thee	512
3:13	Father, Lord of all creation	172
3:23-29	In Christ there is no east or west	353
3:28	I'm black, I'm white, I'm tall, I'm short	346
4:4	God of love	250
4:4-7	At this time of giving	54
4:5-7	Blessèd assurance	75
	Father God, I wonder (*I will sing your praises*)	168
4:6	Abba, Father, let me be	5
	Alleluia (x 8)	29

Galatians

5:1	From the very depths of darkness	211
	Great God, your love has called us	270
	Holy Spirit, truth divine	312
	Jesus, all for Jesus	375
	Jesus, we celebrate your victory	405
	Lord of all being	466
5:22	Come, Lord, to our souls	130
5:22-23	Colours of day (*Light up the fire*)	114
	God, whose city's sure foundation	259
	It's rounded like an orange	366
	Lord of all life and power	468
5:25	One more step along the world I go	595
6:1-10	Jesus, Lord, we look to thee	391
6:2	Help us to help each other, Lord	299
	Long ago, prophets knew	451
6:6	Break the bread and pour the wine	85
6:14	All my days (*Beautiful Saviour*)	18
	How deep the Father's love for us	317
	In the Cross of Christ I glory	358
	Lord, for the years	454
6:14-15	Love divine, all loves excelling	491
	When I survey the wondrous cross	820

EPHESIANS

1:5	Eternal Ruler of the ceaseless round	162
1:7	Glory be to Jesus	224
	Jesus, the name high over all	404
	Lord of lords and King eternal	474
1:10	Have faith in God, my heart	290
1:13	Father of peace, and God of love	175
	God is working his purpose out	246
1:15-23	All praise to our redeeming Lord	22
1:20	Jesus is King	386
1:21	Above all powers, above all kings	7
	Jesus, the name high over all	404
	Ye watchers and ye holy ones	844
1:21-23	Of the Father's love begotten	584
2:1	We give immortal praise	795
2:6	Come, let us with our Lord arise	129
	Lord of all life and power	468
	To God be the glory!	777
2:8	Here on the threshold of a new beginning	305
	Only by grace	598
2:11-18	From the eastern mountains	207
2:11-22	In Christ there is no east or west	353
2:12	All for Jesus! All for Jesus!	11
2:13-22	Bread of heaven, on thee we feed	83
	Christ is made the sure foundation	96
	Christ is our cornerstone	97
2:14	Christ is the world's Light	100
	Put peace into each other's hands	633
2:14-18	Lord of lords and King eternal	474
2:17	Christ is the heavenly food	98
2:18	Father of heaven, whose love profound	174
2:19-21	All praise to our redeeming Lord	22
2:19-22	Let us build a house (*All are welcome*)	432
2:19-23	Come, risen Lord	137
2:20	Blessèd city, heavenly Salem	77
	In Christ alone	352
2:20-22	O, heaven is in my heart	552
2:21-22	For I'm building a people of power	193
	Here on the threshold of a new beginning	305

Ephesians

2:27	Jesus, the name high over all	404
3:6	Christ is the heavenly food	98
3:12	And can it be	36
	Blessèd assurance	75
3:14	I give you all the honour (*I worship you*)	331
3:14-21	Praise God from whom all blessings flow	619
3:17	Bread of heaven, on thee we feed	83
	God be in my head	235
3:17-18	Jesus, Lord, we look to thee	391
	Lord of the boundless curves	475
3:17-21	Lord of beauty, thine the splendour	470
3:18	God's love is deeper	
	(*Deeper, wider, higher*)	261
	It is a thing most wonderful	364
	Jesus' love is very wonderful	393
	Just as I am, without one plea	413
3:18-19	You are beautiful (*I stand in awe*)	847
3:19	All my hope on God is founded	19
	Come, let us with our Lord arise	129
	Jesus, the name high over all	404
	There's a spirit in the air	746
4:1-5	As the disciples	44
4:1-6	Come, risen Lord	137
	God, our Creator	253
4:1-16	Christ is the King!	99
	In Christ there is no east or west	353
4:3	Blessèd city, heavenly Salem	77
4:3-6	God of love	250
4	Father, who in Jesus found us	182
4:4-6	Christ is the heavenly food	98
4:5	The Church's one foundation	702
	Thy hand, O God, has guided	772
4:8	Come, see the Lord	138
4:11	Saint Luke, beloved physician	645
4:11-16	All praise to our redeeming Lord	22
	One is the body	594
4:12-16	Hands that have been handling	284
4:14	Lord of all life and power	468
4:15	Help us to help each other, Lord	299
4:15-16	Christ is the heavenly food	98
	Come, risen Lord	137
4:23-24	Come, let us with our Lord arise	129
4:24	And can it be	36
	For the healing of the nations	198
4:25-32	Jesus, Lord, we look to thee	391
4:32	God forgave my sin (*Freely, freely*)	237
5:1-2	Come on and celebrate	135
	Jesus, Lord, we look to thee	391
	Lord of all life and power	468
5:2	May the fragrance of Jesus fill this place	504
5:6-20	Awake, awake: fling off the night	56
	Awake, my soul, and with the sun	57
5:8	The Spirit lives to set us free	732
	Waken, O sleeper, wake and rise	787
5:14	Longing for light (*Christ, be our light*)	452
5:18	Jesus is King	386
5:19-20	Fill thou my life, O Lord my God	182
	Let all the world in every corner sing	425
5:20	Glory, love, and praise, and honour	225
5:22-33	The love we share	725
	These vows of love are taken	749
	We gather here	794
5:25	Lord, we thank you for the promise	484
5:33	Lord, we thank you for the promise	484

Ephesians

6:1-4	Our Father God in heaven	605
6:4	Eternal God, we consecrate	161
6:10	Here, O my Lord	304
6:10-17	Be thou my vision	66
	Eternal Ruler of the ceaseless round	162
	God of grace and God of glory	248
6:10-18	Stand up, stand up for Jesus	677
6:14	I bind unto myself today	326
6:15	How beauteous are their feet	315
6:17	Lord of lords and King eternal	474
6:18	Holy Spirit, will you be	
	(*One who intercedes*)	313

PHILIPPIANS

1:12	Thanks be to God	696
1:20	For all thy saints, O Lord	191
1:20-26	Lord it belongs not to my care	462
1:21	Lord, we thank you for the promise	484
2:2-11	Above all powers, above all kings	7
2:4	From heaven you came	205
2:5	Help us to help each other, Lord	299
	May the mind of Christ my Saviour	506
2:5-11	All praise to thee	23
	At the name of Jesus	52
	Come, see the Lord	138
	Creator of the starry height	148
	He is Lord	294
	Jesus, humble was your birth	384
	Jesus shall take the highest honour	400
	Name of all majesty	524
	Praise to the Holiest	627
	We believe in God the Father	790
2:6-9	You laid aside your majesty	
	(*I really want to worship you*)	850
2:7	And can it be	36
	Blest are the pure in heart	79
	Christ triumphant	103
	God is our strength from days of old	244
	Hark, the herald-angels sing	289
	Lord, enthroned in heavenly splendour	453
	O Lord, all the world belongs to you	560
	Sing, my tongue, the glorious battle	662
	The advent of our King	699
	Thou didst leave thy throne	766
2:7-9	Jesus Christ (*Once again*)	380
2:8-9	Light of the world (*Here I am to worship*)	441
2:9	Jesus, Name above all names	395
	Jesus, the name high over all	404
2:9-10	Jesus Christ is risen today	381
	Jesus is the name we honour	388
2:10-11	Blessing and honour (*Ancient of Days*)	78
	Come, now is the time to worship	132
	From all that dwell below the skies	203
	Holy, holy, holy is the Lord	309
	How lovely on the mountains	319
	Jesus is Lord! Creation's voice proclaims it	387
2:11	For all the saints	190
	Happy are they, they that love God	285
	Let all the world in every corner sing	425
	Shout for joy and sing	656
	To the name of our salvation	779
2:13	God is here! As we his people	241
	God, whose city's sure foundation	259
3:7-8	God of the Passover	252

Philippians

	Jesus, lover of my soul (*It's all about you*)	394
	When I survey the wondrous cross	820
3:7-11	How deep the Father's love for us	317
3:8-12	All I once held dear (*Knowing you*)	16
3:9	And now, O Father, mindful of the love	38
	Jesus, the name high over all	404
3:10	Come and see	118
3:10-14	Lord of all life and power	468
3:12-14	Christ be with me	94
	Fight the good fight	181
	Lord, you call us to a journey	487
3:14	Jesu, our hope, our heart's desire	370
4:4	Come and celebrate	116
4:4-7	In the Lord I'll be ever thankful	360
	Rejoice in the Lord always	636
	Wait for the Lord	785
4:5	I watch the sunrise (*Close to you*)	338
	Lift up your heads	438
4:7	Like a mighty river flowing	445
4:8	Lord, today your voice is calling	482
4:11	Blessèd be your name	76

COLOSSIANS

1:5	God is working his purpose out	246
1:11-12	Grant us the courage, gracious God	269
1:12-13	Lord it belongs not to my care	462
1:13	Creator of the earth and skies	147
1:13-20	Of the Father's love begotten	584
1:15	Hail to the Lord who comes	279
	One more step along the world I go	595
1:15-17	Above all powers, above all kings	7
	Alleluia, Alleluia, give thanks to the risen Lord	31
1:15-18	Jesu, our hope, our heart's desire	370
1:16	At the name of Jesus	52
	Christ, the fair glory of the holy angels	101
	Creator of the earth and skies	147
	Lord of beauty, thine the splendour	470
	Ye watchers and ye holy ones	844
1:18	Come, risen Lord	137
	Hail the day that sees him rise	277
	Hail to the Lord who comes	279
	Jesus, stand among us	401
	We hail thy presence glorious	796
1:19-20	O Love that wilt not let me go	571
1:27	In Christ alone	352
	Jesus, be the centre	376
	King of kings, majesty	418
	Lord, for the years	454
2:3	All my hope on God is founded	19
2:7	Bread of heaven, on thee we feed	83
2:8-15	In Christ alone	352
2:13	God forgave my sin (*Freely, freely*)	237
2:15	Come, let us with our Lord arise	129
	God of love	250
3:1	To God be the glory!	777
3:1-11	In Christ there is no east or west	353
3:3	Before the throne	70
	Now is eternal life	529
3:4	Thee we adore, O hidden Saviour, thee	737
3:5	Firmly I believe and truly	186
3:11	Jesus calls us here to meet him	378
	Lord of the boundless curves	475
3:12	Hands that have been handling	284

Colossians

3:12-17	All praise to our redeeming Lord	22
	Let all the world in every corner sing	425
3:14	Bind us together, Lord	73
	Come down, O Love divine	120
	Lord, we come to ask your healing	483
3:15	Over all the earth	609
3:15-16	Forth in the peace of Christ we go	200
3:17	Thanks be to God	696
4:14	Saint Luke, beloved physician	645

1 THESSALONIANS

1:1-10	Christ is the King!	99
2:9-13	Jesus, Lord, we look to thee	391
2:19	Fight the good fight	181
4:1-6	Come and celebrate	116
4:13-18	Lord it belongs not to my care	462
4:16	This joyful Eastertide	761
5:8	I bind unto myself today	326
	Stand up, stand up for Jesus	677
5:18	Thanks be to God	696

2 THESSALONIANS

1:7	At the name of Jesus	52
2:10	God is love: his the care	242
2:13	Go wandering in the sun	234
2:17	Fill thou my life, O Lord my God	182
3:16	The peace of the earth be with you	726

1 TIMOTHY

1:17	Immortal, invisible, God only wise	349
	Lord of lords and King eternal	474
	Name of all majesty	524
	The Lord is King!	718
2:5-6	Christ, when for us you were baptized	104
	Father of heaven, whose love profound	174
2:8	Lord, I lift my hands to you in prayer	460
3:16	Name of all majesty	524
4:9-10	I am trusting thee, Lord Jesus	324
4:10	All my hope on God is founded	19
	Glory to God!	227
	I'm black, I'm white, I'm tall, I'm short	346
	Jesus, the name high over all	404
	Thank you for saving me	693
6:12	Fight the good fight	181
6:15	Lord of lords and King eternal	474
6:17-19	Oh, the life of the world	586

2 TIMOTHY

1:10	My Jesus, my Saviour	519
	Name of all majesty	524
1:12	Firmly I believe and truly	186
1:14	Spirit of God (*Mallaig Sprinkling Song*)	672
3:14-17	Lord, for the years	454
3:16	Christians, lift up your hearts	108
	Come, Holy Ghost, our hearts inspire	123
3:16-17	Here on the threshold of a new beginning	305
4:1	The advent of our King	699
4:7	Fight the good fight	181
	For all the saints	190
	Jesu, Son of Mary	371
4:6-8	God be in my head	235
4:7-8	Lord, we thank you for the promise	484
4:11	Saint Luke, beloved physician	645

TITUS

1:11	There's a spirit in the air	746
3:4	The Spirit lives to set us free	732

HEBREWS

1	Hail, gladdening Light	276
1:1	Thanks to God whose word was spoken	698
1:1-4	God has spoken – by the prophets	238
1:3	Jesu, our hope, our heart's desire	370
	Jesus is the name we honour	388
	Lord of beauty, thine the splendour	470
	Rejoice, the Lord is King	638
1:6	Hail to the Lord who comes	279
1:8	The day thou gavest, Lord, is ended	704
1:10	God is love: let heaven adore him	243
2:5	O love, how deep, how broad, how high	570
2:9	All hail the power of Jesus' name	14
	Be still, for the presence of the Lord	62
2:9-10	How deep the Father's love for us	317
2:14	A man there lived in Galilee	3
	Firmly I believe and truly	186
2:17	We hail thy presence glorious	796
3:1	We hail thy presence glorious	796
4:12-13	Holy Spirit, will you be (*One who intercedes*)	313
	Lord of all, to whom alone	469
4:14	How sweet the name of Jesus sounds	321
	Jesus is King	386
4:14-16	Before the throne	70
	Father of heaven, whose love profound	174
	Go wandering in the sun	234
4:15	At the Lamb's high feast we sing	51
4:16	Blessèd assurance	75
	Help us, O Lord, to learn	298
	Thank you for saving me	693
5:12	Break thou the bread	86
7:22	Come, let us use the grace divine	128
7:25	And now, O Father, mindful of the love	38
	Hail the day that sees him rise	277
	Jesus is King	386
	We hail thy presence glorious	796
7:26	Christians lift your hearts and voices	109
7:27	Hail, true body	281
	Once, only once, and once for all	593
8:1	Rejoice, the Lord is King	638
9:5	As with gladness men of old	46
	Hail the day that sees him rise	277
	Hail, thou once despisèd Jesus	278
	Jesus, where'er thy people meet	407
	My God, how wonderful you are	516
	Once, only once, and once for all	593
9:11	Alleluia, sing to Jesus	33
	Father, Lord of all creation	172
9:11-14	Draw nigh and take the body	157
9:13	I am trusting thee, Lord Jesus	324
9:14	All my days (*Beautiful Saviour*)	18
9:24-28	Draw nigh and take the body	157
10:7	Christ, when for us you were baptized	104
10:11-25	Jesu, our hope, our heart's desire	370
10:19-20	Lord, the light of your love	479
10:19-22	Jesus, we celebrate your victory	405
10:19-25	Come, let us with our Lord arise	129
10:21	Come, see the Lord	138
10:22-23	Have faith in God, my heart	290
11	Rejoice in God's saints	635

Hebrews

11:1	Blessèd assurance	75
	Here, O my Lord	304
	Here on the threshold of a new beginning	305
11:3	Of the Father's love begotten	584
	Thanks to God whose word was spoken	698
11:10	Give thanks for those	217
11:13-16	Give thanks for those	217
	In our day of thanksgiving	356
	Though pilgrim strangers here below	768
11:26	For all thy saints, O Lord	191
11:37-40	Give thanks for those	217
11:40	For all thy saints, O Lord	191
12:1	As Jacob with travel was weary one day	41
	Christ is the King!	99
	Give us the wings of faith	221
	Rejoice in God's saints	635
12:2	Christian people, raise your song	106
	Hands that have been handling	284
	Jesus Christ is risen today	381
	Lo round the throne, a glorious band	450
12:14	Come, gracious Spirit, heavenly Dove	122
	For all thy saints, O Lord	191
12:22	As Jacob with travel was weary one day	41
12:23	Jesu, Son of Mary	371
12:24	Glory be to Jesus	224
12:29	Jesus, lover of my soul (*It's all about you*)	394
13:6	Abide with me	6
13:7	For all thy saints, O Lord	191
13:8	Christ is the King!	99
	Yesterday, today, for ever	846
13:12	There is a green hill far away	740
13:13	Christ for the world we sing!	95
13:15	All my hope on God is founded	19
	For the beauty of the earth	195
13:15	Fill thou my life, O Lord my God	182
	When morning gilds the skies	822
	When the music fades (*The heart of worship*)	823
13:16	Praise and thanksgiving	617
13:20-21	Father of peace, and God of love	175
	To God be the glory!	777

JAMES

1:5	From thee all skill and science flow	212
	Grant us the courage, gracious God	269
1:12	Lo round the throne, a glorious band	450
1:17	Abide with me	6
	All my hope on God is founded	19
	Be still, my soul	63
	Fight the good fight	181
	From thee all skill and science flow	212
	Glory, love, and praise, and honour	225
	Great is thy faithfulness	273
	Immortal, invisible, God only wise	349
	Lift up your hearts!	439
	O God beyond all praising	544
	O strength and stay	577
	We plough the fields and scatter	801
1:21	Come, let us with our Lord arise	129
2:19	Jesus, the name high over all	404
3:9	Great God, your love has called us	270
	Lord of the boundless curves	475
3:17	From thee all skill and science flow	212

James

4:7	Jesus, the name high over all	404
5:10-11	For all thy saints, O Lord	191
5:13-20	Father of heaven, whose love profound	174
	Lift up your hearts!	439
5:16	Come, O thou traveller unknown	134
5:19-20	From the eastern mountains	207
5:20	Christ for the world we sing!	95

1 PETER

1:2	O for a heart to praise my God	540
1:3	A brighter dawn is breaking	1
	Christians lift your hearts and voices	109
	Come, all who look to Christ today	115
	Come and celebrate	116
	God forgave my sin (*Freely, freely*)	237
1:6	What a friend we have in Jesus	811
1:10	All hail the power of Jesus' name	14
1:15	Here in this place (*Gather us in*)	302
1:18-19	Blessèd assurance	75
	Come, ye thankful people, come	144
	I believe in Jesus	325
	The Church's one foundation	702
	There is a green hill far away	740
1:19	Bind us together, Lord	73
	Glory be to Jesus	224
	In Christ alone	352
	We give immortal praise	795
1:21	All my hope on God is founded	19
1:25	Lord, thy word abideth	481
2:4-6	Christ is made the sure foundation	96
	Christ is our cornerstone	97
	In Christ alone	352
2:4-7	Blessèd city, heavenly Salem	77
2:9	Eternal God, we consecrate	161
2:9-10	Jesus, we have heard your Spirit	406
2:11-12	Though pilgrim strangers here below	768
2:17	Come, all who look to Christ today	115
2:21	Creator of the earth and skies	147
	Jesus, humble was your birth	384
2:21-22	A man there lived in Galilee	3
	All creatures of our God and King	10
	All hail the power of Jesus' name	14
2:24	Ah, holy Jesu, how hast thou offended	9
	As Jacob with travel was weary one day	41
	Bread of heaven, on thee we feed	83
	How deep the Father's love for us	317
	I'm special	348
	Jesu, our hope, our heart's desire	370
	The strife is o'er, the battle done	733
2:25	Father of peace, and God of love	175
	O Jesus, I have promised	556
3:1	God, whose city's sure foundation	259
3:8	Jesus, Lord, we look to thee	391
3:10-12	Hands that have been handling	284
3:15	Stand up, stand up for Jesus	677
3:18-19	Christ the Lord is risen again	102
	Finished the strife	185
3:21	Eternal God, we consecrate	161
4:10	From thee all skill and science flow	212
	God the Father, name we treasure	257
4:11	Lord of beauty, thine the splendour	470
4:14-16	God the Father, name we treasure	257
5:7	All creatures of our God and King	10
	Come and celebrate	116
	Lord it belongs not to my care	462

2 PETER

1:7	Let there be love	430
1:19	Colours of day (*Light up the fire*)	114
	Give thanks for those	217
3:4	Inspired by love and anger	362
3:5	Thanks to God whose word was spoken	698
3:7	Jesus, Lord, we pray	392
3:8	O God, our help in ages past	547
3:10	Songs of praise the angels sang	668
3:13	Come, let us use the grace divine	128
3:18	It is a thing most wonderful	364

1 JOHN

1:1	God is our strength from days of old	244
	Jesus calls us here to meet him	378
	We love the place, O God	800
1:5	Lead, kindly light	421
1:7	All you who seek a comfort sure	28
	I am trusting thee, Lord Jesus	324
	Lord Jesus, think on me	465
	The Spirit lives to set us free	732
1:8	God is our strength from days of old	244
1:9	Christians, lift up your hearts	108
	Here on the threshold of a new beginning	305
1:16	Glory, love, and praise, and honour	225
1:19	Jesus, humble was your birth	384
2:1	And now, O Father, mindful of the love	38
2:2	All my days (*Beautiful Saviour*)	18
2:8	Creator of the earth and skies	147
2:8-10	Lord of life	473
2:14	May the mind of Christ my Saviour	506
2:16	Be thou my guardian and my guide	65
2:20	Come, Holy Ghost, our souls inspire	124
3:1	God of love	250
	How deep the Father's love for us	317
3:2	Here, O my Lord	304
	How sweet the name of Jesus sounds	321
	Lord it belongs not to my care	462
	It is a thing most wonderful	364
	Once in royal David's city	592
	Thee we adore, O hidden Saviour, thee	737
3:2	My God, how wonderful you are	516
3:2-3	Lord Jesus, think on me	465
3:5	Be still, for the presence of the Lord	62
3:12	Great is the darkness (*Come, Lord Jesus*)	271
3:14	Jesus, Lord, we look to thee	391
	Let there be love	430
3:18	God the Father, name we treasure	257
3:23-24	God, our Creator	253
4:7	Let love be found among us	427
	Let there be love	430
	Ubi caritas	781
4:7-12	Let love be found among us	427
4:7-14	Overwhelmed by love	612
4:7-8	Father of peace, and God of love	175
4:8	Come, O thou traveller unknown	134
4:9	From heaven you came	205
4:9-10	It is a thing most wonderful	364
4:10	Come, wounded healer	141
	Here on the threshold of a new beginning	305
4:12-13	Abide with me	6
4:14	Glory, love, and praise, and honour	225
	Lift up your heads	438

1 John

4:16	God is love: his the care	242
	God is love: let heaven adore him	243
	Ubi caritas	781
	We sing the praise of him who died	804
4:19	It is a thing most wonderful	364
	My God, I love thee	517
	Thank you for saving me	693
5:4	Be bold, be strong	60

2 JOHN

1:12	Let there be love	430

3 JOHN

1:14	Let there be love	430

REVELATION

1:5	Lord, enthroned in heavenly splendour	453
	To God be the glory!	777
1:5-6	Alleluia, sing to Jesus	33
	Lo round the throne, a glorious band	450
1:6	From the sun's rising	210
1:7	Jesus is the name we honour	388
	Lo, he comes with clouds descending	449
1:8	God has spoken – by the prophets	238
	Jesus, lover of my soul (*It's all about you*)	394
	Lord of the boundless curves	475
	Love divine, all loves excelling	491
	Now thank we all our God	532
	Of the Father's love begotten	584
	Unto us a boy is born	782
1:17	Come, see the Lord	138
	Jesus, lover of my soul (*It's all about you*)	394
1:17-18	Heaven is open wide	296
	Rejoice, the Lord is King	638
1:18	I believe in Jesus	325
2:4	At even, ere the sun was set	49
	Lift up your hearts!	439
	Thy kingdom come, O God	774
2:7	From thee all skill and science flow	212
2:10	For all the saints	190
	Lo round the throne, a glorious band	450
2:17	O for a heart to praise my God	540
3:4	How bright these glorious spirits shine!	316
3:7	O come, O come, Emmanuel	535
3:21	Stand up, stand up for Jesus	677
4	Alleluia, sing to Jesus	33
	Come and see the shining hope	119
	Come, see the Lord	138
	Lift up your voice	440
4:1-6	As Jacob with travel was weary one day	41
4:6	I will sing the wondrous story	340
4:6-9	Angel-voices ever singing	40
4:8	Father in heaven, how we love you	
	(*Blessed be the Lord God Almighty*)	171
	Hands that have been handling	284
	Holy, holy, holy	308
	Holy, holy, holy is the Lord	309
	In the bleak mid-winter	357
	Sanctus, sanctus, sanctus	
	(*Holy, holy, holy*)	647
4:8-11	Awake, my soul, and with the sun	57
	Holy, holy, holy! Lord God almighty	310
4:9-12	Alleluia! Alleluia! (*Alleluia!*	
	Raise the Gospel)	30

Revelation

	Blessing and honour (*Ancient of Days*)	78
4:10	Love divine, all loves excelling	491
4:11	All my days (*Beautiful Saviour*)	18
	Hail, gladdening Light	276
4:12	Holy, holy, holy is the Lord	309
5	Come and see	118
5:5	Hail the day that sees him rise	277
	Ye choirs of new Jerusalem	839
5:5-6	Alleluia, sing to Jesus	33
5:6	Christ the Lord is risen again	102
	Come, wounded healer	141
	How bright these glorious spirits shine!	316
	O for a closer walk with God	539
5:6-14	Crown him with many crowns	150
5:8-10	All hail the power of Jesus' name	14
	All heaven declares	15
	From the sun's rising	210
	Now, my tongue, the mystery telling	531
5:9	Alleluia, sing to Jesus	33
	Fill thou my life, O Lord my God	182
	King of kings, majesty	418
	Lift high the Cross	437
	Holy, holy, holy	308
	There is a green hill far away	740
5:9-10	Lo round the throne, a glorious band	450
5:11	All my days (*Beautiful Saviour*)	18
	How shall I sing that majesty	320
5:11-13	Before the throne	70
	Praise God from whom all blessings flow	
	(*Doxology*)	618
5:11-14	From all that dwell below the skies	203
	I cannot tell	327
	Majesty, worship his majesty	498
	Ye servants of God	841
5:12	All hail the Lamb	13
	Come and see	118
	Come, let us join our cheerful songs	127
	Come, ye faithful, raise the anthem	142
	Glorious things of thee are spoken	223
	Sing, my tongue, the glorious battle	662
	We have a gospel to proclaim	798
5:12-13	Come, see the Lord	138
	Hail the day that sees him rise	277
5:13	All heaven declares	15
	Angel-voices ever singing	40
5:14	Jesus, the name high over all	404
	Praise to the Lord, the Almighty	628
6:9-10	All hail the power of Jesus' name	14
	Angels from the realms of glory	39
	Inspired by love and anger	362
7:3	Lift high the Cross	437
7:9	King of kings, majesty	418
7:9-17	How bright these glorious spirits shine!	316
7:10	Ye servants of God	841
7:13-17	Lo round the throne, a glorious band	450
7:14	As we are gathered	45
	At the Lamb's high feast we sing	51
	Blessèd assurance	75
	Only by grace	598
7:14-15	Blessèd assurance	75
7:17	All heaven declares	15
	Have you heard the raindrops	291
	Jesus, be the centre	376
8:4-5	We want to see Jesus lifted high	807

Revelation

11:15	Come and see the shining hope	119
	Crown him with many crowns	150
	From the eastern mountains	207
	Over all the earth	609
12:7-10	Christ, the fair glory of the holy angels	101
14:6	From the sun's rising	210
	We have a gospel to proclaim	798
14:7	Christ is the world's Light	100
	Come, faithful pilgrims all	121
14:13	For all the saints	190
	Jesu, Son of Mary	371
	Lo round the throne, a glorious band	450
15:4	Adoramus te, Domine	8
	Angels from the realms of glory	39
16:33	Glory, love, and praise, and honour	225
17:14	Alleluia, sing to Jesus	33
19:1	From all that dwell below the skies	203
19:1-9	Glory to God (Peruvian Gloria)	226
19:4	Let all mortal flesh keep silence	424
19:6	Alleluia, alleluia, give thanks to the risen Lord	31
	Hallelu, hallelu	283
	The Lord is King!	718
19:6-9	Come, ye thankful people, come	144
	Deck thyself, my soul, with gladness	153
	Glory, love, and praise, and honour	225
19:9	At the Lamb's high feast we sing	51
	At this table we remember	53
19:11-14	He has risen	292
19:16	Alleluia, sing to Jesus	33
	Christ the Lord is risen again	102
	Hosanna, hosanna	314
	Judge eternal, throned in splendour	411
	King of kings and Lord of lords	417
	Let all mortal flesh keep silence	424
	Majesty, worship his majesty	498
	The head that once was crowned with thorns	711
	The Lord is King!	718
20:10	Ye choirs of new Jerusalem	839
20:14	Guide me, O thou great Redeemer	275
21	Songs of praise the angels sang	668
21:1	Creation sings!	146
21:1-2	In the bleak mid-winter	357
21:1-6	Blessèd city, heavenly Salem	77
21:1-27	Light's abode, celestial Salem	442
21:2	I'm not ashamed to own my Lord	347
	The Church's one foundation	702

Revelation

	Ye choirs of new Jerusalem	839
21:3	Deck thyself, my soul, with gladness	153
21:3-5	Blessèd city, heavenly Salem	77
	O comfort my people	536
	O Lord, all the world belongs to you	560
	Ye choirs of new Jerusalem	839
21:3-10	As with gladness men of old	46
	Wake, O wake! with tidings thrilling	786
21:4	From the eastern mountains	207
	From thee all skill and science flow	212
	Great God, your love has called us	270
	Hills of the north, rejoice	307
	Long ago, prophets knew	451
	Oft in danger, oft in woe	585
	Thy kingdom come, O God	774
21:6	Come, see the Lord	138
	Deck thyself, my soul, with gladness	153
	God is our strength from days of old	244
	Have you heard the raindrops	291
	Jesus, lover of my soul (*It's all about you*)	394
21:10	City of God, how broad and far	111
21:21	For all the saints	190
	Wake, O wake! with tidings thrilling	786
21:22-27	From the eastern mountains	207
22:1	Have you heard the raindrops	291
22:1-3	Crown him with many crowns	150
	To thee, O Lord, our hearts we raise	780
22:1-4	All heaven declares	15
	For the healing of the nations	198
	Guide me, O thou great Redeemer	275
22:3-4	How bright these glorious spirits shine!	316
22:4	Lord it belongs not to my care	462
22:4-5	Jesu, Son of Mary	371
22:13	God is our strength from days of old	244
	How good is the God we adore	318
	King of kings, majesty	418
	Love divine, all loves excelling	491
	Of the Father's love begotten	584
	One more step along the world I go	595
22:16	Christ, whose glory fills the skies	105
	O come, O come, Emmanuel	535
22:16-17	Heaven is open wide	296
22:17	Have you heard the raindrops	291
	O, heaven is in my heart	552
22:20	Alleluia (x 8)	29
	Great is the darkness (*Come, Lord Jesus*)	271
22:23	As with gladness men of old	46

Index of Uses

ADORATION AND PRAISE

Father

Abba, Father, let me be	5
Alleluia (x 8)	29
Come and celebrate	116
Dear Lord and Father of mankind	152
Father God, I wonder	168
Father in heaven, how we love you	171
Father, most holy, merciful and loving	173
Father, we adore you	176
Father, we love you	177
Father, who in Jesus found us	180
How deep the Father's love for us	317
I'm accepted, I'm forgiven	345
Our Father God in heaven	605
Praise and thanksgiving	617
The King is among us	714

Godhead

Adoramus te, Domine	8
All creatures of our God and King	10
All people that on earth do dwell	21
All the nations of the earth	25
Alleluia! Alleluia!	30
Alleluia, alleluia, hearts to heaven and voices raise	32
Alleluia (x 8)	29
Amazing grace	34
As the deer pants for the water	43
Ascribe greatness	48
At the Lamb's high feast we sing	51
At this time of giving	54
Awake, awake: fling off the night	56
Before Jehovah's aweful throne	68
Bless the Lord, my soul	74
Blessèd be your name	76
Blessing and honour	78
Bright the vision that delighted	88
Christians, lift up your hearts	108
Christians lift your hearts and voices	109
Clap your hands, all you people	112
Come and celebrate	116
Come and see the shining hope	119
Come into his presence	126
Come, let us with our Lord arise	129
Come, my Way, my Truth, my Life	131
Come, now is the time to worship	132
Come on and celebrate	135
Confitemini Domino	145
Dance and sing	151
Deck thyself, my soul, with gladness	153
Father in heaven, how we love you	171

Fill thou my life, O Lord my God	182
Fill your hearts with joy and gladness	183
Fishes of the ocean	187
For the beauty of the earth	195
For the days when you feel near	196
From all that dwell below the skies	203
From the rising of the sun	209
Give me joy in my heart	215
Give thanks to the Lord	218
Give to our God immortal praise	220
Glorious things of thee are spoken	223
Glory to God above	228
God is here! As we his people	241
God is love: let heaven adore him	243
God of mercy, God of grace	251
God, our Creator	253
God's love is deeper	261
Great is the Lord and most worthy of praise	272
Great is thy faithfulness	273
Guide me, O thou great Redeemer	275
Halle, halle, halle	282
Hallelu, hallelu	283
He's got the whole world in his hand	306
Holy, holy, holy is the Lord	309
Hosanna, hosanna	314
How shall I sing that majesty	320
I am a new creation	322
I give you all the honour	331
I will worship	341
If I were a butterfly	342
Immortal, invisible, God only wise	349
In the Cross of Christ I glory	358
In the Lord is my joy	361
Jesu, our hope, our heart's desire	370
Jesu, the very thought of thee	373
Jesus put this song	397
Jubilate, everybody	410
King of glory, King of peace	416
King of kings and Lord of lords	417
King of kings, majesty	418
Laudate Dominum	420
Let all mortal flesh keep silence	424
Let all the world in every corner sing	425
Let everything that has breath	426
Let the mountains dance and sing	429
Let us praise God together	433
Let us with a gladsome mind	435
Lift up your hearts!	439
Light of the world	441
Lord, for the years	454
Lord of all hopefulness	467
Lord of all life and power	468

Lord of creation, to you be all praise!	471
Lord of the future	476
Lord, today your voice is calling	482
Lord, you created	488
Magnificat	497
Morning has broken	510
My God, how wonderful you are	516
My God, I love thee	517
My heart will sing to you	518
New songs of celebration render	527
Now thank we all our God	532
O for a heart to praise my God	540
O for a thousand tongues to sing	541
O give thanks (Kendrick)	542
O give thanks (Pond)	543
O God beyond all praising	544
O happy day	551
O, how good is the Lord	555
O Lord, my God	563
O Lord, we want to praise you	567
O praise ye the Lord!	574
O worship the King	582
O worship the Lord in the beauty of holiness	583
Of the Father's love begotten	584
On Christmas night all Christians sing	588
One shall tell another	596
Open the eyes of my heart	601
Our God is a great big God	606
Our God is so great	607
Our God loves us	608
Over the mountains and the sea	611
Overwhelmed by love	612
Peace is flowing like a river	613
Praise him on the trumpet	620
Praise him, praise him, all his children	621
Praise, my soul, the King of heaven	623
Praise, O praise our God and King	624
Praise the Lord, ye heavens, adore him	625
Praise to the Holiest	627
Praise to the Lord, the Almighty	628
Rejoice in the Lord always	636
Rise and shine	642
Salvation belongs to our God	646
Sanctus, sanctus, sanctus	647
Send forth your Spirit, Lord	653
Sing of the Lord's goodness	663
Sing praise to God who reigns above	664
Stand up and bless the Lord	676
Surrexit Christus	683
Teach me to dance	691
Tell out, my soul	692
Thanks be to God	696
Thanks to God whose word was spoken	698

Godhead

The Lord is my song	720
There are hundreds of sparrows	738
This is my desire	756
This is the air I breathe	758
This is the day	759
This is the day the Lord has made	760
To be in your presence	776
To God be the glory!	777
We bow down	791
When all thy mercies, O my God	813
When I feel the touch	817
When I look into your holiness	818
When the Spirit of the Lord	824
Who is there like you	830
Ye holy angels bright	840
Ye servants of God	841
You are beautiful	847
You, Lord, are in this place	852
You shall go out with joy	853
Your love is amazing	855
Your love's greater	856

Jesus Christ

All glory, laud and honour	12
All hail the Lamb	13
All hail the power of Jesus' name	14
All heaven declares	15
All I once held dear	16
All my days	18
All praise to our redeeming Lord	22
All praise to thee	23
All that I am	24
Alleluia, alleluia, give thanks to the risen Lord	31
Alleluia, sing to Jesus	33
Alleluia (x 8)	29
As the deer pants for the water	43
At the Lamb's high feast we sing	51
At the name of Jesus	52
Blessèd assurance	75
Christ triumphant	103
Cloth for the cradle	113
Come and see	118
Come and see the shining hope	119
Come into his presence	126
Come, let us join our cheerful songs	127
Come, let us with our Lord arise	129
Come on, let's get up and go	136
Come, see the Lord	138
Crown him with many crowns	150
Father, we adore you	176
Father, we love you	177
Forth in the peace of Christ we go	200
From heaven you came	205
From the sun's rising	210
Glory be to Jesus	224
Glory, love, and praise, and honour	225
Hail, thou once despisèd Jesus	278
Hail to the Lord's anointed	280
He is exalted	293
He is Lord	294

Hills of the north, rejoice	307
How deep the Father's love for us	317
How sweet the name of Jesus sounds	321
I am a new creation	322
I danced in the morning	329
I love you, Lord, and I lift my voice	335
I will offer up my life	339
I'm special	348
In Christ alone	352
Jesu, Son of Mary	371
Jesu, thou joy of loving hearts	374
Jesus, all for Jesus	375
Jesus, be the centre	376
Jesus Christ	380
Jesus Christ is risen today	381
Jesus is greater	385
Jesus is King	386
Jesus is Lord! Creation's voice proclaims it	387
Jesus is the name we honour	388
Jesus, Jesus	389
Jesus' love is very wonderful	393
Jesus, lover of my soul	394
Jesus, Name above all names	395
Jesus shall take the highest honour	400
Jesus, the name high over all	404
Jesus, we celebrate your victory	405
Joy to the world!	409
King kings, majesty	418
King of kings and Lord of lords	417
Led like a lamb	423
Lift high the Cross	437
Lift up your heads	438
Lo, he comes with clouds descending	449
Lord, enthroned in heavenly splendour	453
Lord, I lift your name on high	461
Lord Jesus Christ	463
Lord Jesus Christ, be present	464
Lord, the light of your love	479
Lord, you have my heart	489
Lovely in your littleness	493
Majesty, worship his majesty	498
Make way, make way	500
May the fragrance of Jesus fill this place	504
Meekness and majesty	507
My Jesus, my Saviour	519
My Lord, what love is this	520
Name of all majesty	524
O, heaven is in my heart	552
O let the Son of God enfold you	558
O when the saints go marching in	581
Open our eyes, Lord	600
Peace, perfect peace, is the gift	615
Praise him, praise him, praise him	622
Rejoice, the Lord is King	638
Shout for joy and sing	656
Songs of thankfulness and praise	669
Such love	681
Thank you for saving me	693

There's a quiet understanding	745
Thine be the glory	751
Think of a world without any flowers	753
To the name of our salvation	779
We have a King who rides a donkey	799
We sing the praise of him who died	804
We want to see Jesus lifted high	807
When I feel the touch	817
When morning gilds the skies	822
When the music fades	823
Wonderful, so wonderful	838
Yesterday, today, for ever	846
You are the King of Glory	849
You laid aside your majesty	850

Trinity

All people that on earth do dwell	21
Alleluia, alleluia, hearts to heaven and voices raise	32
Angel-voices ever singing	40
Awake, my soul, and with the sun	57
Blessèd assurance	75
Blest Creator of the light	80
Christ is made the sure foundation	96
Christ is our cornerstone	97
Christ is the world's Light	100
Christ, the fair glory of the holy angels	101
Come, ye faithful, raise the anthem	142
Come, ye faithful, raise the strain	143
Creator of the starry height	148
Disposer supreme	155
Father most holy, merciful and loving	173
Father, we adore you	176
Father, we love you	177
Firmly I believe and truly	186
For all thy saints, O Lord	191
For all your saints still active	192
From glory to glory advancing	204
Gloria (Anderson)	222
Glory to God (Peruvian Gloria)	225
God is our strength from days of old	244
God of life, God of love	249
God, our Creator	253
Holy, holy, holy!	308
Holy, holy, holy! Lord God almighty	310
How good is the God we adore	318
Jesus calls us here to meet him	378
Lead us, heavenly Father, lead us	422
Light's abode, celestial Salem	442
Oh, the life of the world	586
Praise God from whom all blessings flow	618, 619
Praise to God for saints and martyrs	626
Sing to God a song of glory	665
Songs of praise the angels sang	668

Trinity

The God of Abraham praise 706
There is a Redeemer 743
Through all the changing scenes
of life 769
We give immortal praise 795
Ye watchers and ye holy ones 844

GOD

Creation

All creatures of our God and King 10
All the nations of the earth 25
All things bright and beautiful 26
Angel-voices ever singing 40
Before Jehovah's aweful throne 68
Blest Creator of the light 80
Come, let us with our Lord arise 129
Come, ye faithful, raise the
anthem 142
Creation sings! 146
Creator of the earth and skies 147
Creator of the starry height 148
Dance and sing 151
Father, Lord of all creation 172
Fill your hearts with joy and
gladness 183
Fishes of the ocean 187
For the beauty of the earth 195
For the fruits of his creation 197
From all that dwell below the
skies 203
Glory to God above 228
God is good, God is great 240
God is love: his the care 242
God is love: let heaven adore him 243
God is our strength from days of
old 244
God moves in a mysterious way 247
God, our Creator 253
God that madest earth and
heaven 256
God, whose farm is all creation 260
Goliath was big and Goliath
was strong 264
I bind unto myself today 326
I give you all the honour 331
I watch the sunrise 338
If I were a butterfly 341
I'm accepted, I'm forgiven 345
Immortal, invisible, God only
wise 349
Let the mountains dance and
sing 429
Let us with a gladsome mind 435
Like a mighty river flowing 445
Lord of all life and power 468
Lord of beauty, thine the
splendour 470
Lord of creation 471, 472
Lord of the boundless curves 475
Lord, you created 488
Morning glory, starlit sky 509
Morning has broken 510

O give thanks (Kendrick) 542
O God, you search me 549
O Lord, my God 563
O Lord of every shining
constellation 565
O Lord of heaven and earth
and sea 566
O worship the King 582
Of the Father's love begotten 584
Our God is so great 607
Over the earth is a mat of green 610
Push, little seed 632
Send forth your Spirit, Lord 653
Thank you for the summer
morning 694
Thanks to God whose word was
spoken 698
There are hundreds of sparrows 738
Think of a world without any
flowers 753
This day God gives me 754
This is the day 759
This is the day the Lord has made 760
This world you have made 763
Though pilgrim strangers here
below 768
We eat the plants that grow from
the seed 793
We plough the fields and scatter 801
When God made the garden of
creation 815
Who put the colours in the
rainbow? 831
Your love's greater 856

Desire for

As pants the hart for cooling
streams 42
As the deer pants for the water 43
Nearer, my God, to thee 525
Over all the earth 609

Everlasting

God has spoken – by the prophets 237
O God, our help in ages past 547

Faith and Hope

All my hope on God is founded 19
All who would valiant be 27
Be bold, be strong 59
Be still, my soul 63

Faithfulness

Ascribe greatness 48
Faithful One, so unchanging 165
Give thanks to the Lord 218
Great is thy faithfulness 273
How good is the God we adore 318
Let us praise God together 433
Lord, I come before your throne
of grace 457
Praise, my soul, the King of
heaven 623
The God of Abraham praise 706

Father

Be thou my vision 66
Dear Lord and Father of mankind 152
Do not be afraid 156
Father God, I wonder 168
Father, I place into your hands 170
Father most holy, merciful and
loving 173
Father of heaven, whose love
profound 174
Father of peace, and God of love 175
Father, we thank thee 178
Father welcomes all his children 179
Follow me 189
God has spoken – by the prophets 237
God is love: let heaven adore him 243
God of life, God of love 249
God, our Creator 253
God the Father, name we treasure 257
Great is thy faithfulness 273
Hail, gladdening Light 276
Holy, holy, holy! 308
How deep the Father's love for us 317
I'm accepted, I'm forgiven 345
It's rounded like an orange 366
One shall tell another 596
Our Father (Caribbean) 603
Our Father God in heaven 605
Our Father (Wiener) 604
Praise, my soul, the King of
heaven 623
The gracious invitation 709
The King is among us 714
The love we share 725
This is my will 757
When God made the garden of
creation 815

Forgiveness

Bless the Lord, my soul 74
Dear Lord and Father of mankind 152
Father of heaven, whose love
profound 174
Father welcomes all his children 179
Forgive our sins as we forgive 199
Glory to thee, my God, this night 229
God forgave my sin 237
Great is thy faithfulness 273
Hail, thou once despisèd Jesus 278
Here, O my Lord 304
Here on the threshold of a new
beginning 305
I'm accepted, I'm forgiven 345
Let us praise God together 433
Lord, we thank you for the
promise 485
Make me a channel of your peace 499
New every morning is the love 526
O Lord, all the world belongs
to you 560
O Lord of heaven and earth
and sea 566
One shall tell another 596
Only by grace 598

Forgiveness

Our Father (Caribbean) 603
Our Father (Wiener) 604
Rejoice, O land, in God thy might 637
Rise and hear! The Lord is speaking 641
The gracious invitation 709
We turn to you 806

Glory

A great and mighty wonder 2
Angel-voices ever singing 40
Glorious things of thee are spoken 223
God, in the planning 239
God of grace and God of glory 248
Holy, holy, holy is the Lord 309
Hosanna, hosanna 314
Immortal, invisible, God only wise 349
Judge eternal, throned in splendour 411
Lord of beauty, thine the splendour 470
Lord of creation 471, 472
Lord, the light of your love 479
O, how good is the Lord 555
O worship the King 582
O worship the Lord in the beauty of holiness 583
Praise, my soul, the King of heaven 623
Praise the Lord, ye heavens, adore him 625
Rise and hear! The Lord is speaking` 641

Grace and Mercy

Abide with me 6
All creatures of our God and King 10
All people that on earth do dwell 21
Bless the Lord, my soul 74
Blest Creator of the light 80
Christ is our cornerstone 97
Fight the good fight 181
From all that dwell below the skies 203
Give to our God immortal praise 220
Go forth and tell 232
God be with you till we meet again 236
God is the giver of love 245
God moves in a mysterious way 247
God of grace and God of glory 248
God of life, God of love 249
God of mercy, God of grace 251
God, our Creator 253
God save our Gracious Queen 255
God that madest earth and heaven 256
God to enfold you 258
God's love is deeper 261
Great God, your love has called us 270
Great is thy faithfulness 273

Have faith in God, my heart 290
Heaven shall not wait 297
Here on the threshold of a new beginning 305
Holy, holy, holy! Lord God almighty 310
I am a new creation 322
I give you love 332
Jubilate, everybody 410
Let us with a gladsome mind 435
Lift up your voice 440
Lord, have mercy (Ghana) 455
Lord, have mercy (Russian) 456
Lord, I come before your throne of grace 457
Lord, I come to you 458
Lord it belongs not to my care 462
Lord of lords and King eternal 474
Lord of the boundless curves 475
Lord, teach us how to pray aright 478
Lord, we turn to you for mercy 485
Lord, when I turn my back on you 486
Love divine, all loves excelling 491
My God, accept my heart this day 514
My God, how wonderful you are 516
New every morning is the love 526
O for a thousand tongues to sing 541
O God beyond all praising 544
O Lord of heaven and earth and sea 566
O, the love of my Lord 578
O worship the King 582
One shall tell another 596
Only by grace 598
Overwhelmed by love 612
Praise, my soul, the King of heaven 623
Praise to the Lord, the Almighty 628
Put thou thy trust in God 634
Restore, O Lord 639
Tell out, my soul 692
The God of Abraham praise 706
The King of love my shepherd is 715
The Lord's my shepherd (Crimond) 723
The Lord's my shepherd (Townend) 724
The love we share 725
There's a wideness in God's mercy 747
We turn to you 806
When all thy mercies, O my God 813
Who can sound the depths of sorrow 829

Holiness

Give thanks with a grateful heart 219
God of mercy, God of grace 251
Great is the Lord and most worthy of praise 272
Holy, holy, holy! 308
Holy, holy, holy is the Lord 309
Holy, holy, holy! Lord God almighty 310
Praise to the Holiest 627

Judgement

Before the throne 70
Creator of the starry height 148
Disposer supreme 155
Fill your hearts with joy and gladness 183
Immortal, invisible, God only wise 349
Judge eternal, throned in splendour 411
O comfort my people 536
O day of God, draw nigh 537
The Lord will come and not be slow 722
There's a wideness in God's mercy 747
Who can sound the depths of sorrow 829

Love

And can it be 36
Before the throne 70
Bless the Lord, my soul 74
Breathe on me, Breath of God 87
Come and celebrate 116
Come and see the shining hope 119
Come down, O Love divine 120
Come, Holy Spirit, come 125
Come, O thou traveller unknown 134
Come on and celebrate 135
Creator of the starry height 148
Dear Lord and Father of mankind 152
Do not be afraid 156
Eternal Ruler of the ceaseless round 162
Faithful One, so unchanging 165
Father God, I wonder 168
Father, I place into your hands 170
Father, Lord of all creation 172
Father of heaven, whose love profound 174
Father of peace, and God of love 175
Father welcomes all his children 179
Father, who in Jesus found us 180
For all your saints still active 192
From many grains 206
From the very depths of darkness 211
From thee all skill and science flow 212
Gather around, for the table is spread 213
Give me peace, O Lord 216
Give thanks for those 217
Give thanks to the Lord 218
Glorious things of thee are spoken 223
Go wandering in the sun 234
God, in the planning 239
God is good, God is great 240
God is love: his the care 242
God is love: let heaven adore him 243
God is the giver of love 245
God of life, God of love 249
God of love 250
God, our Creator 253
God's love is deeper 261
Gracious Spirit, Holy Ghost 268

Love

Grant us the courage, gracious God	269
Great God, your love has called us	270
Great is the Lord and most worthy of praise	272
Great is thy faithfulness	273
Hail the day that sees him rise	277
Hail to the Lord's anointed	280
Happy are they, they that love God	285
Hark, my soul, it is the Lord	287
Heaven is open wide	296
Help us to help each other, Lord	299
Holy, holy, holy! Lord God almighty	310
How deep the Father's love for us	317
How good is the God we adore	318
I come with joy	328
I give my hands	330
I, the Lord of sea and sky	337
If we only seek peace	343
I'm black, I'm white, I'm short, I'm tall	346
I'm special	348
Immortal, invisible, God only wise	349
Immortal love, for ever full	350
In Christ alone	352
In full and glad surrender	354
In heavenly love abiding	355
It is a thing most wonderful	364
Joy to the world!	409
Let love be found among us	427
Let there be love	430
Lord, I come before your throne of grace	457
Lord, I come to you	458
Lord, I lift my hands to you in prayer	460
Lord of life	473
Lord, today your voice is calling	482
Love divine, all loves excelling	491
Love is his word	492
May the grace of Christ the Saviour	505
Morning glory, starlit sky	509
Moses, I know you're the man	511
My heart will sing to you	518
My spirit longs for thee	522
Name of all majesty	524
New every morning is the love	526
Not far beyond the sea	528
Now is eternal life	529
O for a heart to praise my God	540
O God, unseen but ever near	548
O Lord, all the world belongs to you	560
O Lord, we want to praise you	567
O Lord, your tenderness	568
O love divine, how sweet thou art!	569
O love, how deep, how broad, how high	570
O Love that wilt not let me go	571
O perfect love	573
O, the love of my Lord	578
O worship the King	582
Of the Father's love begotten	584
One shall tell another	596
Open the eyes of my heart	601
Our Father God in heaven	605
Our God is a great big God	606
Our God love us	608
Over the earth is a mat of green	610
Over the mountains and the sea	611
Overwhelmed by love	612
Rejoice, O land, in God thy might	637
Saint Luke, beloved physician	645
Sanctus, sanctus, sanctus	647
Spirit of God, our light amid the darkness	673
Take me, Lord	685
Thanks be to God	696
The God of love my shepherd is	707
The King of love my shepherd is	715
The love we share	725
There is a longing	742
There's a wideness in God's mercy	747
This little light of mine	762
This world you have made	763
Through the night of doubt and sorrow	770
Thy kingdom come, O God	774
To be in your presence	776
Ubi caritas	781
We cannot measure	792
We sing the praise of him who died	804
We turn to you	806
We will lay our burden down	808
When God made the garden of creation	815
Your love is amazing	855
Your love's greater	856

Majesty and Power

As pants the hart for cooling streams	42
Awake, our souls; away, our fears	58
Holy, holy, holy! Lord God almighty	310
How good is the God we adore	318
How lovely on the mountains	319
How shall I sing that majesty	320
I bind unto myself today	326
Immortal, invisible, God only wise	349
Judge eternal, throned in splendour	411
King of kings, majesty	418
Lord of beauty, thine the splendour	470
Lord of creation	471
My God, how wonderful you are	516
New songs of celebration render	527
O Lord, my God	563
O worship the King	582
Of the Father's love begotten	584

Open the eyes of my heart	601
Our God is a great big God	606
Our God is so great	607
Over all the earth	609
Praise the Lord, ye heavens, adore him	625
Restore, O Lord	639
Tell out, my soul	692
The Lord is King!	718

Presence

Give thanks to the Lord	218
God be in my head	235
O God, unseen but ever near	548
O God, you search me	549
Only by grace	598
Praise to the Holiest	627
Show me how to stand for justice	657
The Lord's my shepherd (Crimond)	723
The Lord's my shepherd (Townend)	724
Through the night of doubt and sorrow	770

Protection, Care and Guidance

All my hope on God is founded	19
Be bold, be strong	59
Be still, my soul	63
Be thou my guardian and my guide	65
Be thou my vision	66
Before Jehovah's aweful throne	68
Eternal Father, strong to save	160
Eternal God, we consecrate	161
Faithful One, so unchanging	165
Faithful Shepherd, feed me	166
Father, hear the prayer we offer	169
Father, I place into your hands	170
Fight the good fight	181
Give thanks to the Lord	218
Give to our God immortal praise	220
God be with you till we meet again	236
God is love: let heaven adore him	243
Great is thy faithfulness	273
Guide me, O thou great Redeemer	275
I bind unto myself today	326
In heavenly love abiding	355
Lead, kindly light	421
Lead us, heavenly Father, lead us	422
Lord of beauty, thine the splendour	470
Lord of lords and King eternal	474
Lord, when I turn my back on you	486
Moses, I know you're the man	511
My spirit longs for thee	523
O God of Bethel, by whose hand	545
O God, our help in ages past	547
O God, you search me	549
O worship the King	582

Protection, Care and Guidance

O worship the Lord in the beauty
of holiness 583
Our God is a great big God 606
Praise, my soul, the King of
heaven 623
Praise the Lord, ye heavens,
adore him 625
Praise to the Lord, the Almighty 628
Take me, Lord 685
Thanks be to God 696
The God of Abraham praise 706
The God of love my shepherd is 707
The King of love my shepherd is 715
The Lord's my shepherd
(Crimond) 723
The Lord's my shepherd
(Townend) 724
Thine for ever! God of love 752
This day God gives me 754
Thy hand, O God, has guided 772
When all thy mercies, O my God 813

Provision

Blessèd be your name 76
Come, ye thankful people, come 144
Glory, love, and praise, and
honour 225
Great is thy faithfulness 273
I give you love 332
I, the Lord of sea and sky 337
Let us with a gladsome mind 435
Lord of all life and power 468
O give thanks (Kendrick) 542
O God beyond all praising 544
O Lord of heaven and earth and
sea 566
Praise and thanksgiving 617
Praise God from whom all
blessings flow 619
Praise, O praise our God and
King 624
Push, little seed 632
Thank you, Lord 695
Thanks be to God 696
The King of love my shepherd is 715
The Lord's my shepherd
(Crimond) 723
This day God gives me 754
To thee, O Lord, our hearts
we raise 780
We eat the plants that grow from
the seed 793
We plough the fields and scatter 801
When God made the garden of
creation 815

The Word

Break thou the bread 86
Come, Lord, to our souls 130
Disposer supreme 155
Go forth and tell 232
God has spoken – by the prophets 237
God is our strength from days of
old 244

God the Father, name we treasure 257
God, whose city's sure foundation 259
Lord, I have made thy word my
choice 459
Lord, thy word abideth 481
May the mind of Christ my
Saviour 506
Not far beyond the sea 528
Praise we now the word of grace 629
Rejoice, O land, in God thy
might 637
Rise and hear! The Lord is
speaking 641
Saint Luke, beloved physician 645
Seek ye first 652
Silent, surrendered 659
Tell out, my soul 692
Thanks to God whose word was
spoken 698
The heavens declare thy glory,
Lord 712
We love the place, O God 800

HOLY SPIRIT

Gifts

Come, Holy Ghost, our souls
inspire 124
Come, thou Holy Spirit, come 139
Gracious Spirit, Holy Ghost 268
Holy Spirit, come, confirm us 311
O thou who camest from above 580
One is the body 594
Our blest Redeemer, ere he
breathed 602
The King is among us 714

Presence and Power

All over the world 20
Break thou the bread 86
Breathe on me, Breath of God 87
Christ, when for us you were
baptised 104
Christians, lift up your hearts 108
Colours of day 114
Come down, O Love divine 120
Come, gracious Spirit, heavenly
Dove 122
Come, Holy Ghost, our hearts
inspire 123
Come, Holy Ghost, our souls
inspire 124
Come, Holy Spirit, come 125
Come, thou Holy Spirit, come 139
Creator Spirit, come 149
Eternal God, we consecrate 161
Eternal Ruler of the ceaseless
round 162
Father, Lord of all creation 172
Father of heaven, whose love
profound 174
Father of peace, and God of love 175
Filled with the Spirit's power 184
Follow me 189

For all your saints still active 192
For I'm building a people of
power 193
From the falter of breath 208
Gather around, for the table is
spread 213
Go back, go back to Galilee 231
God is here! As we his people 241
God of love 250
God the Father, name we treasure 257
Gracious Spirit, Holy Ghost 268
Grant us the courage, gracious
God 269
Great is the darkness 271
Holy, holy, holy! 308
Holy Spirit, come, confirm us 311
Holy Spirit, truth divine 312
Holy Spirit, will you be 313
I come with joy 328
I give you all the honour 331
If you believe and I believe 344
Jesus is Lord! Creation's voice
proclaims it 387
Jesus, stand among us in thy risen
power 402
Lead us, heavenly Father, lead us 422
Listen, let your heart keep seeking 446
Lord, I come to you 458
Lord Jesus Christ, be present 464
Lord of all life and power 468
Lord, the light of your love 479
Love divine, all loves excelling 491
May the grace of Christ the
Saviour 505
O Holy Spirit, Lord of grace 554
O, how good is the Lord 555
O King, enthroned on high 557
O let the Son of God enfold you 558
O Lord of heaven and earth and
sea 566
O thou who camest from above 580
On the day of Pentecost 590
Our blest Redeemer, ere he
breathed 602
Send forth your Spirit, Lord 653
She sits like a bird 654
Shepherd divine, our wants relieve 655
Silent, surrendered 659
Sing we of the blessèd Mother 666
Spirit divine, attend our prayers 671
Spirit of God 672
Spirit of God, our light amid the
darkness 673
Spirit of the living God
(Armstrong) 674
Spirit of the living God (Iverson) 675
The King is among us 714
The Spirit lives to set us free 732
There's a quiet understanding 745
There's a spirit in the air 746
This is the day 759
This little light of mine 762
Thou, whose almighty word 767
Veni, lumen cordium 783
We cannot measure 792

Presence and Power

When God of old came down from heaven	816
When Jesus came to Jordan	821
When the Spirit of the Lord	824
You are the centre	848

JESUS CHRIST

Advent and Birth

A great and mighty wonder	2
Angels from the realms of glory	39
At this time of giving	54
Away in a manger	59
Behold, the great Creator	71
Born in the night, Mary's child	81
Christians, awake!	107
Cloth for the cradle	113
Come and join the celebration	117
Ding dong, merrily on high!	154
For Mary, mother of our Lord	194
From heaven you came	205
From the eastern mountains	207
Glory to God!	227
Go, tell it on the mountain	233
God rest you merry, gentlefolk	254
Good Christians all, rejoice	265
Hail, true body	281
Hark, the herald-angels sing	289
I cannot tell	327
I danced in the morning	329
In Christ alone	352
Jesus, good above all other	383
Joy to the world!	409
Like a candle flame	444
Little donkey	447
Little Jesus, sweetly sleep	448
Long ago, prophets knew	451
Lord Jesus Christ	463
Love came down at Christmas	490
Mary had a baby	502
Now, my tongue, the mystery telling	531
O come, all ye faithful	534
O little town of Bethlehem	559
Of the Father's love begotten	584
On Christmas night all Christians sing	588
Once in royal David's city	592
Our Father God in heaven	605
See, amid the winter's snow	649
See him lying on a bed of straw	650
Silent night	658
Sing lullaby	661
Sing we of the blessèd Mother	666
The advent of our King	699
The angel Gabriel from heaven came	700
The first Nowell	705
The God whom earth and sea and sky	708
The holly and the ivy	713
The people that in darkness sat	727
The Virgin Mary had a baby boy	734
Thou didst leave thy throne	766

Unto us a boy is born	782
Virgin-born, we bow before thee	784
We three kings of Orient are	805
What child is this	812
Where is this stupendous stranger?	825
While shepherds watched	827
Who would think that what was needed	832
Ye who own the faith of Jesus	845

Atonement, Suffering and Death

Above all powers, above all kings	7
Ah, holy Jesu, how hast thou offended	9
All praise to thee	23
All you who seek a comfort sure	28
Alleluia, alleluia, hearts to heaven and voices raise	32
And can it be	36
And now, O Father, mindful of the love	38
At the Lamb's high feast we sing	51
At the name of Jesus	52
At this table we remember	53
Before the throne	70
Beneath the cross of Jesus	72
Bread of heaven, on thee we feed	83
Bread of the world in mercy broken	84
Broken for me	90
Christ the Lord is risen again	102
Christ triumphant	103
Come and celebrate	116
Come and see	118
Come, let us join our cheerful songs	127
Come, O thou traveller unknown	134
Come, see the Lord	138
Come, wounded healer	141
Come, ye faithful, raise the anthem	142
Crown him with many crowns	150
Draw nigh and take the body	157
From heaven you came	205
From the very depths of darkness	211
Give us the wings of faith	221
Glory be to Jesus	224
God of life, God of love	249
Hail, thou once despisèd Jesus	278
Hail, true body	281
How bright these glorious spirits shine!	316
How deep the Father's love for us	317
I believe in Jesus	325
I cannot tell	327
I danced in the morning	329
I give you love	332
I will offer up my life	339
I will sing the wondrous story	340
In the Cross of Christ I glory	358
It is a thing most wonderful	364
Jesu, grant me this, I pray	367
Jesu, our hope, our heart's desire	370

Jesus Christ	380
Jesus, Prince and Saviour	396
Just as I am, without one plea	413
Led like a lamb	423
Low in the grave he lay	496
Mary, blessed grieving mother	501
Meekness and majesty	507
Morning glory, starlit sky	509
My God, accept my heart this day	514
My God, I love thee	517
My Lord, what love is this	520
My song is love unknown	521
Name of all majesty	524
Now, my tongue, the mystery telling	531
Now the green blade riseth	533
O dearest Lord, thy sacred head	538
O happy band of pilgrims	550
O love, how deep, how broad, how high	570
O my Saviour, lifted from the earth	572
O sacred head, surrounded	576
On a hill far away	587
On the holy cross I see	591
Once, only once, and once for all	593
One whose heart is hard as steel	597
Onward, Christian pilgrims	599
Praise to the Holiest	627
Rock of ages	643
Sing, my tongue, the glorious battle	662
Sing we of the blessèd Mother	666
Soul of my Saviour	670
The royal banners forward go	729
There in God's garden	739
There is a green hill far away	740
Thou didst leave thy throne	766
To mock your reign, O dearest Lord	778
We sing the praise of him who died	804
Were you there when they crucified my Lord?	810
When I survey the wondrous cross	820
You laid aside your majesty	850
Zip bam boo	858

Baptism

Awake, awake: fling off the night	56
Be thou my vision	66
Breathe on me, Breath of God	87
Christ, when for us you were baptised	104
Come down, O Love divine	120
Come, gracious Spirit, heavenly Dove	122
Crown him with many crowns	150
Do not be afraid	156
Hail to the Lord's anointed	280
Just as I am, without one plea	413
Lord, the light of your love	479
Name of all majesty	524
Now is eternal life	529
O love, how deep, how broad, how high	570

Baptism

O thou who camest from above	580
On Jordan's bank the Baptist's cry	589
Spirit divine, attend our prayers	671
Spirit of the living God (Iverson)	675
Take this moment	688
The people that in darkness sat	727
To the name of our salvation	779
Veni, lumen cordium	783
When Jesus came to Jordan	821

Grace and Mercy

All hail the power of Jesus' name	14
All praise to our redeeming Lord	22
All praise to thee	23
Amazing grace	34
Be still, for the presence of the Lord	62

Incarnation

Ah, holy Jesu, how hast thou offended	9
Christ triumphant	103
For all your saints still active	192
Give thanks with a grateful heart	219
Glory to God!	227
God is love: his the care	242
God is our strength from days of old	244
God of love	250
God the Father, name we treasure	257
Hail to the Lord who comes	279
I, the Lord of sea and sky	337
In Christ alone	352
Jesus is greater	385
Jesus is Lord! Creation's voice proclaims it	387
Let all mortal flesh keep silence	424
Long ago, prophets knew	451
Meekness and majesty	507
Name of all majesty	524
Now, my tongue, the mystery telling	531
O love, how deep, how broad, how high	570
Sing, my tongue, the glorious battle	662
Son of God, eternal Saviour	667
Songs of thankfulness and praise	669
Thanks to God whose word was spoken	698
The advent of our King	699
The God whom earth and sea and sky	708
The great Creator of the world	710
Thou didst leave thy throne	766
Where is this stupendous stranger?	825
Who would think that what was needed	832

Kingship and Kingdom

A brighter dawn is breaking	1
A man there lived in Galilee	3
Above all powers, above all kings	7

All glory, laud and honour	12
All hail the Lamb	13
All hail the power of Jesus' name	14
All heaven declares	15
All my days	18
Alleluia, sing to Jesus	33
At the name of Jesus	52
Born in the night, Mary's child	81
Christ is the King!	99
Christ is the world's Light	100
Christ triumphant	103
Come, see the Lord	138
Crown him with many crowns	150
From heaven you came	205
Give me joy in my heart	215
God is love: his the care	242
Hail to the Lord's anointed	280
He is exalted	293
He is Lord	294
Hosanna, hosanna	314
How lovely on the mountains	319
I cannot tell	327
I will worship	340
I'm not ashamed to own my Lord	347
In full and glad surrender	354
Jesu, our hope, our heart's desire	370
Jesus, good above all other	383
Jesus is King	386
Jesus is Lord! Creation's voice proclaims it	387
Jesus is the name we honour	388
Jesus lives! thy terrors now	390
Jesus shall reign	399
Jesus, we have heard your Spirit	406
Joy to the world!	409
Let all mortal flesh keep silence	424
Lift up your heads	438
Listen, let your heart keep seeking	446
Lord, enthroned in heavenly splendour	453
Majesty, worship his majesty	498
Make way, make way	500
My Jesus, my Saviour	519
O, heaven is in my heart	552
O raise your eyes on high	575
Proclaim, proclaim the story	630
Rejoice, the Lord is King	638
Shout for joy and sing	656
Sing it in the valleys	660
Stand up, stand up for Jesus	677
The head that once was crowned with thorns	711

Life

A man there lived in Galilee	3
At even, ere the sun was set	49
Blest are the pure in heart	79
Christ, when for us you were baptised	104
Come, see the Lord	138
Come, thou long-expected Jesus	140
5000 + hungry folk	188
For all your saints still active	192
Hail to the Lord who comes	279
I cannot tell	327

I danced in the morning	329
Life for the poor was hard and tough	436
Saint Luke, beloved physician	645
Songs of thankfulness and praise	669
When God almighty came to earth	814
When Jesus came to Jordan	821
Zip bam boo	858

Lordship

All hail the Lamb	13
All hail the power of Jesus' name	14
All praise to thee	23
Alleluia, alleluia, give thanks to the risen Lord	31
An upper room did our Lord prepare	35
At the name of Jesus	52
Come into his presence	126
He is Lord	294
He is the Lord	295
Heaven shall not wait	297
Holy, holy, holy is the Lord	309
I cannot tell	327
I'm special	348
Jesu, Son of Mary	371
Jesus is Lord! Creation's voice proclaims it	387
Jesus, Name above all names	395
Jesus shall take the highest honour	400
Jesus the Lord said: 'I am the Bread'	403
Let all mortal flesh keep silence	424
Lord, enthroned in heavenly splendour	453
Men of faith	508
Name of all majesty	524
O raise your eyes on high	575
O when the saints go marching in	581
The great Creator of the world	710
The head that once was crowned with thorns	711

Love

In Christ alone	352
It is a thing most wonderful	364
Jesu, Jesu, fill us with your love	368
Jesu, our hope, our heart's desire	370
Jesu, the very thought of thee	373
Jesus Christ is waiting	382
Jesus, humble was your birth	384
Jesus is greater	385
Jesus' love is very wonderful	393
Jesus, lover of my soul	394
Jesus shall reign	399
Jesus, the name high over all	404
Jesus, we celebrate your victory	405
Just as I am, without one plea	413
Let us talents and tongues employ	434
Lift high the Cross	437
Lord Jesus Christ	463
Lord of all hopefulness	467
Lord, the light of your love	479

Love

Love divine, all loves excelling	491
Love is his word	492
May the mind of Christ my Saviour	506
Men of faith	508
My God, I love thee	517
My Jesus, my Saviour	519
My Lord, what love is this	520
My song is love unknown	521
O love divine, how sweet thou art!	569
O my Saviour, lifted from the earth	572
O sacred head, surrounded	576
On the holy cross I see	591
Peace is flowing like a river	613
Peace, perfect peace, is the gift	615
Spirit of God	672
Stand up, stand up for Jesus	677
Such love	681
There is a green hill far away	740
This is my will	757
Ubi caritas	781
Wide, wide as the ocean	832

Name and Glory

All heaven declares	15
All praise to thee	23
At the name of Jesus	52
For all the saints	190
For all your saints still active	192
God forgave my sin	237
He is the Lord	295
Hosanna, hosanna	314
How sweet the name of Jesus sounds	321
I'm not ashamed to own my Lord	347
Immortal love, for ever full	350
Jesus is King	386
Jesus is the name we honour	388
Jesus, Jesus	389
Jesus, Lord, we look to thee	391
Jesus, lover of my soul	394
Jesus, Name above all names	395
Jesus, Prince and Saviour	396
Jesus shall reign	399
Jesus shall take the highest honour	400
Jesus, the name high over all	404
Jesus, where'er thy people meet	407
Majesty, worship his majesty	498
My Jesus, my Saviour	519
Name of all majesty	524
O for a thousand tongues to sing	541
O let the Son of God enfold you	558
O when the saints go marching in	581
Proclaim, proclaim the story	630
The Lord will come and not be slow	722
There's a quiet understanding	745
Thou art the Christ, O Lord	764
To the name of our salvation	779
We believe in God the Father	790
We have a gospel to proclaim	798

Yesterday, today, for ever	846
You, living Christ, our eyes behold	851

Protection, Care and Guidance

Christ be with me	94
I bind unto myself today	326
I have a friend	333
Jesu, lover of my soul	369
Jesus Christ is waiting	382
Jesus, good above all other	383
Let saints on earth in concert sing	428
Loving Shepherd of thy sheep	495
O Jesus, I have promised	556
Shout for joy and sing	656
Walk with me, O my Lord	788

Resurrection

A brighter dawn is breaking	1
All in an Easter garden	17
All my days	18
All praise to thee	23
Alleluia, alleluia, give thanks to the risen Lord	31
Alleluia, alleluia, hearts to heaven and voices raise	32
At the Lamb's high feast we sing	51
Before the throne	70
Christ the Lord is risen again	102
Colours of day	114
Come and see	118
Come, let us with our Lord arise	129
Come, risen Lord	137
Come, see the Lord	138
Come, ye faithful, raise the anthem	142
Come, ye faithful, raise the strain	143
Father of peace, and God of love	175
Finished the strife	185
For all your saints still active	192
From the very depths of darkness	211
Go back, go back to Galilee	231
God of life, God of love	249
God of love	250
Good Christians all, rejoice and sing	266
Hail the day that sees him rise	277
He has risen	292
He is Lord	294
Holy, holy, holy!	308
How deep the Father's love for us	317
I am the bread of life	323
I believe in Jesus	325
I danced in the morning	329
In Christ alone	352
In the garden Mary lingers	359
Jesu, our hope, our heart's desire	370
Jesus Christ	380
Jesus Christ is risen today	381
Jesus, good above all other	383
Jesus, humble was your birth	384
Jesus is Lord! Creation's voice proclaims it	387
Jesus lives! thy terrors now	390

Jesus, Prince and Saviour	396
Led like a lamb	423
Light's glittering morn	443
Love's redeeming work is done	494
Low in the grave he lay	496
Now is eternal life	529
Now the green blade riseth	533
O love, how deep, how broad, how high	570
Onward, Christian pilgrims	599
Proclaim, proclaim the story	630
Sing we of the blessèd Mother	666
Surrexit Christus	683
The day of resurrection	703
The Lord is risen indeed	721
The strife is o'er, the battle done	733
Thine be the glory	751
This is the day	759
This is the day the Lord has made	760
This joyful Eastertide	761
We have a King who rides a donkey	799
Were you there when they crucified my Lord?	810
Ye choirs of new Jerusalem	839
You laid aside your majesty	850
You stood there on the shoreline	854
Zip bam boo	858

Saviour

A brighter dawn is breaking	1
A great and mighty wonder	2
A man there lived in Galilee	3
All for Jesus!	11
All my days	18
As Jacob with travel was weary one day	41
Be the centre of my life	64
Before the throne	70
Beneath the cross of Jesus	72
Blessèd assurance	75
Break thou the bread	86
Christ is the world's Light	100
Christ the Lord is risen again	102
Come, risen Lord	137
Crown him with many crowns	150
Draw nigh and take the body	157
Fight the good fight	181
For all your saints still active	192
Forgive our sins as we forgive	199
From heaven you came	205
From the very depths of darkness	211
Give to our God immortal praise	220
Gloria (Anderson)	222
Glorious things of thee are spoken	223
Glory, love, and praise, and honour	225
God is love: his the care	242
God is our strength from days of old	244
Good Christians all, rejoice	265
Great God, your love has called us	270
Hail, thou once despisèd Jesus	278
Hail to the Lord who comes	279
Hail to the Lord's anointed	280

Saviour

Hail, true body 281
Hark, my soul, it is the Lord 287
Hark, the glad sound! 288
Have you heard the raindrops 291
He is the Lord 295
Here on the threshold of a new
  beginning 305
Hills of the north, rejoice 307
Holy, holy, holy! 308
How bright these glorious spirits
  shine! 316
How deep the Father's love for us 317
How lovely on the mountains 319
I am the bread of life 323
I am trusting thee, Lord Jesus 324
I believe in Jesus 325
I bind unto myself today 326
I cannot tell 327
I heard the voice of Jesus say 334
I need thee every hour 336
I will offer up my life 339
I will sing the wondrous story 340
I'm special 348
In Christ alone 352
In full and glad surrender 354
In the garden Mary lingers 359
In the Lord is my joy 361
Inspired by love and anger 362
Jesu, lover of my soul 369
Jesu, our hope, our heart's desire 370
Jesu, Son of Mary 371
Jesu, the very thought of thee 373
Jesus, all for Jesus 375
Jesus calls us here to meet him 378
Jesus calls us: o'er the tumult 379
Jesus Christ is risen today 381
Jesus is greater 385
Jesus is King 386
Jesus is Lord! Creation's voice
  proclaims it 387
Jesus lives! thy terrors now 390
Jesus, Name above all names 395
Jesus, Prince and Saviour 396
Jesus shall reign 399
Jesus the Lord said: 'I am the
  Bread' 403
Jesus, the name high over all 404
Jesus, we celebrate your victory 405
Joy to the world! 409
Just as I am, without one plea 413
King of kings, majesty 418
Let all mortal flesh keep silence 424
Lift up your heads 438
Listen, let your heart keep
  seeking 446
Lord, I lift your name on high 461
Lord Jesus Christ 463
Lord of all life and power 468
Lord of all, to whom alone 469
Lord of life 473
Love divine, all loves excelling 491
Love's redeeming work is done 494
Meekness and majesty 507
Men of faith 508

My faith looks up to thee 512
My Jesus, my Saviour 519
My Lord, what love is this 520
My song is love unknown 521
Now is eternal life 529
Now, my tongue, the mystery
  telling 531
O comfort my people 536
O for a thousand tongues to sing 541
O happy band of pilgrims 550
O happy day 551
O, how good is the Lord 555
O Jesus, I have promised 556
O let the Son of God enfold you 558
O love, how deep, how broad,
  how high 570
O my Saviour, lifted from the
  earth 572
O sacred head, surrounded 576
O when the saints go marching in 581
Of the Father's love begotten 584
On a hill far away 587
On Jordan's bank the Baptist's cry 589
Onward, Christian pilgrims 599
Rejoice, the Lord is King 638
Rock of ages 643
Sing it in the valleys 660
Sing, my tongue, the glorious
  battle 662
Sing we of the blessèd Mother 666
Son of God, eternal Saviour 667
Songs of thankfulness and praise 669
Spirit of God 672
Thank you for saving me 693
The great Creator of the world 710
The Saviour will come,
  resplendent in joy 730
The Spirit lives to set us free 732
There in God's garden 739
There is a green hill far away 740
There is a Redeemer 743
This is the day the Lord has made 760
We believe in God the Father 790
Zacchaeus was a very little man 857

Second Coming

Alleluia, alleluia, hearts to heaven
  and voices raise 32
At the name of Jesus 52
Come, ye thankful people, come 144
Eat this bread 159
Great is the darkness 271
Hark! A thrilling voice is calling 286
He has risen 292
In Christ alone 352
O Lord, my God 563
There's a place where the streets
  shine 744

THE CHURCH
The Communion of Saints

All hail the power of Jesus' name 14
And now, O Father, mindful of the
  love 38

Angel-voices ever singing 40
Christ is our cornerstone 97
Come, let us join our cheerful
  songs 127
Disposer supreme 155
Follow me 189
For all the saints 190
From glory to glory advancing 204
From the falter of breath 208
Give thanks for those 217
Give us the wings of faith 221
Holy, holy, holy! Lord God
  almighty 310
Jesus, be the centre 376
Let saints on earth in concert sing 428
Light's abode, celestial Salem 442
Lord, you call us to a journey 487
May the fragrance of Jesus fill this
  place 504
May the grace of Christ the
  Saviour 505
O God, our help in ages past 547
O God, you search me 549
O thou, who at thy Eucharist
  didst pray 579
O when the saints go marching in 581
Songs of praise the angels sang 668
Thanks be to God 696
The Church of God a kingdom is 701
The Church's one foundation 702
Ye holy angels bright 840
Ye watchers and ye holy ones 844

The Serving Community

Brother, sister, let me serve you 91
Christ's is the world 110
For all your saints still active 192
Forth in thy name, O Lord, I go 201
From heaven you came 205
Give me joy in my heart 215
Glory to thee, my God, this night 229
Help us to help each other, Lord 299
Here am I, Lord 300
Here I am 301
I give my hands 330
I, the Lord of sea and sky 337
I will offer up my life 339
If we only seek peace 343
In Christ there is no east or west 352
Jesu, Jesu, fill us with your love 368
Jesus bids us shine 377
Jesus calls us: o'er the tumult 379
Jesus Christ is waiting 382
Jesus, Lord, we look to thee 391
Let us build a house 432
Let us praise God together 433
Longing for light 452
Lord it belongs not to my care 462
Lord of all being 466
Lord of creation 471
Lord of the worlds above 477
My God, accept my heart this day 514
Now let us from this table rise 530
O Jesus, I have promised 556
O Lord, all the world belongs to
  you 560

The Serving Community

O Lord, we want to praise you 567
One is the body 594
Son of God, eternal Saviour 667
Strengthen for service, Lord 680
Take my hands, Lord 686
The world is full of smelly feet 736
This is my body 755
Though pilgrim strangers here below 768
When I needed a neighbour 819

The Witnessing Community

For all your saints still active 192
From the eastern mountains 207
From the sun's rising 210
Go back, go back to Galilee 231
Go forth and tell 232
Go, tell it on the mountain 233
God is working his purpose out 246
God, our Creator 253
God's Spirit is in my heart 262
Great is the darkness 271
Hands that have been handling 284
Happy are they, they that love God 285
Help us, O Lord, to learn 298
Here I am 301
Here in this place 302
I give my hands 330
Jesu, Jesu, fill us with your love 368
Jesus bids us shine 377
Jesus calls us here to meet him 378
Jesus, Lord, we look to thee 391
Now let us from this table rise 530
O Lord, we want to praise you 567
One is the body 594
One shall tell another 596
Praise we now the word of grace 629
Proclaim, proclaim the story 630
Show me how to stand for justice 657
Stand up, stand up for Jesus 677
Strengthen for service, Lord 680
Through the night of doubt and sorrow 770
We are marching 789
We have a gospel to proclaim 798
We'll walk the land 809
Ye that know the Lord is gracious 843

The Worldwide Church

All the nations of the earth 25
Alleluia! Alleluia! 30
Christ for the world we sing! 95
Come, all who look to Christ today 115
Filled with the Spirit's power 184
From the sun's rising 210
Go forth and tell 232
God is the giver of love 245
God is working his purpose out 246
God of mercy, God of grace 251
Great is the darkness 271
How beauteous are their feet 315

In Christ there is no east or west 352
Jesus calls us here to meet him 378
Jesus put this song 397
Let all the world in every corner sing 425
Praise we now the word of grace 629
The Church of God a kingdom is 701
The heavens declare thy glory, Lord 712
You, living Christ, our eyes behold 851

Unity and Fellowship

As we are gathered 45
As your family, Lord 46
Bind us together, Lord 73
Blessèd city, heavenly Salem 77
Brother, sister, let me serve you 91
Christ is made the sure foundation 96
Christ is the heavenly food 98
Christ is the King! 99
Christians, lift up your hearts 108
City of God, how broad and far 111
Come, all who look to Christ today 115
Come, risen Lord 137
Father, Lord of all creation 172
Father, we thank thee 178
Filled with the Spirit's power 184
For all the saints 190
For all thy saints, O Lord 191
For I'm building a people of power 193
Forth in the peace of Christ we go 200
From many grains 206
From the sun's rising 210
Great Shepherd of thy people 274
Hands that have been handling 284
Happy are they, they that love God 285
Heaven is open wide 296
Help us to help each other, Lord 299
Here on the threshold of a new beginning 305
I come with joy 328
In Christ there is no east or west 352
Jesus calls us here to meet him 378
Jesus put this song 397
Jesus, stand among us 401
Let saints on earth in concert sing 428
Let us build a house 432
Let us talents and tongues employ 434
Lord of lords and King eternal 474
Lord, we come to ask your healing 483
May the grace of Christ the Saviour 505
O Holy Spirit, Lord of grace 554
O Lord, all the world belongs to you 560
O thou, who at thy Eucharist didst pray 579
Son of God, eternal Saviour 667
The Spirit lives to set us free 732

This is my body 755
Ubi caritas 781
We have a dream 797

THE GOSPEL

Call to Worship

As we are gathered 45
Come, now is the time to worship 132
Come on and celebrate 135
Crown him with many crowns 150
From the rising of the sun 209
Give thanks to the Lord 218
Holy, holy, holy! Lord God almighty 310
Hosanna, hosanna 314
I believe in Jesus 325
Jesus is Lord! Creation's voice proclaims it 387
Jesus, the name high over all 404
Joy to the world! 409
Jubilate, everybody 410
King of kings and Lord of lords 417
Lift up your heads 438
Light of the world 441
Lord, I lift your name on high 461
Make way, make way 500
O, heaven is in my heart 552
Praise God from whom all blessings flow 618, 619
Praise him on the trumpet 620
Praise, my soul, the King of heaven 623
Shout for joy and sing 656
Tell out, my soul 692
We are marching 789
We believe in God the Father 790
When the music fades 823

Commitment and Consecration

A new commandment 4
Abba, Father, let me be 5
All I once held dear 16
All my hope on God is founded 19
All that I am 24
At the name of Jesus 52
Awake, awake: fling off the night 56
Awake, my soul, and with the sun 57
Be the centre of my life 64
Be thou my vision 66
Blessèd assurance 75
Blest are the pure in heart 79
Breathe on me, Breath of God 87
Come and celebrate 116
Come and see the shining hope 118
Come, let us use the grace divine 128
Come, my Way, my Truth, my Life 131
Father, hear the prayer we offer 169
Father, I place into your hands 170
Filled with the Spirit's power 184
Follow me 189
Forth in the peace of Christ we go 200

Commitment and Consecration

Forth in thy name, O Lord, I go 201
From heaven you came 205
God's Spirit is in my heart 262
Here am I, Lord 300
Here I am 301
I bind unto myself today 326
I, the Lord of sea and sky 337
I will offer up my life 339
I will worship 341
I'm not ashamed to own my Lord 347
In full and glad surrender 354
In heavenly love abiding 355
Jesus Christ is waiting 382
Jesus, lover of my soul 394
Just as I am, without one plea 413
King of kings, majesty 418
Lift high the Cross 437
Lord, for the years 454
Lord, I come to you 458
Lord Jesus Christ, be present 464
Lord, the light of your love 479
Lord, you call us to a journey 487
Lord, you have my heart 489
May the fragrance of Jesus fill
this place 504
Nearer, my God, to thee 525
O happy day 551
O Jesus, I have promised 556
O Lord, my heart is not proud 564
O thou who camest from above 580
One more step along the world
I go 595
Purify my heart 631
Put thou thy trust in God 634
Restore, O Lord 639
Seek ye first 652
Silent, surrendered 659
Spirit of the living God (Iverson) 675
Stand up, stand up for Jesus 677
Take me, Lord 685
Take my hands, Lord 686
Take my life, and let it be 687
Take this moment 688
Take up thy cross, the Saviour
said 689
Teach me, my God and King 690
Teach me to dance 691
Thank you for saving me 693
This is my desire 756
Thuma mina 771
When God almighty came to
earth 814
When I look into your holiness 818
When I survey the wondrous
cross 820
When the music fades 823
Will you come and follow me 834
You stood there on the shoreline 854

Confession and Repentance

At this table we remember 53
Awake, awake: fling off the night 56
Christians lift your hearts and
voices 109
Creator of the earth and skies 147
Father of heaven, whose love
profound 174
Forgive our sins as we forgive 199
Here, O my Lord 304
Here on the threshold of a new
beginning 305
Lord, we come to ask your healing 483
Lord, we thank you for the
promise 485
My faith looks up to thee 512
We turn to you 806
Who can sound the depths of
sorrow 829

Eternal Life

All who would valiant be 27
Be still, my soul 63
Blessèd city, heavenly Salem 77
Breathe on me, Breath of God 87
Come, gracious Spirit, heavenly
Dove 122
Come, ye thankful people, come 144
Eat this bread 159
Every minute of every day 163
For all the saints 190
Forty days and forty nights 202
From glory to glory advancing 204
From the falter of breath 208
From thee all skill and science
flow 212
Give thanks for those 217
How bright these glorious spirits
shine! 316
I am the bread of life 323
Jesus lives! thy terrors now 390
Jesus, lover of my soul 394
Name of all majesty 524
Now is eternal life 529
O holy, heavenly kingdom 553
O Love that wilt not let me go 571
There's a place where the streets
shine 744

Faith and Hope

Amazing grace 34
As Jacob with travel was weary one
day 41
Be still, for the presence of the Lord 62
Born in the night, Mary's child 81
Christ is the heavenly food 98
Christ is the King! 99
Christians, lift up your hearts 108
Come and celebrate 116
Come, faithful pilgrims all 121
Come, Holy Spirit, come 125
Come, Lord, to our souls 130
Come, risen Lord 137
Come, thou Holy Spirit, come 139
Come, thou long-expected Jesus 140
Faithful One, so unchanging 165
Faithful Shepherd, feed me 166
Father, we thank thee 178
Firmly I believe and truly 186
For all the saints 190
For all your saints still active 192
Forth in the peace of Christ we go 200

From the falter of breath 208
From thee all skill and science
flow 212
Gifts of bread and wine 214
Give thanks for those 217
Give us the wings of faith 221
God is our strength from days
of old 244
God of grace and God of glory 248
Gracious Spirit, Holy Ghost 268
Grant us the courage, gracious
God 269
Great Shepherd of thy people 274
Have faith in God, my heart 290
Help us, O Lord, to learn 298
Here on the threshold of a new
beginning 305
I am the bread of life 323
If you believe and I believe 344
I'm not ashamed to own my Lord 347
In Christ alone 352
In heavenly love abiding 355
Jesu, the very thought of thee 373
Jesus, we have heard your Spirit 406
Jesus, where'er thy people meet 407
Let us build a house 432
Life for the poor was hard and
tough 436
Lift up your voice 440
Longing for light 452
Lord of all hopefulness 467
Lord, teach us how to pray aright 478
Lord, we come to ask your healing 483
Lord, you call us to a journey 487
Make me a channel of your peace 499
Men of faith 508
Not far beyond the sea 528
Now is eternal life 529
O day of God, draw nigh 537
O happy band of pilgrims 550
O perfect love 573
Oft in danger, oft in woe 585
Peace is flowing like a river 613
Peace, perfect peace, is the gift 615
Put thou thy trust in God 634
See the holy table, spread for our
healing 651
Shepherd divine, our wants
relieve 655
Spirit of God, our light amid the
darkness 673
Stand up, stand up for Jesus 677
The kingdom is upon you! 716
This little light of mine 762
Thou art the Christ, O Lord 764
Through the night of doubt and
sorrow 770
We believe in God the Father 790
We will lay our burden down 808
Will your anchor hold 835

Forgiveness and Restoration

Be the centre of my life 64
Bread is blessed and broken 82
Christ the Lord is risen again 102

Forgiveness and Restoration

I believe in Jesus	325
Lead us, heavenly Father, lead us	422
Let us build a house	432
Make me a channel of your peace	499
Stand up, stand up for Jesus	677
You stood there on the shoreline	854

Grace and Mercy

And can it be	36
As Jacob with travel was weary one day	41
Author of life divine	55
Come, Holy Ghost, our souls inspire	124
Come, Holy Spirit, come	125
Come, let us use the grace divine	128
Come now, the table's spread	133
Come, O thou traveller unknown	134
Creator of the earth and skies	147
Creator of the starry height	148
Father, Lord of all creation	172
Father of heaven, whose love profound	174
For all your saints still active	192
Forgive our sins as we forgive	199
Forth in thy name, O Lord, I go	201
From many grains	206
Gather around, for the table is spread	213
Give thanks to the Lord	218
Glorious things of thee are spoken	223
Glory be to Jesus	224
Glory, love, and praise, and honour	225
Glory to thee, O God	230
God the Father, name we treasure	257
Great Shepherd of thy people	274
Hark, my soul, it is the Lord	287
Here is bread	303
How sweet the name of Jesus sounds	321
I am trusting thee, Lord Jesus	324
I believe in Jesus	325
I will sing the wondrous story	340
Jesu, lover of my soul	369
Jesu, our hope, our heart's desire	370
Jesu, thou joy of loving hearts	374
Jesus, be the centre	376
Jesus Christ	380
Jesus, good above all other	383
Jesus, Lord, we look to thee	391
Jesus, the name high over all	404
Jesus, we have heard your Spirit	406
Jesus, where'er thy people meet	407
Let us build a house	432
Lord of all hopefulness	467
Lord of all, to whom alone	469
May the grace of Christ the Saviour	505
Men of faith	508
My faith looks up to thee	512
Now let us from this table rise	530
O happy band of pilgrims	550
O happy day	551

O sacred head, surrounded	576
Rock of ages	643
Saint Luke, beloved physician	645
See the holy table, spread for our healing	651
Show me how to stand for justice	657
Thank you for saving me	693
The kingdom of heaven	717
The Saviour will come, resplendent in joy	730
There is a longing	742
This is the day the Lord has made	760
This little light of mine	762
We cannot measure	792
We have a dream	797
With joy we meditate the grace	836

Healing and Renewal

A brighter dawn is breaking	1
At even, ere the sun was set	49
Awake, awake: fling off the night	56
Be still and know that I am God	61
Be still, for the presence of the Lord	62
Bless the Lord, my soul	74
Bread of heaven, on thee we feed	83
Christ, the fair glory of the holy angels	101
Come, Holy Spirit, come	125
Come, thou Holy Spirit, come	139
Come, wounded healer	141
Creator Spirit, come	149
For all your saints still active	192
Forth in the peace of Christ we go	200
God is love: let heaven adore him	243
God to enfold you	258
Great Shepherd of thy people	274
Guide me, O thou great Redeemer	275
Hark, my soul, it is the Lord	287
Here is bread	303
How sweet the name of Jesus sounds	321
I cannot tell	327
Immortal love, for ever full	350
Jesu, lover of my soul	369
Jesu, Son of Mary	371
Jesus Christ is waiting	382
Jesus, humble was your birth	384
Let us build a house	432
Lord, we come to ask your healing	483
Make way, make way	500
Men of faith	508
O, how good is the Lord	555
Oh, the life of the world	586
On Jordan's bank the Baptist's cry	589
One shall tell another	596
Saint Luke, beloved physician	645
See the holy table, spread for our healing	651
The gracious invitation	709
The Saviour will come, resplendent in joy	730

The Spirit lives to set us free	732
There in God's garden	739
There is a longing	742
Thine arm, O Lord, in days of old	750
Thou, whose almighty word	767
Thy kingdom come	773
Walk with me, O my Lord	788
We cannot measure	792
You are the centre	848

Heaven

Come, ye faithful, raise the anthem	142
For all the saints	190
How bright these glorious spirits shine!	316
How shall I sing that majesty	320
O holy, heavenly kingdom	553
There's a place where the streets shine	744

Holiness and Purity

Blest are the pure in heart	79
Breathe on me, Breath of God	87
Christians lift your hearts and voices	109
Come and see the shining hope	119
Come, gracious Spirit, heavenly Dove	122
Dear Lord and Father of mankind	152
For all thy saints, O Lord	191
Forty days and forty nights	202
Hands that have been handling	284
Jesu, lover of my soul	369
Lord Jesus, think on me	465
O Lord, my heart is not proud	564
Purify my heart	631
The kingdom of heaven	717
Thy kingdom come, O God	774

Joy

All I once held dear	16
All people that on earth do dwell	21
All praise to our redeeming Lord	22
Alleluia, alleluia, hearts to heaven and voices raise	32
Amazing grace	34
As the deer pants for the water	43
At the Lamb's high feast we sing	51
At this time of giving	54
Awake, awake: fling off the night	56
Before Jehovah's aweful throne	68
Christ is the heavenly food	98
Christian people, raise your song	106
Christians lift your hearts and voices	109
Cloth for the cradle	113
Come and celebrate	116
Come and see	118
Come, gracious Spirit, heavenly Dove	122
Come, let us with our Lord arise	129
Come, my Way, my Truth, my Life	131
Come on and celebrate	135

Joy

Come, thou long-expected Jesus	140
Come, ye faithful, raise the strain	143
Deck thyself, my soul, with gladness	153
Eternal Ruler of the ceaseless round	162
Father, who in Jesus found us	180
Fight the good fight	181
Fill your hearts with joy and gladness	183
Forth in the peace of Christ we go	200
Forth in thy name, O Lord, I go	201
Give me joy in my heart	215
Give us the wings of faith	221
Glorious things of thee are spoken	223
Glory to God!	227
God is the giver of love	245
God's love is deeper	261
Good Christians all, rejoice	265
Great is the Lord and most worthy of praise	272
Hail to the Lord's anointed	280
Holy Spirit, truth divine	312
How lovely on the mountains	319
I am a new creation	322
I come with joy	328
I give my hands	330
If we only seek peace	343
I'm accepted, I'm forgiven	345
In the Cross of Christ I glory	358
In the Lord is my joy	361
Jesu, our hope, our heart's desire	370
Jesu, the very thought of thee	373
Jesus, good above all other	383
Jesus put this song	397
Jesus, we celebrate your victory	405
Joy to the world!	409
Lead us, heavenly Father, lead us	422
Led like a lamb	423
Let us talents and tongues employ	434
Lift up your voice	440
Lord, I lift your name on high	461
Lord of all hopefulness	467
Love divine, all loves excelling	491
Lovely in your littleness	493
Make way, make way	500
May the grace of Christ the Saviour	505
O happy day	551
O, heaven is in my heart	552
O let the Son of God enfold you	558
O Love that wilt not let me go	571
O perfect love	573
Over the mountains and the sea	611
Peace is flowing like a river	613
Peace, perfect peace, is the gift	615
Shout for joy and sing	656
Teach me to dance	691
Thanks to God whose word was spoken	698
The head that once was crowned with thorns	711
This is the day	759
This is the day the Lord has made	760

We love the place, O God	800
When I look into your holiness	818
You shall go out with joy	853
Your love is amazing	855

Life's Journey

All who would valiant be	27
Come, faithful pilgrims all	121
Eternal Ruler of the ceaseless round	162
Father, hear the prayer we offer	169
For all the saints	190
Forth in thy name, O Lord, I go	201
From the falter of breath	208
God of grace and God of glory	248
Guide me, O thou great Redeemer	275
In heavenly love abiding	355
Jesus, we have heard your Spirit	406
Just a closer walk with thee	412
Lord, we thank you for the promise	484
Lord, you call us to a journey	487
Loving Shepherd of thy sheep	495
O for a closer walk with God	539
O God of Bethel, by whose hand	545
O happy band of pilgrims	550
O Jesus, I have promised	556
O Lord of every shining constellation	565
Oft in danger, oft in woe	585
One more step along the world I go	595
Onward, Christian pilgrims	599
The kingdom is upon you!	716
Through the night of doubt and sorrow	770

Our Love for Others

A new commandment	4
Bind us together, Lord	73
Breathe on me, Breath of God	87
Christ's is the world	110
Come, Holy Spirit, come	125
Father, I place into your hands	170
Father, Lord of all creation	172
For the beauty of the earth	195
Forgive our sins as we forgive	199
Give me joy in my heart	215
Give thanks for those	217
God forgave my sin	237
God is love: his the care	242
God, our Creator	253
Great Shepherd of thy people	274
Jesu, Jesu, fill us with your love	368
Jesus, Lord, we look to thee	391
Jesus, stand among us	401
Let love be found among us	427
Let there be love	430
Let us build a house	432
Lord of lords and King eternal	474
Lord, we come to ask your healing	483
Love is his word	492
Make me a channel of your peace	499
Now let us from this table rise	530

O Holy Spirit, Lord of grace	554
Put peace into each other's hands	633
Son of God, eternal Saviour	667
Take my hands, Lord	686
The love we share	725
This is my body	755
This is my will	757
Though pilgrim strangers here below	768
Ubi caritas	781
We have a dream	797
We turn to you	806
When I needed a neighbour	819

Peace

Alleluia! Alleluia!	30
At this table we remember	53
Beauty for brokenness	67
Calm me, Lord	92
Christ is the world's Light	100
Christ, the fair glory of the holy angels	101
Come, all who look to Christ today	115
Crown him with many crowns	150
Dear Lord and Father of mankind	152
Exaudi nos, Domine	164
Faithful One, so unchanging	165
Faithful vigil ended	167
For all your saints still active	192
For the days when you feel near	196
For the healing of the nations	198
Forth in the peace of Christ we go	200
Forty days and forty nights	202
Gather around, for the table is spread	213
Give me joy in my heart	215
Give me peace, O Lord	216
Gloria (Anderson)	222
Glory to thee, my God, this night	229
God be with you till we meet again	236
God forgave my sin	237
God is the giver of love	245
God is working his purpose out	246
God's love is deeper	261
Good Christians all, rejoice	265
Great is thy faithfulness	273
Great Shepherd of thy people	274
Hail to the Lord's anointed	280
Here is bread	303
Here on the threshold of a new beginning	305
Holy Spirit, truth divine	312
How beauteous are their feet	315
How lovely on the mountains	319
I'm accepted, I'm forgiven	345
In the Cross of Christ I glory	358
In the Lord is my joy	361
Jesus, Lord, we look to thee	391
Let us build a house	432
Like a mighty river flowing	445
Longing for light	452
Lord, I lift my hands to you in prayer	460

Peace

Lord of lords and King eternal	474
Make me a channel of your peace	499
May the mind of Christ my Saviour	506
O day of God, draw nigh	537
O Lord, my heart is not proud	564
O perfect love	573
Peace is flowing like a river	613
Peace, perfect peace, in this dark world of sin	614
Peace, perfect peace, is the gift	615
Peace to you	616
Put peace into each other's hands	633
Saviour, again to thy dear name we raise	648
Son of God, eternal Saviour	667
Spirit of God, our light amid the darkness	673
Sweet sacrament divine	684
The kingdom of heaven	717
The peace of the earth be with you	726
This little light of mine	762
Though pilgrim strangers here below	768
Thy kingdom come	773
Thy kingdom come, O God	774
We will lay our burden down	808
You are the centre	848
You, Lord, are in this place	852

Perseverance and Determination

Awake, our souls; away, our fears	58
Be thou my guardian and my guide	65
For all the saints	190
Forth in thy name, O Lord, I go	201
Forty days and forty nights	202
Grant us the courage, gracious God	269
Lord Jesus, think on me	465
Lord, there are times	480
Lord, you call us to a journey	487
May the mind of Christ my Saviour	506
Oft in danger, oft in woe	585
One more step along the world I go	595
Take up thy cross, the Saviour said	689
Will your anchor hold	835

Prayer and Intercession

All you who seek a comfort sure	28
Alleluia, sing to Jesus	33
Be thou my guardian and my guide	65
Beauty for brokenness	67
Blessèd city, heavenly Salem	77
Brother, sister, let me serve you	91
Christ is made the sure foundation	96
Christ is our cornerstone	97

Come, all who look to Christ today	115
Come, let us with our Lord arise	129
Crown him with many crowns	150
Father, hear the prayer we offer	169
For the days when you feel near	196
Forty days and forty nights	202
Gifts of bread and wine	214
Gloria (Anderson)	222
Glorious things of thee are spoken	223
God is here! As we his people	241
Great Shepherd of thy people	274
Hail, thou once despisèd Jesus	278
Holy Spirit, will you be	313
I give my hands	330
If you believe and I believe	344
It's me, O Lord	365
Jesus, humble was your birth	384
Jesus shall reign	399
Jesus, where'er thy people meet	407
Keep watch with me	414
Kum ba yah	419
Let us praise God together	433
Lord, I lift my hands to you in prayer	460
Lord Jesus Christ	463
Lord of the worlds above	477
Lord, teach us how to pray aright	478
O Lord, hear my prayer	561
O Lord, listen to my prayer	562
Shepherd divine, our wants relieve	655
Spirit divine, attend our prayers	671
Stay with me	678
There is a longing	742
This little light of mine	762
What a friend we have in Jesus	811
Wherefore, O Father	826

Salvation and Redemption

A brighter dawn is breaking	1
Alleluia, sing to Jesus	33
And can it be	36
As Jacob with travel was weary one day	41
Before the throne	70
Bless the Lord, my soul	74
Christ is the world's Light	100
Christ the Lord is risen again	102
Christians, awake!	107
Come and see the shining hope	119
Come, faithful pilgrims all	121
Come, thou Holy Spirit, come	139
Come, wounded healer	141
Come, ye faithful, raise the anthem	142
Creator of the starry height	148
Do not be afraid	156
Draw nigh and take the body	157
Father of heaven, whose love profound	174
Father welcomes all his children	179
From the very depths of darkness	211
Give to our God immortal praise	220
Gloria (Anderson)	222

Glorious things of thee are spoken	223
Glory be to Jesus	224
Go back, go back to Galilee	231
God forgave my sin	237
God is love: his the care	242
God is our strength from days of old	244
God of the Passover	252
Great God, your love has called us	270
Hail, thou once despisèd Jesus	278
Hail to the Lord's anointed	280
Hark, my soul, it is the Lord	287
Hark, the glad sound!	288
Have you heard the raindrops	291
He is the Lord	295
Here on the threshold of a new beginning	305
How beauteous are their feet	315
How lovely on the mountains	319
I am trusting thee, Lord Jesus	324
I bind unto myself today	326
I give you all the honour	331
I heard the voice of Jesus say	334
I, the Lord of sea and sky	337
In the Lord is my joy	361
Just as I am, without one plea	413
Let us praise God together	433
Lord of all, to whom alone	469
My Lord, what love is this	520
My song is love unknown	521
Now is eternal life	529
O comfort my people	536
O for a heart to praise my God	540
O for a thousand tongues to sing	541
O happy day	551
O, how good is the Lord	555
O Lord, my God	563
O love, how deep, how broad, how high	570
O my Saviour, lifted from the earth	572
On a hill far away	587
On Jordan's bank the Baptist's cry	589
Only by grace	598
Onward, Christian pilgrims	599
Rock of ages	643
Salvation belongs to our God	646
See the holy table, spread for our healing	651
Shepherd divine, our wants relieve	655
The gracious invitation	709
The Lord is my light	719
The prophets spoke in days of old	728
The Spirit lives to set us free	732
There in God's garden	739
There's a place where the streets shine	744
There's a wideness in God's mercy	747
These are the days	748
Thou art the Way: by thee alone	765
Thy kingdom come, O God	775
To God be the glory!	777
You, living Christ, our eyes behold	851
Zip bam boo	858

Social Justice

All hail the power of Jesus' name	14
Alleluia! Alleluia!	30
Ascribe greatness	48
Beauty for brokenness	67
Christ's is the world	110
Come and see the shining hope	119
Come now, the table's spread	133
For the fruits of his creation	197
For the healing of the nations	198
From the very depths of darkness	211
God is love: let heaven adore him	243
God is the giver of love	245
God is working his purpose out	246
God's Spirit is in my heart	262
Grant us the courage, gracious God	269
Hail to the Lord's anointed	280
Heaven is open wide	296
Heaven shall not wait	297
Here in this place	302
Here, O my Lord	304
Here on the threshold of a new beginning	305
He's got the whole world in his hand	306
I, the Lord of sea and sky	337
If we only seek peace	343
If you believe and I believe	344
In Christ there is no east or west	353
Inspired by love and anger	362
Jesus Christ is waiting	382
Jesus, we have heard your Spirit	406
Join the song of praise and protest	408
Led like a lamb	423
Let us build a house	432
Longing for light	452
Lord, for the years	454
Lord of lords and King eternal	474
O comfort my people	536
O day of God, draw nigh	537
O Lord, my God	563
Oh, the life of the world	586
Show me how to stand for justice	657
Stand up, stand up for Jesus	677
Take my hands, Lord	686
Tell out, my soul	692
The peace of the earth be with you	726
The Saviour will come, resplendent in joy	730
There is a longing	742
There's a place where the streets shine	744
There's a spirit in the air	746
Though pilgrim strangers here below	768
Thy kingdom come	773
We cannot measure	792
We have a dream	797
We'll walk the land	809
When God made the garden of creation	815
When I needed a neighbour	819
Who can sound the depths of sorrow	829

Suffering and Sorrow

All you who seek a comfort sure	28
Be still, my soul	63
Beauty for brokenness	67
Blessèd be your name	76
Calm me, Lord	92
For all your saints still active	192
God is love: let heaven adore him	243
God, our Creator	253
In the Cross of Christ I glory	358
Jesus bids us shine	377
Jesus calls us: o'er the tumult	379
Lord, I come before your throne of grace	457
Lord Jesus, think on me	465
My faith looks up to thee	512
Now the green blade riseth	533
Put thou thy trust in God	634
Saviour, again to thy dear name we raise	648
The kingdom of heaven	717
There is a longing	742
Through the night of doubt and sorrow	770

Temptations and Trials

Be thou my guardian and my guide	65
Blessèd be your name	76
Calm me, Lord	92
Creator of the earth and skies	147
Forty days and forty nights	202
God be with you till we meet again	236
Guide me, O thou great Redeemer	275
In the Cross of Christ I glory	358
Jesus calls us: o'er the tumult	379
Just a closer walk with thee	412
Just as I am, without one plea	413
Lord Jesus, think on me	465
Lord, there are times	480
Lord, we come to ask your healing	483
O Jesus, I have promised	556
Oft in danger, oft in woe	585
Put thou thy trust in God	634
Shepherd divine, our wants relieve	655
Stay with me	678
Take up thy cross, the Saviour said	689
These are the days	748
Walk with me, O my Lord	788
What a friend we have in Jesus	811
Will your anchor hold	835
With joy we meditate the grace	836

Thanksgiving

Alleluia, alleluia, give thanks to the risen Lord	31
Awake, awake: fling off the night	56
Christians lift your hearts and voices	109
Come and celebrate	116
Come, let us with our Lord arise	129
Come, ye thankful people, come	144
Confitemini Domino	145
Father, we thank thee	178
Finished the strife	185
For the days when you feel near	196
For the fruits of his creation	197
From glory to glory advancing	204
Give thanks for those	217
Give thanks to the Lord	218
Give thanks with a grateful heart	219
Gloria (Anderson)	222
Glory, love, and praise, and honour	225
God is good, God is great	240
God, whose city's sure foundation	259
Great is the Lord and most worthy of praise	272
Great is thy faithfulness	273
I give you all the honour	331
I will offer up my life	339
I'm special	348
In our day of thanksgiving	356
In the Lord I'll be ever thankful	360
It's rounded like an orange	366
Jesus Christ	380
Lift up your voice	440
Lord, for the years	454
Lord, today your voice is calling	482
Lord, we thank you for the promise	484
O give thanks (Kendrick)	542
O give thanks (Pond)	543
O Lord of heaven and earth and sea	566
O praise ye the Lord!	574
Oh, the life of the world	586
Praise and thanksgiving	617
Songs of thankfulness and praise	669
Thank you for saving me	693
Thank you for the summer morning	694
Thank you, Lord	695
Thanks be to God	696
Thanks for the fellowship	697
Thanks to God whose word was spoken	698
There's a quiet understanding	745
Thine be the glory	751
Think of a world without any flowers	753
We plough the fields and scatter	801

Trust

Be still and know that I am God	61
Come and celebrate	116
Dear Lord and Father of mankind	152
Father, I place into your hands	170
Firmly I believe and truly	186
For the days when you feel near	196
God moves in a mysterious way	247
Grant us the courage, gracious God	269
I am trusting thee, Lord Jesus	324

Trust

I'm not ashamed to own my Lord 347
Jesu, lover of my soul 369
Jesus, humble was your birth 384
Lift up your voice 440
Lord of all hopefulness 467
Lord, teach us how to pray aright 478
May God's blessing surround you 503
Oft in danger, oft in woe 585
Put thou thy trust in God 634

Truth

Come, Holy Spirit, come 125
Come, Lord, to our souls 130
Come, my Way, my Truth,
my Life 131
Creator of the earth and skies 147
Disposer supreme 155
Eternal God, we consecrate 161
Eternal Ruler of the ceaseless
round 162
Forty days and forty nights 202
From all that dwell below the
skies 203
Give to our God immortal praise 220
Glory to thee, O God 230
Go back, go back to Galilee 231
God is love: his the care 242
God of life, God of love 249
Here on the threshold of a new
beginning 305
Jesu, thou joy of loving hearts 374
Jesus calls us here to meet him 378
Jesus, good above all other 383
Jesus is greater 385
Lift up your hearts! 439
Lord, the light of your love 479
Lord, you call us to a journey 487
Spirit of God, our light amid the
darkness 673
The gracious invitation 709
The Lord will come and not be
slow 722
Thou art the Way: by thee alone 765
We have a dream 797

THE WORLD

Mission and Evangelism

All for Jesus! 11
Alleluia! Alleluia! 30
Alleluia, alleluia, give thanks to the
risen Lord 31
And did those feet in ancient times 37
Christ for the world we sing! 95
Christians, lift up your hearts 108
Colours of day 114
Come, faithful pilgrims all 121
For all your saints still active 192
From the eastern mountains 207
From the sun's rising 210
Go forth and tell 232
God is working his purpose out 246
God's Spirit is in my heart 262

Great is the darkness 271
Here I am 301
Life for the poor was hard and
tough 436
Praise we now the word of grace 629
The heavens declare thy glory,
Lord 712
These are the days 748
We have a gospel to proclaim 798
We'll walk the land 809
Ye that know the Lord is gracious 843

The Nation

And did those feet in ancient time 37
Here I am 301
Jesus calls us here to meet him 378
Judge eternal, throned in
splendour 411
Let there be love 430
Longing for light 452
Lord, for the years 454
O God of earth and altar 546
Rejoice, O land, in God thy
might 637
Who can sound the depths of
sorrow 829

World Peace

Crown him with many crowns 150
For the fruits of his creation 197
For the healing of the nations 198
Forth in the peace of Christ we go 200
Great is thy faithfulness 273
Hail to the Lord's anointed 280
In Christ there is no east or west 353
Let there be love 430
Like a mighty river flowing 445
Lord, for the years 454
Lord of lords and King eternal 474
Make me a channel of your peace 499
O God, our help in ages past 547
O Lord, my God 563
Peace is flowing like a river 613
Peace, perfect peace, in this dark
world of sin 614
Son of God, eternal Saviour 667
The peace of the earth be with you 726
We turn to you 806
We will lay our burden down 808

TIMES AND SEASONS

Morning

A brighter dawn is breaking 1
All creatures of our God and King 10
All praise to thee 23
Awake, awake: fling off the night 56
Awake, my soul, and with the sun 57
Christ be with me 94
Christ, whose glory fills the skies 105
Colours of day 114
From the rising of the sun 209

Give me joy in my heart 215
God is here! As we his people 241
Holy, holy, holy! Lord God
almighty 310
I watch the sunrise 338
Lord, the light of your love 479
Lord, today your voice is calling 482
Morning has broken 510
My Father, for another night 513
New every morning is the love 526
Thank you, Lord 695
When all thy merices, O my God 813

Evening

Abide with me 6
At even, ere the sun was set 49
Before the ending of the day 69
Blest Creator of the light 80
Glory to thee, my God, this night 229
God that madest earth and heaven 256
God to enfold you 258
Hail, gladdening Light 276
Lead, kindly light 421
Lord, I lift my hands to you in
prayer 460
May God's blessing surround you 503
O strength and stay 577
Round me falls the night 644
Saviour, again to thy dear name
we raise 648
Sun of my soul, thou Saviour dear 682
The day thou gavest, Lord, is
ended 704
The peace of the earth be with you 726
Within our darkest night 837

Advent

Awake, awake: fling off the night 56
Be still, for the presence of the
Lord 62
Christ, whose glory fills the skies 105
Colours of day 114
Come and see the shining hope 119
Come, my Way, my Truth,
my Life 131
Come, now is the time to worship 132
Come, thou long-expected Jesus 140
Creator of the starry height 148
Forth in the peace of Christ we go 200
God has spoken – by the prophets 238
God of mercy, God of grace 251
Great is the darkness 271
Hail to the Lord's anointed 280
Hark! A herald voice is calling 286
Hark, the glad sound! 288
Heaven shall not wait 297
Here in this place 302
Hills of the north, rejoice 307
How lovely on the mountains 319
I heard the voice of Jesus say 334
I, the Lord of sea and sky 337
Immortal, invisible, God only
wise 349
In the Lord I'll be ever thankful 360
It's rounded like an orange 366

Advent

Jesus is the name we honour	388
Join the song of praise and protest	408
Kum ba yah	419
Let all mortal flesh keep silence	424
Let us with a gladsome mind	435
Lift up your heads	438
Light of the world	441
Like a candle flame	444
Lo, he comes with clouds descending	449
Long ago, prophets knew	451
Longing for light	452
Lord, the light of your love	479
Love divine, all loves excelling	491
Make way, make way	500
O come, O come, Emmanuel	535
O comfort my people	536
O worship the King	582
On Jordan's bank the Baptist's cry	589
Restore, O Lord	639
Tell out, my soul	692
The advent of our King	699
The people that in darkness sat	727
The Saviour will come, resplendent in joy	730
The Son of God proclaim	731
Thou didst leave thy throne	766
Thou, whose almighty word	767
Thy kingdom come	773
Thy kingdom come, O God	774
Wait for the Lord	785
Wake, O wake! with tidings thrilling	786
Waken, O sleeper, wake and rise	787
We are marching	789
Ye servants of the Lord	842

Christmas

A great and mighty wonder	2
Angels from the realms of glory	39
At this time of giving	54
Away in a manger	59
Behold, the great Creator	71
Born in the night, Mary's child	81
Christians, awake!	107
Cloth for the cradle	113
Come and join the celebration	117
Ding dong, merrily on high!	154
For Mary, mother of our Lord	194
From heaven you came	205
Glory to God!	227
Go, tell in the mountain	233
God rest you merry, gentlefolk	254
Good Christians all, rejoice	265
Good King Wenceslas	267
Hark, the herald-angels sing	289
I cannot tell	327
In Christ alone	352
In the bleak mid-winter	357
It came upon the midnight clear	363
Joy to the world!	409
Lift up your voice	440
Like a candle flame	444
Little donkey	447
Little Jesus, sweetly sleep	448

Lord Jesus Christ	463
Love came down at Christmas	490
Lovely in your littleness	493
Mary had a baby	502
Meekness and majesty	507
O come, all ye faithful	534
O little town of Bethlehem	559
Of the Father's love begotten	584
On Christmas night all Christians sing	588
Once in royal David's city	592
See, amid the winter's snow	649
See him lying on a bed of straw	650
Silent night	658
Sing lullaby	661
The angel Gabriel from heaven came	700
The first Nowell	705
The holly and the ivy	713
The people that in darkness sat	727
The Virgin Mary had a baby boy	734
Thou didst leave thy throne	766
Unto us a boy is born	782
Virgin-born, we bow before thee	784
What child is this	812
Where is this stupendous stranger?	825
While shepherds watched	827
Who would think that what was needed	832

Baptism of Jesus

Awake, awake: fling off the night	56
Be thou my vision	66
Breathe on me, Breath of God	87
Christ, when for us you were baptised	104
Come down, O Love divine	120
Come, gracious Spirit, heavenly Dove	122
Come, Holy Ghost, our hearts inspire	123
Come, let us use the grace divine	128
Crown him with many crowns	150
Do not be afraid	156
Eternal Ruler of the ceaseless round	162
God is love: his the care	242
Hail to the Lord's anointed	280
I bind unto myself today	326
I danced in the morning	329
Just as I am, without one plea	413
Lord, the light of your love	479
Meekness and majesty	507
Name of all majesty	524
Now is eternal life	529
O let the Son of God enfold you	558
O love, how deep, how broad, how high	570
O thou who camest from above	580
On Jordan's bank the Baptist's cry	589
Spirit divine, attend our prayers	671
Spirit of the living God (Iverson)	675
Take this moment	688
The people that in darkness sat	727
Thou didst leave thy throne	766

Thou, whose almighty word	767
To the name of our salvation	779
Veni, lumen cordium	783
When Jesus came to Jordan	821

New Year

A new commandment	4
All my hope on God is founded	19
All people that on earth do dwell	21
Come, let us use the grace divine	128
Glorious things of thee are spoken	223
God is working his purpose out	246
God of grace and God of glory	248
Have faith in God, my heart	290
Here on the threshold of a new beginning	305
Lord, for the years	454
Lord, I come to you	458
Lord of the future	476
O God of Bethel, by whose hand	545
O God, our help in ages past	547
O Lord, all the world belongs to you	560
One more step along the world I go	595
Put thou thy trust in God	634
Take my life, and let it be	687
Take this moment	688
The Lord is my light	719
Through all the changing scenes of life	769
Ye servants of the Lord	842

Epiphany

Adoramus te, Domine	8
Angels from the realms of glory	39
As with gladness men of old	46
Brightest and best	89
Christ is the world's Light	100
Earth has many a noble city	158
Faithful vigil ended	167
From the eastern mountains	207
God of mercy, God of grace	251
Hail to the Lord's anointed	280
Hills of the north, rejoice	307
In Christ there is no east or west	353
In the bleak mid-winter	357
Jesus shall reign	399
Lift up your voice	440
Lord, the light of your love	479
Love came down at Christmas	490
O worship the Lord in the beauty of holiness	583
See him lying on a bed of straw	650
Songs of thankfulness and praise	669
The first Nowell	705
The Lord is my light	719
The people that in darkness sat	727
The Virgin Mary had a baby boy	734
Thou, whose almighty word	767
To be in your presence	776
We bow down	791
We three kings of Orient are	805
What child is this	812
You are the King of Glory	849

Lent

As pants the hart for cooling streams	42
Be still, for the presence of the Lord	62
Be thou my guardian and my guide	65
Dear Lord and Father of mankind	152
Father, hear the prayer we offer	169
Forgive our sins as we forgive	199
Forty days and forty nights	202
I give you love	332
I need thee every hour	336
Inspired by love and anger	362
It's me, O Lord	365
Jesu, grant me this, I pray	367
Jesus the Lord said: 'I am the Bread'	403
Just as I am, without one plea	413
Lift up your voice	440
Lord, have mercy (Ghana)	455
Lord, have mercy (Russian)	456
Lord Jesus, think on me	465
Lord, teach us how to pray aright	478
Lord, we turn to you for mercy	485
O Lord, hear my prayer	561
Oft in danger, oft in woe	585
Praise to the Holiest	627
Put thou thy trust in God	634
Rock of ages	643
Seek ye first	652
Stay with me	678
Take up thy cross, the Saviour said	689
When God almighty came to earth	814
Will your anchor hold	835
With joy we meditate the grace	836

Mothering Sunday

All things bright and beautiful	26
Bind us together, Lord	73
Come down, O Love divine	120
For Mary, mother of our Lord	194
For the beauty of the earth	195
Glorious things of thee are spoken	223
Happy are they, they that love God	285
He's got the whole world in his hand	306
I come with joy	328
In the Lord I'll be ever thankful	360
Jesus, good above all men	383
Let all the world in every corner sing	425
Lord of all hopefulness	467
Lord, we thank you for the promise	484
Magnificat	497
Make me a channel of your peace	499
May the mind of Christ my Saviour	506
Now thank we all our God	532
Our Father God in heaven	605
Sing we of the blessèd Mother	666
Tell out, my soul	692
The King is among us	714

The King of love my shepherd is	715
Through all the changing scenes of life	769

Passiontide

Above all powers, above all kings	7
Ah, holy Jesu, how hast thou offended	9
All glory, laud and honour	12
All you who seek a comfort sure	28
An upper room did our Lord prepare	35
And now, O Father, mindful of the love	38
At the cross she keeps her station	50
Before the throne	70
Beneath the cross of Jesus	72
Christians lift your hearts and voices	109
Come and see	118
Come, wounded healer	141
Forgive our sins as we forgive	199
From heaven you came	205
Glory be to Jesus	224
How deep the Father's love for us	317
I danced in the morning	329
I give you love	332
I will offer up my life	339
Immortal love, for ever full	350
In Christ alone	352
In the Cross of Christ I glory	358
It is a thing most wonderful	364
Jesu, grant me this, I pray	367
Jesus Christ	380
Jesus, remember me	398
Led like a lamb	423
Lift high the Cross	437
Lord of lords and King eternal	474
Mary, blessed grieving mother	501
My faith looks up to thee	512
My God, I love thee	517
My Lord, what love is this	520
My song is love unknown	521
O dearest Lord, thy sacred head	538
O love, how deep, how broad, how high	570
O my Saviour, lifted from the earth	572
O sacred head, surrounded	576
On a hill far away	587
Once, only once, and once for all	593
One whose heart is hard as steel	597
Overwhelmed by love	612
Praise to the Holiest	627
Ride on, ride on in majesty	640
Rock of ages	643
Soul of my Saviour	670
Stay with me	678
Take up thy cross, the Saviour said	689
Thank you for saving me	693
The royal banners forward go	729
There in God's garden	739
There is a green hill far away	740
To mock your reign, O dearest Lord	778

We have a King who rides a donkey	799
We sing the praise of him who died	804
Were you there when they crucified my Lord?	810
When I survey the wondrous cross	820
You are the King of Glory	849
You laid aside your majesty	850

Palm Sunday

A man there lived in Galilee	3
All glory, laud and honour	12
All hail the Lamb	13
From heaven you came	205
Give me joy in my heart	215
Hosanna, hosanna	314
I danced in the morning	329
Jesus is King	386
Jesus is the name we honour	388
Jesus shall reign	399
Make way, make way	500
Meekness and majesty	507
My song is love unknown	521
Praise him on the trumpet	620
Praise to the Holiest	627
Rejoice, the Lord is King	638
Ride on, ride on in majesty	640
Shout for joy and sing	656
Such love	681
There is a Redeemer	743
This is the day the Lord has made	760
We have a King who rides a donkey	799
When I survey the wondrous cross	820
You are the King of Glory	849
You laid aside your majesty	850

Maundy Thursday

A new commandment	4
Adoramus te, Domine	8
An upper room did our Lord prepare	35
And now, O Father, mindful of the love	38
As we are gathered	45
Bread is blessed and broken	82
Bread of heaven, on thee we feed	83
Bread of the world in mercy broken	84
Break the bread and pour the wine	85
Broken for me	90
Brother, sister, let me serve you	91
Come, now, the table's spread	133
Draw nigh and take the body	157
Eat this bread	159
From many grains	206
Gather around, for the table is spread	213
Gifts of bread and wine	214
God of the Passover	252
Great God, your love has called us	270
Here is bread	303
Here, O my Lord	304
I come with joy	328

Maundy Thursday

In bread we bring you, Lord	351
Jesu, Jesu, fill us with your love	368
Jesus calls us here to meet him	378
Let all mortal flesh keep silence	424
Let there be love	430
Let us break bread together	431
Lord Jesus Christ	463
Love is his word	492
Meekness and majesty	507
My God, and is thy table spread	515
Now, my tongue, the mystery telling	531
O thou, who at thy Eucharist didst pray	579
One whose heart is hard as steel	597
See the holy table, spread for our healing	651
Such love	681
The Son of God proclaim	731
This is my body	755
Ubi caritas	781
We have a King who rides a donkey	799
When I survey the wondrous cross	820
You laid aside your majesty	850

Good Friday

Above all powers, above all kings	7
Ah, holy Jesu, how hast thou offended	9
All you who seek a comfort sure	28
At the cross she keeps her station	50
Beneath the cross of Jesus	72
Broken for me	90
Christians lift your hearts and voices	109
Come and see	118
From heaven you came	205
Glory be to Jesus	224
How deep the Father's love for us	317
I give you love	332
I will offer up my life	339
In Christ alone	352
In the Cross of Christ I glory	358
It is a thing most wonderful	364
Jesus Christ	380
Led like a lamb	423
Low in the grave he lay	496
Mary, blessed grieving mother	501
Meekness and majesty	507
My God, I love thee	517
My Lord, what love is this	520
O dearest Lord, thy sacred head	538
O my Saviour, lifted from the earth	572
O sacred head, surrounded	576
On a hill far away	587
On the holy cross I see	591
Once, only once, and once for all	593
One whose heart is hard as steel	597
Only by grace	598
Praise to the Holiest	627
Sing, my tongue, the glorious battle	662

Thank you for saving me	693
The royal banners forward go	729
There is a green hill far away	740
There is a Redeemer	743
To mock your reign, O dearest Lord	778
We sing the praise of him who died	804
Were you there when they crucified my Lord?	810
When I survey the wondrous cross	820
Who is there like you	830
You laid aside your majesty	850

Easter

A brighter dawn is breaking	1
All hail the Lamb	13
All heaven declares	15
All in an Easter garden	17
All my days	18
Alleluia, alleluia, give thanks to the risen Lord	31
Alleluia, alleluia, hearts to heaven and voices raise	32
Alleluia, sing to Jesus	33
Alleluia (x 8)	29
At the Lamb's high feast we sing	51
Awake, awake: fling off the night	56
Before the throne	70
Christ the Lord is risen again	102
Colours of day	114
Come, ye faithful, raise the anthem	142
Come, ye faithful, raise the strain	143
Father of peace, and God of love	175
Finished the strife	185
From the very depths of darkness	211
Go back, go back to Galilee	231
Good Christians all, rejoice and sing	266
Hail the day that sees him rise	277
He has risen	292
He is Lord	294
Heaven is open wide	296
I believe in Jesus	325
I danced in the morning	329
In Christ alone	352
In the garden Mary lingers	359
Jesus Christ is risen today	381
Jesus is Lord! Creation's voice proclaims it	387
Jesus lives! thy terrors now	390
Jesus, Prince and Saviour	396
Jesus, stand among us in thy risen power	402
Jesus the Lord said: 'I am the Bread'	403
Jesus, the name high over all	404
Led like a lamb	423
Lift up your voice	440
Light's abode, celestial Salem	442
Light's glittering morn	443
Love's redeeming work is done	494
Low in the grave he lay	496

Morning has broken	510
Name of all majesty	524
Now is eternal life	529
Now the green blade riseth	533
Proclaim, proclaim the story	630
Sing of the Lord's goodness	663
Surrexit Christus	683
The day of resurrection	703
The Lord is risen indeed	721
The strife is o'er, the battle done	733
Thine be the glory	751
This is the day	759
This is the day the Lord has made	760
This joyful Eastertide	761
To God be the glory!	777
We have a King who rides a donkey	799
Ye choirs of new Jerusalem	839
You laid aside your majesty	850
You stood there on the shoreline	854

Ascensiontide

All hail the Lamb	13
All hail the power of Jesus' name	14
All heaven declares	15
Alleluia, sing to Jesus	33
At the name of Jesus	52
Be still, for the presence of the Lord	62
Before the throne	70
Christ is the King!	99
Christ triumphant	103
Clap your hands, all you people	112
Come, Holy Spirit, come	125
Come, let us join our cheerful songs	127
Come, ye faithful, raise the anthem	142
Crown him with many crowns	150
Father in heaven, how we love you	171
Forth in the peace of Christ we go	200
Hail the day that sees him rise	277
Hail, thou once despisèd Jesus	278
Hail to the Lord's anointed	280
He is exalted	293
He is Lord	294
Jesus Christ	380
Jesus is King	386
Jesus is the name we honour	388
Jesus shall reign	399
Jesus shall take the highest honour	400
Laudate Dominum	420
Lift up your heads	438
Lift up your voice	440
Lord, enthroned in heavenly splendour	453
Lord, I lift your name on high	461
Majesty, worship his majesty	498
Make way, make way	500
Meekness and majesty	507
Name of all majesty	524
O dearest Lord, thy sacred head	538
One is the body	594
Praise God from whom all blessings flow	618, 619

Ascensiontide

Praise him, praise him, praise him 622
Proclaim, proclaim the story 630
Rejoice the Lord is King 638
Stand up, stand up for Jesus 677
The head that once was crowned
  with thorns 711
Thine be the glory 751
When morning gilds the skies 822

Pentecost

All over the world 20
Alleluia (x 8) 29
Break thou the bread 86
Breathe on me, Breath of God 87
Christians, lift up your hearts 108
Come down, O Love divine 120
Come, gracious Spirit, heavenly
  Dove 122
Come, Holy Ghost, our hearts
  inspire 123
Come, Holy Ghost, our souls
  inspire 124
Come, Holy Spirit, come 125
Come, thou Holy Spirit, come 139
Creator Spirit, come 149
Eternal Ruler of the ceaseless
  round 162
Father, Lord of all creation 172
Filled with the Spirit's power 184
For I'm building a people of
  power 193
Go forth and tell 232
God of grace and God of glory 248
God's Spirit is in my heart 262
Gracious Spirit, Holy Ghost 268
Great is the darkness 271
Holy Spirit, come, confirm us 311
Holy Spirit, truth divine 312
Holy Spirit, will you be 313
If you believe and I believe 344
Listen, let your heart keep seeking 446
Lord of all life and power 468
O Holy Spirit, Lord of grace 554
O King, enthroned on high 557
O thou who camest from above 580
Our blest Redeemer, ere he
  breathed 602
Send forth your Spirit, Lord 653
She sits like a bird 654
Silent, surrendered 659
Spirit divine, attend our prayers 671
Spirit of God 672
Spirit of God, our light amid the
  darkness 673
Spirit of the living God
  (Armstrong) 674
Spirit of the living God (Iverson) 675
The Spirit lives to set us free 732
There's a quiet understanding 745
There's a spirit in the air 746
We are marching 789
We turn to you 806
When God of old came down
  from heaven 816

When Jesus came to Jordan 821
When the Spirit of the Lord 824
You are the centre 848

The Holy Trinity

Angel-voices ever singing 40
As pants the hart for cooling
  streams 42
As we are gathered 45
Before the ending of the day 69
Blessèd assurance 75
Christ is the world's Light 100
Come, Holy Ghost, our souls
  inspire 124
Come, ye faithful, raise the
  anthem 142
Come, ye faithful, raise the strain 143
Eternal Father, strong to save 160
Father in heaven, how we love you 171
Father most holy, merciful and
  loving 173
Father of heaven, whose love
  profound 174
Father, we adore you 176
Father, we love you 177
Firmly I believe and truly 186
Glory to God (Peruvian Gloria) 226
God has spoken – by the prophets 238
God is our strength from days of
  old 244
God of life, God of love 249
God of love 250
God our Creator 253
Heaven is open wide 296
Holy, holy, holy 308
Holy, holy, holy! Lord God
  almighty 310
I bind unto myself today 326
Jesus calls us here to meet him 378
Light's abode, celestial Salem 442
O Holy Spirit, Lord of grace 554
Oh, the life of the world 586
One is the body 594
Praise God from whom all
  blessings flow 618, 619
Praise to God for saints and
  martyrs 626
Sanctus, sanctus, sanctus 647
Sing of the Lord's goodness 663
Songs of praise the angels sang 668
The God of Abraham praise 706
There is a Redeemer 743
Thou, whose almighty word 767
Through all the changing scenes
  of life 769
To God be the glory! 777
We believe in God the Father 790
We give immortal praise 795
We pray thee, heavenly Father 803
Ye watchers and ye holy ones 844

Transfiguration

Christ, whose glory fills the skies 105
Father, in heaven, how we love
  you 171

God of mercy, God of grace 251
Great is the Lord and most worthy
  of praise 272
Heaven is open wide 296
Jesus shall take the highest honour 400
King of kings and Lord of lords 417
Lift up your hearts! 439
Lord, enthroned in heavenly
  splendour 453
Lord, the light of your love 479
Name of all majesty 524
O raise your eyes on high 575
Thy kingdom come, O God 775
We hail thy presence glorious 796

Harvest Festival

All creatures of our God and King 10
All that I am 24
Alleluia, alleluia, hearts to heaven
  and voices raise 32
Angel-voices ever singing 40
Come and see the shining hope 119
Come, now, the table's spread 133
Come, ye thankful people, come 144
Dance and sing 151
Fill your hearts with joy and
  gladness 183
For the beauty of the earth 195
For the fruits of his creation 197
For the healing of the nations 198
From many grains 206
God of mercy, God of grace 251
God, our Creator 253
God, whose farm is all creation 260
Great is thy faithfulness 273
Inspired by love and anger 362
Let us, with a gladsome mind 435
Lord, you created 488
O give thanks (Kendrick) 542
O give thanks (Pond) 543
O Lord of heaven and earth and
  sea 566
Praise and thanksgiving 617
Praise, O praise our God and
  King 624
Push, little seed 632
Send forth your Spirit, Lord 653
Thank you, Lord 695
Think of a world without any
  flowers 753
This world you have made 763
To thee, O Lord, our hearts we
  raise 780
We eat the plants that grow from
  the seed 793
We plough the fields and scatter 801
Who put the colours in the
  rainbow? 831

All Saints

Adoramus te, Domine 8
All hail the power of Jesus' name 14
All heaven declares 15
All praise to our redeeming Lord 22
Bind us together, Lord 73

All Saints

Christ is our cornerstone	97
Disposer supreme	155
For all the saints	190
For all thy saints, O Lord	191
For all your saints still active	192
From glory to glory advancing	204
Give thanks for those	217
Give us the wings of faith	221
Glory to thee, O God	230
God, whose city's sure foundation	259
Here in this place	302
In our day of thanksgiving	356
Let saints on earth in concert sing	428
Light's abode, celestial Salem	442
Lo round the throne, a glorious band	450
Longing for light	452
Lord, you call us to a journey	487
Not far beyond the sea	528
O God of Bethel, by whose hand	545
O thou, who at thy Eucharist didst pray	579
O when the saints go marching in	581
Praise the Lord, ye heavens, adore him	625
Praise to God for saints and martyrs	626
Rejoice in God's saints	635
The people that in darkness sat	727
There is a land of pure delight	741
Thou art the Christ, O Lord	764
Thy hand, O God, has guided	772
Who are these like stars appearing	828
Ye holy angels bright	840
Ye watchers and ye holy ones	844

Remembrance

Be still, for the presence of the Lord	62
Be thou my guardian and my guide	65
Eternal Father, strong to save	160
Father, I place into your hands	170
For the healing of the nations	198
Forgive our sins as we forgive	199
From heaven you came	205
Give thanks for those	217
Great is the darkness	271
Help us to help each other, Lord	299
I will offer up my life	339
I'm black, I'm white, I'm short, I'm tall	346
Jesu, Son of Mary	371
Jesus lives! thy terrors now	390
Join the song of praise and protest	408
Let us talents and tongues employ	434
Lord, I come to you	458
Make me a channel of your peace	499
Mary, blessed grieving mother	501
O God of earth and altar	546
O God, our help in ages past	547
O Lord, my God	563
Seek ye first	652
Take my life, and let it be	687
Take this moment	688

There's a place where the streets shine	744
Through the night of doubt and sorrow	770
Wait for the Lord	785
We will lay our burden down	808

Patronal Festivals

Adoramus te, Domine	8
Christ is the King!	99
For all your saints still active	192
From glory to glory advancing	204
God, whose city's sure foundation	259
In our day of thanksgiving	356
Our Father God in heaven	605
Praise the Lord, ye heavens, adore him	625
Praise to God for saints and martyrs	626
Proclaim, proclaim the story	630
Rejoice in God's saints	635
The Church of God a kingdom is	701

Andrew

For all your saints still active	192
Jesus calls us: o'er the tumult	379

Barnabas

For all your saints still active	192

Bartholomew

For all your saints still active	192

Holy Innocents

For all your saints still active	192

James

For all your saints still active	192

John the Baptist

And can it be	36
Bind us together, Lord	73
Come, thou long-expected Jesus	140
Faithful Shepherd, feed me	166
For all your saints still active	192
God has spoken – by the prophets	238
How sweet the name of Jesus sounds	321
I cannot tell	327
I, the Lord of sea and sky	337
Make way, make way	500
On Jordan's bank the Baptist's cry	589
Purify my heart	631
Restore, O Lord	639

John the Evangelist

For all your saints still active	192

Joseph of Nazareth

For all your saints still active	192

Luke

For all your saints still active	192
Saint Luke, beloved physician	645

Mary Magdalene

All heaven declares	15
All my days	18
Alleluia, alleluia, hearts to heaven and voices raise	32
As the deer pants for the water	43
For all your saints still active	192

From the very depths of darkness	211
Great God, your love has called us	270
I am a new creation	322
It is a thing most wonderful	364
Jesus, stand among us	401
Jesus, stand among us in thy risen power	402
Led like a lamb	423
Let us talents and tongues employ	434
Light's glittering morn	443
Love's redeeming work is done	494
O for a thousand tongues to sing	541
O Lord, your tenderness	568
Thine be the glory	751

Matthew

For all your saints still active	192

Matthias

For all your saints still active	192

Paul

For all your saints still active	192

Peter

For all your saints still active	192

Simon and Jude

A new commandment	4
Bind us together, Lord	73
Christ is made the sure foundation	96
Christ is our cornerstone	97
Come down, O Love divine	120
Disposer supreme	155
Father, most holy, merciful and loving	173
For all your saints still active	192
Heaven shall not wait	297
In Christ alone	352
Jesu, Jesu, fill us with your love	368
Jesus, stand among us in thy risen power	401
Let there be love	430
O, heaven is in my heart	552
Our blest Redeemer, ere he breathed	602
Spirit of the living God (Iverson)	675
There is a Redeemer	743
Ubi caritas	781

Stephen

For all your saints still active	192

Thomas the Apostle

Be still and know that I am God	61
Breathe on me, Breath of God	87
Christ is made the sure foundation	96
Christ is our cornerstone	97
Christ, whose glory fills the skies	105
For all your saints still active	192
Give us the wings of faith	221
Have faith in God, my heart	290
How sweet the name of Jesus sounds	321
I believe in Jesus	325
Jesus, stand among us	401
Jesus, stand among us in thy risen power	402
Lead, kindly light	421
Lead us, heavenly Father, lead us	422

Remembrance

Thomas the Apostle

Light of the world	441
Lord, thy word abideth	481
Open our eyes, Lord	600
Surrexit Christus	683
When I needed a neighbour	819

THE SACRAMENTS

Baptism

All my hope on God is founded	19
All that I am	24
Awake, awake: fling off the night	56
Be bold, be strong	60
Be thou my vision	66
Breathe on me, Breath of God	87
Christ triumphant	103
Christ, when for us you were baptised	104
Christians, lift up your hearts	108
Come down, O Love divine	120
Come, now is the time to worship	132
Come, ye faithful, raise the strain	143
Do not be afraid	156
Eternal God, we consecrate	161
Every minute of every day	163
Father God, I wonder	168
Father welcomes all his children	179
Firmly I believe and truly	186
For all the saints	190
For I'm building a people of power	193
God the Father, name we treasure	257
Have you heard the raindrops	291
He's got the whole world in his hand	306
I bind unto myself today	326
I, the Lord of sea and sky	337
I'm accepted, I'm forgiven	345
I'm not ashamed to own my Lord	347
In Christ alone	352
Jesus, be the centre	376
Jesus call us: o'er the tumult	337
Just as I am, without one plea	413
Lord, I come to you	458
Loving Shepherd of thy sheep	495
Morning has broken	510
My God, accept my heart this day	514
Now is eternal life	529
O God you search me	549
O Jesus, I have promised	556
O let the Son of God enfold you	558
O thou who camest from above	580
O when the saints go marching in	581
Only by grace	598
Spirit of the living God (Armstrong)	674
Spirit of the living God (Iverson)	675
Take my life, and let it be	687
Take this moment	688
The Church's one foundation	702
The wise man	735
There are hundreds of sparrows	738
There's a spirit in the air	746
Thuma mina	771
Veni, lumen cordium	783
We are marching	789
We praise you, Lord	802

Confirmation

All for Jesus!	11
All who would valiant be	27
Amazing grace	34
Be still and know that I am God	61
Be still, for the presence of the Lord	62
Be the centre of my life	64
Be thou my guardian and my guide	65
Be thou my vision	66
Breathe on me, Breath of God	87
Christ be with me	94
Christ is our cornerstone	97
Come, all who look to Christ today	115
Come and celebrate	116
Come down, O Love divine	120
Come, gracious Spirit, heavenly Dove	122
Come, Holy Ghost, our hearts inspire	123
Come, Holy Ghost, our souls inspire	124
Come, Holy Spirit, come	125
Come, let us use the grace divine	128
Father God, I wonder	168
Father, hear the prayer we offer	169
Fight the good fight	181
Fill thou my life, O Lord my God	182
Firmly I believe and truly	186
For all the saints	190
Forth in thy name, O Lord, I go	201
Glorious things of thee are spoken	223
God forgave my sin	237
God is here! As we his people	241
God is our strength from days of old	244
God of grace and God of glory	248
God's Spirit is in my heart	262
Gracious Spirit, Holy Ghost	268
Help us, O Lord, to learn	298
Here I am	301
Here in this place	302
Holy Spirit, come, confirm us	311
Holy Spirit, will you be	313
I give my hands	330
I will offer up my life	339
If you believe and I believe	344
In full and glad surrender	354
Jesu, Jesu, fill us with your love	368
Jesus, we have heard your Spirit	406
Longing for light	452
Lord, I come to you	458
Lord of all being	466
Lord of creation, to you be all praise!	471
Lord of life	473
Lord, the light of your love	479
Lord, you have my heart	489

My God, accept my heart this day	514
Nada te turbe	523
O happy day	551
O how good is the Lord	555
O Jesus, I have promised	556
O Lord, my heart is not proud	564
O thou who camest from above	580
One more step along the world I go	595
Silent, surrendered	659
Spirit of the living God (Armstrong)	674
Spirit of the living God (Iverson)	675
Stand up, stand up for Jesus	677
Take my life, and let it be	687
Take this moment	688
The Lord's my shepherd (Crimond)	723
The Lord's my shepherd (Townend)	724
The wise man	735
Thine for ever! God of love	752
This little light of mine	762
Thuma mina	771
We are marching	789
We believe in God the Father	790
We have a gospel to proclaim	798
When I feel the touch	817
Will you come and follow me	834
Zip bam boo	858

Funerals

Abide with me	6
All my hope on God is founded	19
As with gladness men of old	46
Be still, my soul	63
Bless the Lord, my soul	74
Christ's is the world	110
Do not be afraid	156
Faithful vigil ended	167
Father in heaven, how we love you	171
From the falter of breath	208
God is love: let heaven adore him	243
God to enfold you	258
Going home	263
Guide me, O thou great Redeemer	275
I am the bread of life	323
I heard the voice of Jesus say	334
Immortal love, for ever full	350
In heavenly love abiding	355
Jesu, Son of Mary	371
Jesus lives! thy terrors now	390
Jesus, remember me	398
Jesus, stand among us in thy risen power	402
Jesus the Lord said: 'I am the Bread'	403
Lead, kindly light	421
Lord of all hopefulness	467
Nada te turbe	523
Now is eternal life	529
O Lord, hear my prayer	561
O Love that wilt not let me go	571

Funerals

O strength and stay	577
Rock of ages	643
Surrexit Christus	683
The day thou gavest, Lord, is ended	704
The King of love my shepherd is	715
The Lord is my light	719
The Lord's my shepherd (Crimond)	723
The Lord's my shepherd (Townend)	724
There's a wideness in God's mercy	747
We cannot measure	792
Within our darkest night	837

Holy Communion

All for Jesus!	11
An upper room did our Lord prepare	35
And now, O Father, mindful of the love	38
As the disciples	44
As your family, Lord	46
At the Lamb's high feast we sing	51
At this table we remember	53
Author of life divine	55
Bread is blessed and broken	82
Bread of heaven, on thee we feed	83
Bread of the world in mercy broken	84
Break the bread and pour the wine	85
Break thou the bread	86
Broken for me	90
Christ is the heavenly food	98
Christian people, raise your song	106
Christians lift your hearts and voices	109
Come now, the table's spread	133
Come, risen Lord	137
Draw nigh and take the body	157
Eat this bread	159
Father, who in Jesus found us	180
From many grains	206
Gather around, for the table is spread	213
Gifts of bread and wine	214
Glory to God!	227
God is here! As we his people	241
God of the Passover	252
Here in this place	302
Here is bread	303
Here, O my Lord	304
I come with joy	328
In bread we bring you, Lord	351
Jesus calls us here to meet him	378
Jesus, stand among us	401
Let us break bread together	431
Let us talents and tongues employ	434
Lord, we come to ask your healing	483
Love is his word	492
My God, and is thy table spread	515
Now let us from this table rise	530
Now, my tongue, the mystery telling	531
O God, unseen but ever near	548

O thou, who at thy Eucharist didst pray	579
Our God loves us	608
Put peace into each other's hands	633
See the holy table, spread for our healing	651
Soul of my Saviour	670
Thanks for the fellowship	697
The Son of God proclaim	731
Thee we adore, O hidden Saviour, thee	737
This is my body	755
Ubi caritas	781
We hail thy presence glorious	796
We pray thee, heavenly Father	803

Marriage

A new commandment	4
Bind us together, Lord	73
Brother, sister, let me serve you	91
Christ triumphant	103
Come down, O Love divine	120
Dear Lord and Father of mankind	152
Father of heaven, whose love profound	174
Filled with the Spirit's power	184
Give me joy in my heart	215
God, in the planning	239
God is love: let heaven adore him	243
Gracious Spirit, Holy Ghost	268
Great is thy faithfulness	273
Happy are they, they that love God	285
Help us to help each other, Lord	299
How deep the Father's love for us	317
I will sing the wondrous story	340
Immortal, invisible, God only wise	349
In heavenly love abiding	355
Jesu, Jesu, fill us with your love	368
Jesus, Lord, we pray	392
Jesus, stand among us	401
Just as I am, without one plea	413
King of glory, King of peace	416
Lead us, heavenly Father, lead us	422
Let there be love	430
Lord, for the years	454
Lord Jesus Christ	463
Lord of all hopefulness	467
Lord of life	473
Love divine, all loves excelling	491
Love is his word	492
Make me a channel of your peace	499
May the grace of Christ the Saviour	505
Morning glory, starlit sky	509
My song is love unknown	521
Now thank we all our God	532
O love divine, how sweet thou art!	569
O love, how deep, how broad, how high	570
O perfect love	573
O praise ye the Lord!	574
O thou who camest from above	580

O worship the King	582
Praise, my soul, the King of heaven	623
Praise the Lord, ye heavens, adore him	625
Praise to the Holiest	627
Take my life, and let it be	687
Tell out, my soul	692
The King of love my shepherd is	715
The Lord's my shepherd (Crimond)	723
The Lord's my shepherd (Townend)	724
The love we share	725
These vows of love are taken	749
Through all the changing scenes of life	769
To God be the glory!	777
Ubi caritas	781
We gather here	794
When I needed a neighbour	819

Ordination/Commissioning

All praise to thee	23
An upper room did our Lord prepare	35
Be thou my vision	66
Breathe on me, Breath of God	87
Brother, sister, let me serve you	91
Christ is our cornerstone	97
Christ is the King!	99
Christians lift your hearts	108
Come down, O Love divine	120
Come, Holy Spirit, come	125
Father, hear the prayer we offer	169
Firmly I believe and truly	186
From heaven you came	205
Go forth and tell	232
God has spoken – by the prophets	238
God is here! As we his people	241
Great God, your love has called us	270
Here I am	300
I bind unto myself today	326
I, the Lord of sea and sky	337
I will offer up my life	339
In Christ alone	352
Jesus calls us: o'er the tumult	379
Let us build a house	432
Listen, let your heart keep seeking	446
Longing for light	452
Lord, for the years	454
Lord, I come to you	458
May the mind of Christ my Saviour	506
Meekness and majesty	507
O Jesus, I have promised	556
O thou who camest from above	580
One is the body	594
Silent, surrendered	659
Take me, Lord	685
Take my life, and let it be	687
Take this moment	688
Thanks be to God	696
The Church's one foundation	702
Thuma mina	771

Ordination/Commissioning

We have a gospel to proclaim	798
When God almighty came to earth	814
Will you come and follow me	834
Ye servants of the Lord	842

THE ORDER FOR HOLY COMMUNION

Opening Hymn

All creatures of our God and King	10
All people that on earth do dwell	21
Angel-voices ever singing	40
As we are gathered	45
Awake, awake: fling off the night	56
Awake, my soul, and with the sun	57
Be still and know that I am God	61
Be still, for the presence of the Lord	62
Bless the Lord, my soul	74
Come and celebrate	116
Come, Holy Spirit, come	125
Come, let us join our cheerful songs	127
Come, now is the time to worship	132
Come, ye faithful, raise the anthem	142
From the rising of the sun	209
Give to our God immortal praise	220
God is here! As we his people	241
God of mercy, God of grace	251
I come with joy	328
In the garden Mary lingers	359
Jesus calls us here to meet him	378
Jesus, stand among us	401
Jesus, where'er thy people meet	407
Jubilate, everybody	410
Laudate Dominum	420
Let everything that has breath	426
Let us with a gladsome mind	435
Lord, the light of your love	479
Lord, we come to ask your healing	483
May the fragrance of Jesus fill this place	504
Morning has broken	510
O God beyond all praising	544
O let the Son of God enfold you	558
O worship the King	582
O worship the Lord in the beauty of holiness	583
Only by grace	598
Praise and thanksgiving	617
Spirit of the living God (Armstrong)	674
Spirit of the living God (Iverson)	675
Stand up and bless the Lord	676
Thanks be to God	696
This is the day the Lord has made	759
'Tis good, Lord, to be here	775

To be in your presence	776
To God be the glory!	777
To the name of our salvation	779
Veni, lumen cordium	783
We bow down	791
Ye holy angels bright	840
Ye servants of God	841
Ye watchers and ye holy ones	844

Gradual Hymn

Alleluia! Alleluia!	30
Break thou the bread	86
Come, Holy Ghost, our hearts inspire	123
Dear Lord and Father of mankind	152
God has spoken – by the prophets	238
God is working his purpose out	246
Help us, O Lord, to learn	298
Lord, for the years	454
Lord, the light of your love	479
Lord, thy word abideth	481
Love is his word	492
May the mind of Christ my Saviour	506
Open our eyes, Lord	600
Seek ye first	652
Tell out, my soul	692
Thanks to God whose word was spoken	698
Thou, whose almighty word	767
Thy hand, O God, has guided	772

Offertory Hymn

Abba, Father, let me be	5
All that I am	24
Angel-voices ever singing	40
Before the throne	70
Come, all who look to Christ today	115
Come, now, the table's spread	133
For the beauty of the earth	195
God is here! As we his people	241
I am the bread of life	323
I will offer up my life	339
In bread we bring you, Lord	351
Jesus calls us here to meet him	378
Lift up your hearts!	439
Lord, I come to you	458
O worship the Lord in the beauty of holiness	583
Take my life, and let it be	687
Take this moment	688
When the music fades	823

Communion

Adoramus te, Domine	8
All for Jesus!	11
Alleluia, sing to Jesus	33
And now, O Father, mindful of the love	38
At this table we remember	53
Author of life divine	55

Bread is blessed and broken	82
Bread of heaven, on thee we feed	83
Bread of the world in mercy broken	84
Broken for me	90
Deck thyself, my soul, with gladness	153
Draw nigh and take the body	157
Eat this bread	159
From glory to glory advancing	204
Glory be to Jesus	224
Glory, love, and praise, and honour	225
Hail, true body	281
Here in this place	302
Here is bread	303
Here, O my Lord	304
I am the bread of life	323
I come with joy	328
In bread we bring you, Lord	351
Jesu, thou joy of loving hearts	374
Jesus calls us here to meet him	378
Let all mortal flesh keep silence	424
Let us break bread together	431
Let us build a house	432
Let us talents and tongues employ	434
Lord, enthroned in heavenly splendour	453
Lord Jesus Christ	463
O thou, who at thy Eucharist didst pray	579
Sanctus, sanctus, sanctus	647
Shout for joy and sing	656
Soul of my Saviour	670
Strengthen for service, Lord	680
Sweet sacrament divine	684
The Son of God proclaim	731
Thee we adore, O hidden Saviour, thee	737
We hail thy presence glorious	796
We pray thee, heavenly Father	803
Wherefore, O Father	826

Final Hymn

Christ be with me	94
Glory to thee, my God, this night	229
God be in my head	235
God be with you till we meet again	236
God to enfold you	258
Halle, halle, halle	282
May the grace of Christ the Saviour	505
Peace to you	616
Saviour, again to thy dear name we raise	648
Spirit of the living God (Armstrong)	674
Spirit of the living God (Iverson)	675
The peace of the earth be with you	726
Thuma mina	771

Index of Hymns for the Lectionary

YEAR A

ADVENT

FIRST SUNDAY OF ADVENT - A

Awake, awake: fling off the night 56
Come, thou long-expected Jesus 140
Creator of the starry height 148
Crown him with many crowns 150
For the healing of the nations 198
Great is the darkness 271
Hark! A herald voice is calling 286
Hark, the glad sound! 288
Hills of the north, rejoice 307
How lovely on the mountains 319
I cannot tell 327
Lo, he comes with clouds
descending 449
Make way, make way 500
O come, O come, Emmanuel 535
O day of God, draw nigh 537
Oft in danger, oft in woe 585
Rejoice, O land, in God thy
might 637
Stand up, stand up for Jesus 677
The advent of our King 699
The Lord will come and not be
slow 722
The Spirit lives to set us free 732
Thy kingdom come, O God 774
Wait for the Lord 785
Wake, O wake! with tidings
thrilling 786
We are marching 789
Ye servants of the Lord 842

SECOND SUNDAY OF
ADVENT - A

Christ is the King! 99
Christ, when for us you were
baptised 104
God is working his purpose out 246
Hail to the Lord's anointed 280
Hark! A herald voice is calling 286
Hark, the glad sound! 288
How beauteous are their feet 315
In heavenly love abiding 355
Inspired by love and anger 362
Jesus shall reign 399
Lord, I have made thy word
my choice 459
Lord, thy word abideth 481
Make way, make way 500
May the mind of Christ my
Saviour 506
O come, O come, Emmanuel 535
O day of God, draw nigh 537
On Jordan's bank the Baptist's cry 589
Spirit divine, attend our prayers 671
Thanks to God whose word was
spoken 698
The Lord will come and not be
slow 722

These are the days 748
Thou didst leave thy throne 766
Wait for the Lord 785
When Jesus came to Jordan 821

THIRD SUNDAY OF ADVENT - A

Be bold, be strong 60
Hark! A herald voice is calling 286
Hark, the glad sound! 288
How beauteous are their feet 315
In the Lord I'll be ever thankful 360
It is a thing most wonderful 364
Jesus, the name high over all 404
Little donkey 447
Lord, for the years 454
Magnificat 497
My God, how wonderful you are 516
O day of God, draw nigh 537
O for a thousand tongues to sing 541
Rejoice, the Lord is King 638
Teach me, my God and King 690
Tell out, my soul 692
The people that in darkness sat 727
Thou didst leave thy throne 766
Thy kingdom come, O God 774
Wait for the Lord 785
We have a gospel to proclaim 798

FOURTH SUNDAY OF
ADVENT - A

All hail the power of Jesus' name 14
Away in a manger 59
Come, thou long-expected Jesus 140
For Mary, mother of our Lord 194
From heaven you came 205
Great Shepherd of thy people 274
Immortal, invisible, God only wise 349
Jesus, good above all other 383
Jesus, Name above all names 395
Jesus, the name high over all 404
Lift up your heads 438
Long ago, prophets knew 451
Lord Jesus Christ 463
Magnificat 497
May the grace of Christ our
Saviour 505
O come, O come, Emmanuel 535
O Lord, all the world belongs to
you 560
The advent of our King 699
The Son of God proclaim 731
Thy kingdom come 773
To the name of our salvation 779
Where is this stupendous stranger? 825
Ye who own the faith of Jesus 845

CHRISTMAS

CHRISTMAS EVE -
FOR YEARS A, B AND C

Any of the Christmas Day hymns may
be used on the evening of Christmas
Eve.

CHRISTMAS DAY -
FOR YEARS A, B AND C

A great and mighty wonder 2
Angels from the realms of glory 39
Away in a manger 59
Behold, the great Creator 71
Born in the night, Mary's child 81
Christians, awake! 107
Cloth for the cradle 113
Confitemini Domino 145
Ding dong, merrily on high! 154
Glory to God! 227
God rest you merry, gentlefolk 254
Good Christians all, rejoice 265
Hark, the herald-angels sing 289
In the bleak mid-winter 357
It came upon the midnight clear 363
Joy to the world! 409
Like a candle flame 444
Little Jesus, sweetly sleep 448
O come, all ye faithful 534
O little town of Bethlehem 559
Of the Father's love begotten 584
On Christmas night all Christians
sing 588
Once in royal David's city 592
See, amid the winter's snow 649
See him lying on a bed of straw 650
Silent night 658
The first Nowell 705
The Virgin Mary had a baby boy 734
Thou didst leave thy throne 766
Unto us a boy is born 782
What child is this 812
Where is this stupendous
stranger? 825
While shepherds watched 827
Who would think that what
was needed? 832

FIRST SUNDAY OF
CHRISTMAS - A

A great and mighty wonder 2
A man there lived in Galilee 3
Angels from the realms of glory 39
Give us the wings of faith 221
Glory to God above 228
Good King Wenceslas 267
He's got the whole world in his
hand 306
I'm not ashamed to own my Lord 347
It came upon the midnight clear 363
Let us praise God together 433
Lord Jesus Christ 463
My song is love unknown 521
New songs of celebration render 527
O praise ye the Lord! 574
Praise my soul, the King of
heaven 623
Praise the Lord, ye heavens,
adore him 625

First Sunday of Christmas - A

Unto us a boy is born 782
We hail thy presence glorious 796
Ye holy angels bright 840

SECOND SUNDAY OF CHRISTMAS - FOR YEARS A, B AND C

A great and mighty wonder 2
Angel-voices ever singing 40
As with gladness men of old 46
At the name of Jesus 52
Breathe on me, Breath of God 87
Christ triumphant 103
Come, ye faithful, raise the anthem 142
Confitemini Domino 145
Crown him with many crowns 150
Earth has many a noble city 158
Eternal Ruler of the ceaseless round 162
Father of heaven, whose love profound 174
Father of peace, and God of love 175
Fill your hearts with joy and gladness 183
Give us the wings of faith 221
Go, tell it on the mountain 233
God has spoken – by the prophets 238
God is our strength from days of old 244
God is working his purpose out 246
Hail to the Lord's anointed 280
Hark, the herald-angels sing 289
How sweet the name of Jesus sounds 321
I will worship 341
In the bleak mid-winter 357
It came upon the midnight clear 363
It is a thing most wonderful 364
Jesus calls us here to meet him 378
Jesus' love is very wonderful 393
Jesus, Name above all names 395
Lead us, heavenly Father, lead us 422
Let all mortal flesh keep silence 424
Like a candle flame 444
Little Jesus, sweetly sleep 448
Lord, I lift your name on high 461
Lord, the light of your love 479
Love came down at Christmas 490
Mary had a baby 502
Name of all majesty 524
Now, my tongue, the mystery telling 531
O love, how deep, how broad, how high 570
Of the Father's love begotten 584
See, amid the winter's snow 649
See him lying on a bed of straw 650
Take this moment 688
Thanks to God whose word was spoken 698
The Lord is my light 719
Thou didst leave thy throne 766
Through all the changing scenes of life 769

To the name of our salvation 779
We have a gospel to proclaim 798
What a friend we have in Jesus 811
What child is this 812
Wide, wide as the ocean 833
You laid aside your majesty 850

EPIPHANY

THE EPIPHANY - FOR YEARS A, B AND C

Adoramus te, Domine 8
Angels from the realms of glory 39
As with gladness men of old 46
Brightest and best 89
For I'm building a people of power 193
From the eastern mountains 207
Hail to the Lord's anointed 280
He's got the whole world in his hand 306
In the bleak mid-winter 357
Lord Jesus Christ 463
Lord, the light of your love 479
Love came down at Christmas 490
O worship the Lord in the beauty of holiness 583
See him lying on a bed of straw 650
Songs of thankfulness and praise 669
The first Nowell 705
The Lord is my light 719
The people that in darkness sat 727
The Virgin Mary had a baby boy 734
To be in your presence 776
We bow down 791
We three kings of Orient are 805
You are the King of Glory 849

THE BAPTISM OF CHRIST - A

A man there lived in Galilee 3
Awake, awake: fling off the night 56
Be thou my vision 66
Christ, when for us you were baptised 104
Come down, O Love divine 120
Crown him with many crowns 150
Father, we adore you 176
Father, we love you 177
Father welcomes all his children 179
God forgave my sin 237
Hail to the Lord's anointed 280
I bind unto myself today 326
Jesus Christ is waiting 382
Name of all majesty 524
Now is eternal life 529
O for a closer walk with God 539
O thou who camest from above 580
On Jordan's bank the Baptist's cry 589
Songs of thankfulness and praise 669
Spirit divine, attend our prayers 671
Spirit of the living God (Armstrong) 674
Spirit of the living God (Iverson) 675
Take my life, and let it be 687
The Church's one foundation 702

The people that in darkness sat 727
To the name of our salvation 779
We have a gospel to proclaim 798
When Jesus came to Jordan 821

SECOND SUNDAY OF EPIPHANY - A

All heaven declares 15
Christ, when for us you were baptised 104
Come, let us join our cheerful songs 127
Crown him with many crowns 150
From heaven you came 205
God is working his purpose out 246
God of grace and God of glory 248
Great is thy faithfulness 273
Hail to the Lord's anointed 280
I believe in Jesus 325
Jesus calls us: o'er the tumult 379
Jesus, the name high over all 404
Just as I am, without one plea 413
Like a mighty river flowing 445
Nada te turbe 523
Rock of ages 643
Songs of thankfulness and praise 669
The people that in darkness sat 727
There is a Redeemer 743
We have a gospel to proclaim 798
Will you come and follow me 834
Ye servants of God 841

THIRD SUNDAY OF EPIPHANY - A

Christ is the King! 99
Christ, whose glory fills the skies 105
Crown him with many crowns 150
Dear Lord and Father of mankind 152
Father, Lord of all creation 172
Follow me 189
Forth in the peace of Christ we go 200
From heaven you came 205
Give thanks with a grateful heart 219
God is our strength from days of old 244
God is working his purpose out 246
Guide me, O thou great Redeemer 275
Hail to the Lord's anointed 280
I come with joy 328
I danced in the morning 329
I, the Lord of sea and sky 337
Jesus calls us: o'er the tumult 379
Jesus, Lord, we look to thee 391
Lord, the light of your love 479
Make me a channel of your peace 499
O God beyond all praising 544
O thou, who at thy Eucharist didst pray 579
Peace, perfect peace, is the gift 615
Take my life, and let it be 687
The Church of God a kingdom is 701
The Church's one foundation 702
The Lord is my light 719
The people that in darkness sat 727

Third Sunday of Epiphany - A
This is my body 755
Thy kingdom come 773
Veni, lumen cordium 783
We are marching 789
When God almighty came to
earth 814
When I survey the wondrous cross 820
Will you come and follow me 834

FOURTH SUNDAY OF EPIPHANY - A
Be thou my vision 66
Blest are the pure in heart 79
Breathe on me, Breath of God 87
Christ is our cornerstone 97
Christ's is the world 110
Come on and celebrate 135
Disposer supreme 155
Eat this bread 159
Firmly I believe and truly 186
Forth in the peace of Christ we go 200
Give me joy in my heart 215
Glorious things of thee are spoken 223
Hail to the Lord's anointed 280
How deep the Father's love for us 317
Immortal, invisible, God only
wise 349
In the Cross of Christ I glory 358
Jesus calls us here to meet him 378
Jesus, Lord, we pray 392
Jesus the Lord said: 'I am the
Bread' 403
Joy to the world! 409
Life for the poor was hard and
tough 436
Lift high the Cross 437
Make me a channel of your peace 499
May the grace of Christ our
Saviour 505
O Lord, my God 563
Purify my heart 631
Rejoice in the Lord always 636
Songs of thankfulness and praise 669
We sing the praise of him who
died 804
When I survey the wondrous cross 820

THE PRESENTATION OF CHRIST IN THE TEMPLE - FOR YEARS A, B AND C
Angels from the realms of glory 39
Christ, whose glory fills the skies 105
Colours of day 114
Faithful vigil ended 167
Father welcomes all his children 179
Forth in the peace of Christ we go 200
Glorious things of thee are spoken 223
Gracious Spirit, Holy Ghost 268
Hail to the Lord who comes 279
Jesus bids us shine 377
Lord, the light of your love 479
O, heaven is in my heart 552
O let the Son of God enfold you 558
Of the Father's love begotten 584

Purify my heart 631
Restore, O Lord 639
Sing lullaby 661
The Lord is my light 719
This little light of mine 762
Virgin-born, we bow before thee 784
We bow down 791
With joy we meditate the grace 836

ORDINARY TIME
PROPER 1 - A
Blest are the pure in heart 79
Brother, sister, let me serve you 91
For the healing of the nations 198
Here I am 301
Jesus bids us shine 377
Let us praise God together 433
Lord, the light of your love 479
Men of faith 508
O Jesus, I have promised 556
Praise and thanksgiving 617
The Spirit lives to set us free 732
This little light of mine 762
Thou, whose almighty word 767

PROPER 2 - A
A new commandment 4
Brother, sister, let me serve you 91
Forgive our sins as we forgive 199
Let there be love 430
Lord, when I turn my back on
you 486
My God, accept my heart this day 514
Peace, perfect peace, is the gift 615
The Church of God a kingdom is 701
The Spirit lives to set us free 732

PROPER 3 - A
Beauty for brokenness 67
Blessèd city, heavenly Salem 77
For the beauty of the earth 195
God is love: his the care 242
Make me a channel of your peace 499
O day of God, draw nigh 537
O Lord, all the world belongs to
you 560
Only by grace 598
Peace, perfect peace, is the gift 615
There are hundreds of sparrows 738

SECOND SUNDAY BEFORE LENT - A
All my hope on God is founded 19
Blest Creator of the light 80
Come, Holy Ghost, our hearts
inspire 123
Dance and sing 151
Eternal Father, strong to save 160
From the falter of breath 208
Give to our God immortal praise 220
God is our strength from days of
old 244
He's got the whole world in his
hand 306

Let us with a gladsome mind 435
Lord, the light of your love 479
Morning has broken 510
O give thanks (Kendrick) 542
O give thanks (Pond) 543
Seek ye first 652
She sits like a bird 654
Teach me to dance 691
Thanks to God whose word 698
There are hundreds of sparrows 738
Thine arm, O Lord, in days of old 750
This world you have made 763
Thou whose almighty word 767
Wait for the Lord 785
We want to see Jesus lifted high 807

SUNDAY NEXT BEFORE LENT - A
Adoramus te, Domine 8
All heaven declares 15
Be still, for the presence of the Lord 62
Be thou my vision 66
Christ, whose glory fills the skies 105
For all the saints 190
From glory to glory advancing 204
Glory to God (Peruvian Gloria) 226
God of grace and God of glory 248
Guide me, O thou great
Redeemer 275
Here in this place 302
Immortal, invisible, God only
wise 349
Lord, the light of your love 479
Majesty, worship his majesty 498
Meekness and majesty 507
My God, how wonderful you are 516
Name of all majesty 524
Open our eyes, Lord 600
The Spirit lives to set us free 732
Thee we adore, O hidden
Saviour, thee 737
This little light of mine 762
'Tis good, Lord, to be here 775
You are the King of Glory 849
You, living Christ, our eyes
behold 851

LENT
ASH WEDNESDAY - FOR YEARS A, B AND C
All who would valiant be 27
As the deer pants for the water 43
Be thou my guardian and my guide 65
Be thou my vision 66
Father of heaven, whose love
profound 174
Forgive our sins as we forgive 199
Forty days and forty nights 202
Give thanks with a grateful heart 219
God forgave my sin 237
Jesu, lover of my soul 369
Judge eternal, throned in
splendour 411
Lord Jesus, think on me 465

Ash Wednesday - for years A, B and C

O for a heart to praise my God 540
O God of Bethel, by whose hand 545
O Lord, hear my prayer 561
O love, how deep, how broad, how high 570
Rock of ages 643
Through the night of doubt and sorrow 770

FIRST SUNDAY OF LENT - A

All hail the power of Jesus' name 14
And can it be 36
Awake, our souls; away, our fears 58
Be thou my guardian and my guide 65
Dear Lord and Father of mankind 152
Father, hear the prayer we offer 169
Father of heaven, whose love profound 174
Forty days and forty nights 202
God forgave my sin 237
Jesu, grant me this, I pray 367
Lead us, heavenly Father, lead us 422
Lift up your hearts! 439
Lord Jesus, think on me 465
O happy band of pilgrims 550
O Jesus, I have promised 556
O love, how deep, how broad, how high 570
Praise to the Holiest 627
Restore, O Lord 639
Shepherd divine, our wants relieve 655
There's a wideness in God's mercy 747
What a friend we have in Jesus 811
With joy we meditate the grace 836

SECOND SUNDAY OF LENT - A

Adoramus te, Domine 8
All I once held dear 16
All my hope on God is founded 19
Blessèd assurance 75
Christ for the world we sing! 95
Christ is the world's Light 100
Father, I place into your hands 170
Fill thou my life, O Lord my God 182
Give to our God immortal praise 220
God forgave my sin 237
God's love is deeper 261
Have you heard the raindrops 291
Here I am 301
I heard the voice of Jesus say 334
I'm accepted, I'm forgiven 345
Immortal, invisible, God only wise 349
Immortal love, for ever full 350
It is a thing most wonderful 364
Jesus, Jesus 389
Lead, kindly light 421
Like a candle flame 444
Name of all majesty 524
O praise ye the Lord! 574
Oft in danger, oft in woe 585
Spirit divine, attend our prayers 671
The God of Abraham praise 706
The King of love my shepherd is 715

The Lord is my light 719
Thy hand, O God, has guided 772
To God be the glory! 777
We are marching 789
We give immortal praise 795

THIRD SUNDAY OF LENT - A

As the deer pants for the water 43
Bread of heaven, on thee we feed 83
Come down, O Love divine 120
Father, hear the prayer we offer 169
Glorious things of thee are spoken 223
God is here! As we his people 241
Guide me, O thou great Redeemer 275
Holy Spirit, truth divine 312
How sweet the name of Jesus sounds 321
I am a new creation 322
I cannot tell 327
I heard the voice of Jesus say 334
I'm accepted, I'm forgiven 345
In heavenly love abiding 355
Jesu, lover of my soul 369
Jesu, the very thought of thee 373
Jesu, thou joy of loving hearts 374
Jesus the Lord said: 'I am the Bread' 403
Jesus, where'er thy people meet 407
Lead us, heavenly Father, lead us 422
Let all the world in every corner sing 425
My God, I love thee 517
The King of love my shepherd is 715
Through all the changing scenes of life 769
We cannot measure 792

FOURTH SUNDAY OF LENT - A

Amazing grace 34
Awake, awake: fling off the night 56
Awake, my soul, and with the sun 57
Bind us together, Lord 73
Bless the Lord, my soul 74
Christ, whose glory fills the skies 105
Christ's is the world 110
Come down, O Love divine 120
Come, Holy Ghost, our souls inspire 124
Do not be afraid 156
Faithful Shepherd, feed me 166
For the beauty of the earth 195
God is love: his the care 242
I come with joy 328
I heard the voice of Jesus say 334
I will sing the wondrous story 340
In heavenly love abiding 355
In the Lord I'll be ever thankful 360
Jesu, lover of my soul 369
Jesu, the very thought of thee 373
Just as I am, without one plea 413
Light of the world 441
Love divine, all loves excelling 491
My God, and is thy table spread 515
My song is love unknown 521

O for a thousand tongues to sing 541
Open our eyes, Lord 600
The God of love my shepherd is 707
The King of love my shepherd is 715
Thou, whose almighty word 767
To God be the glory! 777

Or: MOTHERING SUNDAY - FOR YEARS A, B AND C

All things bright and beautiful 26
Bind us together, Lord 73
Come down, O Love divine 120
Do not be afraid 156
For Mary, mother of our Lord 194
For the beauty of the earth 195
Glorious things of thee are spoken 223
Happy are they, they that love God 285
He's got the whole world in his hand 306
I come with joy 328
In the Lord I'll be ever thankful 360
Jesus, good above all other 383
Let all the world in every corner sing 425
Lord of all hopefulness 467
Love divine, all loves excelling 491
Magnificat 497
Make me a channel of your peace 499
May the mind of Christ my Saviour 506
Now thank we all our God 532
Tell out, my soul 692
The King is among us 714
The King of love my shepherd is 715
Through all the changing scenes of life 769

FIFTH SUNDAY OF LENT - A

Beneath the cross of Jesus 72
Breathe on me, Breath of God 87
Christ's is the world 110
Father of heaven, whose love profound 174
From heaven you came 205
Hark, my soul, it is the Lord 287
How deep the Father's love for us 317
How sweet the name of Jesus sounds 321
I am the bread of life 323
I cannot tell 327
In the Cross of Christ I glory 358
It is a thing most wonderful 364
Jesus the Lord said: 'I am the Bread' 403
Jesus, the name high over all 404
Lift high the Cross 437
My Lord, what love is this 520
O for a thousand tongues to sing 541
O Lord, my God 563
Praise to the Holiest 627
Spirit of the living God (Armstrong) 674
Spirit of the living God (Iverson) 675
Such love 681

Fifth Sunday of Lent - A

The royal banners forward go 729
The Spirit lives to set us free 732
There is a Redeemer 743
There's a wideness in God's mercy 747
To God be the glory! 777
We give immortal praise 795
We sing the praise of him who
died 804
When I survey the wondrous
cross 820

PALM SUNDAY - A
Liturgy of the Palms

All glory, laud and honour 12
All praise to thee 23
Clap your hands, all you people 112
Give me joy in my heart 215
Hosanna, hosanna 314
Lift up your heads 438
Make way, make way 500
My song is love unknown 521
Praise to the Holiest 627
Rejoice in the Lord always 636
Ride on, ride on in majesty 640
The royal banners forward go 729
You are the King of Glory 849

Liturgy of the Passion

And now, O Father, mindful of
the love 38
Broken for me 90
From heaven you came 205
Glory be to Jesus 224
Hail, thou once despisèd Jesus 278
I cannot tell 327
I will offer up my life 339
I will sing the wondrous story 340
Meekness and majesty 507
Morning glory, starlit sky 509
My song is love unknown 521
O dearest Lord, thy sacred head 538
O love, how deep, how broad,
how high 570
O my Saviour, lifted from the
earth 572
Such love 681
There is a green hill far away 740
Thou didst leave thy throne 766
We sing the praise of him who
died 804
Were you there when they
crucified my Lord? 810
When I survey the wondrous
cross 820

MONDAY OF HOLY WEEK -
FOR YEARS A, B AND C

Father of heaven, whose love
profound 174
Immortal, invisible, God only
wise 349
Jesu, lover of my soul 369
O God of Bethel, by whose hand 545
Your love's greater 856

TUESDAY OF HOLY WEEK -
FOR YEARS A, B AND C

Come, Holy Spirit, come 125
Disposer supreme 155
Father, we love you 177
For all the saints 190
I'm not ashamed to own my Lord 347
Open our eyes, Lord 600
The Spirit lives to set us free 732
We pray thee, heavenly Father 803

WEDNESDAY OF HOLY WEEK -
FOR YEARS A, B AND C

Christ triumphant 103
Give us the wings of faith 221

MAUNDY THURSDAY -
FOR YEARS A, B AND C

A new commandment 4
Adoramus te, Domine 8
An upper room did our Lord
prepare 35
As we are gathered 45
Broken for me 90
Brother, sister, let me serve you 91
Draw nigh and take the body 157
Eat this bread 159
Great God, your love has called us 270
Here is bread 303
I come with joy 328
In bread we bring you, Lord 351
Jesu, Jesu, fill us with your love 368
Jesus calls us here to meet him 378
Let there be love 430
Let us break bread together 431
Lord Jesus Christ 463
Love is his word 492
Meekness and majesty 507
My God, and is thy table spread 515
Now, my tongue, the mystery
telling 531
O thou, who at the Eucharist
didst pray 579
The Son of God proclaim 731
Ubi caritas 781

GOOD FRIDAY -
FOR YEARS A, B AND C

Ah, holy Jesu, how hast thou
offended 9
At the cross she keeps her station 50
Beneath the cross of Jesus 72
Glory be to Jesus 224
In the Cross of Christ I glory 358
It is a thing most wonderful 364
Jesus Christ 380
Jesus, remember me 398
My Lord, what love is this 520
My song is love unknown 521
O dearest Lord, thy sacred head 538
O sacred head, surrounded 576
Praise to the Holiest 627
Rock of ages 643
Sing, my tongue, the glorious
battle 662

Such love 681
The head that once was crowned
with thorns 711
There is a green hill far away 740
There is a Redeemer 743
Were you there when they
crucified my Lord? 810
When I survey the wondrous cross 820

EASTER EVE -
FOR YEARS A, B AND C
Services other than the Easter Vigil.

All in an Easter garden 17
Alleluia, alleluia, give thanks to the
risen Lord 31
As pants the hart for cooling
streams 42
As the deer pants for the water 43
Awake, awake: fling off the night 56
Be still and know that I am God 61
Breathe on me, Breath of God 87
Christ is the King! 99
Come, ye faithful, raise the strain 143
Great is thy faithfulness 273
Jesus lives! thy terrors now 390
Laudate Dominum 420
Love's redeeming work is done 494
New songs of celebration render 527
Now is eternal life 529
O for a heart to praise my God 540
O Lord, hear my prayer 561
Rejoice, the Lord is King 638
Rock of ages 643
Sing to God a song of glory 665
Surrexit Christus 683
The strife is o'er, the battle done 733
Thou, whose almighty word 767

EASTER
EASTER VIGIL -
FOR YEARS A, B AND C
A brighter dawn is breaking 1
All heaven declares 15
All in an Easter garden 17
All my hope on God is founded 19
Alleluia, alleluia, give thanks to the
risen Lord 31
As pants the hart for cooling
streams 42
As the deer pants for the water 43
At the Lamb's high feast we sing 51
Awake, awake: fling off the night 56
Be still and know that I am God 61
Blest Creator of the light 80
Breathe on me, Breath of God 87
Christ is the King! 99
Come, ye faithful, raise the strain 143
Creation sings! 146
For the days when you feel near 196
From the very depths of darkness 211
Gather around, for the table is
spread 213
Give to our God immortal praise 220
Glorious things of thee are spoken 223

Easter Vigil - for years A, B and C

Go back, go back to Galilee	231
God of life, God of love	249
Great is thy faithfulness	273
Here in this place	302
I, the Lord of sea and sky	337
Jesus, Jesus	389
Jesus lives! thy terrors now	390
Laudate Dominum	420
Let us with a gladsome mind	435
Lift up your voice	440
Lord, the light of your love	479
Love's redeeming work is done	494
My God, and is thy table spread	515
My Jesus, my Saviour	519
New songs of celebration render	527
Now is eternal life	529
O for a heart to praise my God	540
O Lord, hear my prayer	561
Overwhelmed by love	612
Put thou thy trust in God	634
Rejoice, the Lord is King	638
Rock of ages	643
Sing to God a song of glory	665
Surrexit Christus	683
Thanks be to God	696
The Lord is risen indeed	721
The strife is o'er, the battle done	733
Thine be the glory	751
This joyful Eastertide	761
Thou, whose almighty word	767

EASTER DAY - A

All heaven declares	15
All in an Easter garden	17
Alleluia, alleluia, give thanks to the risen Lord	31
Alleluia, alleluia, hearts to heaven and voices raise	32
Alleluia (x 8)	29
At the Lamb's high feast we sing	51
Celtic Alleluia	93
Christ the Lord is risen again	102
Come, let us with our Lord arise	129
Come, risen Lord	137
Come, ye faithful, raise the anthem	142
Come, ye faithful, raise the strain	143
Glory to God (Peruvian Gloria)	226
Good Christians all, rejoice and sing	266
Halle, halle, halle	282
He has risen	292
He is Lord	294
I am the bread of life	323
Jesus Christ is risen today	381
Jesus Christ is waiting	382
Jesus lives! thy terrors now	390
Laudate Dominum	420
Led like a lamb	423
Light of the world	441
Light's glittering morn	443
Love's redeeming work is done	494
Low in the grave he lay	496
Now is eternal life	529

Now the green blade riseth	533
Onward, Christian pilgrims	599
Surrexit Christus	683
The day of resurrection	703
The Lord is risen indeed	721
The strife is o'er, the battle done	733
Thine be the glory	751
This is the day the Lord has made	760
This joyful Eastertide	761
To God be the glory!	777
Ye choirs of new Jerusalem	839
You laid aside your majesty	850

SECOND SUNDAY OF EASTER - A

Amazing grace	34
And can it be	36
Be still and know that I am God	61
Breathe on me, Breath of God	87
Come, ye faithful, raise the strain	143
Guide me, O thou great Redeemer	275
I believe in Jesus	325
Immortal, invisible, God only wise	349
Jesus, stand among us	401
Jesus, stand among us in thy risen power	402
Jesus, the name high over all	404
Lead us, heavenly Father, lead us	422
Lord Jesus Christ	463
Love's redeeming work is done	494
Low in the grave he lay	496
My God, how wonderful you are	516
O God, our help in ages past	547
Open our eyes, Lord	600
Surrexit Christus	683
The Son of God proclaim	731
Thuma mina	771
We have a gospel to proclaim	798

THIRD SUNDAY OF EASTER - A

A brighter dawn is breaking	1
Abide with me	6
All I once held dear	16
Alleluia, alleluia, give thanks to the risen Lord	31
Broken for me	90
Christ is the King!	99
Eat this bread	159
Gather around, for the table is spread	213
Glorious things of thee are spoken	223
I am the bread of life	323
I'm accepted, I'm forgiven	345
In the garden Mary lingers	359
Jesu, thou joy of loving hearts	374
Jesus, stand among us	401
Let there be love	430
New songs of celebration render	527
Now the green blade riseth	533
Open our eyes, Lord	600
Rejoice, the Lord is King	638
Strengthen for service, Lord	680
These are the days	748
Ubi caritas	781

We have a gospel to proclaim	798
We'll walk the land	809

FOURTH SUNDAY OF EASTER - A

As we are gathered	45
Faithful Shepherd, feed me	166
Father, hear the prayer we offer	169
Great is thy faithfulness	273
Great Shepherd of thy people	274
Happy are they, they that love God	285
How sweet the name of Jesus sounds	321
I will sing the wondrous story	340
I'm accepted, I'm forgiven	345
In heavenly love abiding	355
Jesus calls us: o'er the tumult	379
Jesus the Lord said: 'I am the Bread'	403
Jesus, where'er thy people meet	407
Led like a lamb	423
Loving Shepherd of thy sheep	495
O let the Son of God enfold you	558
Restore, O Lord	639
Shepherd divine, our wants relieve	655
Such love	681
The God of love my shepherd is	707
The head that once was crowned with thorns	711
The King of love my shepherd is	715
The Lord's my shepherd	723, 724
There's a wideness in God's mercy	747
Thine for ever! God of love	752
Will you come and follow me	834

FIFTH SUNDAY OF EASTER - A

Be the centre of my life	64
Blessèd city, heavenly Salem	77
Christ is made the sure foundation	96
Christ is our cornerstone	97
Christ is the world's Light	100
Come, my Way, my Truth, my Life	131
For I'm building a people of power	193
Forth in the peace of Christ we go	200
Guide me, O thou great Redeemer	275
How sweet the name of Jesus sounds	321
Jesu, lover of my soul	369
Jesus Christ is waiting	382
Jesus the Lord said: 'I am the Bread'	403
Lord, you have my heart	489
Nada te turbe	523
O for a thousand tongues to sing	541
Put thou thy trust in God	634
The Church's one foundation	702
Thine for ever! God of love	752
Thou art the Way: by thee alone	765
Thy hand, O God, has guided	772
To God be the glory!	777
We are marching	789
When the music fades	823

SIXTH SUNDAY OF EASTER - A

A new commandment	4
All heaven declares	15
All my hope on God is founded	19
Be still and know that I am God	61
Blest are the pure in heart	79
Come down, O Love divine	120
Come, ye faithful, raise the strain	143
Do not be afraid	156
God is love: his the care	242
Great is thy faithfulness	273
I, the Lord of sea and sky	337
Jesu, Jesu, fill us with your love	368
Jesus, where'er thy people meet	407
Let there be love	430
Lord of beauty, thine the splendour	470
Love divine, all loves excelling	491
Love's redeeming work is done	494
Name of all majesty	524
Now let us from this table rise	530
O God of Bethel, by whose hand	545
O Jesus, I have promised	556
O Lord of heaven and earth and sea	566
Our blest Redeemer, ere he breathed	602
Such love	681
There are hundreds of sparrows	738
There is a Redeemer	743
These are the days	748
We have a gospel to proclaim	798

ASCENSION DAY - FOR YEARS A, B AND C

All hail the power of Jesus' name	14
All heaven declares	15
Alleluia, sing to Jesus	33
At the name of Jesus	52
Be still, for the presence of the Lord	62
Christ is the King!	99
Christ triumphant	103
Clap your hands, all you people	112
Come, Holy Spirit, come	125
Come, let us join our cheerful songs	127
Crown him with many crowns	150
Hail the day that sees him rise	277
He is exalted	293
He is Lord	294
How lovely on the mountains	319
Jesus is King	386
Jesus shall reign	399
Laudate Dominum	420
Lord, enthroned in heavenly splendour	453
Majesty, worship his majesty	498
Make way, make way	500
Meekness and majesty	507
Name of all majesty	524
O dearest Lord, thy sacred head	538
Rejoice, the Lord is King	638
The head that once was crowned with thorns	711

SEVENTH SUNDAY OF EASTER - A

All hail the power of Jesus' name	14
Alleluia, sing to Jesus	33
As pants the hart for cooling streams	42
At the name of Jesus	52
Be still, for the presence of the Lord	62
Beauty for brokenness	67
Blessèd assurance	75
Breathe on me, Breath of God	87
Christ is the King!	99
Christ triumphant	103
Christ, whose glory fills the skies	105
Christ's is the world	110
Come and celebrate	116
Come, Holy Ghost, our souls inspire	124
Come, let us join our cheerful songs	127
Crown him with many crowns	150
Father most holy, merciful and loving	173
Fight the good fight	181
Give me joy in my heart	215
Give to our God immortal praise	220
God is love: his the care	242
Hail the day that sees him rise	277
I cannot tell	327
Immortal love, for ever full	350
Jesus shall reign	399
Lord, enthroned in heavenly splendour	453
Nada te turbe	523
O thou, who at thy Eucharist didst pray	579
Rejoice, the Lord is King	638
Son of God, eternal Saviour	667
Take this moment	688
The head that once was crowned with thorns	711

PENTECOST (WHIT SUNDAY) - A

All over the world	20
Breathe on me, Breath of God	87
Christians lift your hearts and voices	108
Colours of day	114
Come down, O Love divine	120
Come, gracious Spirit, heavenly Dove	122
Come, Holy Ghost, our souls inspire	124
Come, Holy Spirit, come	125
Come, thou Holy Spirit, come	139
Filled with the Spirit's power	184
Holy Spirit, come, confirm us	311
If you believe and I believe	344
Lord, the light of your love	479
May the fragrance of Jesus fill this place	504
O King, enthroned on high	557
O thou who camest from above	580

She sits like a bird	654
Spirit of God	672
Spirit of the living God (Armstrong)	674
Spirit of the living God (Iverson)	675
The Spirit lives to set us free	732
There's a spirit in the air	746
This is the day	759
Veni, lumen cordium	783

ORDINARY TIME

TRINITY SUNDAY - A

Christians, lift up your hearts	108
Father in heaven, how we love you	171
Father, Lord of all creation	172
Father most holy, merciful and loving	173
Father of heaven, whose love profound	174
Father, we adore you	176
Father, we love you	177
Filled with the Spirit's power	184
Holy, holy, holy is the Lord	309
Holy, holy, holy! Lord God almighty	310
How shall I sing that majesty	320
I bind unto myself today	326
Immortal, invisible, God only wise	349
Laudate Dominum	420
Lord, the light of your love	479
Majesty, worship his majesty	498
May the grace of Christ our Saviour	505
May the mind of Christ my Saviour	506
My God, how wonderful you are	516
O King, enthroned on high	557
Praise God from whom all blessings flow	618, 619
Sanctus, sanctus, sanctus	647
The God of Abraham praise	706
This day God gives me	754
Thou, whose almighty word	767
To God be the glory!	777
We give immortal praise	795
When I look into your holiness	818

DAY OF THANKSGIVING FOR HOLY COMMUNION

Thursday after Trinity Sunday (Corpus Christi) - for years A, B and C

Adoramus te, Domine	8
All for Jesus!	11
Alleluia, sing to Jesus	33
Author of life divine	55
Be still, for the presence of the Lord	62
Bread is blessed and broken	82
Bread of heaven, on thee we feed	83
Bread of the world in mercy broken	84

Day of Thanksgiving for Holy Communion

Broken for me	90
Deck thyself, my soul, with gladness	153
Draw nigh and take the body	157
Eat this bread	159
Father, we adore you	176
From glory to glory advancing	204
Glory be to Jesus	224
Glory, love, and praise, and honour	225
Hail, true body	281
Here in this place	302
Here, O my Lord	304
I am the bread of life	323
I come with joy	328
In bread we bring you, Lord	351
Jesu, thou joy of loving hearts	374
Jesus calls us here to meet him	378
Let all mortal flesh keep silence	424
Let us break bread together	431
Lord, enthroned in heavenly splendour	453
Lord Jesus Christ	463
My God, and is thy table spread	515
Now, my tongue, the mystery telling	531
O thou, who at thy Eucharist didst pray	579
Sanctus, sanctus, sanctus	647
Soul of my Saviour	670
Strengthen for service, Lord	680
Sweet sacrament divine	684
The Son of God proclaim	731
Thee we adore, O hidden Saviour, thee	737
We hail thy presence glorious	796
We pray thee, heavenly Father	803
Wherefore, O Father	826

PROPER 4 - A

All my hope on God is founded	19
And can it be	36
Bless the Lord, my soul	74
Christ is made the sure foundation	96
Christ is our cornerstone	97
City of God, how broad and far	111
Faithful One, so unchanging	165
Father, hear the prayer we offer	169
Have faith in God, my heart	290
Heaven shall not wait	297
O for a closer walk with God	539
Rock of ages	643
Sing of the Lord's goodness	663
The Lord is my light	719
The wise man	735
There's a wideness in God's mercy	747
Will you come and follow me	834

PROPER 5 - A

All I once held dear	16
At the name of Jesus	52
Christ's is the world	110
Follow me	189

For I'm building a people of power	193
How deep the Father's love for us	317
I believe in Jesus	325
Immortal love, for ever full	350
Jesus calls us: o'er the tumult	379
Jesus' love is very wonderful	393
Just as I am, without one plea	413
Love divine, all loves excelling	491
O Jesus, I have promised	556
O let the Son of God enfold you	558
O Lord, all the world belongs to you	560
O Lord, your tenderness	568
O worship the Lord in the beauty of holiness	583
One more step along the world I go	595
Purify my heart	631
Songs of praise the angels sang	668
Thanks to God whose word was spoken	698
The God of Abraham praise	706
There's a wideness in God's mercy	747
Thou, whose almighty word	767
What a friend we have in Jesus	811
When God almighty came to earth	814
When the music fades	823
Will you come and follow me	834

PROPER 6 - A

All I once held dear	16
All people that on earth do dwell	21
All that I am	24
City of God, how broad and far	111
Come down, O Love divine	120
Come, my Way, my Truth, my Life	131
For the fruits of his creation	197
Forth in the peace of Christ we go	200
From the sun's rising	210
God forgave my sin	237
God is working his purpose out	246
Here I am	301
I am a new creation	322
Jesus calls us here to meet him	378
Let all the world in every corner sing	425
Love divine, all loves excelling	491
Make way, make way	500
Morning glory, starlit sky	509
My God, how wonderful you are	516
O thou who camest from above	580
Peace is flowing like a river	613
Rejoice, the Lord is King	638
Thuma mina	771
We have a gospel to proclaim	798
Will you come and follow me	834
Ye that know the Lord is gracious	843

PROPER 7 - A

Bread of the world in mercy broken	84
Christ for the world we sing!	95

Come, ye faithful, raise the anthem	142
Do not be afraid	156
God is love: his the care	242
Great is the darkness	271
I am trusting thee, Lord Jesus	324
I'm not ashamed to own my Lord	347
In Christ alone	352
Lead, kindly light	421
Lord, for the years	454
My God, accept my heart this day	514
Nada te turbe	523
Now is eternal life	529
Now let us from this table rise	530
O for a heart to praise my God	540
Oft in danger, oft in woe	585
Praise, my soul, the King of heaven	623
Take my life, and let it be	687
Take up thy cross, the Saviour said	689
Teach me to dance	691
The strife is o'er, the battle done	733
There are hundreds of sparrows	738
When God almighty came to earth	814

PROPER 8 - A

And now, O Father, mindful of the love	38
Brother, sister, let me serve you	91
Colours of day	114
Father, I place into your hands	170
God forgave my sin	237
God has spoken – by the prophets	238
God moves in a mysterious way	247
I come with joy	328
I will offer up my life	339
Jesu, Jesu, fill us with your love	368
Jesus, stand among us	401
O for a heart to praise my God	540
O Lord, all the world belongs to you	560
Stand up, stand up for Jesus	677
Strengthen for service, Lord	680
Such love	681
Take my life, and let it be	687
Take up thy cross, the Saviour said	689
Thank you for saving me	693
Thanks be to God	696
The God of Abraham praise	706
To be in your presence	776
We have a gospel to proclaim	798
We'll walk the land	809
When I needed a neighbour	819
Ye servants of God	841

PROPER 9 - A

All you who seek a comfort sure	28
Alleluia, sing to Jesus	33
Amazing grace	34
Be bold, be strong	60
Be still and know that I am God	61

Proper 9 - A

Be thou my vision	66
Beauty for brokenness	67
Forth in thy name, O Lord, I go	201
Give thanks with a grateful heart	219
God forgave my sin	237
Happy are they, they that love God	285
Have faith in God, my heart	290
How sweet the name of Jesus sounds	321
I cannot tell	327
I danced in the morning	329
I heard the voice of Jesus say	334
Jesu, lover of my soul	369
Jesus, remember me	398
Just as I am, without one plea	413
Meekness and majesty	507
O my Saviour, lifted from the earth	572
Sing of the Lord's goodness	663
Thanks be to God	696
The King is among us	714
The strife is o'er, the battle done	733
We cannot measure	792
We will lay our burden down	808
What a friend we have in Jesus	811
You laid aside your majesty	850

PROPER 10 - A

All I once held dear	16
Alleluia, alleluia, give thanks to the risen Lord	31
As the deer pants for the water	43
Before the throne	70
Come, ye thankful people, come	144
Father of heaven, whose love profound	174
Give to our God immortal praise	220
God is working his purpose out	246
I am a new creation	322
I'm accepted, I'm forgiven	345
In Christ alone	352
Jesus lives! thy terrors now	390
Lord, thy word abideth	481
Morning has broken	510
O for a thousand tongues to sing	541
Open our eyes, Lord	600
Over the mountains and the sea	611
Praise we now the word of grace	629
Rise and hear! The Lord is speaking	641
To God be the glory!	777
We give immortal praise	795
We have a gospel to proclaim	798
You shall go out with joy	853

PROPER 11 - A

Abba, Father, let me be	5
As Jacob with travel was weary one day	41
As the deer pants for the water	43
Blessèd assurance	75
Come and see	118
Come, ye thankful people, come	144

Father God, I wonder	168
Fight the good fight	181
For all the saints	190
God forgave my sin	237
God's Spirit is in my heart	262
Happy are they, they that love God	285
Heaven shall not wait	297
Holy Spirit, come, confirm us	311
How deep the Father's love for us	317
In heavenly love abiding	355
In the Cross of Christ I glory	358
Lord, the light of your love	479
May the grace of Christ our Saviour	505
O God you search me	549
O Lord, my God	563
The King is among us	714
The Lord is my light	719
The Spirit lives to set us free	732

PROPER 12 - A

All over the world	20
Father, I place into your hands	170
God is good, God is great	240
God is love: his the care	242
God is love: let heaven adore him	243
God moves in a mysterious way	247
Gracious Spirit, Holy Ghost	268
Hail to the Lord's anointed	280
If you believe and I believe	344
Jesus is King	386
Lord, teach us how to pray aright	478
Lord, thy word abideth	481
New every morning is the love	526
Now is eternal life	529
O for a heart to praise my God	540
O Lord, my God	563
Oft in danger, oft in woe	585
Praise God from whom all blessings flow	618, 619
Seek ye first	652
Teach me, my God and King	690
The kingdom is upon you!	716
Thou art the Way: by thee alone	765

PROPER 13 - A

5000 + hungry folk	188
Alleluia, sing to Jesus	33
As the deer pants for the water	43
Bread of heaven, on thee we feed	83
Break thou the bread	86
Broken for me	90
Come, O thou traveller unknown	134
Eat this bread	159
Gather around, for the table is spread	213
Guide me, O thou great Redeemer	275
I, the Lord of sea and sky	337
In the Lord I'll be ever thankful	360
Jesus the Lord said: 'I am the Bread'	403
Let all mortal flesh keep silence	424
Let us break bread together	431

Let us praise God together	433
Longing for light	452
Not far beyond the sea	528
O God, unseen but ever near	548
Praise, my soul, the King of heaven	623
Restore, O Lord	639
The God of Abraham praise	706
When I needed a neighbour	819

PROPER 14 - A

At the name of Jesus	52
Calm me, Lord	92
Christ is the world's Light	100
Dear Lord and Father of mankind	152
Do not be afraid	156
Eternal Father, strong to save	160
Go forth and tell	232
Guide me, O thou great Redeemer	275
Have faith in God, my heart	290
How sweet the name of Jesus sounds	321
I'm not ashamed to own my Lord	347
Jesu, the very thought of thee	373
Jesus calls us: o'er the tumult	379
Just as I am, without one plea	413
Lead us, heavenly Father, lead us	422
Nada te turbe	523
Name of all majesty	524
Not far beyond the sea	528
Peace is flowing like a river	613
Saviour, again to thy dear name we raise	648
Sweet sacrament divine	684
To the name of our salvation	779
When the music fades	823
Wide, wide as the ocean	833
Will your anchor hold	835

PROPER 15 - A

All hail the power of Jesus' name	14
And can it be	36
Bind us together, Lord	73
Bless the Lord, my soul	74
Christ is made the sure foundation	96
From the sun's rising	210
Glory to God above	228
God is love: his the care	242
God is love: let heaven adore him	243
God of mercy, God of grace	251
He's got the whole world in his hand	306
Immortal love, for ever full	350
In Christ there is no east or west	353
It is a thing most wonderful	364
Jesus is Lord! Creation's voice proclaims it	387
Jesus shall reign	399
Let all the world in every corner sing	425
Let everything that has breath	426
Let us, with a gladsome mind	435
Lord of life	473
Lord, the light of your love	479
O Holy Spirit, Lord of grace	554

Proper 15 - A

O Lord, all the world belongs
  to you   560
There's a wideness in God's mercy 747
Thine arm, O Lord, in days of old 750
To be in your presence   776
We have a gospel to proclaim   798
You are the King of Glory   849

PROPER 16 - A

Amazing grace   34
And can it be   36
As we are gathered   45
Bind us together, Lord   73
Firmly I believe and truly   186
For I'm building a people of
  power   193
God moves in a mysterious way 247
He is Lord   294
Help us to help each other, Lord 299
Holy Spirit, come, confirm us   311
I am the bread of life   323
I believe in Jesus   325
I will offer up my life   339
Jesus shall take the highest
  honour   400
Jesus, where'er thy people meet 407
Laudate Dominum   420
Let us talents and tongues employ 434
O Lord, my God   563
O thou who camest from above   580
One more step along the world
  I go   595
Praise, my soul, the King of
  heaven   623
Take my life, and let it be   687
Tell out, my soul   692
The God of Abraham praise   706
The Lord is my light   719
Thou art the Christ, O Lord   764
Wide, wide as the ocean   833

PROPER 17 - A

All who would valiant be   27
As the deer pants for the water   43
Be still, for the presence of the Lord 62
Beneath the cross of Jesus   72
Brother, sister, let me serve you 91
Christ's is the world   110
Father, hear the prayer we offer 169
Father, Lord of all creation   172
Follow me   189
Gracious Spirit, Holy Ghost   268
Happy are they, they that love
  God   285
He is Lord   294
Holy Spirit, truth divine   312
I, the Lord of sea and sky   337
Jesus Christ is waiting   382
Jesus is Lord! Creation's voice
  proclaims it   387
Jesus, Lord, we look to thee   391
Jesus' love is very wonderful   393
Love divine, all loves excelling   491
O Lord, your tenderness   568

Once, only once, and once for all 593
Take my life, and let it be   687
Take up thy cross, the Saviour
  said   689
Teach me, my God and King   690
Thank you, Lord   695
The head that once was crowned
  with thorns   711
There is a Redeemer   743
Thou art the Christ, O Lord   764
Thuma mina   771

PROPER 18 - A

As we are gathered   45
Awake, awake: fling off the night 56
Christ be with me   94
Dear Lord and Father of mankind 152
Father God, I wonder   168
For the fruits of his creation   197
For the healing of the nations   198
Forgive our sins as we forgive   199
God is working his purpose out   246
Hark! A herald voice is calling   286
Here in this place   302
In bread we bring you, Lord   351
Jesus calls us here to meet him   378
Jesus, where'er thy people meet 407
Let there be love   430
Lord, the light of your love   479
O day of God, draw nigh   537
O God of earth and altar   546
O Lord, your tenderness   568
Only by grace   598
Such love   681
Teach me to dance   691
The King is among us   714
Thy kingdom come, O God   774
Ubi caritas   781
When I needed a neighbour   819
Ye servants of the Lord   842

PROPER 19 - A

Amazing grace   34
And can it be   36
At the name of Jesus   52
Bless the Lord, my soul   74
Brother, sister, let me serve you 91
Dear Lord and Father of mankind 152
Father of heaven, whose love
  profound   174
Forgive our sins as we forgive   199
God forgave my sin   237
God is love: let heaven adore him 243
Great is thy faithfulness   273
How deep the Father's love for us 317
I have a friend   333
I heard the voice of Jesus say   334
I'm accepted, I'm forgiven   345
Jesus lives! thy terrors now   390
Jesus, where'er thy people meet 407
Just as I am, without one plea   413
Lead us, heavenly Father, lead us 422
Make me a channel of your peace 499
O God, our help in ages past   547
O Lord, all the world belongs
  to you   560

Praise, my soul, the King of
  heaven   623
Purify my heart   631
Rock of ages   643
Take this moment   688
There's a wideness in God's mercy 747
Through the night of doubt and
  sorrow   770
When I survey the wondrous
  cross   820

PROPER 20 - A

Amazing grace   34
Bread of heaven, on thee we feed 83
Christ's is the world   110
Fight the good fight   181
For the healing of the nations   198
Forth in the peace of Christ we go 200
Forth in thy name, O Lord, I go 201
From heaven you came   205
God is love: his the care   242
God of life, God of love   249
God, whose farm is all creation 260
Great is thy faithfulness   273
Guide me, O thou great
  Redeemer   275
In the Lord I'll be ever thankful 360
Jesu, the very thought of thee   373
Jesus lives! thy terrors now   390
Lead us, heavenly Father, lead us 422
Lord, enthroned in heavenly
  splendour   453
Lord, for the years   454
Lord, today your voice is calling 482
Make me a channel of your peace 499
May the mind of Christ my
  Saviour   506
Nada te turbe   523
O Lord, all the world belongs
  to you   560
O Lord, hear my prayer   561
Praise to the Holiest   627
Seek ye first   652
Such love   681
Take my life, and let it be   687
The Lord is King!   718
Through all the changing scenes
  of life   769
When I look into your holiness   818
With joy we meditate the grace   836

PROPER 21 - A

All hail the power of Jesus' name 14
All praise to thee   23
And can it be   36
Christ triumphant   103
Christ's is the world   110
Crown him with many crowns   150
God is here! As we his people   241
God is our strength from days
  of old   244
Guide me, O thou great
  Redeemer   275
Heaven shall not wait   297
Help us to help each other, Lord 299

Proper 21 - A

I will offer up my life 339
Jesus is Lord! Creation's voice
  proclaims it 387
Jesus is the name we honour 388
Jesus, remember me 398
Jesus shall take the highest honour 400
Lord Jesus Christ 463
May the mind of Christ my
  Saviour 506
Meekness and majesty 507
O Jesus, I have promised 556
O Lord, all the world belongs
  to you 560
O Lord, my God 563
On Jordan's bank the Baptist's cry 589
Purify my heart 631
Rejoice, the Lord is King 638
Rock of ages 643
The Spirit lives to set us free 732
There is a Redeemer 743
We are marching 789
You laid aside your majesty 850

PROPER 22 - A

Ah, holy Jesu, how hast thou
  offended 9
Christ be with me 94
Christ is made the sure foundation 96
Christ is our cornerstone 97
Come and celebrate 116
Come and see the shining hope 118
Fight the good fight 181
For the fruits of his creation 197
God of life, God of love 249
God, whose farm is all creation 260
I danced in the morning 329
I, the Lord of sea and sky 337
I will offer up my life 339
It is a thing most wonderful 364
Jesu, the very thought of thee 373
Jesu, thou joy of loving hearts 374
Love divine, all loves excelling 491
My Lord, what love is this 520
My song is love unknown 521
O, how good is the Lord 555
O Lord, hear my prayer 561
Praise to the Holiest 627
Thank you, Lord 695
The head that once was crowned
  with thorns 711
To be in your presence 776
Ubi caritas 781
We have a gospel to proclaim 798
We sing the praise of him who
  died 804
When I survey the wondrous cross 820

PROPER 23 - A

Bread of heaven, on thee we feed 83
Dear Lord and Father of mankind 152
Eat this bread 159
Faithful Shepherd, feed me 166
From glory to glory advancing 204
Give thanks with a grateful heart 219

How bright these glorious spirits
  shine! 316
I come with joy 328
Jesu, lover of my soul 369
Joy to the world! 409
Jubilate, everybody 410
Light's abode, celestial Salem 442
Like a mighty river flowing 445
My God, and is thy table spread 515
Put thou thy trust in God 634
Rejoice in the Lord always 636
Rejoice, the Lord is King 638
The King is among us 714
There's a place where the streets
  shine 744
This is my body 755
What a friend we have in Jesus 811
Wide, wide as the ocean 833
Ye watchers and ye holy ones 844

PROPER 24 - A

Abba, Father, let me be 5
Adoramus te, Domine 8
All my hope on God is founded 19
Bless the Lord, my soul 74
Christ is the King! 99
City of God, how broad and far 111
Give to our God immortal praise 220
Glorious things of thee are spoken 223
Great is the Lord and most worthy
  of praise 272
Great is thy faithfulness 273
He's got the whole world in his
  hand 306
I will offer up my life 339
Immortal, invisible, God only
  wise 349
Jesus shall reign 399
Judge eternal, throned in
  splendour 411
Lord, I lift your name on high 461
Nada te turbe 523
Name of all majesty 524
O Lord, all the world belongs to
  you 560
Over the mountains and the sea 611
Praise to the Lord, the Almighty 628
Rejoice, O land, in God thy
  might 637
Rejoice, the Lord is King 638
Take my life, and let it be 687
The Lord is King! 718
Thou, whose almighty word 767
To God be the glory! 777
We have a gospel to proclaim 798

PROPER 25 - A

A new commandment 4
All who would valiant be 27
Be thou my vision 66
Bind us together, Lord 73
Brother, sister, let me serve you 91
Christ's is the world 110
Come down, O Love divine 120
Father of heaven, whose love
  profound 174

For the healing of the nations 198
God's love is deeper 261
Hail to the Lord's anointed 280
How deep the Father's love for us 317
Jesu, Jesu, fill us with your love 368
Lead us, heavenly Father, lead us 422
Let there be love 430
Lord of all being 466
Love is his word 492
Make me a channel of your peace 499
O Jesus, I have promised 556
O thou who camest from above 580
Put thou thy trust in God 634
Take my life, and let it be 687
There is a land of pure delight 741
Through all the changing scenes
  of life 769
Through the night of doubt and
  sorrow 770
Thy hand, O God, has guided 772
Ubi caritas 781

Or: BIBLE SUNDAY - A

All for Jesus! 11
Angel-voices ever singing 40
Christ is the King! 99
Come down, O Love divine 120
God has spoken – by the prophets 238
Hark, my soul, it is the Lord 287
Help us, O Lord, to learn 298
I cannot tell 327
Let all the world in every corner
  sing 425
Lord, thy word abideth 481
May the mind of Christ my
  Saviour 506
Rejoice, the Lord is King 638
Rise and hear! The Lord is
  speaking` 641
Seek ye first 652
Songs of praise the angels sang 668
The Lord is my light 719
The prophets spoke in days of old 728
Thou, whose almighty word 767
You shall go out with joy 853

DEDICATION FESTIVAL - A

Adoramus te, Domine 8
Angel-voices ever singing 40
Be still, for the presence of the
  Lord 62
Be thou my vision 66
Blessèd city, heavenly Salem 77
Christ is made the sure foundation 96
Christ is our cornerstone 97
Christ is the world's Light 100
City of God, how broad and far 111
Father, Lord of all creation 172
For I'm building a people of
  power 193
Forth in the peace of Christ we go 200
Forth in thy name, O Lord, I go 201
Give me joy in my heart 215
Glorious things of thee are spoken 223
Glory be to Jesus 224

Dedication Festival - A

God is here! As we his people	241
Here in this place	302
Holy, holy, holy! Lord God almighty	310
Hosanna, hosanna	314
In our day of thanksgiving	356
Jesus Christ is waiting	382
Jesus, where'er thy people meet	407
Let us build a house	432
Lord, enthroned in heavenly splendour	453
Lord, for the years	454
Lord of life	473
My song is love unknown	521
O God of Bethel, by whose hand	545
The Church's one foundation	702
Thy hand, O God, has guided	772
To be in your presence	776
We bow down	791
We have a gospel to proclaim	798
We love the place, O God	800
Ye that know the Lord is gracious	843
You are the King of Glory	849

ALL SAINTS' DAY - A

All heaven declares	15
All praise to our redeeming Lord	22
All who would valiant be	27
As we are gathered	45
As your family, Lord	47
At the Lamb's high feast we sing	51
Blessèd assurance	75
Blest are the pure in heart	79
Bright the vision that delighted	88
Fill your hearts with joy and gladness	183
For all the saints	190
For all thy saints, O Lord	191
From the falter of breath	208
Give us the wings of faith	221
Glory to thee, O God	230
Help us, O Lord, to learn	298
How shall I sing that majesty	320
How sweet the name of Jesus sounds	321
In the Lord I'll be ever thankful	360
Jesus, be the centre	376
Let saints on earth in concert sing	428
Lord, the light of your love	479
Make me a channel of your peace	499
Make way, make way	500
O when the saints go marching in	581
Only by grace	598
Rejoice in God's saints	635
Saint Luke, beloved physician	645
Seek ye first	652
The Church's one foundation	702
The kingdom of heaven	717
The Lord is my light	719
Thee we adore, O hidden Saviour, thee	737
There is a land of pure delight	741
Through all the changing scenes of life	769

When I look into your holiness	818
Who are these like stars appearing	828
Ye servants of God	841
Ye watchers and ye holy ones	844

FOURTH SUNDAY BEFORE ADVENT - A

All my hope on God is founded	19
At the name of Jesus	52
Blest are the pure in heart	79
Brother, sister, let me serve you	91
God has spoken – by the prophets	238
Great is the darkness	271
Heaven shall not wait	297
He's got the whole world in his hand	306
If you believe and I believe	344
Jesu, Jesu, fill us with your love	368
Jesus, Lord, we look to thee	391
Jesus, where'er thy people meet	407
Judge eternal, throned in splendour	411
Lo, he comes with clouds descending	449
Lord of all hopefulness	467
Love divine, all loves excelling	491
My God, how wonderful you are	516
O Jesus, I have promised	556
The Church's one foundation	702
There's a wideness in God's mercy	747
Thy kingdom come, O God	774
We are marching	789
We have a gospel to proclaim	798
When God almighty came to earth	814
Who can sound the depths of sorrow	829
Within our darkest night	837
Ye servants of God	841
You are the King of Glory	849

THIRD SUNDAY BEFORE ADVENT - A

As the deer pants for the water	43
Awake, awake: fling off the night	56
Be thou my vision	66
Great is thy faithfulness	273
Here, O my Lord	304
Jesus bids us shine	377
Let saints on earth in concert sing	428
Love divine, all loves excelling	491
O for a closer walk with God	539
O worship the Lord in the beauty of holiness	583
Peace is flowing like a river	613
Rejoice, the Lord is King	638
Spirit of the living God (Iverson)	675
The Lord will come and not be slow	722
These are the days	748
This little light of mine	762
Thy hand, O God, has guided	772
Veni, lumen cordium	783
Wake, O wake! with tidings thrilling	786

We are marching	789
Will you come and follow me	834

SECOND SUNDAY BEFORE ADVENT - A

All that I am	24
Be still, for the presence of the Lord	62
Be thou my guardian and my guide	65
Father, I place into your hands	170
For the healing of the nations	198
From heaven you came	205
Great is the darkness	271
Help us to help each other, Lord	299
I will offer up my life	339
Jesus lives! thy terrors now	390
Lead us, heavenly Father, lead us	422
Let us talents and tongues employ	434
Lord, I come to you	458
Make me a channel of your peace	499
O God, our help in ages past	547
O Lord, my God	563
One is the body	594
Seek ye first	652
Take my hands, Lord	686
Take my life, and let it be	687
Take this moment	688
There are hundreds of sparrows	738
There's a place where the streets shine	744
Through the night of doubt and sorrow	770
Wait for the Lord	785

CHRIST THE KING - A

Alleluia, sing to Jesus	33
At the name of Jesus	52
Beauty for brokenness	67
Brother, sister, let me serve you	91
Christ triumphant	103
Crown him with many crowns	150
From heaven you came	205
Great is the Lord and most worthy of praise	272
Hail the day that sees him rise	277
He is Lord	294
In Christ there is no east or west	353
Inspired by love and anger	362
Jesus Christ is waiting	382
Jesus, remember me	398
Jesus, the name high over all	404
Lord, enthroned in heavenly splendour	453
Make way, make way	500
Meekness and majesty	507
My Jesus, my Saviour	519
O King, enthroned on high	557
O worship the King	582
Rejoice, the Lord is King	638
Son of God, eternal Saviour	667
The head that once was crowned with thorns	711
The King of love my shepherd is	715
The kingdom is upon you!	716
Thy kingdom come, O God	774
When I needed a neighbour	819

YEAR B

ADVENT

FIRST SUNDAY OF ADVENT - B
All for Jesus! 11
Awake, awake: fling off the night 56
Be still and know that I am God 61
Come, thou long-expected Jesus 140
Faithful One, so unchanging 165
God is love: his the care 242
Guide me, O thou great
  Redeemer 275
Hail to the Lord's anointed 280
Hark! A herald voice is calling 286
Jesus bids us shine 377
Lo, he comes with clouds
  descending 449
Lord, I come before your throne
  of grace 457
Make way, make way 500
O come, O come, Emmanuel 535
Restore, O Lord 639
Songs of praise the angels sang 668
The advent of our King 699
The Lord will come and not be
  slow 722
Thou didst leave thy throne 766
Wait for the Lord 785
Wake, O wake! with tidings
  thrilling 786
Will your anchor hold 835
Ye servants of the Lord 842

SECOND SUNDAY OF
ADVENT - B
Christ, when for us you were
  baptised 104
Come, thou long-expected Jesus 140
Father, we adore you 176
Great is the darkness 271
Hail to the Lord's anointed 280
Hark! A herald voice is calling 286
Hills of the north, rejoice 307
Jesus bids us shine 377
Judge eternal, throned in
  splendour 411
Long ago, prophets knew 451
Love divine, all loves excelling 491
Make me a channel of your peace 499
Make way, make way 500
Nada te turbe 523
O comfort my people 536
O God, our help in ages past 547
On Jordan's bank the Baptist's cry 589
Thuma mina 771
When Jesus came to Jordan 821
Ye servants of the Lord 842

THIRD SUNDAY OF ADVENT - B
Be thou my vision 66
Give me joy in my heart 215
God is working his purpose out 246
Hail to the Lord's anointed 280
Hark! A herald voice is calling 286
Hark, the glad sound! 288
Heaven shall not wait 297

How lovely on the mountains 319
I, the Lord of sea and sky 337
Jesus' love is very wonderful 393
Jesus, remember me 398
Jesus shall reign 399
Jesus, stand among us 401
Lord, the light of your love 479
Magnificat 497
O thou who camest from above 580
On Jordan's bank the Baptist's cry 589
Rejoice in the Lord always 636
Restore, O Lord 639
Tell out, my soul 692
The people that in darkness sat 727
Thou, whose almighty word 767
Thy kingdom come, O God 774
Wait for the Lord 785

FOURTH SUNDAY OF
ADVENT - B
Amazing grace 34
At the name of Jesus 52
Away in a manger 59
Come, thou long-expected Jesus 140
For Mary, mother of our Lord 194
Hark, the glad sound! 288
Jesus, Name above all names 395
Jesus, the name high over all 404
Long ago, prophets knew 451
Magnificat 497
May the mind of Christ my
  Saviour 506
Of the Father's love begotten 584
Tell out, my soul 692
The angel Gabriel from heaven
  came 700
The God whom earth and sea
  and sky 708
Thou didst leave thy throne 766
Thy kingdom come, O God 774
To the name of our salvation 779
Ye who own the faith of Jesus 845

CHRISTMAS
CHRISTMAS EVE - see YEAR A

CHRISTMAS DAY - see YEAR A

FIRST SUNDAY OF
CHRISTMAS - B
Abba, Father, let me be 5
Alleluia (x 8) 29
Angel-voices ever singing 40
Behold, the great Creator 71
It came upon the midnight clear 363
Joy to the world! 409
Let us praise God together 433
New songs of celebration render 527
O come, all ye faithful 534
O praise ye the Lord! 574
Once in royal David's city 592
Praise, my soul, the King of
  heaven 623
Praise the Lord, ye heavens,
  adore him 625

Thou didst leave thy throne 766
Ye holy angels bright 840

SECOND SUNDAY OF
CHRISTMAS - see YEAR A

EPIPHANY
THE EPIPHANY - see YEAR A

THE BAPTISM OF CHRIST - B
Be thou my vision 66
Breathe on me, Breath of God 87
Christ, when for us you were
  baptised 104
Come down, O Love divine 120
Come, gracious Spirit, heavenly
  Dove 122
Crown him with many crowns 150
Father, we adore you 176
Glory to God (Peruvian Gloria) 226
God forgave my sin 237
Hail to the Lord's anointed 280
Have you heard the raindrops 291
Just as I am, without one plea 413
Let everything that has breath 426
O let the Son of God enfold you 558
O love, how deep, how broad,
  how high 570
On Jordan's bank the Baptist's cry 589
Songs of thankfulness and praise 669
Spirit of the living God
  (Armstrong) 674
Spirit of the living God (Iverson) 675
Take this moment 688
The King is among us 714
The people that in darkness sat 727
To the name of our salvation 779
When Jesus came to Jordan 821

SECOND SUNDAY OF
EPIPHANY - B
All heaven declares 15
All my days 18
Alleluia, sing to Jesus 33
Be still and know that I am God 61
Be thou my vision 66
Bright the vision that delighted 88
Come and see the shining hope 119
Come, let us join our cheerful
  songs 127
Forth in the peace of Christ we go 200
I cannot tell 327
I come with joy 328
I, the Lord of sea and sky 337
I will offer up my life 339
In Christ alone 352
Jesus calls us: o'er the tumult 379
Just as I am, without one plea 413
Lord, enthroned in heavenly
  splendour 453
O worship the King 582
The Lord is my light 719
There is a Redeemer 743
When God almighty came to
  earth 814

Second Sunday of Epiphany - B
Will you come and follow me 834
Ye holy angels bright 840
You are the King of Glory 849

**THIRD SUNDAY OF
EPIPHANY - B**
All hail the power of Jesus' name 14
Alleluia, sing to Jesus 33
Amazing grace 34
At the Lamb's high feast we sing 51
Come on and celebrate 135
Dear Lord and Father of mankind 152
Deck thyself, my soul, with
gladness 153
Forth in the peace of Christ we go 200
Give me joy in my heart 215
Hail to the Lord's anointed 280
How sweet the name of Jesus
sounds 321
I come with joy 328
I will worship 341
Jesus calls us: o'er the tumult 379
Jesus Christ is waiting 382
Jesus, Lord, we pray 392
Jesus' love is very wonderful 393
Jesus, lover of my soul 369
Let all mortal flesh keep silence 424
Life for the poor was hard and
tough 436
Nada te turbe 523
Rejoice, the Lord is King 638
Songs of thankfulness and praise 669
Take up thy cross, the Saviour said 689
The Lord is King! 718
The people that in darkness sat 727
There's a place where the streets
shine 744
This is my desire 756
When God almighty came to
earth 814
When the music fades 823

**FOURTH SUNDAY OF
EPIPHANY - B**
At the name of Jesus 52
Be still, for the presence of the
Lord 62
Christ is our cornerstone 97
Father of heaven, whose love
profound 174
Firmly I believe and truly 186
Give thanks with a grateful heart 219
Hail to the Lord's anointed 280
He's got the whole world in his
hand 306
How sweet the name of Jesus
sounds 321
I give you all the honour 331
Jesus Christ is waiting 382
Jesus shall reign 399
Jesus, the name high over all 404
Judge eternal, throned in
splendour 411
King of glory, King of peace 416
Kum ba yah 419

O for a thousand tongues to sing 541
Son of God, eternal Saviour 667
The kingdom is upon you! 716
The people that in darkness sat 727
There is a Redeemer 743
Thine arm, O Lord, in days of old 750
Thy kingdom come, O God 774

**THE PRESENTATION OF CHRIST
IN THE TEMPLE - see YEAR A**

ORDINARY TIME
PROPER 1 - B
At even, ere the sun was set 49
Be still and know that I am God 61
Be still, for the presence of the
Lord 62
Christ's is the world 110
Come, wounded healer 141
Father, I place into your hands 170
Give thanks with a grateful heart 219
Go forth and tell 232
God is love: his the care 242
God is love: let heaven adore him 243
God to enfold you 258
God's Spirit is in my heart 262
Here in this place 302
Immortal love, for ever full 350
Jesus, the name high over all 404
Lord, I come to you 458
O, how good is the Lord 555
Seek ye first 652
Thine arm, O Lord, in days of old 750
We cannot measure 792
We have a gospel to proclaim 798

PROPER 2 - B
A man there lived in Galilee 3
Bless the Lord, my soul 74
Fight the good fight 181
God forgave my sin 237
Here is bread 303
Inspired by love and anger 362
Jesu, lover of my soul 369
O let the Son of God enfold you 558
Purify my heart 631
Thank you, Lord 695
Thine arm, O Lord, in days of
old 750
Thou, whose almighty word 767
We cannot measure 792
What a friend we have in Jesus 811
When I feel the touch 817
Will you come and follow me 834

PROPER 3 - B
Dear Lord and Father of mankind 152
Father of heaven, whose love
profound 174
Give me joy in my heart 215
Give thanks with a grateful heart 219
Praise, my soul, the King of
heaven 623
Rise and hear! The Lord is
speaking 641

Through the night of doubt
and sorrow 770

**SECOND SUNDAY BEFORE
LENT - B**
Adoramus te, Domine 8
All creatures of our God and King 10
At the name of Jesus 52
Christ be with me 94
Christ is the world's Light 100
Christ triumphant 103
Christ's is the world 110
Father of heaven, whose love
profound 174
God is our strength from days
of old 244
I am a new creation 322
I believe in Jesus 325
If I were a butterfly 342
Immortal, invisible, God only
wise 349
Jesus is Lord! Creation's voice
proclaims it 387
Jesus shall take the highest honour 400
Let everything that has breath 426
Lord of beauty, thine the
splendour 470
Lord, the light of your love 479
Praise to the Holiest 627
The Lord is my light 719
There is a Redeemer 743
Think of a world without any
flowers 753
Thou, whose almighty word 767
To the name of our salvation 779

**SUNDAY NEXT BEFORE
LENT - B**
Adoramus te, Domine 8
And can it be 36
At the name of Jesus 52
Be still, for the presence of the
Lord 62
Be thou my vision 66
Christ, whose glory fills the skies 105
Father of heaven, whose love
profound 174
God is love: his the care 242
God of mercy, God of grace 251
Hail to the Lord's anointed 280
He is exalted 293
Jesus calls us here to meet him 378
Jesus calls us: o'er the tumult 379
Lord Jesus Christ 463
Majesty, worship his majesty 498
Meekness and majesty 507
My God, how wonderful you are 516
Name of all majesty 524
Sing to God a song of glory 665
Thee we adore, O hidden Saviour,
thee 737
'Tis good, Lord, to be here 775
We have a gospel to proclaim 798
You, living Christ, our eyes
behold 851

LENT

ASH WEDNESDAY - *see* YEAR A

FIRST SUNDAY OF LENT - B

And can it be 36
As the deer pants for the water 43
Be thou my guardian and my guide 65
Father, hear the prayer we offer 169
Father welcomes all his children 179
Forgive our sins as we forgive 199
Forty days and forty nights 202
Give thanks to the Lord 218
God forgave my sin 237
I bind unto myself today 326
Jesu, lover of my soul 369
Just as I am, without one plea 413
Lead us, heavenly Father, lead us 422
Lord Jesus, think on me 465
Nada te turbe 523
O Jesus, I have promised 556
O let the Son of God enfold you 558
O love, how deep, how broad,
  how high 570
Purify my heart 631
Songs of thankfulness and praise 669
Take this moment 688

SECOND SUNDAY OF LENT - B

And can it be 36
At the name of Jesus 52
Be thou my guardian and my guide 65
Beneath the cross of Jesus 72
Follow me 189
I, the Lord of sea and sky 337
I'm not ashamed to own my Lord 347
In the Cross of Christ I glory 358
Jesu, grant me this, I pray 367
Jesu, lover of my soul 369
Jesus calls us: o'er the tumult 379
Jesus Christ 380
Lord Jesus, think on me 465
My faith looks up to thee 512
New every morning is the love 526
Take my life, and let it be 687
Take up thy cross, the Saviour
  said 689
The God of Abraham praise 706
Thuma mina 771
Will you come and follow me 834

THIRD SUNDAY OF LENT - B

All my hope on God is founded 19
Be thou my vision 66
Before the throne 70
Beneath the cross of Jesus 72
Bless the Lord, my soul 74
Christ is our cornerstone 97
Father, hear the prayer we offer 169
Father, Lord of all creation 172
God of grace and God of glory 248
How deep the Father's love for us 317
In the Cross of Christ I glory 358
Inspired by love and anger 362
Jesus Christ 380
Jesus Christ is waiting 382

Lift high the Cross 437
Lord, thy word abideth 481
Take up thy cross, the Saviour said 689
Thou art the Way: by thee alone 765
We love the place, O God 800
We sing the praise of him who
  died 804

FOURTH SUNDAY OF LENT - B

All hail the power of Jesus' name 14
Amazing grace 34
And can it be 36
Bread of heaven, on thee we feed 83
From heaven you came 205
How deep the Father's love for us 317
I will sing the wondrous story 340
In heavenly love abiding 355
It is a thing most wonderful 364
May the grace of Christ our
  Saviour 505
My faith looks up to thee 512
Name of all majesty 524
Now thank we all our God 532
O my Saviour, lifted from the
  earth 572
Only by grace 598
Praise to the Holiest 627
Rock of ages 643
Sing, my tongue, the glorious
  battle 662
The King of love my shepherd is 715
We will lay our burden down 808

Or: MOTHERING SUNDAY – *see* YEAR A

FIFTH SUNDAY OF LENT - B

A man there lived in Galilee 3
From heaven you came 205
How deep the Father's love for us 317
It is a thing most wonderful 364
Jesu, lover of my soul 369
Jesus' love is very wonderful 393
Lead us, heavenly Father, lead us 422
Lift high the Cross 437
Meekness and majesty 507
My Lord, what love is this 520
My song is love unknown 521
Now the green blade riseth 533
O Jesus, I have promised 556
O my Saviour, lifted from the
  earth 572
Push, little seed 632
Sing, my tongue, the glorious
  battle 662
Such love 681
The royal banners forward go 729
There is a Redeemer 743
When I survey the wondrous cross 820
Will you come and follow me 834
With joy we meditate the grace 836

PALM SUNDAY - B
Liturgy of the Palms

All glory, laud and honour 12

All praise to thee 23
Christ is made the sure foundation 96
Come, now is the time to worship 132
Confitemini Domino 145
Give me joy in my heart 215
Hosanna, hosanna 314
Jesus is the name we honour 388
Lift up your heads 438
Make way, make way 500
My song is love unknown 521
One whose heart is hard as steel 597
Praise to the Holiest 627
Ride on, ride on in majesty 640
Thanks be to God 696
The royal banners forward go 729
This is the day the Lord has made 760
We have a King who rides a
  donkey 799
You are the King of Glory 849
You laid aside your majesty 850

Liturgy of the Passion

Ah, holy Jesu, how hast thou
  offended 9
All you who seek a comfort sure 28
An upper room did our Lord
  prepare 35
And can it be 36
And now, O Father, mindful of the
  love 38
At the cross she keeps her station 50
At the name of Jesus 52
Be still, for the presence of the
  Lord 62
Be thou my guardian and my
  guide 65
Beneath the cross of Jesus 72
Blest are the pure in heart 79
Broken for me 90
Christ triumphant 103
Come and see 119
Come, wounded healer 141
For all the saints 190
From heaven you came 205
Glory be to Jesus 224
God is our strength from days
  of old 244
Hail thou once despisèd Jesus 278
Happy are they, they that love
  God 285
Help us to help each other, Lord 299
Here is bread 303
How deep the Father's love for us 317
I cannot tell 327
I will sing the wondrous story 340
In the Cross of Christ I glory 358
It is a thing most wonderful 364
Jesu, grant me this, I pray 367
Jesus Christ 380
Jesus, Name above all names 395
Jesus, remember me 398
Jesus shall take the highest
  honour 400
Love is his word 492
May the mind of Christ my
  Saviour 506

Palm Sunday - B

Meekness and majesty	507
Morning glory, starlit sky	509
My song is love unknown	521
O dearest Lord, thy sacred head	538
O love, how deep, how broad, how high	570
O my Saviour, lifted from the earth	572
O sacred head, surrounded	576
Onward, Christian pilgrims	599
Praise to the Holiest	627
Sing, my tongue, the glorious battle	662
Stay with me	678
Take up thy cross, the Saviour said	689
There in God's garden	739
This is my body	755
Thou didst leave thy throne	766
To mock your reign, O dearest Lord	778
To the name of our salvation	779
We believe in God the Father	790
We sing the praise of him who died	804
We turn to you	806
Were you there when they crucified my Lord?	810
When I survey the wondrous cross	820
You laid aside your majesty	850

MONDAY OF HOLY WEEK - *see* YEAR A

TUESDAY OF HOLY WEEK - *see* YEAR A

WEDNESDAY OF HOLY WEEK - *see* YEAR A

MAUNDY THURSDAY - *see* YEAR A

GOOD FRIDAY - *see* YEAR A

EASTER EVE - *see* YEAR A
Services other than the Easter Vigil.

EASTER
EASTER VIGIL - *see* YEAR A

EASTER DAY - B

All heaven declares	15
All in an Easter garden	17
All praise to thee	23
Alleluia, alleluia, give thanks to the risen Lord	31
Alleluia, alleluia, hearts to heaven and voices raise	32
Alleluia (x 8)	29
At the Lamb's high feast we sing	51
Celtic Alleluia	93
Christ the Lord is risen again	102

Come, risen Lord	137
Come, ye faithful, raise the anthem	142
Come, ye faithful, raise the strain	143
From the very depths of darkness	211
Good Christians all, rejoice	265
Halle, halle, halle	282
He has risen	292
He is Lord	294
I am the bread of life	323
I danced in the morning	329
Jesus Christ is risen today	381
Jesus Christ is waiting	382
Jesus lives! thy terrors now	390
Laudate Dominum	420
Led like a lamb	423
Light's glittering morn	443
Low in the grave he lay	496
Now is eternal life	529
Now the green blade riseth	533
Surrexit Christus	683
The day of resurrection	703
The Lord is risen indeed	721
The strife is o'er, the battle done	733
Thine be the glory	751
This is the day the Lord has made	760
This joyful Eastertide	761
Ye choirs of new Jerusalem	839

SECOND SUNDAY OF EASTER - B

At the Lamb's high feast we sing	51
Be still and know that I am God	61
Blessèd assurance	75
Breathe on me, Breath of God	87
Firmly I believe and truly	186
Go forth and tell	232
Help us to help each other, Lord	299
I am trusting thee, Lord Jesus	324
I believe in Jesus	325
Jesus Christ is risen today	381
Jesus is Lord! Creation's voice proclaims it	387
Jesus lives! thy terrors now	390
Jesus, Lord, we look to thee	391
Jesus, stand among us	401
Jesus, stand among us in thy risen power	402
Jesus, the name high over all	404
Light's glittering morn	443
Open our eyes, Lord	600
Our blest Redeemer, ere he breathed	602
Surrexit Christus	683
The Lord is my light	719
The peace of the earth be with you	726
The Son of God proclaim	731
The Spirit lives to set us free	732
To God be the glory!	777

THIRD SUNDAY OF EASTER - B

Alleluia, alleluia, give thanks to the risen Lord	31
Alleluia, alleluia, hearts to heaven and voices raise	32

Be thou my guardian and my guide	65
Be thou my vision	66
Come, ye faithful, raise the anthem	142
Crown him with many crowns	150
Father God, I wonder	168
Father, hear the prayer we offer	169
Father of heaven, whose love profound	174
God be in my head	235
He is Lord	294
How deep the Father's love for us	317
I cannot tell	327
I come with joy	328
It is a thing most wonderful	364
Jesu, our hope, our heart's desire	370
Let all mortal flesh keep silence	424
My Lord, what love is this	520
O for a thousand tongues to sing	541
Peace, perfect peace, is the gift	615
Purify my heart	631
The Lord is risen indeed	721
The Son of God proclaim	731
The strife is o'er, the battle done	733
To the name of our salvation	779
What a friend we have in Jesus	811
Ye choirs of new Jerusalem	839

FOURTH SUNDAY OF EASTER - B

A new commandment	4
Be thou my guardian and my guide	65
Bind us together, Lord	73
Christ is made the sure foundation	96
Christ is our cornerstone	97
Faithful Shepherd, feed me	166
Good Christians all, rejoice and sing	266
How sweet the name of Jesus sounds	321
I will sing the wondrous story	340
In Christ alone	352
In heavenly love abiding	355
Jesus the Lord said: 'I am the Bread'	403
Jesus, the name high over all	404
Let there be love	430
Lord, thy word abideth	481
Love's redeeming work is done	494
Loving Shepherd of thy sheep	495
Nada te turbe	523
O let the Son of God enfold you	558
O thou, who at the Eucharist didst pray	579
Praise, my soul, the King of heaven	623
The King of love my shepherd is	715
The Lord's my shepherd (Crimond)	723
The Lord's my shepherd (Townend)	724
There's a quiet understanding	745
Thine be the glory	751
Thine for ever! God of love	752
Ubi caritas	781

FIFTH SUNDAY OF EASTER - B

Abide with me	6
Alleluia, alleluia, hearts to heaven and voices raise	32
Bread of heaven, on thee we feed	83
Christ be with me	94
Draw nigh and take the body	157
For I'm building a people of power	193
God is love: his the care	242
God is love: let heaven adore him	243
Gracious Spirit, Holy Ghost	268
Happy are they, they that love God	285
Immortal, invisible, God only wise	349
It is a thing most wonderful	364
Led like a lamb	423
Let there be love	430
Lord, I come to you	458
Love divine, all loves excelling	491
Love is his word	492
Now the green bade riseth	533
The Lord is risen indeed	721
We have a gospel to proclaim	798

SIXTH SUNDAY OF EASTER - B

A new commandment	4
Be still and know that I am God	61
Christ the Lord is risen again	102
Come down, O Love divine	120
Deck thyself, my soul, with gladness	153
Father, we adore you	176
Forth in the peace of Christ we go	200
God is love: let heaven adore him	243
Great God, your love has called us	270
I come with joy	328
I danced in the morning	329
I, the Lord of sea and sky	337
In full and glad surrender	354
In heavenly love abiding	355
Jesu, Jesu, fill us with your love	368
Lord, I come to you	458
Lord of all being	466
Love divine, all loves excelling	491
My God, I love thee	517
Now the green bade riseth	533
O God of Bethel, by whose hand	545
O Jesus, I have promised	556
Rock of ages	643
Such love	681
Take my life, and let it be	687
Take this moment	688
The Son of God proclaim	731
There's a spirit in the air	746
Ubi caritas	781
What a friend we have in Jesus	811
When I needed a neighbour	819

ASCENSION DAY - see YEAR A

SEVENTH SUNDAY OF EASTER - B

All hail the power of Jesus' name	14
Alleluia, alleluia, give thanks to the risen Lord	31
Alleluia, sing to Jesus	33
Breathe on me, Breath of God	87
Christ is the King!	99
Christ triumphant	103
Crown him with many crowns	150
Father most holy, merciful and loving	173
Hail the day that sees him rise	277
Help us, O Lord, to learn	298
I, the Lord of sea and sky	337
Jesus Christ is waiting	382
Jesus is Lord! Creation's voice proclaims it	387
Jesus shall reign	399
Lord, enthroned in heavenly splendour	453
Nada te turbe	523
Now is eternal life	529
O for a heart to praise my God	540
O thou, who at thy Eucharist didst pray	579
Rejoice, the Lord is King	638
The head that once was crowned with thorns	711
We will lay our burden down	808
Will you come and follow me	834

PENTECOST (WHIT SUNDAY) - B

All over the world	20
Be still, for the presence of the Lord	62
Breathe on me, Breath of God	87
Christians, lift up your hearts	108
Come down, O Love divine	120
Come, gracious Spirit, heavenly Dove	122
Come, Holy Ghost, our souls inspire	124
Come, Holy Spirit, come	125
Come, thou Holy Spirit, come	139
Filled with the Spirit's power	184
For I'm building a people of power	193
Gracious Spirit, Holy Ghost	268
Holy Spirit, come, confirm us	311
Lord, the light of your love	479
O King, enthroned on high	557
O thou who camest from above	580
On the day of Pentecost	590
She sits like a bird	654
Spirit of God	672
Spirit of the living God (Armstrong)	674
Spirit of the living God (Iverson)	675
The Spirit lives to set us free	732
There's a spirit in the air	746
This is the day the Lord has made	760
Veni, lumen cordium	783
When God of old came down from heaven	816

ORDINARY TIME

TRINITY SUNDAY - B

Angel-voices ever singing	40
Be still, for the presence of the Lord	62
Bright the vision that delighted	88
Come, ye faithful, raise the anthem	142
Father in heaven, how we love you	171
Father, Lord of all creation	172
Father most holy, merciful and loving	173
Father of heaven, whose love profound	174
Father, we adore you	176
Father, we love you	177
Give to our God immortal praise	220
Holy, holy, holy is the Lord	309
Holy, holy, holy! Lord God almighty	310
How shall I sing that majesty	320
I bind unto myself today	326
Laudate Dominum	420
Lead us, heavenly Father, lead us	422
May the grace of Christ our Saviour	505
Meekness and majesty	507
My God, how wonderful you are	516
One is the body	594
Praise God from whom all blessings flow	618
Sanctus, sanctus, sanctus	647
The God of Abraham praise	706
The Lord is King!	718
This day God gives me	754
Thou, whose almighty word	767
Thuma mina	771
We give immortal praise	795

DAY OF THANKSGIVING FOR HOLY COMMUNION

Thursday after Trinity Sunday (Corpus Christi) - see Year A

PROPER 4 - B

Come, let us with our Lord arise	129
Disposer supreme	155
God of grace and God of glory	248
Lord of all hopefulness	467
Lord, the light of your love	479
O God, you search me	549
Our God is a great big God	606
She sits like a bird	654
Take my hands, Lord	686
Take my life, and let it be	687
This is the day the Lord has made	760
You are beautiful	847

PROPER 5 - B

Immortal love, for ever full	350
Jesus' love is very wonderful	393
Lift up your heads	438
Lord of lords and King eternal	474
Only by grace	598
Stand up, stand up for Jesus	677
The God whom earth and sea and sky	708
The King is among us	714
There's a wideness in God's mercy	747

PROPER 6 - B

Blest are the pure in heart	79
For the fruits of his creation	197
God is working his purpose out	246
Great God, your love has called us	270
Hail to the Lord's anointed	280
Love divine, all loves excelling	491
My God, I love thee	517
Now the green blade riseth	533
Rise and hear! The Lord is speaking	641
The Church's one foundation	702
There are hundreds of sparrows	738
Thy kingdom come, O God	774
We give immortal praise	795
Will you come and follow me	834

PROPER 7 - B

All who would valiant be	27
Be still and know that I am God	61
Be still, for the presence of the Lord	62
Be thou my vision	66
Calm me, Lord	92
Dear Lord and Father of mankind	152
Do not be afraid	156
Eternal Father, strong to save	160
Fight the good fight	181
Give thanks with a grateful heart	219
God is love: his the care	242
Holy Spirit, truth divine	312
I bind unto myself today	326
Jesus calls us: o'er the tumult	379
Lead us, heavenly Father, lead us	422
Nada te turbe	523
O Jesus, I have promised	556
Oft in danger, oft in woe	585
Praise the Lord, ye heavens, adore him	625
Praise to the Lord, the Almighty	628
Stand up, stand up for Jesus	677
The Church's one foundation	702
The Lord is my light	719
This day God gives me	754
Walk with me, O my Lord	788
Wide, wide as the ocean	833
Will your anchor hold	835

PROPER 8 - B

All praise to thee	23
Be still and know that I am God	61
Bless the Lord, my soul	74
Christ's is the world	110
Give thanks with a grateful heart	219
I heard the voice of Jesus say	334
Immortal love, for ever full	350
Jesu, the very thought of thee	373
Jesu, thou joy of loving hearts	374
Lord of all, to whom alone	469
New every morning is the love	526
O for a thousand tongues to sing	541
Surrexit Christus	683
Take my life, and let it be	687
Thine arm, O Lord, in days of old	750
Thou didst leave thy throne	766
We cannot measure	792

PROPER 9 - B

At even, ere the sun was set	49
Be thou my vision	66
Father, hear the prayer we offer	169
Give thanks to the Lord	218
Give thanks with a grateful heart	219
God has spoken – by the prophets	238
God is our strength from days of old	244
God's Spirit is in my heart	262
Happy are they, they that love God	285
Have faith in God, my heart	290
How sweet the name of Jesus sounds	321
I believe in Jesus	325
Inspired by love and anger	362
King of glory, King of peace	416
Let us talents and tongues employ	434
Lord of all being	466
Lord, you call us to a journey	487
Make way, make way	500
May the grace of Christ our Saviour	505
O for a thousand tongues to sing,	541
Peace, perfect peace, is the gift	615
Songs of thankfulness and praise	669
Thanks to God whose word was spoken	698
Thine arm, O Lord, in days of old	750
Thy hand, O God, has guided	772
Wait for the Lord	785
We have a gospel to proclaim	798
We will lay our burden down	808
We'll walk the land	809

PROPER 10 - B

Come, ye faithful, raise the anthem	142
Deck thyself, my soul, with gladness	153
God has spoken – by the prophets	238
God is working his purpose out	246
God moves in a mysterious way	247
How bright these glorious spirits shine!	316
If you believe and I believe	344
Jesus, Name above all names	395
Kum ba yah	419
Lead us, heavenly Father, lead us	422
Majesty, worship his majesty	498
O God of Bethel, by whose hand	545
On Jordan's bank the Baptist's cry	589
Praise God from whom all blessings flow	618
Put thou thy trust in God	634
The Church's one foundation	702
Thy hand, O God, has guided	772
Thy kingdom come, O God	774
To God be the glory!	777

PROPER 11 - B

All over the world	20
Be thou my guardian and my guide	65
Christ is made the sure foundation	96

Christ is our cornerstone	97
Dear Lord and Father of mankind	152
Faithful Shepherd, feed me	166
Father, hear the prayer we offer	169
5000 + hungry folk	188
For I'm building a people of power	193
Immortal love, for ever full	350
In Christ there is no east or west	353
In our day of thanksgiving	356
In the Lord I'll be ever thankful	360
Jesus put this song	397
Lord, we come to ask your healing	483
Loving Shepherd of thy sheep	495
O, heaven is in my heart	552
Peace, perfect peace, is the gift	615
Praise to the Holiest	627
The Church's one foundation	702
The God of Abraham praise	706
The King of love my shepherd is	715
The Lord's my shepherd (Crimond)	723
The Lord's my shepherd (Townend)	724
Thy kingdom come, O God	774
To God be the glory!	777
We love the place, O God	800
When I needed a neighbour	819

PROPER 12 - B

All for Jesus!	11
Bread is blessed and broken	82
Bread of heaven, on thee we feed	83
Break thou the bread	86
Come down, O Love divine	120
Creator of the earth and skies	147
Eat this bread	159
Eternal Father, strong to save	160
Faithful Shepherd, feed me	166
5000 + hungry folk	188
For the fruits of his creation	197
Gather around, for the table is spread	213
Gracious Spirit, Holy Ghost	268
Great God, your love has called us	270
Guide me, O thou great Redeemer	275
Happy are they, they that love God	285
I am the bread of life	323
I heard the voice of Jesus say	334
In bread we bring you, Lord	351
Just as I am, without one plea	413
Let all mortal flesh keep silence	424
Let there be love	430
Let us break bread together	431
Let us build a house	432
Let us talents and tongues employ	434
Love is his word	492
Not far beyond the sea	528
O love divine, how sweet thou art!	569
Praise and thanksgiving	617
Restore, O Lord	639

Proper 12 - B

The King of love my shepherd is 715
To God be the glory! 777
Ubi caritas 781

PROPER 13 - B

Adoramus te, Domine 8
Bread of heaven, on thee we feed 83
Bread of the world in mercy broken 84
Break thou the bread 86
Christ is the heavenly food 98
Christ is the King! 99
Come, risen Lord 137
Deck thyself, my soul, with
gladness 153
Draw nigh and take the body 157
Eat this bread 159
Father, Lord of all creation 172
From glory to glory advancing 204
Guide me, O thou great
Redeemer 275
I am the bread of life 323
In Christ there is no east or west 353
Jesu, thou joy of loving hearts 374
Jesus, stand among us in thy risen
power 402
Jesus the Lord said: 'I am the
Bread' 403
Let all mortal flesh keep silence 424
Let there be love 430
Lord, enthroned in heavenly
splendour 453
Lord Jesus Christ 463
Now is eternal life 529
O thou, who at thy Eucharist
didst pray 579
One is the body 594
Praise and thanksgiving 617
Rise and hear! The Lord is
speaking 641
The Church's one foundation 702
There are hundreds of sparrows 738
Through the night of doubt and
sorrow 770

PROPER 14 - B

Alleluia, sing to Jesus 33
As we are gathered 45
Author of life divine 55
Bread of the world in mercy
broken 84
Break the bread and pour the wine 85
Break thou the bread 86
Christ is the heavenly food 98
Eat this bread 159
God is love: let heaven adore him 243
Guide me, O thou great
Redeemer 275
Help us to help each other, Lord 299
I come with joy 328
I, the Lord of sea and sky 337
Jesu, thou joy of loving hearts 374
Jesus, Lord, we look to thee 391
Lead, kindly light 421
Let all mortal flesh keep silence 424

Lord, enthroned in heavenly
splendour 453
Make me a channel of your peace 499
May the mind of Christ my
Saviour 506
My faith looks up to thee 512
My Lord, what love is this 520
O for a closer walk with God 539
Praise him, praise him, praise him 622
Put thou thy trust in God 634
Soul of my Saviour 670
Thee we adore, O hidden Saviour,
thee 737
We hail thy presence glorious 796

PROPER 15 - B

Alleluia, sing to Jesus 33
Angel-voices ever singing 40
Awake, awake: fling off the night 56
Awake, my soul, and with the sun 57
Be thou my guardian and my guide 65
Be thou my vision 66
Bread of heaven, on thee we feed 83
Christian people, raise your song 106
Come, ye faithful, raise the
anthem 142
Draw nigh and take the body 157
Eat this bread 159
Faithful Shepherd, feed me 166
Father, we thank thee 178
Gather around, for the table is
spread 213
Glory, love, and praise, and
honour 225
Hands that have been handling 284
Here is bread 303
In Christ there is no east or west 353
Jesus is King 386
Jesus' love is very wonderful 393
Laudate Dominum 420
Let all the world in every corner
sing 425
Let us break bread together 431
Lord, enthroned in heavenly
splendour 453
My God, and is thy table spread 515
Now is eternal life 529
Now let us from this table rise 530
O God beyond all praising 544
Praise God from whom all
blessings flow 618
Sing to God a song of glory 665
Songs of praise the angels sang 668
Thee we adore, O hidden
Saviour, thee 737
We pray thee, heavenly Father 803
When morning gilds the skies 822

PROPER 16 - B

Adoramus te, Domine 8
As we are gathered 45
Author of life divine 55
Bless the Lord, my soul 74
Break the bread and pour the wine 85
Break thou the bread 86

Christ is made the sure foundation 96
Eat this bread 159
From glory to glory advancing 204
God of grace and God of glory 248
How sweet the name of Jesus
sounds 321
I come with joy 328
In Christ alone 352
Jesus calls us: o'er the tumult 379
Jesus, where'er thy people meet 407
Lord Jesus Christ 463
Now is eternal life 529
Now let us from this table rise 530
O Jesus, I have promised 556
O thou, who at thy Eucharist
didst pray 579
Oft in danger, oft in woe 585
Soul of my Saviour 670
Spirit of the living God (Iverson) 675
Stand up, stand up for Jesus 677
The Son of God proclaim 731
There is a Redeemer 743
We are marching 789
We pray thee, heavenly Father 803
What a friend we have in Jesus 811
You are the King of Glory 849

PROPER 17 - B

Before Jehovah's aweful throne 68
Blest are the pure in heart 79
Christian people, raise your song 106
Dear Lord and Father of mankind 152
Father, who in Jesus found us 180
For the beauty of the earth 195
For the fruits of his creation 197
Hail, true body 281
Happy are they, they that love
God 285
Help us, O Lord, to learn 298
Lord, thy word abideth 481
May the mind of Christ my
Saviour 506
My God, accept my heart this day 514
O for a heart to praise my God 540
Purify my heart 631
Strengthen for service, Lord 680
Teach me, my God and King 690
The Lord is King! 718
There's a spirit in the air 746
Thuma mina 771
Ubi caritas 781

PROPER 18 - B

All people that on earth do dwell 21
All things bright and beautiful 26
As the disciples 44
Beauty for brokenness 67
Dear Lord and Father of mankind 152
Fill your hearts with joy and
gladness 183
From heaven you came 205
Give thanks with a grateful heart 219
God be in my head 235
Happy are they, they that love
God 285

Proper 18 - B

Help us to help each other, Lord	299
I believe in Jesus	325
I heard the voice of Jesus say	334
Jesus Christ is waiting	382
Jesus shall reign	399
Laudate Dominum	420
Listen, let your heart keep seeking	446
Lord of the worlds above	477
O for a thousand tongues to sing	541
O let the Son of God enfold you	558
O my Saviour, lifted from the earth	572
Open our eyes, Lord	600
Praise, my soul, the King of heaven	623
Restore, O Lord	639
Son of God, eternal Saviour	667
The Saviour will come, resplendent in joy	730
Thou, whose almighty word	767
We cannot measure	792

PROPER 19 - B

At the name of Jesus	52
Be still and know that I am God	61
Be thou my vision	66
Christ be with me	94
Christ, whose glory fills the skies	105
Follow me	189
God of love	250
Great God, your love has called us	270
Help us, O Lord, to learn	298
I heard the voice of Jesus say	334
I, the Lord of sea and sky	337
I'm not ashamed to own my Lord	347
Immortal love, for ever full	350
Jesus calls us here to meet him	378
Jesus lives! thy terrors now	390
Just as I am, without one plea	413
King of kings and Lord of lords	417
Lord, for the years	454
O Jesus, I have promised	556
O Lord of every shining constellation	565
Praise, my soul, the King of heaven	623
Rejoice, the Lord is King	638
Stay with me	678
Take my life, and let it be	687
Take up thy cross, the Saviour said	689
Teach me, my God and King	690
There is a Redeemer	743
Thou art the Christ, O Lord	764
We have a gospel to proclaim	798
When God almighty came to earth	814
Wide, wide as the ocean	833
Will you come and follow me	834

PROPER 20 - B

A man there lived in Galilee	3
And now, O Father, mindful of the love	38
Be thou my guardian and my guide	65
Brother, sister, let me serve you	91
Christ's is the world	110
From heaven you came	205
God of grace and God of glory	248
Great God, your love has called us	270
I danced in the morning	329
It is a thing most wonderful	364
Jesu, Jesu, fill us with your love	368
Jesu, lover of my soul	369
Led like a lamb	423
Lord, thy word abideth	481
Make me a channel of your peace	499
Meekness and majesty	507
Morning glory, starlit sky	509
My song is love unknown	521
O perfect love	573
One more step along the world I go	595
Praise to the Holiest	627
Put thou thy trust in God	634
Teach me, my God and King	690
The Lord will come and not be slow	722
Thou art the Way: by thee alone	765
Through all the changing scenes of life	769
Through the night of doubt and sorrow	770
Thuma mina	771
Thy hand, O God, has guided	772
We sing the praise of him who died	804
What a friend we have in Jesus	811
When I needed a neighbour	819

PROPER 21 - B

Be thou my guardian and my guide	65
Be thou my vision	66
Dear Lord and Father of mankind	152
Father, hear the prayer we offer	169
Father of heaven, whose love profound	174
Father welcomes all his children	179
For the beauty of the earth	195
Forth in thy name, O Lord, I go	201
God forgave my sin	237
Great is thy faithfulness	273
Guide me, O thou great Redeemer	275
Here I am	310
How sweet the name of Jesus sounds	321
I heard the voice of Jesus say	334
Jesus calls us here to meet him	378
Lift up your hearts!	439
Lord of all hopefulness	467
Lord, teach us how to pray aright	478
New every morning is the love	526
O God of Bethel, by whose hand	545
O God, our help in ages past	547
O let the Son of God enfold you	558
Praise, my soul, the King of heaven	623
Purify my heart	631
Son of God, eternal Saviour	667

Strengthen for service, Lord	680
There are hundreds of sparrows	738
There's a spirit in the air	746
Through all the changing scenes of life	769
We have a gospel to proclaim	798
When all thy mercies, O my God	813
When I needed a neighbour	819

PROPER 22 - B

A new commandment	4
All creatures of our God and King	10
As we are gathered	45
Bind us together, Lord	73
Blest are the pure in heart	79
Christ triumphant	103
Crown him with many crowns	150
Dance and sing	151
Father, I place into your hands	170
Follow me	189
For I'm building a people of power	193
For the beauty of the earth	195
God has spoken – by the prophets	238
Happy are they, they that love God	285
How deep the Father's love for us	317
Jesus, good above all other	383
Lead us, heavenly Father, lead us	422
Lord Jesus Christ	463
Lord of all hopefulness	467
Love divine, all loves excelling	491
May the grace of Christ our Saviour	505
O Lord, my God	563
Seek ye first	652
The Lord is King!	718
Ubi caritas	781
Who put the colours in the rainbow?	831
Will you come and follow me	834

PROPER 23 - B

All I once held dear	16
All that I am	24
Amazing grace	34
And can it be	36
Be still and know that I am God	61
Be thou my vision	66
Brother, sister, let me serve you	91
From heaven you came	205
Give thanks with a grateful heart	219
Glorious things of thee are spoken	223
I, the Lord of sea and sky	337
I will offer up my life	339
Jesus calls us: o'er the tumult	379
Just as I am, without one plea	413
Lord, enthroned in heavenly splendour	453
Lord, I come to you	458
My God, accept my heart this day	514
O for a closer walk with God	539
O Jesus, I have promised	556
O Lord, all the world belongs to you	560

Proper 23 - B

O Lord of heaven and earth and sea	566
Purify my heart	631
Take my life, and let it be	687
Thou didst leave thy throne	766
Thy kingdom come, O God	774
We will lay our burden down	808
What a friend we have in Jesus	811
When the music fades	823
Will you come and follow me	834
With joy we meditate the grace	836
Ye servants of God	841

PROPER 24 - B

All praise to thee	23
Before the throne	70
Broken for me	90
Brother, sister, let me serve you	91
Christ triumphant	103
Christ's is the world	110
Father of heaven, whose love profound	174
From heaven you came	205
Help us to help each other, Lord	299
I will sing the wondrous story	340
It is a thing most wonderful	364
Jesus is Lord! Creation's voice proclaims it	387
Lead us, heavenly Father, lead us	422
Led like a lamb	423
Lord of beauty, thine the splendour	470
Make me a channel of your peace	499
Meekness and majesty	507
My Lord, what love is this	520
My song is love unknown	521
O dearest Lord, thy sacred head	538
O Lord, all the world belongs to you	560
O worship the King	582
Praise, my soul, the King of heaven	623
Strengthen for service, Lord	680
We sing the praise of him who died	804
Will you come and follow me	834
You laid aside your majesty	850

PROPER 25 - B

All for Jesus!	11
Alleluia, sing to Jesus	33
Amazing grace	34
Be thou my vision	66
Dear Lord and Father of mankind	152
Forth in the peace of Christ we go	200
God moves in a mysterious way	247
Have faith in God, my heart	290
Hills of the north, rejoice	307
How sweet the name of Jesus sounds	321
I heard the voice of Jesus say	334
I watch the sunrise	338
Immortal love, for ever full	350
Jesu, lover of my soul	369

Lord, enthroned in heavenly splendour	453
O for a thousand tongues to sing	541
Once, only once, and once for all	593
Son of God, eternal Saviour	667
The King of love my shepherd is	715
The Spirit lives to set us free	732
There is a Redeemer	743
Thine arm, O Lord, in days of old	750
Veni, lumen cordium	783
We cannot measure	792
We hail thy presence glorious	796
When all thy mercies, O my God	813
Will you come and follow me	834
Ye servants of God	841

Or: BIBLE SUNDAY - B

Break thou the bread	86
Come, Holy Ghost, our hearts inspire	123
God has spoken – by the prophets	238
God's Spirit is in my heart	262
Hark, my soul, it is the Lord	287
Help us, O Lord, to learn	298
Immortal, invisible, God only wise	349
Lord, for the years	454
Lord, I have made thy word my choice	459
Lord, thy word abideth	481
May the mind of Christ my Saviour	506
Not far beyond the sea	528
Rise and hear! The Lord is speaking	641
Seek ye first	652
Thanks to God whose word was spoken	698
The heavens declare thy glory, Lord	712
The Lord is my light	719
The prophets spoke in days of old	728
Thou, whose almighty word	767
We have a gospel to proclaim	798

DEDICATION FESTIVAL - B

Angel-voices ever singing	40
As Jacob with travel was weary one day	41
Be still, for the presence of the Lord	62
Blessèd city, heavenly Salem	77
Christ is made the sure foundation	96
Christ is our cornerstone	97
For I'm building a people of power	193
Forth in the peace of Christ we go	200
Glorious things of thee are spoken	223
God is here! As we his people	241
Here in this place	302
In our day of thanksgiving	356
Jesus, where'er thy people meet	407
Let us build a house	432
Longing for light	452
Lord, for the years	454
O God of Bethel, by whose hand	545

The Church's one foundation	702
Thy hand, O God, has guided	772
We have a gospel to proclaim	798
We love the place, O God	800
Ye that know the Lord is gracious	843
You, living Christ, our eyes behold	851

ALL SAINTS' DAY - B

All who would valiant be	27
Blest are the pure in heart	79
Bright the vision that delighted	88
For all the saints	190
Give thanks for those	217
Give us the wings of faith	221
Glory to thee, O God	230
Help us, O Lord, to learn	298
How bright these glorious spirits shine!	316
Let saints on earth in concert sing	428
Light's abode, celestial Salem	442
Make me a channel of your peace	499
O when the saints go marching in	581
Seek ye first	652
Thanks be to God	696
The Lord is my light	719
There is a land of pure delight	741
Through all the changing scenes of life	769
Who are these like stars appearing	828
Ye watchers and ye holy ones	844

FOURTH SUNDAY BEFORE ADVENT - B

A new commandment	4
All praise to thee	23
Before Jehovah's aweful throne	68
Before the throne	70
Father, Lord of all creation	172
Father, we adore you	176
Father, we love you	177
Fill thou my life, O Lord my God	182
Glory be to Jesus	224
God has spoken – by the prophets	238
God is love: his the care	242
Happy are they, they that love God	285
In bread we bring you, Lord	351
Jesu, Jesu, fill us with your love	368
My God, I love thee	517
Put thou thy trust in God	634
The prophets spoke in days of old	728
There's a wideness in God's mercy	747
Ubi caritas	781
Veni, lumen cordium	783
When I needed a neighbour	819
With joy we meditate the grace	836

THIRD SUNDAY BEFORE ADVENT - B

Amazing grace	34
And can it be	36
And now, O Father, mindful of the love	38
Follow me	189

Third Sunday before Advent - B

Forgive our sins as we forgive	199
God forgave my sin	237
I will offer up my life	339
Jesus calls us here to meet him	378
Jesus calls us: o'er the tumult	379
Just as I am, without one plea	413
Lord, enthroned in heavenly splendour	453
Lord Jesus Christ	463
Lord of all being	466
My Lord, what love is this	520
O Jesus, I have promised	556
O thou who camest from above	580
Once, only once, and once for all	593
Take my life, and let it be	687
We sing the praise of him who died	804
When all thy mercies, O my God	813
When God almighty came to earth	814
Will you come and follow me	834

SECOND SUNDAY BEFORE ADVENT - B

All my hope on God is founded	19
And can it be	36
Christ is our cornerstone	97
Christ, the fair glory of the holy angels	101
Crown him with many crowns	150
Do not be afraid	156
Fight the good fight	181
Forth in thy name, O Lord, I go	201
Glorious things of thee are spoken	223
God moves in a mysterious way	247
He's got the whole world in his hand	306
Jesus is King	386
Jesus' love is very wonderful	393
Lord, the light of your love	479
My Lord, what love is this	520
Oft in danger, oft in woe	585
Rejoice, the Lord is King	638
Restore, O Lord	639
Songs of thankfulness and praise	669
The head that once was crowned with thorns	711
The Lord is my light	719
There is a Redeemer	743
There's a place where the streets shine	744
There's a wideness in God's mercy	747
Through all the changing scenes of life	769
Through the night of doubt and sorrow	770
Wait for the Lord	785
We are marching	789
Wherefore, O Father	826
Who are these like stars appearing	828
You laid aside your majesty	850

CHRIST THE KING - B

All hail the power of Jesus' name	14
All heaven declares	15

All praise to thee	23
Alleluia, sing to Jesus	33
At the name of Jesus	52
Blessing and honour	78
Christ is the King!	99
Christ triumphant	103
Crown him with many crowns	150
From heaven you came	205
He is exalted	293
How shall I sing that majesty	320
I will sing the wondrous story	340
Jesus is King	386
Jesus is the name we honour	388
Jesus, remember me	398
Jesus shall reign	399
King of kings and Lord of lords	417
Laudate Dominum	420
Let all the world in every corner sing	425
Lord, enthroned in heavenly splendour	453
Lord of the boundless curves	475
Majesty, worship his majesty	498
Make way, make way	500
Meekness and majesty	507
Name of all majesty	524
O worship the King	582
O worship the Lord in the beauty of holiness	583
Rejoice, the Lord is King	638
The head that once was crowned with thorns	711
The King is among us	714
The King of love my shepherd is	715
The kingdom is upon you!	716
Thy kingdom come, O God	774
To God be the glory!	777
Yesterday, today, for ever	846
You are the King of Glory	849

YEAR C
ADVENT
FIRST SUNDAY OF ADVENT - C

All my hope on God is founded	19
Be still and know that I am God	61
Come and see the shining hope	119
Come, thou long-expected Jesus	140
Do not be afraid	156
Father, we love you	177
God is working his purpose out	246
Great is the darkness	271
Hark! A herald voice is calling	286
Hark, the glad sound!	288
Hills of the north, rejoice	307
I cannot tell	327
Jesus is the name we honour	388
Kum ba yah	419
Lo, he comes with clouds descending	449
Lord of the future	476
Make way, make way	500
Nada te turbe	523
O come, O come, Emmanuel	535

O day of God, draw nigh	537
Restore, O Lord	639
The advent of our King	699
The God of Abraham praise	706
The Lord will come and not be slow	722
Thy kingdom come, O God	774
Wait for the Lord	785
Wake, O wake! with tidings thrilling	786

SECOND SUNDAY OF ADVENT - C

All praise to our redeeming Lord	22
Awake, awake: fling off the night	56
Bless the Lord, my soul	74
Come, thou long-expected Jesus	140
Dear Lord and Father of mankind	152
Hail to the Lord's anointed	280
Hark! A herald voice is calling	286
Here in this place	302
Hills of the north, rejoice	307
Little donkey	447
Long ago, prophets knew	451
Love divine, all loves excelling	491
Make way, make way	500
On Jordan's bank the Baptist's cry	589
Peace is flowing like a river	613
Purify my heart	631
Restore, O Lord	639
The advent of our King	699
The great Creator of the world	710
Wait for the Lord	785
When Jesus came to Jordan	821
Ye servants of the Lord	842

THIRD SUNDAY OF ADVENT - C

Be bold, be strong	60
Christ is the King!	99
Christ, when for us you were baptised	104
Colours of day	114
Glorious things of thee are spoken	223
Hark! A herald voice is calling	286
Like a mighty river flowing	445
Lord Jesus Christ	463
Make way, make way	500
May the mind of Christ my Saviour	506
O comfort my people	536
O day of God, draw nigh	537
On Jordan's bank the Baptist's cry	589
Purify my heart	631
Rejoice, the Lord is King	638
The Lord will come and not be slow	722
The people that in darkness sat	727
Thy kingdom come, O God	774
To God be the glory!	777
Wait for the Lord	785
We are marching	789
We praise you, Lord	802
What a friend we have in Jesus	811
When Jesus came to Jordan	821
While shepherds watched	827

FOURTH SUNDAY OF ADVENT - C

Away in a manger 59
Father, I place into your hands 170
For Mary, mother of our Lord 194
Hark, the glad sound! 288
Heaven shall not wait 297
Jesus, the name high over all 404
Joy to the world! 409
Lift up your heads 438
Like a candle flame 444
Long ago, prophets knew 451
Lord, the light of your love 479
Magnificat 497
May the mind of Christ my Saviour 506
O come, O come, Emmanuel 535
Of the Father's love begotten 584
See him lying on a bed of straw 650
Take my life, and let it be 687
Tell out, my soul 692
The angel Gabriel from heaven came 700
The God whom earth and sea and sky 708
The Lord will come and not be slow 722
To the name of our salvation 779
Virgin-born, we bow before thee 784

CHRISTMAS

CHRISTMAS EVE - see YEAR A

CHRISTMAS DAY - see YEAR A

FIRST SUNDAY OF CHRISTMAS - C

A great and mighty wonder 2
Angels from the realms of glory 39
Away in a manger 59
Behold, the great Creator 71
Born in the night, Mary's child 81
Christians, awake! 107
Cloth for the cradle 113
Confitemini Domino 145
Glory to God (Peruvian Gloria) 226
God rest you merry, gentlefolk 254
Good Christians all, rejoice 265
Hallelu, hallelu 283
Hark, the herald-angels sing 289
In the bleak mid-winter 357
It came upon the midnight clear 363
Jesus' love is very wonderful 393
Like a candle flame 444
Little Jesus, sweetly sleep 448
Lord, I lift your name on high 461
O little town of Bethlehem 559
Of the Father's love begotten 584
On Christmas night all Christians sing 588
Once in royal David's city 592
See, amid the winter's snow 649
See him lying on a bed of straw 650
Silent night 658

The first Nowell 705
Thou didst leave thy throne 766
Unto us a boy is born 782
What child is this 812
Where is this stupendous stranger? 825
While shepherds watched 827
Who would think that what was needed 832

SECOND SUNDAY OF CHRISTMAS - see YEAR A

EPIPHANY

THE EPIPHANY - see YEAR A

THE BAPTISM OF CHRIST - C

Awake, awake: fling off the night 56
Be thou my vision 66
Breathe on me, Breath of God 87
Christ, when for us you were baptised 104
Come down, O Love divine 120
Come, gracious Spirit, heavenly Dove 122
Crown him with many crowns 150
Do not be afraid 156
Father of heaven, whose love profound 174
Father, we adore you 176
Father, we love you 177
Father welcomes all his children 179
God's love is deeper 261
God's Spirit is in my heart 262
Hail to the Lord's anointed 280
Have you heard the raindrops 291
Jesus, Jesus 389
Just as I am, without one plea 413
Name of all majesty 524
Now is eternal life 529
O let the Son of God enfold you 558
O love, how deep, how broad, how high 570
O thou who camest from above 580
On Jordan's bank the Baptist's cry 589
Spirit divine, attend our prayers 671
Spirit of the living God (Iverson) 675
Take this moment 688
The people that in darkness sat 727
To the name of our salvation 779
Veni, lumen cordium 783
When Jesus came to Jordan 821

SECOND SUNDAY OF EPIPHANY - C

All praise to our redeeming Lord 22
Bread is blessed and broken 82
Filled with the Spirit's power 184
From heaven you came 205
Give me joy in my heart 215
Gracious Spirit, Holy Ghost 268
Heaven shall not wait 297
Holy Spirit, come, confirm us 311
I, the Lord of sea and sky 337

Immortal, invisible, God only wise 349
In the Lord I'll be ever thankful 360
Jesus, Lord, we look to thee 391
Jesus' love is very wonderful 393
Jesus put this song 397
Jesus the Lord said: 'I am the Bread' 403
Joy to the world! 409
Love divine, all loves excelling 491
Name of all majesty 524
O for a heart to praise my God 540
O Lord, your tenderness 568
O thou who camest from above 580
One shall tell another 596
Praise the Lord, ye heavens, adore him 625
Rejoice in the Lord always 636
Sing of the Lord's goodness 663
Songs of thankfulness and praise 669
Take my life, and let it be 687
The Church's one foundation 702
We hail thy presence glorious 796
We have a gospel to proclaim 798

THIRD SUNDAY OF EPIPHANY - C

Christ is the King! 99
Father, Lord of all creation 172
Give thanks with a grateful heart 219
God has spoken – by the prophets 238
God of grace and God of glory 248
God's Spirit is in my heart 262
Hark, my soul, it is the Lord 287
He is the Lord 295
He's got the whole world in his hand 306
I cannot tell 327
I come with joy 328
Jesus Christ is waiting 382
Jesus, Jesus 389
Jesus, Lord, we look to thee 391
Jesus shall reign 399
Jesus, the name high over all 404
Lord, I have made thy word my choice 459
Lord, thy word abideth 481
O for a thousand tongues to sing 541
O thou, who at thy Eucharist didst pray 579
One is the body 594
Seek ye first 652
Songs of thankfulness and praise 669
Thanks to God whose word was spoken 698
The King is among us 714
This is the day the Lord has made 760
Thuma mina 771
We have a gospel to proclaim 798
Will you come and follow me 834

FOURTH SUNDAY OF EPIPHANY - C

A new commandment 4
Breathe on me, Breath of God 87
Christ is our cornerstone 97

Fourth Sunday of Epiphany - C

Christ, whose glory fills the skies 105
Colours of day 114
Faithful vigil ended 167
Forth in the peace of Christ we go 200
Glorious things of thee are
  spoken 223
God of mercy, God of grace 251
Gracious Spirit, Holy Ghost 268
Great is the Lord and most
  worthy of praise 272
Help us to help each other, Lord 299
Immortal love, for ever full 350
Jesus bids us shine 377
Lord, the light of your love 479
Love divine, all loves excelling 491
My God, how wonderful you are 516
Purify my heart 631
Restore, O Lord 639
The Lord is my light 719
This little light of mine 762
Ubi caritas 781
We bow down 791
With joy we meditate the grace 836

**THE PRESENTATION OF CHRIST
IN THE TEMPLE -** *see* **YEAR A**

ORDINARY TIME

PROPER 1 - C

Adoramus te, Domine 8
And can it be 36
Be still, for the presence of the
  Lord 62
Bright the vision that delighted 88
Follow me 189
Forth in thy name, O Lord, I go 201
God of love 250
Holy, holy, holy is the Lord 309
Holy, holy, holy! Lord God
  almighty 310
How shall I sing that majesty 320
I, the Lord of sea and sky 337
I will worship 341
Immortal, invisible, God only
  wise 349
Jesu, lover of my soul 369
Jesus calls us: o'er the tumult 379
Jesus Christ is waiting 382
Let all mortal flesh keep silence 424
Lord Jesus Christ 463
Make way, make way 500
My God, how wonderful you are 516
O thou who camest from above 580
Restore, O Lord 639
Stand up and bless the Lord 676
Take my life, and let it be 687
The strife is o'er, the battle done 733
We give immortal praise 795
We'll walk the land 809
When God almighty came to
  earth 814
Wide, wide as the ocean 833
Will you come and follow me 834

PROPER 2 - C

A new commandment 4
All my hope on God is founded 19
Blessèd assurance 75
Blest are the pure in heart 79
Christ the Lord is risen again 102
Father, hear the prayer we offer 169
Make way, make way 500
Now let us from this table rise 530
O God, our help in ages past 547
Seek ye first 652
The kingdom of heaven 717
Will you come and follow me 834

PROPER 3 - C

A new commandment 4
Brother, sister, let me serve you 91
Lord, we come to ask your
  healing 483
Make me a channel of your peace 499
O Lord, all the world belongs
  to you 560
One more step along the world
  I go 595
Praise to the Holiest 627

**SECOND SUNDAY BEFORE
LENT - C**

All creatures of our God and King 10
Alleluia, sing to Jesus 33
Angel-voices ever singing 40
Be still and know that I am God 61
Calm me, Lord 92
Come, let us join our cheerful
  songs 127
Come, let us with our Lord arise 129
Do not be afraid 156
Eternal Father, strong to save 160
For the beauty of the earth 195
Give to our God immortal praise 220
Great is the darkness 271
I will worship 341
Let us with a gladsome mind 435
Lord, enthroned in heavenly
  splendour 453
Lord of beauty, thine the
  splendour 470
Lord of the boundless curves 475
Morning has broken 510
Nada te turbe 523
Name of all majesty 524
New every morning is the love 526
O Lord of every shining
  constellation 565
Songs of praise the angels sang 668
Sweet sacrament divine 684
This is the day the Lord has made 760
Thou, whose almighty word 767
What a friend we have in Jesus 811
Wide, wide as the ocean 833
Will your anchor hold 835

**SUNDAY NEXT BEFORE
LENT - C**

Adoramus te, Domine 8

Be still, for the presence of the
  Lord 62
Christ, whose glory fills the skies 105
Forgive our sins as we forgive 199
From glory to glory advancing 204
Glory to God (Peruvian Gloria) 226
God of mercy, God of grace 251
Help us to help each other, Lord 299
Immortal, invisible, God only
  wise 349
Jesus bids us shine 377
Jesus shall take the highest honour 400
Light's abode, celestial Salem 442
Lord Jesus Christ 463
Lord, the light of your love 479
Lord, you have my heart 489
Meekness and majesty 507
My God, how wonderful you are 516
Name of all majesty 524
O raise your eyes on high 575
Thee we adore, O hidden
  Saviour, thee 737
'Tis good, Lord, to be here 775
We hail thy presence glorious 796
You, living Christ, our eyes
  behold 851

LENT

ASH WEDNESDAY - *see* **YEAR A**

FIRST SUNDAY OF LENT - C

All who would valiant be 27
Awake, our souls; away, our fears 58
Father, hear the prayer we offer 169
Father of heaven, whose love
  profound 174
Forty days and forty nights 202
He is Lord 294
I bind unto myself today 326
I'm not ashamed to own my Lord 347
Jesu, lover of my soul 369
Jesu, the very thought of thee 373
Jesu, thou joy of loving hearts 374
Lead us, heavenly Father, lead us 422
Lord Jesus Christ 463
My Jesus, my Saviour 519
Name of all majesty 524
O happy band of pilgrims 550
O Jesus, I have promised 556
O Lord, my God 563
O love, how deep, how broad,
  how high 570
Open our eyes, Lord 600
Seek ye first 652
Strengthen for service, Lord 680
Take my life, and let it be 687
To the name of our salvation 779
We are marching 789
What a friend we have in Jesus 811

SECOND SUNDAY OF LENT - C

Ah, holy Jesu, how hast thou
  offended 9
All my hope on God is founded 19

Second Sunday of Lent - C

All you who seek a comfort sure	28
Come, O thou traveller unknown	134
Do not be afraid	156
Faithful One, so unchanging	165
Fight the good fight	181
Have faith in God, my heart	290
In the Cross of Christ I glory	358
Light's abode, celestial Salem	442
Lord Jesus Christ	463
Lord of all hopefulness	467
Lord, you call us to a journey	487
My faith looks up to thee	512
O love, how deep, how broad, how high	570
The God of Abraham praise	706
The Lord is my light	719
There is a land of pure delight	741
There's a wideness in God's mercy	747
To be in your presence	776
We are marching	789

THIRD SUNDAY OF LENT - C

All who would valiant be	27
As the deer pants for the water	43
Beauty for brokenness	67
Bread of heaven, on thee we feed	83
Bread of the world in mercy broken	84
Christ is the heavenly food	98
Draw nigh and take the body	157
Faithful Shepherd, feed me	166
For the fruits of his creation	197
Give me joy in my heart	215
Glorious things of thee are spoken	223
Guide me, O thou great Redeemer	275
How sweet the name of Jesus sounds	321
I come with joy	328
I heard the voice of Jesus say	334
Just as I am, without one plea	413
Meekness and majesty	507
Morning glory, starlit sky	509
O for a closer walk with God	539
O let the Son of God enfold you	558
Purify my heart	631
Rock of ages	643
The Church's one foundation	702
Through the night of doubt and sorrow	770
Who can sound the depths of sorrow	829

FOURTH SUNDAY OF LENT - C

All for Jesus!	11
Amazing grace	34
Bind us together, Lord	73
For the beauty of the earth	195
Forgive our sins as we forgive	199
God forgave my sin	237
God is love: his care	242
Great God, your love has called us	270
Hail, thou once despisèd Jesus	278

Holy Spirit, come, confirm us	311
I cannot tell	327
I will sing the wondrous story	340
In Christ there is no east or west	353
Just as I am, without one plea	413
King of glory, King of peace	416
Lord of all being	466
Love divine, all loves excelling	491
O Lord, all the world belongs to you	560
O Lord, your tenderness	568
O thou, who at thy Eucharist didst pray	579
Our Father God in heaven	605
The Church's one foundation	702
The King of love my shepherd is	715
There are hundreds of sparrows	738
There is a Redeemer	743
There's a spirit in the air	746
Through all the changing scenes of life	769

Or: MOTHERING SUNDAY - see YEAR A

FIFTH SUNDAY OF LENT - C

A man there lived in Galilee	3
And can it be	36
And now, O Father, mindful of the love	38
Be thou my guardian and my guide	65
Beneath the cross of Jesus	72
Christ's is the world	110
Fight the good fight	181
From heaven you came	205
Glory be to Jesus	224
God forgave my sin	237
Have faith in God, my heart	290
Here, O my Lord	304
How deep the Father's love for us	317
In the Cross of Christ I glory	358
Jesu, the very thought of thee	373
Jesu, thou joy of loving hearts	374
Jesus' love is very wonderful	393
Jesus put this song	397
Jesus, remember me	398
Lift high the Cross	437
Lord, for the years	454
Meekness and majesty	507
Morning glory, starlit sky	509
My Lord, what love is this	520
O happy band of pilgrims	550
O love divine, how sweet thou art!	569
Praise to the Holiest	627
Such love	681
The royal banners forward go	729
There in God's garden	739
There is a Redeemer	743
To God be the glory!	777
Ubi caritas	781
We cannot measure	792
We sing the praise of him who died	804
When I survey the wondrous cross	820
You laid aside your majesty	850

PALM SUNDAY - C
Liturgy of the Palms

All glory, laud and honour	12
All praise to thee	23
Clap your hands, all you people	112
Give me joy in my heart	215
Hosanna, hosanna	314
Lift up your heads	438
Make way, make way	500
Rejoice in the Lord always	636
Ride on, ride on in majesty	640
The royal banners forward go	729
We have a King who rides a donkey	799
You are the King of Glory	849

Liturgy of the Passion

And now, O Father, mindful of the love	38
Broken for me	90
From heaven you came	205
Hail, thou once despisèd Jesus	278
I cannot tell	327
I danced in the morning	329
I will sing the wondrous story	340
It is a thing most wonderful	364
Lift high the Cross	437
Meekness and majesty	507
Morning glory, starlit sky	509
My song is love unknown	521
O love, how deep, how broad, how high	570
O sacred head, surrounded	576
Praise to the Holiest	627
There is a green hill far away	740
Thou didst leave thy throne	766
Were you there when they crucified my Lord?	810

MONDAY OF HOLY WEEK - see YEAR A

TUESDAY OF HOLY WEEK - see YEAR A

WEDNESDAY OF HOLY WEEK - see YEAR A

MAUNDY THURSDAY - FOR YEARS A, B AND C

GOOD FRIDAY - see YEAR A

EASTER EVE - see YEAR A
Services other than the Easter Vigil.

EASTER

EASTER VIGIL - see YEAR A

EASTER DAY - C

All in an Easter garden	17
Alleluia, alleluia, give thanks to the risen Lord	31
Alleluia, alleluia, hearts to heaven and voices raise	32

Easter Day - C

Alleluia, sing to Jesus	33
Alleluia (x 8)	29
At the Lamb's high feast we sing	51
Christ the Lord is risen again	102
Christian people, raise your song	106
Come, risen Lord	137
Come, ye faithful, raise the anthem	142
Come, ye faithful, raise the strain	143
From the very depths of darkness	211
Good Christians all, rejoice and sing	266
Halle, halle, halle	282
He has risen	292
He is Lord	294
I am the bread of life	323
Jesus Christ is risen today	381
Jesus lives! thy terrors now	390
Laudate Dominum	420
Led like a lamb	423
Light's glittering morn	443
Low in the grave he lay	496
Now is eternal life	529
Now the green blade riseth	533
Surrexit Christus	683
The day of resurrection	703
The Lord is risen indeed	721
The strife is o'er, the battle done	733
Thine be the glory	751
This is the day the Lord has made	760
This joyful Eastertide	761
Ye choirs of new Jerusalem	839

SECOND SUNDAY OF EASTER - C

Alleluia, alleluia, hearts to heaven and voices raise	32
At the Lamb's high feast we sing	51
At the name of Jesus	52
Be still and know that I am God	61
Breathe on me, Breath of God	87
Christians lift your hearts and voices	109
Forth in the peace of Christ we go	200
Holy, holy, holy! Lord God almighty	310
I believe in Jesus	325
Jesus, stand among us in thy risen power	402
Jesus, the name high over all	404
Light's glittering morn	443
Lord, enthroned in heavenly splendour	453
Love's redeeming work is done	494
Open our eyes, Lord	600
Peace is flowing like a river	613
Peace, perfect peace, is the gift	615
Surrexit Christus	683
The Lord is risen indeed	721
This is the day the Lord has made	760
This joyful Eastertide	761
To God be the glory!	777
We have a gospel to proclaim	798

THIRD SUNDAY OF EASTER - C

All that I am	24
Come, let us join our cheerful songs	127
Come, my Way, my Truth, my Life	131
Come, ye faithful, raise the anthem	142
From all that dwell below the skies	203
God moves in a mysterious way	247
Good Christians all, rejoice and sing	266
Hark, my soul, it is the Lord	287
Heaven shall not wait	297
Holy, holy, holy is the Lord	309
I cannot tell	327
In the Lord I'll be ever thankful	360
Jesus, the name high over all	404
Just as I am, without one plea	413
Lead us, heavenly Father, lead us	422
Lord Jesus Christ	463
Love's redeeming work is done	494
Majesty, worship his majesty	498
My God, I love thee	517
Now the green blade riseth	533
Open our eyes, Lord	600
The Lord is risen indeed	721
There is a Redeemer	743
Thine be the glory	751
To God be the glory!	777
We have a gospel to proclaim	798
Will you come and follow me	834
Ye servants of God	841
You stood there on the shoreline	854

FOURTH SUNDAY OF EASTER - C

All heaven declares	15
All people that on earth do dwell	21
Alleluia, sing to Jesus	33
As we are gathered	45
At the Lamb's high feast we sing	51
Blessèd assurance	75
Faithful Shepherd, feed me	166
He is Lord	294
How bright these glorious spirits shine!	316
How sweet the name of Jesus sounds	321
In heavenly love abiding	355
Love is his word	492
Loving Shepherd of thy sheep	495
Majesty, worship his majesty	498
My God, how wonderful you are	516
O for a thousand tongues to sing	541
One more step along the world I go	595
Shepherd divine, our wants relieve	655
Such love	681
The Church's one foundation	702
The God of love my shepherd is	707
The King of love my shepherd is	715
The Lord's my shepherd (Crimond)	723
The Lord's my shepherd (Townend)	724

There's a wideness in God's mercy 747

Thine for ever! God of love	752
Who are these like stars appearing	828
Ye servants of God	841

FIFTH SUNDAY OF EASTER - C

A new commandment	4
All hail the power of Jesus' name	14
Christ is made the sure foundation	96
Christ's is the world	110
Come down, O Love divine	120
Confitemini Domino	145
Glorious things of thee are spoken	223
Hark, my soul, it is the Lord	287
How bright these glorious spirits shine!	316
I am a new creation	322
Jesus' love is very wonderful	393
Jesus shall reign	399
Let there be love	430
Love divine, all loves excelling	491
O Jesus, I have promised	556
O Lord, your tenderness	568
O thou, who at thy Eucharist didst pray	579
Praise the Lord, ye heavens, adore him	625
There is a land of pure delight	741
There's a place where the streets shine	744
Ubi caritas	781
Ye choirs of new Jerusalem	839

SIXTH SUNDAY OF EASTER - C

Be thou my vision	66
Christ is made the sure foundation	96
Christ is the world's Light	100
City of God, how broad and far	111
Come down, O Love divine	120
Come, let us join our cheerful songs	127
Dear Lord and Father of mankind	152
Give to our God immortal praise	220
God of mercy, God of grace	251
Have faith in God, my heart	290
Inspired by love and anger	362
Jesus calls us: o'er the tumult	379
Jesus Christ is waiting	382
Light's abode, celestial Salem	442
Longing for light	452
Lord of all being	466
Love divine, all loves excelling	491
Men of faith	508
O for a thousand tongues to sing	541
O let the Son of God enfold you	558
Our blest Redeemer, ere he breathed	602
Peace is flowing like a river	613
Peace, perfect peace, in this dark world of sin	614
Peace, perfect peace, is the gift	615
Praise him, praise him, praise him	622
Take this moment	688
The Church's one foundation	702

Sixth Sunday of Easter - C

The day of resurrection	703
There is a Redeemer	743
Ye holy angels bright	840

ASCENSION DAY - *see* **YEAR A**

SEVENTH SUNDAY OF EASTER - C

All hail the power of Jesus' name	14
Alleluia, alleluia, give thanks to the risen Lord	31
Alleluia, sing to Jesus	33
As pants the hart for cooling streams	42
At the name of Jesus	52
Bind us together, Lord	73
Breathe on me, Breath of God	87
Christ be with me	94
Christ is the King!	99
Christ triumphant	103
Come, let us join our cheerful songs	127
Crown him with many crowns	150
From glory to glory advancing	204
Glorious things of thee are spoken	223
Great is the darkness	271
Hail the day that sees him rise	277
Here, O my Lord	304
How shall I sing that majesty	320
Jesus calls us here to meet him	378
Jesus shall reign	399
King of kings and Lord of lords	417
Lord, enthroned in heavenly splendour	453
Love divine, all loves excelling	491
O for a heart to praise my God	540
Praise, my soul, the King of heaven	623
Rejoice, the Lord is King	638
The head that once was crowned with thorns	711
Thine be the glory	751
Thy kingdom come, O God	774
Veni, lumen cordium	783
You are the King of Glory	849

PENTECOST (WHIT SUNDAY) - C

All over the world	20
Be still, for the presence of the Lord	62
Breathe on me, Breath of God	87
Christians, lift up your hearts	108
Come down, O Love divine	120
Come, gracious Spirit, heavenly Dove	122
Come, Holy Ghost, our souls inspire	124
Come, Holy Spirit, come	125
Come, thou Holy Spirit, come	139
Filled with the Spirit's power	184
For I'm building a people of power	193
Holy Spirit, come, confirm us	311

If you believe and I believe	344
Lord, the light of your love	479
Love divine, all loves excelling	491
O King, enthroned on high	557
O thou who camest from above	580
On the day of Pentecost	590
She sits like a bird	654
Spirit of the living God (Armstrong)	674
Spirit of the living God (Iverson)	675
The Spirit lives to set us free	732
There's a spirit in the air	746

ORDINARY TIME

TRINITY SUNDAY - C

Bread of heaven, on thee we feed	83
Come down, O Love divine	120
Come, ye faithful, raise the anthem	142
Father in heaven, how we love you	171
Father most holy, merciful and loving	173
Father of heaven, whose love profound	174
Father, we adore you	176
Father, we love you	177
Holy, holy, holy is the Lord	309
Holy, holy, holy! Lord God almighty	310
Holy Spirit, truth divine	312
How shall I sing that majesty	320
I bind unto myself today	326
Laudate Dominum	420
Lead us, heavenly Father, lead us	422
Lord of all hopefulness	467
Majesty, worship his majesty	498
May the grace of Christ the Saviour	505
May the mind of Christ my Saviour	506
My God, how wonderful you are	516
O King, enthroned on high	557
Praise God from whom all blessings flow	618
Sanctus, sanctus, sanctus	647
The God of Abraham praise	706
This day God gives me	754
Thou, whose almighty word	767
We give immortal praise	795

DAY OF THANKSGIVING FOR HOLY COMMUNION
Thursday after Trinity Sunday (Corpus Christi) - *see* **Year A**

PROPER 4 - C

Come, Holy Ghost, our souls inspire	124
Father of heaven, whose love profound	174
Give thanks with a grateful heart	219
Go, tell it on the mountain	233
Jesus, humble was your birth	384

Just as I am, without one plea	413
O for a thousand tongues to sing	541
One shall tell another	596
Peace, perfect peace, is the gift	615
Praise, my soul, the King of heaven	623
Thank you for saving me	693
To God be the glory!	777
We have a gospel to proclaim	798

PROPER 5 - C

Alleluia, sing to Jesus	33
Christ's is the world	110
Disposer supreme	155
God forgave my sin	237
Great is thy faithfulness	273
Guide me, O thou great Redeemer	275
Here, O my Lord	304
How beauteous are their feet	315
I am the bread of life	323
I believe in Jesus	325
I danced in the morning	329
In Christ alone	352
Jesus' love is very wonderful	393
My Father, for another night	513
Now the green blade riseth	533
O for a thousand tongues to sing	541
Surrexit Christus	683
The King of love my shepherd is	715
There's a wideness in God's mercy	747
Thine arm, O Lord, in days of old	750
We have a gospel to proclaim	798
Will you come and follow me	834

PROPER 6 - C

All I once held dear	16
And can it be	36
As the deer pants for the water	43
Awake, my soul, and with the sun	57
Bless the Lord, my soul	74
Come, O thou traveller unknown	134
Dear Lord and Father of mankind	152
Eternal Ruler of the ceaseless round	162
Forgive our sins as we forgive	199
God forgave my sin	237
Great is thy faithfulness	273
Hail thou once despisèd Jesus	278
How deep the Father's love for us	317
How sweet the name of Jesus sounds	321
I am trusting thee, Lord Jesus	324
I bind unto myself today	326
I'm accepted, I'm forgiven	345
Jesu, lover of my soul	369
Jesu, the very thought of thee	373
Just as I am, without one plea	413
Lead us, heavenly Father, lead us	422
My God, I love thee	517
Now let us from this table rise	530
O for a closer walk with God	539
Open our eyes, Lord	600
Peace, perfect peace, is the gift	615

Proper 6 - C

Praise, my soul, the King of heaven	623
Rock of ages	643
Such love	681
There's a wideness in God's mercy	747
We cannot measure	792
We will lay our burden down	808
Ye that know the Lord is gracious	843

PROPER 7 - C

All hail the power of Jesus' name	14
And can it be	36
As the deer pants for the water	43
Be still and know that I am God	61
Be still, for the presence of the Lord	62
Bind us together, Lord	73
Christ's is the world	110
Dear Lord and Father of mankind	152
For the healing of the nations	198
From thee all skill and science flow	212
God forgave my sin	237
Guide me, O thou great Redeemer	275
In Christ there is no east or west	353
Jesu, the very thought of thee	373
King of glory, King of peace	416
Lord Jesus, think on me	465
Lord, when I turn my back on you	486
O Jesus, I have promised	556
One is the body	594
Peace is flowing like a river	613
Peace, perfect peace, is the gift	615
Rock of ages	643
Thanks to God whose word was spoken	698
To God be the glory!	777
To the name of our salvation	779
Walk with me, O my Lord	788
We cannot measure	792
What a friend we have in Jesus	811

PROPER 8 - C

All I once held dear	16
All that I am	24
Christians, lift up your hearts	108
Come, thou Holy Spirit, come	139
Every minute of every day	163
Filled with the Spirit's power	184
For the fruits of his creation	197
From heaven you came	205
Give us the wings of faith	221
I come with joy	328
I, the Lord of sea and sky	337
In the Lord I'll be ever thankful	360
Jesu, the very thought of thee	373
Jesus calls us: o'er the tumult	379
Lead us, heavenly Father, lead us	422
Let saints on earth in concert sing	428
Lord, for the years	454
Lord, I come to you	458
My song is love unknown	521
O happy band of pilgrims	550

O Jesus, I have promised	556
Thou didst leave thy throne	766
We are marching	789
We have a gospel to proclaim	798
Will you come and follow me	834
Ye holy angels bright	840

PROPER 9 - C

Alleluia, alleluia, hearts to heaven and voices raise	32
Be bold, be strong	60
Beneath the cross of Jesus	72
Colours of day	114
Crown him with many crowns	150
For the fruits of his creation	197
Forth in the peace of Christ we go	200
Forth in thy name, O Lord, I go	201
Glorious things of thee are spoken	223
Go forth and tell	232
God be in my head	235
How deep the Father's love for us	317
I am a new creation	322
I'm not ashamed to own my Lord	347
In the Cross of Christ I glory	358
Jesu, lover of my soul	369
Jesus, Lord, we look to thee	391
Just as I am, without one plea	413
Like a mighty river flowing	445
Love divine, all loves excelling	491
Meekness and majesty	507
O Lord, all the world belongs to you	560
O Lord, my God	563
Peace is flowing like a river	613
Rock of ages	643
Sing praise to God who reigns above	664
Tell out, my soul	692
The Church's one foundation	702
Thuma mina	771
We have a gospel to proclaim	798
We sing the praise of him who died	804
When I survey the wondrous cross	820

PROPER 10 - C

All who would valiant be	27
Brother, sister, let me serve you	91
Come, ye faithful, raise the anthem	142
Father, hear the prayer we offer	169
For all the saints	190
God has spoken – by the prophets	238
Gracious Spirit, Holy Ghost	268
Hark, my soul, it is the Lord	287
Help us to help each other, Lord	299
I will offer up my life	339
Immortal love, for ever full	350
Jesu, Jesu, fill us with your love	368
Jesus, Lord, we look to thee	391
Let there be love	430
Lord of all hopefulness	467
My God, accept my heart this day	514
Not far beyond the sea	528

O Lord, all the world belongs to you	560
O Lord of heaven and earth and sea	566
O thou who camest from above	580
Open our eyes, Lord	600
To God be the glory!	777
Ubi caritas	781
When I needed a neighbour	819
When morning gilds the skies	822
Who can sound the depths of sorrow	829
Ye that know the Lord is gracious	843

PROPER 11 - C

Adoramus te, Domine	8
All heaven declares	15
At the name of Jesus	52
Be still and know that I am God	61
Be still, my soul	63
Be thou my vision	66
Father, we adore you	176
Hail to the Lord's anointed	280
Hark, my soul, it is the Lord	287
I come with joy	328
I will worship	341
It is a thing most wonderful	364
Jesu, Jesu, fill us with your love	368
Jesus shall take the highest honour	400
Just as I am, without one plea	413
Let saints on earth in concert sing	428
Listen, let your heart keep seeking	446
Lord, enthroned in heavenly splendour	453
My God, how wonderful you are	516
My God, I love thee	517
O love divine, how sweet thou art!	569
Overwhelmed by love	612
Peace, perfect peace, is the gift	615
Praise to the Lord, the Almighty	628
Seek ye first	652
Take this moment	688
The God of Abraham praise	706
The Son of God proclaim	731
To be in your presence	776
We bow down	791
What a friend we have in Jesus	811

PROPER 12 - C

Abba, Father, let me be	5
All who would valiant be	27
At the name of Jesus	52
Father God, I wonder	168
Father of heaven, whose love profound	174
Father, we adore you	176
Forgive our sins as we forgive	199
God of love	250
Great is thy faithfulness	273
I believe in Jesus	325
I will offer up my life	339
In Christ alone	352

Proper 12 - C

Jesus, where'er thy people meet	407
Lift high the Cross	437
Lord Jesus Christ	463
Lord, teach us how to pray aright	478
O Lord, hear my prayer	561
O praise ye the Lord!	574
Our Father (Caribbean)	603
Our Father God in heaven	605
Seek ye first	652
Son of God, eternal Saviour	667
Stand up and bless the Lord	676
The Lord is King!	718
Thy kingdom come, O God	774
What a friend we have in Jesus	811
When I survey the wondrous cross	820

PROPER 13 - C

Alleluia, alleluia, hearts to heaven and voices raise	32
Be thou my vision	66
Before the throne	70
Bind us together, Lord	73
Brother, sister, let me serve you	91
Come, let us with our Lord arise	129
Firmly I believe and truly	186
God is love: let heaven adore him	243
God of grace and God of glory	248
Hark, my soul, it is the Lord	287
In Christ there is no east or west	353
In heavenly love abiding	355
Jesus lives! thy terrors now	390
Let all mortal flesh keep silence	424
Love is his word	492
Make me a channel of your peace	499
My God, accept my heart this day	514
My God, how wonderful you are	516
O worship the Lord in the beauty of holiness	583
Purify my heart	631
Put thou thy trust in God	634
Sing praise to God who reigns above	664
Take my life, and let it be	687
The great Creator of the world	710
Ubi caritas	781
When all thy mercies, O my God	813
When God made the garden of creation	815
When I survey the wondrous cross	820

PROPER 14 - C

At the name of Jesus	52
Christ is made the sure foundation	96
Christ is the King!	99
Colours of day	114
Do not be afraid	156
Firmly I believe and truly	186
Glorious things of thee are spoken	223
God is love: his the care	242
Guide me, O thou great Redeemer	275
Have faith in God, my heart	290

How beauteous are their feet	315
I'm accepted, I'm forgiven	345
Jesu, lover of my soul	369
Just as I am, without one plea	413
My Jesus, my Saviour	519
My Lord, what love is this	520
Nada te turbe	523
Now let us from this table rise	530
O God of Bethel, by whose hand	545
O God, our help in ages past	547
O Lord, all the world belongs to you	560
One more step along the world I go	595
Only by grace	598
Seek ye first	652
Strengthen for service, Lord	680
Teach me, my God and King	690
Thanks to God whose word was spoken	698
The God of Abraham praise	706
The Lord is my light	719
There is a land of pure delight	741
There's a place where the streets shine	744
Thou didst leave thy throne	766
Through the night of doubt and sorrow	770
Thy kingdom come, O God	774
Wait for the Lord	785
Ye servants of the Lord	842

PROPER 15 - C

Awake, awake: fling off the night	56
Awake, my soul, and with the sun	57
Be thou my vision	66
Beauty for brokenness	67
Come, Holy Ghost, our hearts inspire	123
Faithful One, so unchanging	165
Fight the good fight	181
Give thanks with a grateful heart	219
Give us the wings of faith	221
God of grace and God of glory	248
Help us to help each other, Lord	299
In Christ there is no east or west	353
Jesus, remember me	398
Let all mortal flesh keep silence	424
Lord of all being	466
May the mind of Christ my Saviour	506
O God, unseen but ever near	548
O thou who camest from above	580
Oft in danger, oft in woe	585
Rejoice in God's saints	635
Such love	681
The God of Abraham praise	706
The head that once was crowned with thorns	711
The Lord is my light	719
There are hundreds of sparrows	738
There is a Redeemer	743
Who can sound the depths of sorrow	829
Ye holy angels bright	840

PROPER 16 - C

Amazing grace	34
Be still and know that I am God	61
Bless the Lord, my soul	74
Christ's is the world	110
Come, Lord, to our souls	130
Do not be afraid	156
Father, hear the prayer we offer	169
Glorious things of thee are spoken	223
Glory be to Jesus	224
Go, tell it on the mountain	233
God be in my head	235
Guide me, O thou great Redeemer	275
Hark, the glad sound!	288
Here in this place	302
I danced in the morning	329
In Christ there is no east or west	353
Jesus, remember me	398
King of glory, King of peace	416
Lord Jesus Christ	463
Lord, today your voice is calling	482
O for a heart to praise my God	540
O praise ye the Lord!	574
Praise, my soul, the King of heaven	623
Purify my heart	631
Rejoice, the Lord is King	638
Restore, O Lord	639
Take my life, and let it be	687
Thine arm, O Lord, in days of old	750
This is my body	755
Thy hand, O God, has guided	772
We cannot measure	792
Ye holy angels bright	840

PROPER 17 - C

A new commandment	4
All my hope on God is founded	19
All praise to thee	23
Angel-voices ever singing	40
Be bold, be strong	60
Beauty for brokenness	67
Brother, sister, let me serve you	91
Christ is the King!	99
Christ's is the world	110
Come down, O Love divine	120
Come, Lord, to our souls	130
For the beauty of the earth	195
Glorious things of thee are spoken	223
God is love: his the care	242
Here in this place	302
How sweet the name of Jesus sounds	321
Jesu, Jesu, fill us with your love	368
Jesu, lover of my soul	369
Jesus, humble was your birth	384
Let all the world in every corner sing	425
Magnificat	497
Nada te turbe	523
O for a heart to praise my God	540
O God beyond all praising	544
O Lord, all the world belongs to you	560

Proper 17 - C

Praise, my soul, the King of heaven	623
Praise the Lord, ye heavens, adore him	625
Rock of ages	643
Such love	681
Tell out, my soul	692
We'll walk the land	809
When I needed a neighbour	819
Wide, wide as the ocean	833
Ye holy angels bright	840

PROPER 18 - C

All that I am	24
All who would valiant be	27
Angel-voices ever singing	40
As the deer pants for the water	43
Before Jehovah's aweful throne	68
Brother, sister, let me serve you	91
Come, let us join our cheerful songs	127
Deck thyself, my soul, with gladness	153
God be in my head	235
Have faith in God, my heart	290
I bind unto myself today	326
I heard the voice of Jesus say	334
I will offer up my life	339
Jesus Christ is waiting	382
Jesus, we celebrate your victory	405
Lord, I come to you	458
Lord, I have made thy word my choice	459
Lord Jesus Christ	463
O happy day	551
O Jesus, I have promised	556
O Lord, your tenderness	568
O thou who camest from above	580
O worship the King	582
One more step along the world I go	595
Only by grace	598
Onward, Christian pilgrims	599
Praise to the Holiest	627
Spirit of the living God (Iverson)	675
Take me, Lord	685
Take my life, and let it be	687
Take up thy cross, the Saviour said	689
The King of love my shepherd is	715
There are hundreds of sparrows	738
Thine for ever! God of love	752
Ubi caritas	781
Will you come and follow me	834

PROPER 19 - C

All people that on earth do dwell	21
Amazing grace	34
Be thou my guardian and my guide	65
Broken for me	90
Come on and celebrate	135
Faithful Shepherd, feed me	166
Father of heaven, whose love profound	174
From all that dwell below the skies	203

Go forth and tell	232
God forgave my sin	237
Good Christians all, rejoice and sing	266
Happy are they, they that love God	285
Hark, my soul, it is the Lord	287
How deep the Father's love for us	317
How sweet the name of Jesus sounds	321
I cannot tell	327
I have a friend	333
I will sing the wondrous story	340
Immortal, invisible, God only wise	349
In heavenly love abiding	355
Just as I am, without one plea	413
King of glory, King of peace	416
Lord Jesus Christ	463
Loving Shepherd of thy sheep	495
Name of all majesty	524
O God of Bethel, by whose hand	545
O thou, who at thy Eucharist didst pray	579
Praise, my soul, the King of heaven	623
Rejoice, O land, in God thy might	637
Songs of praise the angels sang	668
The God of love my shepherd is	707
The King of love my shepherd is	715
The Lord's my shepherd (Townend)	724
There is a Redeemer	743
There's a wideness in God's mercy	747
Thine for ever! God of love	752
This is the day the Lord has made	760
Through all the changing scenes of life	769
We will lay our burden down	808

PROPER 20 - C

Abide with me	6
Beauty for brokenness	67
Father, Lord of all creation	172
Father of heaven, whose love profound	174
Forth in thy name, O Lord, I go	201
Give thanks with a grateful heart	219
Great is the darkness	271
Guide me, O thou great Redeemer	275
Heaven shall not wait	297
Inspired by love and anger	362
Jesus Christ	380
Jesus, Lord, we look to thee	391
Jesus, where'er thy people meet	407
Judge eternal, throned in splendour	411
Lord, for the years	454
Lord, thy word abideth	481
Lord, we come to ask your healing	483
O for a heart to praise my God	540
O Jesus, I have promised	556
Restore, O Lord	639

Son of God, eternal Saviour	667
Stand up, stand up for Jesus	677
Take my life, and let it be	687
Teach me, my God and King	690
The Lord is King!	718
Thou art the Way: by thee alone	765
Thy kingdom come, O God	774
When God made the garden of creation	815
When I survey the wondrous cross	820

PROPER 21 - C

All my hope on God is founded	19
Amazing grace	34
Be thou my vision	66
Bind us together, Lord	73
Blest are the pure in heart	79
Breathe on me, Breath of God	87
Brother, sister, let me serve you	91
Christ is the world's Light	100
Christ's is the world	110
Come, ye faithful, raise the anthem	142
Crown him with many crowns	150
Father, we thank thee	178
Fight the good fight	181
For the healing of the nations	198
Give thanks with a grateful heart	219
Give to our God immortal praise	220
God has spoken – by the prophets	238
God is love: let heaven adore him	243
Heaven shall not wait	297
If you believe and I believe	344
Immortal, invisible, God only wise	349
Immortal love, for ever full	350
Inspired by love and anger	362
Kum ba yah	419
Lord of the worlds above	477
Love is his word	492
Magnificat	497
O God of Bethel, by whose hand	545
O Lord of heaven and earth and sea	566
Oft in danger, oft in woe	585
Rejoice, the Lord is King	638
Tell out, my soul	692
The head that once was crowned with thorns	711
The Lord is King!	718
There are hundreds of sparrows	738
Wait for the Lord	785
When I needed a neighbour	819
Who can sound the depths of sorrow	829
Ye holy angels bright	840
Ye that know the Lord is gracious	843

PROPER 22 - C

All I once held dear	16
All that I am	24
All you who seek a comfort sure	28
As the deer pants for the water	43
Be bold, be strong	60

Proper 22 - C

Dear Lord and Father of mankind 152
Do not be afraid 156
Faithful One, so unchanging 165
Father, hear the prayer we offer 169
Father, I place into your hands 170
Fill thou my life, O Lord my God 182
Firmly I believe and truly 186
Give us the wings of faith 221
God is working his purpose out 246
Great is thy faithfulness 273
Guide me, O thou great
  Redeemer 275
Have faith in God, my heart 290
Help us to help each other, Lord 299
I cannot tell 327
If you believe and I believe 344
I'm not ashamed to own my Lord 347
Nada te turbe 523
Name of all majesty 524
New every morning is the love 526
Now thank we all our God 532
O Love that wilt not let me go 571
O thou who camest from above 580
Put thou thy trust in God 634
Stay with me 678
Strengthen for service, Lord 680
Take this moment 688
Teach me, my God and King 690
Through all the changing scenes
  of life 769
Through the night of doubt and
  sorrow 770
Thy hand, O God, has guided 772
Thy kingdom come, O God 774
We have a gospel to proclaim 798

PROPER 23 - C

A man there lived in Galilee 3
As pants the hart for cooling
  streams 42
Bless the Lord, my soul 74
Christ is made the sure foundation 96
Christ's is the world 110
Give thanks with a grateful heart 219
Go, tell it on the mountain 233
Halle, halle, halle 282
How sweet the name of Jesus
  sounds 321
I give you all the honour 331
I'm accepted, I'm forgiven 345
Immortal love, for ever full 350
Jesu, lover of my soul 369
Just as I am, without one plea 413
Lead, kindly light 421
Lord, I lift your name on high 461
Lord Jesus Christ 463
My Jesus, my Saviour 519
New every morning is the love 526
Now thank we all our God 532
O for a thousand tongues to sing 541
Oft in danger, oft in woe 585
Praise him, praise him, praise him 622
Praise, my soul, the King of
  heaven 623

Praise to the Lord, the Almighty 628
Rock of ages 643
Sing of the Lord's goodness 663
Stand up, stand up for Jesus 677
Take up thy cross, the Saviour
  said 689
Thank you, Lord 695
The head that once was crowned
  with thorns 711
There is a Redeemer 743
Thine arm, O Lord, in days of old 750
Through the night of doubt and
  sorrow 770
To God be the glory! 777
What a friend we have in Jesus 811
When all thy mercies, O my God 813

PROPER 24 - C

A brighter dawn is breaking 1
Amazing grace 34
Author of life divine 55
Be still and know that I am God 61
Be thou my guardian and my guide 65
Christ is the heavenly food 98
Come, O thou traveller unknown 134
Father, hear the prayer we offer 169
Father, I place into your hands 170
Father of heaven, whose love
  profound 174
Give to our God immortal praise 220
Great Shepherd of thy people 274
Hail to the Lord's anointed 280
Help us, O Lord, to learn 298
Here, O my Lord 304
Immortal, invisible, God only
  wise 349
It's me, O Lord 365
Let us, with a gladsome mind 435
Lift up your hearts! 439
Lord, for the years 454
Lord, teach us how to pray aright 478
Lord, thy word abideth 481
O God beyond all praising 544
O Lord, hear my prayer 561
Restore, O Lord 639
Shepherd divine, our wants
  relieve 655
Thanks to God whose word was
  spoken 698
The Church's one foundation 702
Thou, whose almighty word 767
We are marching 789
What a friend we have in Jesus 811

PROPER 25 - C

All praise to thee 23
All who would valiant be 27
Amazing grace 34
And can it be 36
Beauty for brokenness 67
Breathe on me, Breath of God 87
Brother, sister, let me serve you 91
Christ's is the world 110
Come down, O Love divine 120

Father of heaven, whose love
  profound 174
Fight the good fight 181
God forgave my sin 237
Guide me, O thou great
  Redeemer 275
How shall I sing that majesty 320
I will sing the wondrous story 340
Inspired by love and anger 362
Jesu, lover of my soul 369
Jesus, remember me 398
Just as I am, without one plea 413
King of glory, King of peace 416
Let us break bread together 431
Lift up your hearts! 439
Lord, have mercy (Ghana) 455
Lord Jesus, think on me 465
Name of all majesty 524
O for a closer walk with God 539
O God, our help in ages past 547
Praise, my soul, the King of
  heaven 623
Rejoice, O land, in God thy
  might 637
Rejoice, the Lord is King 638
Rock of ages 643
Tell out, my soul 692
The King is among us 714
There are hundreds of sparrows 738
Wait for the Lord 785
When I feel the touch 817
When I look into your holiness 818
Ye holy angels bright 840
Ye that know the Lord is gracious 843

Or: BIBLE SUNDAY - C

Break thou the bread 86
Christians, lift up your hearts 108
Come, Holy Ghost, our hearts
  inspire 123
God has spoken – by the prophets 238
God's Spirit is in my heart 262
Hark, my soul, it is the Lord 287
Help us, O Lord, to learn 298
If you believe and I believe 344
Jesus the Lord said: 'I am the
  Bread' 403
Lord, for the years 454
Lord, I have made thy word my
  choice 459
Lord, thy word abideth 481
May the mind of Christ my
  Saviour 506
Not far beyond the sea 528
Rise and hear! The Lord is
  speaking 641
Seek ye first 652
Thanks to God whose word was
  spoken 698
The heavens declare thy glory,
  Lord 712
The Lord is my light 719
The prophets spoke in days of old 728
Thou, whose almighty word 767
We have a gospel to proclaim 798

DEDICATION FESTIVAL - C

Angel-voices ever singing	40
Be still, for the presence of the Lord	62
Blessèd city, heavenly Salem	77
Christ is made the sure foundation	96
Christ is our cornerstone	97
City of God, how broad and far	111
For I'm building a people of power	193
Forth in the peace of Christ we go	200
Glorious things of thee are spoken	223
God is here! As we his people	241
Here in this place	302
In our day of thanksgiving	356
Let us build a house	432
Longing for light	452
Lord, for the years	454
O God of Bethel, by whose hand	545
The Church of God a kingdom is	701
The Church's one foundation	702
Thy hand, O God, has guided	772
We have a gospel to proclaim	798
We love the place, O God	800
Ye that know the Lord is gracious	843

ALL SAINTS' DAY - C

At the name of Jesus	52
Be thou my vision	66
Beauty for brokenness	67
Blest are the pure in heart	79
Come, Holy Ghost, our souls inspire	124
Come, thou Holy Spirit, come	139
Disposer supreme	155
For all the saints	190
For all thy saints, O Lord	191
Give us the wings of faith	221
How bright these glorious spirits shine!	316
Immortal, invisible, God only wise	349
Let all the world in every corner sing	425
Let saints on earth in concert sing	428
O King, enthroned on high	557
O worship the King	582
Rejoice in God's saints	635
Thanks be to God	696
The head that once was crowned with thorns	711
The Lord is my light	719
There is a land of pure delight	741
There's a place where the streets shine	744
Who are these like stars appearing	828
Ye watchers and ye holy ones	844

FOURTH SUNDAY BEFORE ADVENT - C

All that I am	24
At the name of Jesus	52
Come, risen Lord	137
Dear Lord and Father of mankind	152

Deck thyself, my soul, with gladness	153
God forgave my sin	237
How sweet the name of Jesus sounds	321
I come with joy	328
I heard the voice of Jesus say	334
I'm accepted, I'm forgiven	345
Jesus, remember me	398
Just as I am, without one plea	413
Lo, he comes with clouds descending	449
My Lord, what love is this	520
O day of God, draw nigh	537
O for a closer walk with God	539
O happy band of pilgrims	550
O thou who camest from above	580
Purify my heart	631
Sing of the Lord's goodness	663
Strengthen for service, Lord	680
Take my life, and let it be	687
The Spirit lives to set us free	732
This is the day the Lord has made	760
Thou didst leave thy throne	766
When the music fades	823
Will you come and follow me	834
Zacchaeus was a very little man	857

THIRD SUNDAY BEFORE ADVENT - C

A man there lived in Galilee	3
Alleluia, alleluia, give thanks to the risen Lord	31
Alleluia (x 8)	29
Be still, my soul	63
Be thou my guardian and my guide	65
Come, let us with our Lord arise	129
Come on and celebrate	135
Forth in the peace of Christ we go	200
God of life, God of love	249
Great is thy faithfulness	273
How sweet the name of Jesus sounds	321
I am the bread of life	323
Immortal, invisible, God only wise	349
Jesus the Lord said: 'I am the Bread'	403
Led like a lamb	423
Lord, for the years	454
Love's redeeming work is done	494
My God, accept my heart this day	514
My God, how wonderful you are	516
Now is eternal life	529
Now the green blade riseth	533
O God, our help in ages past	547
O Jesus, I have promised	556
O Lord, hear my prayer	561
Our blest Redeemer, ere he breathed	602
The God of Abraham praise	706
There is a green hill far away	740
Wherefore, O Father	826
Within our darkest night	837
You, living Christ, our eyes behold	851

SECOND SUNDAY BEFORE ADVENT - C

Christ is our cornerstone	97
Christ, whose glory fills the skies	105
Colours of day	114
Confitemini Domino	145
Do not be afraid	156
For the healing of the nations	198
God of love	250
Guide me, O thou great Redeemer	275
Help us to help each other, Lord	299
Hills of the north, rejoice	307
Immortal love, for ever full	350
Jesus' love is very wonderful	393
Jesus, where'er thy people meet	407
Judge eternal, throned in splendour	411
Lead us, heavenly Father, lead us	422
Make me a channel of your peace	499
Nada te turbe	523
New songs of celebration render	527
Now let us from this table rise	530
Strengthen for service, Lord	680
The Lord is my light	719
The people that in darkness sat	727
The Spirit lives to set us free	732
Thou, whose almighty word	767
Through the night of doubt and sorrow	770
To the name of our salvation	779
Wait for the Lord	785
We are marching	789
We turn to you	806
You are the King of Glory	849

CHRIST THE KING - C

All hail the power of Jesus' name	14
All praise to thee	23
At the name of Jesus	52
Be still, for the presence of the Lord	62
Christ is made the sure foundation	96
Christ is the King!	99
Christ triumphant	103
Christ's is the world	110
Crown him with many crowns	150
From glory to glory advancing	204
God is love: his the care	242
God is our strength from days of old	244
God of mercy, God of grace	251
He is exalted	293
How shall I sing that majesty	320
I danced in the morning	329
I will sing the wondrous story	340
Jesus calls us here to meet him	378
Jesus is King	386
Jesus is the name we honour	388
Jesus, remember me	398
Jesus shall reign	399
King of kings and Lord of lords	417
Lord, enthroned in heavenly splendour	453
Lord Jesus Christ	463

Christ the King - C

Lord, teach us how to pray aright	478
Make way, make way	500
Meekness and majesty	507
Name of all majesty	524
O worship the King	582
Rejoice, the Lord is King	638
Stand up, stand up for Jesus	677
The God of Abraham praise	706

The head that once was crowned with thorns	711
The King is among us	714
The King of love my shepherd is	715
The Lord is King!	718
When God almighty came to earth	814
Ye servants of God	841

All-Age Index

All in an Easter garden	17
All over the world	20
All the nations of the earth	25
All things bright and beautiful	26
All who would valiant be	27
Amazing grace	34
Angels from the realms of glory	39
As Jacob with travel was weary one day	41
Away in a manger	59
Be bold, be strong	60
Be the centre of my life	64
Break the bread and pour the wine	85
Clap your hands, all you people	112
Come and join the celebration	117
Come into his presence	126
Come on, let's get up and go	136
Ding dong, merrily on high!	130
Every minute of every day	163
Father God, I wonder	168
Father, we adore you	176
Father, we love you	177
Father welcomes all his children	179
Fishes of the ocean	187
5000 + hungry folk	188
Follow me	189
Gather around, for the table is spread	213
Give me joy in my heart	215
Give me peace, O Lord	216
Go wandering in the sun	234
God forgave my sin	237
God is good, God is great	240
God is love: his the care	242
God rest you merry, gentlefolk	254
God's love is deeper	261
Goliath was big and Goliath was strong	264
Good King Wenceslas	267
Halle, halle, halle	282
Hallelu, hallelu	283
Hark, the herald-angels sing	289
Have you heard the raindrops	291
He is Lord	294

He's got the whole world in his hand	306
I have a friend	333
I'm accepted, I'm forgiven	345
I'm black, I'm white, I'm short, I'm tall	346
I'm special	348
If I were a butterfly	342
In the bleak mid-winter	357
It came upon the midnight clear	363
It's me, O Lord	365
It's rounded like an orange	366
Jesu, Jesu, fill us with your love	368
Jesus bids us shine	377
Jesus is greater	385
Jesus' love is very wonderful	393
Jesus put this song	397
Jesus the Lord said: 'I am the Bread'	403
Kum ba yah	419
Let the mountains dance and sing	429
Life for the poor was hard and tough	436
Little donkey	447
Little Jesus, sweetly sleep	448
Lord of the future	476
Loving Shepherd of thy sheep	495
Make me a channel of your peace	499
Mary had a baby	502
Morning has broken	510
O come, all ye faithful	534
O give thanks (Kendrick)	542
O give thanks (Pond)	543
O little town of Bethlehem	559
O Lord, all the world belongs to you	560
O when the saints go marching in	581
Once in royal David's city	592
One more step	595
Onward, Christian pilgrims	599
Our God is a great big God	606
Our God is so great	607
Over the earth is a mat of green	610
Over the mountains and the sea	611
Praise God from whom all blessings flow	618

Praise God from whom all blessings flow	619
Push, little seed	632
Rise and shine	642
See, amid the winter's snow	649
See him lying in a bed of straw	650
Seek ye first	652
Silent night	658
Steal away	679
Thank you for the summer morning	694
Thank you, Lord	695
The first Nowell	705
The holly and the ivy	713
The King of love my shepherd is	715
The Spirit lives to set us free	732
The Virgin Mary had a baby boy	734
The wise man	735
The world is full of smelly feet	736
There are hundreds of sparrows	738
There is a green hill far away	740
Think of a world without any flowers	753
This little light of mine	762
We are marching	789
We eat the plants that grow from the seed	793
We have a gospel to proclaim	798
We have a King who rides a donkey	799
We'll walk the land	809
We plough the fields and scatter	801
We three kings of Orient are	805
What a friend we have in Jesus	811
When God made the garden of creation	815
When the Spirit of the Lord	824
While shepherds watched	827
Who put the colours in the rainbow?	831
Wide, wide as the ocean	833
Yesterday, today, for ever	846
You shall go out with joy	853
Zacchaeus was a very little man	857
Zip bam boo	858

Index of First Lines and Titles

This index gives the first line of each hymn. If a hymn is known also by a title (e.g. Jerusalem) this is given as well, but indented and in italics.

A

A brighter dawn is breaking 1
A great and mighty wonder 2
A man there lived in Galilee 3
A new commandment 4
A touching place 110
Abba, Father, let me be 5
Abide with me 6
Above all powers, above all kings 7
Adoramus te, Domine 8
Ah, holy Jesu, how hast thou offended 9
All are welcome 432
All creatures of our God and King 10
All for Jesus! All for Jesus! 11
All glory, laud and honour 12
All hail the Lamb 13
All hail the power of Jesus' name 14
All heaven declares 15
All I once held dear 16
All in an Easter garden 17
All my days 18
All my hope on God is founded 19
All over the world 20
All people that on earth do dwell 21
All praise to our redeeming Lord 22
All praise to thee 23
All that I am 24
All the nations of the earth 25
All things bright and beautiful 26
All who would valiant be 27
All you who seek a comfort sure 28
Alleluia (x 8) 29
Alleluia! Alleluia! 30
Alleluia! Raise the Gospel 30
Alleluia, alleluia, give thanks to the risen Lord 31
Alleluia, alleluia, hearts to heaven and voices raise 32
Alleluia, sing to Jesus 33
Amazing grace 34
Amazing love 520
An upper room did our Lord prepare 35
Ancient of Days 78
And can it be 36
And did those feet in ancient time 37
And now, O Father, mindful of the love 38
Angels from the realms of glory 39
Angel-voices ever singing 40
As gentle as silence 578
As Jacob with travel was weary one day 41
As pants the hart for cooling streams 42

As the deer pants for the water 43
As the disciples 44
As we are gathered 45
As with gladness men of old 46
As your family, Lord, see us here 47
Ascribe greatness 48
At even, ere the sun was set 49
At the cross she keeps her station 50
At the Lamb's high feast we sing 51
At the name of Jesus 52
At this table we remember 53
At this time of giving 54
Author of life divine 55
Awake, awake: fling off the night 56
Awake, my soul, and with the sun 57
Awake, our souls; away, our fears 58
Away in a manger 59

B

Be bold, be strong 60
Be still and know that I am God 61
Be still, for the presence of the Lord 62
Be still, my soul 63
Be the centre of my life 64
Be the centre 376
Be thou my guardian and my guide 65
Be thou my vision 66
Beautiful one 838
Beautiful Saviour 18
Beautiful world 763
Beauty for brokenness 67
Because of you 744
Before Jehovah's aweful throne 68
Before the ending of the day 69
Before the throne 70
Behold, the great Creator 71
Beneath the cross of Jesus 72
Bind us together, Lord 73
Bless the Lord, my soul 74
Blessèd assurance 75
Blessed be the Lord God Almighty 171
Blessèd be your name 76
Blessèd city, heavenly Salem 77
Blessing and honour 78
Blest are the pure in heart 79
Blest Creator of the light 80
Born in the night, Mary's child 81
Bread is blessed and broken 82
Bread of heaven, on thee we feed 83
Bread of the world in mercy broken 84
Break the bread and pour the wine 85
Break thou the bread 86
Breathe on me, Breath of God 87
Breathe 758
Bright the vision that delighted 88
Brightest and best 89
Broken for me 90
Brother, sister, let me serve you 91

C

Calm me, Lord 92
Celtic Alleluia 93
Christ be with me 94
Christ for the world we sing! 95
Christ is made the sure foundation 96
Christ is our cornerstone 97
Christ is the heavenly food 98
Christ is the King! 99
Christ is the world's Light 100
Christ, the fair glory of the holy angels 101
Christ the Lord is risen again 102
Christ triumphant 103
Christ, be our light 452
Christ, when for us you were baptised 104
Christ, whose glory fills the skies 105
Christian people, raise your song 106
Christians, awake! 107
Christians, lift up your hearts 108
Christians lift your hearts and voices 109
Christ's is the world 110
City of God, how broad and far 111
Clap your hands, all you people 112
Close to you 338
Cloth for the cradle 113
Colours of day 114
Come, all who look to Christ today 115
Come and celebrate 116
Come and join the celebration 117
Come and see 118
Come and see the shining hope 119
Come down, O Love divine 120
Come, faithful pilgrims all 121
Come, gracious Spirit, heavenly Dove 122
Come, Holy Ghost, our hearts inspire 123
Come, Holy Ghost, our souls inspire 124
Come, Holy Spirit, come 125
Come into his presence 126
Come, let us join our cheerful songs 127
Come, let us use the grace divine 128
Come, let us with our Lord arise 129
Come, light of our hearts 783
Come, Lord Jesus 271
Come, Lord, to our souls 130
Come, my Way, my Truth, my Life 131
Come, now is the time to worship 132
Come now, the table's spread 133
Come, O thou traveller unknown 134
Come on and celebrate 135
Come on, let's get up and go 136
Come, risen Lord 137
Come, see the Lord 138

Come, thou Holy Spirit, come 139
Come, thou long-expected Jesus 140
Come, wounded healer 141
Come, ye faithful, raise the
anthem 142
Come, ye faithful, raise the strain 143
Come, ye thankful people, come 144
Confitemini Domino 145
Creation sings! 146
Creator of the earth and skies 147
Creator of the starry height 148
Creator Spirit, come 149
Crown him with many crowns 150

D

Dance and sing 151
Days of Elijah 748
Dear Lord and Father of mankind 152
Deck thyself, my soul, with
gladness 153
Deeper, wider, higher 261
Ding dong, merrily on high! 154
Disposer supreme 155
Do not be afraid 156
Doxology 618
Draw nigh and take the body 157

E

Earth has many a noble city 158
Eat this bread 159
Enemy of apathy 654
Eternal Father, strong to save 160
Eternal God, we consecrate 161
Eternal Ruler of the ceaseless
round 162
Every minute of every day 163
Exaudi nos, Domine 164

F

Faithful One, so unchanging 165
Faithful Shepherd, feed me 166
Faithful vigil ended 167
Father God, I wonder 168
Father, hear the prayer we offer 169
Father, I place into your hands 170
Father in heaven, how we love
you 171
Father, Lord of all creation 172
Father, most holy, merciful and
loving 173
Father of heaven, whose love
profound 174
Father of peace, and God of love 175
Father, we adore you 176
Father, we love you 177
Father, we thank thee 178
Father welcomes all his children 179
Father, who in Jesus found us 180
Fight the good fight 181
Fill thou my life, O Lord my God 182
Fill your hearts with joy and
gladness 183
Filled with the Spirit's power 184
Finished the strife 185
Firmly I believe and truly 186

Fishes of the ocean 187
5000 + hungry folk 188
Follow me 189
For all the saints 190
For all thy saints, O Lord 191
For all your saints still active 192
For ever 218
For I'm building a people of
power 193
For Mary, mother of our Lord 194
For the beauty of the earth 195
For the days when you feel near 196
For the fruits of his creation 197
For the healing of the nations 198
Forgive our sins as we forgive 199
Forth in the peace of Christ we go 200
Forth in thy name, O Lord, I go 201
Forty days and forty nights 202
Freely, freely 237
From all that dwell below the
skies 203
From glory to glory advancing 204
From heaven you came 205
From many grains 206
From the eastern mountains 207
From the falter of breath 208
From the rising of the sun 209
From the sun's rising 210
From the very depths of darkness 211
From thee all skill and science
flow 212

G

Gather around, for the table is
spread 213
Gather us in 302
Gifts of bread and wine 214
Give me joy in my heart 215
Give me peace, O Lord 216
Give thanks for those 217
Give thanks to the Lord 218
Give thanks with a grateful heart 219
Give to our God immortal praise 220
Give us the wings of faith 221
Gloria (Anderson) 222
Glorify your name 177
Glorious things of thee are
spoken 223
Glory be to Jesus 224
Glory, love, and praise, and
honour 225
Glory to God (Peruvian Gloria) 226
Glory to God! 227
Glory to God above 228
Glory to thee, my God, this night 229
Glory to thee, O God 230
Go back, go back to Galilee 231
Go forth and tell 232
Go, tell it on the mountain 233
Go wandering in the sun 234
Go, tell everyone 262
God be in my head 235
God be with you till we meet
again 236
God forgave my sin 237

God has spoken – by the prophets 238
God, in the planning 239
God is good, God is great 240
God is here! As we his people 241
God is love: his the care 242
God is love: let heaven adore him 243
God is our strength from days
of old 244
God is the giver of love 245
God is working his purpose out 246
God knows me 738
God moves in a mysterious way 247
God of grace and God of glory 248
God of life, God of love 249
God of love 250
God of mercy 485
God of mercy, God of grace 251
God of the Passover 252
God of the poor 67
God on earth 814
God, our Creator 253
God rest you merry, gentlefolk 254
God save our gracious Queen 255
God that madest earth and
heaven 256
God the Father, name we treasure 257
God to enfold you 258
God, whose city's sure foundation 259
God, whose farm is all creation 260
God's love is deeper 261
God's Spirit is in my heart 262
God's surprise 832
Going home, moving on 263
Goliath was big and Goliath was
strong 264
Good Christians all, rejoice 265
Good Christians all, rejoice and
sing 266
Good King Wenceslas 267
Gracious Spirit, Holy Ghost 268
Grant us the courage, gracious
God 269
Great big God 606
Great God, your love has called us 270
Great is the darkness 271
Great is the Lord and most
worthy of praise 272
Great is thy faithfulness 273
Great love 518
Great Shepherd of thy people 274
Guide me, O thou great
Redeemer 275

H

Hail, gladdening Light 276
Hail the day that sees him rise 277
Hail, thou once despisèd Jesus 278
Hail to the Lord who comes 279
Hail to the Lord's anointed 280
Hail, true body 281
Halle, halle, halle 282
Hallelu, hallelu 283
Hallelujah 855
Hands that have been handling 284
Happy are they, they that love
God 285

Hark! A herald voice is calling 286
Hark, my soul, it is the Lord 287
Hark, the glad sound! 288
Hark, the herald-angels sing 289
Have faith in God, my heart 290
Have you heard the raindrops 291
He has risen 292
He is exalted 293
He is Lord 294
He is the Lord 295
Heaven is in my heart 552
Heaven is open wide 296
Heaven shall not wait 297
Help us, O Lord, to learn 298
Help us to help each other, Lord 299
Here am I, Lord 300
Here I am 301
Here I am, Lord 337
Here I am to worship 441
Here in this place 302
Here is bread 303
Here, O my Lord 304
Here on the threshold of a new
  beginning 305
He's got the whole world in his
  hand 306
Hills of the north, rejoice 307
Holy and anointed One 389
Holy, holy 647
Holy, holy, holy 308
Holy, holy, holy is the Lord 309
Holy, holy, holy! Lord God
  almighty 310
Holy Spirit, come, confirm us 311
Holy Spirit, truth divine 312
Holy Spirit, will you be 313
Hosanna, hosanna 314
Hosanna to the Son of David 849
How beauteous are their feet 315
How bright these glorious spirits
  shine! 316
How deep the Father's love for us 317
How good is the God we adore 318
How great thou art 563
How lovely on the mountains 319
How shall I sing that majesty 320
How sweet the name of Jesus
  sounds 321

I

I am a new creation 322
I am the bread of life 323
I am trusting thee, Lord Jesus 324
I believe in Jesus 325
I bind unto myself today 326
I cannot tell 327
I come with joy 328
I could sing of your love for ever 611
I danced in the morning 329
I give my hands 330
I give you all the honour 331
I give you love 332
I give you my heart 756
I have a friend 333
I heard the voice of Jesus say 334

I love you, Lord, and I lift my
  voice 335
I need thee every hour 336
I really want to worship you 850
I stand in awe 847
I, the Lord of sea and sky 337
I watch the sunrise 338
I will offer up my life 339
I will sing the wondrous story 340
I will sing your praises 168
I will worship 341
I worship you 331
If I were a butterfly 342
If we only seek peace 343
If you believe and I believe 344
I'm accepted, I'm forgiven 345
I'm black, I'm white, I'm short,
  I'm tall 346
I'm not ashamed to own my Lord 347
I'm special 348
Immortal, invisible, God only
  wise 349
Immortal love, for ever full 350
In bread we bring you, Lord 351
In Christ alone 352
In Christ there is no east or west 353
In full and glad surrender 354
In heavenly love abiding 355
In love for me 755
In our day of thanksgiving 356
In the bleak mid-winter 357
In the Cross of Christ I glory 358
In the garden Mary lingers 359
In the Lord I'll be ever thankful 360
In the Lord is my joy 361
Inspired by love and anger 362
It came upon the midnight clear 363
It is a thing most wonderful 364
It's all about you 394
It's me, O Lord 365
It's rounded like an orange 366

J

Jerusalem 37
Jesu, grant me this, I pray 367
Jesu, Jesu, fill us with your love 368
Jesu, lover of my soul 369
Jesu, our hope, our heart's desire 370
Jesu, Son of Mary 371
Jesu, tawa pano 372
Jesu, the very thought of thee 373
Jesu, thou joy of loving hearts 374
Jesus, all for Jesus 375
Jesus, be the centre 376
Jesus bids us shine 377
Jesus calls us here to meet him 378
Jesus calls us: o'er the tumult 379
Jesus Christ 380
Jesus Christ is risen today 381
Jesus Christ is waiting 382
Jesus, good above all other 383
Jesus, humble was your birth 384
Jesus is greater 385
Jesus is King 386
Jesus is Lord! Creation's voice
  proclaims it 387

Jesus is our God 388
Jesus is our joy 493
Jesus is the name we honour 388
Jesus, Jesus 389
Jesus lives! thy terrors now 390
Jesus, Lord, we look to thee 391
Jesus, Lord, we pray 392
Jesus' love is very wonderful 393
Jesus, lover of my soul 394
Jesus, Name above all names 395
Jesus, Prince and Saviour 396
Jesus put this song 397
Jesus, remember me 398
Jesus shall reign 399
Jesus shall take the highest
  honour 400
Jesus, stand among us 401
Jesus, stand among us in thy risen
  power 402
Jesus the Lord said: 'I am the
  Bread' 403
Jesus, the name high over all 404
Jesus, we are here 372
Jesus, we celebrate your victory 405
Jesus, we have heard your Spirit 406
Jesus, where'er thy people meet 407
Join the song of praise and
  protest 408
Joy to the world! 409
Jubilate, everybody 410
Judge eternal, throned in
  splendour 411
Just a closer walk with thee 412
Just as I am, without one plea 413

K

Keep watch with me 414
Kindle a flame 415
King of glory, King of peace 416
King of kings and Lord of lords 417
King of kings, majesty 418
Knowing you 16
Kum ba yah 419

L

Laudate Dominum 420
Lead, kindly light 421
Lead us, heavenly Father, lead us 422
Led like a lamb 423
Let all mortal flesh keep silence 424
Let all the world in every corner
  sing 425
Let everything that has breath 426
Let love be found among us 427
Let saints on earth in concert sing 428
Let the flame burn brighter 809
Let the mountains dance and sing 429
Let there be love 430
Let us break bread together 431
Let us build a house 432
Let us praise God together 433
Let us talents and tongues employ 434
Let us, with a gladsome mind 435
Life for the poor was hard and
  tough 436

Lift high the Cross 437
Lift up your heads 438
Lift up your hearts! 439
Lift up your voice 440
Light of the world 441
Light up the fire 114
Light's abode, celestial Salem 442
Light's glittering morn 443
Like a candle flame 444
Like a mighty river flowing 445
Listen, let your heart keep seeking 446
Little donkey 447
Little Jesus, sweetly sleep 448
Living Lord 463
Lo, he comes with clouds
  descending 449
Lo, round the throne, a glorious
  band 450
Long ago, prophets knew 451
Longing for light 452
Lord, enthroned in heavenly
  splendour 453
Lord, for the years 454
Lord, have mercy (Ghana) 455
Lord, have mercy (Russian) 456
Lord, I come before your throne
  of grace 457
Lord, I come to you 458
Lord, I have made thy word my
  choice 459
Lord, I lift my hands to you in
  prayer 460
Lord, I lift your name on high 461
Lord, it belongs not to my care 462
Lord Jesus Christ 463
Lord Jesus Christ, be present 464
Lord Jesus, think on me 465
Lord of all being 466
Lord of all hopefulness 467
Lord of all life and power 468
Lord of all, to whom alone 469
Lord of beauty, thine the
  splendour 470
Lord of creation, to you be
  all praise! 471
Lord of creation, may your will be
  done 472
Lord of life 473
Lord of lords and King eternal 474
Lord of the boundless curves 475
Lord of the Dance 329
Lord of the future 476
Lord of the worlds above 477
Lord, teach us how to pray aright 478
Lord, the light of your love 479
Lord, there are times 480
Lord, thy word abideth 481
Lord, today your voice is calling 482
Lord, we come to ask your
  healing 483
Lord, we thank you for the
  promise 484
Lord, we turn to you for mercy 485
Lord, when I turn my back
  on you 486

Lord, you call us to a journey 487
Lord, you created 488
Lord, you have my heart 489
Love came down at Christmas 490
Love divine, all loves excelling 491
Love is his word 492
Lovely in your littleness 493
Love's redeeming work is done 494
Loving Shepherd of thy sheep 495
Low in the grave he lay 496

M

Magnificat 497
  Magnificat 408
Majesty, worship his majesty 498
Make me a channel of your peace 499
Make way, make way 500
  Mallaig Sprinkling Song 672
Mary, blessèd grieving mother 501
Mary had a baby 502
May God's blessing surround you 503
May the fragrance of Jesus fill this
  place 504
May the grace of Christ our
  Saviour 505
May the mind of Christ my
  Saviour 506
Meekness and majesty 507
Men of faith 508
Morning glory, starlit sky 509
Morning has broken 510
Moses, I know you're the man 511
  My desire 776
My faith looks up to thee 512
My Father, for another night 513
My God, accept my heart this day 514
My God, and is thy table spread 515
My God, how wonderful you are 516
My God, I love thee 517
My heart will sing to you 518
My Jesus, my Saviour 519
My Lord, what love is this 520
My song is love unknown 521
My spirit longs for thee 522

N

Nada te turbe 523
Name of all majesty 524
Nearer, my God, to thee 525
New every morning is the love 526
New songs of celebration render 527
  New Wine 596
Not far beyond the sea 528
  Nothing can trouble 523
Now is eternal life 529
Now let us from this table rise 530
Now, my tongue, the mystery
  telling 531
Now thank we all our God 532
Now the green blade riseth 533

O

O come, all ye faithful 534
O come, O come, Emmanuel 535
O comfort my people 536

O day of God, draw nigh 537
O dearest Lord, thy sacred head 538
O for a closer walk with God 539
O for a heart to praise my God 540
O for a thousand tongues to sing 541
O give thanks (Kendrick) 542
O give thanks (Pond) 543
O God beyond all praising 544
O God of Bethel, by whose hand 545
O God of earth and altar 546
O God, our help in ages past 547
O God, unseen yet ever near 548
O God, you search me 549
O happy band of pilgrims 550
O happy day 551
O, heaven is in my heart 552
O holy, heavenly kingdom 553
O Holy Spirit, Lord of grace 554
O, how good is the Lord! 555
O Jesus, I have promised 556
O King enthroned on high 557
O let the Son of God enfold you 558
O little town of Bethlehem 559
O Lord, all the world belongs to
  you 560
O Lord, hear my prayer 561
O Lord, listen to my prayer 562
O Lord, my God! 563
O Lord, my heart is not proud 564
O Lord of every shining
  constellation 565
O Lord of heaven and earth
  and sea 566
O Lord, we want to praise you 567
O Lord, your tenderness 568
O love divine, how sweet
  thou art! 569
O love, how deep, how broad,
  how high 570
O Love that wilt not let me go 571
O my Saviour, lifted from the
  earth 572
O perfect love 573
O praise ye the Lord! 574
O raise your eyes on high 575
O sacred head, surrounded 576
O strength and stay 577
O, the love of my Lord 578
O thou, who at thy Eucharist
  didst pray 579
O thou who camest from above 580
O when the saints go marching in 581
O worship the King 582
O worship the Lord in the beauty
  of holiness 583
Of the Father's love begotten 584
Oft in danger, oft in woe 585
Oh, the life of the world 586
On a hill far away 587
On Christmas night all Christians
  sing 588
On Jordan's bank the Baptist's cry 589
On the day of Pentecost 590
On the holy cross I see 591
  Once again 380

Once in royal David's city 592
Once, only once, and once for all 593
One is the body 594
One more step along the world I go 595
One shall tell another 596
One who intercedes 313
One whose heart is hard as steel 597
Only by grace 598
Onward, Christian pilgrims 599
Open our eyes, Lord 600
Open the eyes of my heart 601
Our blest Redeemer, ere he breathed 602
Our Father (Caribbean) 603
Our Father (Wiener) 604
Our Father God in heaven 605
Our God is a great big God 606
Our God is so great 607
Our God loves us 608
Our God reigns 319
Over all the earth 609
Over the earth is a mat of green 610
Over the mountains and the sea 611
Overwhelmed by love 612

P

Peace is flowing like a river 613
Peace, perfect peace, in this dark world of sin 614
Peace, perfect peace, is the gift 615
Peace to you 616
Power of your love 458
Praise and thanksgiving 617
Praise God from whom all blessings flow 618
Praise God from whom all blessings flow 619
Praise him on the trumpet 620
Praise him, praise him, all his children 621
Praise him, praise him, praise him 622
Praise, my soul, the King of heaven! 623
Praise, O praise our God and King 624
Praise the Lord, ye heavens, adore him! 625
Praise to God for saints and martyrs 626
Praise to the Holiest 627
Praise to the Lord, the Almighty 628
Praise we now the word of grace 629
Proclaim, proclaim the story 630
Purify my heart 631
Push, little seed 632
Put peace into each other's hands 633
Put thou thy trust in God 634

R

Refiner's fire 631
Rejoice in God's saints 635
Rejoice in the Lord always 636
Rejoice, O land, in God thy might 637

Rejoice, the Lord is King! 638
Reproaches 332
Restore, O Lord 639
Resurrection breakfast 854
Ride on, ride on in majesty! 640
Right where we are 695
Rise and hear! The Lord is speaking 641
Rise and shine 642
Rock of ages 643
Round me falls the night 644

S

Saint Luke, beloved physician 645
Salvation belongs to our God 646
Sanctus, sanctus, sanctus 647
Saviour, again to thy dear name we raise 648
See, amid the winter's snow 649
See him lying on a bed of straw 650
See the holy table, spread for our healing 651
Seek ye first 652
Send forth your Spirit, Lord 653
Send me, Lord 771
She sits like a bird 654
Shepherd divine, our wants relieve 655
Shine, Jesus, shine 479
Shout for joy and sing 656
Shout to the Lord 519
Shout to the north 508
Show me how to stand for justice 657
Show your power 295
Silent night 658
Silent, surrendered 659
Sing hosanna 215
Sing it in the valleys 660
Sing lullaby! 661
Sing, my tongue, the glorious battle 662
Sing of the Lord's goodness 663
Sing praise 420
Sing praise to God who reigns above 664
Sing to God a song of glory 665
Sing we of the blessèd Mother 666
Son of God, eternal Saviour 667
Songs of praise the angels sang 668
Songs of thankfulness and praise 669
Soul of my Saviour 670
Spirit divine, attend our prayers 671
Spirit of God 672
Spirit of God, our light amid the darkness 673
Spirit of the living God (Armstrong) 674
Spirit of the living God (Iverson) 675
Spirit song 558
Stand up and bless the Lord 676
Stand up, stand up for Jesus 677
Stay with me 678
Steal away 679
Story of love 343
Strengthen for service, Lord 680

Such love 681
Sun of my soul, thou Saviour dear 682
Surrexit Christus 683
Sweet sacrament divine 684

T

Take me, Lord 685
Take my hands, Lord 686
Take my life, and let it be 687
Take this moment 688
Take up thy cross, the Saviour said 689
Teach me, my God and King 690
Teach me to dance 691
Tell out, my soul 692
Thank you for saving me 693
Thank you for the summer morning 694
Thank you, Lord 695
Thanks be to God 696
Thanks for the fellowship 697
Thanks to God whose word was spoken 698
The advent of our King 699
The angel Gabriel from heaven came 700
The Beatitudes 717
The candle song 444
The Church of God a kingdom is 701
The Church's one foundation 702
The day of resurrection! 703
The day thou gavest, Lord, is ended 704
The first Nowell 705
The giving song 54
The God of Abraham praise 706
The God of love my shepherd is 707
The God whom earth and sea and sky 708
The gracious invitation 709
The great Creator of the worlds 710
The head that once was crowned with thorns 711
The heart of worship 823
The heavens declare thy glory, Lord 712
The holly and the ivy 713
The King is among us 714
The King of love my shepherd is 715
The kingdom is upon you! 716
The kingdom of heaven 717
The Last Journey 208
The Lord is King! 718
The Lord is my light 719
The Lord is my song 720
The Lord is risen indeed 721
The Lord will come and not be slow 722
The Lord's my shepherd (Crimond) 723
The Lord's my shepherd (Townend) 724
The love we share 725
The old rugged cross 587

The peace of the earth be with you 726
The people of God 511
The people that in darkness sat 727
The prophets spoke in days of old 728
The royal banners forward go 729
The Saviour will come, resplendent in joy 730
The Servant King 205
The servant song 91
The Son of God proclaim 731
The Spirit lives to set us free 732
The strife is o'er, the battle done 733
The Summons 834
The trees of the field 853
The Virgin Mary had a baby boy 734
The wise man 735
The world is full of smelly feet 736
Thee we adore, O hidden Saviour, thee 737
There are hundreds of sparrows 738
There in God's garden 739
There is a green hill far away 740
There is a land of pure delight 741
There is a longing 742
There is a Redeemer 743
There's a place where the streets shine 744
There's a quiet understanding 745
There's a spirit in the air 746
There's a wideness in God's mercy 747
These are the days 748
These vows of love are taken 749
Thine arm, O Lord, in days of old 750
Thine be the glory 751
Thine for ever! God of love 752
Think of a world without any flowers 753
This day God gives me 754
This is my body 755
This is my desire 756
This is my will 757
This is the air I breathe 758
This is the day 759
This is the day the Lord has made 760
This is your God 507
This joyful Eastertide 761
This little light of mine 762
This thankful heart 339
This world you have made 763
Thou art the Christ, O Lord 764
Thou art the Way: by thee alone 765
Thou didst leave thy throne 766
Thou, whose almighty word 767
Though pilgrim strangers here below 768
Through all the changing scenes of life 769
Through the night of doubt and sorrow 770
Thuma mina 771

Thy hand, O God, has guided 772
Thy kingdom come! 773
Thy kingdom come, O God 774
'Tis good, Lord, to be here 775
To be in your presence 776
To God be the glory! 777
To mock your reign, O dearest Lord 778
To the name of our salvation 779
To thee, O Lord, our hearts we raise 780

U
Ubi caritas 781
Unto us a boy is born! 782

V
Veni, lumen cordium 783
Virgin-born, we bow before thee 784

W
Wait for the Lord 785
Wake, O wake! with tidings thrilling 786
Waken, O sleeper, wake and rise 787
Walk in the light 732
Walk with me, O my Lord 788
Water of life 291
We are marching 789
We believe in God the Father 790
We bow down 791
We cannot measure 792
We eat the plants that grow from the seed 793
We gather here 794
We give immortal praise 795
We hail thy presence glorious 796
We have a dream 797
We have a gospel to proclaim 798
We have a King who rides a donkey 799
We love the place, O God 800
We plough the fields and scatter 801
We praise you, Lord 802
We pray thee, heavenly Father 803
We sing the praise of him who died 804
We three kings of Orient are 805
We turn to you 806
We want to see Jesus lifted high 807
We will lay our burden down 808
We worship at your feet 118
We'll walk the land 809
Were you there when they crucified my Lord? 810
What a friend we have in Jesus 811
What child is this 812
When all thy mercies, O my God 813
When God almighty came to earth 814

When God made the garden of creation 815
When God of old came down from heaven 816
When I feel the touch 817
When I look into your holiness 818
When I needed a neighbour 819
When I survey the wondrous cross 820
When Jesus came to Jordan 821
When morning gilds the skies 822
When the music fades 823
When the Spirit of the Lord 824
Where is this stupendous stranger? 825
Wherefore, O Father 826
While shepherds watched 827
Who are these like stars appearing 828
Who can sound the depths of sorrow 829
Who is there like you 830
Who put the colours in the rainbow? 831
Who would think that what was needed 832
Wide, wide as the ocean 833
Will you come and follow me 834
Will your anchor hold 835
With joy we meditate the grace 836
Within our darkest night 837
Within the reign of God 133
Wonderful, so wonderful 838

Y
Ye choirs of new Jerusalem 839
Ye holy angels bright 840
Ye servants of God 841
Ye servants of the Lord 842
Ye that know the Lord is gracious 843
Ye watchers and ye holy ones 844
Ye who own the faith of Jesus 845
Yesterday, today, for ever 846
You are beautiful 847
You are the centre 848
You are the King of Glory 849
You came from heaven to earth 461
You laid aside your majesty 850
You, living Christ, our eyes behold 851
You, Lord, are in this place 852
You shall go out with joy 853
You stood there on the shoreline 854
Your love is amazing 855
You're alive 423
You're worthy of my praise 341
Your love's greater 856

Z
Zacchaeus was a very little man 857
Zip bam boo 858